Pathway
of the Birds

The past is never fully gone. It is absorbed into the present and the future. It stays to shape what we are and what we do.

— Sir William Deane, Governor-General of Australia, 1996

Pathway
of the Birds

The voyaging achievements of Māori and their Polynesian ancestors

ANDREW CROWE

Bateman

*To the forgotten explorers of the Pacific – a vast ocean world
that extends across one third of the surface of the planet.*

Front cover: Hinemoana, *the waka at the heart of the Māori Youth Development waka
voyaging project, Hawaiki Rising.* www.wakavoyages.org/waka

*Back cover: (clockwise from top left) Marquesan cultural performer; Te Aurere;
Kuhl's lorikeet; Aitutaki; moai on Easter Island; Cape pigeons; Nuku Hiva, Marquesas
Islands; birdman motifs, Easter Island; sooty shearwaters.*

Page 1: Te Aurere, *a traditional-style voyaging canoe hollowed out from two giant kauri
trees lashed together in the traditional manner and assembled without the use of bolts or
nails. It is 18 metres long and weighs 8 tonnes.*

*Opposite: (from left) Moai on Easter Island; Fakarava lagoon, Tuamotus; Torlesse Range,
South Island, New Zealand.*

Published with support from

ARTS COUNCIL OF NEW ZEALAND TOI AOTEAROA

Text © Andrew Crowe, 2018
Typographical design © David Bateman Ltd, 2018
Photographs and illustrations © Individual contributors, see Picture Credits

Published in 2018 by David Bateman Ltd
Unit 2/5 Workspace Drive, Hobsonville, Auckland, New Zealand

Reprinted 2019, 2020

www.batemanbooks.co.nz

ISBN 978-1-86953-961-0

Project editor: Tracey Borgfeldt
Book design: Alice Bell
Map and graphic design: Andrew Crowe and Jola Martysz
Design concept and picture research: Andrew Crowe
Printed in China through Colorcraft Ltd, Hong Kong

Contents

List of Maps

Major maps are highlighted below in italics and shown on the globe opposite.

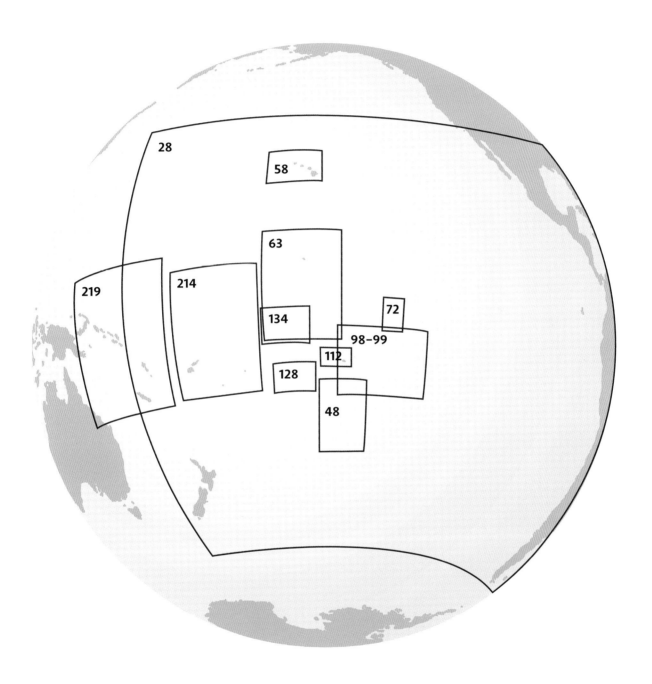

28

58

63

219

214

72

134

98–99

112

128

48

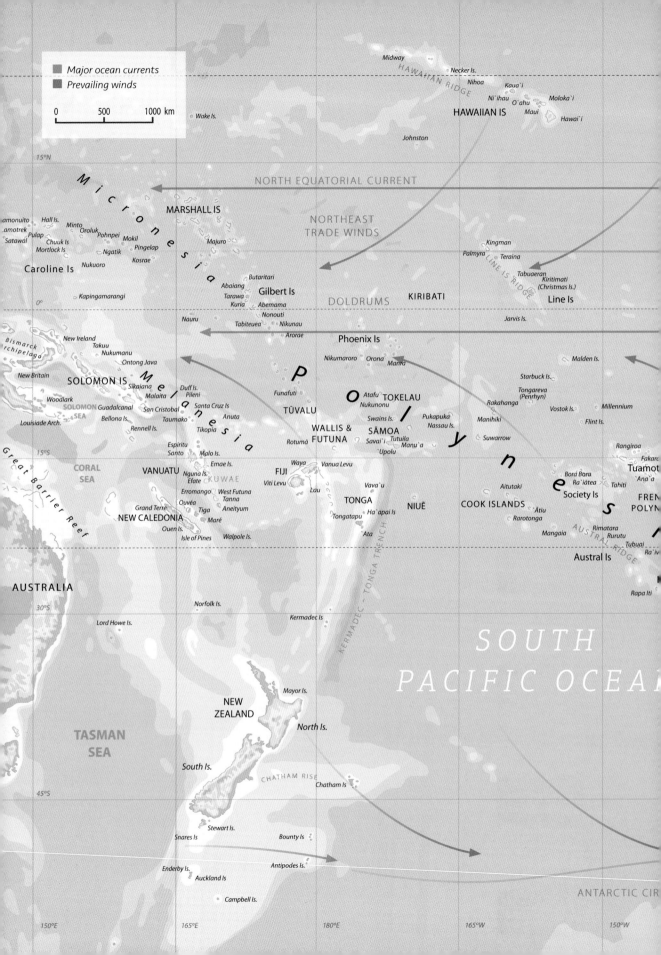

0   500   1000 km

Midway

HAWAIIAN RIDGE

Necker Is.

Nihoa

Kaua`i

Ni`ihau    O`ahu   Moloka`i

Maui

HAWAIIAN IS

Hawai`i

Johnston

Wake Is.

15°N

Micronesia

NORTH EQUATORIAL CURRENT

MARSHALL IS

NORTHEAST
TRADE WINDS

amonuito   Hall Is.   Minto
amotrek   Pulap   Oroluk   Pohnpei   Mokil
Satawal   Chuuk Is   Ngatik   Pingelap
Mortlock Is   Kosrae
Caroline Is   Nukuoro

Majuro

Kingman
Palmyra   Teraina

LINE IS RIDGE

Tabuaeran
Kiritimati
(Christmas Is.)

Line Is

Kapingamarangi

0°

Butaritari
Abaiang
Tarawa   Abemama
Kuria
Nonouti
Nauru   Nikunau
Tabiteuea   Arorae

Gilbert Is

DOLDRUMS   KIRIBATI

Jarvis Is.

Phoenix Is

Nikumaroro   Orona   Manra

Malden Is.

Starbuck Is.

Tongareva
(Penrhyn)

Rakahanga

Vostok Is.

Millennium

Flint Is.

Bismarck
rchipelago

New Ireland   Takuu
Nukumanu
Ontong Java

Melanesia

New Britain
SOLOMON IS   Sikaiana   Duff Is.
Woodlark   Santa Cruz Is
SOLOMON   Guadalcanal   Taumako   Anuta
SEA   Bellona Is.   Tikopia
Louisiade Arch.   Rennell Is.

Funafuti

TUVALU

Atafu   TOKELAU
Nukunonu

Swains Is.

P
o
l
y
n
e
s
i
a

Pukapuka
Nassau Is.

Manihiki

Suwarrow

Espiritu
Santo   Malo Is.

Emae Is.
Nguna Is.   KUWAE
Efate

WALLIS &
FUTUNA

Rotumā

SĀMOA
Savai`i   Tutuila
Manu`a
`Upolu

Rangiroa

Fakarav
`Ana`a

Tuamot

15°S

CORAL
SEA

VANUATU

Erromango   West Futuna
Ouvéa   Tanna
Grand Terre   Tiga   Aneityum
NEW CALEDONIA   Maré
Ouen Is.   Isle of Pines   Walpole Is.

Waya   Vanua Levu

FIJI

Viti Levu   Lau

Vava`u

Ha`apai Is

Tongatapu
Ata

TONGA

NIUĒ

COOK ISLANDS

Aitutaki

Rarotonga

Mangaia

Bora Bora
Ra`iatea   Tahiti

Society Is

`Ātiu

AUSTRAL RIDGE

Rimatara
Rurutu
Tubuai

FREN
POLYN

Ra`iv

30°S

AUSTRALIA

Great Barrier Reef

Norfolk Is.

Lord Howe Is.

Kermadec Is

KERMADEC – TONGA TRENCH

Austral Is

Rapa Iti

SOUTH
PACIFIC OCEA

NEW
ZEALAND

Mayor Is.

North Is.

TASMAN
SEA

South Is.

CHATHAM RISE

Chatham Is

45°S

Snares Is   Stewart Is.
Enderby Is.
Auckland Is

Bounty Is
Antipodes Is.

Campbell Is.

ANTARCTIC CIR

150°E   165°E   180°E   165°W   150°W

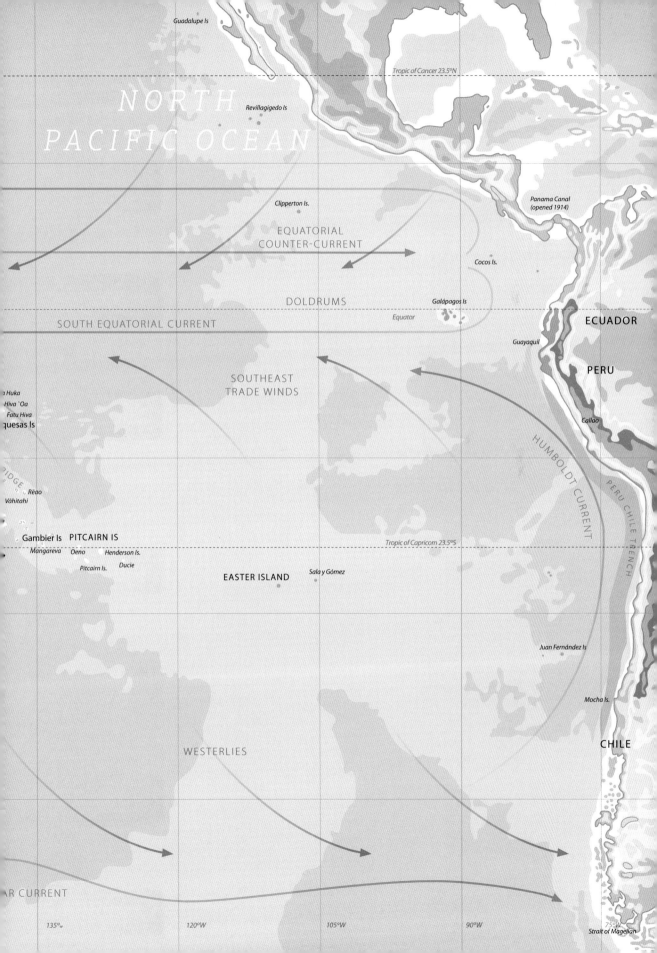

NORTH
PACIFIC OCEAN

Guadalupe Is

Tropic of Cancer 23.5°N

Revillagigedo Is

Clipperton Is

EQUATORIAL
COUNTER-CURRENT

Panama Canal
(opened 1914)

Cocos Is.

DOLDRUMS

Galápagos Is

ECUADOR

Equator

SOUTH EQUATORIAL CURRENT

Guayaquil

PERU

Huka

Hiva `Oa

Fatu Hiva

quesas Is

SOUTHEAST
TRADE WINDS

Callao

IDGE

Rēao

Vāhitahi

Gambier Is   PITCAIRN IS

HUMBOLDT CURRENT

PERU CHILE TRENCH

Tropic of Capricorn 23.5°S

Mangareva   Oeno   Henderson Is.

Pitcairn Is.   Ducie

EASTER ISLAND   Sala y Gómez

Juan Fernández Is

Mocha Is.

CHILE

WESTERLIES

AR CURRENT

135°W   *120°W*   *105°W*   *90°W*   *75°W*
Strait of Magellan

Author's Note

This book tells of one of the most expansive and
rapid phases of human migration in prehistory, a
period during which Polynesians reached and settled
nearly every archipelago scattered across some
28 million sq km of the Pacific Ocean, an area now
known as East Polynesia. *Pathway of the Birds* is not
the work of an academic, but the sincere effort of a
science writer to summarise in an accessible way
what is currently known about this largely neglected
epoch of world history. It is the fruit of many years of
gathering research from a wide range of specialists
and assembling their findings as if they were pieces
of one enormous jigsaw. In presenting the picture
that emerges from this, my focus is primarily on
the journey, or enquiry, rather than on promoting
any particular theory. I want to convey some idea of
the skills, innovation, resourcefulness and courage
of the people that drove this extraordinary feat of
maritime exploration.

Foreword

The famous Māori anthropologist Te Rangi Hīroa (Sir Peter Buck), writing of his ancient Polynesian ancestors, justly called them 'the supreme navigators of history.' Sailing across vast swaths of the Pacific Ocean centuries before Vasco da Gama cautiously ventured around the Cape of Good Hope to India, before Columbus crossed the far smaller Atlantic to the Caribbean, the Polynesians in their double-hulled, sewn-plank canoes propelled by woven mat sails explored the far reaches of the Earth's greatest ocean. By the 13th century A.D., the Polynesians had discovered virtually every island and archipelago that lay east, north or south of their homeland in the tropical islands of Tonga and Samoa. On these isolated lands – some tiny like cliff-bound Pitcairn, others verdant like Tahiti and Hawai'i, and some vast like New Zealand – they established permanent settlements. In time, the descendants of these intrepid explorers would multiply, each archipelago developing its own variant of Polynesian culture.

When Europeans eventually entered the Pacific realm, beginning with Magellan in AD 1520, they found every island they encountered already inhabited. Captain James Cook, who between 1769 and 1779 visited more Polynesian islands than any other European explorer before him including the apices of the Polynesian Triangle (New Zealand, Hawai'i and Easter Island), expressed his great admiration for this island 'Nation' as he called it. Cook had the privilege of meeting and befriending one of the great Polynesian navigators, or 'wayfinders' as we now prefer to call them, for their methods did not depend upon or use instruments. On his first voyage to observe the transit of Venus in Tahiti in 1769, Cook encountered the Ra'iatean priest and wayfinder Tupaia. Tupaia enumerated more than one hundred islands for which he claimed to know the star paths that would take one there. The encyclopedic wayfinding knowledge held in Tupaia's head is only hinted at in the famous chart that bears his name.

But in the decades after Tupaia, Polynesian voyaging and wayfinding entered a period of tragic decline. Devastating epidemics, the effects of missionization and colonial oppression, and the adoption of new ideas and technologies, all took their toll. By the mid-20th century, the great voyaging history of the Polynesians had been largely forgotten. Some scholars ventured to claim that the Polynesians had largely settled their islands through a series of accidental 'drift voyages'.

The restoration of the Polynesians into their rightful place in the history of world exploration and seafaring has been the outcome of two main efforts over the past five decades. One has been the gradual work of archaeologists and other scholars who have painstakingly accumulated the empirical evidence documenting the steady advance of the Polynesians and their Lapita ancestors out from the 'voyaging nursery' of Near Oceania and across the vast expanse of Remote Oceania, even to touch upon the shores of South America. The other has been the remarkable reinvention of ancient seafaring and wayfinding skills, beginning with the 1976 voyage of *Hōkūle'a* from Hawai'i to Tahiti and culminating most recently with her epic circumnavigation of the globe.

In *Pathway of the Birds*, Andrew Crowe has brought together these complementary sources of knowledge, along with insights from other disciplines including linguistics and ethnobotany, in a new synthesis of the Polynesian past. Te Rangi Hīroa, whose own book *Vikings of the Sunrise* engagingly brought the Polynesian story to the public some 80 years ago, would be astounded by how much new knowledge has been accumulated and new insights generated. This is truly one of the great sagas of world history, and Crowe tells it superbly. Hīroa would be justly proud.

Patrick Vinton Kirch
Chancellor's Professor Emeritus
University of California, Berkeley

Chance or Skill?

The Polynesian Voyaging Debate

By surpassing the achievements of the Phœnicians in the Mediterranean and the Vikings of the north Atlantic, [Polynesians] are worthy of being called the supreme navigators of history.

– Te Rangi Hīroa (Sir Peter Buck), *Vikings of the Sunrise* 1938

When Europeans first entered the world's largest ocean, they were understandably puzzled to find people of a single race, culture and language already settled on virtually every inhabitable island scattered across it. Had all these people managed to locate and colonise many hundreds of Pacific islands merely by chance, or had they acquired some kind of inexplicable navigational skill? Had they colonised this vast region through a deliberate process of planned exploration or had they merely drifted into the unknown in fully laden canoes to happen upon these widely scattered islands? There were, and still are, proponents of both views.

In *Tangata Whenua* (2014) for example, a recent history of Māori, we find Polynesian colonisation of the Pacific attributed primarily to a people on the run from internal conflict and self-induced collapse of resources, 'setting off into the unknown' in fully laden canoes, effectively into exile.[1]

This conjures up a very different scene from that portrayed by Sir Peter Buck (Te Rangi Hīroa) in his classic history of the region, *Vikings of the Sunrise* (1938), where he claimed that fairly frequent two-way voyaging contact between distant islands of the Pacific continued for centuries after settlement. Polynesians were deliberate voyagers, he asserted – a conclusion based not on any written record (of which there is none) but on oral history, language, legends, genealogies and all the other culture products of the islands concerned. 'We have a glorious heritage,' he wrote of his own people, 'for we come of the blood that conquered the Pacific with stone-age vessels that sailed ever toward the sunrise.'[2]

Many anthropologists of Buck's generation were not convinced. With Pacific archaeology still in its infancy, one young Norwegian adventurer and ethnographer, Thor Heyerdahl, outlined an alternative scenario. Many of the greatest human achievements that remain evident in Polynesia today, such as their colossal stonework found on Easter Island, were in his view attributable not to the Polynesians themselves but to people of a South American culture who had reached these islands by sailing downwind on rafts.

Although his idea proved very popular, few scholars took it seriously for there was too much evidence against it. This tendency to downplay the voyaging achievements of the Polynesians remained, nonetheless. In *Ancient Voyagers in Polynesia* (1964), Andrew Sharp presented his own view very clearly, that 'in the days before navigation instruments, deliberate navigation to and from distant ocean islands was impossible in any form of sailing or paddling craft . . .'[3] Māori 'came by accident on New Zealand,' he declared, 'after being lost at sea as the result of storms or voluntary or enforced exile' – a view that was subsequently endorsed by *An Encyclopaedia of New Zealand* (1966).[4]

This idea of 'settlement by chance' did not convince

everyone. In 1962, archaeologist Jack Golson took the trouble to test how credible such drift scenarios really were by compiling a map of more than 150 records of accidental voyages made prior to that date. From this a clear pattern emerged, showing that almost all such unnavigated voyages had occurred within the tropics and that they had been primarily westbound – that is, in the direction of prevailing trade winds and in the opposite direction to that from which the islands had been settled.[5]

Other evidence in support of deliberate navigation followed. In November 1965, New Zealand navigator David Lewis set out aboard his catamaran *Rehu Moana* to sail from Rarotonga to New Zealand without recourse to navigational instruments, applying only traditional wayfinding methods learned from Micronesians in the western Pacific. Without checking any navigational instruments for over 3000 km, he arrived at his destination to find himself in error by only 26 sea miles (48 km). It was an important demonstration of how previously discovered islands such as New Zealand could be re-found, and of how explorers might find their way back again to their home islands.

Despite such graphic findings, the theory of settlement by unnavigated voyages continued to hold sway through the 1970s and 80s. As Lewis himself pointed out, his voyage did not throw any light on how hitherto unknown islands might have been discovered in the first place. In *New Zealand's Heritage* (1971) – a major source of New Zealand history knowledge at the time – Sharp stuck to his view that 'unnavigated one-way voyages give a simple explanation of the discovery and settlement of distant islands, more acceptable than elaborate theories of two-way navigation'.[6]

The idea of unnavigated one-way voyages endured, but so too did the debate. In 1972, Michael Levison and colleagues applied more sophisticated computer models to the problem. After running thousands of simulations based on accumulated information on winds, currents and gales, they conceded that settlement-by-drift was highly unlikely in the tropics and, more importantly, that settlement of more remote islands such as New Zealand, Hawai`i and Easter Island was virtually impossible by this means.

But it was not until 2006 that the public would be treated to a really accessible and enlightening

Te Rangi Hīroa (Sir Peter Buck), 1935.

introduction to how the settlement of the Pacific was actually achieved. In that year, Auckland Museum launched *Vaka Moana*, a major international travelling exhibition and book of the same name. Here, at last, the public could find displays that illustrated traditional boatbuilding and navigation in the Pacific, and the proud renaissance in Polynesian voyaging that had been going on since 1976 aboard modern versions of the original Polynesian craft. As sailor-archaeologist Geoffrey Irwin explained, Polynesians had explored west to east across the Pacific from Asia, with an eye to personal safety, making use of anomalies in the winds, secure in the knowledge that the resumption of predominating easterlies would facilitate a safe return to their home islands. It made more sense than this idea of simply setting off into the unknown – and it fitted the evidence.

The message was important, for the question of whether or not Polynesians were highly skilled in their voyaging deeds is relevant not just to historians, but to society as a whole. In Western culture we are commonly urged to look to the future, rather than look back. But the past is never fully gone; it is absorbed into the present and the future. It stays to shape what we are and what we do.[7] Or, in the idiom of Māori, 'kia whakatōmuri te haere whakamua' (we walk backwards into the future with our eyes fixed on the past).

That is, the past is important for it helps us make sense of the present.

How New Zealand was settled

And it is for the same reason that it is important to resolve this bewildering variety of contradictory explanations as to how New Zealand was first settled.

In the most widely disseminated version, taught in New Zealand schools until very recently, settlement was attributed to the arrival of a single fleet of canoes following the directions of a Polynesian explorer named Kupe. Yet we hear a very different claim: that settlement occurred by accident. The antecedents of Māori were setting off into the unknown in fully laden voyaging canoes in desperate circumstances in the hope that they might make landfall somewhere before succumbing to a storm, exhaustion, exposure, hunger or thirst.[8] Somehow these two contradictory ideas seemed to coexist.

As to where the antecedents of Māori came from, *An Encyclopaedia of New Zealand* (1966) suggested that they set out for New Zealand from 'the Society Group of islands'.[9] Then, as it became increasingly clear that the immediate homeland of Māori was not necessarily confined to a single island group, this Hawaiki (or homeland) grew. Before long, it was being more accurately referred to as 'an East Polynesian interaction sphere',[10] a region of regular interarchipelago trade that included the Society Islands, Southern Cook Islands, Austral Islands and the Tuamotus, at least.

Polynesian settlement history in the media

In many ways, it is easier to trace the antecedents of Māori much further back, to Asia, and in this way appreciate that they sailed island by island from that continent right across the Pacific. However one views it, it is a mind-boggling dispersal of humanity, and it was achieved more than two centuries before Europe's own so-called 'Age of Exploration' began. It is certainly an epic history, but one that sadly receives scant coverage in the media, other than on Māori Television. Rather, it is not unusual to see Māori and their settlement history portrayed in a manner that is condescending, distorted or muddled. Although one might charitably attribute this to ignorance, it is a 'sanctioned ignorance'.

Sanctioned or not, it is an ignorance born of the idiom 'history is written by the victors' – i.e., subsequent colonisers from Europe. This book aims to address this by summarising in a simple way what

is actually known about this fascinating period of history and what is not – and, in particular, to try and establish whether or not the voyages of Māori and their ancestors were necessarily skilful.

The wider context

This will involve reviewing evidence not just from archaeology, but from poetry, ecology, seasonal wind changes, navigation, transequatorial bird migration, astronomy and the parameters of human survival. In an effort to understand what these deep-sea voyages were like and to put them in context alongside the skills of Polynesians in many other spheres, we will investigate how Polynesians acquired and cultivated their traditional crops, manufactured their tools and oceangoing canoes, practised non-instrument wayfinding, and shifted enormous quantities of earth and stone to construct megalithic platforms, statues, irrigation systems and canals. We will enter a world that has been largely forgotten to explore such themes as:

- Whether return voyages of exploration generally preceded those of settlement
- How navigators could discern the presence of remote islands, such as New Zealand, from enormous distances, well before they reached them
- What was carried aboard the voyaging canoes, how these were navigated and how long individual voyages are likely to have taken
- Why the canoes coming to New Zealand brought no pottery, skin drums, Polynesian pigs or chickens, nor the traditional Polynesian practice of archery or building stone marae platforms
- The overall ingenuity of Polynesians and the ways in which they are linked to one another by language, culture and DNA
- The evidence that, before Europeans arrived, Polynesians had already reached the Americas and possibly Australia
- The origins of Polynesians and, more specifically, the points from which canoes carrying the immediate ancestors of New Zealand Māori are likely to have set sail
- Why long-distance voyaging stopped and how so much of the story was lost.

The islands of tropical East Polynesia will be introduced along three voyaging routes

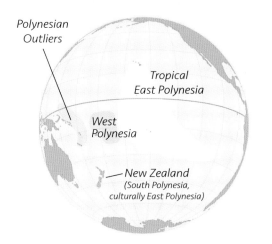
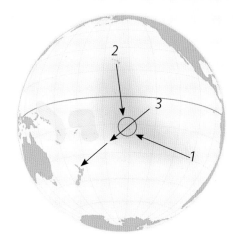

Left, the major cultural regions of Polynesia. Right, three potential voyaging routes through tropical East Polynesia.

East Polynesia

To do this, we will be focusing on a huge expanse of the Pacific known as East Polynesia, the same region from which the ancestors of Māori are understood to have set sail for New Zealand, and where the most ambitious long-distance voyages were evidently undertaken. This region extends east from New Zealand to Easter Island and north to the Hawaiian Islands. To help maintain a sense of orientation across this vast cultural region, and to facilitate an appreciation of the navigational considerations, islands will be visited along three main voyaging routes, sections of which are all known to have been sailed at one time or another by Polynesians.

1. West with the summer easterlies from Easter Island through the Pitcairn Islands to the Austral Islands,
2. South across the prevailing winds from the Hawaiian Islands via the Line Islands across the equator to the Society Islands, and
3. West-southwest with the trade winds from the remote Marquesas Islands through the Tuamotus and Society Islands to the Cook Islands.

This means that we will be tracing these three routes through the Pacific in the opposite direction to that in which the region is understood to have been colonised. This approach will help challenge a common misconception that the first inhabitants of these islands remained thereafter in isolation, lacking the capability of getting back.

As we come to each island we will investigate the origins of its 'first peoples', and why it is almost certain that explorers made a return voyage to report back on the island before any preparations were made to settle it. In each case, this is followed by an assessment of the capability and motives of the inhabitants to maintain interarchipelago contact – at least in the early years of settlement.

Along the way we will review the basic principles behind making an exploratory voyage, wayfinding at sea, traditional boatbuilding, and recent attempts to retrace some of the original voyages – all of which provide the context for reconstructing a deliberate voyage to New Zealand.

We begin with one of the most culturally disenfranchised of all Polynesian long-distance navigators, the inhabitants of Rapa Nui (Easter Island).

CHAPTER ONE

Easter Island

Out On a Limb

[Easter Islanders] are certainly of the same race of People as the
New Zealanders and the other islanders, the affinity of the Language,
Colour and some of their customs all tend to prove it.

Captain James Cook, *Journal*, 17th March 1774

Master masons from Peru?

When Europeans first reached Easter Island in 1722 they were understandably astonished to find the island encircled by enormous stone statues, for this destination is so exceedingly remote – indeed, it is one of the most remote inhabited islands in the world. How had such an isolated place been found by humans, when, and by whom?

In the 1950s, Norwegian ethnographer Thor Heyerdahl felt that he had solved the mystery. Credit for discovery of the island lay with a fair-skinned people from Peru, he wrote, who had sailed there aboard rafts from South America and who had erected these statues centuries before Polynesians arrived. In his view, Polynesians were a primitive people who did not reach the island until 'perhaps only a hundred years or so' before Europeans. They fought the island's original inhabitants and toppled their statues, bringing all cultural life on the island to an abrupt end with 'a wave of war and cannibalism'. The remarkable statues, he declared, were 'not the work of a canoe-load of Polynesian wood-carvers', but that of master masons from Peru.[1]

To be fair, we can thank Heyerdahl for effectively introducing this island and its statues to the world, but the success of his books – published in more than 65 languages with sales of over 20 million –

had a downside. It served to give disproportionate influence to his views, largely overshadowing a more evidence-based approach to the history of the island, one in which the culture of Polynesians emerges in a far more positive light.

An enigmatic destination

Easter Island stands alone in the southeastern Pacific, the summit of a volcanic mountain that pokes out of the ocean some 3500 km west of the South American coastline. Its nearest inhabited neighbours are the tiny islands of Henderson and Pitcairn, which lie some 2000 km further west, as distant from the island as Mexico is from Canada. As a navigational target it is minuscule, with a coastline so short that it can be walked in a day and an extent no more than about half that of New Zealand's Great Barrier Island. Not only is its highest point visible from no more than 90 km away, but there is no surrounding archipelago here to help navigators locate it.[2] Given such formidable challenges to finding it, it is intriguing to learn that most of the traditional crops grown here originated in Southeast Asia, and that one – the sweet potato – came from the other side of the Pacific, from South America.

The settlement of Easter Island is puzzling for other reasons: the island lacks a safe natural

Right: All the giant statues (moai) face inland. Here, a back view of Ahu Tongariki shows what navigators see on approach from the southeast.

NORTH PACIFIC OCEAN

Hawai`i

MICRONESIA

Marshall Islands

Line Islands

New Guinea

Tokelau

Tūvalu

Sāmoa

Society Islands

Marquesas

Vanuatu

Fiji

Tonga

Cook Islands

Tuamotus

Pitcairn Islands

New Caledonia

Austral Islands

Kermadec Islands

SOUTH PACIFIC OCEAN

New Zealand

Chatham Islands

`Anakena Bay

Tongariki

Rano Kao

Easter Island

Below: At 163 sq km, Easter Island is about half the size of New Zealand's Great Barrier Island. Current population: less than 6000, of whom some 60 percent are descendants of the indigenous population.

Easter Island, Rapa Nui or Rapanui?

Indigenous names for Easter Island are unknown prior to 1862, the year in which some of its inhabitants visited the smaller Polynesian island of Rapa (now known as Rapa Iti, or 'Little Rapa') aboard the Peruvian schooner Cora. It was this contact that inspired the name Rapa Nui ('Big Rapa') – the name used for Easter Island today, subsequently translated as Te Pito `o te Henua – 'The End of the Land'. For reasons of grammar, the island itself is known as Rapa Nui, but its people as Rapanui.[3]

Above: A man from Easter Island in 1777, with extended earlobes and wearing a headdress of rooster feathers, drawn by William Hodges. Below: An Easter Islander today.

harbour, and – at least when found by Europeans – was devoid of trees, permanent streams or rivers, with freshwater confined to lakes within its craters, and its climate was too cool to produce two of the most important staple crops of Polynesians: coconuts and breadfruit. Further, when the Dutch Admiral Jacob Roggeveen arrived here on Easter Sunday 1722, he found nothing to suggest that these people had ever been deep-sea navigators. On the contrary, he was struck by the 'poor and flimsy construction' of the local canoes made from small planks stitched together and not caulked, and by the lack of any tree on the island more than 10 feet (3 m) tall. The 'great many canoes [that] came off to the ships,' he reported, were capable of carrying just one or, at most, two people, and were so leaky that half their time was spent bailing. Many of those who came to the Dutch ships reached them by swimming.

The island's extreme isolation has always seemed hard to reconcile with its sophisticated culture. Roggeveen wrote of how the islanders lit fires in front of enormous carved statues, reverentially 'squatting on their heels with heads bowed down,' bringing the palms of their hands together and alternately raising and lowering them. Some of these sculptures, he added, 'were a good 30 feet in height and broad in proportion'. How was it possible, he wondered, 'that people who are destitute of heavy or thick timber, and also of stout cordage, out of which to construct gear, had been able to erect them'?

Roggeveen was impressed by the island's horticultural productivity and rich soil; he described Easter Island at that point as being 'exceedingly fruitful, producing bananas, [sweet] potatoes, sugar-cane of remarkable thickness, and many other kinds of the fruits of the earth'. Although the island was prone to drought, its inhabitants had met the challenge with a horticultural innovation known as 'stone mulching', a practice that helped protect their crops not only from loss of moisture but also from erosion and swings in soil temperature. Such was the bounty of the harvest that, on orders from the chief, 'a great abundance' of sugarcane, about 60 fowls, yams and 30 bunches of bananas were laid before them.

Roggeveen left no doubt that the people here were at that time healthy and thriving. He saw no evidence of malnutrition. The islanders 'have well proportioned limbs,' he wrote, 'with large and strong muscles; they are big in stature, and . . . have also snow-white teeth, with which they are exceptionally well provided, even the old and hoary, as was evidenced by the cracking of a large and hard nut, whose shell was thicker and more resisting than our peach stones'.[4]

A flourishing society settled in such a remote place, and without seaworthy craft, left us with a puzzle as to how the islanders had reached here, and from where.

A downwind voyage from Peru?

This was really the mystery that prompted Thor Heyerdahl to set off with some friends in 1947 aboard a raft named *Kon-Tiki* on a downwind voyage into the Pacific from Peru. He was keen to prove that the island could have been first settled from South America. He made no bones about it, either, that he considered Polynesians incapable of such a high degree of cultural development. In his opinion, Easter Island must have been first settled by a more 'civilised race'.

The story of his archetypal adventure, as narrated in his own book and film about the 101-day voyage, *The Kon-Tiki Expedition*, was certainly well told, and yet it paid scant attention to the bulk of linguistic, ethnographic and ethnobotanical evidence contradicting his views.[5] It paid little heed to the fact that the Tuamotuan atoll of Raro`ia, where his raft wrecked, is no closer to Easter Island than Callao, where he began the voyage; and the fact that reaching Easter Island from that atoll would have required him to sail as far again along the very course he had originally argued against for Polynesians.[6] To avoid getting swept too far north by the powerful northbound Humboldt Current off South America, his raft had been towed through the first night of the voyage for over 90 km by a Peruvian Navy tug, without which he would have ended up further away still from Easter Island.[7] In fact, the chances of reaching Easter Island from anywhere in South America without prior knowledge of its whereabouts are very low – around 6 percent, according to sailor–archaeologist Geoffrey Irwin.[8]

How Polynesian?

In fact, the Rapanui people are of Polynesian descent.[9] Captain Cook, who reached Easter Island some 50 years after Roggeveen, in 1774, immediately understood this – from the moment the first islander stepped aboard the *Resolution*. 'Tahi, rua, toru, hā, ka-rima . . .' called out the man as he strode the deck, counting off the fathoms as he measured its length.[10] Here were the same numbers that the British captain had heard in Tahiti and New Zealand – 'tahi, rua, toru, hā, rima . . .' in Tahitian, or 'tahi, rua, toru, whā, rima . . .' in New Zealand Māori.

As Cook summarised, on turning his ship to leave the island, these people:

> are certainly of the same race of People as the New Zealanders and the other islanders, the affinity of the Language, Colour and some of their customs all tend to prove it, I think they bearing more affinity to the Inhabitants of [Tongatapu in Tonga] and New Zealand, than those of the more northern [Society] islands … It is extraordinary, that the same nation should have spread themselves over all the isles in this Vast Ocean from New Zealand to this Island, which is almost one-fourth part of the circumference of the Globe.

It was a powerful conclusion to reach, but one that was fully supported by the Polynesian character of their artefacts and crops. 'They have . . . a weapon made of wood, like the Patoo [patu] of New Zealand' he wrote, and 'several plantations of [sweet] potatoes, plantains, and sugar-canes . . . some fowls,' and paper mulberry trees, taro and yams, 'but so very few [gourds], that a cocoa-nut shell was the most valuable thing we could give

Heyerdahl and the *Kon-Tiki*

Thor Heyerdahl (1914–2002) declared that the remarkable statues on Easter Island were 'not the work of a canoe-load of Polynesian wood-carvers', but that of master masons from Peru. In an attempt to prove that Polynesian presence on the island could have been preceded by that of Peruvians, he set out in 1947 from Callao, Peru, on a downwind voyage into the Pacific aboard a balsa raft named the Kon-Tiki, *above. After 101 days, his raft wrecked on the Tuamotuan atoll of Raro'ia, no closer to Easter Island than where he began.*

Patu (hand clubs)

Cook noted many affinities in the language, customs and artefacts of Rapanui and Māori, noting 'They are certainly of the same race of People as the New Zealanders and the other islanders... They have ... a weapon made of wood, like the Patoo [patu] of New Zealand.'

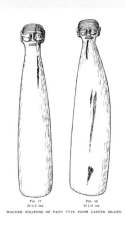

Fig. 17   Fig. 18
20 3/4 ins.   22 1/4 ins.
WOODEN WEAPONS OF PATU TYPE FROM EASTER ISLAND.

Above: Two wooden paoa (hand clubs) of Easter Island, some 50 cm long, with human faces.
Below: Patu parāoa (whalebone club) from New Zealand.

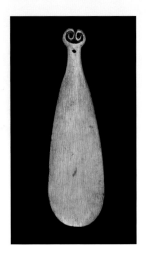

them'. In his list of crops lies a compelling clue as to where these people originated, for all but one of these imports are native to Southeast Asia. And all – in addition to the Pacific Island cabbage tree – are traditionally grown elsewhere by Polynesians. Each crop, along with the humanly-introduced Pacific rat, is known locally by a traditional Polynesian name: kūmara, maika, tōa, moa, mahute, taro, uhi, hue, tī and kio`e.[11] The same Polynesian link is found in Rapanui terms for wild plants, birds, invertebrates and fish.[12] The language of the island's early indigenous literature[13] is likewise unambiguously Polynesian, as is their traditional method of cooking in underground ovens (umu), rather than using any kind of pottery.[14]

A similar ethnic signature is found in maternally inherited DNA from 12 human skeletons buried in two of the stone platforms; this too was found to be typically Polynesian.[15]

The remarkable statues

As for the statues (moai or mo`ai), who made them and how, a closer investigation reveals that these are made from volcanic tuff, a rock not much harder than chalk, shaped with basalt adzes in a manner similar to Polynesian woodcarving. They are depictions of Polynesian ancestors and were carved and erected AD 1200–1600, a period recently determined from remains of coral files used in the final stages of shaping them, and from algae, whose white nodules can still be found growing on the platforms.[16] With subsequent weathering, the surface of this kind of rock becomes steel-hard, which explains why sparks were sent flying when Europeans later struck at the statues with iron tools.

The largest of the movable ones is over 10 m tall, weighs about 74 tonnes and was transported over 5 km. Many have puzzled over how Rapanui managed to handle such immense weights and in such quantities. In all, some 12,700 tonnes of stone were moved here, including hundreds of multi-tonne statues transported over rugged terrain from the quarry sites up to 18 km away.[17] Polynesians were no strangers to shifting immense weights though; they were used to using pivots, slipways and rollers[18] for beaching and launching their canoes and dragging them overland. In New Zealand, for example, Māori made huge canoe hulls out of solid tree trunks, some weighing far more than the statues,[19] and moved these by dragging them over slipways. When transporting large canoes across the Auckland isthmus, for example, the slipway was lubricated with the slime-oozing branches of the five-finger tree (whauwhaupaku).[20] Elsewhere, the hefty hulls were hauled over wet seaweed with thick ropes woven from dried cabbage tree leaves, to the rhythm of collective chants. In this way, and with the aid of as many as 2000 people, large bodies of timber could be hauled overland for 30 km or more.[21]

But the megalithic grandeur on Easter Island extends well beyond the carving and transport of its statues. It includes more than 300 stone ahu (platforms) dotted along the coast, some up to 150 m long and 3 m high, built with facing slabs, each weighing up to 10 tonnes and infilled with rubble. The style of their construction is again recognisably Polynesian,

Moving a statue akin to moving a canoe

Polynesians were familiar with moving heavy weights. Māori dragged canoes with the aid of plant 'lubricants' along a 1-km course across the Auckland isthmus from the Tāmaki River to the Manukau Harbour. Similar methods were trialled on Easter Island. In one trial bark-fibre rope was used to tow large rocks from the quarry over a skidway along old transport 'roads' on wooden sledges with the aid of rollers and mashed reeds or palm fronds as 'lubricants'. Another trial involved 'walking' the statues in a manner similar to that traditionally used by Polynesians to draw large canoes up onto the beach, by pivoting the hull and swinging it.[22] In 2012 a team of 18 people on Hawai`i quickly manoeuvred a five-ton concrete replica of one of the Easter Island statues 'refrigerator-style' a few hundred metres with the aid of three hemp ropes. Erecting the statues is thought to have been achieved with a combination of ropes, levers and earthen ramps. Comparable feats elsewhere in Polynesia

include erecting stone pillars c. AD 1200 for the five-metre-tall Stonehenge-style trilithon 'Ha`amonga `a Maui' on Tongatapu (Tonga).

Right: Map showing the old transport 'roads' used on Easter Island for moving large rocks or statues from the main quarries – reminiscent of the canoe-hauling tracks in New Zealand.[23] These roads are still visible today from satellites.[24]

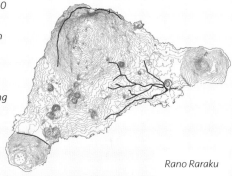

Rano Raraku

as is the Rapanui term for them: ahu is a specifically East Polynesian word, applied in New Zealand, for example, to the 'foundation of a marae site', a 'sacred mound' or 'altar'.[25] Constructions of a similar style and scale can be seen on the Marquesas, Society and Hawaiian islands. The foundations of Ili`ili`opae on Moloka`i (Hawaiian Islands), for example, involved the cartage of some 15,750 cubic metres of stone[26] – equivalent to the entire contents of more than six Olympic-size swimming pools.

Which islands did the people come from?

The culture of Rapanui is Polynesian. This is evident in their patu (ceremonial clubs), whose style is shared with New Zealand, the Chatham Islands and Society Islands, and in their traditional houses, which resembled 'a large canoe upside down',[27] much like those that were found on neighbouring Mangareva, Rapa Iti and the Tuamotus. Strong ties with Mangareva, Hawai`i and the Marquesas are palpable also to linguists. Similarly, many Rapanui place names are shared with the Marquesas, Hawai`i, Society Islands, Austral Islands or New Zealand.[28] The stone

Above: Within the walls of the Rano Raraku crater more statues can still be seen standing among yellow lupins.

Sooty tern (manu-tara)

*The sooty tern, or manu-tara of Easter Island (Onychoprion fuscatus; syn. Sterna, below), almost certainly played a major role in the traditional location and relocation of the island. As shown on the globe below, these long-ranging terns are known right across Polynesia as **tara** – a term applied in New Zealand to the white-fronted tern (Sterna striata).*

Sooty terns breed in dense communities on predator-free islets and atolls. Egg incubation takes 26–30 days, after which the chicks remain dependent for up to 70 days on being fed by the adults, which may forage for 480 km or more. In season, sightings of them within this radius would have helped guide voyagers to the island – a potential origin of a 'birdman cult' ritual practised on the island.

statues and platforms, and more portable artefacts such as fishhooks, stone adze styles, harpoons and coral files are likewise strongly reminiscent of those of early Marquesans, Mangarevans and Pitcairn Islanders.

In short, all the evidence – including the DNA of humanly-transported Pacific rats (kiore) – points to an East Polynesian origin for Rapanui, with an immediate origin in the region of Mangareva, some 2600 km to the west.[29]

Locating the island without navigational instruments

And yet, coming from Mangareva, the mind boggles at the challenge of locating this tiny, remote island; indeed, doing so by purely traditional means without the aid of roaming seabirds seems nigh impossible. So it is worth trying to envisage what the birdlife was like here in the period during which the island was first settled.

Ornithologist David Steadman went through the subfossil evidence to discover that the island's seabird fauna 'probably exceeded 30 resident species when Polynesians arrived, making it the richest seabird island in the world'.[30] About half of these species were petrels, prions and shearwaters, many of which are known for making transequatorial migrations. In spring, these tireless oceanic wanderers return to their birthplace to breed in enormous colonies, such as on this island, from where they will continue to undertake long-distance foraging flights.[31] At least one of the species that formerly bred here is known to range as far north as Hawai`i.[32]

Since that time, though, there has been a dramatic change in the island's ecology. From being the richest seabird island in the world, the main island now supports just one native species – the red-tailed tropicbird.[33] Even if we factor in the offshore islets, colonies of more than half the island's original seabird species have been lost. The demise of so many birds is partly due to the Polynesian introduction of rats, which ate the eggs, but large quantities of bones in early remains of domestic waste (middens) reveal that much of the loss is directly attributable to their having been harvested for meat.[34]

In other words, when the island's first inhabitants arrived, seabirds were coming and going in extraordinary numbers. Even if we care to wind the calendar forward to as late as the 18th century, we find reports from Captain Cook's approach to the island in March 1774 of his sighting the island's first frigatebirds about 750 km away, and a sharp increase in overall bird numbers at around 500 km.[35] From this we can perhaps get a glimpse of what these waters might have looked like some five centuries earlier, when seabirds may often have been present in sufficient numbers to serve traditional navigators as a powerful 'locator beacon' for finding and refinding the island.

In this regard, there is one bird that stands out. For much of the year, the sooty tern (manu-tara) is away roaming on the wing, but in spring it makes its way back to predator-free atolls and islands such as this one to breed. Their population in the mid-central Pacific alone – even as late as the 1960s – was estimated at some 30 million. In spring, they have settled back into their nesting colonies, from where they will continue to disperse on daily foraging flights of up to 480 km or more, with particularly high densities of birds evident within 40 to 80 km of the colony.[36] Such was the value of these birds to Polynesian navigators that we find their pride of place in traditional wayfinding immortalised in the lines of a Polynesian voyaging song:

> The black tern –
> The black tern is my bird,
> Bird in whom my eyes are gifted with unbounded vision . . .

So declares this Tuamotuan chant, in recognition of this bird's uncanny ability to refind its home island from so far afield.[37]

For any navigator heading for Easter Island from Mangareva, at least in the birds' September–March nesting season, tern sightings might then serve to widen the navigational target some thirtyfold. For this reason, the traditional navigator's ability to find and refind this particular island may have been largely dependent on these birds being in residence.[38] This may also have been the season in which Easter Island was originally discovered, for it is in August that the most favourable winds begin to blow from the west.[39] Indeed, this phenomenon may well be connected with the well-known Rapanui 'birdman cult' ritual practised on the island, in which the return of this bird in September was ritually celebrated by contestants swimming out to the offshore islet of Motu Nui to retrieve the first egg of this same bird.

Active blue-water sailors

By 5 April, the day in 1722 on which Jacob Roggeveen arrived, most of these birds would have left the island and there were no oceangoing vessels to be seen. Roggeveen would be struck more by the flimsiness of the local canoes and a lack of trees with which to build them, an observation substantiated over 50 years later, in 1774, by Cook. 'Barren and without wood' was how he described the island; he noted that the only prominent wild tree remaining on the steep inner crater slopes was toromiro, 'not exceeding six or seven feet in height'. By this time, Rapa Nui seems to have been cut off from the world again.

And yet we can be sure that Rapanui had previously possessed oceangoing canoes and that they were at one time active bluewater sailors. This is evident from the crumbling remains of numerous canoe ramps on the island and in the subfossil record of the islanders' deep-sea fisheries catch. More than a third of vertebrate bones unearthed from old middens on the north coast are of dolphin, a creature that is almost impossible to harpoon without the use of a seaworthy vessel.[40]

Equally telling and no less intriguing is the fact that, when Roggeveen arrived, Rapanui were wearing neck pendants made from mother-of-pearl shell, a raw material that is not locally available. The nearest island where these attractive oyster shells are found is the atoll of Ducie, over 1500 km to the west.[41] Maybe Easter Island was not as cut off from neighbouring islands as it seemed.

Toromiro

The toromiro of Easter Island (Sophora toromiro, above), a small tree that was highly valued on Easter Island for woodcarving and which is now considered identical with the New Zealand kōwhai (S. microphylla). The globe shows the distribution of this name **toromiro**, *which is applied in New Zealand not to this plant but to a much larger forest tree with similar leaves, a plant better known today as miro (Prumnopitys ferruginea).[42] Such differences suggest that if any direct contact occurred between Easter Island and New Zealand, it was minimal.*

Easter Island forest

*The original forest of the island consisted primarily of a large Easter Island palm that was either identical to the Chilean wine palm (Jubaea chilensis, above) or a similar but unique species, Paschalococos disperta. Yet when Europeans reached the island it was almost devoid of trees. Today, most of the species that originally grew here are now either scarce or extinct, largely due to the twin impacts of fire used for clearing land for agriculture, and the introduction of Pacific rats, which consumed many of the tree seeds, preventing regeneration. The globe below shows the distribution of the word **rākau** for tree. By the time Europeans arrived in Rapanui, this term applied only to 'riches, wealth, goods or property' in general.*

A source of shipbuilding timber

The likely source of their shipbuilding timber was discovered in the early 1990s when researchers bored through undisturbed columns of sediment in a local swamp to find prehistoric pollen and carbonised wood fragments from over 20 vanished plant species. From these and from seed remains, we now know that most of the island was previously covered in forest dominated by various species of palm, including more than 16 million now-extinct giant Easter Island palms.[43]

By the time Europeans reached the island, almost all its trees had vanished – and, with them, their indigenous names. The Polynesian word rākau for 'tree' survived nonetheless, though by then it referred only to 'riches, wealth, goods or property' – a faint echo of the high commodity value Polynesians placed on wood.

So what had happened? In the popular version, promoted through the mid-1990s by science writer Jared Diamond,

> Easter's growing population was cutting the forest more rapidly than the forest was regenerating. The people used land for gardens and wood for fuel, canoes, and houses – and of course, [as rollers] for lugging statues. As forest disappeared, the islanders ran out of timber and rope to transport and erect their statues . . .

'What were they thinking when they cut down the last palm tree?' Diamond asks[44] – here hinting at a parallel with the predicament of modern humans today.

Archaeo-ecologists today, though, are confident that, in the case of Easter Island at least, Diamond is on the wrong track.[45] The main culprits in this case turn out to be a combination of fire and the dire ecological impact of some two million Pacific rats.[46] The evidence is found in large areas of burnt palm stumps and burnt soil layers containing charred palm seeds, and in many subfossil palm nuts that show clear signs of having been nibbled by rats in such a way as to prevent germination. In the early stages of settlement it is clear that many of the palms were felled and burnt, most likely to clear potentially productive land for taro cultivation.[47]

For the forest as a whole, this combination – the impact of fire and gnawing rats – proved devastating. The palms of Easter Island are unlikely to have been suitable for canoe-building anyway – gauging by the properties of related palms elsewhere – but suitable trees certainly grew here in the past. One is a tree that is known over much of Polynesia as toi (*Alphitonia zizyphoides*). This can reach heights of 20–25 m and produces a very hard wood that was traditionally valued by shipbuilders elsewhere in Polynesia for the manufacture of canoes and paddles.[48] When it came to the task of caulking any gaps between the planks (or hauling the statues, for that matter) the requisite fibre is understood to have come from the remarkably strong inner bark of a small, formerly dominant native shrub known locally as hauhau. In other words, we now know that Rapanui had previously possessed sizeable ships of some kind and were in a position to build them from local materials.

Sail-making material

But what had Rapanui used for making their sails? Their own native palm fronds, perhaps? On 19th-century Mangareva, for example, makeshift sails were made by joining several coconut fronds at the butt end, splaying them out and lacing the leaves together.[49] Although the coconut itself was not grown on Easter Island before European contact, perhaps Rapanui experimented with the fronds of their local palms. And yet, even if they did, such rudimentary sails would hardly have survived the rigours of long-distance voyaging.

Sails may also have been made from the rush-like leaves of the tall bulrush (ngā`atu) that grow in thick stands in the large crater lakes, and which are known to have been used for house thatching, mats, baskets and simple rafts. But here again, sails made from them are highly unlikely to have withstood a long voyage.[50]

And likewise, although Rapanui produced 'a fair quantity of bark cloth', tapa cloth has not proven rugged enough to survive use as a sail for any distance at sea.[51]

In summary, there may have been no practical alternative to using pandanus leaves, the same material used by islanders almost everywhere else in the Pacific. The snag here is that pandanus never grew on Easter Island; the climate is too cold for it.[52]

Voyaging contact with the rest of Polynesia

This leads one to ask whether Rapanui obtained their customary sail-making material from elsewhere. The nearest island where pandanus is known to grow is Henderson Island, where two varieties grew at the northern end.[53] The distance involved in a voyage to reach it – some 1925 km each way – is immense. But there were other incentives to go. Important commodities of interest to Polynesians on Henderson Island include coconuts and candlenuts (for lighting), neither of which was available on Easter Island. Just 170 km to the WSW of Henderson, Pitcairn Island produced breadfruit, a tree greatly valued by Polynesians not only for its fruit – a staple food – but also for a sticky sap, traditionally used by Polynesians for caulking gaps between the planks of oceangoing canoes.[54] The inhabitants of these two tiny islands could supply Polynesian pigs too, a resource from Southeast Asia that Rapanui lacked.[55] Whether such commodities were actually traded with Easter Island we do not know, but en route lies the atoll of Ducie, the nearest known source of the mother-of-pearl oyster shells that Roggeveen saw being worn as neck pendants by Rapanui in 1722.

All we can say with certainty is that such valued commodities were available to anyone prepared to sail this far.[56]

Contact with South America

There is stronger evidence, though, that Rapanui set out from Easter Island in the opposite direction, to the east, for there was evidently some kind of contact – direct or indirect – with South America. Both Roggeveen and Cook refer to plantations of kūmara on the island, a vegetable that is

Local sources of timber and fibre

Alphitonia zizyphoides, *above, is now extinct on Easter Island, but produces a very hard wood that is valued across much of Polynesia for making canoes and paddles; its original Rapanui name is unknown, but elsewhere in Polynesia it is known as toi.*
Hauhau (Sacramento bur, Triumfetta semitriloba, below), is a small shrub (1–1.5 m) that has been growing in the Easter Island craters for at least 35,000 years. The bark produces a tough fibre that was used for making rope and fishing lines. The globe shows the distribution of the name **hauhau** *for small shrubs or trees of the* Malvaceae *family with spiky fruits and serrated, heart-shaped leaves – applied in New Zealand to whau (Entelea arborescens).*

Above: *Chief's breast ornament made of pearl oyster shell and sennit (coconut fibre) in a style typical of much of Polynesia.*

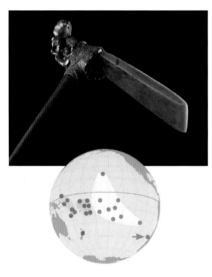

Above: **Toki** *(ceremonial adze) from New Zealand; the globe shows how the distribution of this term for an adze or axe extends east to the Mapuche of South America (arrow).*

native only to that continent.

Some have questioned whether the seeds or tubers might have reached the island by natural means, but this has been ruled out. A thorough search across the Pacific has failed to find any wild population of the plant, either here or elsewhere, whose presence might predate its rapid adoption as a crop across East Polynesia.[57] It clearly reached these islands with the help of people, but who were they? Did their voyage originate in the Americas or in the Pacific?

As we know, Heyerdahl favoured a vessel from the Americas, but his reasoning failed to address one of the most basic questions: what would motivate Peruvians – with no shortage of land and no deep-sea voyaging traditions of their own – to set out on a downwind voyage into unknown seas entrusted with a wealth of planting material?[58]

Meanwhile, others who continued to engage with a broader suite of evidence came to a very different conclusion: kūmara was introduced to the Pacific by Polynesians.[59] Polynesians tick all the boxes: they possessed the motive, and had developed the voyaging technology and the navigational expertise to re-locate tiny, remote islands. All three factors are reflected in the extraordinarily widespread distribution of their oceanic horticulture.

Support for contact along this route includes the remains of Polynesian chickens that were unearthed from an archaeological site in Chile in 2007.[60] And the word used by the indigenous Mapuche people of central Chile for a polished stone axe, toki, is identical with the Polynesia-wide term for a stone adze: both artefacts are stylistically similar, and have similar functional and ceremonial prestige uses.[61]

But what would prompt Polynesian voyagers, as yet unaware of the existence of the kūmara, to venture so far to the east? Besides the perennial attraction of finding new land, there was a more specific lure: the annual migrations of oceanic birds, including petrels and shearwaters. In autumn, huge flocks of them are riding the westerly winds just to the south of Easter Island, eager to exploit the extraordinarily rich marine life of the Humboldt Current running up the west coast of South America. With their nesting duties now over, the drawcard for them lies in the cold, nutrient-rich waters of the Pacific hitting the continental shelf and creating a strong upwelling that sustains what is believed to be the most productive marine ecosystem in the world. That is, this current is teeming with food. By following the birds, Polynesians too would find an uncommonly rich source of meat: mackerel, sardines, anchovies, turtles, marine mammals and Humboldt penguins.[62]

A circuitous return

How, though, might a voyager from Easter Island get back to it once they had entered the Humboldt Current – a current so strong that it would sweep their craft swiftly north along the rocky southern coast of Chile?

According to two recent reviews of multidisciplinary knowledge about the kūmara and its oceanic distribution, an indirect route of return is likely: the voyagers would continue to sail some 3500 km north to where the South Equatorial Current veers sharply west. It is at this latitude that they would encounter their first safe port, a natural harbour with plentiful freshwater,

Birdman art

Birdman motifs on a rock on Easter Island, above. The offshore islet in the background is Motu Nui, to which contestants in the Rapanui 'birdman cult' ritual once swam to retrieve the first egg of a sooty tern.

An undated stone bead, right, shown at actual size, just 12 mm across, and three times magnified, with birdman motif found on

Puná Island, Gulf of Guayaquil, Ecuador (now housed in the Kon-Tiki Museum, Oslo), which one archaeologist suggests may be an old Manteño-style spindle-whorl (for spinning fibre), taking the birdman design on it as proof of early contact with South America. However, very sharp edges to the carving suggest that it may have been carved with a modern knife.[63]

good fishing and timber for repairs – the Gulf of Guayaquil, Ecuador.[64] The location of the harbour is significant, for a genetic analysis of historical collections of kūmara plant material has shown this to be the precise region of origin of the kūmara traditionally grown across East Polynesia.[65] This is consistent with evidence from language that identifies this as the area from which the Polynesian term for the tubers originated. Indeed, the Gulf of Guayaquil is where the territory occupied by the Cañari people extended from the highlands of Ecuador down to the coast; their word for these tubers is *comal*, a variation of *cumar* in the Quito dialect of Quechua, spoken in the northern highlands of Ecuador.[66] It is from this that the Polynesian term for them, kūmara, is evidently derived.

The above scenario is based largely on the prevailing winds and currents,

POLYNESIAN VOYAGERS:
Contact with the Americas

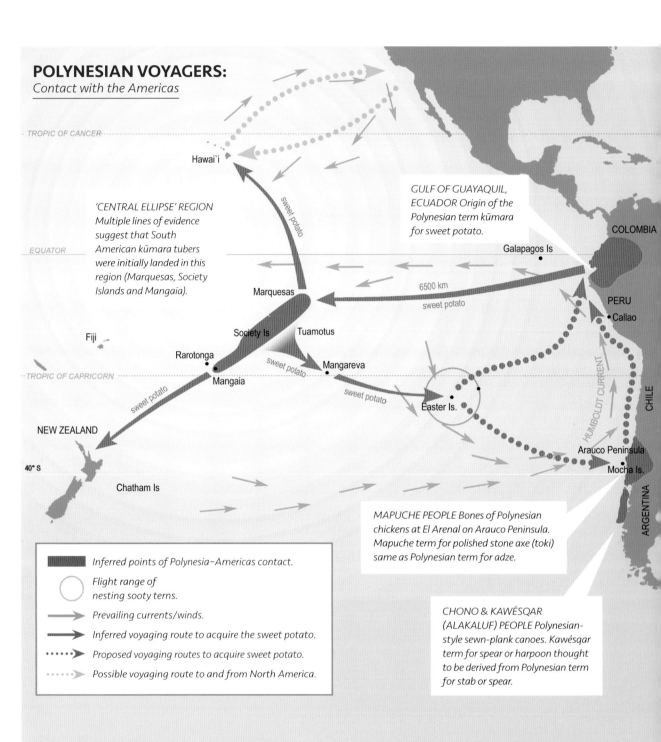

TROPIC OF CANCER

Hawai`i

'CENTRAL ELLIPSE' REGION Multiple lines of evidence suggest that South American kūmara tubers were initially landed in this region (Marquesas, Society Islands and Mangaia).

GULF OF GUAYAQUIL, ECUADOR Origin of the Polynesian term kūmara for sweet potato.

COLOMBIA

EQUATOR

Galapagos Is

PERU
• Callao

Marquesas

6500 km
sweet potato

Society Is   Tuamotus

Fiji

Rarotonga   Mangareva

TROPIC OF CAPRICORN   sweet potato

Mangaia   sweet potato

sweet potato   HUMBOLDT CURRENT

sweet potato

Easter Is.   CHILE

NEW ZEALAND

Arauco Peninsula

40° S

Mocha Is.

Chatham Is

ARGENTINA

MAPUCHE PEOPLE Bones of Polynesian chickens at El Arenal on Arauco Peninsula. Mapuche term for polished stone axe (toki) same as Polynesian term for adze.

Inferred points of Polynesia–Americas contact.

Flight range of nesting sooty terns.

Prevailing currents/winds.

Inferred voyaging route to acquire the sweet potato.

Proposed voyaging routes to acquire sweet potato.

Possible voyaging route to and from North America.

CHONO & KAWÉSQAR (ALAKALUF) PEOPLE Polynesian-style sewn-plank canoes. Kawésqar term for spear or harpoon thought to be derived from Polynesian term for stab or spear.

Four main lines of evidence allow the spread of kūmara into the Pacific to be traced: (1) plant genetics; (2) sailing probabilities; (3) evolution of traditional terms for it;[67] and (4) the early distribution and range of varieties of it in Polynesia. From such evidence, archaeologists deduce that tubers were first landed in the region of the Marquesas, Society Islands and Mangaia (Southern Cook Islands)[68] and dispersed from there to Easter Island via the horticulturally-marginal region of the Tuamotus and Mangareva. Prior to European contact, its tubers had also reached New Zealand and Hawai`i.[69]

which switch direction at the latitude of Ecuador. This suggests that kūmara is likely to have been introduced to the Pacific from that region via the Marquesas Islands, with the tubers then being transferred on to Easter Island via the Tuamotus, Mangareva and Pitcairn Islands (see map). Whether or not the entire round trip from Easter Island back home to Easter Island was undertaken by the same crew in the same craft we do not know but, if it was, they would have sailed at least 18,000 km – further than from one side of the Pacific to the other. In any case, Easter Island remains the likely departure point for those who obtained the tubers from South America. Broad support for this scenario comes from a multidisciplinary team working in the fields of archaeology, ethnobotany, linguistics and palynology (the study of plant pollen and starch particles).[70] As summarised by Geoffrey Irwin, this is 'an established view and not controversial'.[71]

Whether or not the introduction of kūmara to Easter Island was the result of a single voyage, the mind-boggling spans of ocean involved serve to put the long-distance voyaging capabilities of East Polynesians in a proper perspective. This South American vegetable would be distributed not only to Easter Island but to the Hawaiian Islands and New Zealand – all well before Europeans knew any of these islands existed.

Easter Island's subsequent isolation

And yet Rapanui evidently lived in relative cultural isolation from an early period. This can be inferred from the Rapanui language, which can be traced back to old Polynesian roots with little, if any, signs of subsequent influence.[72] Geneticists have identified similar evidence in creatures that Polynesians introduced to the island; examining the DNA in archaeological remains of Pacific rats here, they note remarkably little variation.[73]

We have some clues, too, as to when this contraction in Rapanui voyaging is likely to have occurred. It would seem that any major episode of contact predates the spread through tropical East Polynesia of such cultural artefacts as sharkskin drums, formal stone food pounders and the Polynesian sport of archery.[74] It also seems likely that any break with the rest of Polynesia occurred somewhat later in Rapa Nui than in New Zealand, for while both lack drums, formal stone food pounders and archery, the East Polynesian practice of building stone marae platforms – a practice adopted by Rapanui – failed to reach New Zealand. Of course the break, when it did come, may not have been absolute – which might help to explain the prevalence in 1722 of introduced pearl-shell artefacts on the island, as reported by Roggeveen.

As for what caused the contact to break down, there are several possibilities.[75] One is a decline in available shipbuilding timber on Easter Island that becomes evident from around 1500. Another is the growing challenge of re-locating the island in the face of a marked decline in its nesting seabird populations. One might add to these two factors a change in the winds or a reduced demand for imports. However, there is one, more dramatic factor to consider: the impact of major inundation waves or surges generated by one or more large tsunami.

As it turns out, direct evidence for past catastrophic inundations on

The Galápagos Islands

Despite lying close to the route by which kūmara is believed to have entered the Pacific (see map opposite), the Galápagos Islands were evidently not found by Polynesians. In 1953 Thor Heyerdahl and two archaeologists, Arne Skjölsvold and Erik Reed, unearthed 2000 pottery fragments here, from which they inferred that Peruvians must have reached here aboard sailing rafts. However, subsequent radiocarbon dating of these sites implies that this pottery reached here after European discovery in 1535; these fragments are now thought to be from quince marmalade jars brought by early European pirates.[76]

Stone food pounders (penu), such as this one from the Society Islands (height, 20 cm), are absent from Easter Island, suggesting a period of isolated cultural development.

Local impact of the 1960 tsunami from Chile

Below: A tsunami from the largest instrumentally-recorded earthquake in the world, centred in Chile on 23 May 1960, affected coasts throughout the Pacific. On Easter Island, the resulting inundation carried statues more than 150 m inland, as seen above in this photo of Ahu Tongariki taken shortly after the destruction of the ahu.

Sediments of gravel and sand carried inland by tsunami can generally be distinguished from those left by major storms by the fact that they become finer inland and upwards within the deposit. In many cases it is even possible to distinguish the individual signatures of the run-up and backwash of each high-energy wave. Dating the tsunami event often relies on the examination of other layers in the sandwich – above and beneath the sediment – in search of microscopic charcoal, spores and pollen that can be identified, dated and linked with episodes of human settlement. In the case of more recent events, such dates can sometimes be matched with historical records of earthquakes elsewhere.

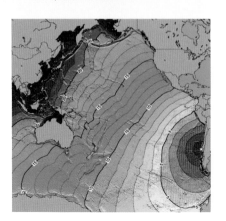

Easter Island is hard to identify with any confidence, for much of the island's coastline has been too well dug over by archaeologists. But there is indirect evidence from the wider region, including that of a submarine landslide off the south coast of Mangaia (Southern Cook Islands) in 2010 that generated a run-up there of 12 m, lifting boulders 10 m and carrying them inland for 60 m.[77] As palaeotsunami researcher James Goff points out, similar phenomena off the flanks of Easter Island can be expected to have occurred at some stage too.[78]

The island is known to be vulnerable to the effects of distant earthquakes. For example, a tsunami from the 1946 Aleutian earthquake caused the sea at Easter Island's main settlement of Hanga Roa to rise by 8.6 m.[79] And in 1960 a tsunami from a major earthquake off Chile generated a run-up of around 6 m along the eastern and southeastern coasts of the island, sending an inundation wave into the low bay of Hanga Nui and surrounding lowlands that completely destroyed the main stone platform of Ahu Tongariki, pushing some of the statues more than 150 m inland and spreading remains over an area of more than four hectares (see photo).[80]

These are just two instances of inundations experienced here in the past 60 years or so, but historical records from South America allow us to date tsunami generated off Chile and Peru right back to the 15th century, revealing that inundations of a similar scale were almost certainly occurring on Easter Island every few decades, at least in 1471, 1513, 1575 and 1604.[81]

Events of this magnitude would have had the capacity to destroy large canoes beached on the white coral sands at `Anakena Bay on the island's north side. Canoes elsewhere around the island are likely to have been hauled out; hence the numerous, now rapidly deteriorating paved ramps down to the sea. And yet even these craft may not have been completely out of reach of a freak wave.[82] With no real harbour on the island, the force of a single train of waves of the magnitude just described might easily wipe out an entire fleet.

In reality, we do not know what triggered the ultimate break in regional voyaging. But it is clear that Easter Island's inhabitants were not always isolated.

Contact with further afield?

Such are the extraordinary distances over which kūmara tubers were ultimately distributed – to Easter Island, New Zealand and the Hawaiian Islands – that it must raise the question of whether the inhabitants of these distant islands were ever in direct contact with one another. In the early stages of settlement, at least – from around AD 1200[83] – it is not hard to identify a potential motive: to share horticultural knowledge and planting material. All three destinations (or parts of them) shared challenging climatic conditions that were either cooler or drier than most of tropical Polynesia. This is particularly true of New Zealand and Easter Island, where cooler temperatures precluded the growing of Polynesian staples such as coconut and breadfruit, but where kūmara would ultimately be adopted as the main crop.[84]

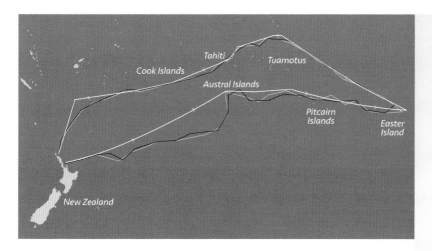

Practicable routes for
sailing between Easter
Island and New Zealand

*Despite the formidable distance
between Easter Island and New
Zealand (over 7000 km), seasonal
wind shifts facilitate sailing in
either direction. In late winter,
westerly winds favour sailing to
Easter Island from New Zealand at
a southerly latitude, before turning
north into the large intermediate
target of the Tuamotus, and
continuing via Mangareva and
the Pitcairn Islands. In the reverse
direction, a voyage from Easter
Island to New Zealand would
involve leaving a little later in
the year potentially via Pitcairn
Island.[90] On 17 August 2012, Te
Aurere (green line) and Ngāhiraka
Mai Tawhiti (red line) sailed from
New Zealand for Easter Island
via Tupua`i (Austral Islands) and
Mangareva; on 18 May 2013 they
left for the return voyage via Tahiti
and Rarotonga (Cook Islands).
Intended theoretical course shown
in white.[91]*

And yet there is very little evidence of contact. In the case of voyages between Easter Island and New Zealand, for example, contact is likely to have been either minimal or non-existent. This much might be inferred from limits in the distribution of New Zealand flax, for example, for imported cuttings of this plant would certainly have been valued on Easter Island to generate a local supply of strong fibre for sail-making. Despite the fact that Polynesians introduced the plant successfully to Raoul Island (Kermadecs) at around the same latitude, there is no evidence that this plant was ever grown on Easter Island.[85]

Another reason to doubt major contact between Easter Island and New Zealand is that, although these islands share at least one conspicuous native plant, it is known in these two locations by different names. On Easter Island, the tree that is known to New Zealand Māori as kōwhai is known as toromiro.[86]

Of course, neither point rules out the possibility of voyaging contact altogether, for, despite the huge loss of wildlife on Easter Island, the Rapanui language does share with New Zealand many other indigenous terms for birds, trees, fish and invertebrates. The two also share at least 90 place names – a high number given the size of the island.[87] What we can say with some confidence is that the inhabitants of these two destinations share many fascinating aspects of a common culture and ancestry, and that their crops link their history to places as far-flung as Asia, Hawai`i and South America.

Oral tradition and human DNA

To continue with our investigation into the history of Easter Island, we might also turn to Rapanui oral traditions, or at least what is recorded of them; and to evidence from human DNA samples taken from the modern population. But before doing so, we need to look at some harsh realities about the postcolonial fate of the island's original population.

When Europeans arrived, Rapanui are thought to have numbered 3000–4000;[88] this is consistent with the 'thousands of islanders' that are reported to have come out to greet Roggeveen in 1722.[89] And yet, by 1877, just 111

Heyerdahl's evidence revisited

Pictured above is the Rano Kao volcanic crater, where evidence of much of the island's original flora lies preserved. Some of the plants found in the crater swamps of Easter Island also grow in the Americas.

*Thor Heyerdahl took this as evidence of a visit by Peruvians; however, these plants are now known to be native to the island and go by indigenous names that are unquestionably Polynesian. This is true of the giant bulrush (Scirpus californicus; syn. Schoenoplectus, below, left) whose pollen remains indicate its native presence on the island for at least 30,000 years. On Easter Island, this is known as **ngā`atu**, a name that links all three corners of the 'Polynesian*

Triangle' (see globe below).[92]

*Similarly with **tavai** (tapertip smartweed, Polygonum acuminatum, below, right), which forms a thick floating bog in the crater lakes, and whose pollen evidence confirms that it too is native to the island; its name is Polynesian (see globe), and refers to plants used to produce a black dye.*[93]

Hauhau (Triumfetta semitriloba, page 25) is another plant that Heyerdahl assumed had been introduced; however, pollen evidence reveals that it has been growing here for at least 35,000 years. It belongs to the same family as its namesake whau (Entelea arborescens) in New Zealand, both with serrated, heart-shaped leaves and small seed capsules covered

in spines – further confirmation of a link to other Polynesian cultures.

Despite Heyerdahl's claim, the presence of these plants on Easter Island does not constitute evidence of a visit by Peruvians, for all are native to the island and are known there by a name that is unambiguously Polynesian.

Heyerdahl saw similarities between some of the 'characters' used in rongorongo texts and those found in several South American scripts. These rongorongo 'characters' (carved on Rapanui battle staffs and driftwood tablets) have since been traced to a visit by the Spanish in 1770, when the chiefs were invited to respond to a proclamation of annexation of the island by signing 'by a mark in the form of their characters', which they did with motifs from their rock art. Over the next three generations, this inspired the carving of staffs and wooden tablets in a similar style.[94]

A mid-section of the so-called 'Santiago Staff' (126 cm long), below, covered with glyphs, the longest of the two dozen surviving rongorongo texts.

The myth of self-destruction

In the popular version of Easter Island history – promoted by science writer Jared Diamond in his book Collapse *– the human population self-destructed here due to overexploitation of resources.*

Using an inflated estimate of the pre-contact population;[95] a rise in the use of obsidian flakes; charred human bones; and the presence of human remains in middens, Diamond infers a pre-contact period of endemic warfare, cannibalism and famine, which he links to the toppling of statues and a societal collapse. However, plant remains found on the **mata`a** *(stemmed obsidian artefacts, above right, with globe showing distribution*

of this Polynesian term) reveal that these were used on Easter Island not as spear points but for cutting and scraping fibrous plant materials.[96] Similarly, a review of remains of human bones found few fatalities that were directly attributable to violence, and no unambiguous evidence for cannibalism. Researchers had evidently failed to take into account the local practices of cremation and the use of human bone to make fishhooks and needles.[97] There is nothing in the reports by Roggeveen to suggest famine, and no early observer refers to the statues as having been toppled. Indeed, Roggeveen describes them

as being ritually venerated.[98] In other words, the demise came later, after European contact.

inhabitants remained. It is remarkable but true that every native Rapanui alive today can claim descent from just 36 individuals.[99] Under such circumstances, it is not hard to appreciate why oral traditions collected on the island might be hard to cross-check for authenticity, and why similar limitations are inherent in local human DNA studies.

Such a dramatic drop in population requires an explanation.

When Roggeveen's three ships arrived in 1722 with 223 crew, over 100 men marched inland, each armed with a musket, pistols and cutlass. In response to what were described as 'threatening gestures', some 35 shots were fired, 'leaving 10 or 12 dead, besides the wounded'.[100] On this occasion no mention is made in the reports of the customary diversions of the sailors during their five-day visit; but during a comparable five-day visit made by 814 crew aboard two ships led by Felipe González de Haedo in 1770, we learn that 'the women [went] to the length of offering with inviting demonstrations all the homage that an impassioned man can desire'.[101] Whether it was quite like that is unclear, but we do know that syphilis was the price. Many, if not most, of the 85 more foreign ships that continued to arrive in the years leading up to 1861 brought with them alcohol, weapons and disease. The Peruvian 'slave or labour' raids followed in 1862–63, taking 1407 men and women from the island,[102] of whom only a few would be later deemed fit for 'repatriation'. And even then, their return would bring the seeds of annihilation for their kin: tuberculosis, dysentery and smallpox.

The popular explanation that this calamitous collapse in the Easter Island population can be attributed to ecological mismanagement by Rapanui is not only patently wrong, but serves to distract from the horticultural and long-distance voyaging skills of Polynesians, and their unique megalithic achievements.

Below: Rapanui women with just a few of a 220-man French crew aboard two ships led by La Pérouse in 1786, showing the customary diversions of sailors.

CHAPTER TWO

Pitcairn, Mangareva, Rapa and the Austral Islands

Dark Horses of the South

'We may never pin the Maori Hawaiki, or place of origin, down to a single island…. [however,] Rapa and Mangareva Islands, south of the Austral and Tuamotu Archipelagoes, are dark-horse possibilities, as is Pitcairn.'

Historian James Belich, *Making Peoples* 1996

When Captain Cook reached Easter Island, he was so struck by the cultural affinities between that island and New Zealand that he raised the possibility 'that there lies a chain of isles in about this Parallel or under…'[1] connecting the two. And in a very loose sense this is true and every one of this 'chain of isles' was indeed either inhabited or visited by Polynesians.

Sailing west from Easter Island, most likely in the summer months when prevailing winds blow from the east,[2] the first in this 'chain of isles' is Ducie Atoll, followed by Henderson and Pitcairn Islands, Oeno Atoll, Mangareva, then Rapa Iti and the Austral Islands.[3] Several of these islands have already been mentioned, but here we will be attempting to retrace a southerly route between them, presenting evidence along the way that all were either occupied or visited at some point.

The main intention here is to evoke an appreciation of the challenges Polynesians faced in finding and re-finding these islets, many of which are tiny and extremely remote (see map on pages 8–9).

Ducie Atoll, a haven en route

The first haven navigators would encounter along this route is one of the most southern atolls in the world, stunningly remote and rarely visited today. Ducie Atoll is just 3 km wide, and lies over 1500 km from Easter Island, thus presenting to the Rapanui navigator a target arc of truly miniscule proportions, just 0.1 degrees wide.

One might wonder how it was possible at all, but Portuguese navigator Pedro Fernández de Quirós gives us a clue. In January 1606, he was sailing in these waters when he was led to this atoll through his observations of seabirds and floating seaweed.[4] The full significance of such navigational indicators cannot be fully grasped until one comprehends that Ducie is home to almost one million nesting seabirds.[5] In the nesting season, many continue to forage over vast distances, thereby serving the traditional navigator by considerably expanding an otherwise elusive target. With the nesting season over, most abandon Ducie, with some migrating across the equator as far as the Hawaiian Islands and the west coast of North America.

We know that Quirós was not the only one to follow such clues, for Pacific rats found on the atoll (prior to their eradication in 1997) were almost certainly introduced by Polynesians, as were two introduced lizard species.[6] For navigators sailing to or from Easter Island, the atoll's 16-m-deep lagoon provided the possibility of shelter, with access via a shallow channel on the southwestern side. Mother-of-pearl shells traditionally worn by Rapanui as neck pendants may have been collected here.[7] Other reasons to stop here include a chance to collect fresh food: the chicks and eggs of Murphy's petrel, Kermadec and Herald petrels, shearwaters and terns, plus an abundance of edible hermit crabs, and to harvest tail feathers from at least 500–1000 pairs of red-tailed tropicbirds for adorning headdresses.

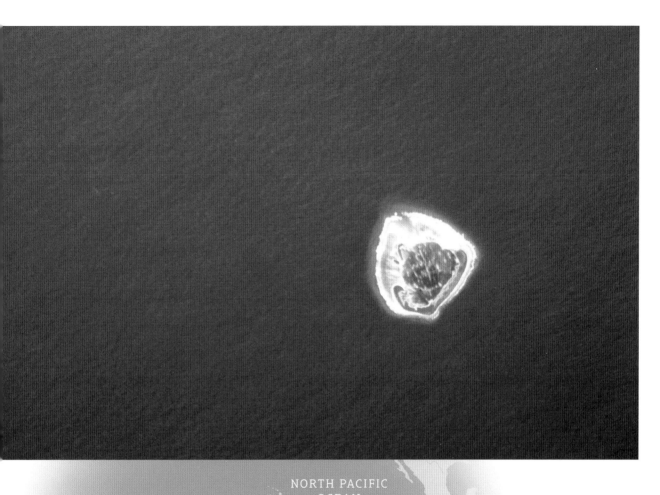

NORTH PACIFIC
OCEAN

Hawai'i

MICRONESIA

Marshall
Islands

Line Islands

NEW GUINEA

Tūvalu   Tokelau

Sāmoa

Marquesas

Vanuatu   Fiji

Cook   Society
Islands Islands Tuamotus

Tonga

Pitcairn
Islands

New Caledonia

Austral
Islands

Easter
Island

Kermadec
Islands

SOUTH PACIFIC
OCEAN

New Zealand

Chatham
Islands

Rurutu
Rimatara   Tupua'i
        Ra'ivavae

Gambier Islands

Mangareva

Henderson

Oeno   Ducie

Easter
Island

Austral
Islands

Pitcairn

Rapa Iti

Pitcairn
Islands

Above: Ducie Atoll (4 sq km, including the lagoon) is the first in a chain of islands that stretches west from Easter Island across the Pacific. This atoll is home to about 90 percent of the world population of Murphy's petrel (Pterodroma ultima), below.[8]

Above: Henderson Island was formerly inhabited by Polynesians. At 37 sq km, it is slightly larger than New Zealand's Little Barrier Island. Today, access is by permit only.

Below: Before humans arrived, some 5 million pairs of Henderson petrel (Pterodroma atrata) are estimated to have bred on Henderson Island, numbers that have since dropped to around 16,000 pairs, due largely to predation by the Polynesian-introduced Pacific rat (Rattus exulans). Visits by the migratory New Zealand long-tailed cuckoo are also known from subfossil bones.[9]

Henderson, a tough place to live

The next way-station along this route is Henderson Island, a flat-topped chunk of uplifted coral (makatea) some 360 km west of Ducie. Although Henderson has no natural harbour, and much of it is bounded by steep 30 m cliffs, it is larger than Ducie and hence more easily locatable, again partly on account of its enormous bird population. Before the impact of human settlement, its original tally of Henderson petrel is estimated at around ten million.[10]

Few would consider this island a place to try and survive for long, let alone a place where Polynesians might establish a settlement. Not only does it lack running water, but even the simple act of walking across its 37 sq km is rendered hazardous by numerous pits and crevices up to 7 m deep. Polynesians were extraordinarily resourceful though, a phenomenon that is perhaps best illustrated by weighing up the ability of Polynesians to thrive here against an aborted attempt here in 1820 by the crew of the American whaleship *Essex* to simply survive.

In that year, the *Essex* was rammed twice by an unusually large sperm whale and was sinking, forcing the crew to clamber into three small whaleboats. With the aid of improvised sails, they managed to reach Henderson Island, where one week on the island was enough to convince most to return to their leaky boats and head out to sea once more. Only three chose to remain. When they were rescued from the island over three months later, they had barely remained alive due largely to a paucity of freshwater, limited to a brackish spring and drips found in caves.

That Polynesians were able to thrive in this environment is evident to archaeo-zoologists from a number of creatures they found on the island that could only have been brought earlier aboard canoes. These include one species of gecko, three species of skinks[11] and several smaller creatures that are understood to have reached the island in soil adhering to the roots of planting material – one species of jumping spider, at least seven species of ant (rōroro or rō), and at least three of tiny landsnails just 2–4 mm high.[12] The researchers were also able to ascertain that some forty percent of the island's native landsnail fauna was lost at around the same time, due to competition from the new snails, predation by introduced Pacific rats, or modification of their original habitat by fire.

Not only had people come and tried to settle here, they had also succeeded in raising several Polynesian crops – giant swamp taro, coconut, candlenut and pandanus, the last three of which were not grown on Easter Island.[13] Indeed, two ancient human skulls found in the rockshelters suggest that Henderson may once have served as a way-station linking Easter Island with the rest of Polynesia to the west, skulls that forensic anthropologist Vincent Stefan believes 'may reflect a close biological affinity, and genetic relationship, between the prehistoric populations of Henderson and Easter Islands'.[14]

As for voyaging links from Henderson to the west, basalt used for making adze blades found on the island can be geochemically traced back to a source quarry on Pitcairn Island some 170 km to the WSW.

Also, because pearl shell from which local fishhooks were made is not locally available, it is thought by archaeologist Marshall Weisler to have been imported from even further away, Mangareva, almost 700 km to the west.[15]

Trade with Pitcairn and Mangareva can also be confirmed from remains of fish, sea turtles, crabs, thousands of birds and shellfish found in habitation caves here. Enough of these remains can be dated to show that interarchipelago trade flourished here AD 1200–1450.[16] From such evidence, archaeologist Marshall Weisler has deduced that around 50 people are likely to have lived on the island at any one time.[17] And yet, when Portuguese navigator Quirós reached here in 1606, he found it uninhabited. Whether the islanders left voluntarily in search of somewhere less dependant on interarchipelago trade, or were wiped out is not known, but there is at least one clue to be found at an abandoned occupation site, where a layer of fine sand and vegetation overlying the site at 22 m above sea level points to a major tsunami. Shell from the occupation layer beneath this sand provides a maximum age of AD 1260–1430, suggesting that an inundation from the sea occurred some time after that.[18]

Were the islanders' canoes smashed or washed away, or did Henderson Island simply lose its viability as a place to live? Mangareva is nearby, and clues exist to know of land further afield, evident from the spring migrations of the island's New Zealand long-tailed cuckoo.[19] What exactly happened in the mid-15th century, we will never know, but what we do know is that prior to 1450, Henderson Islanders maintained voyaging contact with their neighbours. There is indeed nothing here to suggest that they arrived on a voyage of exile or that they were living here in a state of isolation.

Above: Henderson lorikeet (Vini stepheni), a source of sought-after red feathers.

Below: Cave Dwellers of Henderson – miniature sheet of four Pitcairn Island postage stamps (2006).

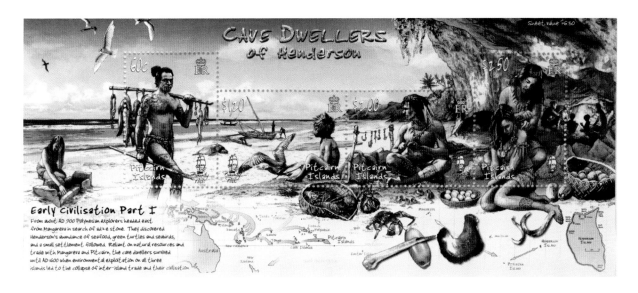

Pitcairn and its quarries

Continuing west now, the next port of call is just 170 km to the WSW of Henderson. Here we come to Pitcairn Island, a destination of which Europeans were unaware until the arrival in 1790 of the mutineers of the *Bounty*. Their steep climb up from the island's only landing place is here re-envisaged for us by Te Rangi Hīroa (Sir Peter Buck):

> 'They had seen no canoes or smoke, but in the rich vegetation they saw breadfruit trees which warned them of human occupation. On a peak near the edge of the cliff facing Bounty Bay they saw an arresting sight. Rocks had been carefully placed together to form a quadrangular platform, and on each corner a stone image with its back to the sea gazed disapprovingly at the intruders on their sacred domain. But the temple and the gods were mute, for the people who had created them had mysteriously disappeared.'[21]

The mutineers were quick to dismantle the temple (marae) platforms and roll the stone statues over a nearby cliff, and yet petroglyphs of men, animals, birds and geometrical figures remain on the cliffs to speak of the Polynesians that had lived on the island from around AD 1300.[22] Here again, the island is remote and tiny (just 5 sq km; altitude 347 m) and, like Easter Island, vulnerable to drought, devoid of reefs for fishing and lacking a safe harbour. So what possessed the first Pitcairn Islanders to live here?

The answer is to be found in an abundance of fine-grained basalt for adze-making of such quality for this purpose that it would be exported from quarries here to at least three other islands, including an atoll in the NW Tuamotus some 2050 km away. Obsidian-like volcanic glass from Pitcairn was also shipped to neighbouring islands for use as cutting tools. In this way Pitcairn and neighbouring Henderson Island can be seen to have served as an important trading hub in southeastern Polynesia for at least 200 years.[23] The climate and soil of Pitcairn also proved suitable for producing breadfruit, pandanus and candlenut, commodities that may have

Opposite left: Pitcairn Island was formerly inhabited by Polynesians. At just 4.6 sq km, it is about twice the size of Tiritiri Matangi Island in New Zealand's Hauraki Gulf.

Opposite, top right: A fishhook from Pitcairn Island made from pearl shell, presumed to have been imported from neighbouring Mangareva.

Above: A hafting tool from Pitcairn, whose style has been likened by anthropologist Kenneth Emory to that of hafted knives of Easter Island and the Chatham Islands.[20]

Below: Cave Dwellers of Pitcairn – miniature sheet of four Pitcairn Island postage stamps (2006).

been in demand on other islands such as Easter Island, where none of these could be grown.[24]

Whether the Pitcairn population dwindled to zero, or simply abandoned the island we do not know. Where else might they go? Again, Mangareva is a possibility and a clue to land further afield can be seen in the spring departures from the island of overwintering long-tailed cuckoos heading for New Zealand.[25] Interestingly, prehistorian Janet Davidson notes that many of the adzes and other stone tools found on Pitcairn 'reveal close similarities to New Zealand examples – almost to the point of suggesting direct contact between the two' areas.[26]

Whether or not such direct long-distance contact occurred we do not know. What is clear though is that Pitcairn Islanders did not live here in a state of isolation, for they were exporting rock for distances of at least 2000 km.

Shelter at Oeno Atoll

Continuing some 345 km northwest of Pitcairn along this southern chain of isles, we come to the tiny atoll of Oeno, a coral reef that encircles a 5 km-wide lagoon with a tiny forested islet, less than 1 sq km in area. We know that Polynesian canoes landed from the presence here of Pacific rats (eradicated in 1997) and two humanly-transported lizard species, and the discovery in 1858 of a blue-grey basalt adze-head which anthropologist Kenneth Emory judges to be Mangarevan.[27]

Even though Oeno is a tiny speck in the ocean, it would have provided shelter for voyagers and a chance not only to harvest eggs, chicks and feathers, but also to access freshwater, obtainable here by digging in the sand. Leaves from the local pandanus trees were available here for the repair of storm-damaged sails, and timber from 9-m-tall pukatea (*Pisonia*) trees on the south end of the main islet for repairs to the hull and rig.[28]

It seems here again that Oeno served as some kind of way-station on this route, with locally-nesting birds helping seafarers locate the atoll.[29] Canoes could enter the 3 m-deep lagoon through a passage on the northern side to wait out a passing storm, providing a degree of shelter that both Pitcairn and Henderson lacked.

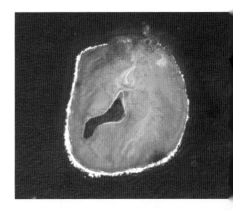

Oeno Atoll

The tiny atoll of Oeno, above, contains a forested islet within a 5 km-wide lagoon that offers shelter for canoes.

Landing by Polynesians is evidenced by an adze head (below), humanly-transported lizards and the Pacific rat. Migratory long-tailed cuckoos from New Zealand have been sighted here.[30]

Mangareva (Gambier Is.), a regional hub

All the islands we have visited since leaving Easter Island are small, with only Henderson and Pitcairn ever actually settled by Polynesians. And life on these would prove sufficiently marginal for them to be abandoned in around 1450, some two centuries after they were first settled and well before Europeans reached here. With respect to their size and the sustainability of their settlements, they differ greatly from the next island we come to, one that lies some 440 km west of Oeno.

Unlike its neighbours, 18-sq-km Mangareva is a 'high island'. It is essentially a mountain rising to 441 m from within an extensive 24-km-wide lagoon. This lagoon has long served the region as a safe natural harbour, which gave the island strategic importance both to Polynesians and to the French military in connection with their nuclear testing programme on the nearby atolls of Mururoa and Fangataufa. The island is effectively a gateway to the southeast Pacific. Today, it is connected by air to Tahiti, and a supply ship also plies from here to Pitcairn Island, a thirty-hour boat ride away.

Clues as to the origin of the island's inhabitants can be found in the Mangarevan language. According to linguist Steven Roger Fischer, Mangarevan includes 'one of the largest collections of doublets' of all Polynesian languages, a doublet being where two words for the same thing in a language reflect two waves of immigration from a single region. Examples in English are words like 'cow' and 'beef', or 'sheep' and 'mutton', with the first of each pair entering English via German, the second via French – evidence of two distinct waves of immigration into England from mainland Europe.[31] Similarly in Mangarevan, the words 'kōiro' and 'kōere' for eel reflect two waves of immigration into Mangareva from the Marquesas, probably via the Eastern Tuamotus.[32] Archaeologists can also identify a Marquesan influence in the style of many ruined marae platforms on Mangareva.[33] In other words, the language and culture of these islands is closely linked.[34]

One can trace the ultimate origin of most of the island's traditional

Above and below: The main island of Mangareva is 18 sq km, about the size of New Zealand's Kapiti Island. It rises to 441 m from within a 24-km wide lagoon that provides a large, safe natural harbour. When Captain James Wilson sighted the island in 1797, he named the entire group the 'Gambier Islands' in honour of Admiral James Gambier. Actual European contact did not come until 1825, with the arrival of Captain Beechey. Including neighbouring islands in the Gambier group, the current population is approximately 1640. To this day, Mangareva is regularly visited by the New Zealand long-tailed cuckoo.

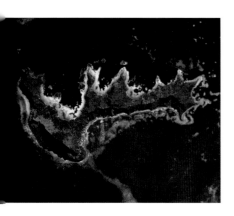

crops – bananas, taro, yam and breadfruit (fermented here as a staple food) – to SE Asia. All but the breadfruit are known to have been carried on through to Easter Island. Of the animals introduced to the island by Polynesians – chickens, Pacific rats, pigs and dogs – all are likewise from Asia, of which only the chickens and Pacific rats were transported right through to Easter Island.[35] Only the kūmara here is South American.

Mangarevans evidently maintained voyaging contact across a wide area too, for the sources of basalt used for making Mangarevan adze heads can be geochemically traced to quarries on the Marquesas and Society Islands to the north, and to Pitcairn and Henderson Island to the east.[36] Strong similarities between the earliest artefacts here and those from Easter Island have also been identified.[37] Mangareva, as we saw, is also understood to be the origin of Easter Islanders, and also of those who settled Pitcairn and Henderson Islands.[38] In this sense, the large harbour of Mangareva appears to have served as a southern sailing hub comparable to the Society Islands in the more northerly trade wind belt.[39]

However, a major change occurred in the mid-15th century that would curtail long-distance voyaging across this whole southeastern region.[40] This is evident from an archaeologically visible contraction in trade between Mangareva, Pitcairn and Henderson. The cause for this is not known, but may be attributable to conflict, to ecological change such as a major loss of forest around this time for building canoes,[41] or to one or more tsunami. Certainly, one tsunami was generated around the same time (1450) by an earthquake along the Tonga-Kermadec trench to the west, while others were produced from the east off Chile and Peru, as mentioned with respect to Easter Island.[42]

With the arrival of Europeans came missionaries in 1834, who

Above: Ancient temple at Rikitea, Mangareva, showing a large deified statue in the foreground, as seen in 1838 during a visit to the island by Capt Jules Dumont d'Urville on the second voyage of the Astrolabe. *Drawing by Louis Le Breton.*

instigated the destruction or removal of the regalia and symbols of spiritual and temporal power. The old traditions were broken with most of the old Mangarevan marae platforms being dismantled and wooden images of the local gods (tiki) burnt. The fanatical 37-year-rule of Father Honoré Laval, brought a staggering toll of deaths from starvation and overwork; more than half of the island's original 2100 or so inhabitants perished.[44] Others succumbed to introduced diseases, including tuberculosis. And with this dreadful human and cultural loss went much of the island's oral history record, leaving us struggling today to piece the story together.

Notwithstanding the fact that Mangareva lies some 5000 km from New Zealand, much of their culture and language is shared. Indeed, linguist Edward Tregear described the Mangarevan language as 'nearly identical with [that spoken by] Māori of New Zealand',[45] resembling 'a blending of Maori and Rarotongan dialects.'[46] Also, some 88 New Zealand place names can be recognised here, many more in proportion to land area than are found on Rarotonga.[47] However one looks at it, Mangareva was a major voyaging hub with strong cultural ties to New Zealand.

To continue west from here, there are two main options. Navigators could either leave to the northwest through the many closely-spaced atolls of the Tuamotus, or continue along a more southerly route via a cluster of high islands – Rapa Iti, Ra`ivavae, Tupua`i, Rurutu and Rimatara.

Above: Drawing of four-legged wooden figure (90 cm high) depicting Tū, the principal god of Mangareva, and Rogo (left). The first was collected in 1834–36 and taken to the Vatican Missionary-Ethnological Museum in Rome. Images of Rogo (Rongo) were dispersed as far afield as London, Rome, New York, La Rochelle and Cahors in France, and one of Rao to Paris.[43]

Above: Traditional drummers on Mangareva (Gambier Islands).

Right: Traditional dancers on Mangareva in 2008, with French police in the background.

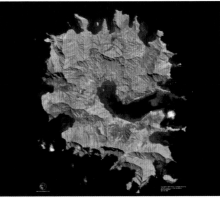

*Rapa Iti, above, is just 40 sq km and rises to 650 m. Its name means 'Little Rapa', distinguishing it from 'Big Rapa' or Rapa Nui, which is about four times larger. It boasts a good all-weather harbour and many sheltered bays. The original population of 2000–3000 had crashed by 1867 to 120, and currently stands at around 500. Tevaitau pā (fortification), left, is terraced, like 15 or so similar sites on Rapa, with steep ramparts and defensive ditches. These pā began appearing in around AD 1450, increasing in number until 1650, and again during the 1700s, just before European contact in 1791.[51] Many therefore predate similar fortified hilltop settlements (**pā**) in New Zealand that were being constructed from around AD 1500.[52] The globe shows the distribution of the term, originally applied to a fence or wall (frequently an enclosure for animals), but which in New Zealand, Tahitian, Ra`ivavae and Rapa refers to a fortification.*

Rapa Iti, with many natural harbours

In months other than August, prevailing winds from the ENE to NNE allow navigators to continue WSW along the more southerly option,[48] where the next destination is Rapa (or Rapa Iti), a small, high island some 1060 km away. While there is as yet no archaeological evidence of voyaging between Mangareva and Rapa, Rapan narratives do nevertheless speak of recurring contact along this route.[49]

Indeed, the island's extreme isolation today is deceptive, for it seems that Rapans and their neighbours were at one time engaged in deliberate two-way voyaging over immense distances. This is evident both from local narratives and from uniquely shared nature vocabulary that point to contact with Rarotonga (see panel, page 44). Support for contact over this wider region has also been identified in the Old Rapan language, where shared grammar and vocabulary reflect ongoing contact between Rapa Iti and Mangaia to the west, implying a network of contact that once stretched east from Mangaia through Rapa Iti to Mangareva and Easter Island.[50]

Admittedly, the island's remoteness today makes all this very hard to imagine. To maintain contact with the outside world, Rapa is nowadays almost entirely dependent on the supply ship *Tuhaa Pae II*, which calls in from Tahiti every two to three months, stopping on the island for just a few hours. Like Pitcairn, the island has no airstrip.

Rapa Iti is also known to have remained in contact with other archipelagos to the north. This is evident from Tahitian narratives that speak of visits to Rapa by East Polynesian navigator Hiro,[53] and from course directions from Rapa to Vāhitahi (SE Tuamotus), Tahiti and Rarotonga/Rotumā, Pukapuka (N. Cook Is.) and Savai`i (Sāmoa) given to Captain Cook in 1769 by Tahitian navigator Tupa`ia.[54] Also, rock used to fashion a basalt adze head found on Takaroa (NW Tuamotus) is geochemically traceable to quarries on Rapa – despite the distance between them of 1450 km.[55]

Rapa provided Polynesians with more than quality basalt for adze manufacture. It also possessed good soil for horticulture, many reliable year-round sources of freshwater and exceptionally good shelter for voyaging canoes in the shape of a well-protected crater harbour on the east side and 10 other deep bays.

And yet on a map of the region, Rapa appears as little more than a dot. At just 40 sq km, it is scarcely more than twice the size of New Zealand's Kapiti Island, with a 650-m peak that is visible on a clear day from not much

Rapan nature vocabulary

The nature vocabulary of Rapa reflects a strong association with East Polynesia, in particular with New Zealand and the Southern Cook Islands.

NEW ZEALAND MĀORI	RAPAN	KNOWN ELSEWHERE?
kotakota (*cockle shellfish*)	**kotakota**	*unknown elsewhere*
kea (*a bird*)	**kea**	*unknown elsewhere*
ōi (*petrel or shearwater*)	**oioi**	*Hawaiian Is*
hangehange (Geniostoma *shrub*)	**ange**	*Austral Is, S. Cook Is*
ngaio (Myoporum *tree*)	**ngaio**	*Austral Is, S. Cook Is, Tuāmotu, Hawai`i*
raupō (*a kind of bulrush*)	**raupō**	*S. Cook Is*
para (Marattia *fern*)	**para**	*Rarotonga, Tahitian, Marquesas, Hawai`i*
whekī (*tree fern*)	**`akī**	*Rarotonga, Marquesas, Hawai`i*
taketake (*landfinding bird*)	**taketake**	*Niuē, Tūvalu*
ngoio (*landfinding bird*)	**ngoio**	*Cook Is (N. & S.), Tuāmotu, Mangareva*
tāmure (*snapper fish*)	**tamure**	*Austral Is, Tuāmotu, N. Cook Is*

*Below: The **hangehange** (Geniostoma rupestre) of New Zealand with globe depicting distribution of this name for Geniostoma shrubs or trees, applied on Rapa to ange (Geniostoma rapense).*

*Far right: The **ngaio** (Myoporum laetum) of New Zealand with globe depicting distribution of this name for various trees of the Myoporum genus, applied on Rapa to Myoporum rapense.*

more than 100 km – or a little further with the aid of its frequent cap of cloud. Its nearest neighbour, Ra`ivavae to the northwest, lies 530 km away. Perhaps voyagers were led to find Rapa while exploiting a fishing hotspot over an underwater seamount range that extends in this direction from the Southern Cooks. The roaming flights of local seabirds would doubtless have helped. In spring, black-winged petrels are returning from the subtropical North Pacific to nest here in large numbers on nearby rookery islets. While raising their chicks, parent birds may be absent from their nesting grounds for 4 to 5 days, implying that they forage over considerable distances.[56]

To date when the island was first discovered, researchers have used a suite of ecological indicators contained within core soil samples. From taking these samples, they can identify a sudden increase in charcoal around AD 1200, coinciding with the extinction of many native plants and invertebrates. At around this date, native palm pollen and tree fern spores suddenly give way to pollen from taro, grasses and sedges, and spores of introduced tangle fern (*Dicranopteris*), and remains of an introduced earwig species appear along with a range of introduced beetles.[57] These abrupt changes in the island's ecology mark the first discernible impact of humans.

So, despite the island's remoteness, we now know it was discovered by Polynesians more than two centuries before Portuguese mariners began their exploration of the west coast of Africa. This is indeed true of most of Polynesia.

Like Rapa Nui (Easter Island), Rapa Iti lies just outside the tropics, in waters too cool for the formation of coral reefs. While the climate is warm enough here for growing banana, yam, gourd, Malay apple, kūmara and taro, low winter temperatures and frequent fog precluded the growing of other important Polynesian crops, such as coconut, breadfruit and plantain. In this sense, Rapans and New Zealand Māori were up against very similar challenges, both with respect to horticulture and resisting the cold and wet conditions of their winters. Both introduced Pacific rats and dogs, but neither would acquire pigs or poultry.[58]

As on Easter Island, efforts to cross-check Rapan oral history record for authenticity are seriously compromised by a calamitous collapse in population. When Europeans found the island in 1791, over 2000 people lived here and yet, in just six years (1824–1830), three quarters of the population succumbed to introduced diseases.[59] By 1867, numbers had plummeted to just 120. A full 95 percent of the original population were lost. Hence, it is hard to know how much further Rapan voyaging may have extended.

However, from an extensive study of the island, environmental archaeologist Matiu Prebble, makes an interesting point that, 'Rapa is really the island which stands out as a connecting point [in pre-European times between New Zealand and] the rest of Polynesia'.[60] Indeed, Rapa lies 'just' 3640 km ENE of East Cape, North Island, which is closer to New Zealand than better-known homelands of Māori, such as the Society Islands.[61] Many New Zealand place names can be recognised on the island, occurring at a density far higher than that recorded for the Society Islands.[62] In many senses, Rapa can be considered part of the regional homeland of Māori.

Above: Drawing of a young Rapan man, 1820.

Winters on Rapa

In the winter on Rapa, traditional clothing consisted of 'two pieces the size and shape of a very large door mat… One… they fasten around the neck which reaches the loins. The other is made fast to the loins so that the upper one covers the lower one a few inches. These… cloaks are very heavy, [made from paper mulberry bark]… by which means they can withstand the rain for a month and not get wet'. Hugh Cuming goes on to describe their houses as being like a 'large wagon having the wheels and the shafts taken off, the roof neatly thatched with rushes of about two feet thick, having a door at each end and three feet high, and two small windows a foot square. The fire place nearly at one end. Each house about 14 feet long and 10 broad'.[63]

The Austral Islands

The Austral Islands are here introduced, from east to west.

Ra`ivavae – 8.5 km long; peak 435 m

Some 100 marae platforms here, at least 25 of which were orientated to the rising and setting points of significant stars – a phenomenon that archaeologist Edmundo Edwards attributes to the island's proximity to the Tropic of Capricorn.[64] Entry into the lagoon is via a pass in the north side. The 2.3 m female stone figure (tiki) on the right (since removed to the Gauguin Museum in Tahiti) is one of more than 60 huge stone tiki statues that once stood here. Its style conforms to the classic East Polynesian hands-on-belly tiki pose.

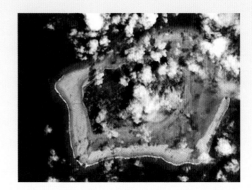

Tupua`i (Tubuai) – 9.5 km long; peak 422 m

Entry into the lagoon is via a pass on the north side. The first Europeans to land were the mutineers of the Bounty *in 1789. Finding some 3000 inhabitants, they purchased land with 'a quantity of red feathers' brought from Tahiti, and introduced 312 pigs, which quickly rooted up the existing gardens. After killing 60 locals, the mutineers fled.*

Rurutu – 11 km long; peak 384 m

A small, raised makatea platform (32 sq km) surrounded by steep, coral cliffs that drop onto white sandy beaches, protected by a narrow fringing reef. Two passes – one on each side of the island – permit sizeable craft to enter. Rurutuan basalt was exported to Ra`ivavae, Aratika (Tuamotus) and Ma`uke (S. Cook Islands).[65] Excavations in  *the dune valley of Peva on the east coast reveal settlement from the late 13th century.[66] Besides harvesting the existing fauna,[67] Rurutuans brought pigs, chickens, Pacific dogs and rats, along with a wide range of traditional crops, including breadfruit, wetland taro and kūmara. Some of the many caves here were previously occupied; however, by the time Captain Cook passed through these waters, Rurutuans were living in large, oval-ended houses, each capable of housing a large family group of about 20 people.[68]*

A 3 cm-long, whale-tooth tiki pendant found here, dating from the 1700s (right), is carved in human form, with eyes notched in the head, a chiefly collar, folded arms and legs represented by chevrons, and fanning toes.

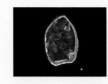

Rimatara – 3.5 km across; peak 86 m

The westernmost inhabited island of the group – a tiny, circular, coral plateau (makatea). Although anchoring is hard, the island's Kuhl's lorikeet (`ura), below, are understood to have attracted Tahitians in search of red feathers.[69] According to the pollen record, the original pandanus swamp forest was burnt soon after the island was settled, probably for growing taro. Rimatara was not found by Europeans until 1811.

Austral Islands, another homeland of Māori

Some 525 km northwest of Rapa comes a much larger and more reliable target: a cluster of four volcanic islands known as the Austral Islands, a southeastern extension of the Southern Cook Islands,[70] that are today linked by air to Tahiti. Of the four that are inhabited, two (Rurutu and Rimatara) are raised platforms of coral, with the others (Ra`ivavae and Tupua`i) being 'high islands' that rise to over 400 m from within beautiful lagoons. While the largest is no bigger than New Zealand's Rangitoto and Motutapu Islands combined, all except Rimatara offer safe natural harbours.

Voyaging between the Australs and Southern Cooks is evident from the transfer of tool-making basalt from Rurutu to Ma`uke (S. Cook Is.),[71] a distance of some 675 km.[72] Further support for contact along this route can be seen in shared nature vocabulary and place names.[73] An adze head made of basalt from a quarry on Rurutu has also been found on Aratika (NW Tuamotus), evidence of contact with the Tuamotus some 980 km to the northeast.[74] Voyaging links to the Society Islands, some 550 km to the north, are also evident. Confirmation is found in strong affinities in language and culture, and in the ability of Society Island navigator Tupa`ia to give Captain Cook an accurate bearing from Meheti`a (Society Is.) to Tupua`i (Austral Is.). Contact with the Society Islands can also be independently corroborated from the DNA of a tiny endemic Pacific island tree snail.

This snail occurs naturally only on the island of Tahiti, where the shells are either white or dark brown. Polynesians selected only the white shells to make necklaces, transporting live snails by canoe to establish populations on other islands.[75] An analysis of local lineages of genotyped DNA reveals that populations of these snails were transferred from Tahiti to all four inhabited islands of the Australs, and at least two of the Southern Cook Islands.

A high degree of interarchipelago contact is consistent with Austral traditions, which speak of Tute of Rurutu voyaging throughout the Society Islands, Tuamotus and to Mangareva.[76] Austral Island navigators evidently retained interarchipelago voyaging skills right through to the end of the 18th century, when the first European navigators to reach these islands witnessed large double canoes still in use for long-distance voyaging, and outrigger canoes with raised sterns and made of split planks sewn together. Te Rangi Hīroa elaborates, telling us that these canoes were 'decorated with sea-birds' feathers held under the lashings of the topstrake in apparently the same technique as in New Zealand war canoes'.[77]

Carbon-dating of archaeological remains allows settlement of the Austral Islands to be traced back to AD 1200–1450,[78] when pigs, chickens, Pacific dogs and rats were introduced to many, along with a wide range of traditional Polynesian crops, including breadfruit, wetland taro and kūmara. The former importance of Rurutu and Ra`ivavae is evident from archaeological remains, including that of some 100 marae platforms and more than 60 huge stone tiki statues on Ra`ivavae, and many similar tiki that were removed from Rurutu by missionaries in 1826.[79] On Ra`ivavae, archaeologists have also identified, several terraced, defensive (pā) sites.

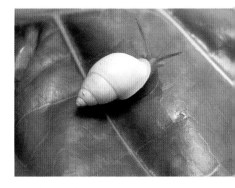

Above: Polynesian tree snails (Partula hyalina) are typically the size of a small fingernail, and were transported from Tahiti to several islands in the Southern Cooks and Austral Islands.

Above: Wooden figure, 117 cm high, from Rurutu depicting A`a in the act of creating other gods and men, 30 of which cover the surface of his body. (This is a replica from Moera`i; the original is held in the British Museum, London). A cavity within contained 24 small figures that were removed in 1882, but researchers believe that the original function of A`a may have been to serve as a reliquary for the skull and long bones of a human being.[80]

AUSTRAL ISLANDS: *Languages and trade*

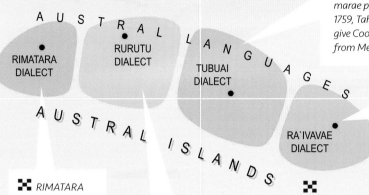

■ TUPUA'I (TUBUAI) *Numerous stone marae platforms. Resources: pearl shell. In 1759, Tahitian navigator, Tupa'ia, was able to give Cook accurate directions to this island from Meheti'a (Society Is.).*

TROPIC OF CAPRICORN

■ RA'IVAVAE *Stone marae platforms and defensive terraces (pā); large stone tiki statues. Resources: sandalwood, pearl shell. Basalt imported from Rurutu for adzes.*

25°

■ RIMATARA *Stone marae platforms. Resources: Kuhl's lorikeet red feathers sought after as ornament.*

■ RURUTU *Stone marae platforms. Resources: basalt exported to Ra'ivavae, Ma'uke and NW Tuamotus; whales, turtles, red-tailed tropicbirds.*

■ RAPA (RAPA ITI) *At least one stone marae platform. Inhabited since circa AD 1200 with defensive terraces (pā) from AD 1450. Resources: basalt exported to NW Tuamotus; turtles, crayfish, sandalwood.*

B A S S
I S L A N D S

RAPAN LANGUAGE

■ *Islands with archaeological remains of marae platforms.*

➡ *Interarchipelago trade of basalt.*

⇨ *Interarchipelago trade of white tree snails.*

MAROTIRI
Tiny group of uninhabited rocks. Important seabird rookery.

145° W

SOCIETY IS.
TAHITI

20° S

■ AITUTAKI

MA'UKE

S. COOK IS

■ RAROTONGA

MANGAIA

■ MARIA

RIMUTARA   RURUTU

TUPUA'I

RA'IVAVAE

Maria Atoll is believed to have provided a prehistoric voyaging link between the Austral Islands and the Southern Cook Islands.

AUSTRAL IS.

160° W

150° W

RAPA ITI ■

0   50   100 km

The first Europeans to visit these islands reported on a large and healthy population;[81] however, with their continued arrival through the early 1800s came unfamiliar diseases – flu or smallpox or both – ultimately wiping out 90 percent of the population.[82] As in much of Polynesia, the wholesale loss of storytellers and cultural heirlooms broke many strands of the lineage of oral history. However, by piecing together these fragments of evidence, we can fortunately still see that, prior to the impact of European contact, the inhabitants of these islands were not isolated and that they were indeed long-distance two-way voyagers. Further, archaeologists are now confident in including the Austral Islands in the homeland region of New Zealand Māori, the area from which their ancestors set sail.[83]

Cook's chain of southern isles reviewed

Every island mentioned in this chapter was visited by Polynesians, and all but the tiniest also supported permanent Polynesian settlements. All lie more or less along the same latitude,[84] near the 'Tropic of Capricorn' (at about 23°S), the highest latitude at which the sun passes directly overhead.[85] To the traditional navigator, this is potentially significant, for at this latitude a seasonal alternation in wind regimes occurs, allowing the route to be sailed in either direction, depending on the month.

Heading west, as we have done, navigators are likely to have departed in the warmer months. Whether any single navigator sailed the entire route through to New Zealand is not known, but if they did, they are likely to have departed on the final leg either via the Southern Cook Islands or Austral Islands.[86]

Contact with New Zealand?

In the early stages of settlement, the inhabitants of these southern isles had a compelling motive to maintain some kind of contact to exchange cool-climate horticultural material and knowledge. Some very important Polynesian crops, such as coconut and breadfruit, could not be grown in New Zealand, Rapa Iti or Easter Island, and yet kūmara could. The inhabitants of all three had to learn how best to adapt from the tropics to endure their cold winters.

By the time Cook reached Easter Island, he had seen enough of Polynesia to appreciate the extraordinary dissemination of a single culture across such widely separated islands.

He was as yet unaware of another major Polynesian archipelago that he had yet to find – one that lay over 5500 km to the north of these islands, way across the equator: the Hawaiian Islands, the subject of our next chapter.

Navigation along the Tropic of Capricorn

The Tropic of Capricorn, the southernmost latitude at which the sun passes directly overhead (about 23°S), is marked on the map below as a red line. Mangareva lies on it and 'is unique in Polynesia in [that] paired stones were set up on mountain ridges to define exactly the northern or southern limits of the sun's course.'[87] One such solar observatory has been identified by archaeologist Patrick Kirch – a 23 m long stone platform at Atituiti Ruga.[88] From end of November through to the first week of January, the sun is seen to pass directly overhead along this latitude, a likely aid to navigators in daylight hours at this time of year. At night, latitude can be maintained with reference to various zenith stars. Sirius passes directly overhead at 16°S and Antares at 25°S. Pairs of stars such as Betelgeuse & Sirius, or Pollux & Castor, are seen to rise together at 30°S.[89] These latitudes can be compared with Easter Island and Rapa Iti at 27°S; Ducie and Pitcairn at 25°S; Henderson, Oeno and Ra`ivavae at 24°; and Mangareva at 23°S.

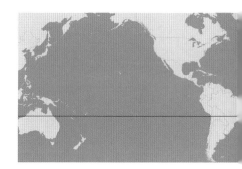

CHAPTER THREE

The Hawaiian and Line Islands
Maui's Hook

The inhabitants of the [Hawaiian] Islands are undoubtedly of the same race with those
of New Zealand, the Society and [Tongan] Islands, Easter Island, and the Marquesas.

Captain James King in *Cook's Journal*, 12th March 1779

Almost a fifth of the way around the planet from Easter Island, over 7000 km to the northwest of it, lie the Hawaiian Islands.[1] Despite the enormous distance, Cook would find many of the same crops here as on Easter Island, known by what were essentially the same names: the kūmara (sweet potato), maika (plantain), tōa (sugarcane), mahute (paper mulberry), taro, uhi (winged yam) and tī (Pacific cabbage tree) of Easter Island were known here as `uala, mai`a, kō, wauke, kalo, uhi and kī.

How did these people get here and how had they obtained such a wide range of Polynesian crops, including the South American kūmara? How much was skill, and how much was chance? We cannot help but wonder what the full extent of the original navigational range of these people might have been.

At least, that was the question that arose in my mind on a visit to the Hawaiian forests of Kaua`i in 1986, where I first learnt that the Hawaiian `ie`ie vine corresponds so closely to the kiekie vine of New Zealand (see page 52). In other respects, too, the cultures of these distant islands are extraordinarily similar. This is despite the 6800 km stretch of ocean that lies between them.

This tropical archipelago lies over 2000 km north of the equator and comprises eight main islands, all of which are just the peaks of a great undersea mountain range. Of these, Hawai`i, with its two active volcanoes,

is the largest. The whole group has become a popular tourist destination nowadays, and its beaches, surfing and high-rises clustered in the modern capital of Honolulu are often featured in movies. The main port of Honolulu serves merchant ships plying between North America and Asia, while its airport is a major Pacific hub – a gateway to reach the Line Islands, Fiji, Sāmoa, Tahiti, Chuuk, Guam and Pohnpei. Flights connect Honolulu further afield too, to Asia, mainland North America, Australia and New Zealand. Despite the links, Honolulu has been ranked the most remote city of its size in the world, and second only to Auckland as the most populous city in Polynesia: over 1.4 million people live in these islands today, of whom about 10 percent are Polynesian.

A major centre for Polynesians too
In view of the remoteness the Hawaiian Islands from the rest of inhabited Polynesia, its traditional society was surprisingly sophisticated. This is evident not only from the grandeur of the stonework here, but also from Hawaiian achievements in the fields of horticulture, aquaculture and sports, including stand-up surfing[2] and tobogganing. In terms of the original size of the population,[3] level of industry and interisland trade, it is clear that these islands constituted a major centre of Polynesia. According to archaeologist Patrick Kirch, its contact-period society rates as 'one of the

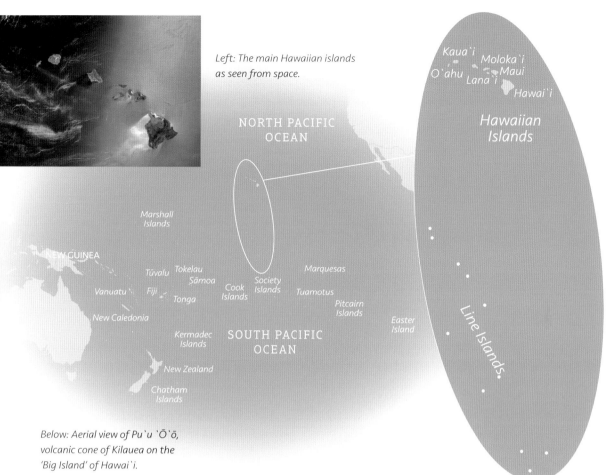

Left: The main Hawaiian islands as seen from space.

NORTH PACIFIC OCEAN

Kaua`i
O`ahu
Moloka`i
Lana`i
Maui
Hawai`i

Hawaiian Islands

Marshall Islands

NEW GUINEA

Tūvalu
Tokelau
Sāmoa
Marquesas
Vanuatu
Fiji
Cook Islands
Society Islands
Tuamotus
Tonga
Pitcairn Islands
New Caledonia
Easter Island

Kermadec Islands

SOUTH PACIFIC OCEAN

Line Islands

New Zealand

Chatham Islands

Below: Aerial view of Pu`u `Ō`ō, volcanic cone of Kilauea on the 'Big Island' of Hawai`i.

Right: Kaua`i, where Captain Cook first learnt of the existence of the Hawaiian Islands.

Kiekie/`ie`ie

*The Hawaiian `ie`ie (Polynesian freycinetia, Freycinetia arborea, below) with New Zealand kiekie (Freycinetia banksii, bottom), and globe showing distribution of the term **kiekie** for plants in the Pandanaceae family, whose leaves are used for making sails, clothes and mats (applied in West Polynesia to fibre trees and in East Polynesia to freycinetia vines).*

most sophisticated, complex, and developed of the many hundreds of indigenous societies and cultures dispersed throughout the Pacific'. Kirch, who is a specialist in Pacific cultural history, adds that 'Hawai`i had achieved a status that many would argue deserves the appellation "civilization"'.[4]

By the time Europeans reached these islands, kūmara – known locally as `uala or `uwala – had not only reached here, but was already well established, despite the immense distance from its source in Ecuador some 8500 km away. Those who have studied the subject surmise that the most likely route of introduction of kūmara to these islands is via the Marquesas or Society islands.[5]

Prior to Captain Cook's arrival on these islands on 20 January 1778, their existence was unknown to Europe. At that point the eight major islands were politically divided between four to six competing chiefdoms, centred on the islands of Kaua`i, O`ahu, Maui and Hawai`i. There was a hierarchical division between several grades of chief, land managers and commoners, in which the latter farmed the valleys and slopes and harvested the resources of reef and sea. These commoners were required to prostrate themselves before the high chiefs, and to provide labour to construct the immense stone marae platforms, many of which can still be seen on these islands today.[6]

A mutual amazement

Following a failed attempt to find a passage around the top of North America, Captain Cook returned to the Hawaiian islands in 1779, where he was met at Kealakekua Bay, on the western side of the 'Big Island' of Hawai`i by 'ships very much Crouded with Indians.' Cook was 'agreeably surprised to find them of the same Nation as the people of Otahiete [Tahiti] and other islands we had lately visited' – a surprise fostered by the fact that Tahiti lies more than 4000 km from here, as distant as Baghdad is from London. James King, second lieutenant on the *Resolution*, elaborated: 'what more than all suprisd us, was, our catching the Sound of Otaheite words in their speech, & on asking them for hogs, breadfruit,

yams, in that Dialect, we found we were understood, & that these were in plenty on shore'.

Next morning, the canoes kept coming. 'I never saw Indians so much astonished at the entering a ship before,' wrote Cook. 'Their eyes were continually flying from object to object, the wildness of their looks and actions fully express'd their surprise and astonishment at the several new objects before them and evinced that they never had been on board of a ship before.'[7]

After nine years of Pacific exploration, Cook had finally found the largest archipelago in all of tropical Polynesia.[8] It was with this discovery that he was brought to the realisation that Polynesians inhabited a territory greater at that time than that occupied by any other race on Earth. 'How shall we account for this Nation spreading itself so far over this Vast ocean?' he wrote. 'We find it from New Zealand to the South, to these islands to the North, and from Easter Island to the Hebrides [Vanuatu].'[9]

The amazement was no doubt mutual, as Hawaiian historian and scholar Samuel Kamakau describes:

> A man named Moapu and his companions who were out fishing with heavy lines, saw this strange thing move by and saw the lights on board. Abandoning their fishing gear, no doubt through fright, they hurried ashore and hastened to tell Ka-`eo and the other chiefs of Kauai about this strange apparition . . . The valley of Waimea [on the island of Kaua`i] rang with the shouts of the excited people as they saw the boat with its masts and its sails shaped like a gigantic sting ray.[10]

Swimming about the ships like shoals of fish

Cook was struck by the sheer number of people living here. On their return the following year, Cook wrote of their arrival at the 'Big Island' of Hawai`i:

> I have no where in this Sea seen such a number of people assembled at one place, besides those in the Canoes all the Shore of the bay was

Above: Captain Cook's reception in 1779 at Kealakekua Bay on the western side of the 'Big Island' of Hawai`i.

Above: Portrait of Kanaina, one of the first two chiefs to greet Captain Cook and, below, King Kamehameha Parade 2012 in Honolulu, Hawai`i.

Cook is killed on Hawai`i

Cook was initially venerated as Lono, the Hawaiian god of rain and weather or an eponymous ancestor returning from Tahiti – or both.[11] But as the weeks passed, the expectations of neither group could match the cultural framework of the other. Respect soon turned to mistrust and disdain. Then a fracas broke out over the theft of a large cutter used to ferry stores and crew to shore. Cook was hit from behind with a club: 'while he staggered he was stabbed in the neck, or the shoulder, with one of the iron daggers – a blow which, not in itself fatal, was enough to fell him, strong as he was, face down in the water. There was a great shout, and a rush to hold him under and finish him off with daggers and clubs . . .'[12] It was 14 February 1779, and Cook's 10 years of recording what were generally sympathetic portraits of Polynesian life were over.

covered with people and hundreds were swimming about the Ships like shoals of fish . . .

The people far outnumbered those of any Pacific archipelago Cook had seen: some 300,000 inhabitants in all, about three times that of Māori, as estimated by him and others for the whole of New Zealand.[13] With good justification, he proudly declared the find 'in many respects, to be the most important [discovery] that had hitherto been made by Europeans, throughout the extent of the Pacific Ocean'.

Midshipman George Gilbert elaborates on the tumult:

> As we approached near the shore we were surrounded with upwards of 1000 canoes at the mean rate of six people in each; and so very anxious were they to see us, that those who had none swam off in great numbers, and remained alongside in the water, both men, women, and children, for four or five hours, without seeming tired; the decks both above and below were entirely covered with them; so that when we wanted to work the ships we could not come at the ropes without first driving the greatest part of them overboard; which they bore with the utmost cheerfulness and good nature, jumping from every part of her into the water, as fast as they could, appearing to be much diverted at it, and would come on board again when the business was over.[14]

Hawaiian grandeur

The level of industry here at that time was no less impressive. Near the 4206-m summit of Hawai`i, the island on which Cook was later killed, we find the largest neolithic adze quarry complex in all of the Pacific Islands. Here on Mauna Kea, the heap of basalt fragments discarded by the quarry workers alone stands 7 m high by some 18–20 m across. Archaeologists describe this as a factory, one with a spiritual focus, for they found ritual offerings of branch coral among the shrines here. To bring these here, someone had gone to a lot of trouble: this site lies more than 45 km from the sea, at 3750 m – equivalent in altitude to New Zealand's highest peak of Aoraki Mt Cook.

Archaeologists can even say when this occurred. Using a new technique called thorium dating, they can determine with extraordinary precision when the living coral was collected from the reef. By this means, they have determined that the shrine was dedicated in AD 1441±3.[15]

The extraordinary energy expended in these islands is evident in the remains of more than 800 heiau (temple) sites constructed throughout the Hawaiian Islands, ranging from simple earth terraces to elaborately constructed stone platforms.[16] The largest and most architecturally complex is on the neighbouring island of Maui: the enormous stone heiau platform of Pi`ilanihale on the east coast. Its footprint extends over 12,000 sq m (equivalent to almost two rugby fields), with a northern wall five storeys high[17] – enough to dwarf even the tallest statues on Easter Island. The style of construction is very similar to that of stone plazas on Easter

Left: An estimated 128,150 labour-days were required to build this, the largest stone platform in Polynesia – the heiau (marae) of Pi`ilanihale on the east coast of Maui. It covers an area 126 m x 103 m, with a northern wall five storeys (13.4 m) high.

Island, and on the Marquesas and Society islands. And yet, by comparison, Pi`ilanihale still stands out as being by far the largest.[18] It was built in several stages, much of it – along with the rock-lined 'king's trail' that circumscribes this island – under the reign of high chief Pi`ilani, who unified and ruled Maui from around 1570 to 1630.[19]

With the benefit of labour-investment research carried out in other areas of the world, archaeologist Michael Kolb has assessed the labour involved in building Pi`ilanihale. There are early descriptions of how workers would form a chain from the quarry to the construction site, passing the rocks along hand to hand. From this and from the total volume and weight of rock involved, Kolb calculated that the task of quarrying, transporting and constructing this particular platform ran to 128,150 labour-days, equivalent to the input of around 350 people every day for a year.[20]

At such sites, Hawaiian chiefs would sacrifice pigs – or sometimes humans – and offer a large quantity of food to one of the gods before publicly consuming it amid lavish displays of wealth.[21]

The relevance of these grand projects to long-distance voyaging is that all of the above required centralised decision-making and an ability by the chiefs to command resources and organise a large labour force.

Hawaiian canoes

According to Kirch, the canoes used here for interisland voyaging were frequently double-hulled, constructed from large koa (*Acacia koa*) logs with separate gunwales (boards) lashed on, and rigged with sails of pandanus matting.[22] An early eyewitness description is provided by

Largest adze quarry in the Pacific

Near the 4206 m summit of the 'Big Island' at Keanakako`i, at the largest neolithic adze quarry complex in all of the Pacific Islands, lies a massive pile of chipped adze rejects, some 18–20 m wide by 7 m high (above). Below, restored shrine at 3675 m, showing where the well-preserved ritual offering of branch coral (inset) was found – more than 45 km from the sea.

For their boatbuilding, Hawaiians used koa (Acacia koa) above, a fast-growing endemic tree to 15–25 m. Sails were woven from pandanus, which is thought to be indigenous here – although Polynesians probably introduced additional varieties.

Dr David Samwell, who accompanied Captain Cook as surgeon aboard the *Discovery*:

> The double canoe consists of two large ones joined together by cross-pieces of wood, forming an arch between them, on which a platform is erected, where the chiefs generally sit, and where they carry their hogs and other articles of trade. On one of these cross-pieces, near the middle of the canoe, the mast rests, and is secured by shrouds and stays… The sail is made of strong matting sewed together, and is joined to the mast and the yard, and at the upper end forms a half-moon, which gives their canoes, when under sail, a very singular appearance. They generally have a bunch of black feathers at the mast-head, and at the end of the yard a kind of pendant flying, made of cloth. In the stern of their canoes they carry small wooden images, which they call etee. Some of the double canoes are twenty yards long . . . and the largest will hold . . . about sixty or seventy men.[23]

Origins of the Hawaiians

Current research suggests that the ancestors of Hawaiians arrived from the Marquesas[24] and the Society Islands,[25] some 3500 km and 4000 km away, respectively. This has been inferred from characteristic archaeological artefacts, language affiliations and oral tradition,[26] and from the high incidence of Hawaiian place names shared with the Society Islands and southeast Marquesas Islands.[27] This conclusion is consistent with genetic analysis of humanly introduced `iole (Pacific rats), which reveal diverse lineages traceable to both the Society Island/Cook Island region and the Marquesas Islands.[28]

Given the immense distances, it seems likely that Polynesian explorers discovered the Hawaiian Islands by paying attention to tangible clues, such as the return flights of locally nesting seabirds.[29] This is especially so in the northern spring, when Bulwer's petrel, Hawaiian petrel, Hawaiian shearwater and wedge-tailed shearwater are all converging on these islands from across a wide area of the tropical Pacific.[30]

On account of prevailing winds, one of the best places in Polynesia from which to locate the Hawaiian Islands is the Marquesas Islands.[31] Their subsequent *re-location* without the aid of navigational instruments has been proven practicable by heading north from the Marquesas using the North Star as a guide, with the aim of arriving to the east and upwind of them, so as to be able to sail downwind into the 'island screen' of the Hawaiian Archipelago. The critical latitude at which to make this turn is indicated, at least on clear nights from January to June, by Arcturus (Hōkūle`a) as zenith star ('star on top')[32] – a star that subsequently gave its name to one of the Hawaiian replica sailing canoes.[33]

Over the years, the dates put forward for the timing of first settlement of these islands have varied widely, to as early as AD 300; however, a particularly robust and recent review of carbon-dating data found no reliable evidence of human impact earlier than about AD 940–1130.[34] The date – approximate though it is – is significant, for it coincides with the earliest accepted timing of settlement of much of East Polynesia: that is to say, this is around the time when the presence of humans shows up in the palaeoenvironmental record on all three corners of the Polynesian Triangle. If the dates are correct, the spread of Polynesians through this region was more or less contemporaneous. Such a scenario would seem to preclude fully laden canoes simply setting off into the unknown; a safer, more efficient, approach seems more likely.

In the Hawaiian Islands, for example, the dateable impact of human arrival includes the extinction of several hundred species of landsnail – either through the destruction of their lowland forest habitat[35] or through predation by the Pacific rats people brought. Add to this the extinction of around 40 species of endemic birds, including petrels, several species of large geese and geese-like ducks,[36] one small hawk, a sea eagle, seven flightless rails, three owls, two large crows, one honeyeater and at least 15 Hawaiian finches. Although the loss of many of the smaller birds can be attributed to habitat change, hunting by humans and their dogs is to blame for the demise of the flightless and groundnesting birds.[37] Of course, reef fish, shellfish and deepwater fish were also harvested, but marine populations – as elsewhere – proved less vulnerable. Comparable ecological impacts are found on many Pacific islands, but the parallel with the Hawaiian wildlife is particularly striking in the case of New Zealand, where many giant flightless birds also succumbed to hunting by humans.

The rats led to the loss of more than just native snails. As on Easter Island, they bred rapidly and consumed vast quantities of tree seeds, particularly those of the native Hawaiian *Pritchardia* palms. Much of the forest cover was lost from this alone;[38] but the Hawaiians followed this by clearing areas for agriculture with the aid of stone adzes and fire, before breaking up the soil with wooden digging sticks. Their horticultural skill is evident from the survival of a wide range of cultivated plants that continued

Above: turtle-jawed moa-nalo (Chelychelynechen quassus), a now-extinct giant, flightless, goose-like duck of Kaua`i (up to 7.6 kg). Top: three Hawaiian geese, from front to back, the endangered nene (Hawaiian goose, Branta sandvicensis), extinct nene-nui (greater nene, Branta hylobadistes), and an extinct giant Hawaiian goose (Branta rhuax).

Hawaiian imports

The ancestors of Hawaiians arrived well prepared. The full inventory of their known settlement cargo is impressive. Besides the rats and dogs already mentioned, they brought with them domestic chickens and Polynesian pigs,[39] and the seeds, corms and cuttings of some 25 plant species.[40] To get these well enough established to produce a surplus for replanting may have required more than one introduction. The South American sweet potato has already been mentioned; the origins of the remaining crops, however, lie on the other side of the Pacific – in Southeast Asia or the Western Pacific.

FRUIT AND NUT TREES
Coconut (niu, Cocos nucifera); banana (mai`a, Musa species); breadfruit (`ulu, Artocarpus altilis); Indian mulberry (noni, Morinda citrifola) ; Malay apple (`ōhi`a `ai, Syzygium malaccense)

OTHER TREES AND SHRUBS
Fish poison plant (`auhuhu, Tephrosia purpurea); Polynesian bamboo (`ohe, Schizostachyum glaucifolium); Pacific Island cabbage tree (kī, Cordyline fruticosa); Polynesian mahogany (kamani, Calophyllum inophyllum); paper mulberry (wauke, Broussonetia papyrifera); beach hibiscus (hau, Hibiscus tiliaceus); candlenut (kukui, Aleurites moluccana); kava (`awa, Piper methysticum)

STARCH CROPS
Taro (kalo, Colocasia esculenta); giant taro (`ape, Alocasia macrorrhizos); winged yam (uhi, Dioscorea alata); bitter yam (hoi or pi`oi, Dioscorea; bulbifera); finger-leaf yam (pi`a, Dioscorea pentaphylla); sweet potato (`uala, `uwala, Ipomoea batatas); Polynesian arrowroot (pia, Tacca leontopetaloides)

OTHER CROPS
Sugarcane (kō, Saccharum officinarum); turmeric (`ōlena, Curcuma longa); shampoo ginger (`awapuhi, Zingiber zerumbet); bottle gourd (ipu, Lagenaria siceraria)

Above: Loulu (Pritchardia species), one of 23 indigenous fan palm species in the Hawaiian Islands.

to thrive until the time Europeans arrived to record them.

Hawaiians went to considerable trouble to achieve this success. To enhance productivity, they built stone walls along the coast and inland to form agricultural terraces, and constructed extensive systems of irrigation, many of them connected to walled fishponds at the outlet for raising mullet and milkfish. They dug ditches to bring water from springs and streams high in the valleys to irrigate terraced pondfields of taro. These were ingeniously engineered so as to allow cool water to circulate among the crops and between terraces, effectively controlling stagnation and overheating from the sun, which would otherwise have rotted the corms. Anthropologist Marion Kelly finds an element of genius in their choice of fish species to breed in the ponds: all were herbivorous kinds that feed directly on minute algae, diatoms and organic detritus.[41]

In the case of Moloka`i, the fifth largest of the Hawaiian islands, such intensification of food production involved some 9 sq km of irrigated pondfields and 8 sq km of intensive dryland systems. This particular aquaculture project is estimated to have yielded some 18 metric tonnes of fish protein a year.[42]

Such achievements serve to highlight the advanced nature of Hawaiian society. By the time Cook arrived, 80 percent of the Hawaiian Islands below about 460 m had been modified for horticulture.[43] He and his crew were clearly impressed: they noted that Hawaiian taro was 'much superior

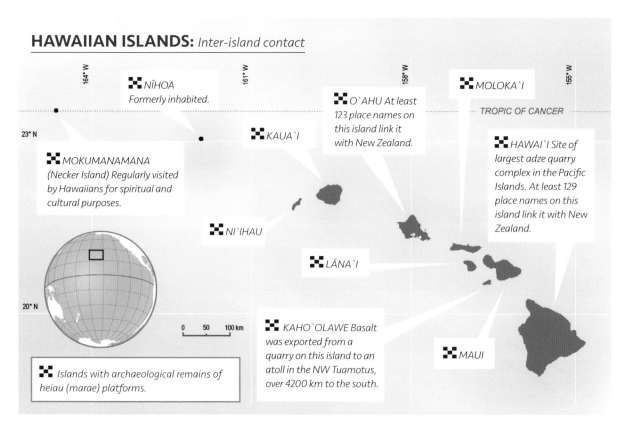

HAWAIIAN ISLANDS: *Inter-island contact*

NĪHOA
Formerly inhabited.

O`AHU At least 123 place names on this island link it with New Zealand.

MOLOKA`I

TROPIC OF CANCER

KAUA`I

HAWAI`I Site of largest adze quarry complex in the Pacific Islands. At least 129 place names on this island link it with New Zealand.

MOKUMANAMANA (Necker Island) Regularly visited by Hawaiians for spiritual and cultural purposes.

NI`IHAU

LĀNA`I

KAHO`OLAWE Basalt was exported from a quarry on this island to an atoll in the NW Tuamotus, over 4200 km to the south.

MAUI

0   50   100 km

Islands with archaeological remains of heiau (marae) platforms.

to any we had before tasted', that breadfruit trees here 'produce double the quantity of fruit they do on the rich plains of Otaheite', and that the sugarcane grew to unheard-of dimensions, 'eleven inches and a quarter in circumference, and having fourteen feet eatable'. Also, the tubers of one variety of kūmara (`uala) here were judged to be the biggest they had seen in Polynesia, some 'as big as a man's head' and 'infinitely superior to any others we ever met with'.[44] In the words of Lieutenant King, the kūmara here thrives prodigiously, in 'such Plenty that the poorest natives would throw them into our Ships for Nothing'.[45]

In the more marginal, relatively arid soils of Hawai`i, O`ahu and Maui, this last crop, kūmara, proved to be of particular value. The Hawaiian Islands are also one of the few regions of Polynesia where the plant is known to have set seed,[46] facilitating the production of new varieties. This fact may have been of interest to Polynesians elsewhere in the Pacific, especially in the early years of settlement. In the case of Māori, for example, it is interesting to note that in their search for new varieties of this vegetable, the return voyage to Hawai`i would have been shorter than one to South America. It is therefore intriguing to find that at least two of the 24 or more named kūmara varieties traditionally grown on the Hawaiian Islands – moi and hamo – go by names that are also recorded in New Zealand, though not elsewhere.

The same is true of gourd names: two – omo and pāha`aha`a – are shared only between these widely separated destinations.

Local interisland voyaging

It is not known how far voyaging contact extended from these islands, but the Hawaiian Islands themselves certainly remained in contact within one another. This is evident from the fact that a single language is spoken throughout the archipelago, with little dialectical variation between the islands;[47] and from geochemical evidence indicating the ongoing interisland transfer of basalt rock and volcanic glass for tool-making.[48]

The scope of regular two-way voyaging extended further, though, beyond the main islands of Hawai`i to two tiny islets to the northwest, so remote from them that they are left off most maps of the region. Nowadays these islets serve as isolated havens for green turtles, Hawaiian monk seals and vast numbers of seabirds, but archaeologists have found clear evidence of prehistoric human presence on both.

Nīhoa, the nearest of the two, lies some 250 km west of Kaua`i. Despite its size (just 0.7 sq km) and sheer cliffs, some 35 prehistoric house sites, 15 heiau (marae platforms) and 28 agricultural terraces have been found here, revealing that Nīhoa was occupied by gardeners from the earliest times of Hawaiian settlement.

Continuing some 300 km further WNW we come to Mokumanamana (Necker Island), an even tinier and more remote rocky islet that was evidently used for ceremonial purposes – possibly linked to its position on the Tropic of Cancer. Here, Hawaiians had constructed at least 33 heiau, where they arranged many small stone tiki statues.[49]

Hawaiians may have been deliberately exploring for land in this

Kūmara/`uala

While kūmara (sweet potato, Ipomoea batatas), above, is generally propagated from tubers (or vine cuttings), it may also be grown from tiny seeds (shown above at twice life-size). The Hawaiian islands are among the few in Polynesia where seed is set.

Above left, a drawing of a stone carving in the Bishop Museum depicts the Hawaiian god of kūmara; right, an equivalent stone figure of Māori – taumatea atua – placed in New Zealand kūmara fields to increase productivity.

NW Hawaiian Islands

Beyond the main islands of Hawai`i lie two tiny islets, so remote that they are left off most Hawaiian maps. Above right, Nīhoa (0.7 sq km), some 250 km west of Kaua`i, was formerly occupied by Hawaiian gardeners. Then comes Mokumanamana (Necker Island), below, some 300 km further WNW. Despite being rocky, and even tinier than Nīhoa (just 0.18 sq km), and devoid of soil or trees, it was visited by Hawaiians for spiritual and cultural purposes, perhaps because of its location on the Tropic of Cancer (where the sun passes directly overhead at the summer solstice). In 1894 many stone tiki (ki`i pōhaku, tiki pōhatu) were found on one of the 33 stone marae platforms here. In this selection shown right, the largest is just 40 cm high.

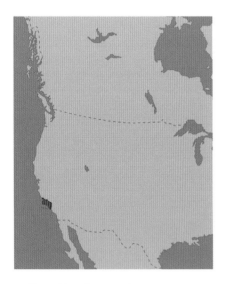

Above: Hawaiians may have ventured to North America. Red marks the location of the Chumash people near Los Angeles, some 4130 km east of Hawai`i, where Polynesian-style sewn-plank canoes were found; however, this may be an independent innovation.

direction, or perhaps they were out here exploiting the rich fishing grounds over a great undersea mountain range that extends in this direction. Either way, it was almost certainly the clouds of birds swirling over these islets that caught their attention,[50] and they continued to navigate here from the main islands, over a distance of some 550 km each way.

Voyages to North America?

There is evidence that Hawaiians ventured further still. Archaeologist Terry Jones and linguist Kathryn Klar believe that they may even have reached the west coast of North America, some 4130 km to the east. Their conclusion is based largely on maritime technology and vocabulary shared between central East Polynesia and the Chumash and Gabrielino Indians of the Los Angeles region. They note that, along the entire North American coastline, this is the only region where Polynesian-style sewn-plank canoes have been recorded, and where the Polynesian words 'tumu-rākau' ('tree trunk'), 'tia' (to sew) and 'tarai' (to carve) are found.[51] They note that return voyaging between the two is facilitated by prevailing winds, with departures to the north from Hawai`i to approach the Santa Barbara Channel from WNW and returns to the SW from that region to approach Hawai`i from the east (see map).[52]

Many scholars are not convinced, though. Archaeologists such as Jeanne Arnold believe that Chumash canoe technology is more likely to have developed independently and that apparent links in vocabulary may be no more than coincidence.[53]

And yet Hawaiians were presumably aware of land to the east, for American pine logs commonly drift to the Hawaiian coast, where they were used for building gigantic war canoes.[54] Captain George Vancouver reports seeing one of these in the 1790s that had been fashioned from a drift log of American pine 61 ft (18.6 m) long.[55]

Hawaiian surfing

In March 1779, Europeans witnessed the sport of surfing for the first time. Lieutenant King: 'The first wave they meet, they plunge under, and suffering it to roll over them, rise again beyond it, and make the best of their way, by swimming out into the sea. The second wave is encountered in the same manner as the first; the great difficulty consisting in seizing the proper moment of diving under it, which, if missed, the person is caught by the surf, and driven back again with great violence, and all his dexterity is then required to prevent himself from being dashed against the rocks. As soon as they have gained, by these repeated efforts, the smooth water beyond the surf, they lay themselves at length on their board, and prepare for their return.

As the surf consists of a number of waves, of which every third is remarked to be always much larger than the others, and to flow higher on the shore, the rest breaking in the intermediate space, their first object is to place themselves on the summit of the largest surge, by which they are driven along with amazing rapidity toward the shore.'

Above: Poeta, Hawaiian wife of Kanaina, 1779.

South to Tahiti and the Tuamotus

To the south, Hawaiian oral tradition speaks of return voyages to Tahiti,[56] some 4135 km away, and the findings of both linguists and geneticists support this. According to archaeologist Roger Green, ongoing contact is evident in 'lexical borrowings' in the Hawaiian vocabulary that can be traced back to Tahitic languages.[57] And this is consistent with the findings of geneticist Lisa Matisoo-Smith and co-workers who have extracted DNA from local remains of Pacific rats, showing 'that the Hawaiian archipelago did not remain completely isolated after initial human arrival'.[58] More specifically, these researchers found evidence for one-way contact from the Marquesas and for return voyaging between Hawai`i and the region of Tahiti, Cook Islands and Tuamotus.[59] In fact, recent voyaging experiments using traditional techniques of non-instrument navigation suggest the use of a triangular route Marquesas–Hawai`i–Tahiti.[60]

Perhaps the strongest support for ongoing voyaging from the Hawaiian Islands to the south came in 2007 from the findings of archaeologist Marshall Weisler and earth scientist Kenneth Collerson. By checking the trace element and isotope chemistries of an adze head collected in the 1930s from Nāpuka in the Tuamotus, they determined that the basalt used to fashion it was quarried in the Hawaiian Islands. The adze head had been worked to a style typical of the Tuamotus but unknown from Hawai`i, suggesting that it was unworked rock that had been carried from Hawai`i to the Tuamotus as ballast – hard evidence of a voyage of some 4200 km.[61] For such a long voyage, the most likely route would have been via the Line Islands and Tahiti.

Below: An adze head found in the 1930s on Nāpuka in the Tuamotus. Isotope and trace element data indicate that the source rock to make it was obtained from the Hawaiian Islands, 4000 km away.

Line Islands

The Line Islands are individually tiny and extremely remote. Together, though, they constitute one of the longest island chains in the world, presenting to Polynesians an enormous transequatorial navigational target. Each offers a useful resource. Tereina, Kiritimati and Tabuaeran all supported the Kuhl's lorikeet, above. And Jarvis Island (Central Line Islands), below, is home to some 2 million sooty terns.

Below: Flint Island (Southern Line Islands) sports five small freshwater lakes.

The Line Islands en route

The Line Islands are not well known; indeed, they scarcely feature on most maps of the Pacific, due to the minute scale of each and the vast distance over which they are scattered – a transequatorial string of atolls and coral islands that extends in a line some 2300 km long; hence the name.

Most 18th-century visitors to these isles overlooked the telltale signs of former Polynesian settlement. This is true of Captain Cook, who landed on Kiritimati (Christmas Is) in 1777, and Captain Fanning during his visits to Teraina (Washington Is) and Tabuaeran (Fanning Atoll) in 1798.[62] Archaeologists have since identified remains of coral marae platforms and/or village complexes on all three, though – and on Malden, Millennium Atoll and Flint Island. These remains are dateable as far back as the 14th century, and show that the inhabitants of the Line Islands were more than just castaways. This conclusion is supported by the presence on these isles of humanly-introduced Kuhl's lorikeet and/or Pacific rats.[63]

Every one of these atolls and coral islands had resources to offer, but the jewel in the region's crown was Tabuaeran, with its safe harbour, relatively high rainfall, luxuriant vegetation, a freshwater marsh and good gardening soils. Its regional importance is evident from locally discovered adze heads, the basalt for which has been traced to at least three distinct sources, including a quarry on Eiao (Marquesas Is), over 2400 km away.[64]

Such findings are a powerful challenge to the popular image of isolation and paucity of resources available to the inhabitants of remote atolls.

Tabuaeran was not the only Line Island to offer a wide range of resources. Nearby Teraina features a 2-sq-km freshwater lake, coconuts and a population of over 1000 introduced Kuhl's lorikeet. These birds were a major source of the red feathers traditionally used by Polynesians for cloaks and headdresses. At the southern end of the chain, Flint Island has migratory ducks, shorebirds, the occasional green turtle and literally millions of coconut crabs, a Polynesian delicacy. Most of these atolls could supply coconut fibre for lashing and rigging, and pandanus leaves for sail-making. Many also support forest trees of sufficient size for canoe planking.

These islands and atolls are individually so small that they might seem almost impossible to find. However, collectively they support one of the largest seabird colonies in the world. Kiritimati (Christmas Is) alone is home base for up to 6 million seabirds – mostly red-footed boobies and sooty terns. In the nesting season, the former disperse from this island on flights of up to 150 km, while the latter range up to 500 km.[65]

Of course, all this is relevant to the history of Hawai`i, for every isle in this immense chain is likely to have served Polynesians at one time or another as a 'stepping stone' on voyages between adjacent archipelagos, including the Hawaiian, Society, Northern Cook and Marquesas islands.

And yet, by the time Cook and Fanning reached the Line Islands in the late 1700s, they had all been abandoned. What led to this? It can hardly have been a case of resource depletion. The Line Islanders were

LINE ISLANDS: *Prehistoric habitation and traditional resources*

PALMYRA ATOLL
12 km long. No evidence of prehistoric habitation. Traditional resources: forest; world's second-largest colony of red-footed boobies; plus 750,000 sooty terns, migratory seabirds and shorebirds; large population of red-tailed tropicbirds for tail feathers.

KINGMAN REEF
7.5 km long. Awash most of the time.

 **TERAINA** (Washington Is.) 12 km long. Prehistorically inhabited: stone walls, and basalt artefacts. Traditional resources: large freshwater lake; Kuhl's lorikeet (currently 1000 birds), nesting turtles.

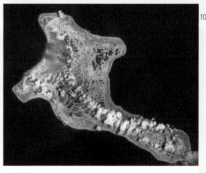
10° N

KIRITIMATI (CHRISTMAS) ISLAND
53 km long. Prehistorically inhabited: canoe house; tombs; basalt artefacts. Traditional resources: enormous bird population including world's largest colonies of sooty terns (15 million in the 1960s) and Phoenix petrels; plus coconut crabs, turtles and feathers from thousands of red-tailed tropicbirds and Kuhl's lorikeet.

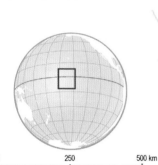 **TABUAERAN** (Fanning Atoll) 18 km long. Prehistorically inhabited: tombs, basalt adzes imported from three distant sources, and pearl shell fishhooks. Traditional resources: good harbour; freshwater marsh; good soils; formerly important for seabirds and Kuhl's lorikeet.

LINE ISLANDS

— EQUATOR —————

MALDEN ISLAND
8 km across. Prehistorically inhabited: graves, artefacts. Traditional resources: large population of grey-backed terns, sooty terns, breeding turtles and migratory shorebirds.

JARVIS ISLAND 3.3 km long. No evidence of prehistoric habitation. Traditional resources: two million sooty terns.

MILLENNIUM ATOLL (Caroline Is) 13 km long. On the same latitude as Hiva 'Oa (Marquesas Is) to the east. Prehistorically inhabited: basalt adzes and 'highly polished' greenstone found. Traditional resources: turtles; one of the world's largest populations of coconut crabs.

STARBUCK ISLAND
9 km long. No evidence of prehistoric habitation. Traditional resources: over three million sooty terns.

VOSTOCK ISLAND
1.3 km long. Traditional resources: green turtles, coconut crabs, and forest.

0   250   500 km

 Evidence of coral marae platforms.

◯ Flight ranges of nesting sooty terns, indicating the range over which each island is visible to navigators. Satellite images are shown at 1:1,000,000.

PENRHYN (TONGAREVA)

RAKAHANGA

 FLINT ISLAND 4 km long. Prehistorically inhabited: basalt adzes found. Traditional resources: migratory ducks and shorebirds; five fresh-water lakes; coconut crabs, turtles.

PUKAPUKA

MANIHIKI

NORTHERN COOK ISLANDS

165° W

150° W

10° S

Pānānā (sighting wall)

*At Hanamauloa, Kahikinui, on the
Hawaiian island of Maui, stands
a notched sighting wall (pānānā),
above. From mid-December to
mid-May, it is thought that this
may have served as a navigational
guide for setting off on the correct
course to reach the Line Islands.
This neatly constructed wall
(8.75 m x 1.5 m) and its associated
upright slab are positioned in such
a way that, when the slab is viewed
through the notch, the stars of
the Southern Cross are aligned
when the cross reaches an upright
position. At this point, the Cross
marks celestial south, the bearing
for Kiritimati (Christmas Island).*

vulnerable not only to drought and inundation by the sea, but also to any
major disruption to long-distance trading links with the wider region.

But prior to this, Hawaiians had evidently maintained contact with
the Society Island region and beyond. As for the actual bearing for such a
southbound voyage, Patrick Kirch and his collaborators believe that they
have found evidence for one on the Hawaiian island of Maui in the form
of a notched 'sighting wall' (pānānā) at Hanamauloa, Kahikinui. It turns
out that this neatly constructed wall and associated upright slab are
positioned in such a way that, when the slab is viewed through the notch,
the stars of the Southern Cross are framed when the cross reaches an
upright position above the slab.[66] This constellation reaches the requisite
position during the hours of darkness only between mid-December and
mid-May, when it stands some 10 degrees above the horizon, directly
above celestial south – which would guide the navigator departing from
this island toward Kiritimati. If Kirch's team is correct in their reasoning,
then ritual offerings of branch coral found here, dateable to AD 1444 (± 4),
imply that deliberate long-distance return voyages from here were still
being made as late as the 15th century.[67]

Subsequent isolation

Yet by the time Cook reached the Hawaiian Islands in 1778, its
inhabitants were evidently cut off from the rest of Polynesia. It is hard
to say precisely what caused the break, but oral traditions do make
reference to major conflict in the Society Islands; and low-lying atolls
en route are vulnerable to inundation from a tsunami. For example,
a seismic event of requisite magnitude is known to have affected the
southern coast of the Hawaiian island of Kaua`i AD 1430–1665. This is
evidenced by many lumps of peaty sand, found on the landward side of a
3-m-high dune, that had been ripped up and carried inland for up to 120
m, along with gravel and boulders, some weighing over 100 kg.[68]

Although the cause of isolation may never be known, its timing can
perhaps be inferred from the fact that, although the custom of using
formal stone food pounders and skin drums reached the Hawaiian
Islands, neither was adopted on Easter Island or in New Zealand.[69] This
would seem to suggest that Hawaiians retained some kind of contact
with central East Polynesia (e.g. the Society Islands) after Easter Island
and New Zealand broke away.[70]

Is Hawai`i a Hawaiki of Māori?

Despite suggestions back in the early 1900s that the ancestors of New
Zealand Māori had come from Hawai`i,[71] historians soon dismissed the
idea, largely because of the enormous distance involved and significant
differences in their cultures and languages. The obvious association
between the indigenous name for the 'Big Island' of Hawai`i and
'Hawaiki', the traditional homeland of Māori, was understood for what it
was:[72] the true meaning of the word Hawaiki is more generic, applying
to a number of ancestral homelands. Here, the name applies to the most
prominent, large, high island, Hawai`i. By itself, this name alone does not

imply that the ancestors of Māori sailed from here, although this is what many New Zealanders still believe.[73]

Further, although direct contact between the Hawaiian Islands and New Zealand might conceivably be picked up from a DNA analysis of Pacific rats, genetic analysis has failed to turn up any evidence of a transfer of these creatures along this route.[74] This alone does not rule out indirect voyages, though, where rats may have had a chance to disembark at an intermediate stop en route.[75]

Despite the objections, some compelling cultural ties between Hawai`i and New Zealand remain. Anthropologist Roland Dixon has identified an apparently close relationship in shared 'myth-incidents', 'very nearly as great' in number as between New Zealand and the Cook Islands.[76] Nor are the Hawaiian and Māori languages as different as was first thought: from a recent review of East Polynesian languages, linguist Mary Walworth concluded that 'for several generations there was regular contact among all of the islands of east Polynesia, except Rapa Nui'.[77]

It seems that we should at least remain open to the possibility of prehistoric contact between the two regions. One viable route of sailing via the Society Islands was ably demonstrated by the Hawaiian voyaging canoe *Hōkūle`a* in 1985. Alternatively, voyagers may have been led along a more direct, wind-assisted route by millions of sooty shearwaters and other seabirds heading through Hawaiian waters in October across the Northern Cook Islands to New Zealand – where the majority of these birds still nest; see map (page 148).[78]

Population loss

When it comes to the Hawaiian oral history record, we run up against the same inherent limitations as elsewhere and for the same reason: the enormous crash in population that occurred here soon after European contact. From the original estimate of 300,000 or so native Hawaiians, a head count by missionaries in 1823 found less than half this number – just 142,050.[79] By 1853 the population had halved again, to just over 70,000. And by 1872, a census found just 56,897 Hawaiian residents (including some 5300 foreigners) – down to less than 20 percent of the pre-contact figure.[80]

The unpalatable implications of the loss have previously been evaded by dismissing the original estimates as being wildly exaggerated. However, the pre-contact figure has recently found strong support from an archaeological assessment of the extent of Hawaiian agriculture, along with physical counts of house terraces and ceremonial sites. That is, the figure of 300,000 is no exaggeration; in the course of little more than 100 years of European contact, a staggering loss of 80 percent of the native population did indeed occur.

Again, this loss can be attributed primarily to the spread of unfamiliar diseases, including syphilis and deadly epidemics of measles and smallpox.[81] This tragedy and the consequent loss of tradition has given impetus to the formation of a Polynesian Voyaging Society. By navigating replicas of traditional double-hulled canoes without the use of modern instruments, this local nonprofit research and educational corporation is helping to keep traditional Polynesian voyaging methods alive.

Some shared vocabulary

*Winter snow on Mauna Kea ('white mountain'), above, a dormant volcano on the Big Island of Hawai`i. At 4207 m, its peak is higher than that of New Zealand's Mt Cook (3754 m). The globe shows the distribution of the Hawaiian term for snow, **hau kea** ('white dew'), shared only with New Zealand.[82]*

*Above: The **hōlua** in Hawai`i, used on carefully constructed stone ramps, some of which were over 900 m long. The globe shows the distribution of this term for 'to toboggan down a slope', shared only between the high islands of Hawai`i, Tahiti and New Zealand.[83] On atolls – which lack slopes – the term is unknown.*

CHAPTER FOUR

The Marquesas Islands

Statues in the Forest

The most likely points of departure [for the ancestors of New Zealand Māori] are the Society, Cook or Austral Islands, with the more distant Tuamotu and Marquesas groups . . . also being possibilities.

Archaeologist Nigel Prickett *Maori Origins*, 2001

Up until this point, we have retraced two routes toward central East Polynesia from the outer reaches of the region – one from Easter Island, the other from the Hawaiian Islands. We will now embark on a third course, with the trade winds from the Marquesas Islands toward the setting sun through this same central region, following much of the route by which the Ecuadorian kūmara is understood to have reached New Zealand from South America.

The Marquesas

The Marquesas, like so many of the islands we have visited thus far, are remote – a tiny group of 10 high islands situated about halfway between New Zealand and Panama.

I visited the group via Tahiti in 2006, flying in from the west aboard a 48-seater. We crossed empty ocean for about an hour before passing over the turquoise lagoons of the Tuamotus, then continued for two more hours in the direction of Central America before the tiny Marquesan island of Hiva `Oa appeared. As the plane spiralled in on its descent, I could see the craggy black walls of three large volcanic craters. There was no protective coral reef or gentle beach on which to land a canoe – just mountainous slopes rising steeply from the waves. From the point of view of a Polynesian navigator, it seems a particularly tough destination.

The 10 main islands are mere peaks of sunken volcanoes, their lonely, knife-like ridges plummeting from up to 1230 m above sea level to a base almost 4000 m beneath the ocean surface. The overall effect is stunning, with streams cutting through deep, steep-sided valleys, spilling out over spectacular waterfalls. With no coastal plains on these islands there is often no easy access from one radiating valley to the next, except by sea. This effectively split Marquesans into rival groups living in separate valleys, which, along with life-threatening droughts, fuelled outbreaks of war between neighbouring clans.

Despite the spectacular landscape, few know of these islands. The exceptions are generally either tattoo enthusiasts, archaeologists or sailors, or those who have read Herman Melville's novel *Typee*, based on the Marquesan island of Nuku Hiva. Indeed, prior to the completion of the Panama Canal in 1914, which opened up a direct link between the Atlantic and the Pacific, few sailors knew of these islands either. It was only then that the Marquesas became a relatively easy stop-off on a westbound voyage around the globe, sailing with the trade winds. From here, round-the-world sailors generally continue via the Tuamotus, Society Islands and Cook Islands through to New Zealand, a route very similar to that by which the Ecuadorian kūmara is understood to have reached New Zealand and the rest of East Polynesia.

The Marquesas Islands are typically precipitous, as seen at Fatu Hiva, above, and Nuku Hiva, below. The task of locating them is likely to have been aided by migratory shorebirds, including the bristle-thighed curlew and Pacific golden plover, or oceanic birds such as Bulwer's petrel, Phoenix petrel, Tahiti petrel, Herald petrel, Christmas shearwater and Audubon's shearwater.

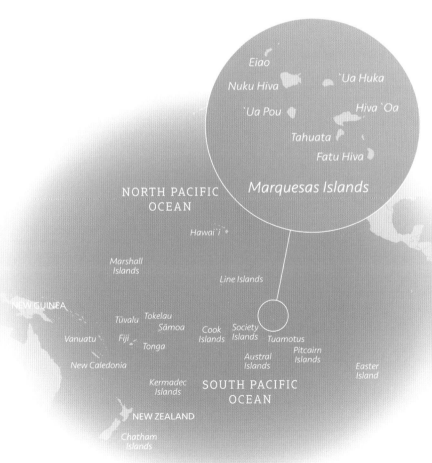

Eiao

Nuku Hiva

`Ua Huka

`Ua Pou

Hiva `Oa

Tahuata

Fatu Hiva

Marquesas Islands

NORTH PACIFIC OCEAN

Hawai`i

Marshall Islands

Line Islands

NEW GUINEA

Tūvalu

Tokelau

Sāmoa

Cook Islands

Society Islands

Tuamotus

Vanuatu

Fiji

Tonga

Austral Islands

Pitcairn Islands

New Caledonia

Easter Island

Kermadec Islands

SOUTH PACIFIC OCEAN

NEW ZEALAND

Chatham Islands

Colossal tiki

Tiki *are familiar in New Zealand as stylised pendants ('hei tiki') carved in the form of a human embryo, below. However, the term embraces larger carved representations of the human figure that are found over much of tropical East Polynesia (see globe below). The largest of these stand in the Marquesas at Me`ae (marae) I`ipona near Puama`u on the remote northeast coast of Hiva `Oa, including Takai`i (2.6 m), above (with author), the largest stone tiki in Polynesia.[1] Over 60 such tiki have been found in the forests of Hiva `Oa alone, most of them chiselled with basalt tools from soft volcanic tuff.*

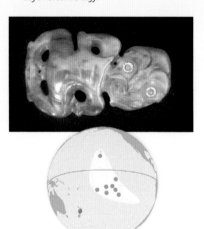

It was Thor Heyerdahl's time here in 1937–38 that spawned his theory that the South American kūmara must have been introduced to the Pacific by Peruvians. An old man here, Tei Tetua, told Heyerdahl that his ancestors had come from Te-Fiti, 'nodd[ing] toward that part of the horizon where the sun rose'. Heyerdahl took this to mean South America,[2] apparently unaware Te Fiti is an old Polynesian name for islands to the west, including Tahiti[3] and Fiti, the Polynesian form of the name Fiji.[4] Heyerdahl found further support for his theory in the giant stone statues on these islands in his observation that, 'The giants of the cliff-girt Puamau Valley displayed such a contrast to the lazy people down on the beach that the question inevitably came to mind: Who put these red stone colossi there, and how?'[5] In Heyerdahl's eyes, Polynesians were incapable of such achievements.

First contact

Prior to the completion of the Panama Canal, the only route by which European mariners could enter the Pacific went right around the southern tip of South America, the route by which they discovered the existence of these islands on 22 July 1595 – an event that constitutes the very first contact between the people of Polynesia and Europe.[6]

Álvaro de Mendaña of Spain had been sailing west from Peru aboard the *San Jerónimo* for over three months on his second voyage of Pacific exploration when his crew spotted the Marquesan island of Fatu Hiva. In thanks to God for the mercy of sighting land, all fell to their knees, chanting *'Te Deum laudamus'*.

Their navigator Pedro Fernández de Quirós describes the scene they encountered the next day when they dropped anchor offshore:

> There came out seventy small canoes [from the forest]… The least number they had in a canoe was three, the greatest ten, some swimming, and others hanging on altogether, four hundred [naked men, their faces and bodies tattooed in blue]… a strong and healthy race, and indeed robust… pointing with their fingers to their port and land, speaking loudly, and often using the words atalut and analut.[7] They came to our ships, and… gave us cocoa-nuts, a kind of food rolled up in leaves, good plantains, and large canes [of bamboo] full of water.

These words, 'atalut and analut' would turn out to be the first utterance by a Polynesian to a European – subsequently deciphered as an expression of hospitality: an invitation, `a tāve`e uta ('come on shore!').[8] Their welcome proved ironic in view of what followed.

Mendaña did not understand their language, but was reassured by their gifts. He judged these strange, long-haired men 'friendly and gentle', so let them aboard. In keeping with their own custom of reciprocity, the Marquesans soon began taking things, to which Mendaña took offence and ordered that a gun be fired. Startled by the strange blast, their hosts jumped overboard . . . pursued by the crew, who began shooting Marquesans on sight. One 'old man who [was said to have] made the menaces was shot in the forehead, and fell dead'. Seven or eight others suffered the same fate.

First contact with Europe

Spanish navigator and explorer Álvaro de Mendaña de Neira, top right. With his arrival in 1595 came the first known contact between the civilisations of Polynesia and Europe – and this new name for the islands, Marquesas, in honour of Mendaña's benefactor Mendoza, Marquis of Cañete.

Above: Fatu Hiva, where first contact with Europe occurred (in the foreground is Mary Vorgan, the yacht in which the author sailed).

Right: Honu, a chief from the island of Tahuata, with large, whale ivory ear ornaments secured with a spur inserted through a large hole in the ear (1774).

In the fortnight that followed, the 378 crew aboard Mendaña's four ships killed more than 200 men: they hanged three from trees on nearby Tahuata, where they also left three large crosses; syphilis; and the date of their visit cut into a tree. This date marks the likely first introduction into Polynesia of European genes.

In the words of Te Rangi Hīroa, 'No branch of the Polynesians has suffered more for its kindness and hospitality to Europeans than have the Marquesans.'[9] Indeed, while conservative estimates put the original population of these 10 islands at about 45,000, subsequent counts in 1920 found just 2255: introduced diseases, alcohol and firearms had reduced the Marquesan population by a staggering 95 percent.[10] Te Rangi Hīroa, in his attempts to re-envisage the history of these islands, asks: 'Can we ever see the throbbing past except in dreams? I do not wish to awake, for when I do, I will see but a line drawing in a book that conjures up a lone terrace overgrown with exotic weeds, and sad stone walls crumbling to decay.'[11]

However, from the evidence still available to us, we can at least make some attempt to appreciate the former voyaging capabilities of Marquesans.

Above: A fragment of Marquesan pottery found on Nuku Hiva. The clay in it originated on Fiji, 4500 km to the west.

Imported plants

Thirty-three traditional Marquesan crop plants, grouped by region of origin:

SOUTHEAST ASIA (18)

*Banana and plantain (*Musa x paradisiaca*)*
*Bitter yam (*Dioscorea bulbifera*)*
*Candlenut (*Aleurites moluccana*)*
*Finger-leaf yam (*Dioscorea pentaphylla*)*
*Fish poison plant (*Tephrosia purpurea*)*
*Giant taro (*Alocasia macrorrhizos*)*
*Malay apple (*Syzygium malaccense*)*
*Pacific Island cabbage tree (*Cordyline fruticosa*)*
*Paper mulberry (*Broussonetia papyrifera*)*
*Polynesian wax gourd (*Benincasa hispida*)*
*Red hibiscus (*Hibiscus rosa-sinensis*)*
*Shampoo ginger (*Zingiber zerumbet*)*
*Spiny-base yam (*Dioscorea nummularia*)*
*Stink lily (*Amorphophallus paeoniifolius*)*
*Sugarcane (*Saccharum officinarum*)*
*Taro (*Colocasia esculenta*)*
*Turmeric (*Curcuma longa*)*
*Winged yam (*Dioscorea alata*)*

SOUTHEAST ASIA TO WESTERN PACIFIC (5)

*Coconut (*Cocos nucifera*)*
*Indian mulberry (*Morinda citrifolia*)[12]*
*Ironwood (*Casuarina equisetifolia*)*
*Mountain banana (*Musa troglodytarum*)*
*Polynesian arrowroot (*Tacca leontopetaloides*)*

WESTERN PACIFIC (7)

*Barringtonia (*Barringtonia asiatica*)*
*Breadfruit (*Artocarpus altilis*)*
*Cannibal tomato (*Solanum viride*)*
*Kava (*Piper methysticum*)*
*Polynesian bamboo (*Schizostachyum glaucifolium*)*
*Polynesian chestnut (*Inocarpus fagifer*)*
*Tahitian gardenia (*Gardenia taitensis*)*

WESTERN PACIFIC THROUGH TO TUAMOTUS (1)

*Polynesian mahogany (*Calophyllum inophyllum*)*

TROPICAL AMERICA (1)

*Kūmara or sweet potato (*Ipomoea batatas*)*

TROPICAL AMERICA AND/OR SOUTHEAST ASIA (1)

*Bottle gourd (*Lagenaria siceraria*)*

Right: **Kahika** *(Malay apple, *Syzygium malaccense*) flowers and edible fruit (3–7 cm).[13] Its seeds were almost certainly brought to New Zealand, too, where the tree would have been insufficiently frost-hardy to survive. The globe depicts the distribution of its Polynesian name, which in New Zealand was transferred to the kahikatea tree (*Dacrycarpus dacrydioides*), another prolific bearer.*

*Right: Nono or noni (Indian mulberry, *Morinda citrifolia*), a relative of coffee [*Rubiaceae*].[14] Seeds and/or cuttings were introduced to the Marquesas for the edible fruit. The odd taste is described by several alternative names – cheese fruit, vomit fruit or starvation fruit. The tree will not tolerate temperatures below 12°C, so could not be grown in New Zealand; however, the name survives for a close relative, *Coprosma grandifolia* [*Rubiaceae*], known to Māori as manono, kanono or kānonono.*

Marquesan canoe plants

In the past, many have assumed that the island's original population arrived on an accidental voyage. However, this would be hard to reconcile with the wide range of seeds, corms and cuttings they introduced to these islands – sufficient to establish over 30 crop species.[15]

As elsewhere in Polynesia, almost all – in addition to the Pacific rats, chickens, pigs and dogs that Marquesans introduced – originate from the west, either from Southeast Asia or from the Western Pacific. As we saw, their kūmara (or `ūma`a as it is known here) is an exception; it arrived from Ecuador, some 6500 km to the east.

To Marquesans, kūmara proved to be an important secondary crop, largely on account of its lower water requirements and shorter maturation period;[16] but the main crop here was breadfruit. The evidence for this remains today in many large pits in the forest, the largest of which are some 12 m in diameter.

These are estimated to have stored breadfruit sufficient to feed several thousand. Root suckers of the breadfruit tree were distributed by canoe all across East Polynesia, as evidenced by the fact that all breadfruit trees across this region are seedless and share a similar DNA fingerprint.[17]

The origin of their seed material alone constitutes strong support for human migration from west to east, despite this being against the prevailing winds – an intriguing phenomenon that will be explored more fully in the next chapter.

At least two origins likely

We can understand something of Marquesan origins, too, from their traditional method of cooking – one that is commonly employed right across Polynesia. This involves wrapping the food in leaves and placing it along with very hot rocks in a pit, sprinkling water over it, covering the pit and leaving the contents to steam. These underground cooking pits are known locally as umu – a term recorded right across Polynesia (West and East), including New Zealand, where these pits are also known as hāngī.

More surprisingly, pottery was at one time also used here, as evidenced by 14 fragments of early hand-formed plainware recovered from lower levels of Marquesan archaeological sites. Petrographic analyses reveal that the clay to make them came from Fiji.[18]

Contact with the Western Pacific is also evident in the West Polynesian styles of Marquesan adze heads and fishhooks,[19] and in the strikingly high incidence of place names shared between the Marquesas and Sāmoa.[20]

All this points to a West Polynesian origin for the ancestors of Marquesans, but some may have come from still further afield.

Based on shared innovations in vocabulary and grammar, Hawaiian linguist William Wilson believes that some may have arrived from atolls in the Northern Polynesian Outliers, such as Ontong Java (or Luangiua), north of the Solomon Islands, reaching the Marquesas via a northern chain of atolls in the Phoenix and Line islands.[21]

Breadfruit, and fire for cooking

The kuru of the tropical Pacific (breadfruit, Artocarpus altilis*), above; its bread-like fruit, when cooked, provided a staple food for Marquesans. The leaves were used here as roofing, the inner bark for making bark cloth (tapa), the timber for canoe building and the sticky white latex for caulking.*

To cook the breadfruit, an ability to generate fire was a basic necessity. Below is a fire plough, known locally as `ounati (Māori: kaunati). Globe highlights the East Polynesian distribution of the term **kaunati** *for the fire plough or its two components, the pointed fire-stick and friction base.*

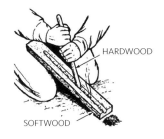

HARDWOOD

SOFTWOOD

If so, this may account for the two language groups found in the Marquesas – one spoken in the NW group, the other in the SE,[22] despite the two island groups being separated from one another by no more than an overnight sail. What remains clear, in any case, is that the origin of Marquesans lies in the Western Pacific.

Marquesan tattoos

The Marquesas Islands are well known to tattoo enthusiasts for their particularly striking and distinctive motifs, as shown above, a Marquesan cultural performer (2006) and below, a tattooed Marquesan warrior (1880).

MARQUESAS ISLANDS: *Languages and history*

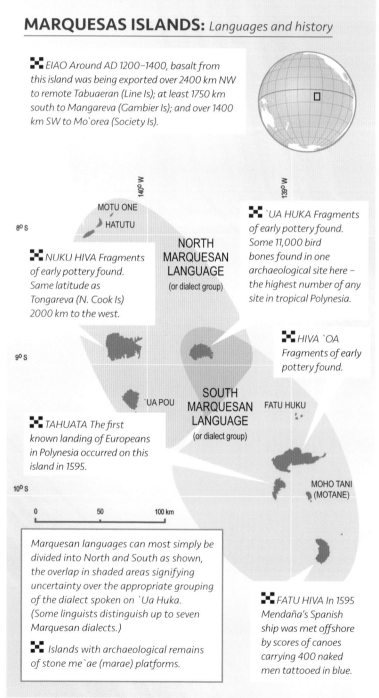

EIAO Around AD 1200–1400, basalt from this island was being exported over 2400 km NW to remote Tabuaeran (Line Is); at least 1750 km south to Mangareva (Gambier Is); and over 1400 km SW to Mo'orea (Society Is).

'UA HUKA Fragments of early pottery found. Some 11,000 bird bones found in one archaeological site here – the highest number of any site in tropical Polynesia.

NUKU HIVA Fragments of early pottery found. Same latitude as Tongareva (N. Cook Is) 2000 km to the west.

NORTH MARQUESAN LANGUAGE (or dialect group)

HIVA 'OA Fragments of early pottery found.

SOUTH MARQUESAN LANGUAGE (or dialect group)

TAHUATA The first known landing of Europeans in Polynesia occurred on this island in 1595.

MOTU ONE
HATUTU
8° S
'UA POU
FATU HUKU
9° S
MOHO TANI (MOTANE)
10° S

0   50   100 km

Marquesan languages can most simply be divided into North and South as shown, the overlap in shaded areas signifying uncertainty over the appropriate grouping of the dialect spoken on 'Ua Huka. (Some linguists distinguish up to seven Marquesan dialects.)

Islands with archaeological remains of stone me'ae (marae) platforms.

FATU HIVA In 1595 Mendaña's Spanish ship was met offshore by scores of canoes carrying 400 naked men tattooed in blue.

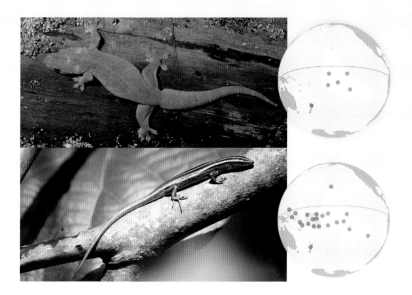

Accidental cargo

*Top left: **Ngārara** (gecko), with
globe showing the East Polynesian
distribution of this term for gecko.
Bottom left: **Moko** (skink) with
globe showing the widespread
distribution of the term moko
for lizard.*

*Below: **Weri** (centipede). A
common 15 cm-long ve`i of the
Marquesas (Scolopendra species),
with globe showing distribution of
the name for venomous centipedes
and sea centipedes.*

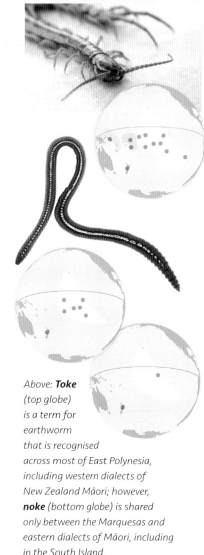

Accidental stowaways

When the ancestors of Marquesans arrived, they had onboard more than just
pottery, planting material, rats, pigs, dogs and chickens. Their sailing canoes
carried lizards – both skinks (moko) and geckos – whose DNA can be used to
help establish former voyaging routes.[23] The origin of both lizard groups can
again be traced to Southeast Asia, from where they were evidently spread
eastward across the Pacific against the prevailing currents.[24]

The oceanic field crickets found on these islands today also reached
here aboard canoes, possibly as eggs. This has been deduced partly from
an analysis of their DNA, which indicates that these insects are native to
the New Guinea/Australia region, from where they reached Vanuatu, Fiji,
Sāmoa, Southern Cooks, Society Islands, Marquesas and Hawaiian Islands
against the prevailing winds, before the arrival of Europeans, and in a
sequence that closely mirrors the spread of Polynesians.[25]

The giant centipede, found on all but the tiniest islands of the
Marquesas, is understood to have arrived here aboard Polynesian craft too
– most likely as eggs among planting material – having entered the Pacific
region again from Asia.[26] The painful poison these creatures can inject
from their hardened fangs suggests that their introduction was accidental.
Indeed, they are known across most of Polynesia as weri, meaning
'disgusting' or 'repulsive'.

Some of the canoes arriving here evidently had earthworms aboard, or
their eggs, in soil adhering to Polynesian crops. Their indigenous names
are instructive: while the term to`e, from the island of Hiva `Oa, is familiar
across much of East Polynesia and New Zealand (as toke), earthworms are
known on the northwestern Marquesan island of Nuku Hiva as noke – a
term that is shared only with eastern dialects of Māori, including New
Zealand's South Island.[27] This link between northwestern Marquesas and
South Island Māori is evident in other words, too: to linguists Ray Harlow
and Ross Clark it suggests direct contact between the two regions.[28]

*Above: **Toke**
(top globe)
is a term for
earthworm
that is recognised
across most of East Polynesia,
including western dialects of
New Zealand Māori; however,
noke (bottom globe) is shared
only between the Marquesas and
eastern dialects of Māori, including
in the South Island.*

Above: `Ua Pou (Marquesas Is), site of one of the earliest settlements in East Polynesia. From the sea, its gigantic, cathedral-like spires or volcanic 'plugs' stand out from well over 40 km away; the tallest rises vertically through the clouds to 1203 m. A comprehensive review of carbon-dating protocols saw the timing of first settlement of this island brought forward more than 1000 years from 150 BC (± 95 years) to AD 1180 (± 50).*

Carbon dating

The principle behind carbon dating is that the Earth's upper atmosphere is continuously producing carbon-14 (^{14}C, a radioactive isotope of carbon), which is absorbed by growing plants as carbon dioxide (CO_2). This ^{14}C decays at a predictable rate, thus allowing the age of the plant (or animal that ate it) to be estimated from the remaining ^{14}C. The technique works only for dating organic matter.

Dating the arrival of the first canoes

A lot of work has gone into attempts to date first human settlement on each of the islands, in part to help establish the order in which they were settled – and hence where their inhabitants are likely to have come from – but also the overall speed of dispersal of the Polynesian people. This contributes to our understanding of the nature and extent of Polynesian voyaging.

Hence the excitement when American archaeologists Robert Suggs and Yosihiko Sinoto in the 1960s found early settlement evidence on the Marquesan islands of Nuku Hiva and `Ua Huka, which they initially dated to around AD 300.[29] More excitement followed in 1981, when French archaeologist Pierre Ottino found even earlier evidence: a piece of charcoal from a disused fireplace in a rockshelter at Anapua on the southwest coast of `Ua Pou. Dated to 150 BC (± 95 years), this constituted what was at that time the earliest known evidence of human settlement in all of East Polynesia.[30] It suggested that the Marquesas may have been the centre from which this whole East Polynesian region was settled.

However, there turned out to be a problem with the dates. In 1992, shell from the same section of Ottino's Anapua site was dated, and produced a very different age of AD 1180 (± 50),[31] a full 1300 years younger than the first date. It was at this point that similarly serious dating anomalies began coming to light all over the Pacific. To find out which dates to accept, researchers needed to find out what was going wrong.

As it turned out, they identified a number of factors that can easily skew the dates:

Stone marae platforms

Left: Stone me`ae (marae) platform on Hiva `Oa.

Below: Ao`a (banyan fig, Ficus prolixa), a centrepiece of most sacred sites here, and commonly used to secrete skulls.[33]

Besides this and tī (Pacific Island cabbage tree – page 187), other trees traditionally associated with Marquesan marae include at least one toa (ironwood, Casuarina equisetifolia, below). Indeed, both toa and tī were distributed across the Pacific by Polynesians.[34]

*Ironwood is an emblem of great warriors; its strong timber was used for spears and clubs. Indeed, **toa** means 'courageous', 'hero' or 'warrior'. The globe shows the distribution of this name, transferred in New Zealand to celery pines (toatoa, tānekaha, Phyllocladus species) that are likewise associated with the warrior, its strong wood valued for spears.*[35] *Both trees are traditional sources of red dye.*[36]

1. a creature may have consumed a source of carbon much older than itself
2. long-lived plant materials will inevitably give an imprecise result, and
3. unidentified charcoal may well include residue from old wood.

In short, when attempting to carbon date remains of first settlement, it was surprisingly easy to come up with dates that were too old. Some 'chronometric hygiene' protocols were clearly required to exclude samples of dubious value. The testing needed to focus more on bones and eggshell from land birds and short-lived plant remains (e.g. twig charcoal or wood, bark, seeds or leaves).

All settlement dates published prior to 1999 had to be rechecked with these new protocols in mind. As a consequence, the earliest sites in East Polynesia were found to be shared between a number of archipelagos – the Marquesas, Society, Cook, Hawaiian and Gambier islands – at around AD 1000.[32] In other words, there was a contemporaneous expansion of voyaging across the entire region.

This correction in carbon-dating protocols is reflected in all the settlement dates presented in this book, and effectively compresses the timeframe within which East Polynesia was settled. So, rather than represent the pattern of migration as a sequence of one-way arrows on a map, it may be more accurately envisaged as a criss-cross of ripples from stones being thrown into a pond, with the steadily expanding ripples representing overlapping spheres of purposeful, two-way interaction.

Eiao

The tiny quarry island of Eiao (Marquesas Is), above right. At 44 sq km, this is slightly larger than New Zealand's Rangitoto and Motutapu islands combined. Basalt was transported from here over enormous distances of up to 2500 km or more, see map on page 231.

Above left is a Marquesan toʻi (toki, stone adze) blade about 8.5 cm long, made from basalt.

Interarchipelago trade

Although Marquesan oral tradition spoke of ongoing trade with other islands, archaeologists have been able to confirm this only recently.

Marquesan traditions collected in 1897 speak of westbound voyages over distances of some 2500 km to Rarotonga (S. Cook Is) to obtain red feathers for garlands, headdresses and girdles;[37] while accounts collected in the 1930s from Pukapuka (N. Cook Is) tell of voyaging in the return direction, to the Marquesas from the west.[38]

On the basis of shared styles of fishhooks, octopus lures and adzes, archaeologists had long suspected trade between the Marquesas and the Society Islands, but it was not until 1998 that hard evidence for long-distance voyaging came to light.

It was a technique called X-ray fluorescence that provided the breakthrough, enabling researchers to accurately determine the geochemistry of basalt,[39] the volcanic rock from which many common Polynesian artefacts are made. As each individual flow of basalt carries a unique geochemical signature, this technique opened up the possibility of matching an artefact collected from an archaeological site with the specific quarry from which the rock had originated.

This is, of course, the same technique by which the raw material for adze heads mentioned in earlier chapters were traced back to distant

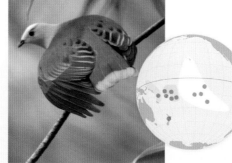
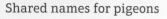

Shared names for pigeons

*In New Zealand, Māori names recorded for the local pigeon (Hemiphaga novaeseelandiae) include kererū, rupe, kūkū and kūkupa. Of these, the first is a local innovation; the other three were introduced from the tropics. The Māori term **rupe**, used for large (or mythical) New Zealand pigeons,[40] applies to similarly large pigeons (Ducula species) throughout most of tropical Polynesia (see globe above), e.g., the ʻupe of*

the Marquesas (Marquesan imperial-pigeon, Ducula galeata, above left).

* **Kūkū**, on the other hand – the Tainui (Waikato Māori) term for the New Zealand pigeon – is applied throughout most of Polynesia to smaller fruit-doves, including the white-capped fruit-dove (Ptilinopus dupetithouarsii of the Marquesas, above), but is not recorded in the Cook Islands (see adjacent globe).*

* To Northland Māori, however,*

*the New Zealand pigeon is known as **kūkupa** – a term for tropical fruit-doves (Ptilinopus species) that is recorded in the Cook Islands and much of central East Polynesia, e.g., on Rarotonga and ʻĀtiu for the Cook Islands fruit-dove (Ptilinopus rarotongensis, above right).*

basalt quarries on the islands of Pitcairn, Rapa, Rurutu and Hawai`i.

Here in the Marquesas, the primary local source of basalt is Eiao, a tiny island in the northwestern corner of the group. This is a 576-m-high plateau, hemmed in almost entirely by steep cliffs, that nowadays serves as an uninhabited wildlife sanctuary. But archaeologists tell us that a small bay at Vaituha on the western side once provided canoe access to the island's quarries and two small villages.

It was long known that the island's basalt was locally important, but this X-ray technique brought to light the interarchipelago trade: it transpires that Eiao was the source of raw material used in the manufacture of early, dateable adze heads found on islands as distant as Mo`orea (near Tahiti) and Mangareva. Here was hard evidence of voyages in the 13th to 15th centuries, over distances of at least 1425 km and 1750 km respectively.[41]

Evidence for even longer voyages followed, showing that basalt from Eiao had been transported as far as Tabuaeran (in the Northern Line Is) some 2426 km to the NW;[42] Tubuai (Austral Is) 1950 km to the SSW;[43] and over 2500 km WSW to Rarotonga – more than halfway to New Zealand.[44] Not only did this evidence deal a blow to any notion of prehistoric isolation, it also implied deliberate voyages in the opposite direction to that of settlement, i.e., two-way interarchipelago navigation.

From DNA research into lineages of Pacific rats, we saw earlier that at least one canoe must have headed north from the Marquesas to the Hawaiian Islands.[45] Not only were Marquesans not isolated, they were in contact with islands scattered over a vast area of the Pacific.

Marquesan voyaging canoes

As for the craft used for such voyages, Marquesan canoes seen by Europeans were all small and mostly without sails. Captain David Porter provides details in 1813 of their construction:

> The canoes of these people . . . are formed of many pieces of the breadfruit-tree, cut into the form of planks, and sewed together with the fibres of the outside shell of the coconut. The seams are covered inside and out with strips of bamboo, sewed to the edge of each plank, to keep in a stuffing of [caulking] . . . The keel consists of one piece, which runs the whole length [and] is hollowed out.[46]

When it comes to the original long-distance voyaging craft, we find a hint of their true grandeur on a map of the region drawn under the direction of Cook's Tahitian navigator Tupa`ia in 1769. Against the Marquesan island of Tahuata appears a note that reads, 'Mā`a te ta`ata, pahī rahi, iti te pahī no Britanne'[47] ('people eaten, double canoes long; small [by comparison] are the ships of Britain'). Cook's *Endeavour* was about 30 m long, so a literal interpretation suggests that the original Marquesan voyaging craft were longer still.

Cannibal tomato

*It is important to note when
introducing the so-called cannibal
tomato, that the main motive for
Polynesians consuming human flesh
was not nutritional, but rather one
of revenge, to appease the gods or
to assimilate the victim's strength.[52]
One plant was cultivated specifically
for accompanying this meat: poro
(cannibal tomato, Solanum viride
cv. 'anthropophagorum').[53] Its seeds
were carried from island to island
from the region of Fiji, Sāmoa and
Tonga to the Marquesas, where it
is known as oupo`o or porohito,
from **poro**, a term applied to
Solanum species throughout much
of the Pacific. The distribution of
this name, shown in the globe,
was applied in New Zealand (as
poroporo) to related plants such
as S. aviculare or S. laciniatum,
whose ripe fruits European colonists
collected to make a sweet relish
or jam.*

Contact with New Zealand?

It would seem from this that New Zealand (some 5500 km from here) was
at one time within reach of Marquesan navigators, as it is via these islands
that the South American kūmara is thought to have reached New Zealand.
We also have hard evidence now that Marquesan basalt was being
transported at least halfway in this direction, to the Cook Islands.

New Zealand Māori clearly belong to the same cultural region as
Marquesans. In particular, linguists have identified a specific link between
NW Marquesan and South Island Māori,[54] which is reflected in a switch
from 'ng' in North Island Māori to a 'k' typical of the South Island and the
adjacent Chatham Islands.[55] According to Ray Harlow, this southern form of
Māori is likely to have occurred as a consequence of multiple settlement in
the south, involving the NW Marquesan islands.[56] And yet the differences
between Marquesan and Māori languages are sufficient to suggest that
any contact between these regions is likely to have been relatively minor,
a conclusion that is consistent with the relatively low incidence of shared
place names.[57] In any event, New Zealand Māori clearly belong to the same
wider cultural region as Marquesans, namely East Polynesia.

Marquesan nature terms shared with New Zealand Māori[58]

NEW ZEALAND MĀORI	SE MARQUESAS	SOUTH ISLAND MĀORI	NW MARQUESAS
inanga *(a kind of juvenile fish)*	inana (?)	inaka	inaka
mangō *(shark)*	mano	mako, makō	mako
ongaonga *(nettle)*	onaona	okaoka[59]	okaoka
pūngāwerewere *(spider)*	punave`eve`e	pūkāwerewere	pukave`eve`e
toke *(earthworm)*	to`eto`e	noke	noke, toketoke

*As this table shows, the language of Māori as a whole is linked to SE
Marquesan, whereas NW Marquesan can be more clearly linked with South
Island Māori.*

Finding Eiao

Until the development of the first sextant, maritime compass and
maritime clock, European navigators were unable to ascertain their
location with any accuracy. So how were voyagers without any tools
of navigation able to find and re-locate such remote locations?[60] The
Marquesan quarry island of Eiao is no bigger than New Zealand's Rangitoto
and Motutapu islands combined; from the nearest inhabited island to the
west, the target arc for refinding it is minuscule.[61] How this was achieved is
the subject of our next chapter.

Marquesan ceremony

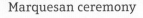

Above: A photo montage from 2006 showing further cultural similarities between here and New Zealand. Here, a traditional Marquesan reception is being given on Hiva ʻOa to the French Minister of Overseas Territories, François Baroin. He is initially greeted by men performing a haka (traditional war cry), uttering a deep, blood-curdling throat-breath while brandishing short wooden clubs – a challenge accompanied by wailing women.

The women wear flowers

On such ceremonial occasions, the women wear flowers: top, the perfumed tiaʻe or tiare (gardenia, Gardenia taitensis); middle, pua (perfume flower tree, Fagraea berteroana); and bottom, maire (alyxia, Alyxia stellata), a white-flowered shrub or shrubby vine with scented leaves and bark. All three Marquesan terms are shared across much of the Pacific. In New Zealand, **pua** *applies to flowers in general but in particular to the native clematis (puapua or puawānanga), whose flowers women traditionally wore as elegant headdresses; the term* **tiare** *applies to 'scent' generally; and the term* **maire** *was transferred to the scented maire-taiki (Mida salicifolia tree) and the mairehau shrub (Leionema nudum syn. Phebalium), and to several unscented plants with similar leaves.*

- CHAPTER FIVE -

Traditional Wayfinding at Sea

Expanding the Target

The objectives toward which Polynesian and Micronesian navigators have to steer are tiny in relation to the vast areas of sea that surround them. It has therefore been crucial for them to develop, as an adjunct to their systems of star steering and dead reckoning, techniques for 'expanding' their targets into sizable objectives.

David Lewis, *We, the Navigators*, 1972

To re-locate a tiny island such as Eiao in the Marquesas from afar, the navigator needs to know not only how to steer toward it, but also how to pass between hidden reefs and low-lying atolls en route. To explore how a traditional navigator achieves both, we will now take the example of a voyage toward and through an enormous group of atolls known as the Tuamotus, the first destination en route from the Marquesas to New Zealand.

In this chapter we will elaborate on the many non-instrument navigation techniques employed and the kinds of craft that were traditionally used for voyaging over such long distances.

A modern context

In this age of satellite phones and satnav, it is important to appreciate the difference between sailing aboard a modern yacht and the navigation of a traditional craft by purely non-instrument means. As an example of the former, we can take life aboard the yacht on which I crewed in 2006 on my own voyage from the Marquesas Islands via the Tuamotus through to the Society Islands.

Mary Vorgan (13.4 m) is about half the length of a Polynesian voyaging canoe, single-masted and single-hulled with synthetic sails and a crew of three. In light

or contrary winds, or when manoeuvring close to shore, we simply started up our inboard diesel motor. Like most contemporary 'bluewater sailors', we had the ship's laptop to guide us and keep us up to date with weather reports. Satellites orbiting the globe showed us our position in relation to the ocean floor to within one-metre accuracy. A battery of screens gave our sideways drift caused by the swell, wind and local current, the depth of ocean beneath us and the distance remaining to our chosen waypoint. With the yacht's laptop programmed, we could watch an image of our craft on screen, seeking out its virtual target like a guided missile.

It is not until the satnav fails that most modern sailors get a glimpse of what it is like to be at sea without this technology – and then only if a freak storm takes away the ship's compass and charts.

Polynesian ships

We need to clear away some of the confusion surrounding the kind of vessels Polynesians used to colonise the Pacific. Even today, many Māori children in my neighbourhood are under the misconception that their ancestors reached New Zealand aboard single-hulled canoes that were paddled. This incongruous notion is now thankfully being addressed by a

Left: Te Aurere, *a Polynesian-style twin-hulled 18-m sailing canoe under sail off New Zealand.*

Above: Globes showing (left) the distribution of the name **pahī** *for a large seagoing canoe, and (right) of the term* **hourua** *for a twin-hulled canoe (or – on Lau – an outrigger canoe). Note that both names are recorded in New Zealand Māori.*

renaissance in Polynesian voyaging using modern versions of the old canoes – a tangible reminder that the migration craft of old were in fact twin-hulled vessels or outriggers that bore sails.

This notion that Polynesians had somehow paddled across the Pacific arises partly from confusion surrounding the Polynesian term waka, which is commonly defined simply as 'a canoe' – which, if taken literally, would mean 'a narrow, single-hulled craft propelled by paddling'.

In reality – and this is true right across the Pacific – the term 'waka' includes sailing craft. The confusion can to some extent be avoided, in East Polynesia at least, where large, twin-hulled, seagoing sailing canoes (waka moana) were often distinguished as pahī or hourua. Both these terms were brought to New Zealand too, and are remembered in the Māori language. If we use the word 'canoe' for any kind of sailing craft, we should at least qualify it as being a 'sailing canoe' or 'voyaging canoe'. Otherwise, we risk confusing ourselves and our children.

Although there is no question that the main means of propulsion for long-distance voyaging was the sails, Polynesian craft were ingeniously designed so that they could also be paddled if becalmed or when manoeuvring close to shore. Paddling these craft over really long distances is not practicable, though – as demonstrated in the 1960s by a crew of physically fit and experienced paddlers aboard a reconstructed Hawaiian double canoe. They proved unable to sustain paddling for more than a couple of days, enabling them to cover over 90 km, but by that time they had, in the words of the experimenters, been brought 'close to their physiological limit'.[1]

When is a ship a canoe?

(Definitions from Oxford Dictionary *and Williams,* A Dictionary of the Maori Language*).*

ENGLISH

Ship – a large boat for transporting people or goods by sea

Catamaran – a yacht or other boat with twin hulls in parallel

Canoe – a light, narrow boat with pointed ends and no keel, propelled with a paddle or paddles

MĀORI

Pahī – 'large sea-going canoe; hence, ship'

Hourua – 'double canoe'

Waka – 'canoe in general, different forms being distinguished by epithets or distinct names'

Ama – 'outrigger on the windward side of a canoe'

Above: David Lewis (1917–2002), sailor, navigator and anthropologist, who sailed his catamaran Rehu Moana *from Rarotonga to New Zealand in 1965 using only traditional methods of navigation, i.e. with no instruments.*

Below: Two standing stones (the second one visible in the middle distance, marked by the arrow) mark the bow and stern of the Tainui *canoe, where it was interred at Te Ahurei on Kāwhia Harbour. These stones are 21 m apart. Photo from the early 1900s.*

The voyaging canoes that Cook saw in Tahiti in 1769 were generally double-hulled and up to 24 m in length; they had a large steering paddle, and carried a matting sail (or two) of woven pandanus leaves. These large Polynesian craft were almost as long as Cook's 32-m *Endeavour*, which carried a crew of 94.[2] With a deck joining the two hulls, they were essentially catamarans. Some were capable of accommodating 80–100 crew; however, when sailing in rough seas between archipelagos and loaded up for settlement, they are likely to have carried half this number or fewer.[3] Accounts from this same period also speak of interisland voyaging aboard much smaller outrigger canoes (waka ama, page 102).[4]

It is important to appreciate that the designs of both types of vessel were in many respects superior to those of Europeans. They enjoyed far greater manoeuvrability, due partly to an unusually shallow draught, narrow beam and movable keel that doubled as a steering paddle; this enabled them to be sailed much closer to shore than a European ship, to safely cross shallow reefs and then be simply drawn up onto the beach. No doubt Polynesians were impressed by the load-carrying capacity of European vessels, but these must still have seemed very clumsy by comparison.

The Polynesian craft that Cook saw were generally sewn-plank canoes with a dugout log for the base,[5] and sides of timber, split and shaped into planks with stone adzes, drilled with shark's teeth or shell, then lashed together and to the frames with sennit cord made from coconut-husk fibre. The remaining gaps between the planks were caulked with this same fibre mixed with sticky breadfruit sap, and occasionally overlaid with strips of turtle shell or bamboo. We have many descriptions of such sailing canoes from central East Polynesia dating from the late 18th century. But to learn whether these are really comparable to the craft in use for long-distance migration several centuries earlier, we must turn to independent forms of evidence.

To establish the nature of vessels that were in use during the original settlement period, some of the most compelling proof comes from excavations by archaeologist Yoshiko Sinoto and co-workers on Huahine (Society Is). In 1977 and 1981 they uncovered remains here of waterlogged canoe decking or side planks, a steering paddle and mast. From these, Sinoto and his team could confirm that the kind of double-hulled canoes being built in the settlement period were not dissimilar to those seen by Cook and 'could easily have been 25 metres long'.[6]

This size is consistent with the inferred 21-m length of the Māori migration canoe *Tainui*, as measured from the span between two standing stones near Maketū on the shores of Kāwhia Harbour that were purportedly erected at either end of its resting place, and with a tradition that gives the length of this canoe as 'twelve prone men with their arms stretched forward' ('ko *Tainui* waka e kīa ana te roa tekau ma rua takoto o nga tāngata roroa nei').[7]

We know that vessels from this early period carried sails, yet we know very little of their actual rig.[8] But when it comes to their range and how long Polynesians were willing to remain at sea in them, we do have some clues. We know that the transfer of Ecuadorian kūmara into the Pacific from South America, for example, involved a minimum open-sea voyage of 6500 km; and, from reports by Cook in 1769, that one-way passages of 30 days were being undertaken at that time by Tahitians.

Zenith stars for latitude

As for how these craft were navigated, this art was not only vastly different from that of modern navigation, it took far longer to learn. One Samoan wayfinder describes an apprenticeship of over 20 years – a training that required him to spend 'a great deal of time at sea, alone in a small canoe' until 'the mind [is] . . . filled with the sea as the body is filled with blood'. Another wayfinder, a Tahitian, describes how he learned to follow the rise and fall of his vessel with his breath until he could 'breathe with the feet' and 'see with the heart'.[9] Information concerning the natural phenomena that was required to navigate would be imprinted on the mind with the aid of a series of traditional chants.

But if I can return now to our own yacht: all I aimed to do on this voyage from the Marquesas to the Tuamotus was acquire a basic grasp of non-instrument navigation. Gazing up into the darkening sky, I searched for the first star of the night and saw it emerge almost directly above the mast. From my star chart, I confirmed that this unusually brilliant star was Sirius – a star that appears bright because of its relative closeness to Earth. From a preliminary study of the subject I had come to understand that, if Sirius appeared directly overhead, it meant that we were at latitude 17°S.[10] The principle behind this is that a star appears to reach a point directly overhead (as a 'zenith star' or 'star on top') only when viewed from the corresponding parallel of Earth's latitude. From our position, though, Sirius appeared to be standing a little to the south of the mast, indicating that we were still north of 16°S, the latitude of our destination atoll of Raro`ia. To ascertain how far north, I reached my arm up to the sky, gauging that Sirius appeared roughly four finger-widths (around 7°) south of vertical. From this, I estimated that our latitude was around 10°S, which turned out to be about right.

Much the same principle was applied by New Zealander David Lewis (author of We, The Navigators) while sailing without instruments in this region aboard the Polynesian-style Hōkūle`a in 1976. At the time, the crew were trying to avoid hitting a known reef. Lewis began by adjusting the aft mast to make it more or less perpendicular, then lay down with his head at its base. From this vantage, the mast tip appeared to dance around Spica with the gentle rocking movement of the boat, which reassured Lewis and the crew that they were at this point already some 30 nautical miles (about 55 km) clear of danger.[11]

The principle here is not unlike that employed by European-trained navigators, when they ascertained their latitude by measuring the elevation

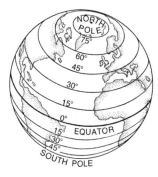

Latitude

A sextant (top) for measuring latitude; these were first used by Europeans in 1757. (Although a more basic navigational instrument, the backstaff, was already in use by 1594.)

The globe above shows lines of latitude, used as a reference for north–south position. Europeans and Polynesians alike learned to judge their latitude from the elevation of stars. One useful example is Spica; the globe below shows the distribution of the term **Whiti-kaupeka**, *recorded in New Zealand as the bright star Spica, but in Marquesan as 'one of a trinity of sky deities'.[12]*

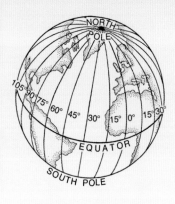

Longitude and time

This globe above shows lines of longitude, a reference for west–east position. The ability to judge longitude at sea with any accuracy was made possible only with John Harrison's marine timekeeper H4, shown below, first used in 1761. To gauge west–east position, non-instrument navigators such as Tupa`ia were reliant on an alternative form of estimation known as 'dead-reckoning'.

of a given star above the horizon with the aid of a sextant. Thus, establishing approximate latitude (north/south position) is relatively easy and well within the grasp of the non-instrument navigator – at least on a clear night.

The value of latitude sailing

Establishing longitude (or west/east position) is quite another matter, though – a skill that requires the traditional navigator to have some way of estimating position in relation to a known location. And the further one travels from that known point, the trickier this gets. For Europeans, the real breakthrough came in the 1700s with the invention of a clock capable of keeping time at sea: equipped with this, it became possible for them to interpret the elevation of the sun, or other stars, as indicators of longitude.

Without this knowledge, a navigator can also play it safe by attempting to approach his destination from due east or due west – that is, along its line of latitude. This is known as 'latitude sailing', a navigational technique that is understood to have played a strong role in the initial stages of Pacific exploration and settlement.

The ability of Polynesians to refind the Marquesan quarry island of Eiao will serve as an excellent example. To keep the navigator on the right latitude to reach it, one of the most useful stars is Spica used as the island's zenith star – the same star that Lewis was using in 1976 to avoid hitting a reef. Today, a navigator doing this would be guided to the southernmost island in the group (Fatu Hiva at 11°S), but in AD 1350, Spica stood at 8°S, making it a zenith star for Eiao. In a very real sense then, one could say that this star would have represented home to Marquesans;[13] and in that sense, it *belonged* to the island over which it passed.[14]

To any navigator approaching the Marquesas along this latitude – from west or east – the group presents a kind of 'island screen' some 300 km wide. Although there is theoretically a risk that one might sail right through without seeing an island, this risk is greatly reduced by the concentration of seabirds that nest on these islands, including the petrels, shearwaters and some millions of sooty terns (tara) that nest on tiny islets such as Teuaua and Hemeni, off the southwest tip of `Ua Huka. A degree of security exists even in the dark from the calls of sooty terns, which can often still be heard after nightfall. Throughout the long nesting season of these birds – September to December – they are based in such colonies, from where they continue to disperse on extraordinarily long foraging flights. As described previously with respect to Easter Island and the Line Islands, navigators approaching within a 480 km radius at this time of year may use increased sightings of them as a guide to the whereabouts of land.[15] In this way, the entire archipelago serves as a single target, or island screen, that is effectively widened to as much as 1000 km. Theoretically, the target arc for finding the quarry island of Eiao from the nearest inhabited island to the west is a minuscule 0.268 degrees, but with the aid of birdlife, this objective can be widened almost a hundredfold to a far more manageable 26 degrees. David Lewis has coined a useful term to describe this traditional landfinding technique: he calls it: 'expanded target landfall'.

Horizon stars to steer by

Stars were no less important to Pacific navigators for holding course. This is something that Europeans initially found hard to grasp, for the stars continue to track across the heavens throughout the night in much the same way as the sun does by day. Elsdon Best, for one, in his treatise on the astronomical knowledge of Māori (1922), found it hard to see how this could work: 'at what juncture in the movement of a star or other body on its course did the steersman commence to steer by it . . .?'[16]

By this time, much of the original wayfinding knowledge of Polynesians had been lost, so the answer was not immediately apparent.[17] However, in the Western Pacific, a few Micronesian navigators from the Caroline and Marshall islands, northeast of New Guinea, had maintained their original lineage of wayfinding skills and still practised them. By the early 1970s they were still able to demonstrate the finer practical details – namely, that any star can serve as a reliable direction indicator as long as it remains low in the sky. As it lifts away from the horizon, its compass direction changes, obliging the navigator to switch his attention to a new star lower in the sky. In other words, a star is useful as a 'steering star' only so long as it is lying close to the horizon. Within an hour or so of its rising or setting, its compass bearing remains surprisingly constant, so can serve as a precise guide to steer by.

On our own voyage between the Marquesas and Tuamotus, I tried this out. Having scanned the horizon for a good reference star, I picked Altair rising to port (left side), close to the cardinal point of east, and Vega (Whānui), a little further left along the horizon at NE (see graphic). I then noted points on the gunwale and rigging with which I could align these stars, before shifting my attention away from the yacht's compass.

Aware that these stars might easily disappear at some point behind a cloud, I scanned along the horizon for other steering stars that I might use as a back-up. This is really only the first step, the start of a process that will

Above: Tara (sooty tern, Onychoprion fuscatus; was Sterna), a species that proved highly useful in the tropics as a long-distance landfinder, especially during the bird's very long nesting season.

*Left: The eastern horizon viewed from 10°S, near the Marquesas on 4 April 2006 at 2.30am, where the bright stars of Whānui (Vega) and Altair are seen rising either side of the Milky Way. When such stars lie close to the horizon like this, they can be relied upon as directional guides. The globe below draws attention to the East Polynesian distribution of the name **Whānui** (recorded in New Zealand for Vega).[18]*

Lightning at night

*A mariner must keep watch at night for the distant flicker of storm lightning, signalling a possible change in wind or an approaching storm. Māori refer to lightning not only by the widespread Polynesian term uira, but also as **kanapu**, a name shared only with distant Tokelau and Hawai`i (see globe).[19]*

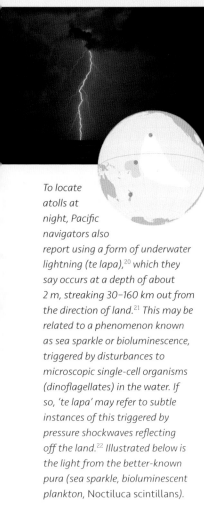

To locate atolls at night, Pacific navigators also report using a form of underwater lightning (te lapa),[20] which they say occurs at a depth of about 2 m, streaking 30–160 km out from the direction of land.[21] This may be related to a phenomenon known as sea sparkle or bioluminescence, triggered by disturbances to microscopic single-cell organisms (dinoflagellates) in the water. If so, 'te lapa' may refer to subtle instances of this triggered by pressure shockwaves reflecting off the land.[22] Illustrated below is the light from the better-known pura (sea sparkle, bioluminescent plankton, Noctiluca scintillans).

continue through the night, with the navigator keeping track of a series of stars. As each new star is seen to rise out of the sea to the east, another horizon star to the west drops back into the sea.

The stars are steadily tracking across the sky through the night by up to 15° an hour, so holding course through a single night generally requires a minimum sequence of about 10 horizon stars. As the nights proceed, each star rises about four minutes earlier each night than it did the night before, so the set of stars relevant to steering any particular course is also slowly changing. Over several months, therefore, the steering stars for a single course change; this requires an experienced navigator to recognise, and commit to memory, many more than just 10 stars. Lest the reader doubt that Polynesians possessed the requisite grasp of astronomy to do this, evidence is provided by a 'snapshot' of the state of Tahitian star knowledge in 1769 as recorded by Cook's botanist Joseph Banks:

> Of these [stars, the Tahitians] know a very large part by their Names and the clever ones among them will tell in what part of the heavens they are to be seen in any month when they are above the horizon; they know also the time of their annual appearing and disappearing to a great nicety, far greater than would be easily believed by an European astronomer.[23]

Indeed, according to Lewis, 'Polynesian wayfinders had names for, and knew the courses of, some 150 stars'.[24]

Horizon stars have the potential to serve as a way of establishing latitude, too. This is particularly true of neighbouring pairs of stars, such as Vega and Altair, which are seen to rise or set simultaneously only from a particular latitude. On our own voyage from the Marquesas to the Tuamotus, I noticed that Vega rose before Altair; this told us that we lay north of 26°S, the latitude at which they rise together. This particular pair of stars is therefore useful to the navigator for keeping on track when attempting to refind Pitcairn Island (at 25°S), Rapa Iti (Bass Is at 27°S) and Rapa Nui (Easter Island at 27°S).[25]

Steering by the wind

According to Lewis there are, in practice, very few nights in the Pacific when cloud will obscure every star right throughout the night; but the navigator must still be able to fall back at times on other wayfinding methods, especially during the day. Of these, by far the most important involves the art of reading the wind and ocean swell.

So that same night I made some rudimentary attempts to do this. To ascertain wind direction, I closed my eyes and slowly turned my head from side to side until I could feel the wind flowing equally past both cheeks; I then opened my eyes to note the horizon star directly ahead of me. I repeated this several times and found the result surprisingly consistent. This ability to 'face the wind' in a literal sense can be highly useful out at sea for maintaining orientation, especially in the tropical Pacific where the wind direction can often remain stable over long periods, day and night.

Above: **Peau** (rolling swell of the open sea), with globe showing distribution of the term.

The technique has its limitations, of course, especially near the coast. On an earlier occasion off Fiji, I witnessed a local captain relying solely on the wind to steer while heavy rain obscured our vision. When the rain lifted half an hour later, there was a moment of disorientation before we realised that our faithfulness to the wind direction had achieved nothing more than to slowly rotate us almost 180 degrees as we followed the twist of a passing squall. This turns out to be much less of a problem further out to sea. However, one is still required to keep track of local wind changes. So next I wanted to understand how this is achieved.

Navigator's best friend, the swell

When far from land, the single most reliable reference for orientating a vessel – day or night, in dull weather or in fog – is the rolling swell (peau) of the deep ocean. This background swell of the sea is slow and continues to roll along for hundreds of kilometres after the wind that generated it has died away. It not only gives the sea its underlying surface texture, it also permits a navigator to steer by feel alone. Any slight deviation in course is felt as a change in pitch and roll of the vessel – something a skilled navigator remains conscious of, even in a semi-alert state of sleep. Many sailors today are aware of this, and I have experienced it myself. This phenomenon is one that non-instrument navigators commonly refer to as their 'best friend'.

The clearest example of this in the South Pacific is a rolling swell generated by the notorious westerlies that blow across the Southern Ocean, more or less in line with New Zealand's South Island. On account of the latitudes at which these westerlies blow, they are commonly known as the 'Roaring Forties' and 'Furious Fifties'. The swell they generate is so powerful that its effects reach over 2000 km to the north. In the region of the Society and Cook islands, it can still be clearly seen and felt as a background swell coming up from the southwest.

The intriguing thing here, though, is that on our approach to the Tuamotus from the northeast, I could not pick up any sign of this swell;

Other wave types

Karekare (breaking wave), above, with globe showing distribution of the term.

Ngaru (local wind waves, as distinct from sea swell generated at a distant source), below, with globe showing distribution of the term.

Below, Ngaru whenua (bounce-back waves, diffracted by the nearby presence of land).

indeed I was unable to do so until we had passed through the entire archipelago into open ocean on the western side. I later learned why. It turns out that, on our approach to this archipelago from the northeast, we were sailing in its 'swell shadow', and that this phenomenon is one that navigators approaching from this side have been able to pick up from up to 650 km away.[26] So the swell can serve to indicate not only one's orientation, but also one's location.

Much the same principle can be used to discern the presence of individual atolls – and not just from their 'swell shadow', but also from 'bounce-back waves' (ngaru whenua) and diffraction waves. The latter phenomenon is set up by the swell dividing and curling around the atoll as it passes, creating a distinctive pattern of intersecting waves that can be felt and seen on the far side of the atoll.[27]

By paying attention to the ocean texture alone, Pacific navigators have demonstrated an ability to locate land at night from distances of up to 55 km. This ability is not something that comes straight away, though. In the Marshall Islands, for example, the requisite training may involve the navigator lying in the water at different locations to familiarise himself with how it feels to be on the north side of a particular atoll or on the south side; east or west. In this way, he learns to use his own body as a kinaesthetic instrument to distinguish how the water acts at different distances and orientations from land. Only later will he learn to use the rocking, rolling and pitching of the craft itself to identify his whereabouts, before going on to identify wave signs by sight alone. Feel comes first.

Other wave types

Wave types are distinguished by name.[28] True ocean swells generated from distant origins, like those just described, are known as peau. This type is relatively constant; it rises and falls slowly, is smooth and rounded, and has a long interval between crests.

Wind waves (ngaru), on the other hand, are generated by a local wind; they tend to be temporary, shorter and steeper, and have breaking crests.

In reality, though, the situation is a bit more complex than this. Wave patterns are often set up by several systems moving across one another in different directions, each differing in height, length, shape and speed. In my own efforts to untangle this tapestry, I found it easiest to first identify the wave system that matched the local wind direction, and then assign any remaining large swell to one generated by a distant source.

Those are two main wave types. But there is also a third, a breaking wave or karekare, characterised by white surf or spray, that frequently serves as an early warning sign for shallow water, a reef or sandbank. The term is a familiar component of several New Zealand place names associated with rough water, e.g. Karekare and Waikaremoana; it is a Māori term that is in this case strictly East Polynesian.[29] Such agitated waters represent danger. In the words of master seaman, shipbuilder and nautical chronicler Charles G. Davis, 'out of sight of land the sailor feels safe. It is the beach that worries him.'

When sailing in coastal waters – especially at night or in fog – the navigator is alert for the sound of this surf, and for the telltale cries of birds, many of which continue after dark. Birds whose cries may warn in this way of a dangerous proximity to land include Pacific golden plovers, shearwaters, tropicbirds and sooty terns.

Temperature, taste and colour

Once the navigator is fully trained, he is being called to use all his senses. He can even distinguish local currents through subtle changes in the colour of the sea, or its taste; and he dips his arm in at times to test for cool flows.[30]

Although such phenomena have rarely attracted much attention from Europeans, in 1817 Russian Lieutenant Otto Kotzebue recorded a spot between the Marshall Islands and Guam where the sea had 'a paler blue colour, had a greater salt content, and deep under the surface had a noticeably lower temperature than elsewhere at the same latitude in the [Pacific] Ocean'.[31] From this he deduced that the ocean here was less deep; he observed that, as they steered north toward Guam, the sea colour returned to normal, as did its salt content and subsurface temperature.

These kinds of observations seem to be more common among traditional navigators. For example, in the early 1980s, when Scottish navigator James Barr sailed with Captain Moi of Sāmoa, he noticed Moi tasting the water repeatedly as an aid to wayfinding. 'I have no idea how it is [possible to navigate by these means],' adds Barr. 'I tried it, but could only taste brine. Tasting the sea is an art.'[32] And yet the fact is that regional variations in the temperature and salinity of the top 1–2 cm of the world's oceans are sufficiently distinctive that these can be readily picked up from space, as depicted in the accompanying NASA satellite maps.

The 'scent of land'

The navigator is also alert to the distinctive smell of a distant forest or reef, and can be forewarned of land in this way. In 1769, Joseph Banks demonstrated this when sailing from Rio de Janeiro to Tierra del Fuego: he noted 'a singular smell from windward . . . like rotten seaweed and at some times very strong' – a smell that he was in this case able to pick up from some 400 km off the Argentinean coast.[33] Similarly, in the same century, when Scottish immigrants were sailing to North America, they were able to pick up their first sweet whiff of spruce and pine on the west wind well before sighting land.

Reading the flotsam

During Captain Cook's search for Easter Island in 1774, in the days leading up to his first sighting of it, he was able to determine his proximity to land from spotting 'several pieces of sponge, and a small dried leaf not unlike a bay one'.[34] For Pacific peoples and Europeans alike, sightings of driftwood,

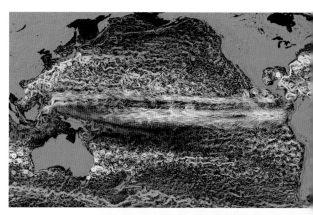

Surface temperature and saltiness of the sea

Above: Traditional navigators used local variations in sea surface temperatures to keep track of their location. Here, sea surface current flows and eddies in the Pacific are shown in detail, coloured according to sea surface temperatures – from hot (red) to cold (blue).

Below: Traditional navigators also tasted the sea for its salt content, shown here from high salinity (orange and yellow) to lower salinity (dark blue), as determined from space. High salt concentrations are generally found away from the mouths of rivers, or in regions with little rain. Toward the poles, salinity is low, partly due to the diluting effect of melting ice.

Current boundaries

Above: Current boundaries may show up on the surface of the sea as lines of drift debris, here illustrated by a line of Sargassum seaweed.

Below: Ocean currents conform to a pattern that changes predictably with the seasons. On this map of ocean circulation, dashed lines show the major current boundaries for August to September.

leaves and seaweed carried by the wind and currents have long been interpreted in this way.

This type of observation was further refined by Polynesians and Micronesians. They noted that, when drifting debris accumulates in bands out at sea, this usually marks the location of a boundary between major ocean currents. Although the locations of these boundaries do not remain fixed, they do move around in a predictable manner with the seasons – which makes them useful as another tool for determining the navigator's whereabouts. On approach to New Zealand, for example, one major flotsam-marked current boundary running east–west lies to the north of the land mass, while others further south extend to the west and east of it.[35]

Such bands can often be spotted from surprisingly large distances, as the small fish that gather for shelter beneath the drifting material attract predatory fish such as mahimahi and skipjack tuna, which in turn draw sharks and fish-feeding birds such as terns and shearwaters.[36] In many cases, the clash of currents associated with these bands of flotsam brings nutrients welling up from the deep; these provide sustenance for surface phytoplankton and zooplankton, which attract not only flying fish but also feeding seabirds and whales. The manner in which this flurry of activity can stand out from the desert-like nature of much of the deep ocean was aptly described in 1872 by yachtsman C.F. Wood when crossing the equator from New Guinea to Pohnpei:

> We passed through immense quantities of driftwood. Huge trees and logs of wood . . . Among this driftwood, we saw immense flocks of terns and [tropicbirds]. The water was alive with fish of all sizes. Large [bluefin tuna] splashed and jumped on all sides, evidently in pursuit of the smaller fish that hung round the large floating trees . . . Above them all fluttered vast flocks of terns, incessantly darting down in pursuit of small fry.[37]

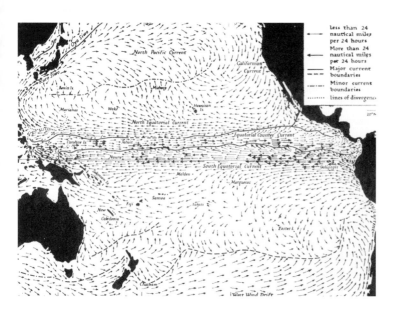

Featureless though much of the deep ocean may seem, it is not entirely so, certainly to the observant navigator, fisherman or naturalist. When viewed in its entirety as one organic whole, it is seen to have its own geography and to be inseparably intertwined with the life in and upon it.

In this sense, traditional wayfinders were not 'working in the dark' or merely drifting into the unknown; they were in effect 'reading a map'.

Looking to the sky

To find his way, the navigator also looked to the sky for the presence, form and colour of clouds. Two main cloud types are distinguished in Māori, for example.

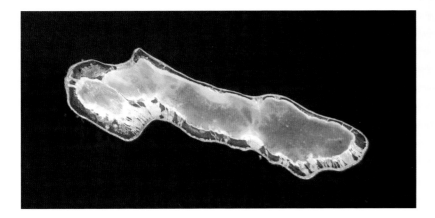

Left: `Ana`a (NW Tuamotus). The colour of its unusually shallow lagoon is so intense that navigators seeing this hue reflected onto the underside of clouds may pick up its presence from up to 70 km away.

Ao clouds, below, may appear as if tethered over land like a stationary balloon and are associated with fine weather. The globe depicts the distribution of the term.

Kapua refers to a misty cloud that spreads over, surrounds or envelops, like a mist, fog or haze. It is a familiar component in several New Zealand place names, including Ō-Tū-Kapua-Rangi (the Pink Terraces) – a name that referred to the proximity of this place to the steamy hot vents here, so typical of the Rotorua region.

Such misty clouds are readily distinguished from ao, a more compact type that is frequently seen piled up by the trade winds over high islands such as Tahiti and Hawai`i, as if tethered over land like a balloon. This kind of cloud often hangs over some or all of New Zealand. When present, such clouds can greatly increase the distance from which the navigator is able to locate an island, from say 90 km to over 150 km.[38]

Another important sign is the blue of the sky as reflected in the sea. The precise shade of blue can be used to locate a reef (akau) and gauge its depth up to 30 fathoms (55 m),[39] by distinguishing the light green or turquoise of shallow water (as in lagoons) and darker shades, through to the dark blue of the deep sea. In the case of a particularly shallow lagoon, the navigator even may be guided to it by the turquoise tint of the water reflected up onto the underside of a cloud.[40] Striking examples of this include the unusually shallow lagoons of Aitutaki (S. Cook Is) and `Ana`a (Tuamotus),[41] where the presence of these low-lying atolls can be discerned in fine weather from up to 70 km away.[42] This kind of phenomenon can show up in other cases, too, where the destination island can even be distinguished by the colour of the cloud hanging over it – a green tinge in the case a forested island; an unusually bright cloud over white sand or surf; or a pink tinge warning of a reef.[43]

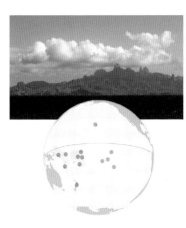

A **kapua** cloud, below, spreads over, surrounds, or envelops, like a mist, fog or haze; globe depicts distribution of the term.

Fish are another indicator

The full repertoire of navigational indicators includes not only an increase in the prevalence of fish and fish-finding birds,[44] but also a change in fish species. In 1947, for example, when Thor Heyerdahl and his crew had been crossing the southeastern Pacific for many months aboard *Kon-Tiki* without sign of land, they noticed that a larger species of flying fish had begun throwing itself on board. From this species they could correctly deduce that they were approaching their first island.[45]

Landfinding birds

Below: Kiva (kōtaha, mokohe, frigatebird or man-o'-war bird, Fregata species), which Polynesians often carried aboard their canoes to help with landfinding. These birds were said to take their 'rightful place, poised upon the towering prow' as the 'eyes' of the navigator. New Zealand sightings are rare.

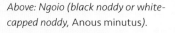

Above: Ngoio (black noddy or white-capped noddy, Anous minutus).

Right: Kena (brown booby, Sula leucogaster).

*The red-footed booby (Sula sula), above left, tends to roam more widely and is hence less useful for landfinding. Its counterpart in New Zealand waters is the look-alike Australasian gannet (Morus serrator), above right. Both are known as **tākupu** — a name shared with East Polynesia and Tokelau, see globe below.*

Landfinding birds

But it is the land-based birds that provide the strongest indication that land is close, and this is particularly so on approach to low-lying atolls, where brown boobies can often be seen from up to 55 km offshore. At this distance, traditional navigators can generally count on sighting small groups of them.[46]

On our own approach to the Tuamotus, I had a chance to try this out. It had been three days since we had left the Marquesas, so I knew we must be getting close by now. I came up on deck before sunrise and waited, and indeed, some 15 minutes after the sun came up, two brown boobies appeared from the south. This early in the day, it seemed almost certain that they had just left their roosting site in that direction to begin the day's fishing.[47] Just in case they were early starters heading home, I double-checked to see whether either of them had fish in their mouths.

Soon, their numbers began to increase. Then large, pterodactyl-like birds appeared and started to harass them. With wingspans of over 2 m, these piratical creatures are known as frigatebirds for their habit of swooping on other birds in an effort to rob them of their catch. Such was the usefulness of these birds for landfinding that Polynesians and Micronesians often carried them as pets aboard their canoes. When released, the birds could be relied on to either fly off in the direction of land, or return to the canoe after a while until land was within reach. At least two traditional Polynesian sea shanties honour this, specifically the manner in which these birds would take their 'rightful place – poised upon the towering prow' as the 'eyes' of the navigator.[48] Frigatebirds have proven so reliable for landfinding because they are very reluctant to get their unoiled feathers wet, and hence rarely roam more than 80–100 km from land before returning at night to roost on shore (or onboard the canoe).[49]

A wide range of other bird species were evidently carried aboard canoes for the same purpose. According to a traditional voyaging chant from the Tuamotus, these included rails, plovers, red-tailed tropicbirds, herons and sooty terns.[50] I kept a lookout for other birds. As the boobies and frigatebirds continued to increase in numbers, small, tight flocks of white terns appeared. These elegant birds have a dispersal range no greater than 45 km.[51] They were soon joined by black noddies – confirmation that we were now within about 40 km of land.[52]

Spotting an atoll before hitting it

This might well make the process sound easier than it is, for spotting an atoll before hitting it is harder than it looks. All the shipwrecks that litter these reefs today are testament to that – a reminder of all the captains who have been caught unawares by the strong tidal currents that frequently race between the atolls. At mid-tide, when the sea is surging at its strongest in and out of the lagoons here, the currents in the passes can reach speeds of up to 8 knots (15 kph).

Given that such a large proportion of the Pacific consists of such atolls, it is understandable that Polynesians and Micronesians designed their craft to be highly manoeuvrable in shallow water, and that they acquired considerable skill at navigating in such treacherous conditions.

As with most atolls, there was nothing at all to see on our own approach to the Tuamotuan atoll of Raro`ia until we were just 15 km away. It is at this point that I could detect a faint smudge appearing to dance on the horizon, an apparition on the water that had to be the tops of the tallest coconut palms here. But even as these 'smudges' began to grow in number across the horizon, there was still no way to know whether the gaps between them marked a safe entry into the lagoon or a treacherous stretch of barren reef.

On Heyerdahl's approach to this same atoll in 1947, he was confronted with a very similar situation when his balsa raft *Kon-Tiki* was driven ashore on the eastern side of Raro`ia and smashed to pieces. Miraculously, he and the crew survived. 'We felt the *Kon-Tiki* being lifted up in the air,' he wrote of his historic arrival.

> We were riding on the wave-back at breathless speed, our ramshackle craft creaking and groaning as she quivered under us . . . In an instant hell was over us again, and the *Kon-Tiki* disappeared completely under the masses of water . . . The vessel we knew from weeks and months at sea was no more; in a few seconds our pleasant world had become a shattered wreck.

The destruction of their raft did not detract from the point that the Norwegian archaeologist and his five companions had sought to make: that it was indeed possible to sail downwind for over 7000 km on a raft from Callao, Peru to an atoll in the Pacific.[53] It was a brave adventure and one that would catch the attention of the world.

Another landfinding bird

As one draws closer to land, one of the most useful of all the landfinding birds used by Pacific navigators is the akiaki or taketake (white tern or fairy tern, Gygis alba), above. At nightfall, these birds can generally be relied upon to return to their home island to rest in trees or in low vegetation, where Polynesians caught them for food or to keep as pets. Globes show the distribution of the two names for them: **akiaki** *(left-hand globe) and* **taketake** *(right). In New Zealand Māori, both forms of the name were transferred to the local equivalent landfinding bird, the red-billed gull (Larus novaehollandiae).*

Raro`ia Atoll is so low-lying that the tops of the coconut palms (up to 15 m tall) cannot be spotted from more than 15 km. Above is a very close-up view of the atoll on a clear day.

CHAPTER SIX

The Tuāmotu Archipelago

Crossroads of East Polynesia

In the Tuamotu archipelago, we cannot sail into there and not find an island.
This box [navigational target] is four hundred miles wide.

Hawaiian navigator Nainoa Thompson

Most people who have heard of the Tuamotus have learned of them either through Thor Heyerdahl's voyage, or through the more than 180 nuclear tests that were conducted between 1966 and 1996 by the French military on two of the southern atolls in the group, Mururoa (or Moruroa) and Fangataufa.

The Tuāmotu Archipelago is the largest chain of atolls in the world, consisting of numerous sunken remains of volcanic peaks. It includes 78 atolls and raised coral reefs scattered over a region of the Pacific some 500 km wide and 1600 km long, an extent almost as great as that of all of Spain and France combined.

To the Tuamotuans, their archipelago was a collection of 'numerous islets' (tuā-motu),[1] but Europeans have opted for more pejorative terms. To Ferdinand Magellan, who sighted the Tuamotuan atoll of Pukapuka in 1521, they were the *Islas Infortunadas* (unfortunate islands), while Captain Cook, who sailed through here in 1774, referred to them as the 'drowned isles'. To European eyes, such atolls have seemed scarcely habitable, a perception reinforced today by 'reality' TV shows featuring make-believe castaways struggling to survive on them. Rarely is any heed paid to the fact that Micronesians and Polynesians not only sought out and settled such environments deliberately, but refined a culture and way of life on them that has proven sustainable for a thousand years or more. Thus, Tuamotuans and other atoll-dwellers are frequently dispossessed of their settlement history, all too easily relegated in the popular mind to being no more than descendants of hapless castaways.

To do these atoll dwellers justice, we should therefore begin by acknowledging the considerable challenges they faced and then go on to demonstrate their resourcefulness in meeting these challenges. How, for example, did they build their ships, make footwear, establish gardens and harvest the marine resources around them? How long have they been here and how far did they voyage? In other words, what was the traditional life here on these atolls really like?

Lacking freshwater and soil

From a physical point of view, atolls consist largely of rubble, a kind of volcanic moonscape over which the gravel-like remains of years of broken coral lie scattered. Soil and freshwater are almost completely lacking. For hydration, atoll dwellers tapped into a lens of brackish water that accumulates beneath the coral and which floats on a denser layer of saltwater beneath it. They gained access to this by digging wells through the coral; however, the water that can be retrieved in this way is generally so salty as to be virtually undrinkable to anyone but a local. (It has since become common here to rely on rainwater collected from roofs, stored in PVC tanks.)

Wild food

Traditionally the Tuamotuan diet consisted of fish, crayfish, the occasional turtle, and birds. They had many ingenious means of catching birds, all of which New Zealand Māori also used. They caught the birds with nets, or lured them into a noose held on a pole,

NORTH PACIFIC
OCEAN

Hawai`i

Marshall
Islands

Line Islands

GUINEA

Marquesas

Tūvalu   Tokelau
         Sāmoa
Vanuatu Fiji   Cook   Society
         Tonga   Islands Islands

New Caledonia   Austral
                             Islands

Pitcairn
Islands

Easter
Island

Kermadec
Islands

SOUTH PACIFIC
OCEAN

New Zealand

Chatham
Islands

Rangîroa

Raro`ia

Tuāmotu
Archipelago

Mururoa

Above left: Tuāmotu Archipelago,
as seen from space.

Above: Tuamotuans at the festival
of Tuamotuan culture in Tahiti.

Below: Raro`ia Atoll, where Thor
Heyerdahl's raft, Kon-Tiki, was
wrecked in 1947. Like most atolls,
it is a kind of 'moonscape' of
practically barren coral, lacking
both soil and fresh water.

Local wild foods

Local wild foods available to Tuamotuans include not only fish and coconut, but also, top to bottom, the native pōkea (pigweed or purslane, Portulaca lutea);[2] nau (native peppergrass, Lepidium bidentatum); flightless chicks, such as these of tavake (tropicbird),[3] and tōua (bird eggs).

or waited at night to grab a bird when it returned exhausted from the sea. Young birds could simply be struck off a branch with bare hands or a stick.[4] The most popular edible species – at least nowadays on Raro`ia – are tropicbirds, frigatebirds, boobies, noddies and terns.[5] It was also traditional to eat seabird eggs (tōuo).

On atolls, edible wild plants are very few: the smaller-fruited native coconuts, the tough, fibrous fruits of pandanus trees, the unappetising woody roots of sprawling hogweed (rūnā, *Boerhavia tetrandra*),[6] and the more palatable leaves of pigweed (pōkea) and native pepper grass (nau, page 101).

In other words – and this is an important point – almost all the food plants found on these isles today were introduced by people. As such, they constitute a kind of 'transported landscape' brought here aboard the sailing canoes to render their new colonies habitable.

Horticultural innovation

To raise crops in such extreme conditions required ingenuity. Tuamotuans would begin by selecting a spot sufficiently far back from the sea and the edge of the lagoon to escape the damaging effects of salt spray. They then set to work with a wooden digging stick to excavate a pit in the loose coral up to 100 m long by 40 m wide by 1–2 m deep. They gathered leaves and other plant debris from around the atoll, placed this mixture in the pit and broke it up, sieving and mixing it with sand to make soil. By this means they were able to supply their crops with the requisite moisture and nutrients to propagate a range of edible tubers – taro, yam, kape (a kind of giant taro), atoll taro[7] and Polynesian arrowroot.

Other traditional crops Polynesians introduced to these atolls include sugarcane, turmeric, Polynesian bamboo, nono (Indian mulberry, page 70), a larger-fruited strain of coconut and – on some atolls – even breadfruit, candlenut and banana. In addition to these plants, Tuamotuans also introduced Pacific dogs and Pacific rats. And again, the origin of every one of these lies to the west, either in the Western Pacific or in Asia.[8]

History disappears quickly

Settlement of the Tuamotus is understood to date from around AD 1000,[9] not long after this entire chain of atolls emerged from the sea in around AD 900.[10] Even today, many of the atolls stand no more than 4 m above sea level, leaving Tuamotuans highly vulnerable to inundation from tsunami and major storms. In the 1960 Chilean earthquake, for example, the local fluctuation in sea level was 1 m; and a series of five cyclones between January and April 1983 led to storm surges of 3–4 m or more that submerged inhabited parts of most of the atolls by more than 1 m.[11] There are many accounts here of islanders surviving only by tying themselves and their children to coconut trees, or taking refuge in the tops of the trees.[12] Under such conditions it is not easy to find archaeological evidence – so much of it has been washed away, often more than once.

Even so, archaeologists have been able to identify remains of stone marae platforms on almost every atoll in the archipelago (see map, pages 98–99).[13] A survey by anthropologist Kenneth Emory in 1934 identified 344

Atoll horticulture

Crops traditionally grown here include, left to right: kape (giant taro or elephant ear taro, Alocasia macrorrhizos) from the Philippines; atoll taro (giant swamp taro, Cyrtosperma merkusii), widely known as puraka, from New Guinea; pia (Polynesian arrowroot, Tacca leontopetaloides) from Southeast Asia and New Guinea, whose tubers are traditionally grated and washed as a starchy thickener for puddings; tō (sugarcane, Saccharum officinarum) from New Guinea, whose stem was chewed and the leaves used for thatching roofs;[14] renga (turmeric, Curcuma longa) from Southeast Asia, whose root-like rhizomes provide a yellow dye, culinary spice and medicine;[15] and kohe (Polynesian bamboo, Schizostachyum glaucifolium) from tropical Asia, used as water containers, for house walls, roof framing, ladders, bridges, fencing and gutters, fishing rods, rafts, canoe masts and booms, or split to make simple knives for cutting tough meat and conducting minor surgery (e.g., severing the

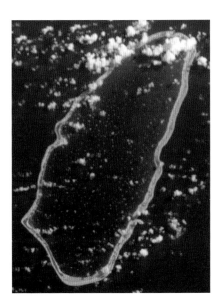

umbilical cord of newborn babies and performing traditional circumcision). This last – bamboo – was indeed so useful to Polynesians that archaeologists use groves of it to help locate former habitation sites.[16]

of them, some roughly constructed, but many with neatly fitted coral slabs and megalithic slab uprights up to 2.4 m tall that had evidently served as ceremonial backrests for chiefs and ritual officiants, or were places of honour for ancestral gods. Some Emory described as 'shaped in the semblance of the human form' with a simple rounded flange at the top to represent the head, reminiscent of the stone statues of Easter Island.

Many of the old stones have since been removed by villagers for house foundations and church-building; most sites are now either damaged or overgrown. And yet in 1952, anthropologist Bengt Danielsson was able to report of Raro`ia alone: 'old men still point out and name 42 marae sites on which they had witnessed ceremonies when they were young. Today, on half a dozen of these sites an overturned and broken slab or two can still be found, but in all the other sites not a trace is left.'[17]

Fortunately, we have a first-hand description from 1765 of one of these old marae still in use on Takaroa Atoll, where John Byron saw the 'figure of a dog' adorned with feathers hanging from the branches of one of the lofty trees, and 'a great number of the heads and bones of turtles and a variety of fish, enclosed in a kind of basketwork of reeds'. From the 'many neat boxes full of human bones' he found nearby he surmised that the people had a great veneration for the dead.[18]

Above: As on many atolls, the lagoon of Raro`ia is too wide to see from one side to the other.

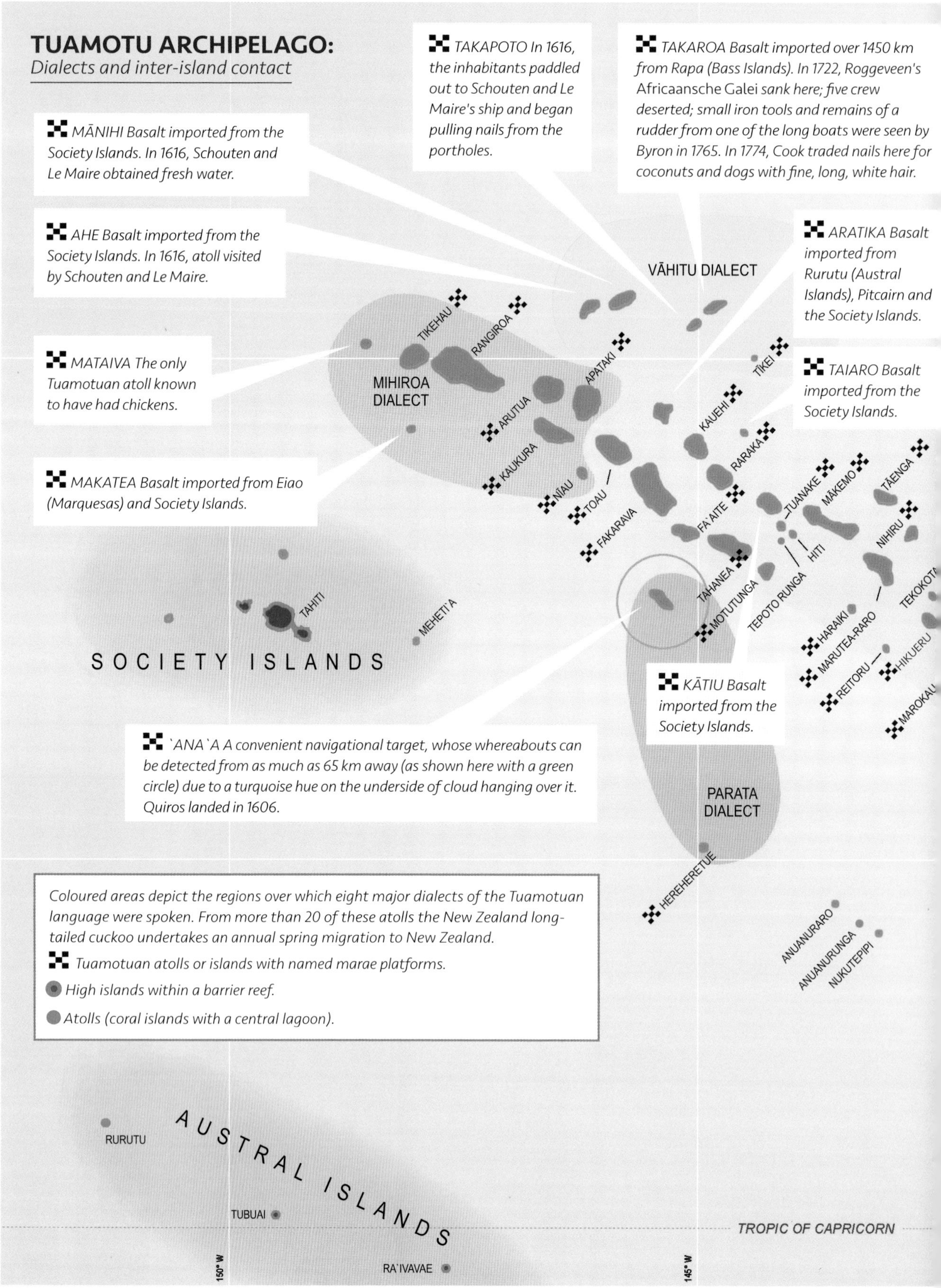

TUAMOTU ARCHIPELAGO:
Dialects and inter-island contact
MĀNIHI Basalt imported from the Society Islands. In 1616, Schouten and Le Maire obtained fresh water.
AHE Basalt imported from the Society Islands. In 1616, atoll visited by Schouten and Le Maire.
MATAIVA The only Tuamotuan atoll known to have had chickens.
MAKATEA Basalt imported from Eiao (Marquesas) and Society Islands.
TAKAPOTO In 1616, the inhabitants paddled out to Schouten and Le Maire's ship and began pulling nails from the portholes.
TAKAROA Basalt imported over 1450 km from Rapa (Bass Islands). In 1722, Roggeveen's Africaansche Galei sank here; five crew deserted; small iron tools and remains of a rudder from one of the long boats were seen by Byron in 1765. In 1774, Cook traded nails here for coconuts and dogs with fine, long, white hair.
ARATIKA Basalt imported from Rurutu (Austral Islands), Pitcairn and the Society Islands.
TAIARO Basalt imported from the Society Islands.
KĀTIU Basalt imported from the Society Islands.
`ANA`A A convenient navigational target, whose whereabouts can be detected from as much as 65 km away (as shown here with a green circle) due to a turquoise hue on the underside of cloud hanging over it. Quiros landed in 1606.
VĀHITU DIALECT
MIHIROA DIALECT
PARATA DIALECT
TIKEHAU
RANGIROA
APATAKI
ARUTUA
KAUKURA
NIAU
TOAU
FAKARAVA
TĪKEI
KAUEHI
RARAKA
FA`AITE
TUANAKE
MĀKEMO
TĀENGA
NIHIRU
HITI
TAHANEA
MOTUTUNGA
TEPOTO RUNGA
TEKOKOTA
HARAIKI
MARUTEA-RARO
REITORU
HIKUERU
MAROKAU
HEREHERETUE
ANUANURARO
ANUANURUNGA
NUKUTEPIPI
SOCIETY ISLANDS
TAHITI
MEHETI`A
AUSTRAL ISLANDS
RURUTU
TUBUAI
RA`IVAVAE
TROPIC OF CAPRICORN
150° W
145° W
Coloured areas depict the regions over which eight major dialects of the Tuamotuan language were spoken. From more than 20 of these atolls the New Zealand long-tailed cuckoo undertakes an annual spring migration to New Zealand.
Tuamotuan atolls or islands with named marae platforms.
High islands within a barrier reef.
Atolls (coral islands with a central lagoon).

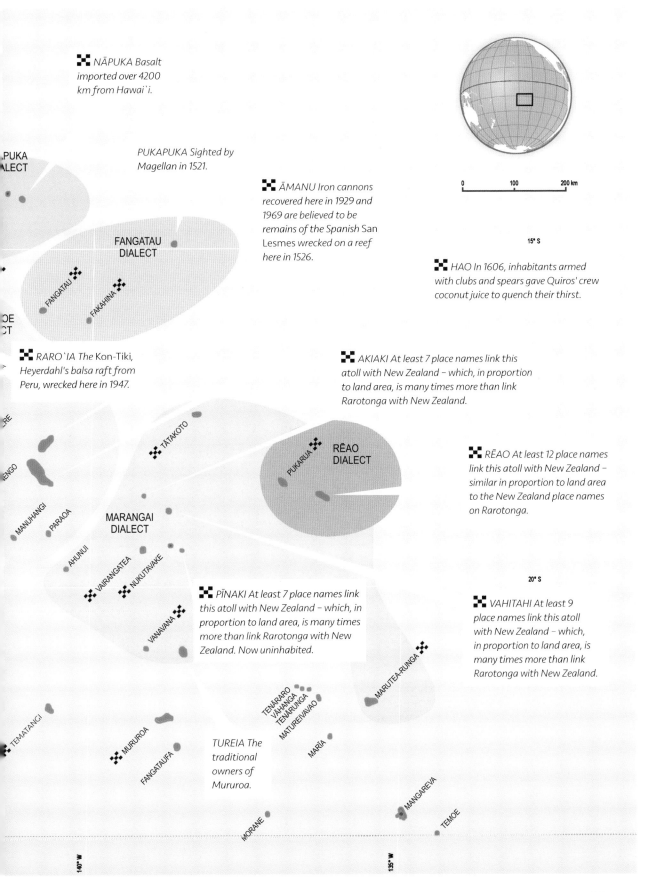

NĀPUKA Basalt imported over 4200 km from Hawai`i.

PUKAPUKA Sighted by Magellan in 1521.

ĀMANU Iron cannons recovered here in 1929 and 1969 are believed to be remains of the Spanish San Lesmes wrecked on a reef here in 1526.

HAO In 1606, inhabitants armed with clubs and spears gave Quiros' crew coconut juice to quench their thirst.

PUKA ALECT

FANGATAU DIALECT

FANGATAU

FAKAHINA

OE CT

RARO`IA The Kon-Tiki, Heyerdahl's balsa raft from Peru, wrecked here in 1947.

AKIAKI At least 7 place names link this atoll with New Zealand – which, in proportion to land area, is many times more than link Rarotonga with New Zealand.

RE

ENGO

TĀTAKOTO

RĒAO DIALECT

PUKARUA

RĒAO At least 12 place names link this atoll with New Zealand – similar in proportion to land area to the New Zealand place names on Rarotonga.

MANUHANGI

PARAOA

MARANGAI DIALECT

AHUNUI

VAIRANGATEA

NUKUTAVAKE

PĪNAKI At least 7 place names link this atoll with New Zealand – which, in proportion to land area, is many times more than link Rarotonga with New Zealand. Now uninhabited.

VAHITAHI At least 9 place names link this atoll with New Zealand – which, in proportion to land area, is many times more than link Rarotonga with New Zealand.

VANAVANA

MARUTEA-RUNGA

TENĀRARO
VĀHANGA
TENĀRUNGA
MATUREIVAVAO

TEMATANGI

MURUROA

FANGATAUFA

TUREIA The traditional owners of Mururoa.

MARIA

MORANE

MANGAREVA

TEMOE

15° S

0   100   200 km

20° S

140° W

135° W

The coconut

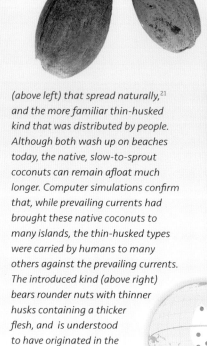

Every part of the coconut palm provides something useful. The thick white flesh lining the inside of the nut can be eaten fresh or dried, or grated and pressed to extract coconut cream, or rendered into oil for cooking or for the skin.[19] 'Water' contained in the immature nut is drunk, and the tender heart at the top of the trunk can be eaten raw. Sennit for string and rope is supplied by 'coir' fibre torn from the outer husk of the nut, used for nets and rigging, and for lashing canoes, fences and buildings, and the shell itself serves as a water container, bowl or ladle. Wood from the base of the trunk is useful for house building, bridges, canoe hulls, oars, drums, containers and firewood, while the tough roots are used to make fish traps and lashing. To attract fish at night, bundles of dried leaflets are burned as torches, and the stiff midribs supply cooking skewers or needles for threading rope, or are tied into bundles as brooms. The heavy bases of the fronds provide stakes and war clubs, or are doubled over for use as tongs for handling hot oven stones. So how did coconuts (Cocos nucifera) reach here? Did they float or were they brought?[20] It seems that the answer is both, for Pacific coconuts include a thick-husked native of the Pacific

(above left) that spread naturally,[21] and the more familiar thin-husked kind that was distributed by people. Although both wash up on beaches today, the native, slow-to-sprout coconuts can remain afloat much longer. Computer simulations confirm that, while prevailing currents had brought these native coconuts to many islands, the thin-husked types were carried by humans to many others against the prevailing currents. The introduced kind (above right) bears rounder nuts with thinner husks containing a thicker flesh, and is understood to have originated in the Philippines,[22] and been bred in SE Asia or Indonesia, from where it was transported across the Pacific by canoe. Its importance to Polynesians is reflected in the vocabulary of the coconut that was brought to New Zealand. For example, the East Polynesian term for 'coconut frond', **nīkau** (see globe) was transferred to the New Zealand palm (Rhopalostylis sapida), above,

for while the latter bears no edible nuts, its fronds could still be used, just like those of its tropical counterpart, for roofing, mats and baskets. Below are some of the many similar examples of shared coconut vocabulary.

MĀORI	MEANING IN TROPICAL POLYNESIA	MEANING IN NEW ZEALAND
kaha	coconut husk fibre (coir) or sennit rope made from it	rope, or top-strake lashings of a canoe[23]
kaka	cloth-like fibre surrounding the base of a coconut frond	fibre, or single hair
kārawa	fibre from coconut frond midrib	line of flax with nooses for snaring birds
pora	plaited coconut leaf as a mat, panel, thatch or basket	floor mat or coarse cloak
rau	a kind of net made from coconut fronds	catch, as in a net
roi/roroi	food cooked in coconut cream	various local foods;[24] to grate into a pulp
tahā	coconut shell used as a water container	a bottle gourd with a narrow mouth
takapau	mat plaited from coconut fronds	plaited floor mat
tāpora	basket plaited from a single coconut frond	basket in which whitebait is cooked
whē	coconut stick insect	stick insect generally

Tuamotuan plant names shared with Māori

*Of six Tuamotuan native plants whose indigenous names are shared with Māori, five are strictly East Polynesian, of which the three above are not shared with other islands. Above, from left, the Tuamotuan **mairehau** (scented fern,* Phymatosorus grossus*), with globe, above right, showing the very limited distribution of this term for plants with fragrant leaves, applied in New Zealand to* Leionema nudum; *the Tuamotuan **mikimiki** (*Pemphis acidula*), a term with similarly limited distribution for small-leaved shrubs growing 4–5 m, applied in New Zealand to* Leucopogon fasciculatus, Cyathodes juniperina *or* Coprosma propinqua; *the **ongaonga** of the Tuamotus (woodnettle,* Laportea ruderalis*), whose Polynesian name was transferred in New Zealand to related nettles (*Urtica*).*[25]

*Centre right: The edible **nau** (native peppergrass,* Lepidium bidentatum*), with globe showing the East Polynesian distribution of the name, applied in New Zealand to Cook's scurvy grass (*Lepidium oleraceum*). Bottom right: The **piripiri** of tropical East Polynesia (sandbur,* Cenchrus *species) with globe showing the East Polynesian distribution of this name for bur plants, applied in New Zealand to* Acaena anserinifolia. *Below: The **tainoka** of the tropical Pacific (lovevine,* Cassytha filiformis*), with globe showing distribution of this name for leafless plants, applied in New Zealand to the leafless New Zealand broom (*Carmichaelia australis*).*

Tuamotuan marae

Upright coral slabs, above, at Ramapohia marae on Fangatau Atoll stand on a raised platform (ahu) about 15 m long, constructed at one end of an unpaved court some 50 m long. (Photo from 1929–1930). The centrepiece of most Tuamotuan marae is a reliquary tree, **pukatea** (Pisonia grandis), right, with globe alongside depicting distribution of this term for a large, buttressed reliquary tree, generally Pisonia, but applied in New Zealand to another reliquary tree, Laurelia novae-zelandiae.[26]

Below: **Honu** (turtle), which were seasonally harvested by Tuamotuans for sacrifice to the gods, and ritually consumed by the chiefs and priests. Polynesians ate the eggs, too, and fashioned the bones into blades, scrapers and needles. Despite turtles being very rare in New Zealand's cooler waters, the Polynesia-wide term for them is remembered in Māori – see globe.

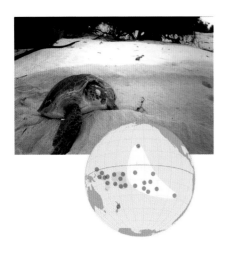

Stonework on such a scale serves as hard evidence that Tuamotuans were not mere castaways – a conclusion that is reinforced by their shipbuilding skills.

Tuamotuan shipbuilding

Tuamotuan shipbuilders built many different shapes and sizes of craft. In the words of French explorer Jacques-Antoine Moerenhout in 1842, 'The most significant were those they call pahi (ship), which are used only for long sea voyages.' These, he reports, were double-hulled sailing canoes up to 23 m long, whose hulls were joined by a deck up to 8.5 m wide.[27] James Hornell, an acknowledged expert on the canoes of Polynesia, Fiji and Micronesia, later judged 'the double-canoes of the Tuamotus [as being] perhaps the finest ever built in Polynesia'.[28]

Early 19th-century accounts from the region also report the use of much smaller outrigger canoes (waka ama) for long-distance voyaging.[29] With their superior manoeuvrability and speed, these smaller craft were suited not only to coastal sailing but also to exploration. And while outriggers can be more tiring to sail and are more easily overturned than a double canoe, recovery from capsize is also easier.

As atolls do not generally support large trees, Tuamotuans became particularly adept and ingenious at fitting and lashing small planks together with coconut fibre. In view of such constraints, one wonders how sustainable the local timber supply would have been to keep building large canoes. To find out, archaeologists Anne Di Piazza and Erik Pearthree set up a computerised simulation in which they tested the area of forest required to build and maintain a fleet of outrigger canoes for both local and long-distance use. From this they learned that it was perfectly feasible to supply sufficient timber for this purpose from a typical inhabited atoll.[30] This is significant, for it shows that long-distance voyaging was not the prerogative of residents of high islands. And this, in turn, contributes to our appreciation of the likely scale of Pacific exploration, for atolls comprise some 70 percent of East Polynesia.[31]

Vital though it was for Tuamotuan shipbuilders to have access to enough timber, they still had to find tools. Anyone who has ever found themselves on an atoll trying to dehusk a coconut without a tool of their own will appreciate the predicament. There is not even a piece of volcanic stone here from which to fashion a simple adze. We know that Tuamotuans imported basalt for this purpose from elsewhere, but they also fashioned adze heads from the tough shells of giant clams, aged in seawater.

The logs they cut would first be seasoned by rolling them into the shallows of a lagoon, where the ebb and flow of the tide would expose them to alternating dampness and heat. Once the logs had been cured in this way, wedges were hammered in to split them. The original wooden tools have long since decayed, but their traditional use can be inferred from the widespread distribution of a Polynesian term for them – ora, a term that is familiar in Māori, too, for a timber-splitting wedge.

Gouges were required for working the wood. These were at least sometimes supplied by human bones, generally 'the thin bone of the upper arm', according to Cook's naturalist Joseph Banks:

> these they grind very sharp and fix to a handle of wood, making the instrument serve the purpose of a gouge by striking it with a mallet made of a hard black wood [ironwood], and with them would do as much work as with Iron tools was it not that the brittle Edge of the tool is very liable to be broke.[32]

Files and abraders were needed, too, and were made here from pieces of coral (punga) and bunches of heavy sea-urchin spines ('Echinoid spine abraders', page 132).[33] 'Sandpaper' was supplied by the rough skin of a shark, stingray or manta ray; the skin of an old stingray (whai) was used for the coarse work, the skin of a young one for fine work, and a shark fin for polishing.[34] The canoe planks had to be drilled in preparation for being sewn together. For this, a pump drill was used, with the tooth of a shark or rat as a point, or the spine of a stingray, the point of a long-spired shell or the heavy spine of a slate-pencil urchin.[35]

Population and voyaging capacity

The nature and extent of Tuamotuan voyaging is likely to have depended to some extent on the size of the local population. Unfortunately there is no early census, but we do know that in 1842, more than two centuries after the first known European contact in 1606, the northwestern atoll of `Ana`a alone still boasted some 2000 inhabitants and a fleet of 60 double

Tuamotuan shipbuilding

A Tuamotuan double canoe (15 m long), 1847, top.[36]
Above: Tou (Cordia subcordata), which provided the timber for most Tuamotuan boatbuilding.[37]
Below: **Pāua** *(giant clam, Tridacna species) of the tropical Pacific, whose shell was used for making shipbuilding tools. Its Polynesian-wide name was transferred in New Zealand to an equivalent shellfish (Haliotis species) whose large, strong shell was used by Māori for making much smaller adze-like tools.*

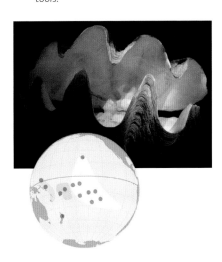

More atoll tools

Whai (stingray), left, were speared not only for meat, but also for two hoto (tara whai, tail spikes, below left), which serve as drill bits and points for spears; stingray skin also served as sandpaper. The Māori stingray name, whai, is conspicuously absent from the Southern Cook Islands, where stingrays are known as tāmanu.

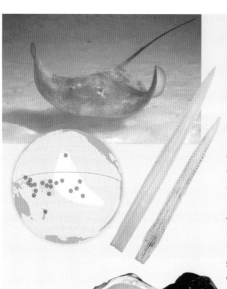

Punga (coral rock), below right, lumps of which were widely used in the tropical Pacific as canoe anchors, with globe showing the distribution of this term, transferred in New Zealand to any kind of anchor.

A **kahi** of the tropical Pacific (tropical freshwater mussel, Batissa violacea), left, with globe showing distribution of this term for bivalve shellfish used for scraping tubers and breadfruit, transferred in New Zealand to local kākahi shells used for scraping kūmara, freshwater mussel (Hyridella menziesi) and pipi (Paphies australe).

An edible **kuku** of the tropical Pacific (winged mussel, Modiolus auriculatus), left, whose shells are used as a scraper or made into fishhooks and needles for sewing leaf mats.[38] Globe shows the distribution of this term, applied in New Zealand to the equivalent saltwater mussel used for the same purposes.[39]

A **pipi** of the tropical Pacific (Asaphis deflorata), right, whose shells are used for cutting, sawing and scraping. Globe shows the distribution for this term, which generally refers to a bivalve used as scraping and cutting tools, coconut graters and taro scrapers,[40] applied in New Zealand to Paphies australe, a similarly prized tool for scaling fish or for scraping flax leaves for weaving.

A **tio** (oyster), left, with globe showing distribution of this term for oysters. The shell has a knife-like edge used for cutting hair and performing minor surgery, including removing a spear point from a person's leg.

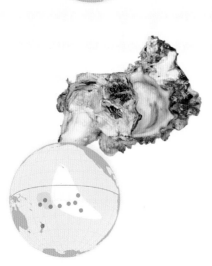

Pā (pārau, black-lipped pearl oyster, Pinctada margaritifera), right, containing the pearls that provide the basis of a pearl farming industry today. Traditionally, its shells were to fashion into breast ornaments, spear points, tattoo needles, crescent-shaped vegetable scrapers, fishhooks and fishing lures. The globe shows the distribution of the term pā for pearl oyster or fishing lure, transferred in New Zealand to a corresponding lure from pāua shell (Haliotis).

canoes;[41] and that, around this time or earlier, `Ana`a and neighbouring atolls of Fakarava and Rangiroa formed a powerful military confederation that dominated much of the Tuamotus.[42]

Tuamotuan traditions refer to voyages beyond the archipelago, too – at least as far as the Society Islands,[43] where Tuamotuans exchanged shells, red tropicbird tail-feathers, white dogs' hair and shipbuilding skills for high-island bark cloth and basalt for making adzes.[44] Long-distance contact can be independently verified from basalt adze heads recovered from several northern Tuamotuan atolls: the basalt was imported from at least five distant archipelagos, including the Marquesas, Pitcairn Island, Rurutu (Austral Is), Rapa Iti (Bass Is), and even the Hawaiian Islands.[45]

Clearly, the archipelago was an important voyaging destination – and with good reason.

Largest navigational target in Polynesia

In the previous chapter we saw how the 'swell shadow' of this archipelago enables navigators to discern its presence from up to 650 km to the northeast, and the vast area over which the archipelago extends – two factors that contribute to its strategic role in East Polynesian navigation. It is practically impossible to sail through the group unwittingly, as most atolls within the archipelago lie sufficiently close to their neighbour that the flight ranges of their local landfinding birds overlap. As Captain Cook noted while exploring this region in 1774, the water between the atolls is also noticeably smoother than in the open ocean. On rediscovering the swell of the open ocean on the western side, it was clear to him – as it was to other navigators – that they had passed right through the archipelago to reach the other side. In a sense, its 78 scattered atolls and raised coral reefs can be likened to the knots of one enormous net, one that presents by far the largest navigational target in tropical Polynesia.

And it is for this very same reason that the atolls of the Tuamotus were found by almost every European explorer that passed through this region, from the Spanish and Portuguese mariners who came this way in the 250 years before Cook, to Heyerdahl aboard his *Kon-Tiki* raft.[46]

In other words, when traditional navigators headed into this region, they could be reasonably confident of making landfall on an inhabited atoll, where they might – with due attention to the appropriate protocols – restock on fresh provisions and confirm their location before setting out on the next leg of their voyage. In this way, the archipelago is likely to have played a key role for voyagers sailing to and from Hawai`i, Tahiti, the Marquesas Islands and Mangareva, perhaps Easter Island, South America and – as we shall see – also New Zealand.[47]

We know that Tuamotuans had the requisite knowledge of neighbouring atolls to offer this kind of navigational assistance from an 1839 report by American naval officer Charles Wilkes, in which he records a local supplying him with the names of 62 isles in the archipelago as he marked out their relative positions on the deck of the captain's bridge with a piece of chalk.[48]

Mosquito eggs onboard

Despite a lack of freshwater on these atolls, the Polynesian mosquito (Aedes polynesiensis) was already well established before PVC rainwater tanks were installed, for it develops from egg to adult in rainwater collecting in natural containers such as tree holes, coconut husks and land crab burrows. It was evidently distributed from its native Fiji – Sāmoa/Tonga region to the Cook Islands and French Polynesia aboard Polynesian sailing canoes – probably as eggs.[49] Although it did not reach New Zealand, its Polynesian names – namu, naonao, nono – did. The globes below show (top) distribution of the name **namu**; *and (bottom) distribution of the term* **naonao** *or nono.*

Local migratory birds

*Of the three migrating birds that might reveal the existence to Tuamotuans of unknown lands, the species with the greatest potential is the **kārevareva**, left, of the Tuamotus (New Zealand long-tailed cuckoo, koekoeā or kawekaweā, Urodynamis taitensis), a bird that flies from most of these atolls – and indeed from most islands in tropical Polynesia – to New Zealand in Sep–Oct each year. The globe shows the distribution of this term.[50]*

*In April two shorebird species also depart from here (and from elsewhere in the tropical Pacific) to nest in Alaska. One is the **kivi** (bristle-thighed curlew, Numenius tahitiensis), above, a large shorebird which has an extremely long, downward-curving bill and a loud 'weoo-weet' call. The globe shows the East Polynesian distribution of its name,[51] transferred in New Zealand to a forest bird with a similarly long bill and call, kiwi (Apteryx). The other is the tōrea (or turi, Pacific golden plover, Pluvialis fulva), left. Language globes show the distribution of the name **turi** for migratory waders (left, applied in New Zealand to the stilt and dotterel); and the strictly East Polynesian distribution of the name **tōrea** (right, applied in New Zealand to the oystercatcher and stilt).*

'Mine is the migrating bird'

We also know from Tuamotuan poetry that observations of migrating birds told them of land still further afield. 'Mine is the migrating bird,' declares one of their voyaging songs, 'Pathway of the Birds' – a bird that reveals 'the road of the winds coursed by the Sea Kings to unknown lands'.[52] In general, such chants are judged reliable historical sources because of their structured form, which is resistant to accidental or deliberate alteration. So which kind of birds might Tuamotuans follow?

Two local shorebirds – the curlew and the Pacific golden plover – regularly head up from here to Alaska in April to breed during the northern summer. Although Tuamotuans may have taken this as a cue to explore to the north, it is highly unlikely that they followed these birds as far as Alaska.[53]

The bird that stands out for its potential to guide Tuamotuan navigators to unknown land is a forest species known as the New Zealand long-tailed cuckoo. During the southern hemisphere winter it is resident on at least 20

Tuamotuan fish and crab names shared with Māori

Of the many Tuamotuan fish names shared with Māori, the following are exclusively East Polynesian.[54]

*Left, from top: A local **pātiki** (flounder, Bothus species), with globe showing the distribution of this term for flounder; a **kōkiri** of tropical East Polynesia (Picasso triggerfish, Rhinecanthus aculeatus), with globe showing the distribution of this term for triggerfish or leatherjackets; a **kōura** of the tropical Pacific (spiny lobster, Panulirus penicillatus), with globe showing the distribution of this term for crayfish or lobster; **kōperu** (mackerel scad, Decapterus macarellus), with globe showing the distribution of the term kōheru or kōperu for local species of mackerel scad.*

*Right, from top: A **tōtara** (common porcupine fish, Diodon hystrix), with globe showing the distribution of this term for porcupine fish, recorded as kōpūwaitōtara or kōpūtōtara for its equivalent fish in New Zealand; a **tāmure** of the Tuamotus (scribbled snapper, Lutjanus rivulatus), with globe showing the distribution of this term, generally applied to snapper.*

Tuamotuan atolls, yet all these birds will leave around early October. Their 'swhooeesht' calls are not heard on these atolls for the next four months, until the birds reappear at the same spot as before between January and April. A similar phenomenon can be observed on many Pacific Islands, including the Marquesas, Society, Cook and Austral islands, Rapa Iti, Pitcairn Island and most of West Polynesia.[55] Over this entire region, the bird vanishes and reappears with remarkable regularity.

I had come across these birds many times in New Zealand, but it was not until I reached the Tuamotus that I had the thrill of seeing them in their winter home. It was early May when we anchored at the Tuamotuan atoll of Tahanea, and I had gone ashore to explore the coconut forest when a pair flew past me through the branches and settled just above my head. From the month, I knew that they must have just flown in from New Zealand, the only place where these cuckoos breed, despite the incredible distance – some 4300 km. It felt like a very tangible connection with home.

Sharks

Sharks are as central to the life of the tropical Pacific as the coconut, providing the islanders not only with meat, but also teeth and skins which served as tools, such as drill points and sandpaper. Beyond the confines of the lagoon, the larger man-eating species were also a significant source of danger. It is no surprise, then, to see that Polynesian names for them are widely shared. Of the five Tuamotuan shark names that are shared with New Zealand Māori, the distribution of three are strictly East Polynesian.

The taniwha of the tropical Pacific – a dangerous, man-eating tiger shark (Galeocerdo cuvier), left, up to 5.5 m long, known in the Tuamotus as ngutukao. The left-hand globe shows distribution of the term **taniwha**, whose meaning in New Zealand extended to include a fierce mythical monster that lurks in deep water. Right, distribution of **ngutukao**, the Tuamotuan tiger shark name.[56]

Niuhi (great white shark, Carcharodon carcharias), right, up to 6 m, with globe showing the East Polynesian distribution of the name niuhi or **ninihi**, applied to very large sharks, particularly the great white or the tiger shark.

Parata (oceanic whitetip, Carcharhinus longimanus), right – another dangerous 'man-eating' shark common in tropical waters, with globe showing the East Polynesian distribution of this term, generally for the oceanic whitetip, transferred to New Zealand to a mythical sea monster, a creature so vast that the opening and shutting of its jaws causes the ebb and flow of the tides – the daily 'long breathing' of the ocean.[57]

An **arawa** of the tropical Pacific (silvertip shark, Carcharhinus albimarginatus), left, 3 m long, with globe showing distribution of the term, recorded in New Zealand as a 'species of shark', the name of a canoe and of a tribe.

Mangō (blacktip reef shark, Carcharhinus melanopterus), left, 1.8 m long, with globe showing distribution of the term, applied in New Zealand to Isurus oyrinchus, which Māori hunted for meat and its teeth, which were drilled as necklaces or ear ornaments.

Episodes of migration

Even if one is inclined to doubt that this is the bird in the song, there can be little doubt that Tuamotuans had long-distance voyaging capability, and that they were well placed to hear from other navigators of the existence of 'unknown lands' – including New Zealand. As with the inhabitants of all low-lying atolls, they also had a perennial motive to look beyond their own shores – not only because of their vulnerability to inundation from the sea and to drought, but because of local outbreaks of ciguatera, a type of fish poisoning.[58]

This poison enters the food chain when reef-grazing fish ingest a toxin (ciguatoxin) that is produced in tropical and subtropical waters by algae-like dinoflagellates. The toxin accumulates in the predators of those fish, making it difficult to know which kinds of fish to avoid. Typically, ciguatera causes nausea, vomiting, diarrhoea, weakness, numbness, itchiness, muscle pain and occasionally paralysis or death; and unfortunately, it is not destroyed by cooking.

Local outbreaks are not unusual here, and when they did occur, ciguatera-free islands situated in cooler waters would have been attractive destinations. This would include places like Easter Island and New Zealand – locations that also have many other advantages over atolls.

Contact with New Zealand?

There are many striking cultural links between Tuamotuans and New Zealand Māori. In mythology, for example, the Tuamotuan marakihau – in reference to mermaid-like demons, human above the waist, fish-like below, with a spiralling tail – recurs in traditional carving of New Zealand's southern Bay of Plenty and the Urewera region. And the greedy, menacing Tūhoropunga ('The Ever Greedy One'), mentioned in songs, sayings and myths of Māori, is the same Tuhoropunga who rules the ocean in the Tuamotus.[59]

Many New Zealand place names can be recognised here – more than for the Northern and Southern Cook Islands combined. Among them are such culturally important names as Havaiki (Hawaiki), a marae on the atoll of Nukutavake and an ancient name for the atoll of Fakarava; and the name Taputapuātea, identified as an origin of the Te Arawa Māori of the Bay of Plenty,[60] is recorded in the Tuamotus for marae on both Fakarava and Hao.[61]

As linguist Bruce Biggs explains, the Tuamotuan language is indeed 'closely related to Maori, and a good deal more familiar to a Maori speaker than is modern Tahitian'.[62] Voyaging contact between the Tuamotus and Society Islands[63] was sufficiently frequent that migration from either location seems equally likely.[64] Both are part of the same voyaging sphere.

Whereas anyone leaving to the west from the southern Tuamotuan atolls is likely to have sailed via the Austral Islands, craft leaving from the northern Tuamotus are more likely to have headed for the Southern Cook Islands via the Society Islands – the focus of our next chapter.[65]

Inside/outside

Until coming to the Tuamotus, I had often been puzzled as to why, in New Zealand, the Māori term roto for 'inside' referred also to a lake. Here, it was clear. On an atoll, the lake-like lagoon, roto (inside), stands in clear contrast with 'outside, in the open sea' (moana), representing two distinct worlds with respect to food resources and level of protection from man-eating sharks and rough seas. On high islands with no lagoon (e.g., Tikopia, Niuē, Hawai`i, Marquesas and New Zealand), the meaning of roto (inside) was evidently transferred to a pool, pond or lake, and on islands with both lakes and lagoons (e.g., the Cook Is and Society Is), roto can mean either.

CHAPTER SEVEN

The Society Islands

One Hawaiki Among Many

Māori and Pākehā alike have wondered about the true location of Hawaiki.
The actual location has never been confirmed, and it is uncertain if it is a real, physical island
or a mythical place. Some have associated Hawaiki with the Tahitian island Ra'iātea
(Rangiātea, in Māori).

Māori scholar Te Ahukaramā Charles Royal, *Te Ara – The Encyclopedia of New Zealand*, 2015

A Society of Islands

Continuing towards New Zealand, we arrive next at the Society Islands – a name given by Captain Cook in recognition of the fact that every isle within the group lies close enough to its neighbour to maintain easy contact.[1] This is reflected in the fact that the same dialect of Tahitian is spoken by all inhabitants of the archipelago.

Even so, this archipelago is often divided into two parts – the 'Windward Islands' of Tahiti and Mo`orea in the southeast and, some 135 km downwind to the northwest, the 'Leeward Islands' of Ra`iātea, Porapora (Bora Bora), Huahine and Maupiti.

As with the Marquesas and Hawaiian islands, all are peaks of a ridge of underwater volcanoes, many with slopes that drop down to narrow coastal strips, or directly into lagoons protected from the sea by an encircling barrier reef.

Today, these islands are widely promoted as a tourist destination, with photos of 'aqua-centric luxury resorts' in the turquoise lagoon of the island of Borabora. Tahiti, the highest and largest island in the group, rises to 2241 m above sea level – almost as high as New Zealand's Mt Taranaki – and is a transport hub today for much of East Polynesia, connected by trans-Pacific flights to Los Angeles, Honolulu, Tokyo, Santiago (via Easter Island) and Auckland. It is also an important stopover for round-the-world yachts such as ours: it offers one of the best boat-repair facilities in the South Pacific, and an excellent opportunity to stock up on provisions.

From the oral history record and archaeological evidence we know that the group had previously served as an important voyaging hub for East Polynesians, too.

Origins and long-distance contact

According to carbon-dating evidence, this group of islands is likely to have been among the earliest in this East Polynesian region to be settled – in around AD 1000.[2] This comparatively early date, and the wealth of large natural harbours here, lend support to the idea that these islands originally served as a base for regional exploration and settlement – consistent with the variety of traditional crops grown here. At the time of European contact, these numbered 47 species – a figure that does not include the very large number of horticultural varieties of each crop. Of these, the origins of all but kūmara lie to the west, in the Western Pacific and/or Southeast Asia.[3]

Indeed, local traditions tell of widespread voyaging:

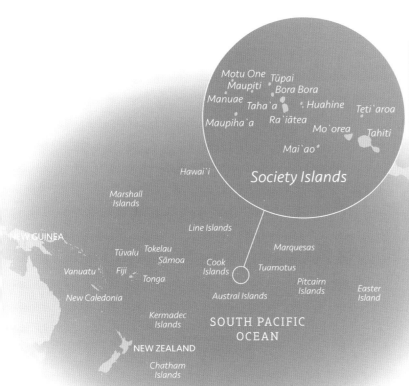

Motu One
Maupiti Tūpai
         Bora Bora
Manuae Taha`a  `Huahine
Maupiha`a  Ra`iātea Teti`aroa
                Mo`orea Tahiti
           Mai`ao

Society Islands

Hawai`i

Marshall
Islands

Line Islands

NEW GUINEA

Tūvalu Tokelau
        Sāmoa   Marquesas
Vanuatu Fiji   Cook   Tuamotus
         Tonga   Islands
New Caledonia   Pitcairn   Easter
              Austral Islands   Islands   Island

            Kermadec
            Islands   **SOUTH PACIFIC**
                        OCEAN
        NEW ZEALAND

        Chatham
        Islands

Above: Huahine, Society Islands – a typical scene today.

Below: The island of Bora Bora (Tahitian: Porapora, Havai`i or Vavau), which sits within a stunning turquoise lagoon, today features in almost every tourist brochure of the region.

SOCIETY ISLANDS: *Inter-island contact*

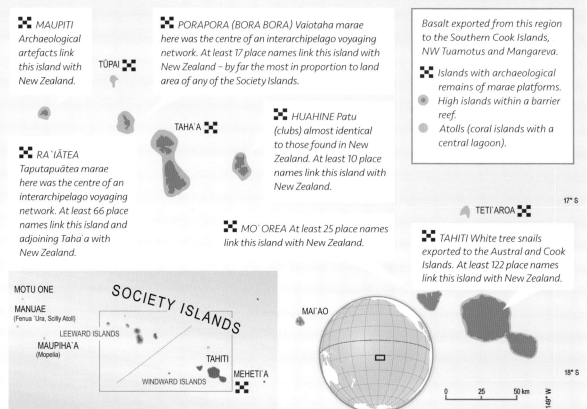

■■ *MAUPITI Archaeological artefacts link this island with New Zealand.*

TŪPAI ■■

■■ *PORAPORA (BORA BORA) Vaiotaha marae here was the centre of an interarchipelago voyaging network. At least 17 place names link this island with New Zealand – by far the most in proportion to land area of any of the Society Islands.*

TAHA`A ■■

■■ *RA`IĀTEA Taputapuātea marae here was the centre of an interarchipelago voyaging network. At least 66 place names link this island and adjoining Taha`a with New Zealand.*

■■ *HUAHINE Patu (clubs) almost identical to those found in New Zealand. At least 10 place names link this island with New Zealand.*

■■ *MO`OREA At least 25 place names link this island with New Zealand.*

Basalt exported from this region to the Southern Cook Islands, NW Tuamotus and Mangareva.

■■ *Islands with archaeological remains of marae platforms.*
● *High islands within a barrier reef.*
● *Atolls (coral islands with a central lagoon).*

17° S

TETI`AROA ■■

■■ *TAHITI White tree snails exported to the Austral and Cook Islands. At least 122 place names link this island with New Zealand.*

MOTU ONE

MANUAE
(Fenua `Ura, Scilly Atoll)

LEEWARD ISLANDS

MAUPIHA`A
(Mopelia)

SOCIETY ISLANDS

MAI`AO

TAHITI

WINDWARD ISLANDS

MEHETI`A ■■

18° S

0   25   50 km

149° W

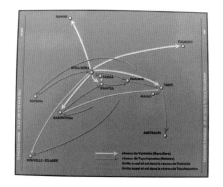

Above: Signage at Taputapuātea marae depicts voyaging networks spoken of in local traditions of Bora Bora, Tahiti, Taha`a and Ra`iātea.[4] Ongoing contact along many of these routes can be confirmed from adze blades whose source can be traced back to basalt quarries on distant archipelagos (see page 231).

south from here to the Austral Islands, west to the Cook Islands, east to the Tuāmotu Archipelago and Marquesas, and north to Hawai`i[5] – traditions that can be independently corroborated from early oral records collected from each of these destinations. They also speak of voyages by Society Island navigators to Mangareva and Rapa.[6]

There is further support for such an extensive voyaging network in the verifiable transfer of basalt for tool-making, either to or from the Marquesas Islands, Tuamotus, Mangareva, Pitcairn and Austral Islands and several of the Southern Cook Islands – and, as previously mentioned, indirectly from the Hawaiian Islands to the Tuamotus. Tahitian ethnologist and folklorist Teuira Henry maintains that Porapora (Bora Bora) was also in voyaging contact with Rotumā to the west in West Polynesia, and with New Zealand to the south.[7] It is worth glancing at a globe or map to fully appreciate the extraordinary reach of this network (page 8–9).

However, by the time Captain Cook reached the Society Islands in 1769, its inhabitants had evidently lost contact with more distant destinations, including the Hawaiian Islands and New Zealand. And yet they retained their long-distance, two-way voyaging skills, for Tahitian navigator Tupa`ia was able to supply Cook with accurate sailing directions from the Society Islands to destinations as far afield as Rotumā to the west, east to the Marquesas and south to the Austral Islands – a region of the Pacific some 4800 km wide[8] (see map on page 213).

Cook and his crew were also clearly impressed by the scale of local shipbuilding activities. Joseph Banks describes the local craftsmen at work on the island of Ra`iātea in 1769:

> Dr Solander and myself walkd out this morn and saw many large Boathouses. On these the inhabitants were at work making and repairing the large Canoes calld by them Pahee, at which business they workd with incredible cleverness tho their tools certainly were as bad as possible.[9]

A description of the long-distance voyaging craft in use at the time, and the care bestowed on them, was left to us by Cook's botanical illustrator Sydney Parkinson:

> This people are very ingenious in building their Proes or Canoes and seem to take as much Care of them having large Sheds or houses to put them in built for the Purpose. . . There is a great number of boathouses all round the bays built with a Catanarian arch, thatched all over; and the boats kept in them are very long, bellying out on the sides, with a very high peaked stern, and are used only at particular seasons.[10]

According to Tupa`ia, these large double-hulled canoes were used to sail out of sight of land for 20 days or more. Cook elaborates:

> In these Proes, or Pahies as they call them, from all the accounts we can learn, these people sail in those Seas from Island to Island for several hundred Leagues [suggesting well over 1000 km],[11] the Sun serving them for a compass by day and the Moon and Stars by night. When this comes to be prov'd we Shall be no longer at a loss to know how the Islands lying in those Seas came to be people'd, for if the inhabitants of [Ra`iātea] have been at Islands laying 2 or 300 Leagues to the westward of them it cannot be doubted but that the inhabitants of those western Islands may have been at others as far to westward of them and so we may trace them from Island to Island quite to [Southeast Asia].[12]

Above: Captain Cook was impressed to learn of long-distance, two-way voyaging by Tahitians over distances of more than 1000 km each way. Cook's crew described Tahitian boatbuilding in 1769 and the care taken to house their sailing canoes in 'a great number of boathouses all round the bays'. Here illustrated is just such a scene from the island of Ra`iātea.

Below: Archaeologist Yosihiko Sinoto at Fa`ahia on Huahine in 1979, with excavated mast from an ancient Polynesian canoe, one of the items that provided the archaeological basis for a reconstruction of an early Society Island voyaging canoe.

Right: A twin-masted, double-hulled canoe at Matavai Bay, on the north coast of Tahiti, 1769.

Above: Mo`orea, where pollen evidence reveals human presence for over 1000 years.

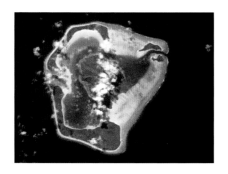

Above: Maupiti, where burial artefacts were found matching those from an early archaeological site on Wairau Bar, South Island, New Zealand.

Below: Huahine Island, home to more than 100 marae sites and some of the most significant archaeological sites in Polynesia.

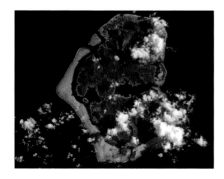

A contraction in long-distance voyaging

Some three centuries before Cook's arrival, though – soon after AD 1450 – voyaging to the more remote islands of the Polynesian Triangle had ceased. This is evident from the dateable archaeological context in which many tradeable items have been found, including tools made of basalt, and fishhooks and ornaments made of pearl shell unearthed on archipelagos where the living shellfish does not occur.[13]

Several explanations for this contraction in long-distance voyaging have been proposed: an abrupt change in climate; a reduction in available resources; conflict; and one or more major tsunami. And indeed there is dateable archaeological and ecological evidence for all four:

1. A change in climatic conditions around AD 1300 is evident in fossil coral, whose prehistoric growth is responding at this point to a change in local sea temperature, reflecting a change in wind regimes and a period of stormier sea conditions.[14]

2. By this time, all worthwhile land in the Pacific had been discovered. A regional shortage of timber for building canoes shows up in the pollen record from around AD 1500, on Mangareva and Easter Island at least; and deposits of subfossil bones on many islands show a marked depletion of birds.

3. Increasing conflict is evident from a proliferation of fortifications 1300–1500 on the Marquesas, Mangareva and Rapa Iti and in New Zealand.[15]

4. There is evidence along the New Zealand coastline and throughout much of the Southern Pacific for at least two mega-tsunami, dateable to around AD 1450.[16] With Polynesian settlements concentrated largely on the coast at that time, such events are likely to have led to major loss of life and canoes.[17]

In reality, several or all of these factors may have worked together to outweigh the rewards of long ocean journeys. Irrespective of the reasons behind the shrinking extent of long-distance voyaging, archaeologists agree on the timing: that this was occurring in the Pacific around AD 1450 – before Europeans arrived.

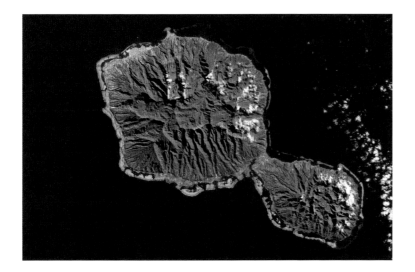

Left: Tahiti is a twin island, sometimes referred to as Tahiti-nui and Tahiti-iti. It is the largest and highest of the Society Islands, rising to 2241 m – a similar elevation to Mt Taranaki in New Zealand; and with a land area of 1045 sq km – less than two-thirds that of Stewart Island. The current population is about 194,000, of whom some 70 percent are of Polynesian descent.

The island of Tahiti

As we saw, Tahiti is the main island in the group; in terms of land area, it accounts for over two-thirds of the Society Islands. It was also – and still is – the most populous island in the region. Its lagoon, which encircles the island and is protected from stormy seas by an encircling barrier reef, would have provided ample shelter for a maritime fleet. For these two reasons alone, the island was virtually guaranteed a prominent place in Polynesian history.

The number of people living here, and the extent of the island's agriculture, would make a deep impression on George Robertson, master of the *Dolphin*, when he arrived in 1767:

> [T]he country hade the most Beautiful appearance its posable to Imagin, from the shore side, one two and three miles Back there is a fine Leavel country that appears to be all laid out in plantations, and the regular built Houses seems to be without number, all allong the Coast, they appeared lyke long farmers Barns and seemd to be all very neatly thatched, with Great Numbers of Coca Nut Trees. . .– from the foot of the Mountains half way up the Country appears to be all

Left: Part of the Tahitian naval fleet that Captain Cook saw at Pare, northwest Tahiti in 1774, with 330 double sailing canoes (160 large and 170 small), poised for battle with their bows drawn up onto the beach. In Cook's efforts to gauge the size of the island's population, he estimated seeing at least 7760 men here alone, drawn from just two districts of the island.

Tahitian nature terms

Of the many Tahitian nature terms that are shared with New Zealand, at least four are evidently shared only between these two regions.

Above: Māori aihe (driftwood); Tahitian āiha.

Below: Māori kokoea (long-tailed cuckoo);[18] Tahitian `ō`ōvea. Māori tawhiwhi (native jasmine vine); Tahitian tāfifi.[19]

Above: Māori rarauhe (for a fern); Tahitian rarauhe.[20]

fine pasture land, except a few places which seemd to be plowed or dug up for planting or sowing some sort of seed… This appears to be the most populoss country I ever saw, the whole shore side was lined with men, women and children all the way that we Saild along.[21]

According to Robertson, over 100,000 people were living on this island at that time – more than the estimated number of Māori living in all of New Zealand.[22]

Cook's party was no less astonished by the island's megalithic architecture. At Paparā on the south side, he and his crew came across the largest temple ever constructed in the Society Islands, Marae Maha`iatea, and set to work measuring the stone platform. It turned out to be 81.4 m x 26.5 m at the base (almost as long as a rugby field), rising in a stepped pyramid to the height of a modern four-storey building. Cook described it:

> There were eleven. . . steps, each of which was four feet high, so that the height . . . was forty-four feet; each course . . . formed . . . of white coral stone, which was neatly squared and polished; the rest of the mass, for there was no hollow within, consisted of round pebbles, which, from the regularity of their figure, seemed to have been wrought [by hand]. Some of the coral stones were very large; we measured one of them, and found it three feet and a half by two feet and a half . . . The quarry stones, as we saw no quarry in the neighbourhood, must have been brought from a considerable distance; and there is no method of conveyance here but by hand; the coral must also have been fished up from under the water, where, though it may be found in plenty, it lies at a considerable depth, never less than three feet.[23]

In tones of the same incredulity as the Europeans expressed on Easter Island, Banks added: 'It is almost beyond belief that Indians could raise so large a structure without the assistance of Iron tools to shape their stones or mortar to join them . . . it is done tho, and almost as firmly as a European workman would have done it.'[24]

Many Tahiti (*lit.*, 'distant place')

NZ MĀORI	Tawhiti	traditional homeland, distant place
HAWAIIAN IS	Kahiki	any foreign land
MARQUESAS	Tehiti	any foreign land
N. COOK IS (PUKAPUKA)	Tawiti	Tahiti
S. COOK IS (RAROTONGA)	Ta`iti	Tahiti
TAHITIAN	Tahiti	Tahiti
TUĀMOTU	Tahiti	Tahiti, remote place

Clearly, Tahiti was a major centre of Polynesia. And this is consistent with the fact that it, along with neighbouring Ra`iātea and Porapora, were traditionally known as Havai`i (Māori: Hawaiki, 'homeland').

Hawaiki (homeland)

Both these names for the island – Hawaiki and Tahiti (Māori: Tawhiti) – occur in Māori origin traditions;[25] however, Te Rangi Hīroa cautions us not to assume too much from this. 'It is due to post-European study,' he writes, 'that [Hawaiki and Tawhiti] have been located in the Society Islands.'

His caution is based on the fact that Tahiti can refer simply to a 'distant place'; and, similarly, 'Hawaiki' applies to a number of East Polynesian homelands,[26] distant or local, including Northland, New Zealand, and several other homeland locations in the North and South Islands.[27]

A literal interpretation of the term can be misleading for another reason, too. In Māori songs, chants, proverbs and genealogies, Hawaiki may also refer to the realm from which the spirit of the newborn emerges, and to which it returns after death. In this sense, life is a journey from Hawaiki to Hawaiki,[28] the unfathomable realms prior to birth and after death.

We find much the same thing in English, where the corresponding word 'home' can refer either to 'the place of one's affections, peace, or rest' or 'one's native place or country'. It, too, appears in many homeland place names, in the Old English form of the word 'hām': Nottingham, Birmingham or Buckingham. For this reason, we cannot identify a Hawaiki origin as a single island on account of the name alone.

Below: Aerial view from the north of Taha`a (lower) and Ra`iātea (upper), showing both islands encircled by a single reef enclosing a navigable band of sheltered coastal water that offered canoes an enviable degree of protection from the sea – and from warriors.

Many Hawaiki (lit., 'an ancestral homeland, spiritual or physical')[29]

NEW ZEALAND MĀORI	Hawaiki	the traditional homeland or spiritual homeland[30]
TUĀMOTU (VĀHITAHI, RARO`IA)	Havāiki	the name of an ancestral homeland[31]
TUĀMOTU	Havaiki	Fakarava Atoll; marae on Nukutavake[32]
MARQUESAS (NW)	Havaiki	the regions below; the invisible world
MARQUESAS (SE)	Havai`i	the regions below; the invisible world
TAHITIAN	Havai`i	previously applied to **Ra`iātea**, **Porapora** and **Tahiti**
HAWAIIAN IS	Hawai`i	largest island in the Hawaiian group (the 'Big Island')
S. COOK IS (RAROTONGA)	`Avaiki	ancestral homeland (Rarotonga/ Society Islands/?)[33]
S. COOK IS (MANGAIA)	`Avaiki	ancestral homeland to the west[34]
GAMBIER IS (MANGAREVA)	`Avaiki	place often mentioned in songs and legends
SĀMOA	Savai`i	the largest island in Sāmoa

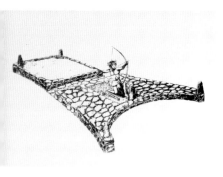

Above: Stone archery platforms, found on all the main Society Islands, were used by the nobility (ari`i and ra`atira): the aim was to shoot the arrow as far as possible, not at a specific target. The absence of similar platforms, and of the sport itself, in New Zealand suggests that contact with the Society Islands had broken off by AD 1500, when the construction of these platforms evidently began.

Twin voyaging hub

Besides Tahiti, local tradition speaks of another major hub of long-distance voyaging some 200 km downwind of Tahiti, centred on Ra`iātea and neighbouring Porapora (Bora Bora), just 30 km to the northwest of it.[35]

We sailed through to Ra`iātea to visit the main marae here – an impressive complex of stone platforms on the southeast coast. Its name speaks for itself, for Taputapuātea implies 'a very sacred space' – a term that is again shared across much of East Polynesia. In New Zealand, for example, it refers to several sacred sites, including one at Whitianga (Te Whitianga o Kupe) on the Coromandel Peninsula.[36]

This is understood to be the same Taputapuātea that is named as an origin of the Te Arawa people of the Bay of Plenty in New Zealand.[37] And yet those voyagers may not have seen the stone platforms themselves, for the custom of building them appears to have begun much later. This is the conclusion of archaeologists Reidar Solsvik and Paul Wallin, from a careful review of construction dates of stone marae and archery platforms from all over the Society Islands. They suggest that these paved marae are unlikely to have played an important role in the Society Islands until after AD 1500.[38] By this time, voyaging to New Zealand is understood to have been over.[39] From the name, it is clear that the site was sacred at that time; it just may not have looked as it does today.

Sacred birds of the marae

Māori are linked to East Polynesia by the names of sacred birds of the marae. Cook's scientists recorded the veneration for the birds when they coined the names Egretta sacra ('sacred egret') for the reef heron, and Todiramphus venerata for the Tahiti kingfisher.

Top right: The `ōtu`u of the Society Islands (or kōtuku of Rarotonga, reef heron Egretta sacra), with globe showing that this name is East Polynesian, transferred in New Zealand to the sacred **kōtuku** (white heron, Ardea alba). Elsewhere, the reef heron is known as matuku, a name shared by Māori but not recorded in the

Society Islands. This suggests that, although some canoes sailed from the Society Islands, others came from elsewhere. Reef herons were kept as pets and were carried on canoes as an aid to landfinding.

Below right: The sacred `ōtātare of Tahiti (or **kōtare** of Rarotonga, chattering kingfisher, Todiramphus tuta), with globe depicting the very limited distribution of this term for kingfishers, applied in New Zealand – as kōtare – to Todiramphus sanctus; this name links New Zealand Māori strongly with the inhabitants of the Society Islands and/or Rarotonga.

Ra`iātea (Rangiātea)

In fact, Ra`iātea (Rangiātea in Māori) has been identified as the departure point of several of the Māori migration canoes.[40] Although it is true that this name can refer to several other places in Polynesia (see below),[41] the location can be independently confirmed through a local legend shared between the northern South Island and the twin islands of Ra`iātea and Taha`a.

In the New Zealand version, one of the main heroes who helps slay a taniwha (mythical monster) that devours travellers between Tākaka and Motueka is identified as Te Kai-Whakaruaki from Arahura. In the Society Island version, the dreaded `Ai-fa`a-rua`i and local forms of these three place names recur together as Motue`a, Ta`a`a and Ara`ura.[42]

Many Rangiātea (lit., 'clear sky')

NZ MĀORI	Rangiātea	reputed source of Tainui and Te Arawa canoes
	Rangiātea	islet near Russell and place near Ōtorohanga, NI
S. COOK IS	Rangiatea	ancient name for Matavera, Rarotonga
SOCIETY IS	Ra`iātea	island in the leeward group of the Society Is
TONGA	Langiatea	tomb on Nomuka Is (Ha`apai group)
HAWAIIAN IS	Laniākea	beach and spring at Kawailoa on O`ahu
	Laniākea	location at Kailua on the 'Big Island' of Hawai`i

Taputapuātea marae

The main marae complex on Ra`iātea is Taputapuātea, where Cook's botanical illustrator Sydney Parkinson described the scene in 1769: besides altar offerings of roasted pig and fish and large skin drums, he saw 'several large cages of wood, having awnings of palm-leaves upon them . . . [for the sacred] grey heron, and a blue and brown king-fisher'.[43] The marae platform was edged with flowering shrubs and, on a pavement facing the sea, a pyramid faced with large rough stones displayed many long boards carved with various figures. He noted that the priests wore feather capes ornamented with round, polished pieces of mother-of-pearl; semicircular breastplates of wickerwork covered with green pigeon feathers, sharks' teeth and fine white dog's hair; and high hats of bamboo decorated with feathers (far right). Their object of worship was the rainbow, closely associated with `Oro, the god of war.[44] The main marae platform (42.5 m long), has been dated by archaeologists to no earlier than AD 1600.[45] An adjacent marae platform, Hauviri, is pictured top, along with the complex as it appears on approach from the sea (above left).

Many Taputapuātea (lit., 'the very sacred space'), with globe showing the East Polynesian distribution of the name.

NZ MĀORI	Taputapuātea	traditional place name in the old homeland
	Taputapuātea	several local sacred sites in NZ
S. COOK IS	Taputapuātea	marae near Avarua on Rarotonga
	Taputapuātea	marae on the NW coast of `Ātiu
SOCIETY IS	Taputapuātea	famous marae on Ra`iātea
	Taputapuātea	marae at Papetoai on Mo`orea
	Taputapuātea	several marae on Tahiti
TUĀMOTU	Taputapuātea	marae on Fakarava Atoll
	Taputapuātea	marae on Hao Atoll
GAMBIER IS	Taputapuātea	marae on Mangareva
HAWAIIAN IS	Kapukapuākea	heiau (marae) site at Waialua on O`ahu
	Kapukapuahakea	heiau (marae) site on Moloka`i

Population crash

At the first known contact of these islands with Europe on 17 June 1767, when Lieutenant Samuel Wallis brought HMS *Dolphin* into Matavai Bay on the north side of Tahiti, George Robertson described Tahiti from the shore as the most populous country he had ever seen. After making a fuller exploration of the island, he elaborated, 'I dare venter to say there is upward of a hundred thousant Men Women and Children on it.'

Above: The missionary zeal of 1815 saw the 'old heathen idols' burned, and, before long, the marae were all abandoned.

If anything, his estimate seems to have been conservative. Johann Forster, who reached here seven years later, in 1774, came up with a slightly higher figure from an extrapolation of the number of fighting men he saw taking part in a 'great naval expedition' at Pare, cross-checking this number against the 'carrying capacity' of the island's breadfruit trees; his estimate was 121,500 inhabitants. And Cook came up with a higher figure still, basing his estimate on this same fleet of 160 large double canoes attended by 170 smaller double canoes: 'the whole Island cannot contain less than two hundred and four thousand inhabitants'.[46]

Even if we accept only the most conservative of these estimates of the Tahitian population and its fleet, the figures are revealing. Both have a bearing on the likely voyaging capacity and ambitions of the inhabitants; and on the scale of losses that followed – for just 25 years later, in 1799, district-by-district head counts found only 16,050; and 30 years later, in 1829, just 8658.

Many historians have attributed the huge disparity between populations at European contact and those counted subsequently to over-enthusiastic estimates by early observers. However, a recent re-examination of the archaeological evidence supports the accuracy of the original estimates – at least the more conservative ones. We now know that, within 60 years of European contact, some 93 percent of the Tahitian population died, a loss attributable almost entirely to the introduction of new diseases.

Contact with New Zealand?

There is a consensus that at least some of the ancestors of Māori left from these islands, a conclusion supported by oral history, shared place names,[47] artefact styles, indigenous names of wild plants (page 116) and the Tahitian language in general,[48] and the maternal DNA of Pacific rats showing that many of these creatures reached New Zealand from this region.[49] Indeed, the Society Islands are likely to have played a strong role in the discovery and settlement of much of the East Polynesian region.

- CHAPTER EIGHT -

Rarotonga and the Cook Islands

En Route to New Zealand

The most considerable element in the settlement of the East Coast from Opotiki
round to Gisborne came from Rarotonga, Mangaia, and so on.

Tribal historian Sir Āpirana Ngata, *Journal of the Polynesian Society*, 1950

Continuing toward New Zealand, we arrive next at the Southern Cook Islands, a likely departure point for the last leg of most voyages to New Zealand from East Polynesia; this was their last chance to reprovision.

The Cook Islands as a whole comprises 15 islands and atolls. These fall into two distinct groups that are separated by some 1000 km: the Northern Cooks with six low atolls; and the Southern Cooks including Rarotonga, whose peak rises to 652 m. Rarotonga is the largest of the Cook Islands, equivalent in land area to the Hauraki Gulf islands of Rangitoto, Motutapu and Little Barrier combined. The remaining Southern Cook islands, in diminishing order of size, are Mangaia, Miti`āro, `Ātiu, Ma`uke and Aitutaki. Of these, Rarotonga and Aitutaki stand out, both for the safe anchorages they offer and for sites for hauling out canoes.[1]

About 15,000 people live in the Cook Islands, some 85 percent of them of Polynesian descent, with the island of Rarotonga nowadays linked by air to Auckland, Christchurch, Sydney, Tahiti and Los Angeles. Onward links to the remaining Cook Islands are provided by local Air Rarotonga flights, and this is how I reached Rarotonga, `Ātiu and Aitutaki.

Origins of the people
Rarotonga means 'southwest' or 'downwind and to the south', an apparent reference to its position in relation to Tahiti. Indeed, Rarotongan oral history refers to immigration from Tahiti, and also from Sāmoa.[2] As for when, the latest review of carbon-dating evidence from the island of Mangaia reveals that the Southern Cook Islands are likely to have been first settled around AD 1000 – a couple of centuries before New Zealand.[3]

The ultimate origin of almost all the islanders' settlement cargo can once again be traced back to Southeast Asia: not just their chickens, Pacific rats, Polynesian pigs, Pacific dogs and crops, but also several kinds of lizards and snails. These lizards and snails, or their eggs, are presumed to have been hidden in the thatching of the canoe hut, or among the crop material. Among the species that are understood to have reached Rarotonga by this means are at least two species of geckos and three of skinks.[4]

Of the herbs, shrubs and trees that were introduced, the ultimate origin of at least 30 likewise lies in the west; and the same is true of several species of tiny landsnails. These range from the 8-mm graceful awlsnail down to species not much bigger than a pinhead. Two of them originate from Asia, one from Indonesia and the tropical western Pacific, and one from the Indonesia–New Guinea region.[5] In other words, all reached these islands from the west, and are understood to have done so before European shipping arrived.

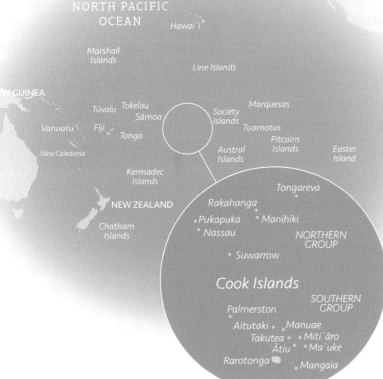

NORTH PACIFIC
OCEAN

Hawai`i

Marshall
Islands

Line Islands

NEW GUINEA

Tūvalu Tokelau
Sāmoa   Society   Marquesas
                         Islands
Vanuatu   Fiji   Tuamotus
          Tonga
New Caledonia   Pitcairn
                         Austral   Islands   Easter
                         Islands   Island
          Kermadec
          Islands

                                    Tongareva
NEW ZEALAND   Rakahanga
              Pukapuka   Manihiki
Chatham   Nassau
Islands   NORTHERN
                                     GROUP
                  Suwarrow

             Cook Islands
                                  SOUTHERN
              Palmerston   GROUP

              Aitutaki   Manuae
              Takutea   Miti`āro
                 Ātiu   Ma`uke
           Rarotonga
                        Mangaia

Rarotonga, above and below,
the main island of the Southern
Cooks, covers 67 sq km and rises
to a peak of 652 m. Its traditional
importance to Polynesians remains
evident in an ancient road that
runs for almost 32 km around
the island, constituting one of
the largest archaeological sites
in Polynesia.

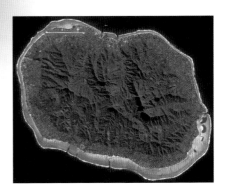

Canoe cargo

Besides people, chickens, Pacific rats, Polynesian pigs, Pacific dogs and crops, the sailing canoes brought several less well-known creatures to the Cook Islands. Above, graceful awlsnails (Allopeas gracile) from Asia, just 12 mm long – one of several small landsnail species that were introduced by Rarotongans. And several lizard species, including the oceanic gecko (Gehyra oceanica) and mournful gecko (Lepidodactylus lugubris, below); and coastal blue-tailed skink (Emoia cyanura, bottom), snake-eyed skink (Cryptoblepharus cf. poecilopleurus), and moth skink (Lipinia noctua). For all the islands east of Sāmoa on which these lizards are found, their presence is attributed to introduction aboard Polynesian canoes.

The local voyaging sphere

Basalt imported to the Southern Cooks for making adze blades was brought from both sides: from quarries in the Society Islands and Marquesas up to 2500 km to the ENE,[6] and from Sāmoa some 1400 km to the WNW.[7] Confirmation of very early contact with the west comes from a pottery fragment found on Ma`uke, the clay for which evidently came from Tongatapu, the main island of Tonga, some 1840 km to the west.[8] This much of the voyaging story is told by the hard evidence.

Local traditions collected here by Te Rangi Hīroa likewise refer to voyages to Tahiti and the Marquesas; and similarities in artefacts, in his view, 'reveal that there must also have been some communication between the Cook and Austral Islands'.[9] Contact a little further afield with Rapa Iti is also evident in shared terms for specific types of fish, shellfish, birds, trees, ferns and shrubs (see page 44).

A voyage, or series of voyages, from South America can also be deduced from the prehistoric presence on Mangaia of kūmara, a Cook Island crop that is known only from this particular island and not Rarotonga, for example.

There can be little doubt, then, that inhabitants of the Southern Cook Islands were capable two-way voyagers – or were at least in regular contact with those who were.

Rarotonga, high island with cloud forest

Rarotonga stands out among the Cook Islands, not just for its size but for its three harbours: two in the north and an all-weather one on the east coast. Being a high island, it is well endowed with running water and timber for shipbuilding. Crops such as taro could be grown in the wetlands bordering the coastal plain and in pond fields constructed in the valleys, and the island's protected reefs and lagoons provided ready access to fish.

Rarotonga is a popular tourist destination nowadays, especially in winter for New Zealanders, who generally come for the swimming, snorkelling and scuba diving. A few go cycling along an ancient road that encircles the island – perhaps unaware that its construction predates the arrival of Europeans on the island. This road provides a tangible clue to the island's former cultural importance: for along it, Rarotongans built more than 50 marae platforms, including the island's main marae of Arai-te-tonga.

Originally, Ara Metua (Te Ara Nui o Toi, the great road of Toi) was paved for about two-thirds of its length with flat pieces of basalt and coral. Unfortunately, much of the old stonework has since been destroyed or buried by modern roading. This paved route is about 5 to 6 m wide and some 30 km long, which makes it one of the largest archaeological sites in Polynesia.[10] The basalt employed in building it was carried from extensive outcrops of volcanic stone on the island – outcrops that also supplied stone for adzes found throughout the archipelago.[11]

Rarotongan plant names

Of the many native Rarotongan plant names that are shared with New Zealand, it is significant that at least three are unrecorded from elsewhere, namely Cook Island equivalents of the Māori **kōtukutuku** (for a shrub that flags its presence with white); **neinei** (for a small forest tree)[12] and **pōhutukawa** (for a coastal tree with spray-resistant leaves).

Above, from left: The Rarotongan kōtuku (Pacific flag-tree, Mussaenda raiateensis), whose white sepals are reminiscent of the white underside of leaves of New Zealand's kōtukutuku (Fuchsia excorticata); neinei (Rarotongan fitchia, Fitchia speciosa), with leaves in tufts at the tip and stems encircled by leaf scars, like the New Zealand neinei (Dracophyllum latifolium); and pō`utukava of the Southern Cook Islands (silverbush, Sophora tomentosa), a coastal tree with a whitish underside to its leaves, as on the coastal New Zealand pōhutukawa tree (Metrosideros excelsa). All three Cook Island plant names are shared only with New Zealand.

Other Rarotongan names subsequently transferred to New Zealand are more widely shared. Above, from left: The local rātā tree (Polynesian metrosideros, Metrosideros collina) of Rarotonga, Austral Islands and Tahiti; the `ākē of Rarotonga or `ake of Mangaia (Dodonaea viscosa); the para of the Pacific (king fern, Ptisana salicina); and, right, the ponga or panga tree fern of Rarotonga (Cyathea affinis). All are either identical, or almost identical, to namesake plants in New Zealand.

Rarotongan fish

The vocabulary of high islands can be distinguished from that of atolls, which lack running water and associated lifeforms. Top right: **Kōurā vai** (freshwater bracelet prawn, Macrobrachium lar) occur in Rarotongan streams but are absent from other Cook Islands; its name is shared with the New Zealand freshwater crayfish (kōura wai, Paranephrops species) — both traditional foods. Right: The freshwater **kōkopu** of Rarotonga (brown gudgeon, Eleotris fusca), with globe showing the East Polynesian distribution of this name for small freshwater fish, applied in New Zealand to the banded kōkopu (Galaxias fasciatus), both again traditionally eaten. While the name tuna (freshwater eel) and puhi (moray eel), are widely used across East and West Polynesia, the name **kōiro** or **ngōiro** (the marine conger eel, right) is again specifically East Polynesian — see globe.

Eel traps

Right: A basket-like pot for catching eels, with globe depicting the distribution of the term **hīnaki** used for them, this one made from the woody stem of the Cook Island **pirita** vine (native jasmine, Jasminum didymum, far right) typical of `Ātiu, Ma`uke, Miti`āro and Mangaia. The adjacent globe shows the distribution of this name for woody vines used for making eel traps, applied in Tahiti to the tough roots of `ie`ie (Freycinetia) and in New Zealand to supplejack vines (Ripogonum scandens).

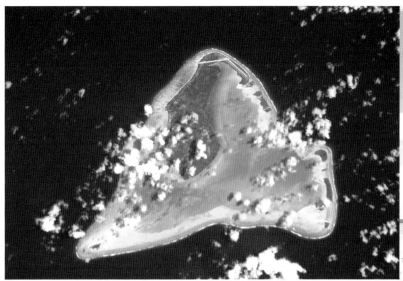

Freshwater life

The vocabulary of high islands and atolls differs in other ways too. A case in point is kōkopu – a term that refers to local species of brown gudgeon right across East Polynesia, but which is naturally recorded only from islands high enough to generate streams. The fact that this particular term is remembered in New Zealand Māori for a similar endemic freshwater fish is an indication that their ancestors are of East Polynesian origin, and that some were familiar with high islands in this region. In the case of the Cook Islands, for example, this term is recorded only from Rarotonga.

Aitutaki – an 'almost-atoll'

To the north of Rarotonga lies Aitutaki, the second most visited island of the Cook Islands. From the plane window on the short flight there from Rarotonga, its wide shallow lagoon looks stunning – a vast aquarium of tropical turquoise. Its hue is indeed so brilliant that navigators, seeing it reflected onto the underside of clouds, were able to identify and locate the island from afar. This lagoon accounts for more than half the total area of Aitutaki; yet high land on the northwestern side rises to an elevation of 123 m, making this a high island and atoll rolled into one – sometimes termed an 'almost-atoll'.

Local traditions tell that the island was first settled from ` Avaiki by Rū,[13] who climbed to the highest point and subdivided the land into 20 parts, one each for his royal maidens. When his four brothers and their wives learnt that they were to receive nothing, they were incensed and promptly left.

From the ecological impact of human presence, first settlement can be dated to AD 1225–1430.[14] This refers to evidence of deforestation, a diminishing range of fish species and the loss of several birds: Rimatara lorikeet, sooty crake, red-footed booby, Tahitian petrel and a now-extinct, undescribed species of giant whistling duck. At this point, introduced species of snail appear in the archaeological record, while native tree-climbing snails are lost, along with the island's native fruit bats.[15]

Likewise, on this island, voyaging contact was maintained over a wide area: the basalt used for making the local adzes was introduced from both Sāmoa to the west and the Society Islands to the east.[16]

Aitutaki

The large turquoise lagoon of Aitutaki (12 km by 15 km) is bordered on the northwestern side by a high island rising to 123 m, and is hence sometimes termed an 'almost-atoll'. Land area: 18 sq km. The lagoon is so vivid that traditional navigators could locate it from afar by the glow reflected onto the underside of clouds. Archaeological evidence confirms pre-European contact with Sāmoa, some 1500 km to the west, and with the Society Islands, some 1100 km to the east. Current population: 2200; and nowadays a popular winter holiday destination for New Zealanders.

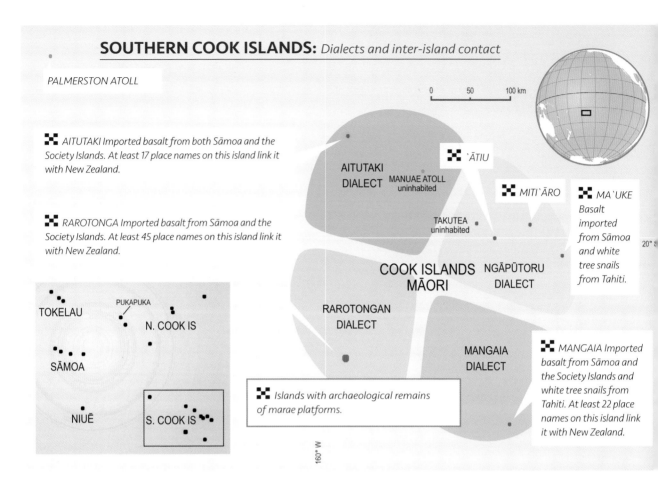

SOUTHERN COOK ISLANDS: *Dialects and inter-island contact*

PALMERSTON ATOLL

▨ *AITUTAKI Imported basalt from both Sāmoa and the Society Islands. At least 17 place names on this island link it with New Zealand.*

▨ *RAROTONGA Imported basalt from Sāmoa and the Society Islands. At least 45 place names on this island link it with New Zealand.*

TOKELAU

PUKAPUKA

N. COOK IS

SĀMOA

NIUĒ

S. COOK IS

AITUTAKI DIALECT

MANUAE ATOLL
uninhabited

TAKUTEA
uninhabited

COOK ISLANDS MĀORI

RAROTONGAN DIALECT

▨ `ĀTIU

▨ MITI`ĀRO

▨ MA`UKE
Basalt imported from Sāmoa and white tree snails from Tahiti.

NGĀPŪTORU DIALECT

MANGAIA DIALECT

▨ *MANGAIA Imported basalt from Sāmoa and the Society Islands and white tree snails from Tahiti. At least 22 place names on this island link it with New Zealand.*

▨ *Islands with archaeological remains of marae platforms.*

20° S

160° W

Above: On `Ātiu and Mangaia (S. Cooks), women search the coastal forest floor after rain for a small (6 mm) bright yellow landsnail, pūpū (yellow necklace shell, Orobophana pacifica). They pierce these shells with a needle and thread them into highly prized shell necklaces (pūpū `ei); a single strand typically requires some 400–500 shells. The pūpū `ei are offered as traditional gifts.

More intriguing still, though, is a find in the 1930s by a local man, Panga Rio. In a small local creek called Vaitekea he spotted a fragment of greenstone. When this was sent off to anthropologist Henry Devenish (H.D.) Skinner, past curator of the Otago Museum, he provided a careful description: he noted that it was 12 cm long by 4.5 cm wide, with 'one surface showing a small amount of grinding'. Geologist Frank J. Turner of the University of Otago went on to examine it and confirmed that 'the rock perfectly resembles the typical *tangiwai* serpentines from Anita Bay, Milford Sound' in the South Island.[17] Panga Rio's find naturally raised the possibility of a voyage to Aitutaki from New Zealand before Europeans arrived. Intriguing though this idea is, there is no way to rule out the possibility that it arrived later aboard a European ship, for we have no 'secure archaeological context' from which to date the find.

'Pancake islands'

Before the late 19th century, when the Cook Islands became a single political entity, each island maintained its own dialect, customs and traditions (see map). This is evident on the four remaining islands of the Southern Cooks: Mangaia, Miti`āro, `Ātiu and Ma`uke. Unlike Rarotonga, these are raised platforms of dead coral, the geological equivalent of 'pancakes'. The Polynesian term for them is 'makatea'.

With no sandy beaches or lagoons to attract holidaymakers and with few other sources of income, many residents have left these islands to seek work

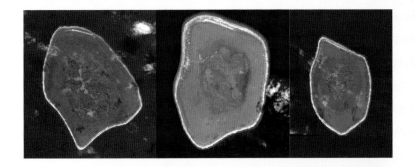

Makatea islands

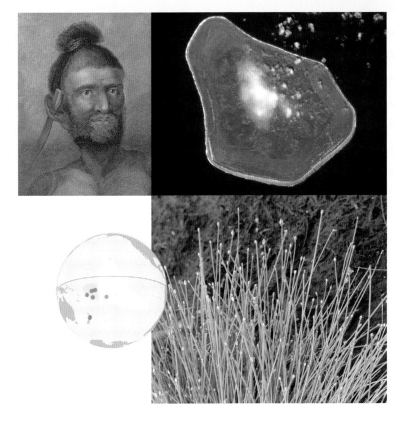

elsewhere – in Rarotonga, New Zealand or Australia.[19] For much of the year the middle generation is largely missing, leaving the old and young behind to lead a more or less subsistence life.

Of these four makatea islands, Mangaia and `Ātiu were historically the most dominant.

Atiuans had the reputation of being great warriors, and made regular raids on neighbouring Ma`uke and Miti`āro and (with less success) on Rarotonga and Mangaia. The pre-eminence of `Ātiu is reflected in such culturally important marae names as Taputapuātea on the northwest coast[20] and Ōrongo on the western side – names that are shared with several Hawaiian islands and with the northern North Island of New Zealand.[21]

Mangaia is the southernmost of the group and is much higher and more

The mountainous terrain of Rarotonga (above) contrasts sharply with the flat makatea island of 'Ātiu, as seen (below) from the 15-seater interisland plane.

Throughout the Southern Cooks, the preferred boatbuilding timber was tamanu (Polynesian mahogany, Calophyllum inophyllum), a native tree to 8–20 m, that grows along the coast and nearby lowland forests.

Red parrot feathers

From Santa Cruz Islands in the west[22] to the Marquesas in the east,[23] red feathers were valued as a kind of currency. During Captain Cook's visit to 'Ātiu in 1777, he found the women and chiefs wearing bunches of red feathers in their ears, despite the fact that kura (Kuhl's lorikeet, Vini kuhlii), above, were already extinct here by this time – a species that has since been reintroduced. In New Zealand, which lacks bright red parrots, this Polynesian-wide term **kura** (globe) came to mean 'precious'.

The corresponding parrot of Fiji (kakā, red shining parrot, Prosopeia tabuensis), right, with globe showing the distribution of this parrot name, applied in Tahitian to two species that are now extinct. This term reached New Zealand, too, where it was given to a number of indigenous parrots known nowadays as **kākā**, kākāriki ('small parrot') and kākāpō ('night parrot').[24]

`Ātiu games and fibre

On `Ātiu, I spoke with local children about their own tradition of playing cat's cradle string games (`ai), a game that is found throughout the Pacific.[25] These games were used when recounting traditional stories to represent houses, canoes or people, some figures so complex that they required the hands, feet and teeth of several people. The globe shows the strictly East Polynesian distribution of the name (**whai** in Māori).

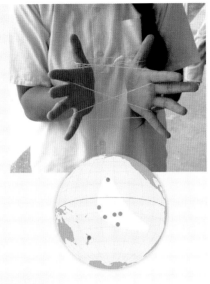

Spears, kites, rafts, roofs

The local spear for the sport described left consists of the stem of a large native reed, kāka`o (fernland reed, Miscanthus floridulus), above, which is used also for house walls.[29] Its New Zealand namesake is **kākaho** (the cane-like stem of toetoe-kākaho or toetoe Cortaderia species), which served Māori likewise as a lightweight spear and for lining walls, but also for making the frames of kites.

Likewise, their sport of distance-throwing of lightweight spears (**teka**), which is played right across the Pacific, goes by a name that is restricted to the cultural region of East Polynesia.[26]

One of the local school children brought me a treasured pair of traditional bark-fibre sandals made from the shrubby beach hibiscus (`au, Hibiscus tiliaceus), below, whose tough, stringy bark was also used for making rope, the lightweight wood providing fishing floats and canoe outriggers.[27] Although its seeds do spread naturally by floating, they were also distributed by canoe across much of the Pacific, where the tree shares a single name (see globe). Its New Zealand namesake is a small, look-alike coastal tree, **whau** (corkwood, Entelea arborescens), whose soft lightweight wood is likewise used as floats for fishing nets and for outriggers of canoes.[28]

The kite frames were interwoven with the lightweight leaves of **raupō** (bulrush, Typha orientalis), which were also bundled to make rafts or thatched as sails.[30] The very same uses apply to their namesake here in the Cook Islands, where raupō refers to giant bulrush (Schoenoplectus californicus), above: its stems and leaves were bundled as rafts or used as thatching. The name in this case, though, is shared only with `Ātiu, nearby Mangaia and Rapa (south of the Austral Islands), and not with Rarotonga where the plant is not recorded.[31]

Out on the reef

On makatea islands, such as `Ātiu, which lack lagoons, much of the local food is collected from the encircling reef flats. Right, a small `eke (octopus) is taken from one of the rock pools.[32] Its indigenous name is shared right across Polynesia, including New Zealand, where it is known as wheke. Sea urchins are cracked open for the edible egg mass. Top right, the local `atuke (slate-pencil urchin, Heterocentrotus species); bunches of the robust spines were used as abrasion tools. Bottom right, kinakina (pale burrowing urchin, Echinometra mathaei); its needles, like those of its New Zealand namesake kina (common urchin), are too weak for this purpose.

Above: Top section (12 cm x 60 cm) of a Cook Island atua rākau (staff god), carved c. 1800. The original staffs were often more than 2 m long.

fortress-like, reaching 169 m – more than twice the elevation of `Ātiu, and not much smaller in land area than Rarotonga. Captain Cook, who met Mangaians in 1777, likened them to New Zealand Māori rather than to Tahitians. Likewise, lexicographer Frederick Christian, who made an early study of the island's native vocabulary, noted a special affinity between the two languages: 'the language of Mangaia is considerably closer to the Maori speech of New Zealand than that of Rarotonga, but it has some archaic words peculiar to itself'.[33] For example, the Mangaian word Mokoroa-i-Ata for the Milky Way has been recorded elsewhere only in New Zealand; and the term kuta for spike-sedges, whose stems are woven into soft sleeping mats, is shared only with New Zealand and West Polynesia.[34] This is consistent with tribal historian Sir Āpirana Ngata's claim that some ancestors of Māori actually came from this island.[35]

Mangaia is also the most probable final staging post for bringing kūmara to New Zealand. This is the conclusion of archaeologist Roger Green,[36] who conducted decades of research into the subject, from early fragments of kūmara found during an archaeological dig in 1990 in a major rockshelter on this island. Here, at Tangatatau, among old stone adzes, shell fishhooks and bone tattooing needles, were large quantities of old animal and plant remains, including several ancient, carbonised fragments of kūmara tubers. These fragments were dated to AD 1210–1400,[37] which qualifies them as the oldest known evidence of sweet potato in Polynesia. Mangaia has thus emerged as the closest island to New Zealand to have possessed tubers in the period during which New Zealand was being settled.

Voyaging canoes

Te Rangi Hīroa tells us that Cook Island canoes were generally made from tamanu (Polynesian mahogany), a hard, strong wood from a tree that grows in coastal forest on all the Southern Cook Islands.[38] Although Captain Cook reported seeing double canoes at ʿĀtiu in 1777, these were only about 6 m long, so were probably only for local use. However, in 1823 English missionary John Williams did see a large double canoe off Rarotonga and another at ʿĀtiu in 1821;[39] and trader W. Bonar reported seeing one of the last of the old double-hulled seagoing canoes on the island of Maʿuke in about 1890, with hulls about 18 m in length made 'in three pieces, with butt joints for sewing together'.[40]

Contact with New Zealand?

Shared use of the term Māori for the native peoples and language of the Cook Islands and New Zealand might seem to imply migration between the two; however, the use of the term māori is common to many Polynesians, from its original use as an adjective, meaning 'true, right or genuine'. It applied to things such as 'stars, water and face' that were regarded as 'normal' or 'standard'. Its use by Polynesians to differentiate themselves from non-native people can be traced no further back than about 1800 in New Zealand,[41] around which time it was adopted not only by Cook Island Māori, but also by the Maoʿi of the Marquesas, Maoli of Hawaiʿi[42] and the Māʿohi of Tahiti.[43]

And yet a very close affinity in culture between Cook Island Māori and New Zealand Māori is evident in other, more specific and therefore more compelling links in vocabulary (see Rarotongan plant names, page 125). The same is true of shared place names.[44] Tākitumu, a region in southeastern Rarotonga, is a dialectical variation of *Tākitimu*, the name of one of the founding canoes of Māori, whose crew are understood to be the ancestors of Ngāti Kahungunu of the East Coast of the North Island, and whose traditions are associated with that region. Others have pointed out that ʿIkurangi, the main peak on Rarotonga, recurs as Hikurangi in the North Island, including near Ruatōria on the East Cape – the sacred mountain of Ngāti Porou. However, this particular name also occurs in Tonga, Sāmoa, Tahiti and the Tuamotus, and applies in New Zealand to at least 40 peaks – most in the North Island.[45]

On Aitutaki we find an even higher density of New Zealand place names. For example, this island's original name of Araʿura recurs as Arahura near Greymouth on the West Coast of the South Island; and the name of its western subdistrict of Ureia recurs in the Firth of Thames as a taniwha (mythical monster), an important symbol of fertility and prestige in the Hauraki region.[46]

It is these kinds of cultural links that prompted Ngata to conclude that many Māori who settled on the East Coast came from the Southern Cook Islands of 'Rarotonga, Mangaia, and so on'.[47]

This is consistent with evidence from the DNA of Pacific rats found in New Zealand; researchers identified a lineage that reached here aboard canoes from the Southern Cook Islands/Society Islands region.[48]

'Garden of Seven Stones'

Near the harbour of Ngātangiʿia (Avana Harbour) on the east coast of Rarotonga is a 'Garden of Seven Stones'. It was created to commemorate seven of the migration canoes that are understood to have sailed to New Zealand: Tainui, Tākitumu, Te Arawa, Mātaatua, Aotea, Kurahaupō and Tokomaru.
It is often said that New Zealand was found by a Polynesian voyager named Kupe, and that news of his discovery inspired others in Tahiti to follow his directions several centuries later via Rarotonga in a single fleet of seven canoes.[49] However, this Kupe-and-fleet story turns out to be a 'cut-and-paste' version of history, dating from an attempt in the late 1800s by New Zealand ethnologist S. Percy Smith to 'tidy up' the diversity contained in the original Māori traditions. Ethnologist David Simmons subsequently dubbed it 'the Great New Zealand Myth', for, as Michael King put it in The Penguin History of New Zealand, *'the story had no sound basis in Māori tradition'.[50]*

NORTHERN COOK ISLANDS: *Languages and history*

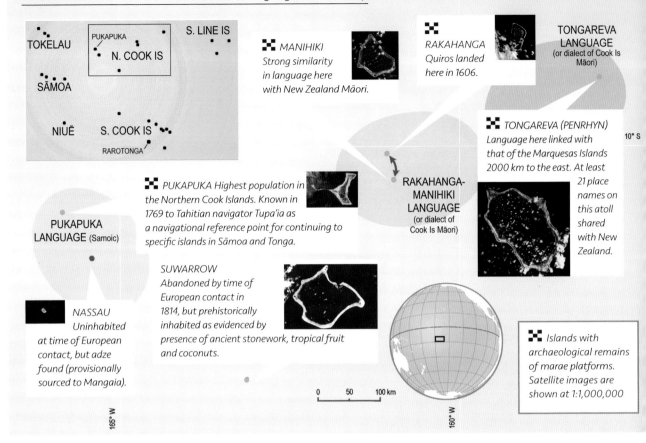

TOKELAU

PUKAPUKA

N. COOK IS

S. LINE IS

SĀMOA

NIUĒ   S. COOK IS

RAROTONGA

MANIHIKI
Strong similarity
in language here
with New Zealand Māori.

RAKAHANGA
Quiros landed
here in 1606.

TONGAREVA
LANGUAGE
(or dialect of Cook Is
Māori)

TONGAREVA (PENRHYN)
Language here linked with
that of the Marquesas Islands
2000 km to the east. At least
21 place
names on
this atoll
shared
with New
Zealand.

10° S

PUKAPUKA Highest population in
the Northern Cook Islands. Known in
1769 to Tahitian navigator Tupa'ia as
a navigational reference point for continuing to
specific islands in Sāmoa and Tonga.

RAKAHANGA-
MANIHIKI
LANGUAGE
(or dialect of
Cook Is Māori)

PUKAPUKA
LANGUAGE (Samoic)

SUWARROW
Abandoned by time of
European contact in
1814, but prehistorically
inhabited as evidenced by
presence of ancient stonework, tropical fruit
and coconuts.

NASSAU
Uninhabited
at time of European
contact, but adze
found (provisionally
sourced to Mangaia).

Islands with
archaeological remains
of marae platforms.
Satellite images are
shown at 1:1,000,000

0   50   100 km

165° W

160° W

The Northern Cooks – a world apart

So far, we have discussed only the Southern Cook Islands. Because these are separated from the Northern Cook Islands by some 1000 km, the two groups inevitably have a very different history. Even today there are no ferries between the two regions, and the cost of flying between them is more than the price of a flight from Auckland to London. As a consequence of this extreme remoteness, their significance in pre-European times has often been overlooked, despite the fact that Pukapuka, Manihiki, Rakahanga and Tongareva were all previously very densely inhabited.

The importance of these northern atolls in Polynesian history lies largely in the fact that most are located between 9°S and 11°S, along an important 'latitude sailing' route that connects Sikaiana in the west[51] (a Polynesian Outlier off the Solomon Islands) through Tūvalu and Tokelau to Hiva `Oa in the Marquesas Islands.[52] Contact along this northern voyaging corridor is evident from affinities in language, culture and place names, and is supported by computer modelling of wind patterns.[53] Along this corridor, the atolls of the Northern Cooks served not only as important way stations or 'stepping stones', but also in some cases as voyaging hubs.

Pukapuka, the westernmost atoll of the Northern Cooks, was a connecting hub linking West and East Polynesia – a role that is reflected in its material culture,[54] and its language, which is Samoic with a Tokelauan influence, rather than Rarotongan. Its original population is likely to have numbered 1000 or more.[55] They were evidently great voyagers in their own right, for Pukapukan traditions speak of frequent passages to Tūvalu, Tokelau, Niuē, Tonga, Rarotonga and Tahiti,[56] and the basalt that was used for many of their adze blades can be geochemically traced to a quarry on Tutuila (Sāmoa).[57] Tahitians are known to have passed through Pukapuka en route to islands in Sāmoa and Tonga, as evidenced by navigational details that the Tahitian navigator Tupa`ia gave to Cook in 1769.[58] As Pukapuka was evidently one of the first locations in East Polynesia to be settled,[59] it is likely to have served as a base from which to explore much of the region.

From the next atoll, Rakahanga, some 450 km east of Pukapuka, we have an early account of life on the Northern Cooks. In 1606 Portuguese navigator Quirós and his Spanish crew describe being greeted on the beach by some 500 inhabitants, and finding a well-built village of houses with gables and high lofts where the people slept, and outrigger canoes made from coconut palms. Quirós saw large double canoes here, about 18 m long with a deck between the two hulls, capable of carrying 50 people, with masts like cross-trees and sails of matting, 'in which they navigate for great distances'.[60] The description is useful here for it implies purposeful two-way voyaging at the time, and gives us some idea of the size of voyaging craft, their carrying capacity and rig.

Long-distance voyaging in the region is consistent with traditions collected on neighbouring Manihiki that refer to visits to 'Arapata' (Teraina, N. Line Is) 1700 km to the north,[61] and with accounts of ancestor Mahuta settling on Tongareva, 360 km to the ENE. Such links between Manihiki and Tongareva can be independently corroborated from Tongarevan tradition, genealogy and shared place names.[62]

Tongareva (or Penrhyn) is in fact the largest of the Northern Cooks and was formerly one of the most densely inhabited atolls in Polynesia. In 1816, when navigator Otto von Kotzebue arrived, he found its people 'so numerous, in proportion to the island' that he could not think how so many could 'find subsistence'.[63] Even, some 30 years after this first encounter with Europeans, a count in 1853 estimated 2500 people.[64] Many of these people subsequently died of introduced diseases; and of those who survived, Peruvian slave traders removed a further 472 in 1863. By 1906, just 420 were left – a staggering loss of 76 percent of the original population of this atoll.

The main point here is that, despite the remoteness of these atolls and their small populations today, their inhabitants were formerly numerous, and were capable long-distance voyagers.

Pukapuka

Despite being remote and tiny, with just 3 sq km of land, Pukapuka (or 'Danger Island' on some maps) once served as an important voyaging hub connecting East and West Polynesia. Its population has recovered from extremely low numbers more than once. Oral traditions refer to at least two episodes of civil war,[65] and inundation of the atoll from a major tsunami or cyclone, in which only two women and 15 men survived.[66] After numbers recovered, a raid in 1863 by Peruvian slave traders took 145 men and women, of whom only two returned; and yet in 1866 the estimated population was 750.[67] (Current population: 500.)

Contact between the Northern Cooks and New Zealand?

As with all atolls, the marginal, low-lying nature of the Northern Cooks supplied their inhabitants with a motive to explore. Such is the known contact between these northern atolls and other islands, including the Society Islands,[68] that news of unclaimed land would undoubtedly have reached them. Perhaps some were lured as far as New Zealand – as frequently occurs today. If so, one practicable route for such a southbound voyage is indicated by enormous flocks of sooty shearwater and Cook's petrel that are passing along the 'Hawai`i–New Zealand flyway' through this group of atolls in spring, via Tonga and the Kermadecs, to nesting sites around New Zealand. Another cue is the spring departure of New Zealand long-tailed cuckoos from Pukapuka and Tongareva.[69]

A second practicable route is via Rarotonga, some 1300 km to the south, with two little-known way stations en route.[70] The first is Suwarrow, an atoll that was located in 1814 by Russian explorer Mikhail Lazarev by the same means that Polynesians would have used, by following clouds of birds dispersing from resident colonies of sooty terns, brown boobies, red-tailed tropicbirds and lesser frigatebirds.[71] The island was uninhabited at the time, so his crew helped themselves to the 'tropical fruit and coconuts which abounded on the [islets]', evidently unaware that these trees had been planted. Polynesians had used Suwarrow for more than just harvesting

Tongareva (or Penrhyn)

The atoll of Tongareva (or Penrhyn, after the Lady Penrhyn, the ship from which it was first sighted by Europeans in 1788) may once have supported some 2500 people. (Current population: just 200.) The Tongarevan language is very similar to Māori, and many local place names are shared with New Zealand. The preferred timbers for canoe hulls on Tongareva and other atolls of the Northern Cook Islands came from tou (Cordia subcordata, above left), a coastal tree that grows to 7–10 m; and hano (Guettarda speciosa, right) a coastal shrub or small tree that grows to 2–6 m. The timber was seasoned, then cut into planks using giant clam shells. Holes were bored into the planks with pointed shells such as crenulated auger shells. The planks were then sewn together with sennit and caulked with fibre from coconut husks.[72]

seabirds, eggs, red tail-feathers, turtles and coconut crabs: this atoll had evidently supported a resident community that had almost certainly served voyagers passing through the region.

The same is true of Palmerston Atoll, just over 500 km south of Suwarrow. When Captain Cook reached here in 1777 he likewise found no one here, yet noted remains of an old canoe, groves of coconuts and the presence of rats that could only have reached here with human help.[73] Subsequently, 12 ancient graves were found, along with 'thirty to forty' stone adzes imbedded in the roots of the palms,[74] all of which spoke of a former community here.

Whether voyagers from the Northern Cooks did actually reach New Zealand – by either route – is not known, but Te Rangi Hīroa, who was a fluent speaker of Māori, drew attention to strong similarities in language. In 1929, during a visit to Rakahanga and Manihiki, he was impressed by 'closer affinities with Maori than with the dialects of Tongareva, Tahiti, and the Cook Islands'.[75]

On a visit to Tongareva the same year, Te Rangi Hīroa made a similar observation, noting that he 'had no difficulty in speaking and understanding Tongarevan, whereas [he] experienced much more trouble with Samoan and Tahitian'.[76] New Zealand place names also occur on Tongareva at a density more than three times that found in the Southern Cook Islands.[77]

The discovery in 1905 of a greenstone adze on Pukapuka also raises the possibility of contact in the reverse direction, from New Zealand to the Northern Cooks. According to Skinner, this adze was unearthed by a local while planting taro 'in circumstances which [seemed to] indicate that it came there in pre-European times'.[78] Again, this is unfortunately not enough to constitute proof that the adze did actually reach Pukapuka in pre-European times.

So, although one can question the evidence for voyagers from the Northern Cooks reaching New Zealand, we do have firm evidence that they were not previously so isolated, and that they were in contact with the region from which the ancestors of New Zealand Māori are understood to have sailed.

Every one of these atolls lies closer to New Zealand than does Tahiti.[79]

Suwarrow – 'a stepping stone'

Suwarrow, about 930 km NNW of Rarotonga, was so named by Russian explorer Mikhail Lazarev in 1814 after his ship, the Suvorov. *The atoll was formerly inhabited by Polynesians, and is now a wildlife refuge.*

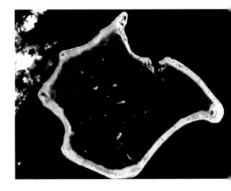

CHAPTER NINE

Exploration and Discovery

Nature's Signposts to the Kermadecs and Beyond

Mine is the migrating bird
flying on even-beating wings to lands revisited,
Ever searching out the road of the ocean.
It is the road of the winds
coursed by the Sea Kings to unknown lands!
Mine is the bird.

Traditional Tuamotuan voyaging chant, trs. Frank Stimson 1957

The traditional wayfinding techniques discussed back in chapter five are pertinent to voyages of settlement or trade to known destinations. However, until the whereabouts of the destination is known, it could be argued that many of these skills are largely irrelevant. Indeed, for these skills to flourish, knowledge of the destination and a prior voyage of exploration is implied – one that is likely to have required a very different set of skills, motives and stamina.

Exploration is the subject of this chapter, and since most canoes sailing to New Zealand from East Polynesia are likely to have done so via Rarotonga or neighbouring islands, we will take the example of the methods by which New Zealand is likely to have been first discovered from that region.

Motives – pushed or pulled?
What impelled Polynesians to keep on exploring? Were they in flight mode, forced to face high risks by a need to escape pressures at home; or were they just generally entrepreneurial? In other words, were they being pushed or pulled? The question is highly relevant when it comes to understanding the level of skill, confidence and risk that was involved in settling the Pacific.

It turns out that there is evidence for both 'push' *and* 'pull'. In oral tradition, we can find many references to people fleeing conflict,[1] and yet it is hard to attribute to such voyages of exile alone the remarkable rapidity with which almost every scrap of habitable land in the Pacific was discovered. With such vast tracts of this huge ocean devoid of islands, this would imply little concern for safety and huge losses. The rapidity of discovery implies a degree of skill in predicting where to look, and a more judicious approach to risk management. From the range of traditional crops that Polynesians established on almost all the islands they settled, we might also infer that a return voyage of exploration typically preceded one of settlement.

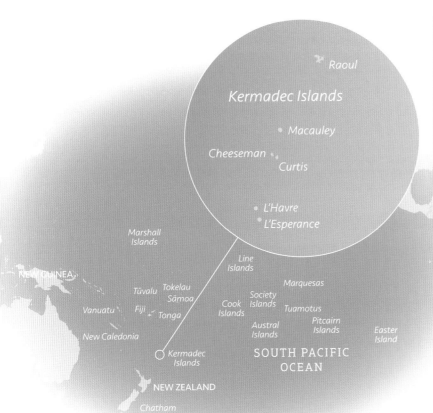

Raoul
Kermadec Islands
• Macauley
Cheeseman
Curtis
• L'Havre
• L'Esperance
Marshall
Islands
Line
Islands
NEW GUINEA
Marquesas
Tūvalu Tokelau
Sāmoa
Society
Islands
Cook
Islands
Tuamotus
Vanuatu Fiji
Tonga
Austral
Islands
Pitcairn
Islands
Easter
Island
New Caledonia
Kermadec
Islands
SOUTH PACIFIC
OCEAN
NEW ZEALAND
Chatham
Islands

Raoul Island (Sunday Island), above and below, the main island of the Kermadec group, lies at 29°S, halfway between Tonga and New Zealand. It rises to over 500 m and is heavily forested, with small lakes and lagoons, and a land area of just 29 sq km – similar in size to New Zealand's Little Barrier Island.

Polynesians were typically adventurous. In 1774, Mai (Omai, above) from Raʻiātea (Society Islands) ventured with Captain James Cook as far as London.

Even in the case of genuine voyages of exile, these are far more likely to have been to known destinations. Not only would this involve less attrition, it is consistent with the archaeological evidence – conflict and a shortage of resources do not show up until around 1450, by which time the whereabouts of habitable islands were already known. Indeed, a common tendency – even among the 'experts' – to conflate the exploratory phase of Polynesian settlement with voyages of exile may stem more from the reluctance of a dominant culture to attribute agency to indigenous peoples. The successful establishment of any *initial* settlement is far more likely to have involved careful planning, instigated by a cooperative parent community with surplus resources – including a good range of planting material from which vigorous strains could be selected according to whether the known destination was an atoll or a high island.

Voyages of exploration to find and 'fish up' new islands in the first place had very different imperatives. In Polynesian society, where the eldest son inherited the lion's share of his family's goods and privileges, younger brothers were frequently spurred to upstage the senior line with heroic acts such as finding uncontested new territory. Finding a pristine new environment meant not only kudos, but access to a bonanza of meat from creatures unaccustomed to being hunted.

The risks were indeed high – but so too were the gains. It was not necessary for Polynesians to be desperate. A keen taste for adventure among Polynesians is evident from those that volunteered to join 18th-century European ships. This was how Society Island navigator Tupaʻia reached Jakarta; how Ahutoru and Mai (Omai) made return trips to Paris and London respectively; and how Tuamotuan navigator Puhoro made the round trip to Lima. Similarly, many early European explorers and missionaries were struck by the eagerness of Polynesians to apply for jobs as sailors and guides, and by their keen interest in stories from other lands.[2]

This spirit of exploration is reflected in some of their deep-sea voyaging chants:

> The handle of my steering paddle thrills to action,
> My paddle named Kautu-ki-te-rangi.
> It guides to the horizon but dimly discerned.
> To the horizon that lifts before us,
> To the horizon that ever recedes,
> To the horizon that ever draws near,
> To the horizon that causes doubt,
> To the horizon that instils dread,
> The horizon with unknown power,
> The horizon not hitherto pierced.
> The lowering skies above,
> The raging seas below,
> Oppose the untraced path
> Our ship must go.[3]

A more credible driving force behind the pulses in Pacific exploration is *opportunity* – a healthy level of cooperation, advances in sailing technology and navigational expertise, episodes of favourable winds, and experience gained over many generations that there might be more islands yet to be found.

There are other reasons to differentiate between the processes of exploration and subsequent settlement, for the two types of voyage are likely to have required not only different crew and cargo, but also different vessels. A voyage of exploration is more likely to have involved a relatively small and physically fit crew prepared for a round trip of indeterminate length, steering a faster, more manoeuvrable and lightly laden craft, such as an outrigger canoe. Major voyages of settlement, on the other hand, were almost certainly navigated aboard slower, more stable craft, heavily laden with elders, women, children, and the accoutrements of settlement, including dogs, pigs, chickens and a range of planting material – suitably provisioned in accordance with the anticipated length of the voyage.

In other words, voyages of trade and exile are likely to have occurred only after voyages of exploration and return had already occurred.

Accidental voyages

As we saw in the introduction, the widespread distribution of Polynesians has often been attributed to a series of accidents – canoes getting blown off course.[4] While it is true that accidental voyages were not uncommon in the Pacific, both before and after European contact, it is important to appreciate that such voyages generally fit a predictable pattern that fails to account for human settlement. This was the finding of archaeologist Jack Golson, who made a study of the history of accidental voyages and found that almost all had occurred within the tropics and had been westbound – that is, in the direction of prevailing trade winds.[5] This is not so surprising, but the point is that Polynesians, on the other hand, are now known to have settled the Pacific in the opposite direction, from Asia. So although it is possible for new land to have been discovered aboard canoes blown off course while fishing, this cannot realistically have applied to many islands, and can hardly account for the horticultural success that Polynesians ultimately achieved on them.

Others suggested that settlement might still be accounted for by a plethora of canoes engaged in a great many accidental voyages. To test this idea out, Michael Levison and colleagues set up an elaborate computer simulation, running many thousands of simulated 'drift voyages' (voyages not steered along a predetermined course), factoring in various starting seasons, accumulated data of winds, currents, gales and even life expectancies. What their results revealed was that certain significant stages of Pacific settlement could have resulted only from *intentional* voyages. In the case of Easter Island, New Zealand and the Hawaiian Islands, in particular, discovery by accident proved virtually impossible.[6] These more ambitious phases of Polynesian exploration had evidently involved a more deliberate process – adhering to a chosen course and searching in a methodical way.

What about accidental voyaging?

Over the centuries, accidental voyages have not been uncommon in the Pacific; however, most of these fit a predictable pattern. This was the finding of archaeologist Jack Golson, who in 1962 compiled records of 152 accidental voyages that had occurred in the South Pacific between the late 1700s and the 1960s. His conclusion: although such unplanned voyages were not unusual in an eastbound direction, over most of tropical Polynesia they have been predominantly westbound – that is, in the direction of prevailing winds and opposite to the direction in which the region was actually settled. In other words, accidental voyaging fails to account for the Polynesian achievement: their discovery of almost all of the Pacific.

Global winds

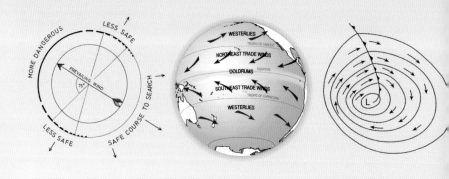

In reality, searching for land upwind is safer because of better prospects for making a return (right). The trade winds are dependable (centre), due to the global forces that drive them: when warm air over the equatorial ocean rises to a high altitude, it spreads north and south to the poles, where it cools and descends. This cool air passes back toward the equator as surface winds, receiving a westerly twist from the eastward spin of the Earth. In the southern tropics, these trade winds curve from the southeast – a pattern that is regularly interrupted, however, by passing southern hemisphere low-pressure systems (as shown far right), with rotating wind direction and a trailing cold front.[7] The resulting reversals in wind direction typically last two to four days. Longer-lasting wind shifts can also be triggered by seasonal changes in ocean temperature, for example from El Niño–Southern Oscillation (ENSO), caused by changing ocean temperatures off South America.[8] Long eastbound voyages were certainly possible. For example, in 1830, John Williams of the London Missionary Society sailed from 370 km west of Niuē to Tahiti, a distance of over 2700 km to the east, in just 15 days.[9] According to Tahitian navigator Tupa`ia, Polynesians made their eastbound voyages 'during the Months of Novr, Decembr & January [when] Westerly winds with rain prevail', though it 'took 10 to 12 days going [to islands to the west of Tahiti], and 30 or more coming back'.

The hard way is really the easy way

Part of the confusion around settlement arises from the fact that European trade vessels, and modern yachts generally, cross the tropical Pacific from east to west with the so-called trade winds in their favour. To Thor Heyerdahl and others, it seemed logical that Polynesians had done the same. On the assumption that Polynesians were one-way voyagers, it seemed to them that the Pacific must have been settled in the same direction, from South America. However, what the trade winds really imply is that exploration was more practicable in the opposite direction. 'The hard way is really the easy or safe way,' explains Geoffrey Irwin. In the days before radio, no explorer could share his discovery unless he was also able to get back. It was consequently far wiser to set out into unknown seas during atypical winds, confident in the return of a prevailing wind to carry him back home. The circumstances surrounding Heyerdahl's own downwind raft voyage were very different: when ready to publicise his trip, he had only to dry out his radio equipment and call home for help.

There is widespread confusion, too, as to what distinguishes a genuinely deliberate voyage of exploration from an accidental one. In the words of navigator David Lewis:

> [Discovery] must always be a largely accidental event, since the most an explorer could have to suggest the existence and bearing of an unknown land would be the clues afforded by drifting objects, migratory bird flight paths, and the like. But currents can carry floating branches in a circle, and the first stop of migrating birds could well be Siberia.[10]

To investigate how Polynesians might ascertain the existence and whereabouts of land they had not yet seen, we can use the Kermadec Islands as an example and explore how they and New Zealand may have been first discovered.

The Kermadecs

The Kermadecs are a tiny group of islands that lie about halfway between New Zealand and Tonga. They are high, with desolate cliffs dropping straight into the sea, and have a combined land area of just 33 sq km, similar to that of New Zealand's Little Barrier Island.[11] When Europeans came upon this

Kermadec cargo

Raoul Island was formerly inhabited by Polynesians. Some of the items they brought came from the tropics; others from New Zealand. Items from the tropics include the seeds of tuitui (candlenut tree, Aleurites moluccana), above left and centre, a native of the Indo-Malaysian region that was introduced to most islands inhabited by Polynesians; indeed groves of

them can often be used to locate archaeological sites.[12] Although candlenut seeds were almost certainly brought to New Zealand too, here they would have failed to thrive as the tree will not tolerate temperatures below about 8°C.

Above right: One of several obsidian flakes from Tūhua (Mayor Island), off Tauranga, New Zealand, that were found on the Kermadecs.

This piece (33 mm x 25 mm) was collected in 2011 on Macauley Island, a remote speck of land covering just 3 sq km, about 110 km south-southwest of Raoul Island (where similar pieces from Tūhua have also been found). Such finds serve as hard archaeological evidence that Polynesians travelled back into the Pacific from New Zealand.

group in 1788, they found them uninhabited.[13] However, these islands had not always been that way, as evidenced by the presence of Polynesian crops on Raoul (the main island in the group) and by artefacts and Pacific rats on this island and on nearby Macauley.

Perhaps these people had been drawn to these islands originally as a place to restock on water, birds' eggs and chicks, while waiting out unfavourable winds or undertaking repairs,[14] but some went on to actually establish a settlement on Raoul. Their outriggers or twin-hulled sailing canoes were presumably landed through the surf on the southwestern side of the island and dragged up onto the sands of Denham Bay, for there is no natural harbour here.[15] As for where they came from, there are some clues: adze heads unearthed here in the 1960s, which ethnologist Roger Duff judged to be of a type made in the 14th and 15th centuries in the Southern Cook Islands.[16] Of the four Polynesian crop species that botanists tell us were introduced to the island in pre-European times, two – candlenut and Pacific Island cabbage tree – originate from the tropics. With the cabbage trees it is possible to be more specific: biologist Anya Hinkle demonstrated that these are a sterile cultivar genetically characteristic of East Polynesia – which implies importation of cuttings specifically from that cultural region.[17]

However, the remaining two crops are known to have come from the south. Karaka seeds can only have been introduced from the northern North Island of New Zealand, the region to which the tree is now

Six million birds

*In spring, some 6 million oceanic birds converge on the Kermadecs, including some 5 million black-winged petrels (*Pterodroma nigripennis*, top), which reach Macauley Island (Kermadecs) from the north, central and eastern Pacific in mid-October, before dispersing from the island in May. From October, too, around half a million Kermadec petrels (*Pterodroma neglecta*, above) arrive on these islands, along with a similar number of white-naped petrels (*Pterodroma cervicalis*, below). Together, their spring migration helps flag the presence of the Kermadecs.*

known to be native. The New Zealand flax found here was presumably introduced as cuttings, and most likely from the same region.[18] Further evidence of voyages from New Zealand came in 1978 when a 14th-century archaeological site on Raoul was excavated: archaeologists found numerous flakes of obsidian (matā) – a kind of volcanic glass used as cutting tools, some sharp enough to cut hair. Although most of the flakes appeared to be of local origin, the distinctive colouring of six translucent, olive-green pieces pointed to a distant origin. Like basalt, obsidian contains a cocktail of minerals that are uniquely characteristic of its source eruption. An X-ray fluorescence (XRF) technique is used to determine the geochemical signature of the pieces, and hence their origin. These tests revealed that all six pieces had been brought here from quarries on Tūhua (Mayor Island) off Tauranga, New Zealand – over 1000 km to the southwest.[19]

Clearly, Raoul had received voyagers from both north and south. Indeed, biological anthropologist Lisa Matisoo-Smith and colleagues found evidence from variations in maternally inherited DNA of Pacific rats to suggest that it had formerly served as a way station in two-way and multiple voyaging between New Zealand and the tropics.[20]

Remains of Pacific dogs were also found on Raoul, but none of chickens or pigs – mirroring the suite of Polynesian animal introductions to New Zealand.

The main point here is that these islands, remote and tiny though they are, were located by Polynesians not just once but many times, and from both the north and the south.

So how was the original discovery made?

Finding Raoul

The nearest inhabited neighbour of Raoul – the southern tip of Tonga – lies almost 1000 km away; and yet, on a fine day, its 520 m peak is visible from no more than about 80 km.[21] As with many islands settled by Polynesians, the Kermadecs are mere 'needles in a haystack'; the target angle for locating Raoul from its nearest inhabited neighbour is less than 0.6 degrees.[22]

However, the dozen or so islets that go to make up the Kermadecs span some 260 km north to south, each close enough to its neighbour for the flight ranges of their permanently resident seabirds, such as noddies, to overlap. This effectively expands the target into an island screen. As on many islets in the Pacific, these resident birds are joined in spring and summer by oceanic birds that come to nest in numbers that seem way out of proportion to the available land area. In the case of sooty terns, for example – even after the considerable impact of introduced rats and cats – about 200,000 nest here.[23] In fact, the overall count of seabirds returning to these islands in spring currently runs to around six million, similar to the estimated bird population for all of the Hawaiian Islands put together.

Most prominent among these returning seabirds are more than five million black-winged petrels, which will remain in the Kermadecs until May[24] before returning to seas around Fiji, the Cook Islands, Society Islands, Marquesas and even across the equator to seas around Hawai`i. In mid-October, as the sun is returning to the south, their flight paths again converge from across this vast region toward the Kermadecs and other remote islets.[25] From October to December, these are followed by around half a million Kermadec petrels[26] and some 100,000 white-naped petrels.[27]

The flocks are impressive enough now, but in the voyaging era they were larger still: this is a period when some 10 million or more birds would have been making fast swoops low to the water, heading to these islands. In spring the spectacle would have been striking to witness from a canoe. It can have left no doubt as to the presence of land in this direction and the promise here of millions of eggs and flightless chicks, both of which Polynesians traditionally sought as food.

In other words, Polynesians had only to follow this enormous spring migration to find the Kermadecs, tiny as they are.

Intriguing flotsam

Having reached Raoul, it is not hard to picture the voyagers searching for unfamiliar drift items along the strand, perhaps noticing small, bright-yellow seeds from New Zealand kōwhai trees, which frequently float enormous distances with the ocean currents and which regularly wash up here,[28] along with many worn fragments of two highly distinctive types of seaweed – bladder kelp and bull kelp.[29] Such novel finds would be of interest to the traditional navigator, for they spoke of undiscovered land up-current.[30]

The same is true of any novel kinds of driftwood (aihe), a sought-after commodity among Polynesians, who traditionally used it for building and repairing their craft. Its usefulness is reflected in specific terms recorded in several Polynesian languages for different kinds of unfamiliar driftwood and for whole floating trees.[31]

In comparison with other Pacific islands, the quantity of driftwood generated by New Zealand stands out. This is due to its extensive land area, dense cover of large trees and unusually long rivers that carry fallen trunks and branches out to the west coast, from where they are swept northward by ocean currents. When the driftwood reaches the northern tip of the North Island, the direction in which it is carried depends on the season. In summer, the current here turns sharply to the east or southeast, but in winter it sweeps to the northeast, carrying the occasional large log as far as Raoul. Among this flotsam is one of New Zealand's most majestic native trees, kauri.

In the 1880s, for example, over 40 kauri logs were counted along the Raoul coast. Many of them bore brands with the various dates on which they had been felled for the mill – confirming that this accumulation was not the result of a single freak event.[32] Any such find would have aroused considerable interest among Polynesians, for kauri was destined to become the preferred timber for constructing Māori canoes.

Any navigator seeing all this winter flotsam is likely to have tried to ascertain the direction from which it was coming. It is not until spring, though, that they would witness the most compelling indicator of land to the south: tens of millions of oceanic birds flying southwest through these waters from the tropics toward their main nesting sites in and around New Zealand. At this same time of year, long-tailed cuckoos from the tropical South Pacific gather here briefly, en route to the same destination.

Flotsam

Among the flotsam that occurs along the Raoul Island shoreline are seeds of kōwhai (Sophora species), above, and fragments of bladder weed (Carpophyllum species), below, both of which are regularly carried northeast from New Zealand on surface currents. The same currents bring ribbons of rimurapa (bull kelp, Durvillaea species) bottom. Such a find on the Kermadecs is likely to have triggered an interest in the prevailing currents that brought them here.

Heading for New Zealand

*In September, over a million Cook's petrel (**tītī**, Pterodroma cookii, above) head south from the central northern Pacific to offshore islands around the North Island of New Zealand, particularly Little Barrier Island; the globe shows the East Polynesian distribution of its Māori name. And about 2.5 million Buller's shearwaters (Puffinus bulleri syn. Ardenna, below) join them as they head from the North Pacific to the Poor Knights Islands off Northland, New Zealand. The globe below shows how its Māori name **rako** is shared only with the Tuamotus.*

Seabird capital of the world

Included in this mass migration are some 20 million sooty shearwaters that are heading southwest through this region in early October.[33] Here, in the waters around the Kermadecs, individual flocks feeding en route can reach sizes of up to 500,000. Impressive though these numbers are, they again represent a mere fraction of those that would have been seen passing through here when Polynesians arrived, for although New Zealand shearwater breeding sites are nowadays confined to offshore islets, their colonies previously extended to the mainland, which was then rat-free.[34]

In the course of a single year, these shearwaters are tracing one enormous figure-of-eight across most of the Pacific (see satellite map), exploiting seasonal abundances of food en route – fish, squid and shrimp-like krill. They leave their northern Pacific foraging zones in huge flocks in the southern spring to return to their breeding sites, most of which lie in and around New Zealand. On crossing the equator, they funnel along a narrow corridor, passing through the Northern Cook Islands, Niuē and the Kermadec Islands, all within a 10-day period in early October.[35]

The seasonal wanderings of these birds are timed and routed to make maximum use of prevailing winds – hence their figure-of-eight course. At high latitudes they ride on the westerlies, and when they reach the tropical zone they take advantage of the easterly trade winds. For this reason, their approach to New Zealand in spring is made from the northeast. For navigators ascertaining viable voyaging routes and the optimal time for sailing them, there was every reason to pay attention to such mass migrations. We also know that tropical East Polynesians and New Zealand Māori shared an interest in these so-called muttonbirds (shearwaters and petrels), from the fact that they used the same indigenous terms for them: tītī and ōi.[36]

South of Tonga, these enormous migratory flocks are joined by a million or so mottled petrels.[37] Other species, flying a little earlier or later in the season, are also arriving from the northeast. These include over a million Cook's petrels[38] and around 2.5 million Buller's shearwaters, which are returning from north of the equator up to a month earlier, and thousands of black petrels (tāiko) returning a little later to New Zealand at the end of their foraging season off the coast of Central and South America.[39] In other words, this massive movement of low-flying oceanic birds continues over a period of some two months.

Indeed, New Zealand has been ranked 'seabird capital of the world', for a quarter of all seabird species on the planet continue to nest in this region today. To grasp the true grandeur of spring seabird migrations in the 13th century, we need to extrapolate back from the current population sizes quoted above to try and visualise the size of these flocks before the arrival of humans and their introduced pests, when a full 51 species of petrels alone were nesting in and around New Zealand.[40]

With such immense flocks of birds heading toward New Zealand in spring, there was really no need for voyagers to simply set off into the unknown to find it by chance.

More seabirds heading for New Zealand

In early October, some 20 million sooty shearwaters (tītī, ōi, Puffinus griseus syn. Ardenna grisea), above, converge on New Zealand, as shown in the satellite map (above right). In the course of a single year, these birds trace a giant figure of eight across the Pacific, covering between 54,000 and 74,000 km. On this map, the light blue lines trace return flights made during the nesting season; yellow marks their routes of departure from New Zealand (by early April); and orange records their activity in three northern Pacific foraging zones and the narrow corridor along which they all pass across the equator toward New Zealand within a period of just 10 days.

The upper globe shows distribution of the name **tītī** for species of petrel or shearwater; and the lower one shows distribution of the alternative name **ōi**. Both Māori names are shared only with East Polynesia, though with different island groups within this region; note that the name ōi is shared only with the island of Rapa Iti (as oioi).

By early November, thousands of **tāiko** (black petrel, Procellaria parkinsoni), below, are returning to New Zealand from waters off Panama and Central America,

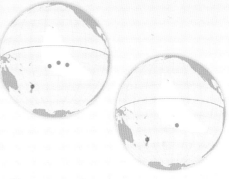

flying via East Polynesia, Niuē and Tonga, as shown in the map (below right). The globe below shows the distribution of this term for species of petrel or shearwater.

Together, all these birds provide a powerful indicator in spring of land and food in the direction of New Zealand.

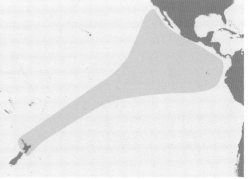

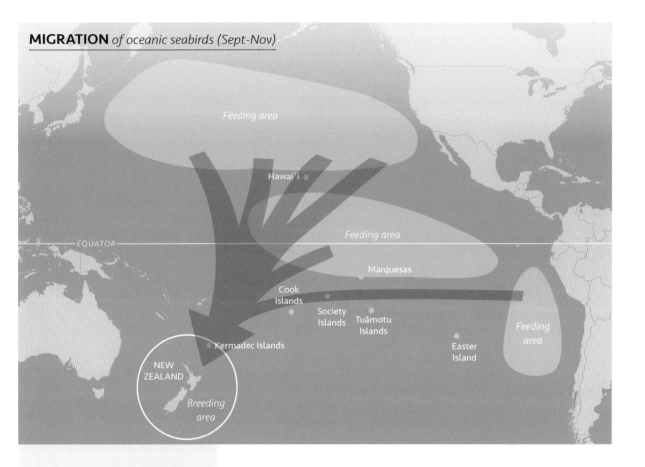

MIGRATION *of oceanic seabirds (Sept-Nov)*

Feeding area

Hawai'i

EQUATOR

Feeding area

Marquesas

Cook
Islands

Society
Islands   Tuāmotu
Islands

Easter
Island

Feeding
area

Kermadec Islands

NEW
ZEALAND

Breeding
area

This map is a compilation of seabird migration data for the Pacific and depicts the mass convergence, between September and November, of tens of millions of oceanic birds flying to New Zealand at close to sea level in preparation for their spring breeding season. It is based on the satellite data below, in which eight seabird species were tracked: mottled petrel (orange dots), sooty shearwater (brown), black-winged petrel (light orange), Chatham petrel (lime green), flesh-footed shearwater (dark green), Pycroft's petrel (blue), Cook's petrel (pink) and Gould's petrel (black).

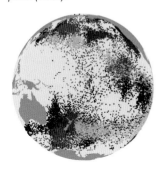

Migratory waders

While these oceanic wanderers live out their lives far out at sea and seek land only to nest, another group – the migratory shorebirds, or waders – feed close to shore. In spring, several are flying high over the Pacific to New Zealand along a similar course. With the onset of the southern spring, their Arctic nesting grounds are heading into winter and food there is becoming scarce. Of the many species making this trans-Pacific flight each year, by far the most conspicuous are bar-tailed godwits (kūaka).

Here again, the current estimate of godwits making this flight today is deceptive – just 125,000 or less – for, when New Zealand ethnologist and surveyor Percy Smith aimed his shotgun into a rising flock of them on Kaipara Harbour in preparation for his Christmas meal in 1861, he downed 43 with a single shot; and New Zealand surveyor Captain Gilbert Mair was able to kill 97 on the Tauranga coast with a single shot.[41] These birds were still being harvested then by Māori using traditional methods, including the strategic deployment of nets.[42] Estimates of flock sizes at the time suggest that these were at least 15 times larger than those of today,[43] from which we might try to extrapolate the number of godwits migrating during the voyaging era and say that their numbers may have run to more than one million.

Although the season of their migration to New Zealand is similar to that of the oceanic birds – mid-September to early October – spotting the godwits en route is considerably more difficult. This is not only because they fly much faster, at around 80 kph, but flocks of up to several thousand typically pass over the Pacific at altitudes of between 2000 and 5000 m – similar to that of

light aircraft. Indeed, over the past 80 years of observations, birdwatchers have rarely recorded more than about 50 birds a year across Oceania.[44] Only now, with the use of satellite tracking of individual birds, do we have a clear picture of their remarkable non-stop flights, which typically last eight days and nights and are again timed to make use of seasonal tailwinds.[45]

Such high-altitude migrations might seem to preclude godwits from guiding the ancestors of Māori to New Zealand;[46] however, the prospect of their playing a minor guiding role is not out of the question. In the 1870s, when more birds were migrating, individual godwits were observed on Suwarrow, Manihiki and Niuē, exhausted and unable to fly any distance, as if they had been unable to keep up with the migratory flocks.[47] From Raoul onwards, a few godwits have also been seen flying low, and the occasional exhausted bird has been known to drop onto a boat to rest. If such a bird were carried for a few days on this last leg of the voyage, then released, it may well have admirably served the needs of both bird and navigator.

Pacific cuckoos

Spring also brings two land birds back to New Zealand: two species of cuckoo.

The shining cuckoo approaches from the NNW, so is never encountered in East Polynesia, but the much larger long-tailed cuckoo almost certainly served Polynesians as an indicator of the whereabouts of an unknown land. This cuckoo has an extraordinarily wide winter distribution – from Palau near New Guinea to Pitcairn Island – and almost every one of these birds will return to New Zealand to breed.

Godwits crossing the Pacific

From mid-September to early October, bar-tailed godwits (kūaka) migrate across the Pacific to New Zealand, typically flying at altitudes of light aircraft.

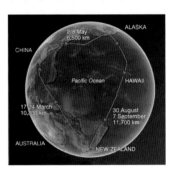

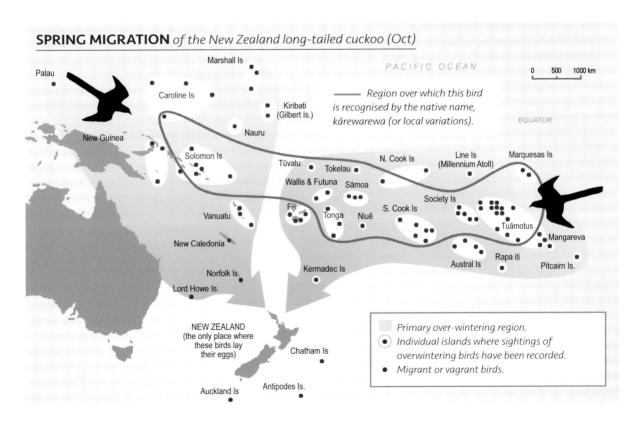

SPRING MIGRATION *of the New Zealand long-tailed cuckoo (Oct)*

—— Region over which this bird is recognised by the native name, kārewarewa (or local variations).

PACIFIC OCEAN

EQUATOR

0   500   1000 km

Palau
Marshall Is
Caroline Is
Kiribati (Gilbert Is.)
Nauru
New Guinea
Solomon Is
Tūvalu
Tokelau
N. Cook Is
Line Is (Millennium Atoll)
Marquesas Is
Wallis & Futuna
Sāmoa
Society Is
Vanuatu
Fiji
Tonga
Niuē
S. Cook Is
Tuāmotus
New Caledonia
Mangareva
Norfolk Is.
Kermadec Is
Austral Is
Rapa iti
Pitcairn Is.
Lord Howe Is.

NEW ZEALAND (the only place where these birds lay their eggs)
Chatham Is
Auckland Is
Antipodes Is.

Primary over-wintering region.
Individual islands where sightings of overwintering birds have been recorded.
Migrant or vagrant birds.

Long-tailed cuckoos

*In October the New Zealand long-
tailed cuckoo (*Urodynamis taitensis;
syn. Eudynamys), *below, sets off for
New Zealand from islands scattered
all across the South Pacific. Across
most of this region, this bird shares
a single name – kārewarewa, or
variations of this. Although the
chances of actually spotting one out
at sea are slim, Polynesians almost
certainly noted their seasonal arrivals
and departures at either end of their
migration. En route to New Zealand,
most evidently pass through the
Kermadec Islands, where they are
frequently seen in large numbers.*

These cuckoos typically fly at speeds of up to 80 kph – like the godwits – and continue to arrive in New Zealand over a period of two or three weeks,[48] usually in October. Unlike the godwits, but like the shearwaters, they generally fly low over the ocean. They call loudly to one other as they go – *zzhweeep*, often followed by a strident *pe-pe-pe-pe-pe-pe-pe* – a call that can still be heard from sea level in the dark.[49] Early 20th-century lighthouse keepers record seeing many of these birds arrive in New Zealand 'in groups and a few solitarily, usually at night from the northeast' – that is, from the direction of the Kermadecs.[50]

Again, their numbers were formerly far more impressive. Even as late as 1872, when 40 percent of New Zealand's forest cover had already been lost, and ship rats and Pacific rats were already well established, Captain Gilbert Mair described his astonishment at the enormity of the flocks:

> During the three days that we were making the passage [down the Hurukareao River in the Urewera Mountains], I saw some hundreds of them, swarming about in the air like large dragonflies, as many as twenty or thirty of them being sometimes associated together. The loud clamour of their notes became at length quite oppressive.[51]

Polynesians took a keen interest in these birds; we know this because they shared a single traditional name for them right across the Pacific, from outlying islands of the Solomons in the west to the Marquesas in the east (see map page 149).[52] Over this vast region, some 7400 km wide, Polynesians identified the New Zealand long-tailed cuckoo as kārewarewa, or variations of this name.[53] This is remarkable, for it implies that the bird was recognised as the same species right across the South Pacific. This in turn implies that its distinctive habits – such as the fact that its eggs are always laid elsewhere – were noted. In October, almost every long-tailed cuckoo leaves these tropical isles, and anyone witnessing this could deduce, from their unwebbed feet and habit of perching in trees, that they were heading for a forested land to nest.

There are many references in Polynesian tradition to the navigational practice of following birds to land. In several Tuamotuan voyaging chants, for example, specific mention is made of frigatebirds, red-tailed tropicbirds, sooty terns, rails and plovers.[54] And in Samoan tradition, Tagaloa sent his daughter Sina to Earth in the form of a bird, Tuli, to find dry land.

So anyone seeing these cuckoos fade from view over the sea may well have wondered where they were headed. Perhaps they grabbed a couple of rocks on the beach and placed them so as to mark the bearing of the birds' departure, returning at sunset to note the corresponding horizon star to sail by. Analogous practices are recorded from the Tuamotuan atoll of Nukutavake, for example, where navigational stones were erected and aligned as guides for canoes departing for the neighbouring atoll of Vairangatea.[55]

In the course of a single year, many of the cuckoos overwintering in East Polynesia are now understood to follow an anticlockwise loop migration, aided by prevailing winds.[56] By passing through the Kermadec region to reach New Zealand, the birds can avoid a direct flight into prevailing westerly winds.

The point is that there is a major pathway of birds leading to New Zealand, one that is being used in spring by some 20 million birds or more. As most of these birds are flying low over the sea through East Polynesia, they are highly conspicuous to the inhabitants of this region. East Polynesians therefore had every reason to know not only of the existence of land in this direction, but also when the most favourable winds blow to reach it. From this alone – but also from the quantity of wood drifting north in winter, as we saw – it would have been equally obvious that this was a land worth finding. In this sense, the Polynesian discovery of this, the last major habitable land mass on Earth, would seem almost inevitable.[57]

A land worth finding

Not until the first navigator sailed along the coastline might anyone appreciate the full extent of this new land mass, for the total land area of New Zealand exceeds by about 10 times the combined extent of all the islands hitherto known to Polynesians. Even a single offshore island, such as Great Barrier Island off the east coast of Auckland, covers an area greater than that of all of the Southern Cook Islands combined. The main islands of this, their latest, discovery stretch in an almost unbroken line north to south for 1600 km, far further than the voyage from Rarotonga to Tahiti. From methods traditionally used by Polynesians to refer to long distances at sea, the scale of this find is likely to have been assessed and communicated by counting off the number of days it took to sail along the shoreline.

Despite the cooler climate, this must have been an attractive destination for, unlike atolls that constitute so much of Polynesia, the islands of New Zealand are high, with reliable rainfall, year-round rivers, good soil and a wide range of quality stone suited to the manufacture of tools. And, unlike the Kermadecs, Easter Island, Pitcairn, Marquesas and the makatea islands of the Southern Cooks, its coastline abounds with large, safe, natural harbours and gently sloping sandy beaches for landing canoes.

Kupe, a circumnavigator

Left: Statue of Kupe on the Wellington waterfront, with his wife and tohunga (priest or guide). Kupe was an important ancestor but, as Michael King points out in The Penguin History of New Zealand, *he is unlikely to have discovered New Zealand.[58] Genealogical evidence shows that he – like Ngāhue of Te Arawa, and Toi in the Bay of Plenty and East Coast[59] – was a contemporary of other settlers, an early circumnavigator of the country and the founder of a community. The wealth of place names associated with him cannot be taken as evidence that Kupe was the first, any more than those commemorating James Cook, whose arrival in New Zealand was preceded by that of Abel Tasman by more than 100 years. Many stretches of coastline are named (and claimed) for Kupe, especially around Hokianga Harbour, Mercury Bay, Cook Strait, and the top of the South Island. For example, his sails (Ngā Rā-o-Kupe) are represented by this distinctive rock formation (above left) just north of Cape Palliser, near Wellington.[60]*

Above: Pārengarenga Harbour, near the northernmost tip of the North Island, is identified in tradition as a landing point for the Kurahaupō and Māhuhu canoes. In northern New Zealand, such large, safe natural harbours and gently sloping sandy beaches abound.

The opportunities for hunting, fishing, timber and horticulture would have been enviable. Unless the first navigators had already visited the Hawaiian Islands, the megafauna in New Zealand, its active volcanoes and many peaks permanently covered in snow would have been something entirely new. There were vast estuarine swamps here too, extensive inland lakes and large fertile plains – all novel sights even to them.

Massive trees

Just as the British and Dutch were drawn to the wooded southern shores of the Baltic Sea in the 17th century, any maritime power is heavily dependent on good sources of timber for shipbuilding and repairs.

*Above: When the first people reached New Zealand, over 80 percent of it was covered in **ngahere** (forest): the globe above left shows the strictly East Polynesian distribution of this term; the globe right, the much wider distribution of the alternative Māori term for forest, **wao**, whose use is reserved for more poetic, sacred or tapu contexts.*

When New Zealand was first discovered, over 80 percent of it was still in forest (compared with just 25 percent today).[61] Many of the trees were of unheard-of dimensions, some up to 60 m high, with trunk diameters of more than 8 m.[62] Here, the traditional method of splitting trunks into planks, drilling them and sewing them together was redundant; large single trunks of tōtara, kauri, mangeao, rimu, kahikatea and matāi could be felled and hollowed out to produce a hull that was far stronger. A row of small fires would be lit along the length of the log and left to burn until the wood charred. Then the fires would be removed and the charred wood chipped away with stone adzes – a process that was repeated until the desired hull shape was achieved.[63] This was no clumsy process; as Joseph Banks observed of Tahitian boatbuilding: 'They hollow out with their stone axes as fast, at least, as our carpenters could do.'[64]

One can well imagine samples of such timber being worth taking back to the tropics.

The kauri and the sperm whale

Polynesians may have first encountered floating logs of New Zealand kauri (Agathis australis) as far north as the Kermadecs. To Northland Māori, this forest giant was the father of parāoa (sperm whale, Physeter macrocephalus). Not only do the two grow to similar proportions with similar 'skin', but pieces of kauri gum (kāpia, pictured) washed up on the beach also look remarkably similar to ambergris (pakake, pakaka, mīmiha, right) from sperm whale intestines and both are flammable.[65] In the 'Legend of the kauri and the sperm whale', the whale came ashore, inviting the tree to join it in the fresh cool sea. It is quite conceivable that the kauri was indeed first encountered as a floating log, like a whale; larger ones are equivalent in bulk to the body of an adult sperm whale.[66]

Shells and feathers to take home

*Any explorer who found New Zealand is almost certain to have returned with evidence to confirm the find. This might include unfamiliar feathers, such as those from New Zealand kākā, left, and potentially useful shells, such as the New Zealand pāua (Haliotis iris), left. The use of pearl oyster shells as ornamental breastplates has been mentioned. These, far left, are known in the Cook Islands as ti`a, a term transferred in New Zealand to pāua shell inlaid into the eyes of wooden carvings (**tiwha**, below). Note that, within tropical East Polynesia, this term tiwha is known only from the Southern Cook Islands.*

A wealth of stone

The value of the stone available in New Zealand for tool-making is evident from the enormous distances over which it was ultimately carried. Basalt (karā) was shipped from quarries at Tahanga near Whitianga on the Coromandel Peninsula over distances of up to 350 km, to North Cape, East Cape and the central North Island, for use in the manufacture of adze heads and chisels. For the same purpose, metamorphosed argillite (pakohe), a hard, flinty kind of rock, was carried from Nelson over a distance of some 500 km to Haast on the West Coast of the South Island. Other kinds of rocks were evidently valued more highly still. Greenstone (pounamu) collected from the West Coast of the South Island – used originally for making a variety of fine tools – was transported some 1000 km to the northern tip of the North Island.[67] And obsidian (mātā) for cutting implements was carried, as we saw, from Mayor Island (Tūhua, off the Coromandel Peninsula) to Raoul Island in the Kermadec Islands, a distance of over 1100 km.

Samples of such rocks would have been worth carrying back to tropical Polynesia, either as exhibits or for trade – and yet no incontestable examples of this have yet been identified.[68]

Feathers and shell

Polynesians were on the lookout for interesting feathers, too. Tahitians and Hawaiians, in particular, sought red and yellow feathers for decorating cloaks, aprons and wicker helmets worn mainly by people of rank, or for decorating images of important gods.[69] At the time of European contact,

Moa

*New Zealand's moa were extraordinary. Some of their eggs were larger than rugby balls (below) and would be worth taking away as samples. In the tropics, the term **moa** originally applied to look-alike chickens (domestic fowl, Gallus gallus), which were carried across the Pacific by Polynesians and bred on the islands for meat, cock fighting and headdress feathers. The globe shows the distribution of this Polynesian name, which would be applied in New Zealand to nine species of giant birds (Dinornis species), including the South Island giant moa (Dinornis robustus, right), the female of which weighed up to 242 kg and stood 1.7 m high. A femur (thigh) bone (below) would serve as evidence of the unprecedented size of some of these birds.*

the main colour of Māori cloaks was brown,[70] but other colours were available here. Māori plucked bright red feathers from the red-crowned kākāriki and the underside of kākā wings, and bright yellow ones from the shoulders of male hihi (stitchbird), metallic blue from tūī, black-and-white tail feathers from the now-extinct huia, and green plumes from native parrots and pigeons.[71] To the first navigators, all would have been worth collecting.

The same is true of seashells. The internal, iridescent lustre of pāua shell was valued by Māori in the manufacture of fishing spinners, cloak pins and pendants, and to represent eyes in carved wooden figures. Indeed, this material would become the New Zealand counterpart of the pearl shell used in the tropics for making tools and breast ornaments.

These are just some of the items that would have been worth stowing aboard a canoe for transport back to the tropics as confirmation of the discovery, not only of new land, but of some of its natural resources.

Birds to look up to

Wherever Polynesians discovered new land, they would encounter a bounty of birds, chicks and eggs, especially in spring and summer when many Pacific islands are teeming with petrels and shearwaters; and it was the same in New Zealand. The difference here was the discovery of so many kinds of giant flightless land birds. It is worth trying to imagine the impression this made – even for someone who had already encountered goose-like ducks on the Hawaiian Islands, weighing up to 7.6 kg, for even the smallest of New Zealand's nine species of moa weighed double that of a Hawaiian duck, and the largest moa weighed up to 240 kg – equivalent in weight to four men – and reached 3 m high, tall enough to look down on a human.[72] Moa eggs were no less impressive: each one could weigh up to 7 kg, equivalent to more than 10 dozen chicken eggs – so big that an old-fashioned tophat might serve as an eggcup.[73]

Above: Size comparison between three species of moa and a human.

It would certainly have been tempting for a navigator to select a moa eggshell to take back to the tropics,[74] or, better still, a 1-m-long moa thigh bone to hold next to his own leg to show that a single bone could reach to his waist. This would have been evidence enough to his compatriots that there was no need to bring the domestic chicken (moa) to New Zealand. Indeed, no archaeological evidence of a pre-European introduction of chickens has ever been found here, despite Polynesians having transported them across the Pacific from Asia to Easter Island and perhaps beyond to South America. New Zealand had enough giant 'native chickens' of its own.

No need of a canoe to hunt these

Easy sources of meat were equally abundant right along the shoreline. When the first people arrived here, there were huge breeding colonies of New Zealand fur seal (kekeno) lolling half-asleep on the rocks. We know something of how they were perceived from the terms Māori coined for them: some refer to their nervous behaviour on land, while others liken them to whales.[75] They were unlike dolphins, though, as no canoe was required to hunt them; when hauled out onto the rocks, a simple club was all that was needed to kill them. Their importance to Māori is evident in kitchen middens around the country, and from the fact that they formerly bred much further north.[76]

A single seal can weigh up to 200 kg – equivalent to two Polynesian pigs (puaka) – so there was little need to give up space on any of the settlement canoes to introduce a pair of these animals.[77] And indeed, despite the fact that Polynesians distributed these Southeast Asian animals as far east as Henderson Island and north to the Hawaiian Islands, no subfossil evidence of them has ever been found in New Zealand. The abundance of wild meat here not only rendered pigs redundant, it saved them from becoming a liability to gardeners as they frequently were in the tropics – especially on larger islands, where escaped animals often proved hard to retrieve.[78]

Indeed, during the first 150 years of settlement, seals are known to have been a far more important source of food to Māori than birds; at many early prehistoric sites they are estimated to have contributed

Coastal megafauna

New Zealand's coastal megafauna provided an unusually abundant source of meat. When the first people arrived, kekeno (New Zealand fur seals, Arctocephalus forsteri, up to 140 kg) above, were common along not only South Island coasts, but also the east coast of the Coromandel Peninsula, and up into the Far North. There was an endemic species of whakahao (New Zealand sealion, Phocarctos species, now extinct), too, that ranged along the coast from Stewart Island up to the Far North; with their demise has come an expansion

in the range of the Hooker's sea lion, Phocarctos hookeri (above right), which weighs up to 400 kg and is today encountered only around the extreme southeast of the country.[79]

Penguins were likewise traditionally eaten by Māori, and ranged from the 1-kg kororā (blue penguin, Eudyptula minor), to the 5.5-kg hoiho (yellow-eyed penguin, Megadyptes antipodes, right) and an almost identical, but now-extinct, bird known as the Waitaha penguin (Megadyptes waitaha).

around 60 percent of the meat consumed.[80] Scientist–explorer J. R. Forster commended the taste, declaring that he preferred seal steaks to wild duck, 'by far more tender & juicy than beefstakes,' he added, 'their good taste soon got the better of my prejudice'.[81]

Until Polynesians reached New Zealand, few would have seen penguins.[82] Even the smallest of these flightless swimmers, the blue penguin (kororā),[83] can weigh over 1 kg. Here again, the hunter's job was easy. At night they had only to wait for them to walk out of the surf onto dry land; and during moulting season (2–5 weeks in summer and autumn) they would find them huddled in caves. Other species that were hunted here include the much larger Fiordland crested penguin, the yellow-eyed penguin and the now-extinct Waitaha penguin (which was hunted out by around AD 1300–1500).[84] The value of penguin meat is evident from remains found in archaeological sites, where these considerably exceed food remains from ducks, petrels or rails.[85]

Any report of a wealth of assets such as this – the harbours, beaches, soil, timber, stone and meat – would have been worth taking back to the tropics as a guide to what was needed in this new land and what could be left behind. And news of such an extraordinary find would almost certainly have spread quickly across a wide area.

Polynesian pigs

With such plentiful sources of meat in New Zealand, there was little need to bring Polynesian pigs (Sus species, below right). DNA from jaw bones and teeth collected from archaeological sites and museums across the Pacific reveals that all share a single genetic heritage,[86] with antecedents traceable via Indonesia to mainland Southeast Asia – ultimately to the wild boar of Vietnam. This pig evidently entered Polynesia along a route south of Borneo and New Guinea,[87] with a separate introduction via a northern route into Micronesia (shown in blue on the map). The globe (far right) shows the distribution of the Polynesian term for pig, **puaka**, which was remembered in New Zealand even though the animal itself was not brought. (Puaka is not to be confused with the modern Māori term 'poaka', which is simply a transliteration of 'porker' or pig.) Nor was this pig brought to any of the more southerly islands of Norfolk, Kermadecs, Austral Islands, Rapa Iti or Easter Island; indeed, this breed may not have tolerated cold conditions.[88] Even on islands where pig bones and teeth have been excavated, pork does not seem to have been particularly important in the diet during the early phases of Polynesian settlement[89] – perhaps because of an initial abundance of protein from other sources, or because of pigs not being widely available until later. As no pure Polynesian pig exists today, the creature in the photograph above is actually a so-called 'Near' Polynesian pig from Mangaia (Southern Cook Islands).

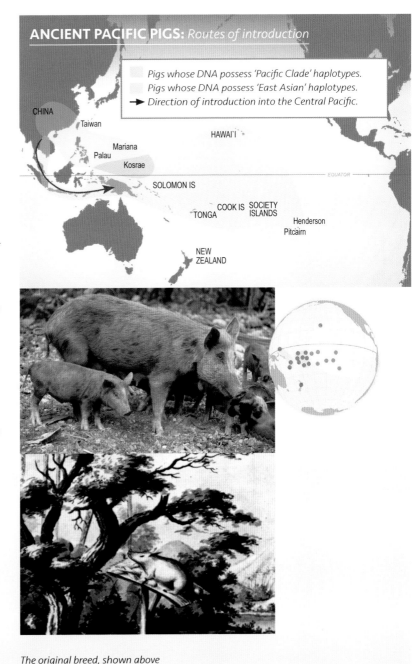

ANCIENT PACIFIC PIGS: *Routes of introduction*

Pigs whose DNA possess 'Pacific Clade' haplotypes.
Pigs whose DNA possess 'East Asian' haplotypes.
➡ Direction of introduction into the Central Pacific.

CHINA
Taiwan
HAWAI'I
Mariana
Palau
Kosrae
EQUATOR
SOLOMON IS
COOK IS SOCIETY ISLANDS
TONGA
Henderson
Pitcairn
NEW ZEALAND

The original breed, shown above in a drawing by Sydney Parkinson from 1769, was smaller than the European one, with a proportionately longer snout, arched back and straight tail, a bristled black coat with underwool and short, erect, pointed ears.

- CHAPTER TEN -

Passage to New Zealand

Planned Voyages of Settlement

Every cord is tied, all is firmly lashed in place.

Bird-carved prows strain for the long voyage of the Sea Kings!

Now the breeze holds steadily from the land, and proudly

the great ships ride eager upon the waves –

Oh, heart-stirring sight!

Traditional East Polynesian sea chant, trs. Frank Stimson 1957

Having reviewed what an original voyage of exploration might look like and what it might achieve, we can now turn to voyages of settlement, investigating how long such a deliberate voyage might take, and the planning required. Polynesians are unlikely to have been any more willing than anyone else to embark in a craft heavily laden with people, tools and planting material, without some idea of their destination and what it might take to reach it. In this chapter, the focus will be on an intentional voyage of settlement from Rarotonga to New Zealand.

Timing

We saw earlier how the tropical Pacific was settled from west to east, against the trade winds, requiring Polynesians to have an intimate understanding of seasonal anomalies in prevailing winds. In the case of voyages to New Zealand, it therefore seems likely that they made efforts to learn the optimal season in which to sail this course, too. Entering waters south of the Kermadec Islands without such knowledge, there was an increased risk in the cooler months from westerlies driving canoes too far east of New Zealand and missing landfall altogether.[1]

It is not until the sun moves south of the equator in November to March that these potentially troublesome westerlies retreat to the south, making way for increasingly common easterly winds immediately east and northeast of the North Island.[2] With a greater chance of tropical cyclones in the last three of these months (January–March) there is really only a narrow window of opportunity to sail this last leg of the voyage, namely November and December.[3]

So is this the season in which the ancestors of Māori actually sailed? It seems that the answer may be 'yes'; that is, if we can accept Māori migration traditions as mythologised history, for these speak of a pod of whales that guarded the wake of the *Tākitimu* canoe.[4] Of the whales encountered in this region, the most likely candidate here is the humpback, which is regularly seen on southern migration from the Kermadecs onward in these very same months – November and December.

It seems that the *Tainui* and *Te Arawa* canoes sailed to New Zealand together, as the traditions and genealogies associated with them are clearly linked,[5] with both arriving when the pōhutukawa tree was in full flower. It is said that Tauninihi, the chief onboard

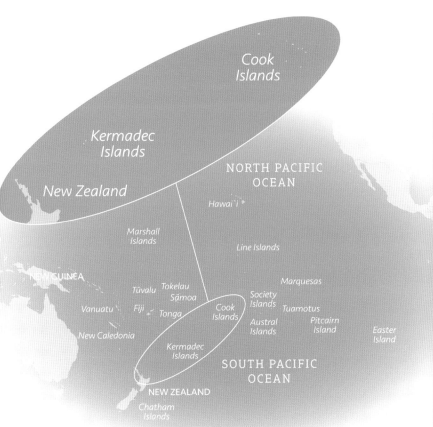

Te Arawa, was so moved by the sight of its deep red blossoms along the cliffs that he tore off his scarlet feather headdress and cast it into the sea.[6] This tells not only of the euphoria of arrival, but that this canoe touched shore in northern New Zealand in the very brief period during which these flowers are sufficiently prolific to make a striking impression from offshore, which implies the last two weeks of December.

Assuming there is an historical basis to these accounts, it would seem that all three voyages were underway in late spring, with at least two canoe arrivals toward the end of December.

Setting off from Rarotonga

If we are to try and visualise the departure of the settlement canoes, we might turn to an account from 1837 by English missionary John Williams of a traditional navigational technique still in use at the time:

> The natives, in making their voyages, do not leave from any part of an island, as we do, but, invariably, have what may be called starting-points. At these places they have certain landmarks, by which they steer, until the stars become visible; and they generally contrive to set sail so as to get sight of their heavenly guides by the time their land-marks disappear.[7]

When Polynesians embarked on long voyages, it was traditional to do so at sunset; this allowed their chosen course to be tied not only to specific

When the chief of the Te Arawa migration canoe saw the deep red blossoms of the pōhutukawa (Metrosideros excelsa, above) he is said to have torn off his scarlet feather headdress (kura) and cast it into the sea. The flowers would not have been unfamiliar to him, for similar trees are common throughout much of tropical East Polynesia; his headdress was most likely made from the 40-cm-long tail feathers of tawake (red-tailed tropicbird, Phaethon rubricauda), top.

From Rarotonga, New Zealand presents an unusually large target

A navigator sailing this route to New Zealand at the end of November will find the sun setting close to WSW – in close alignment with his course to the northern tip of the North Island – identified on the graphic, right, with a photo of the Cape Rēinga lighthouse.[8] In comparison with most other Polynesian wayfinding targets, the entire arc for locating the coastline of New Zealand from Rarotonga is enormous (16°).

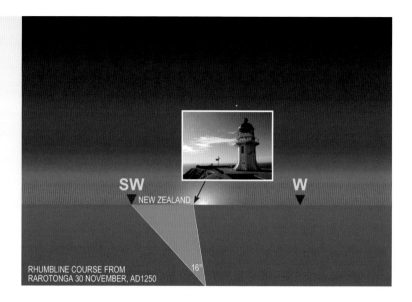

SW
NEW ZEALAND
W
16°
RHUMBLINE COURSE FROM RAROTONGA 30 NOVEMBER, AD1250

stars rising or setting along the horizon, but also to the feel of the craft's orientation to the existing wind and swell.

If they were setting out for New Zealand from Rarotonga in spring, they would find their prow pointing directly toward the setting sun, its reflected light quivering on the waves effectively illuminating a pathway to their destination.

Tied to the 'sky ropes'

Looking back in the fading light, the crew would see the island of Rarotonga retreating into darkness. Or, as one traditional voyaging chant puts it:[9]

> Ho! The ship leans to the freshening breeze! . . .
> Flying sea foam dashes high!
> The ship is tossed upon the waves . . .
> Ho! The land is lost to view! . . .
> Drive on before the wind.

From now on there would be little else to guide them through the night but the wind, swell and stars.

As we saw in chapter 5, night navigation to a known destination involves following a sequence of horizon stars, a sequence for any particular voyage that is aptly described by author Jeff Evans as a 'sky rope'.[10] We saw that the sky rope for any given voyage changes slowly through the year, and also, to a tiny extent, through the centuries. In other words, it is quite specific to a particular route and time.

In the case of the *Tākitimu*, the guiding stars recorded for its voyage to New Zealand were Canopus, Orion's Belt, Rigel, Sirius, Venus as Morning and Evening Star, Pleiades, Tail of Scorpion, and the Milky Way.[11] If this is a faithful record of the original sequence of horizon stars, it is theoretically possible to show that a voyage of settlement was deliberately navigated with foreknowledge of the destination; and to ascertain something about when it took place.[12] This is partly because there are months in which any given star will not appear near the horizon during the hours of darkness,

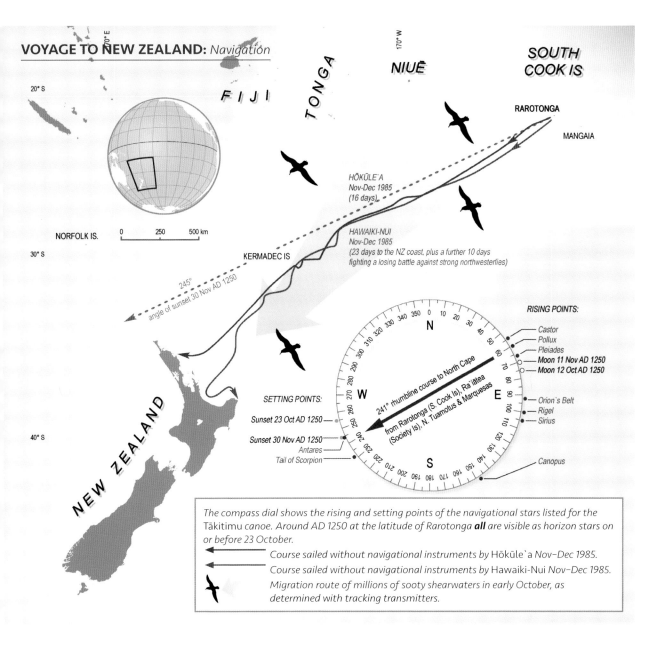

The compass dial shows the rising and setting points of the navigational stars listed for the Tākitimu canoe. Around AD 1250 at the latitude of Rarotonga **all** are visible as horizon stars on or before 23 October.

Course sailed without navigational instruments by Hōkūle'a *Nov–Dec 1985*.

Course sailed without navigational instruments by Hawaiki-Nui *Nov–Dec 1985*.

Migration route of millions of sooty shearwaters in early October, as determined with tracking transmitters.

and because the points at which steering stars rise and set are not randomly orientated. In fact, planetarium software can be used to wind back time to search through various calendar dates and hours, latitudes, longitudes and elevations for a valid match.

What this exercise reveals is that the best fit for guiding stars associated with the *Tākitimu, Tainui* and *Aotea*, for example, would lead all three canoes along a bearing from, or via, Rarotonga shortly before the end of October.[13] This direction of approach to New Zealand, and the timing of it, is consistent with other evidence already reviewed from language, culture, winds and wind indicators such as migrating birds.

With this in mind, we will now attempt to recreate what the navigators of these three craft, at least, may have seen on a typical night sailing this course over the next month.

This map depicts the requisite course and horizon stars for reaching New Zealand from Rarotonga, and the course being flown by millions of seabirds heading for New Zealand on their spring migration.

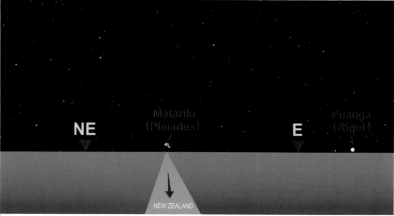

Right: While still low to the eastern horizon, up to an hour after sunset, Matariki (Pleiades, or 'Seven Sisters' in Taurus), a tight cluster of stars, rose at 67° (in the 13th century) almost aligned with the stern.

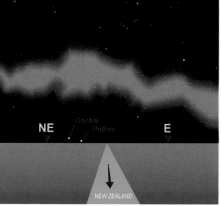

Above: Four hours after sunset, Whakāhu (Pollux and Castor, the twin stars of Gemini) rose just east of northeast (at 58° and 53° in AD 1250), behind the waka. The 'wispy cloud' lying close to the horizon here is Te Mangōroa (the Milky Way).

Guided through the night . . .

An hour after the sun had set in front, they would see a tight cluster of stars behind them: Pleiades (Matariki, or Seven Sisters in Taurus) which is just beginning to appear over the horizon and neatly aligned with the stern. To help appreciate just how small this cluster of stars is, stretch out your arm: this cluster occupies a space no wider than your little fingernail. Most people with reasonable eyesight can distinguish six or seven stars within it, hence the European name.[14] Its importance to Polynesians is evident from the fact that its Māori name, meaning 'little eyes' or 'eyes of the ariki' (chief), is shared throughout Polynesia.[15]

If the navigator turned back to face the prow of his vessel and scanned along the night horizon near where the sun had gone down, he would find Venus, the brightest of the planets, as an 'evening star' (Meremere). For now, this bright planet would replace the sun as his guide.[16] In fact, in the idiom of Māori, Venus is described as 'a companion of the sun', for, although it 'wanders' in relation to the true stars, it never strays more than two hand spans from the sun.[17]

Now Venus too drops over the horizon, and he sees another guiding star rising to the left. Canopus (Autahi, near the Large Magellanic Cloud) serves not only as a guiding mark but – according to tradition – to help foretell the weather, perhaps because it lay upwind for much of the voyage; so when this star was obscured, it signalled the approach of clouds.[18]

Up ahead, near the prow, Antares (Rehua) is now dropping slowly back into the sea. The recorded guiding stars for the *Aotea* are specific on this point, for its navigator is said to have rested the course of his waka on the place of its 'eyes'. (Eyes are a common Polynesian designation for stars.)[19]

Next, the navigator would find Rigel (Puanga, the bright star of Orion)[20] off to the left and behind, at a bearing of around 100°, and – just to its left, in the same constellation – a string of three bright stars known as Orion's Belt or Tautoru.[21]

These are just a small selection of the stars traditionally used by Polynesians; the full inventory is thought to run to over 150.[22] Among them is a vast scattering of stars that appears as a long 'cloud' arching across the night sky: the Milky Way, the outer edge of our home galaxy. Even in bad weather, the navigator can usually rely on seeing this at some point in the night. Its changing orientation in the night sky not only provides an indication of direction, it also helps the navigator keep track of the hours as they pass through the night. In the migration narrative of the *Tākitimu*, this myriad of stars is aptly referred to as 'the long fish' (Te Ikaroa), and in that of *Māmari* as 'the long shark' (Te Mangōroa).

Māori terms for Pleiades and the sun are known throughout all of Polynesia; however, the rest are specifically East Polynesian; this sheds more light on the immediate ancestry of Māori and the direction from which their canoes arrived.

As the accompanying graphic shows, the stars remembered for *Te Arawa*, *Tākitimu*, *Tainui* and *Aotea*, at least, are consistent with a departure in spring or early summer from the direction of Rarotonga/Tahiti.[23] This implies that their navigators knew where they were going and were in a position to choose the season in which they set sail. This in turn implies a prior return voyage to establish the correct course and guiding instructions that were deemed sufficiently important to be remembered centuries later.

Above: The centre of the swirl in this time-lapse star image represents the south celestial pole. The milky blurs on the left and top depict the Large Magellanic Cloud and Small Magellanic Cloud respectively.

. . . and guided on through the day

As the night drew to a close and the stars began to fade, the glow of dawn returned in the east. For the first hour or two, the sun remained low enough in the sky to resume its guiding role; the navigator had to align it with a chosen point on the washboards of his canoe, just as he had with other guiding stars.[24] But as the sun lifted further from the horizon, the navigator was again obliged to orientate his vessel by the swell and wind alone. These would be his guides until late in the day, when he could again align the prow of his vessel with the setting sun in the WSW.

Māori star names point to an East Polynesian origin

NEW ZEALAND MĀORI	NAME RECORDED ELSEWHERE?
Rā *(sun)*	*throughout Polynesia*
Matariki *(Pleiades)*	*throughout Polynesia*
Meremere *(Venus, a planet)*	*East Polynesia and some Polynesian Outliers*
Rehua *(Antares)*	*East Polynesia*
Puanga *(Rigel, the bright star in Orion)*	*East Polynesia*
Takurua *(Sirius, the Dog Star)*	*East Polynesia*
Whakāhu *(Pollux and Castor)*	*East Polynesia*[25]
Te Mangōroa *(The Milky Way)*	*East Polynesia*
Te Ika-roa *(The Milky Way)*	*East Polynesia (Tuāmotu, Hawai`i)*
Te Mokoroa-i-ata *(The Milky Way)*	*East Polynesia (Mangaia)*

Guided by rainbows

Several migration traditions speak of canoes being guided by kahukura or āniwaniwa (a rainbow).

In at least one migration tradition, the canoe was guided at nightfall by hinekōrako (a 'moonbow', true lunar rainbow or kurahaupō) in front of the bow. This kind of rainbow, below, is a relatively rare phenomenon that requires light rain or mist and a (near) full moon low in the sky.

Note that a true lunar rainbow is quite different from the far more common 22-degree lunar halo, below, that sometimes appears around the moon and which is caused by ice crystals suspended in the atmosphere.

Rainbows day and night

According to Elsdon Best in his treatise on the astronomical knowledge of the Māori, navigators were guided by many signs and mythological beings. As to the faith Māori placed in these, Best was apt to inject a note of irony. 'Such are the quaint beliefs of the Maori;' he wrote, 'and any voyager of wide seas who believes that hordes of beings are guiding and guarding him should surely be of tranquil mind' – a comment that refers specifically to the use of rainbows to guide the canoes:

> As night fell Kahukura [a rainbow] returned to the stern of 'Takitumu', and his sister, Hine-korako [a pale luminous arch in the heavens], was sent forward to take his place.[26]

Such rainbows are also said to have guided the *Uruao* and *Horouta* canoes. Best's scepticism may not be entirely warranted, though; for in this twilight period between day and night, rainbows do indeed have potential to serve as precise directional guides. The governing principle here is that an observer who faces the centre of a rainbow's arc will always find the sun directly behind.[27] In other words, finding a rainbow behind the canoe in the evening is the poetic equivalent of having the sun setting directly in front.

As night fell the rainbow behind would naturally vanish, at which point its place was taken by Hinekōrako in front – a term that refers to a pale luminous arch, commonly known as a 'lunar rainbow' or 'moonbow' (not to be confused with a lunar halo that is commonly seen *encircling* the moon). Such night rainbows are not common and are seldom noticed, as they are often very faint; they occur only in fine rain when the moon is low in the sky, within a few days of it being full.[28] And yet, with the spray produced by the bow of the canoe and perhaps a keener night-adapted vision, these more subtle rainbows may have been observed more frequently.

From my own experience I can confirm that they appear far more muted in colour than their daytime counterpart – they seem silvery or whitish in such low light, a soft effect that is evidently produced as a result of the relatively poor functioning of the colour receptors in our eyes. So it seems worth investigating whether such night rainbows might serve any useful purpose for guiding a canoe on this course. To find out, we can return to the planetarium software and run it on over the next few nights until the next full moon is rising. In this way, we can watch it rise at ENE, directly opposite the sun, and see that any 'moonbow' (hinekōrako) cast by it would, in the chosen idiom, have gone 'to the front as a guide'. In other words, steering for the centre of its arc would indeed keep their ship on the correct WSW course.

So, even if one makes a generous allowance in Māori migration traditions for heroic embellishments and other mythologised elements, once again we see the traditions lending support to voyages of settlement having been deliberately navigated.

Dead reckoning and the moon

Although New Zealand is by far the biggest solid target in Polynesia, the navigator could still miss it, for it was not enough for him to be able to

Nights of the moon

None of the Māori names for nights of the moon are known to be shared with West Polynesia, indeed, the practice of giving names to individual nights of the moon is primarily an East Polynesian one.

NEW ZEALAND MĀORI	NAME RECORDED ELSEWHERE?
whiro *(1st night of the moon)*	*East Polynesia only*
hoata *(3rd night of the moon)*	*East Polynesia only*
huna *(10th night of the moon)*	*East Polynesia only*
ōhua *(14th night of the moon)*	*East Polynesia only*
hotu *(15th night of the moon)*	*East Polynesia only*
ōturu *(16th night of the moon)*	*East Polynesia only*
rākau-nui *(18th night of the moon)*[29]	*East Polynesia only*
ōtāne *(27th night of the moon)*	*East Polynesia only*

hold a predetermined course and check his north–south position (latitude); nor would this ability alone tell him *where* he actually was. Without some means of estimating east–west position (longitude), there was a risk in the latter part of the voyage of being driven too far east by westerlies, and unable to tack back to land. In that event, the navigator could be left with little option but to continue east for over 3000 km before finding land again in, say, the Austral Islands or the Tuamotus.

We saw how European navigators had faced similar challenges until the invention of a reliable maritime clock in the 1760s. It was this invention that finally enabled them to interpret their east–west position from the east–west position of the sun. Estimating east–west position is a skill that otherwise required navigators to keep track of their east–west movements in relation to their port of departure – or a known reference point en route, such as the Kermadecs. It involved maintaining an awareness day and night of the course being sailed, drift, speed, passing time and distance covered.[30] This skill is known as 'dead reckoning' and it can become remarkably intuitive, as Tupa`ia demonstrated to Cook on several occasions. In 1769–70, the Tahitian navigator repeatedly impressed the captain by pointing accurately back toward Tahiti, even after following a convoluted route around New Zealand to reach Australia.[31] It seems that, even without instruments, he was fully capable of keeping tabs on where they were.

To keep track of the days that have passed since leaving the last reference point, East Polynesians used the nights of the moon (marama), which they named individually.[32] They distinguished these by the shape of the moon as it waxes and wanes – in effect creating a kind of lunar calendar.[33]

As several Māori names for nights of the moon are shared with Easter Island and Hawai`i, but none with West Polynesia, where very few nights of the moon were individually named, this would seem to imply that this form of timekeeping is peculiar to East Polynesians and that it perhaps reflects a specialisation in long-range voyaging.

Hydration

On planned voyages, named 'nights of the moon' may well have helped with rationing supplies, too – including water, which was traditionally carried in hollow lengths of bamboo with a plug of green leaves to stop up the filling hole.[34] Of course, if and when rain came, this too would have been collected, either as brackish water scooped up from the hull with bailers, or collected in spare receptacles from a trickle running off the angled tip of the 'inverted' pandanus sails.

To keep a large crew hydrated on long voyages must have been a challenge, nonetheless. From bitter experience during World War II, those condemned to protracted life-raft voyages learnt that the critical point below which the intake of drinkable water led to deaths was 110–220 ml (a quarter to half a cupful) per day.[35] At this point, those who remained alive were suffering headaches and irritability, followed by delirium, hallucinations, loss of fingernails and toenails . . . and ultimately death. Survival manuals for life-raft emergencies at sea consequently advocate rationing to no less than 500 ml of freshwater a day, and it seems unlikely that voyaging Polynesians drank much less than this. Even with rationing and catching rainwater, modern 'replica' of Polynesian craft with crews of just 10 typically carry 720 litres (0.72 tonnes) for 43 days at sea,[36] or 1.67 litres per person per day.

To get some insight into what life on the original migration canoes was like, it is worth reviewing the logistics of carrying enough water.

Polynesian bamboo – the type of bamboo used to make the containers – is typically one metre between the internodes, with a stem diameter of up to 8 cm: one section might contain up to 5 litres, or a 10-day ration for one crew member. Other types of container from bottle-gourd skins or coconut shells (tahā) closed off with leaves or a wooden stopper have a similar capacity.[37] And immature green coconuts[38] typically hold 300–600 ml of coconut water each: it would take some 12 coconuts to provide the equivalent 10-day ration.

These figures may well have a bearing on the voyaging range of migration craft, their crews, and planning required; for, to keep delirium and death at bay, the minimum ration of water for a crew of 20 for one month would weigh close to half a tonne. If they were relying solely on coconut water, the same canoe would need to carry over 600 coconuts, which would weigh even more.[39]

The alternative – drinking seawater – is of little value. Survival manuals are unequivocal that drinking seawater for any length of time will lead to death,[40] and this is borne out by statistically fewer deaths among the crew of life rafts who resisted the temptation to drink it. This is because the sea contains about 3.5 percent salt, while urine can carry no more than about 2 percent, so imbibing pure seawater can only hasten dehydration in the long run. Drinking it in small amounts for short periods, or mixing it with freshwater to stretch out water rations, is not necessarily harmful, though.[41] The ability of individuals to tolerate saltwater also varies.[42] On coral atolls such as the Kiribati island of Malden that lack freshwater, Polynesians survived long periods on silty or brackish water.[43] In 1616, Dutch explorers Schouten and Le Maire report their surprise at witnessing Polynesians off the Tuamotus drinking pure seawater.[44] And likewise in 1774, Captain Cook's crew expressed their surprise at seeing Easter Islanders drinking 'pretty plentifully' not only brackish water, but also 'real salt water'.[45] In the Mangarevan language, there is even a specific word, mai, meaning 'to drink saltwater'.[46]

Another source of drinkable fluid is fish, for their salt content is similar to that of human blood – or about one quarter of that found in the sea itself. This liquid can be obtained by twisting pieces of fish in a cloth, or – in the case of large fish – by cutting holes in the side and letting a liquid ooze from the lymphatic glands. Some sailors even report sucking or chewing on fish eyes or drinking fluid in the spinal column, collected by holding the head end down, cutting through the spine near the tail and tipping out the meagre juice.[47]

All this implies that it would be unwise to set off into the unknown with a large crew without any foreknowledge of how long the voyage would be. It seems easier to envisage careful planning on a voyage of settlement, and careful rationing according to the anticipated length of the voyage. And much the same argument can be made regarding the quota of food that settlement voyages are likely to have carried.

Provisioning

Of course, there is always the possibility of finding food on the way. Whenever deep-sea fish such as mahimahi (the so-called dolphinfish), flying fish, oceanic bonito (skipjack tuna) or sharks were available, these would have been caught and eaten, and perhaps an occasional passing turtle or exhausted bird that landed on the canoe. Even so, food provisions would have been carried and strictly rationed for the anticipated length of the journey. Otherwise, there was an increased risk that the tubers the gardeners had selected for planting would not actually reach their destination. As a rule, on any voyage, there are fresh supplies at the start: in this case, cooked taro and breadfruit, bananas, possibly yams or even kūmara. Once this was consumed, the fare is likely to have turned to fermented breadfruit, taro paste wrapped in leaves, bird eggs, dried provisions,[48] coconuts and stalks of sugarcane sealed at either end with breadfruit gum. And, according to Te Rangi Hīroa, it was traditional for a fireplace to be provided on the canoes for cooking, laid on a bed of sand.[49]

Maintaining body heat

Out at sea it is not always easy to keep warm, even in the tropics, a challenge that increases as one continues south toward New Zealand. For example, when the crew of the *Hōkūle`a* attempted to replicate this passage in the early summer of 1985, they complained of the cold south of the Kermadecs, despite being equipped with special, fast-drying sleeping bags and heavy foul-weather gear designed for North Atlantic conditions: 'As we moved farther and farther south, the nights

Food for the voyage

Traditional Polynesian voyaging foods included provisions they carried with them: taro, breadfruit, banana, coconut and pandanus fruit. Besides these, deep-sea fish available en route would include sharks and mahimahi, above, (common dolphinfish, Coryphaena hippurus); at up to 100–180 cm long, it can provide a sizeable meal. And atu, below, (oceanic bonito or skipjack tuna, Katsuwonus pelamis), which can reach 1 m; in the warmer months, great shoals (rere) of these are encountered as far south as the northern edge of the continental shelf off New Zealand.

Above: Like this Inuit family from above the Arctic Circle (1929), Polynesians are generally better adapted to the cold.

especially felt cold, and we wondered about the hardships pioneering voyagers must have experienced.'[50] In these cooler conditions, the elderly, the women and young children would have been particularly vulnerable, even if well shielded from the wind with rain capes of tapa cloth, or woven mat ponchos of pandanus leaves. And all the more so in heavy night rain or when the crew were forced to paddle into drenching head seas. For this reason alone, navigators with mixed crews almost certainly aimed to sail this last leg of a settlement voyage in summer to avoid hypothermia.

It is perhaps worth describing what an ill-prepared crew experiencing an extreme drop in body temperature might face: first, a powerful involuntary shivering, followed by feeling clumsy and increasingly careless. If the body remains cold and the shivering stops, it is a sure sign that death is close, for this involuntary reflex of alternately contracting and relaxing the muscles serves the vital function of generating heat to help maintain core body temperature.

Polynesians were evidently somewhat adapted to this kind of stress by their large average body size, which is understood to have helped them cope with the cold out at sea. In 1995, to investigate how well different body types cope with the stress of exposure typically encountered on a Pacific voyage, physical anthropologist Philip Houghton ran thousands of computer simulations. Using weather data collected in summer and winter at different latitudes in the tropical Pacific, he set in motion a series of virtual 10-day voyages at latitudes 10°, 15° and 22°, factoring in heat gain by the crew from the sun and heat loss to wind chill. Whenever the wind speed reached 15 knots, or when rain fell persistently, the virtual crew could huddle into groups to offset loss of body heat. Although brain death seldom occurs until our core temperature falls to 20°C, our capacity to shiver ceases at 32°C, making this the effective cut-off point for survival, so any crew member in the experiment whose core body temperature fell below 32°C was deemed to have died.

Houghton then compared the results from male and female members of three racial physiques – Karkar (from off the NE coast of New Guinea), Lau (from Malaita in the Solomon Is) and Hawaiian. What this exercise revealed was that the Hawaiian (Polynesian) group demonstrated a consistently superior ability to survive; and men survived slightly better than women.[51]

In fact, this adaptation is thought to explain the large average body weight and muscle mass of Polynesians today, a physique closely associated elsewhere with cold-climate peoples such as Inuit (Eskimos). In both instances, a large ratio of body mass to skin area, and extra muscle mass with which to shiver, is understood to contribute to an enhanced ability to survive the cold conditions faced in daily life.

Stormy seas

The hardships of voyaging are frequently expressed in Polynesian poetry, for conditions at sea can change quickly and dramatically. 'If the sea ever gives up its dead,' writes Te Rangi Hīroa, 'what a parade of Polynesian mariners will rise from the depths when the call of the shell trumpet summons them to the last muster roll! … For them no human songs were sung, but the sea croons their requiem in a language that they understand.'[52] Or, in the lines of one Tuamotuan voyaging song:

> Torrents of driving rain fall from the cloven skies
>   into the storm tossed heavens below;
> A deluge descends from the sundered skies
>   into the raging gale below!
> The god of the elements overturns all ships
>   now venturing forth upon the sea . . .[53]

The danger of storms features in the migration narratives of Māori too. On the *Kurahaupō* and *Aotea* canoes, the planks and lashings began to separate. *Te Rīrino* did not make it through. Sometimes the greatest hazard was the land itself: the *Tākitimu* finally succumbed in this way at Te Waewae Bay on the southernmost shores of the South Island; the *Āraiteuru* wrecked at Moeraki; and the *Māmari* foundered at Maunganui Bluff, near Hokianga.

   And yet the Polynesian voyagers had faith; they rendered 'the sea calm by a spell' (rotu) or recited karakia (spells or prayers) to ensure a safe passage. No fewer than six karakia are recorded for the *Aotea* alone – to ensure calm seas; receive water; speed the sailing and paddling; save the craft while being swamped; and to aid the bailing. And here again, both Māori terms – rotu and karakia – are strictly East Polynesian, further evidence of the cultural origin of Māori.[54]

   In these extreme conditions, the crew would redistribute their body weight around the craft to avoid capsize, busy themselves bailing and lowering and stowing the sails to save the precious rigging and matting.[55] In the event of capsize, some or all of the provisions and water rations are likely to have been lost, along with settlement cargo, bailers, anchor stone and paddles – and perhaps crew. For any crew left floundering for long, there was a risk in tropical waters from shark attacks; and in cooler waters south of the Kermadecs there was the danger of immersion hypothermia.[56]

   All these hardships were very real, but so too were the joys:

> My ship now sails
>   for the seas of the Great Dark Ocean,
> Ever she is slapped by toppling waves
>   while the wake seethes and whispers.
> Battered by dark-blue billows
>   she bathes in the waters of that ocean rip
> Where tossing crests collide,
>   while the gliding advance of my ship
>   gathers speed like the flight of a bird![57]

Far from land, Polynesians had faith. At least six karakia ('spells' or 'prayers') are recorded for the voyage of the Aotea. *It is significant for an understanding of Māori origins that both this term and the Māori term rotu ('to render the sea calm by a spell') are again shared only with East Polynesia.*

Whales encountered en route

South of the Kermadec Islands, the voyagers are likely to have encountered more whales. Again, as shown on the globes, Māori terms pertaining to them are not all shared with the same islands.

By November and December, the **tohorā**, (humpback whale, Megaptera novaeangliae), *above,* are heading south along this route via the east coast of New Zealand to enjoy rich summer feeding grounds around Antarctica.

From the Kermadecs south, the **parāoa** (sperm whale, Physeter macrocephalus, *the largest of the toothed whales*), *above right, also becomes increasingly common.*[58]

Note that this term for whale (or dolphin) is again East Polynesian, a word that is, in this case, shared between New Zealand, Hawai`i, Marquesas and Tuāmotu,[59] but not with the Southern Cook Islands or the Society Islands.

Pupuha (explosive spouting of a whale), *right,* may be heard from almost one kilometre away – a sight and sound that must have been reassuring to any mariner intentionally following their migration route. The globe shows this Māori term for the spouting of a whale and how it is shared with Tahiti and the Tuamotus, but not with the Cook Islands.

Wayfinders of the deep . . .

At this time of year (November–December), humpback whales (tohorā) are migrating in the same direction from tropical waters around Tonga to their summer feeding grounds around Antarctica. Their course follows a deep ocean canyon – the Kermadec Trench – to New Zealand, where they pass along the east coast.[60] Several migration traditions of Māori refer to such whales, including the pod mentioned earlier that is said to have 'guided, preceded, followed, and surrounded' the *Tākitimu* canoe.[61]

The magnificence of the original encounters is impossible to imagine without a grasp of the fact that, before the onset of large-scale commercial whaling in the region, the whale population here was 60 times greater than now.[62] Only with this in mind can we imagine the scene of them streaming slowly past, many of them more than half the length of a voyaging canoe.[63] Even when their presence is obscured by thick fog or heavy rain, or at night, their explosive exhalations can still be heard from almost a kilometre away as they resurface from the deep. This spouting (pupuha) may well have been a reassuring indication that they were on track.

Meeting new birds

South of the Kermadecs, tītore (Cape pigeon or Cape petrel, Daption capense), left, become increasingly common, flying close to the waves in large numbers, frequently following ships.[64]

Another unfamiliar bird that is likely to have been seen from the Kermadecs south is the majestic **toroa** *(black-browed mollymawk, Thalassarche melanophris; syn. Diomedea), left. The globe shows the distribution of this term for large, ocean-going seabirds, applied in New Zealand to albatrosses and mollymawks [Diomedeidae], which have enormous 2-m or more wingspans – further evidence of an East Polynesian ancestry for Māori.*[65]

. . . and now more wayfinders above

South of the Kermadecs, new species of birds appear, many of which would have been noticed following the canoe. Most striking are the albatrosses and mollymawks (toroa) – large, ocean wanderers that seldom flap their wings.[66] Aboard the *Hawaiki-Nui*, Jeff Evans tells of how one 'latched onto' their waka for the final 10 days of their voyage to New Zealand, 'swooping down into the troughs, catching fish without even landing'.[67] Even today, sailors approaching New Zealand from the north commonly remark on a sudden increase in bird numbers at around 370 km (200 nautical miles) away.

Among the petrels, shearwaters and prions, they are often struck by the sight of small flocks of common diving-petrel (kuaka) either entering the waves or exploding from them, in full flight, or swimming about like miniature penguins. In spring, they also encounter large flocks of fairy prion heading back from subtropical waters around the Kermadecs to New Zealand's offshore islands.

A little closer still, at about 300 km off, Jeff Evans records seeing insects

Right: Within some 150–200 km of the coast, navigators may have seen their first karoro (adult black-backed gull, Larus dominicanus).[68]

landing on the canoe.[69] From early references to New Zealand's unusually abundant insect life, this phenomenon is again likely to have been far more striking during the migration era. We can picture swarms of insects blown out to sea, settling on the sails or floating past, as seen by Captain Cook on his approach to Tierra del Fuego in 1769: 'thirty leagues [some 150 km] off land, swarms of butterflies, moths and other insects blown out to sea [that] settled on the deck or floated past the ship'.[70]

It must have been very clear by now that they were close to land.

More new birds

About 370 km north of New Zealand, a new bird that begins to stand out is this stubby little kuaka (common diving-petrel, Pelecanoides urinatrix), above left, which is seen entering and exploding from the waves in full flight, or swimming around rather like a miniature penguin.

About 320 km north of New Zealand, tītī wainui (fairy prion, Pachyptila turtur), above right, are becoming common too. From September, over two million of them are returning from this region to nest on offshore islands, from where they will continue to forage by day, streaming back to their colonies at dusk.

And around 200 km northeast of New Zealand, there is often a sharp increase in numbers of another unfamiliar bird, kororā (blue penguin, Eudyptula minor), above.

Long white cloud

We saw earlier how Polynesians were in the habit of looking out for stationary clouds as an indication of land over the horizon. In this case, these may have been spotted at around 180 km from the North Island, the distance from which sailors arriving from the north often notice these clouds today.[71]

This is the theme of a well-known story in which Hine-i-te-aparangi pointed in the direction of New Zealand and exclaimed to her husband Kupe, 'He ao! He ao!' (A cloud! A cloud!). This is often recounted as the origin of the name 'Aotearoa' for New Zealand, commonly translated as the (Land of the) 'Long White Cloud'.[72] However, historians question the story's authenticity; they point out that, prior to European contact, the islands of New Zealand did not actually have a collective name. The North Island and South Island were then known separately by other names, such as Te Ika a Māui ('the fish of Māui') and Te Wai Pounamu ('the waters of greenstone'), respectively.[73]

There is another kind of 'long white haze' that is often overlooked – a phenomenon that is likely to have guided subsequent navigators, at least those that arrived during the first 100 years or so of settlement, when about 40 percent of New Zealand's original forest cover was in the process of being cleared by fire.[74] In this early period it is likely that smoke haze was visible from hundreds of kilometres out to sea, just as smoke from large Australian bushfires drifts downwind to cloud the skies over New Zealand today. In the case of New Zealand such smoke plumes may have extended east for 1000 km or more.[75]

Shorebirds, flotsam and fish

It is at around 200 km from land, too, that the crew are likely to have noticed a change in the ocean swell and more fragments of vegetation floating by[76] – leaves, the odd floating mangrove propagule,[77] a broken branch or uprooted tree, or lines of floating seaweed, all of which may be noticed up to 200 km east of the North Island.[78]

The navigator's eyes would have been keenly attuned by now, lest they miss the land and sail right past, as in the lines of a Tuamotuan arrival chant:

> The gods are watching through your eyes;
> Theirs are the eyes keeping a sharp lookout!
> Now the far cries of land birds are heard as they swoop
>   into the troughs of the waves upon the horizon . . .[79]

Off the north and east of New Zealand, about 100 km from land, adult black-backed gulls are likely to have appeared, a few perhaps resting in the rigging. At around 80 km, a few white-fronted terns may have joined them. The presence of both these birds marks an increase in fish near the edge of the continental shelf, where the ocean floor off New Zealand suddenly drops away.

The first sighting of land itself is likely to have been made at around 50 km[80] – in clear weather at least. By the time a deep red smudge of

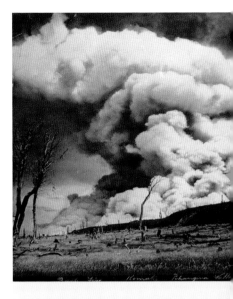

Smoke haze

During the first 100 years or so of Polynesian settlement, scenes like this from the Pohangina Valley (in 1904, above) would have been common, the smoke drifting far out to sea just as it does from Australian bushfires today – as seen in this satellite image (below) from February 2014.

Above: From some quarter of a mile offshore Sir Joseph Banks described the sound of korimako (bellbird, Anthronis melanura): 'They seemed to strain their throats with emulation and made, perhaps, the most melodious wild music I have ever heard, almost imitating small bells, but with the most tunable silver sound imaginable.'

pōhutukawa blossoms appeared along the cliffs, welcoming expanses of white sand could be seen, and soon the enchanting sound of forest birds would come wafting toward them.

Even as late as 1770, this is something that struck Cook's botanist Joseph Banks when their ship was anchored in Queen Charlotte Sound in January that year. 'I was awakened by the singing of the birds ashore, from whence we are distant not a quarter of a mile,' he wrote, 'perhaps, the most melodious wild music I have ever heard.'[81] We can only close our eyes and imagine the melody that would have greeted the original settlers as they hauled their sailing craft up onto the beaches some five centuries earlier.

While it is not hard to imagine the euphoria of arrival, the crew may have been more torn, like all true sailors, between a love of the sea and a longing for land. Perhaps a land-based culture will never fully appreciate the achievements of what was essentially an amphibious one. In reality, the challenge of reaching New Zealand with a settlement crew may have lain less in locating it than in adequate planning to keep everyone warm, fed and hydrated en route, and with their planting material intact.

How long at sea?

Estimates vary wildly as to how long these voyages are likely to have lasted. Modern replicas of Polynesian craft sailing from Rarotonga to New Zealand, averaging about four knots, have taken a little over two weeks; while others claim that the original craft sailed faster still. Captain Cook and other late 18th-century observers saw Polynesian outriggers passing them at estimated speeds of up to 22 knots, sailing circles around their vessels 'with the same ease as if we had been at anchor'.[82]

However, as archaeologist Atholl Anderson points out, heavily loaded settlement craft from some five centuries earlier would certainly have been far slower in the open sea than the lightly-built outriggers seen by Cook in sheltered waters.[83] As for the performance of modern Polynesian replica craft, these canoes differ on many counts from the original migration craft with respect to hull technology and rigging, sails and sail sizes. Because pandanus sails are far more apt to tear than synthetic ones, especially when wet, and sennit rigging is far more vulnerable to abrasion and breaking under strain than its synthetic equivalent, it would have been reckless to 'push' a 13th-century migration craft anywhere near as hard as its modern counterpart.[84]

Their speed of progress towards New Zealand would depend on wind direction and how close to the wind these early vessels could sail. Here, the archaeologists disagree. While Anderson holds to a more conservative view that these vessels may have been largely limited to running before the wind,[85] Geoffrey Irwin argues that they could also sail across the wind, with the wind at around 90 degrees to the hull ('beam reach'), or even with the bow pointing a little closer into the wind.[86] The distinction may seem trivial, yet it has a major bearing on our understanding of how the Pacific was settled, particularly with regard to the practicality of making two-way voyages.

How close to the wind?

The question of how close to the wind a Polynesian craft could sail is directly relevant to the ability of early navigators to make return voyages. Recent wind tunnel experiments provide some answers, confirming that Polynesian sailing canoes of traditional design were more versatile than many had thought; they were not limited to 'running before the wind'. Right, a one-fifth scale model of a 14-m Polynesian sailing canoe is mounted on a balance embedded in a turntable in the Twisted Flow Wind Tunnel at the University of Auckland. During performance tests, the sail was adjusted by small onboard electric winches and data recorded by computer and cameras.

To establish which view is correct, Irwin teamed up with aerodynamics engineer Richard Flay to design a one-fifth scale model of a 14-m canoe, based on ethnohistoric sources, and subjected it to wind-tunnel testing. 'Sailing boats conform to the laws of physics,' explains Irwin, 'and there is a well-established science of sailing.'[87] (Indeed, Flay had already applied this science of sailing to help Team New Zealand win the America's Cup in 1995 and 2000.) Their test was designed to compare the performance of three types of Polynesian hull and traditional V-shaped sail (Oceanic spritsail), small and medium-sized sails, and sailcloth made from modern Dacron and from finely-woven pandanus mat. Their findings: the Dacron sail performed slightly better than the equivalent pandanus one up to a wind angle of around 110°, but performance thereafter was much the same. All three traditional hull profiles they tested could be sailed at 75° or better to the wind.

From this it is clear that Polynesians were not limited to 'running before the wind'. Consequently, Polynesians were far less dependent on wind shifts than many had believed, and two-way voyaging was well within their grasp.

But back to the original question of how long the migration voyages are likely to have lasted: Anderson estimates that the average speed of migration craft, well laden with settlement cargo and passengers, is likely to have been less than two knots – similar to a mean speed of two knots for Cook's *Endeavour*. If so, the voyaging time to New Zealand from Rarotonga is likely to have been around 35 days.[88] This would seem to agree with what can be gleaned from the navigational stars recorded for the *Tākitimu*, for these would seem to imply a voyage lasting a little over one month.[89]

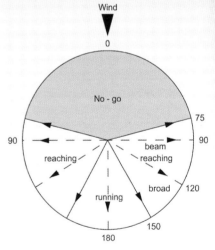

Above, a wind rose depicts the sailing terms commonly used for points of sail. The shaded no-go area makes it clear that no one is suggesting that canoes could sail closer than 75° to the direction the wind is coming from. Rather, the wind tunnel experiment was set up to learn whether canoes could sail 75°–120° to the wind.

CHAPTER ELEVEN

Settling New Zealand

Adapting to a Cool Land

*One must be saturated with the atmosphere of tropical Polynesia
to fully appreciate what the first Maori settlers lost and what they
gained in their new country.*

Te Rangi Hīroa (Sir Peter Buck), *Vikings of the Sunrise*, 1938

Canoe landing sites

From dateable charcoal fragments created by the
first forest fires and from sudden changes in pollen
composition, we know that migration canoes from this
early period landed on both main islands of New Zealand.[1]
Pacific prehistorians can indeed be more specific still from
archaeological finds of two tools that had been held in the
hands of the first crews to reach here.

One is a pearlshell fishing lure unearthed in the
1960s at Tairua on the Coromandel Peninsula, whose use
could be radiocarbon dated to the late 13th to mid-14th
century.[2] It had been made to an early East Polynesian
design from a shell that occurs neither in New Zealand
nor in the Kermadec Islands, only in the clear waters of
a tropical lagoon – that is, from an atoll.[3]

The other item aboard one of the original canoes
is a small shell chisel unearthed at Wairau Bar near
Blenheim in the South Island. It was found in the 1940s,
but lay in the Canterbury Museum for 70 years before
its significance was recognised. Closer scrutiny in 2010
revealed that it had been made from a 10-cm-long
crenulated auger shell that occurs only in coarse sand in
shallow tropical waters. Its sharp end had been ground off
in a manner typical of similar shell chisels in the Society
Islands, Marquesas, Southern Cooks and Austral Islands.[4]

Here was tangible evidence of early arrivals from
tropical East Polynesia – one found in the northern
North Island, the other in the northern South Island.

In fact, Māori tradition speaks of more than 70
landing places[5] – although not necessarily all of canoes
arriving directly from the tropics. As is customary, many
are marked by an instance of 'transfigured landscape'.
When the *Āraiteuru* capsized at Moeraki Beach on the
east coast of the South Island, its cargo of kūmara
and gourds is said to have scattered and remained in
petrified form as the giant round boulders seen there
today. Other canoe landings are commemorated by
place names – Ōmāmari (Hokianga) for where the
Māmari wrecked, and Aotea (Great Barrier Island) and
Aotea Harbour (west of Hamilton) to identify the first
and second major landing sites of the *Aotea*.

How many canoes?

In the familiar 'Great Fleet' version of Māori history,
a flotilla of seven founding canoes are individually
named, but with no mention of the *Māmari* and
Āraiteuru, or of the *Horouta*, *Nukutere*, *Māhuhu*, *Tīnana*
and *Uruao*. One might add to these the names of at
least 35 other canoes[6] – although it is not always clear
which of these were locally built and which originated
from the tropics.

Te Rangi Hīroa gives estimates for the number

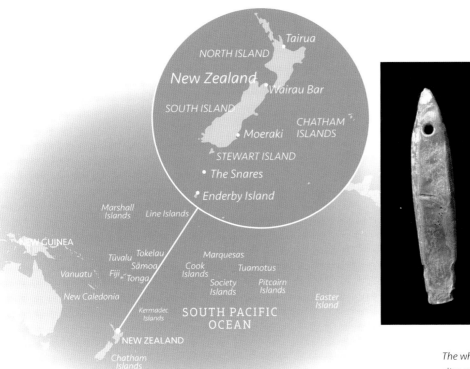

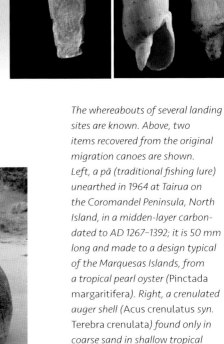

of crew aboard a typical migration craft as high as 60–70, based on oral tradition;[7] but tribal historian Rāwiri Taonui cautions us against taking these figures too literally, as canoe traditions 'express authority and identity, and define tribal boundaries and relationships. They merge poetry and politics, history and myth, fact and legend.'[8] Here, we must turn to independent forms of evidence.

In 1606, Quirós described large double canoes at Rakahanga (N. Cook Is) that he reported were capable of carrying 50 people for 'great distances'.[9] And in 1847 Captain Henry Martin reported seeing a 15-m Tuamotuan double canoe in which 38 men, women and children had voyaged about 400 km to the Society Islands.[10]

The whereabouts of several landing sites are known. Above, two items recovered from the original migration canoes are shown. Left, a pā (traditional fishing lure) unearthed in 1964 at Tairua on the Coromandel Peninsula, North Island, in a midden-layer carbon-dated to AD 1267–1392; it is 50 mm long and made to a design typical of the Marquesas Islands, from a tropical pearl oyster (Pinctada margaritifera). Right, a crenulated auger shell (Acus crenulatus syn. *Terebra crenulata) found only in coarse sand in shallow tropical waters, alongside a 69 mm-long shell chisel made from this type of shell, unearthed from an archaeological site at Wairau Bar, northeastern South Island in the 1940s.*

Above left: Several canoe landing sites are remembered in Māori tradition: here the unusually large, spherical, mudstone concretions known as the Moeraki Boulders, on the east coast of the South Island, are said to be the petrified remains of kūmara and gourds that scattered when Āraiteuru capsized.

Tainui landing site

Perhaps the most ingenious 'memory anchor' for a canoe landing site is that used for Tainui: an erect-growing 4 m namesake shrub, tainui (Pomaderris apetala subsp. maritima, right), whose natural distribution marks the canoe's last known landing site at Kāwhia Harbour. Upright stones were erected at nearby Te Ahurei, too, at either end of its final resting place. The shrub reportedly sprouted from the mat-like flooring (whāriki) of the canoe after it was taken up and used as a skidway for hauling up their craft.[11] It is also sometimes said that the branches of this shrub were brought from 'Hawaiki',[12] so it is intriguing to find tainui growing naturally only along this one short stretch of the west coast of the North Island – at Kāwhia Harbour, Mōkau and Mohakatino.

Te Rangi Hīroa suggests that an erroneous explanation of the source of the plant may have subsequently crept into the original account, for the fossil pollen record reveals that tainui has been growing in New Zealand for over 23 million years.[13] It occurs naturally elsewhere only in Tasmania and parts of the Victorian coast of Australia. The genius of the story remains, nonetheless, for – without recourse to the written word – it has effectively preserved a significant moment in New Zealand's history for some 700 years.

Kāwhia Harbour

However, on longer, deep-sea settlement voyages, large crew numbers seem unlikely. Allowing space to stow paddles, bailers, spare sails, a spare mast perhaps, anchor stone and ropes, harpoons, other utensils, spare clothing, dogs, crop material, water, provisions and firewood, a 25-m double-hulled voyaging canoe cannot reasonably be expected to have carried more than 40, so a crew of 20 is probably more realistic. This would allow space for the crew to lie down at times to sleep, to move around while fishing, toileting, preparing food and having a small fire on board.[14] In Taonui's estimation, 'the most manageable long-distance canoes were about 20 metres long, with an ideal crew size of five to 15'[15] – which is similar to what we find with modern reconstructions of Polynesian-style craft. When provisioned, the 18.7-m double-hulled *Hōkūle`a* takes up to 16 crew; and the 18-m double-hulled *Te Aurere* typically carries a crew of 8–12.

If these more conservative estimates for crew numbers in each canoe are correct, this has important implications for the number of craft arriving in New Zealand, especially in view of the total number of *women* who are now estimated to have been among the founding ancestors of Māori. An analysis by molecular biologist Adele Whyte and co-workers of variation in maternally inherited DNA in the hair and blood of present-day Māori reveals that around 190 women came,[16] 'with possibly as many as 400 females migrating, depending on how rapid[ly] population expansion occurred after arrival'.[17]

If a similar number of men accompanied them, and we allow 20 crew per canoe, then we should be thinking in terms of the arrival of at least 20–40 canoes.

First impact

When the first of these canoes reached New Zealand, all but the high alpine regions and areas affected by volcanic eruptions were forested. These forests accounted for some 80 percent of the total land area.

The new arrivals lit fires to clear the land for settlement and crops, and to drive out large huntable birds. The blazes may have gone further than intended, for huge tracts of kauri and rimu across the Waikato Plains were lost to fire, matai and tōtara in the Hawke's Bay, and native beech along the east coast of the South Island. This is evident from core samples of soil

Forest cover

When the first people reached New Zealand, it was almost entirely forested. The maps above and below compare the original extent of forest (dark green, above) with forest cover in 1840 (below). The difference represents the loss of forest resulting from Māori settlement.

taken in these areas, which reveal a sudden change in pollen composition and an increase in bracken spores that occurred over five centuries ago, coinciding with a sharp increase in charcoal fragments in the soil. The scale of this loss of tree cover is such that it can be clearly differentiated from that due to natural causes, including fires ignited by the volcanic eruption of Taupō in AD 232 – the largest eruption to have occurred in New Zealand in the last 20,000 years.[18] As we saw in the previous chapter, about 40 percent of the country's original tree cover was lost in this way during the first 100 years of settlement,[19] an impact that is dateable and which began around AD 1250–1300.[20]

Independent means can be used to cross-check the date. These include tephrochronology, where the position of archaeological records can be noted in relation to dateable layers of geochemically distinctive volcanic ash. When Kaharoa, near Rotorua, erupted in the winter of AD 1314 (± 12), ash from it spread over the northern and eastern North Island, thereby providing a precise chronological framework. Although no cultural artefacts have been found beneath this layer, a sudden increase in charcoal and bracken spores has; and this serves as evidence of fire that may predate the eruption by up to 50 years. It seems likely that this eruption was in fact witnessed by a small number of Māori who had arrived here as early as AD 1250.[21] This is the date – give or take a few decades – that is now understood to mark the arrival of the first canoes in New Zealand.

Kiore (Pacific rat)

*Kiore (Pacific rats, Rattus exulans, above) are originally from Flores in Indonesia,[22] from where they reached almost every Pacific Island but only with the aid of humans, for they cannot swim far. Globe shows the distribution of the Māori term for them, **kiore**. The timing of their arrival in New Zealand can be ascertained by dating early remains of rat-gnawed seeds and landsnails, below.[23]*

Might a faint footprint precede this?

Bearing in mind that European voyages of settlement of New Zealand postdated their own discovery of it by some 180 years,[24] it seems reasonable to ask whether anyone reached this land much earlier than AD 1250, dismissing it initially as a land too cool to settle, or to grow most Polynesian crops.

The idea of a much earlier visit by explorers found some favour in the 1990s when palaeoecologist Richard Holdaway radiocarbon-dated subfossil bones of Pacific rats excavated from caves in both the North and South islands to AD 50–150. These much earlier dates were certainly intriguing and inspired other researchers to try and replicate them; however, they could find none earlier than 1250–1300. The very early dates were evidently another example of contamination of the bone by ancient carbon (page 74).

So the date for the arrival of rats and their first impact on the environment still stands at AD 1250, consistent with the findings of tephrochronology and pollen evidence, and with dated remains of rat-gnawed seeds of native trees, and remains of rat-gnawed landsnails.[25] Indeed, archaeologists have been unable to find any evidence of people in New Zealand before 1150–1250,[26] which differs little from the date estimated by counting back through remembered generations of Māori. Most tribal genealogies place arrival at 24 to 27 generations ago; assuming 25 years per generation, this produces a date of 1325–1400.[27]

These dates coincide more or less with those for initial human impact across most of East Polynesia, which implies a contemporaneous expansion over this entire region. The speed and efficiency of this pulse of colonisation is sufficient to suggest that a long pause between the discovery and settlement of New Zealand is unlikely. Once such a vast tract of land was found, it is unlikely to have remained unclaimed for long.

For how long did canoes keep coming?

Atholl Anderson identifies this period of New Zealand history as the 'Colonisation phase, AD 1200–1400',[28] for it seems that few canoes were continuing to arrive in New Zealand after this. It is around the end of this phase that stone ceremonial platforms were first being built in the Society Islands – a striking cultural development that was never adopted by Māori. Contemporaneously, around 1450 a contraction in long-distance voyaging was occurring across much of tropical Polynesia.[29] Judging by a proliferation of Māori fortifications in around 1500, crews arriving from elsewhere may have risked a hostile reception anyway.[30]

Canoes hauled up onto the beach

If we are to try and picture the arrival of these canoes, we must first appreciate that Polynesian twin-hulled vessels and outriggers were typically far less clumsy in their approach to land than the cumbersome single-hulled vessels of Europe. While the latter were obliged to anchor in deep water to let the crew disembark into smaller craft to row ashore, Polynesians could sail or paddle their vessels into very shallow harbours or even right up onto the beach to leap out and wade ashore. On the high

tide, their craft could then be hauled out along a makeshift skidway.

On arrival, their dogs doubtless leapt off and raced through the surf to harass the seals, which they would find lolling innocently on the rocks, strangely tame and trusting.[31] As for the birdlife, it is scarcely possible to conceive of their naïveté without first turning to a more recent but comparable 'first contact' event, such as occurred on Lord Howe Island in the Tasman Sea.

Naïve and flightless

Until 1788, no human had set foot on Lord Howe Island, a tiny island that lies between New Zealand and Australia. It has the distinction of being one of the very few Pacific islands that remained undiscovered by Polynesians. In May that year, Arthur Bowes Smyth, surgeon aboard the *Lady Penrhyn*, wrote of his odd encounter with its wildlife:

> The sport we had in knocking down birds was very great … the Pidgeons were the largest I ever saw … [there were] boobies in thousands, together with a curious brown bird about the size of the landrail in England, walking totally fearless and unconcerned in all parts around us so that we had nothing more to do than stand still a minute or two and knock down as many as we pleased with a short stick – if you throwed at them and missed them, or even hit them without killing them, they never made the least attempt to fly away and indeed they would only run a few yards from you and be as quiet and unconcerned as if nothing had happened. The pigeons also were tame as those already described and would sit upon the branches of the trees till you might go and take them off with your hand, or if the branch was so high on which they sat, they would at all times sit till you might go and take them off with your hands. Many hundreds of all sorts together with Parrot and Paroquets, Magpies and other Birds were caught and carried on board our ship with the *Charlotte*.

Captain Thomas Gilbert from the *Charlotte* penned a similar report that same day:

> Several of these [birds] I knocked down, and their legs being broken, I placed them near me as I sat under a tree. The pain they suffered caused them to make a doleful cry which brought five or six dozen of the same kind to them, and by that means I was able to take nearly the whole of them.[32]

Giant birds

Besides moa, kiwi, seals and penguins, there was an abundance of other huntable megafauna in New Zealand when the first people arrived. There were many birds that are now extinct, including, left to right, the North Island adzebill (Aptornis otidiformis), weighing 16 kg and up to 80 cm tall, and the North Island goose (Cnemiornis gracilis), weighing 15 kg and up to 1 m tall. By about 1400, both had been hunted to extinction, along with their South Island counterparts. The now-extinct New Zealand coot (Fulica prisca), weighing 2 kg, was likewise hunted for food. When harvesting all this meat, the only real competition Māori had was the world's largest eagle (Haast's eagle, Harpagornis moorei; syn. Aquila), below, with a wingspan of up to 2.6 m – or possibly more. This giant weighed up to 14 kg, and could tackle prey up to 200 kg. Talon puncture marks through fossil moa pelvises reveal that it attacked moa from behind. It may even have tackled young children. Although Māori hunted this eagle for food and made tools and ornaments from its bones, the bird's demise may have been caused at least partly to a loss of its usual sources of prey. In any case, by AD 1500 all were gone.

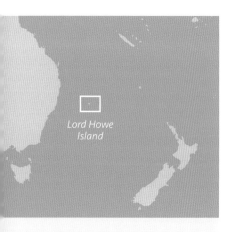

Lord Howe Island

*Worldwide, first encounters
between humans and naïve wildlife
led to extinctions, especially on
islands. In 1788, for example, when
the* Supply, Charlotte *and* Lady
Penrhyn *reached Lord Howe Island,
a remote island between Australia
and New Zealand, first contact
led to the demise of many birds,
including the Lord Howe swamphen
(or white gallinule,* Porphyrio
albus), *pictured below.*

First contact extinctions

Such poignant accounts of first contact between humans and naïve
wildlife not only convey the nature of the original encounters on islands
throughout the Pacific, they remind us that the response of Europeans to
these opportunities differed little from that of Polynesians. In this way, they
serve to challenge the cultural stereotype of Polynesians as being unduly
environmentally irresponsible. The fact is that wildlife proved vulnerable
to the superior hunting skills of humans worldwide, and especially so
on oceanic islands. Such massive losses are therefore more accurately
referred to by the culturally neutral term 'first contact extinctions' – and
there were many. Right across the tropical Pacific, the impact on birds of
first human contact is plainly evident in archaeological remains of food
waste: these reveal that the number of land birds wiped out, directly or
indirectly, by humans runs to well over 1000 species – mostly flightless rails.
Contact resulted in a loss not only of species but of thousands of individual
populations, particularly of seabirds, rails, pigeons and parrots.[33]

In New Zealand, first contact impacted particularly heavily on seals during
the first 150 years of settlement. This is evident from large piles of remains
concentrated not only in areas where they roost today (from Taranaki, around
Cook Strait to the southeast of the South Island), but also along the east coast
of Coromandel Peninsula and right up into the Far North.[34]

Another easy target for Māori was the wide range of moa species, weighing
from 15 kg up to 242 kg. These flightless giant birds were found from coastal
sand dunes right up into the mountains, and even out on larger offshore
islands. Their value as meat is evident in over 300 prehistoric butchering
sites located from North Cape to Stewart Island, some of them of staggering
proportions. At the Waitaki River mouth near Ōamaru, over 8700 moa were
slaughtered and cooked, and some 2400 giant moa eggs consumed. This site
alone is estimated to have covered over 120 hectares, and was – according
to author Quinn Berentson – 'easily the largest prehistoric killing site in the
world'.[35] Even though a single bird is likely to have provided enough meat to
feed 50 people for a day,[36] the number of birds killed across the whole of New
Zealand is thought to be around 100,000.[37] These birds were so easy to hunt
that, by AD 1400, all their main populations were extinct.

Other kinds of flightless birds here are less well known; many of them
were not much smaller than the moa, but all were likewise lost to extinction
by about 1400. This includes two rail-like species that stood waist-high to a
human, and roamed more open habitats: the South Island adzebill, weighing
up to 19 kg, and its North Island counterpart (16 kg). Two enormous species
of native geese were slightly taller and of a similar weight (18 kg) – more
than three times the weight of a modern goose, or twice that of the Hawaiian
goose-like ducks.

As night fell, more giant birds would appear. These included kākāpō –
enormous flightless, owl-like parrots that weighed up to 3.4 kg, more than 10
times that of a ruru (morepork owl), and which were found running along
the ground of both mainland islands. Other similarly meaty ground birds
included many large and unique flightless species of rail, some of which
weighed up to 4 kg;[38] and, of course, kiwi – the most numerous of all: around

Lost rails

*Rails [Rallidae] proved particularly vulnerable; those few that survived the arrival of people in the Pacific were generally species with strong powers of flight. Two common Polynesian terms for them, **moho** (the distribution of which is shown in the globe above) and **weka** (shown in the globe right), probably referred originally to rails in general, most of which are flightless, or tend to run rather than fly, allowing them to be caught with a simple noose laid along their habitual running routes. Their importance to Polynesians is evident in*

subfossil kitchen remains, which reveal that hundreds of unique Pacific Island species were lost to extinction, primarily through human consumption.[39] Above left: A surviving moho of the tropical Pacific (spotless crake, Zapornia tabuensis; syn. Porzana), whose name was transferred in New Zealand to other rails. Above right: The weka of the tropical Pacific (banded rail, Hypotaenidia philippensis; syn. Gallirallus), whose name survives in New Zealand for a large, flightless native rail (woodhen, Gallirallus australis), right.

12 million kiwi,[40] each weighing up to 3 kg. For comparison, the average chicken weighs just 1.5 kg, so every one of these flightless birds could supply enough meat to feed an entire hunting party.

Creatures aboard the canoes

While there was little or no need to bring Polynesian chickens and pigs to New Zealand, the Pacific dog (kurī), on the other hand, would prove useful when hunting. In the tropics these dogs had already proved their worth to Polynesians as an accomplice when fishing in the shallows. In Tahiti, Hawai`i and New Zealand they were kept as pets, and bred as food. Their taste was described by Captain Cook as 'little inferior to an English lamb . . . their excellence . . . probably owing to their being kept up and fed wholly upon vegetables'. The vegetarian dogs he was referring to were Tahitian dogs; in New Zealand they were fed primarily on fish, moa and seals. Their skins supplied material for mats and cloaks (which were reversible, like the sealskins), and their bones and teeth provided Māori with raw material for making fishhooks, awls, pendants and necklaces. Pacific dogs were of different colours; the fine long hair from white dogs was particularly valued in the Society Islands for decorating warrior breastplates.[41] By about 1830 the last of these Pacific dogs had died out, largely through interbreeding with other strains introduced to the Pacific by Europeans. However, from DNA extracted from archaeological remains we know that at least two lineages were brought aboard canoes, again from mainland Southeast Asia.[42]

Kurī (Pacific dog)

Kurī (Pacific dog, Canis lupus familiaris), above, was closely related to the dingo or New Guinea dog. The map depicts one route of introduction into the Pacific, inferred from DNA; and the globe shows the distribution of its Māori name. (The kurī never reached Easter Island; and in Hawai`i they were known as `īlio).

Kutu (lice)

*The tiny **kutu** (adult human head louse, Pediculus humanus capitis) was carried inadvertently across the Pacific. The globe shows the distribution of this indigenous term, which occurs also in Malay and from whence the slang word cootie is derived.*

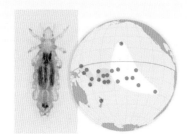

As we saw, it was from Southeast Asia, too, that Pacific rats (kiore) were introduced – as they were to all inhabited Pacific Islands. Their DNA has proven so useful for establishing the routes sailed by the canoes that distributed them that we should look at how and why they were carried: whether they travelled as stowaways or were carried deliberately.[43]

In the case of New Zealand, deliberate transport was hardly necessary, at least in the 13th century, given the abundance of wild meat and skins here. Transferring them intentionally is equally hard to reconcile with the DNA evidence showing that rats were not only brought to New Zealand, but taken in the reverse direction – from New Zealand back up into the tropics.[44] In the tropics, Pacific rats were already known as pests, particularly in coconut and sugarcane plantations, and they would prove no less troublesome to Māori in their gardens and foodstores.[45] It would seem odd if rats were being delivered to their destinations intentionally.

And yet it is equally hard to imagine stowaway rats remaining undetected by crew or dogs on an open canoe or outrigger over many weeks at sea, especially in cases where vulnerable seed crops such as kūmara tubers or gourd seeds were being carried. Perhaps Polynesians were prepared to tolerate them on many of the other voyages, though, with an eye to their potential as a food supply en route, and relied on their dogs to keep the rats from nibbling at the provisions. In this scenario, the rats are likely to have been free to get on and off the craft each time the canoe stopped en route for reprovisioning.[46]

The point here is that, although shared lineages of distinctive DNA extracted from rats is highly useful for confirming instances of voyaging contact, the absence of a shared lineage cannot be used to demonstrate a lack of contact.[47]

In the case of New Zealand, though, we can go as far as to list many of the creatures that were attached to the rats that did reach here: at least 13 species of tiny invertebrates, including specific mites, a flea, a louse and a 'kiore fluke'. The lineages of at least seven can be traced and, of these seven, all again point to an ultimate origin in Southeast Asia.[48]

Attached to the crew came human lice too – an introduction traditionally attributed to Ruaeo who is said to have brought them to New Zealand inside a bag strung around his neck to smear in the hair of Tamatekapua (captain of the *Te Arawa* canoe) in punishment for stealing his wife. Apart from the obvious challenge of keeping them in a bag, a literal interpretation is hardly necessary for lice had been inadvertently carried right across the Pacific in much the same way as they are spread by cramped crews of boats today. They came from Southeast Asia, as is evident from the fact that both Māori and Malay employ the same Pacific-wide terms for adult lice (kutu) and their eggs (riha).

For the sake of completeness mention could also be made of a second human parasite aboard the canoes, the human scabies mite, known to Māori as hakihaki or harehare – a parasite found worldwide that burrows under the skin, causing severe itching.[49]

Canoe plants

Despite early archaeological evidence in New Zealand for a heavy reliance on hunting, especially in the south of the country, the evidence in the north suggests that horticulture was established there almost immediately.[50] Indeed, the ability of Polynesians to colonise new landscapes is linked to the efficiency with which they distributed traditional crops; consignments of planting material carried aboard the canoes have even been dubbed the 'transported Polynesian landscape'. Their full inventory runs to an impressive 50–60 species, 47 of which have been recorded under traditional cultivation in the Society Islands, at least 26 of which reached the Hawaiian Islands,[51] and at least six were brought to New Zealand. All six were identified by early European botanists from neatly laid out communal gardens: paper mulberry, Pacific Island cabbage tree, taro, winged yam, bottle gourd and kūmara.

Although the New Zealand growing season is much shorter than in the tropics, the settlers almost certainly tried to establish other crops, too, for, at that time the growing season was 6–10 weeks longer in the North Island and the South Island was correspondingly warmer, allowing many crops to be grown slightly further inland and further south than now.[52] It therefore seems likely that the settlers brought suckers or seeds of other crops, and attempted to establish banana, breadfruit, pandanus, sugarcane, coconut,[53] arrowroot, giant taro (kape), smaller types of yam, ginger, turmeric, kava, Polynesian bamboo and Malay apple.[54] This is particularly true of fruiting bananas, which are

Vocabulary of the banana

Although fruiting varieties of banana are grown nowadays as far south as Gisborne and suckers were almost certainly brought aboard the migration canoes, whatever strains were brought did not thrive. And yet vocabulary associated with bananas still survived in the Māori language.

māika *banana variety (māika/ meika). In Māori: a native orchid (Orthoceras) with starchy edible tuber.*

tā *hand of bananas. In Māori: tā- whara – sweet, edible flower bracts of kiekie vine (Freycinetia).*

Weeds aboard the canoes

In soil adhering to some tubers aboard the canoes it seems that there were the seeds of at least one Polynesian weed, punawaru (Indian weed, Sigesbeckia orientalis, above),[55] a plant spread in this way from Asia as far east as the Marquesas.[56]

Aute

*Below, **aute** (paper mulberry, Broussonetia papyrifera). In the tropics, trees are cut when 2–4 m tall, and readily resprout to yield the fibrous inner bark used to make tapa cloth. In New Zealand, Cook observed, 'this plant must be very scarce among them, as the Cloth made from it is only worn in small pieces by way of Ornaments at their ears, and even this we have seen but very seldom'. Tapa was also used by Māori for making kites and loincloths. Its cultivation here is also known from pollen and other fragments found in a Bay of Islands swamp at Rangihoua Bay,[57] and from trees that Cook saw much further south, at Anaura Bay north of Gisborne,[58] where its cultivation must have been marginal. The original aute plants became extinct in New Zealand about 1846, when the last of them were destroyed by cattle in the Hokianga district. The globe shows distribution of the indigenous name.*

currently grown as far south as Gisborne, and which were successfully cultivated by Polynesians on the cooler isles of Norfolk Island, Rapa Iti and Easter Island. Much the same case can be made for sugarcane, which will tolerate light frosts; it is currently grown in northern New Zealand, and was successfully grown by Polynesians in the relatively cool climate of Easter Island.

Whatever planting material was brought aboard the canoes, it would have been carefully selected for quality as it was a long way to go back to reintroduce more. In the case of the edible crops, there was the additional imperative to bring enough to ensure the production of a worthwhile surplus from which to select viable planting material for the following year. All of it would have been treated with exceeding care. To protect the slips, cuttings, tubers, seeds and young plants from the potentially deadly effects of sun and salt spray, they are likely to have been wrapped in leaves or tapa cloth and stored well clear of the canoe floor, perhaps slung from the roof of the canoe hut.

Captain Cook failed to bestow a similar level of care on the taro he took aboard the *Endeavour* in the Society Islands; he lost many of them to rot within weeks, well before they reached New Zealand.[59]

Polynesians could not afford to make the same kind of mistake.

Success with six

Despite the challenges, Māori successfully propagated at least six crops continuously for some 500 years, cultivating many of them on a vast scale: some of their gardens extended over 16–20 hectares (40–50 acres).[60] All six of these crops contribute to an appreciation of the horticultural skill – and the ultimate origins – of the people who brought them.

In 1769 Captain Cook's crew spotted about half a dozen paper mulberry (aute) trees on an island in the Bay of Islands. This small tree was introduced to the Pacific from Taiwan and distributed to volcanic islands as distant as Hawai`i, Easter Island and New Zealand for the production of bark fibre for making tapa cloth for clothing and as ritual gifts. It produced no seeds, as its branches were cut and harvested before flowering, so planting material distributed by Polynesians consisted solely of the rootstock and stems of male clones. Indeed, their DNA reveals that all ancient Pacific samples belong to a single, distinct group.[61]

In the Far North, botanists identified small specimens of Pacific Island cabbage tree (tī) at Waimate North and Ahipara. This tree is native to New Guinea and perhaps also to West Polynesia. In East Polynesia it occurs only as a male sterile cultivar, so can only have reached all three corners of the Polynesian Triangle as bundled cuttings arriving aboard canoes. In the Society Islands alone, 13 varieties have been recorded, selected mostly for their sugary, carrot-like rhizomes.[62] The fact that New Zealand plants do not fruit, either, suggests that all cuttings were introduced from this same cultural region of East Polynesia.

In damper areas of Māori gardens in the north, Joseph Banks spotted taro. This plant is originally from Indonesia, but genetic studies suggest that domestication of Pacific cultivars began in New Guinea and the Solomons, by pinching off small offset shoots for replanting,[63] and ultimately distributed from this region to all three corners of the Polynesian Triangle. In Māori, more than 40 named varieties are recorded,[64] one of which, 'pongi' (applied to a dark-coloured variety), is shared only with the Hawaiian Islands, Marquesas and Niuē. However, early taro plants found in New Zealand include stock with two different chromosome numbers: one shared with all of Polynesia; the other with the region of New Caledonia and Timor.[65] This might suggest that canoes coming to New Zealand were bringing planting stock from more than one quarter of the Pacific.

In the Bay of Islands, Banks noted very large plantations of winged yam (uwhi), and Cook saw plantations of them at Tolaga Bay. This crop was grown for its massive underground tubers and was likewise distributed from Southeast Asia to islands as distant as Hawai`i, Easter Island and New Zealand, either as small aerial tubers or, possibly, as a large underground tuber to be broken up later for planting.

In 1769 William Monkhouse, surgeon aboard the *Endeavour*, reported seeing bottle gourd (hue) vines growing over houses near Tolaga Bay on the East Coast. This plant was highly valued by a number of cultures that did not adopt pottery, for the hard dry skins of the fruit, which they used as containers. Varieties grown by Polynesians were indeed sufficiently tough and woody to be used for storing both food and water, and were of particular value on Easter Island and New Zealand, where a cooler climate precluded the cultivation of alternative containers from coconuts or Polynesian bamboo.

With a 10,000-year history of cultivation, the bottle gourd's origin is hard to trace, but probably lies in Africa. In the Pacific, its origins are similarly complex, for there is a so-called 'bottle-gourd gap' in West Polynesia, where the plant was not grown. It is intriguing, then, to find Māori varieties that bear the genetic hallmark of introduction from both sides of the Pacific – from Asia *and* the Americas. Again this suggests canoes arriving in New Zealand from different quarters of the Pacific – from either side of this so-called 'bottle-gourd gap'.

But the one crop that would present Māori with their greatest horticultural challenge, and ultimately their greatest success, was the Ecuadorian sweet potato (kūmara). Banks reported seeing very large plantations of them in the Far North. According to Māori tradition, its tubers were not onboard the original settlement canoes; return voyages were made later to fetch them.[66] Indeed, the almost 100 traditional variety names recorded in Māori are thought to refer to a dozen or so original introductions,[67] most likely via Mangaia (S. Cook Is) or the Society Islands.[68]

Considered together, these six crops speak of a chain of prehistoric voyages that link Māori ultimately with both sides of the Pacific and all three corners of the Polynesian Triangle. Since all six are of tropical origin, success with them in New Zealand may not have been immediate – possibly necessitating subsequent introductions of planting material from cool-climate sites elsewhere.

Tī pore

Tī pore (tī, Pacific Island cabbage tree, Cordyline fruticosa *syn.* terminalis, *above) is grown on islands right across the tropical Pacific. Its leaves are used as headdresses, garlands, skirts and roofing thatch, for wrapping food, and making rope and fishing nets. In the tropics, long, fat, sugar-laden, carrot-like rhizomes are produced, a food enhanced by Polynesians through selective breeding.[69] Its introduction to New Zealand is traditionally attributed to the* Aotea *and* Nukutere *canoes.[70] Although this tī proved less productive here, the leaves of the native tī kōuka (*C. australis*) were found to be sufficiently strong and durable to plait into sandals, rope, baskets, rough rain capes and warriors' cloaks and Māori bred a sterile cultivar from it, a dwarfed, weak-stemmed kind called tī para (or tī tawhiti), whose soft rhizomes could be cooked and eaten in the same way as its tropical counterpart (which they then called tī pore, 'the short tī').[71] Globe shows distribution of the Polynesian term* **tī***, whose use in New Zealand was extended to include all four native cabbage trees (*Cordyline *species), tī ngahere ('forest' tī), tī rauriki ('small-leaved' tī) and tī kōuka ('wind-resistant' tī).*

Four more canoe plants of Māori

Taro (Colocasia esculenta), *right, is grown for its short, swollen underground stem (corms), young leaves and leaf stems, all of which are cooked and eaten. Despite being slightly less cold-tolerant than kūmara, microbotanical evidence confirms its prehistoric cultivation as far south as the northern South Island.[72] It had the advantage over kūmara of not needing to be lifted and stored over winter. Its introduction is often attributed to the Mātaatua;[73] however, the presence of more than 40 named varieties suggests more than one introduction. The globe shows the original distribution of the Polynesian term for it, taro.*

Hue (*ipu, bottle gourd,* Lagenaria siceraria), *right, was grown primarily for its tough skins, which were used as containers; however, the bitter flesh of the gourd was also eaten as a vegetable. In 1769, William Monkhouse, surgeon aboard the* Endeavour *saw vines growing over houses near Tolaga Bay on the East Coast, and microfossil pollen grains have since been found in Harataonga swamp on Great Barrier Island and in a small stone mound at Pouerua, near the Bay of Islands.[74] On noticing that male and female flowers are borne separately, Māori took pains to collect pollen and fertilise plants by hand. Tradition speaks of its introduction from the north aboard the Māhuhu by Ngāti Whātua of Kaipara;[75] however, DNA analysis points to more than one introduction.[76] Indeed, Elsdon Best collected 13 traditional names for them, some of which he could distinguish by the form of their fruits.[77] The process of selectively breeding the original wild gourd for more useful skins began with members of non-pottery cultures some 10,000 years ago – a process continued by Polynesians, who bred them for thicker-skinned and more durable fruit.[78] These skins were used in New Zealand largely for storing and preserving rats, sea mammals and birds in their own fat; some were large enough to hold up to 180 small birds or 'several gallons' of water.[79] The globe shows distribution of the Māori term hue, which clearly excludes West Polynesia – a so-called 'bottle-gourd gap'.*

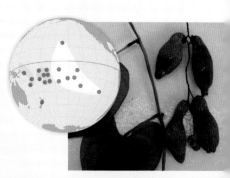

Uwhi (*winged yam or greater yam,* Dioscorea alata) *vines, right, were seen by Cook's botanist, Joseph Banks in northern New Zealand; and microscopic starch residues of the tubers have been identified in a wetland ditch at an archaeological site at Motutangi in the Far North, and from Anaura Bay on the East Cape.[80] Canoes that reportedly introduced the crop include the Horouta.[81] In the tropics, its underground tubers can reach lengths of up to 2 m and weigh up to 60 kg (though more often around 2.5 kg).[82] The plant requires a minimum growing season of eight months and is not recorded south of Hawke's Bay. With the introduction of the more easily grown potato in 1769, its cultivation was promptly abandoned. Globe shows the distribution of the Māori term. (Compare with 'ubi' for yam in both Malay and Malagasy, the language of Madagascar – see page 224.)*

The **kūmara** (*sweet potato,* Ipomoea batatas), *right, that Māori traditionally grew were not the purple-skinned varieties commonly seen today; they produced elongated tubers with white skin and a whitish flesh,[83] like the Taputini variety (right). Their growth habit is more erect and bushy than the familiar, purple-skinned kind that were introduced in the 19th century by Europeans. Globe shows distribution of the Māori term kūmara, which extends to Ecuador, South America; the hollow circles show locations where the name is recorded but where the plant is unknown prior to European contact.*

Multiple introductions of kūmara

The one crop that speaks most profoundly of the voyaging achievements of Māori and their ancestors is of course the kūmara – not just because its origins lie in South America, but because their ultimate success in growing the original pre-European varieties of it here almost certainly required several introductions. (Note that the same constraints would not apply to the purple-skinned varieties subsequently introduced by Europeans in the 19th century, as these are far more tolerant of cool conditions.)

In the tropics, where kūmara originates, it remains in the ground year round. But in New Zealand tubers of pre-European varieties left in the ground over winter will spoil; and even in spring, tubers forming in soil at low temperatures are apt to rot. Low soil temperatures in late summer and early autumn can also adversely affect the viability of the tubers by limiting the harvest that can be obtained from them the following year.

For this reason, Māori would almost certainly have faced serious losses in their first growing season, and would have had to conduct repeated trials to ascertain the correct timing and requisite storage protocols. From this they learned to get the tubers into the ground early and harvest them before winter frosts came, and to carefully sort and store them in waterproof, rat-proof, well-drained, semi-subterranean huts or pits to keep them within a narrow temperature range – never less than about 4°C.[84]

In the words of archaeologist Louise Furey, a specialist in Māori gardening, 'to multiply the available tubers to a number that could produce enough for eating as well as storing for the next year's seed crop must have been a test of skills and a result of trial and error over several years, on the part of the early gardeners'.[85] Recent trials conducted with pre-European Māori varieties show that the tubers need five continuous months in soil warmer than 15°C to supply a reasonable crop – which means they needed to be in the ground by the end of October.[86]

For Māori, their eventual success came from selecting coastal sites with north-facing slopes to catch the sun. To improve drainage and fertility and to maintain moisture and increase ground temperatures, they mulched the plots; mixed gravel, sand, charcoal and wood ash into the soil and heaped it up; and erected fences and stone walls to shelter the crop from wind.

Even though average temperatures in 13th-century New Zealand may have been up to 2–3°C warmer than today,[87] success with kūmara in the first year seems unlikely. This would suggest that they were introduced to New Zealand more than once until enough tubers could be produced locally for replanting the following October. Any voyage to obtain fresh tubers is likely to have involved a hardy crew and faster outriggers returning to New Zealand in September – earlier than the prime voyaging season. To reduce the risk of losing these tubers, they may have been carefully propagated initially in nurseries on frost-free offshore islands.

The exact process by which Māori achieved their initial success with this tropical crop is not known; but by the time Europeans arrived, Māori had established enormous plantations of kūmara, and had succeeded in growing it as far south as Banks Peninsula, over 1000 km further south than it had been grown anywhere else in the world.[88]

Māori potato

It is commonly assumed that the dark-fleshed Māori potato (rīwai, Solanum tuberosum, below)[89] was introduced by Māori. However, at European contact, the plant was not seen in New Zealand or anywhere else in the Pacific, and almost none of the 20 or more Māori names by which it is known are recorded from elsewhere.[90] Nor is there any mention of it in Polynesian tradition. The earliest potatoes known to have been planted in New Zealand were those introduced by Captain Cook to Tolaga Bay and Mercury Bay in 1769 and to Queen Charlotte Sound in 1773. The impact these introductions had on Māori horticulture was immediate, implying the novelty of the crop at this point.[91] How then do we account for so many named varieties – many of which are distinctly different from European ones? The answer lies partly in the novel techniques Māori used to selectively breed it. Rather than propagate from tubers alone, as Europeans do, Māori also saved seed from the large, infrequently produced yellowish-green berries (about 2 cm across), thereby spawning altogether new varieties.[92] So although Māori potatoes were not actually introduced by Māori, they are certainly an authentically Māori innovation.

The southern limit of Polynesian horticulture

Horticultural success this far south hinged on being able to predict the change of seasons. For this, Māori used the flowering and fruiting of native trees, and (where the eastern horizon was unobstructed) the observation of morning stars. The beginning of spring is marked by the flowering of kōwhai (Sophora, above left) and puawānanga (clematis, above centre), rangiora, karaka, kōtukutuku (tree fuchsia) and puahou (five finger); the increasingly vocal riroriro (grey warbler), and the return of the migratory pīpīwharauroa
(shining cuckoo). *This is followed by the flowering of rewarewa (Knightia excelsa, above right), and hīnau, then rātā (Metrosideros robusta, right) and tāwari; then emerging 'manu o Rehua' (grass grub beetles and the loud call of male crickets and cicadas), and ripening karaka berries.*[93] *Because the order in which horizon stars rise at sea in a single night is identical with that of 'morning stars' appearing through the year on the eastern horizon, this aspect of traditional navigational knowledge could be transferred to marking the seasons.*

Undeterred by cold

As Māori continued to venture south, they were required to make many other other adaptions. In the tropics their ancestors had worn cloaks, ponchos and short kilts of tapa cloth, shredded coconut leaflets or plaited pandanus leaves,[94] but on the cooler islands of Polynesia – Easter Island, Rapa Iti and New Zealand – it was necessary to adapt both their clothing and their housing. This is especially true in New Zealand, where winters in the mountains can be very harsh, and where Māori proved to be surprisingly hardy. At Matuku, near Taihape, the Rev. William Colenso records his astonishment at finding, in 1847, 'the natives . . . almost insensible to cold, the majority of them being but poorly clad, each in a single loose shoulder mat, – and yet they go sauntering about the village in the snow, barefooted and barelegged and barebreeched!'[95]

Māori kept warm on the whole by wearing finely twined fibre from scraped New Zealand flax leaves, or thick cloaks made from the skins of birds, dogs, rats or seals. Sandals were made from the leaves of flax or cabbage trees, or from the bark of five finger trees;[96] sandals from cabbage tree leaves were particularly suited to walking in snow.

Here, too, as on Rapa Iti and Easter Island, the open style of housing so familiar in the tropics was abandoned in favour of enclosed, weatherproof

Clothing and housing

For warmth, Māori made thick cloaks with finely twined fibre from scraped harakeke (New Zealand flax) leaves, adding tags of flax to some to shed the rain; and feathers and dyed cords to others for formal use (pictured far left). Cloaks were also made from leaves of kiekie, tī (cabbage tree), pīngao[99] (golden sand sedge, Ficinia spiralis, above centre), the split and scraped leaves of kuta (bamboo spike-sedge, Eleocharis sphacelata, centre), or from the skins of birds, dogs, rats and seals. In place of coconut fibre and bark from hibiscus trees for making sandals, Māori used flax leaves (above), the bark of whauwhaupaku (five finger) and leaves of tī kōuka (cabbage tree).[100] Māori wove floor mats from flax leaves, and a soft grade of sleeping mat from kuta, and constructed sturdy, weatherproof sleeping houses and enclosed marae buildings with a door to keep out the cold winds, as seen here (left) in 1777 at the south- west point of Motuara in Queen Charlotte Sound. On winter nights, a stone-lined charcoal fire would be lit. In place of coconut fronds for the walls and roofs, nīkau fronds were used, or the inner bark of tōtara or mānuka, lined with a thick thatch of kākaho (toetoe stems), oioi (jointed wire rush) or raupō (bulrush). Lacking sennit cord to lash the components together, various forest vines were used, or strips of inner bark torn from mākaka (native ribbonwood) or houhere (lacebark).[101] Every one of these Māori terms can be traced back to functionally equivalent plants in the tropics.[102]

buildings. Communal sleeping houses were made of timber, lined with rushes and bark, with a sliding shutter for the door, a thatched roof and an earthen floor covered with mats.[97]

With such clothing and dwelling innovations, Māori were able to continue moving south down the east coast of the South Island, past Banks Peninsula, to enter a region that would prove too cold for any Polynesian crop to grow. Here, a more transient way of life developed, where they relied more on hunting moa, seals and muttonbirds. They spent the winters by the coast, and moved inland only after the frosts had finished to fish the rivers for eels. With no cultivated sources of starch, they relied more heavily on the edible rhizomes of cabbage tree and bracken fern. And when they discovered that the growth of both responded well to fire, they turned to 'fire-stick farming'.[98]

This nomadic way of life, with its strong focus on seal meat and muttonbirds, went on to fuel an even more ambitious phase of expansion, with voyages south to Stewart Island and beyond.

Enderby and The Snares

Enderby Island, above, in the subantarctic Auckland Islands, some 400 km south of Stewart Island, covers less than 5 sq km and is a particularly challenging destination, yet there is evidence of prehistoric Polynesian presence at Sandy Bay on the south side of the island, at a breeding site for New Zealand sealions (Phocarctos hookeri).

The Snares (Tini Heke), below, with a total land area of just 3.5 sq km, lie some 200 km south of the South Island and are en route to Enderby. In spring, 5.5 million sooty shearwaters arrive here to breed. The island is also used as a haul-out by sealions and is a major breeding area for penguins, as shown in this old photograph from 1909. An early Māori adze was unearthed here.

Subantarctic Enderby

Some 400 km south of Stewart Island lies the tiny subantarctic island of Enderby in the Auckland Islands, the southernmost outpost of Polynesia at almost 51°S. It hardly seems a hospitable destination, let alone one to attract a tropical-bred people, for its mean minimum temperatures fall below freezing for more than six months of the year.[103] However, in 1998 and 2003, when archaeologists excavated sand dunes at Sandy Bay, a landing site on the south side of the island, they came upon unambiguous evidence of prehistoric Polynesian presence. Here, among stone oven pits dating to about AD 1300, they found flaked stone tools of basalt and chert. From the bones they found, it was clear that Polynesians and their dogs had survived on the island for at least one summer by eating fur seals, sealions and nesting seabirds such as yellow-eyed penguins, albatrosses and sooty shearwaters.[104]

The prospect of an accident arrival can be virtually ruled out on account of the prevailing winds; more likely these people had set off from southern New Zealand on a hunting expedition, perhaps led in this direction by seabirds, for an adze of early type has been unearthed en route on the Snares Islands,[105] where an astounding 5.5 million sooty shearwaters come to breed in spring.[106] Some two million of the same species can be seen continuing further south still to the Auckland Islands to nest there, and an increase in seal numbers can be seen along the way.

Whatever led these people to Enderby, returning to the mainland in a traditional craft would have presented a challenge. Depending on the sophistication of their rig, stiff westerlies at this latitude – the Furious Fifties – might sweep their craft too far east.[107] Perhaps they headed northeast into warmer waters to reach the Chatham Islands, or beyond to a destination in tropical East Polynesia; but if they were swept too far downwind they would not find landfall until South America, over 7000 km away.

Whatever their fate, these people ventured further south than any other Polynesian is known to have done, and appear to have done so deliberately – providing additional evidence of the sailing capabilities of Māori in around AD 1300.

The Moriori of the Chatham Islands

Another seemingly poor candidate for Polynesian settlement is a remote cluster of tiny islands that lie some 870 km east of Christchurch. The climate on the Chatham Islands is milder than on Enderby, but still windy, damp and cool. The first inhabitants are known as Moriori.[108] Claims are sometimes made that these people are racially distinguishable from Māori, and that they preceded Māori in the settlement of New Zealand; however, the evidence suggests that the Chatham Islands were settled at around the same time – or possibly even later than New Zealand.[109] 'Moriori' (the word) is understood by linguists to be no more than a dialectical variation of the word 'Māori'.[110] According to current research, Moriori came to the Chatham Islands from New Zealand in about 1500. Moriori traditions, however, hold that there were people on the island before the canoe voyagers arrived.[111]

By 1835, about 2000 people were living here, most of them in small communities of oblong huts on Chatham and Pitt islands.[112] Favourable winds for a return from these islands to mainland New Zealand are so rare that one wonders what prompted the first settlers to come here. Perhaps they were lured in this direction by the rich fishing grounds that extend east from Banks Peninsula along the Chatham Rise, a region renowned for sperm whales and seabirds. Or was their mission more ambitious? Were they perhaps riding the westerlies from New Zealand with the aim of returning to the tropics – as was British Lieutenant William Broughton aboard the HMS *Chatham* in 1791?

Broughton and his crew were en route to Tahiti from Dusky Sound in the South Island on 27 November when they sighted large congregations of seabirds and patches of floating seaweed. Sailing on for two more days, they spotted the northwest corner of the main island of the Chatham Islands – traditionally known as Rēkohu, after the mists (kohu) that often surround these islands.[113] Had they arrived in fine weather, the presence of these low-lying, windswept islands might have been equally evident from an almost permanent cap of cloud, or – at dusk – from enormous flocks of white-faced storm petrels and other seabirds streaming back to their nest burrows.[114]

Origins of Moriori

Whatever it was that led the ancestors of Moriori to find this place, archaeologists believe that most, if not all, arrived from mainland New Zealand.[115] Certainly, several lines of evidence point to contact of some kind along this route.

By comparing the languages of Moriori and Māori, linguists have been able to determine that, while speakers of both languages shared a period of common history, they subsequently diverged. 'Their separation, however, cannot be very recent,' explains Ross Clark, 'since we find both a considerable number of innovations peculiar to Moriori, and a number of items that have been lost or altered in all New Zealand Maori dialects but retained in Moriori.'[116]

For an independent line of evidence, we can turn to the items they brought with them, including kōpi (karaka) seeds from a tree that is native to the North Island of New Zealand.[117] This suggests not only the region of origin of the canoe bringing the seeds, but a prior 'voyage of discovery' to warrant having such seeds on board in the first place.[118] Obsidian flakes used as tools on Pitt and Chatham islands are likewise known to have originated from the North Island and are indeed geochemically traceable to specific quarry sites on Tūhua (Mayor Is), Aotea (Great Barrier Is) and the Taupō–Rotorua region. All this is consistent with multiple computer simulations of voyages in traditional craft – demonstrating that the best chance of a safe return to the Chathams involves sailing SE from the North Island.[119]

However, other evidence points to contact with the South Island. According to linguists, the Moriori language is an offshoot of Māori spoken in the South Island,[120] and it is likewise with here that the closest match in DNA is found with archaeological remains of the Pacific rats (kiore) found on the Chatham Islands.[121] Some of the Chatham Island adzes are made of argillite from the South Island, specifically from the Nelson–Marlborough

Chatham Islands

The Chatham Islands consist of a cluster of tiny islands (total land area 966 sq km), by far the largest of which is Chatham Island (shown below viewed from a satellite). On the map beneath, orange dots denote high densities of seabirds following behind fishing vessels. Note the band of orange dots that follows a shallow rise in the ocean floor, extending over 500 km due east of Christchurch, and a similar cluster of dots south of Stewart Island that extends to the Auckland Islands. To Polynesians, such congregations of birds would have signalled the presence of food and – in spring – of land, where the birds would be heading to nest.

Above: Chatham Island taik (magenta petrel, Pterodroma magentae) was a major item in the Moriori diet, along with seals.[126] Its Moriori name, taik, is shared with Māori (taikō) and with tropical Polynesia. However, many other nature terms, right, are shared only between Moriori and Māori; this serves as evidence of direct contact between the two.

region.[122] Finding the Chathams from Banks Peninsula, near Christchurch, would have been relatively easy for navigators by following a dense band of seabirds that congregate over the Chatham Rise (see seabird map on the previous page).[123] Indeed, Moriori tradition does speak of more than one voyage to these islands.[124]

With substantial trees in short supply on the Chathams, such voyages did not necessarily involve locally built canoes, though.[125] Indeed, in the case of coastal fishing, Moriori are known to have manoeuvred the coastline in wash-through rafts, as described by Broughton's clerk: 'not unlike the body of a common Wheelbarrow, their sides. . . made of small sticks lash'd tightly with withs upon one another about eight or nine feet long'. The floor and sides of these craft consisted of dried flowerstalks (kōrari) of local New

Moriori vocabulary shared with Māori

MĀORI	MORIORI	OTHER NAMES
aruhe	eruhe	bracken fern 'root' – unknown in the tropics[127]
harakeke	harapepe	New Zealand flax – plant unknown in the tropics
kahawai	kawhai	A fish unknown in the tropics
kōkō	kōkō	tūī – a bird unknown in the tropics
kōmako	kōmako	bellbird (korimako)– unknown in the tropics
kōpī	kōpi[128]	karaka – a tree unknown in the tropics[129]
kōrari	kōrari	flower stem of NZ flax – unknown in the tropics
kawau	kuau	shag – a bird unknown in the tropics
pākura	pākura	pūkeko – a bird name unknown in the tropics
parea	parea	endemic NZ pigeon (kererū, kūkūpa)
rimurapa	rimurapa	bull kelp – a seaweed unknown in the tropics
tāiko	taik (t'chaik')[130]	petrel – a bird name shared with the tropics

Moriori at sea

Timber was in short supply here: below, a local waka kōrari, a wash-through raft with a base of rimurapa (bull kelp, left) and sides of kōrari (flax stalks) interwoven with rarauhe (bracken stems), traditionally used for coastal fishing.

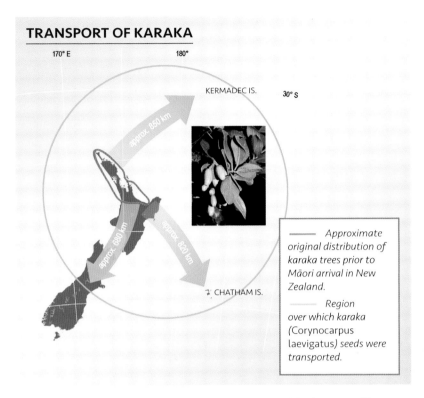

TRANSPORT OF KARAKA

170° E 180°

KERMADEC IS. 30° S

approx. 850 km

approx. 680 km

approx. 820 km

CHATHAM IS.

——— *Approximate original distribution of karaka trees prior to Māori arrival in New Zealand.*

——— *Region over which karaka (Corynocarpus laevigatus) seeds were transported.*

Karaka seeds on the canoes

From fossilised wood and layers of pollen in the soil we know that, within recent history, the karaka tree (kōpi, Corynocarpus laevigatus) is native only to the northern North Island, and that it has been present in New Zealand for at least five million years.[135] *Indeed, all karaka trees in the lower North Island and the whole of the South Island are the result of plantings, and all such sites are strongly linked with other evidence of Māori settlement. The seeds of this tree were distributed still further, to the Chathams and Kermadecs – see map. Tribal narratives associated with the Aotea, Kurahaupō and Nukutere canoes all contain references to carrying karaka seeds.*[136] *If these narratives are based on historical fact, all must refer to voyages whose most immediate departure point lay not in the tropics, but within New Zealand. Shown below is a traditional Moriori dendroglyph (tree carving) on a Chatham Island kōpi (karaka) from 1900.*

Zealand flax, with a base of inflated bull kelp (rimurapa) for buoyancy.[131]

By 1791 when Broughton arrived, Moriori had already lost contact with the mainland.[132] When and why is not known; but regional tsunami research reveals that, because of the nature of the surrounding ocean floor, the Chatham Islands are – and always have been – particularly vulnerable to tsunamis originating from Peru and North Chile. This is reflected in many deposits of tsunami debris found on the island, including a major deposit that is dateable, from pollen changes associated with settlement, to AD 1500–1700. This, according to palaeotsunami researcher James Goff, would seem to implicate a tsunami generated by the Chilean earthquake of AD 1604.[133] Some idea of its likely impact is provided by a comparable tsunami generated off Chile in 1868, which caused the sea to rise here by about 7 m, shifting large stones weighing up to 500 kg, and totally destroying the settlement of Tupunga on the northern side of the main island.[134] In such an event, neither of the island's two harbours at Kaingaroa and Whangaroa is likely to have offered much protection to canoes.

Whatever the cause or causes of their subsequent isolation, there was evidently a period prior to that when Moriori were in two-way voyaging contact with their neighbours.

The voyaging capabilities of Māori

Although some debate remains as to the kind of rig available to Māori, their capacity for long-distance sailing is beyond question from evidence of the voyages they made – not only to the Kermadecs but to the subantarctic and Chatham islands.

CHAPTER TWELVE

Voyages of Return

The Cuckoos Depart

Return voyaging is not very credible for New Zealand.

Historian James Belich, *Making Peoples*, 1996

Potential motives

As archaeologist Barry Rolett has pointed out, on recently settled islands there was a heightened need among small populations to remain in contact with their original homeland: 'Voyaging may have served as a lifeline that allowed contact with people on other islands, providing access to marriage partners and facilitating the transfer of domestic plants or animals not introduced at the time of initial colonization.'[1]

For Māori there was an ongoing demand for fresh introductions of kūmara, as we saw; and a need too for large, strong-skinned, cold-tolerant varieties of bottle gourds to supply containers, for Māori – like Rapanui – lacked both Polynesian bamboo and coconuts.[2]

With the approach of winter, the prospect of a trip back to the tropics must have been tempting, and especially so in the early years of settlement, when Māori were still adapting to the much cooler climate.

Scepticism

But did Māori have the capacity to return to the tropics? In *New Zealand's Heritage* (1971) – New Zealand's main source of historical knowledge in the 1970s and 80s – author Andrew Sharp is emphatic: 'there was no credible method whereby Maori ancestors, having found New Zealand, could have navigated back to their home islands and then relocated their discovery'.[3] Twenty-five years later, historian James Belich, in the quote above, expressed similar doubts.

The sceptics raise four main objections. First, prevailing winds tend to hinder a return voyage from New Zealand to tropical East Polynesia. Second, no craft fit for such a long voyage was seen by Europeans in New Zealand waters. Third, there is a lack of unambiguous archaeological evidence of items transferred from New Zealand back to the tropics. And fourth, distinctive developments in Māori art, language, social structure, religion and material culture that suggest relatively early isolation of New Zealand from tropical East Polynesia.[4]

Some scholars do not go along with this scenario of isolation, though. Historian Michael King, for example, allows the logic of at least one return voyage: 'It seems most likely that . . . New Zealand was located during a voyage of discovery and settled as a result of subsequent and deliberate voyages . . .'[5] And Māori historian Peter Adds concurs that the settlement of New Zealand 'more than likely involved an initial voyage of discovery to find somewhere to move to before risking women and children on a voyage that might easily produce a negative result'.[6] Archaeologist Douglas Sutton has put the case for return voyaging a little more strongly: he argues that 'New Zealand was not a *cul de sac* prior to contact'.[7]

This question is important for several reasons. If no return voyage occurred, the implication is that New Zealand was settled by desperate people setting off in canoes fully laden with crops on the off-chance of

Autumn exodus to the NNW

At the sprawling harbour of Pārengarenga, near the northern tip of the North Island, small flocks of 30–80 kūaka (godwits, Limosa lapponica), left, are seen in March making a spiralling ascent in preparation for their flight to the NNW over New Caledonia to the shores of the Yellow Sea (see the globe on page 149).

finding suitable land. This would in turn imply that navigational stars and other traditional knowledge associated with the migration voyages is a subsequent invention, and that New Zealand was a kind of 'dead end' in the exploration of the Pacific by Polynesians. On the other hand, if a return voyage did occur, news reaching the tropics of such a vast unclaimed land would almost certainly have spread across much of Polynesia, triggering migratory voyages from many islands.[8]

So, in this chapter, we will be reviewing the practicalities of returning to tropical Polynesia from New Zealand; the sailing capabilities of Māori; and the four main points of scepticism outlined above.

Signposts from the natural world

First, we will look at the seasonal movement of the sun and its impact on the winds.

With the shortening days and increasingly cool nights of autumn, a pull to head north toward the retreating sun is felt not only by humans but also by whales and many birds – including godwits (kūaka), which gather in the north of New Zealand at this time in preparation for their flight back to warmer climes. We know that Māori understood the implication of this phenomenon from a traditional saying, 'me he kāhui kūaka',[9] used for when many people die at the same time: the departure of their spirits to the north is likened to that of a flock of godwits. And it is indeed from the northernmost tip of New Zealand, Cape Te Rēinga, that the spirits of the dead are traditionally farewelled.

The local gathering place for the godwits in March is the nearby harbour of Pārengarenga, where small flocks of 30–80 make spiralling ascents before heading NNW over New Caledonia to the shores of the Yellow Sea, en route to the Arctic to nest in the Alaskan summer.[10] As with many migratory birds, the spectacle of their departure is likely to have

In March and April, hundreds of pīpīwharauroa (shining cuckoo, Chrysococcyx lucidus), above, assemble at Maunganui Bluff, south of the Hokianga Harbour, in readiness for their annual departure to the tropical rainforests of the Solomon Islands. In October, single birds have been seen arriving in the same region.[11] The route of some may be direct, but others are known to fly in either direction via northeastern Australia.[12]

Right: It is traditional among Northern Māori that the spirits of the dead depart to the north from Te Rēinga, North Cape (Te Rerenga Wairua or Cape Rēinga) to reach 'Hawaiki', the spiritual homeland.[13]

Te Rēinga traditions

Te Rēinga – *at right and also two peaks on the East Cape, North Island, New Zealand.*

Te Rēinga o Pora & **Te Rerenga Vairua** – *on the west coast of Rarotonga, S. Cook Is.*

Reinga Vaerua – *four leaping-off places of spirits of spirits on Mangaia, S. Cook Is.*

Te Reinga – *marae on Tongareva, N. Cook Is.*

Rēinga – *a jumping-off place Vāhitu dialect, NW Tuamotus.*

**Rēi`a** – *islet, Taha`a, Society Is.*

Rerēinga Ku`ane – *place where spirits leap into the sea, Mangareva, Gambier Is.*

Te Reinga Take – *on Easter Island*[14]

**Leina-a-ka-`uhane** – *point from which spirits leap, O`ahu, Hawaiian Is.*

Ka Leina A Ka `Uhane – *leaping place of spirits, Maui, Hawaiian Is.*

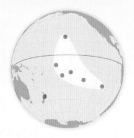

*The globe shows the distribution of '**Te Rēinga**' as a place name. Note that, here again, all known instances are from East Polynesia – further evidence of the origin of Māori.*

made a deep impression, and especially so back in the 13th century. Even as late as the 1870s, Captain Gilbert Mair 'observed [the godwits] flying northward [from near the North Cape] in tens of thousands, and always in considerable flocks, numbering from 700 to 1,200 birds in each'.[15] A similar scene is described by ornithologist Walter Buller in 1877:

> Rising from the beach in a long line and with much clamour, they form into a broad semi-circle, deployed forwards, and, mounting high in the air, generally take a course due north. Sometimes they rise in a confused manner, and, after circling about at a considerable height in the air, return to the beach to reform, as it were, their ranks, and then make a fresh start on their distant pilgrimage. The departure from any fixed locality usually begins on almost the exact date year after year; and for a week or ten days after the migration has commenced fresh parties are constantly on the wing, the flight generally taking place just after sunset. The main body fly in silence, but the straggling birds cry out at intervals, while endeavouring to overtake the flock in advance.[16]

We can be sure Māori witnessed similar scenes as they hunted godwits for food, setting up elaborate snares and nets on beaches, sandbanks and mudflats to catch flocks as they rose en masse. They knew that their

TE RĒINGA: *The way home*

Arrival points recorded in Māori tradition.

Direct rhumbline courses from Te Rēinga. (Prevailing winds would require any vessel heading for these destinations to take less direct routes.)

NORFOLK IS.

FIJI

HAWAI'I
SAMOA
TONGA

KERMADEC IS. | RAROTONGA | RA'IATEA | NW TUAMOTU | MARQUESAS

AUSTRAL IS. | SE TUAMOTU

MANGAREVA
RAPA ITI | PITCAIRN IS.

EASTER IS.

TAKAPAUKURA (TOM BOWLING BAY) Tropical flotsam common here: coconuts, chambered Nautilus shells, seeds of both Entada vines and Barringtonia trees.

TE RĒINGA Cape from which the spirits of the dead are felt to depart for Hawaiki.

PĀRENGARENGA HARBOUR Migrating long-tailed cuckoos and godwit flocks seen here.

DOUBTLESS BAY Long-tailed cuckoos are seen arriving here from the tropical Pacific. In 1769, Cook's Tahitian navigator and interpreter, Tupa'ia, learns from locals of one-month voyages by their ancestors to the NNW.

CAPE MARIA VAN DIEMEN Long-tailed cuckoos observed arriving here from the tropical Pacific.

WHANGAROA HARBOUR Recorded as a major arrival and departure point of migration canoes.

WHĀNGĀPĒ HARBOUR

WHANGARURU HARBOUR

HOKIANGA HARBOUR

RANGAUNU HARBOUR Huge flocks of migrating godwits visit here in the summer.

MAUNGANUI BLUFF Major arrival and departure point for shining cuckoo migrating up to Solomon Islands.

WHĀNGĀREI

0   25   50 km

---

nesting sites lay elsewhere: 'Kua kite te kōhanga kūaka?' (Who has seen the nest of the kūaka?) asks one Māori proverb, alluding to things that are hard to find. Another asks, 'Ko wai ka kite i te hua o te kūaka?' (Who has seen the egg of the kūaka?) Because sailors share with birds a need of favourable winds, Māori may also have noted that birds arriving in spring, and those leaving in autumn, do so via different routes.

It is not hard to picture Polynesian navigators finding tangible reminders of the tropics among the flotsam at nearby Takapaukura (Tom Bowling Bay): chambered *Nautilus* shells, the odd coconut shell, large seed capsules of the *Barringtonia* tree and distinctive, dark brown, bean-like seeds of the *Entada* vine – flotsam brought down from the tropics by the ocean currents in summer. The observant navigator may have deduced from this a seasonal reversal of ocean currents to the north of New Zealand, and that the direction of flow swings back in favour of a voyage to the tropics in autumn.[17]

With the cooler weather, large flocks of shining cuckoos are gathering by the hundred at Maunganui Bluff (south of the Hokianga Harbour), ready to embark on their own migration back up to the tropical rainforests of the Solomon Islands.[18] We know that Māori were aware of their oceanic crossings made in autumn and spring from the name they gave them: wharauroa or pīpīwharauroa, meaning 'bird of the long ocean journey'.[19]

Humpback whales are heading back up from Antarctic waters at this

Te Rēinga lighthouse (top) with adjacent signage (2010). The absence of any reference to the Pacific is conspicuous.

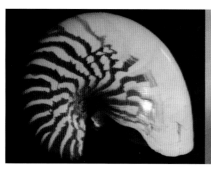 

In summer, items of tropical flotsam are frequently thrown up at nearby Takapaukura (Tom Bowling Bay): left to right, worn nautilus shell (Nautilus macromphalus); niu shell (coconut, Cocos nucifera); seed capsule of hutu (fish poison tree, Barringtonia asiatica); and seed of kākā vai vine (entada, Entada phaseoloides).

time, too, passing along the New Zealand coastline to warmer breeding grounds off southern New Caledonia.[20] We can infer that Māori were aware of this migration from the value they placed on whale strandings as a source of meat, teeth and bones. The trigger for this mass autumn exodus of wildlife heading NNW is, of course, the cooling of the southern hemisphere climate, spurring creatures to follow the warmth of the sun in search of a seasonal abundance of food elsewhere.

The same pull is felt by many oceanic birds, which employ a different strategy at the same time of year, departing from further south in New Zealand to head east initially on prevailing westerly winds. In April the entire world population of Cook's petrel[21] depart: some will head right on through to the west coast of South America; others will veer north along the way and head up over the equator to the North Pacific. In April and May, some 20 million sooty shearwaters follow a similar pathway, taking a wide sweep over the southeast Pacific before turning north to make use of the SE trade winds, again with the aim of crossing the equator to the North Pacific.[22]

In April, too, the majority of New Zealand long-tailed cuckoos leave for their winter feeding grounds, starting off along a similar route.[23] Interestingly, Māori were aware that most long-tailed cuckoos follow a

Another cue as to when, and by which route, to catch the winds to sail back to the tropics is provided by the mass departure from New Zealand of tens of millions of oceanic birds, which head away at the close of their southern breeding season (March–May). The transequatorial flight paths of eight species are shown, with intermediary locations marked. Together, such birds signal to the mariner two effective strategies for heading back to warmer climes in autumn.

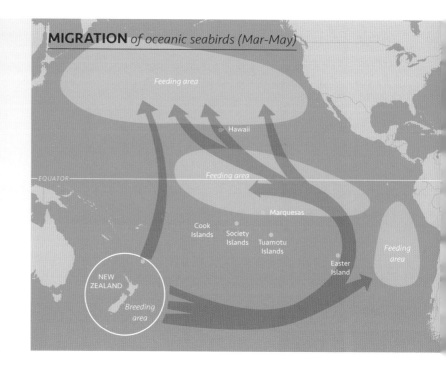

MIGRATION *of oceanic seabirds (Mar–May)*

Feeding area

Hawaii

EQUATOR

Feeding area

Marquesas

Cook Islands
Society Islands
Tuamotu Islands

Easter Island

Feeding area

NEW ZEALAND

Breeding area

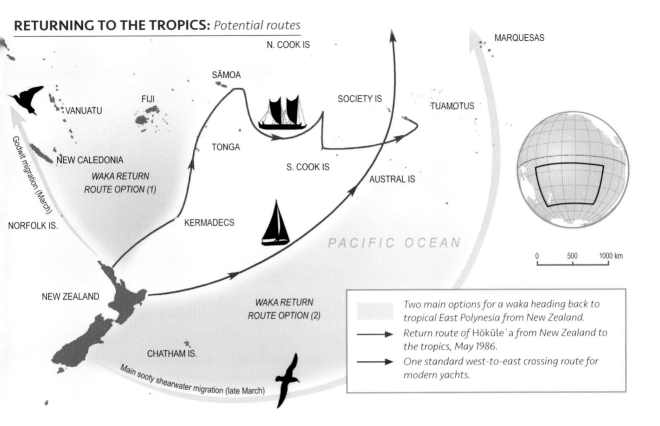

RETURNING TO THE TROPICS: *Potential routes*

MARQUESAS

N. COOK IS

SĀMOA

FIJI

SOCIETY IS

TUAMOTUS

VANUATU

Godwit migration (March)

NEW CALEDONIA

TONGA

S. COOK IS

AUSTRAL IS

**WAKA RETURN
ROUTE OPTION (1)**

NORFOLK IS.

KERMADECS

PACIFIC OCEAN

NEW ZEALAND

**WAKA RETURN
ROUTE OPTION (2)**

CHATHAM IS.

Main sooty shearwater migration (late March)

0   500   1000 km

Two main options for a waka heading back to tropical East Polynesia from New Zealand.

Return route of Hōkūle`a from New Zealand to the tropics, May 1986.

One standard west-to-east crossing route for modern yachts.

different route from shining cuckoos;[24] this is evident from a traditional saying, 'Kahore te kawekaweā i mōhio ki te haerenga mai o te wharauroa'[25] (The long-tailed cuckoo knows not how the shining cuckoo got here).[26]

In other words, the pathways of migrating birds and whales indicate two viable sailing routes from New Zealand, both of them indirect, wind-sensitive, specific to autumn, and likely to have been observed by Māori.

Two route options

Canoes taking the first option of heading north might make landfall in New Caledonia, Fiji or Tonga, but to reach East Polynesia from any of these islands would involve sailing against prevailing easterly winds, To continue from here, would require a wait for the onset of summer westerlies (November–January), or prolonged El Niño westerlies triggered by episodes of warm ocean temperatures off South America.[27] So while this option is doable it is probably slow, and involves a lot of waiting.

The second option – leaving New Zealand from further south – would involve riding the westerlies along with the shearwaters and petrels. This is a standard sailing route even today: yachts leave to the east or northeast in May and turn north near the Austral Islands to sail on up to Pape`ete; and it is essentially the same route that was sailed by Broughton aboard the *Chatham* in 1791.[28]

As Irwin points out in *The Prehistoric Exploration and Colonisation of the Pacific*, there is a challenge for the traditional navigator in knowing when or where to turn[29] a risk offset by the wide 'island screen' of the Tuamotus, and by the uncanny 'dead reckoning' skill of Polynesians. This is a skill that Tupa`ia convincingly demonstrated to Cook by pointing out the true

Below: A map of averaged southern hemisphere winds, centred on Antarctica, shows the overall pattern of westerlies prevailing at southerly latitudes and easterlies at more tropical latitudes.

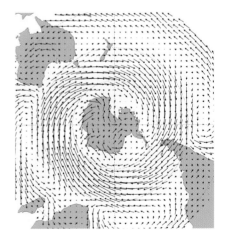

Types of Māori craft

Europeans saw no long-distance voyaging craft in New Zealand waters, but did see double-hulled sailing canoes, such as this war canoe, right, (seen near Tolaga Bay in 1769). Similar sailing craft were seen around the South Island.[30]

Better known are the single-hulled waka of Māori, such as this waka taua (war canoe), below; these were paddled rather than sailed.

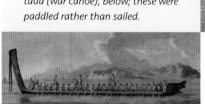

Vessels used by Māori to reach offshore destinations such as the Chatham Islands, Enderby Island and the Kermadecs, almost certainly employed a sturdy and more versatile sailing rig. Double-hulled voyaging canoes of this ocean-going kind were known as hourua or pahī. Until the recent find of the Anaweka canoe, opposite, we could only guess what these were like.

direction of Tahiti nearly a year after leaving it.[31] This ability to keep track of his location left such a deep impression on the Europeans that their onboard naturalist, Johann Reinhold Forster, took the trouble to elaborate on the intervening twists and turns in the course they had sailed:

> The *Endeavour*, in which ship Tupaya sailed to [Jakarta], sailed first from Taheitee into forty Degrees South Latitude, then she came by a North West course into twenty-eight Degrees, after this she came by a South West course to about thirty-eight Degrees, and by a Western run to New Zeeland, which islands were circumnavigated in runs of various directions to forty-eight Degrees South Latitude, till by another Westerly course the coasts of [Australia] were reached, along which she sailed North and North West, up to about four Degrees North Latitude, and then West to Savu [in Indonesia], and lastly by the Streights of Sunda to Batavia. However, Tupaya was never at a loss to point to Taheitee, at whatever place he came, even at Batavia at more than 2000 Leagues distance [or over 11,000 km].[32]

The point here is that the navigational challenges were not insurmountable and that prevailing winds do not, in themselves, constitute a valid reason for ruling out a return voyage to tropical East Polynesia – especially in view the complex routes of return sailed by Polynesians to and from South America and the Hawaiian Islands.[33]

Armed conflict

Another challenge faced by those making an indirect route of return is the need for 'safe passage' – entailing cooperation from host communities en route; the availability of safe anchorages; and chances to reprovision and make repairs. Although Polynesians were no strangers to 'raid rather than trade', this carried its own risks; indeed it is for this reason that unheralded strangers were frequently challenged or attacked.[34]

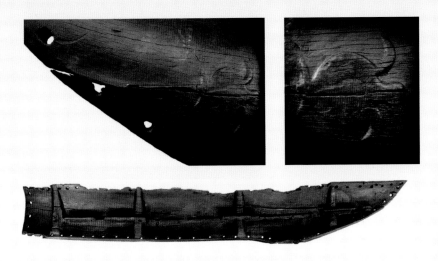

The Anaweka canoe

In 2012, a harsh storm uncovered part of a wooden sailing canoe (three views of which are shown on the left) from a sand dune near the Anaweka River on the northwest coast of the South Island. Fortunately, it had remained waterlogged and hence free of contact with the air, so it was remarkably well preserved. Archaeologists determined that the hull was locally made, as it had been fashioned from mataī, a tree found only in New Zealand. And yet a sea turtle carved in raised relief (top left) spoke of recent cultural contact with the tropics, for turtles are rare in pre-European New Zealand carvings, yet common as artistic motifs in tropical Polynesia. When caulking material still attached to the wood was radiocarbon dated, it revealed that the canoe had made its last voyage around AD 1400. Below is an artistic representation of the whole canoe, showing the likely position (shaded) of the piece that was found. Its design was effectively an adaptation of an East Polynesian sewn-plank canoe constructed by sewing together several substantial hollowed-out parts, with carved ribs and stringers (see photos). The whole canoe is understood to have been about 16 m long. The workmanship is impressive, as no doubt was its performance.

Tongan and Samoan traditions speak of a protracted Tongan war to control Sāmoa, dateable through genealogy to around the 13th to 14th century; and in the Southern Cook Island group and the Society Islands, too, traditions speak of frequent interisland conflict. Both would have a bearing on the viability of the first route option above.

Along the second route, Tuāmotu tradition refers to several centuries of armed conflict. 'Bravely we endure the constant perils of the sea, Ever spears are brandished in defiance,' runs the chorus of one traditional voyaging chant; its verses ingeniously identify a series of hostile atolls that extends some 1700 km from Mangareva through the entire Tuamotuan Archipelago to the Marquesas Islands.[35] In one example of an arrival here from the west in about 1650, the crew of a canoe were massacred and decapitated and the captain, Manavarere, was tortured.[36] Such hostility cut both ways, for a similarly grim treatment was being meted out at around that time to crew arriving in New Zealand.[37]

But things may not have always been this way; archaeological evidence for conflict does not begin until around 1450.

Technological capacity

Having addressed the issue of winds, we come to the second point of scepticism: craft fit for the return voyage. Although the deep-sea voyaging canoes of Māori had evidently fallen into disuse by the time Europeans reached New Zealand, coastal sailing vessels were still in use, as were a number of the old sailing terms, including ama (outrigger float), amatiatia (canoe with an outrigger), hourua (double canoe) and pahī (large seagoing canoe). Double sailing canoes were seen by Abel Tasman at Golden Bay, South Island, in 1642 and by Cook over a century later, in 1769, off Tolaga Bay, North Island. And in 1773 Georg Forster recorded seeing both outrigger canoes and double-hulled craft at Queen Charlotte Sound in the South Island.[38] Some of these craft, including the double-hulled sailing canoes, were fast enough to overtake the *Endeavour*.[39]

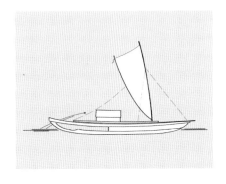

Māori boatbuilding

To build canoes, Māori needed to fell and move large trees, for which they employed several traditional methods, including the use of a ballista (far right), rolling the logs and dragging them along a slipway.

In the Pacific, sails were traditionally made from the strap-like leaves of **hara** (screwpine, Pandanus tectorius, above left), whose local equivalent in New Zealand proved to be harakeke (hard or 'strong hara', New Zealand flax, Phormium tenax, above right). The globe shows the distribution of this term, transferred in New Zealand not only to hara-keke, but to other plants with strap-like leaves: whara-riki, whara-whara etc. (Compare with the Malay word for pandanus, haragh-hagh.) Varieties of the tropical hara were selected for their tough, long leaves, and carried island to island to make not only sails but baskets, clothes and mats.[40] For all these uses, harakeke would prove a worthy replacement.

We can infer something of the range and sailing capability of the craft formerly used by Māori for long-distance voyaging from the fact that they carried people and their commodities over 800 km to the Chatham and Kermadec islands, and some 500 km south into the Furious Fifties to reach the subantarctic island of Enderby. Wind-tunnel evidence confirms that these craft were not limited to running before the wind.[41] It is clear that at one time Māori were building seaworthy sailing canoes.

To do so required some local shipbuilding innovations. In this land of massive trees, hulls could be made from whole trunks. Forest giants such as kauri, tōtara or matai were felled and whole logs shifted, hollowed out, and a topstrake added. In place of breadfruit sap or coconut fibre to caulk and seal any gaps, they used pounded wads of tree bark.[42] They also employed a hybrid boatbuilding technique – a combination of both planked canoe and dugout[43] – as shown by part of a hull of an old 16-m double-hulled sailing canoe uncovered by a storm on the northwest coast of the South Island in 2012 (the Anaweka canoe, page 203). The canoe's construction was as sophisticated as anything known at European contact; yet it was contemporary with the colonisation of East Polynesia for it had made its last voyage around AD 1400.[44]

Just such a craft may have been used by a navigator heading up to the tropics; or perhaps they had opted for a more lightly built outrigger canoe, as there would have been little need on a return voyage to move large numbers of people and settlement cargo.

For sails, Māori had to find an alternative to pandanus, whose strap-like leaves were used for this purpose throughout the Pacific. The long, waxy leaves of New Zealand flax filled the bill. When scraped, these yield a fibre that is far superior to pandanus – stronger, more easily worked and more versatile.[45] With no coconuts or bamboo – and until locally grown gourd skins became available – Māori had to find alternative materials for making water containers, which they did from wood, sealskin and the thick blades of bull kelp, protected within a basket of tōtara bark.[46] Lacking breadfruit and banana, they provisioned with dried fish (including shark), crayfish tails, bird eggs, and other meats (from birds, rats and marine mammals) preserved in their own fat.[47]

VOYAGING ROUTES: *As told by rat DNA*

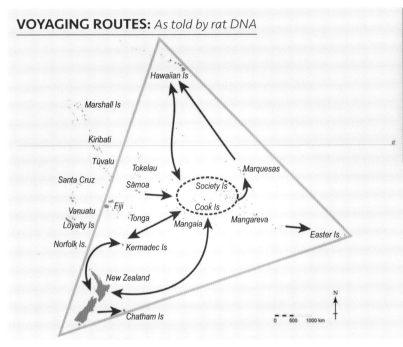

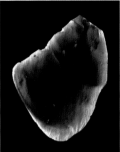

Search for hard evidence

Obsidian flakes (above left) of an identifiably New Zealand origin have been found en route to the tropics, on both the Chatham Islands and the Kermadec Islands. The situation is less clearcut in the case of New Zealand greenstone (above right), pieces of which were found in the 1930s on Aitutaki (S. Cook Is), Pukapuka (N. Cook Is) in 1905, and on Millennium Atoll (S. Line Is) 'some years prior to 1883'. Because none was recovered from 'a secure archaeological context', it is not possible to be sure when or how they reached there.

The most convincing archaeological support for voyage(s) from New Zealand to the Society Islands/Cook Islands region is still the mitochondrial DNA (MtDNA) of Pacific rats (Rattus exulans), from which some of the routes and direction of voyaging can be inferred, as depicted on the map at left.[53]

Where is the archaeological evidence?

We have addressed two of the four main points of scepticism regarding return voyaging and come now to the question of archaeological evidence.

We saw evidence of Māori having transported New Zealand obsidian (matā) over 800 km along two viable routes of return – that is, as far as the Kermadecs and the Chatham Islands,[48] but if Māori continued along either of these routes, there is as yet no archaeological evidence for it. In the case of New Zealand obsidian, no artefacts from it have been found in the tropics.[49]

A similar argument could be made for greenstone (pounamu), but here the evidence is more equivocal. Although we know that greenstone from the West Coast of the South Island was discovered during the first wave of exploration, it was not carried far until the late 1300s,[50] by which time there may have been little need for voyaging back to the tropics. Despite this there have been several finds of this highly attractive stone in tropical East Polynesia: a greenstone adze found on Pukapuka (N. Cook Is) in 1905; and a piece of worked greenstone found on Aitutaki (S. Cook Is) in the 1930s – both mentioned earlier.

A third item was found earlier still, 'some years prior to 1883' on Millennium Atoll (Caroline Island in the southern Line Islands). The owners of the atoll had been digging for guano at the time, when they came upon some 50 graves that contained 'stone axes, and highly polished green stones, such as are used by the Maoris of New Zealand, and spears of the same description'.[51] The unfortunate thing is the lack of what archaeologists call a 'secure archaeological context': without this, there is no way of ascertaining whether this, or the other two items of greenstone, actually reached the tropics prior to European contact.[52]

Te Ika a Māui and Te Wai Pounamu

When Europeans came on the scene, Māori had no collective name for New Zealand; the North and South Islands were referred to individually by separate names such as Te Ika a Māui, Teatea or Aotea for the North Island, and Te Wai Pounamu for the South Island.[54] It was thus intriguing when early European navigators collected these same island names 'Teatea' and 'Pounamu' from native speakers in central East Polynesia. However, it has since transpired that these names were collected only after Tahitians had already travelled around the Pacific on British and Spanish vessels;[55] that is, the possibility remains that these names became known in the tropics only after European contact.

In other words, none of this constitutes hard proof of a return voyage. However, this lack needs to be weighed against how little excavation has been conducted in the tropical Pacific; in reality, the statistical chance of finding hard evidence from a few voyages to the tropics is intrinsically low. Such poor odds are reflected in the fact that just two tools (a pearl-shell fishing lure and a shell chisel, page 177) have so far been found from all the voyages made in the reverse direction, from the tropics to New Zealand. In the words of Irwin, the lack of corresponding items found in the tropical Pacific is 'hardly significant'.[56]

On inundation-prone atolls en route, such as Pukapuka (N. Cooks) and the Tuamotus, the chances of finding stone tools that were traded or left behind would seem to be particularly low.[57] This is especially true when many of the objects used by Polynesians were made of organic materials that deteriorate easily. As Pacific archaeologists Patrick Kirch and Roger Green point out, 'about 82 percent' of the kinds of items used 'in a traditional Polynesian culture would not be expected to survive in a normal open-site archaeological context'.[58]

From archaeological evidence alone, all we can say is that voyagers from New Zealand ventured as far as the Chathams and Kermadecs, which leaves us with a tantalising gap of just 900 km to the next islands, in a region where landfall was not particularly hard to achieve.

Māori tradition

And yet several tribal accounts do make reference to return voyages, often to fetch kūmara tubers. In one from the Bay of Plenty, 'Toi sent the canoe *Te Aratāwhao* to Hawaiki captained by Tama-ki-hikurangi, charging him with retrieving more kūmara'. Others left on similar voyages aboard the *Horouta*, *Mānuka* and *Āraiteuru* canoes.[59] The routes are not specified, but acquisition of kūmara would seem to imply a destination somewhere in East Polynesia or in South America.[60]

There are other traditions of return voyages to the tropics, including one that points along an altogether different course. Intriguingly, this is also the only account of a voyage by Māori to the tropics collected at European contact. Since it has been almost entirely overlooked, it is worth elaborating here.

The account was collected on 9 December 1769 in the Far North, during Captain Cook's visit to Doubtless Bay near North Cape, when six Māori canoes drew alongside the *Endeavour*. The exchange that ensued is here reported by Joseph Banks:

> Finding [their crew] so intelligent [we] desird [Tupa`ia, the navigator] to enquire if they knew of any Countries besides this or ever went to any. They said no but that their ancestors had told them to the NW by N or NNW was a large country to which some people had saild in a very large canoe, which passage took them up to a month: from this expedition a part only returnd who told their countreymen that they had seen a country where the people eat hogs, for which animal they usd the same name (Booak) as is used in the Islands. 'And have you no

hogs among you?' said Tupaia – 'No.' – 'And did your ancestors bring, none back with them?' – 'No.' – 'You must be a parcel of Liars then, said he, and your story a great lye for your ancestors would never have been such fools as to come back without them.'[61]

On the surface it was a smart use of logic and yet it is a shame for us that Tupa`ia chose to use the occasion like this to assert his authority rather than pursue further the veracity of the account he was charged with relaying.[62] He failed to enquire of the Māori crew whether pigs were, (1) considered an asset at this point by their ancestors, rather than a liability; (2) procurable; and (3) likely to survive for a month in an open canoe this far south. Elsewhere, Polynesian pigs frequently rooted up the gardens;[63] and there is no instance anywhere in the Pacific of one surviving south of latitude 25°S.[64] But Tupa`ia had made his point. It nevertheless seems likely, from his proven prowess as a navigator, that he paid more careful heed to the actual sailing course, which was NNW.

Cook refers to this route again later in his own journal of the voyage, where he records a traditional name for the main destination along the route: 'Ulimaroa'.[65] In a series of papers on the subject, linguists Paul Geraghty and Jan Tent have deciphered 'Ulimaroa' as 'Rimaroa' (or 'long arm'), which they have identified as the Melanesian island of Grande Terre, the main island of New Caledonia[66] – the only island on this course within a month's sailing that qualifies as being a 'large countrey'.[67]

Norfolk Island

En route to Grande Terre along this NNW course, we first encounter Norfolk Island about halfway, where archaeologists have identified unambiguous evidence of Polynesian presence. Although Captain Cook found the island uninhabited in October 1774, early stone adzes and fragments of two old Polynesian canoes were subsequently discovered on the beaches, and thick clumps of fruiting 'plantain or bananas' in the forest. In 1995 archaeologists uncovered remnants of a small Polynesian

Norfolk Island – en route to the tropics

Norfolk Island – a former penal colony and nowadays a popular holiday destination – lies about half way between New Zealand and New Caledonia. Cook gave the island its current name in 1774 after the Howard family, dukes of Norfolk, describing the island as 'near a kin to New Zealand . . .' He adds, 'The Flax plant,[68] many other Plants and Trees common to that country was found here but the chief produce of the isle is Spruce Pines which grow here in vast abundance and to a vast size.' The island is largely encircled by cliffs and has no safe harbour; however, canoes could land on a gently sloping beach at Emily Bay on the southeastern side (below left), where the site of a former Polynesian settlement is found. Here again, seabirds are likely to have helped Polynesians locate the island: from mid-April, clouds of them are seen in the surrounding seas, a vestige of the more than two million Providence petrel (Pterodroma solandri, below) that formerly nested here.

Walpole Island

Another Polynesian outpost in this NNW quarter is the now uninhabited island of Walpole, which lies just 150 km east of Grande Terre, the main island of New Caledonia. This spectacular uplifted coral platform, right, is encircled by steep cliffs that drop 80 m into the sea. In calm weather, landing is nevertheless possible along narrow flat areas on the southwestern and northwestern sides. The island is like Henderson Island in that it lacks permanent streams; rainwater drains through the porous soil to accumulate in freshwater pools deep inside caves. Remains of former taro plantations with high walls built to shield them from the incessant wind speak of the former presence of a permanent community. Perhaps their ancestors were drawn from neighbouring islands by the black-winged petrels (Pterodroma nigripennis, below) and red-tailed tropicbirds – or did the island once serve voyagers as a place to await a change in winds? Perhaps both, for archaeologists see evidence for occupation of the island in two distinct phases; skeletal remains from the most recent phase, around AD 1250–1500, suggest that at least some inhabitants were Polynesian.[69]

village hidden beneath the dunes at Emily Bay, along with shell and bone tools, the remains of a house; ovens in which fish, shellfish, turtles and muttonbirds had been cooked; and the remains of an East Polynesian-style marae platform with an upright stone in the centre. The island's original settlement was dated, from charcoal deposits and subfossil rat bones, to about AD 1200–1300.[70]

Who were these people and where had they come from? And did they meet those ancestors of Far North Māori? The bananas spoke of contact with the tropics, and the marae platform pointed more specifically to a cultural influence from tropical East Polynesia in the period during which these were being constructed there.

Other clues included pieces of obsidian. Most of these could be geochemically traced to an origin some 1400 km to the east, on Raoul Island (Kermadecs), but one flake may have come from Tūhua (Mayor Island) in the Bay of Plenty – although this proved harder to confirm.[71] From 'the nature and morphology of the artefacts', archaeologists Atholl Anderson and Peter White concluded that the most likely source of the settlement was 'New Zealand or the Kermadec Islands'.[72] And yet the island had clearly served a wide region, for an analysis of Pacific rat DNA identified as many as five strains of DNA, whose affiliations suggest arrivals not only from New Zealand, the Kermadecs and East Polynesia, but also from elsewhere.[73] It seems that voyagers were arriving from several quarters, presumably using Norfolk Island as some kind of 'stepping stone' to other islands. Indeed, voyagers from this island are even known to have reached Australia (see sidebar opposite).

Norfolk Island itself is small (35 sq km) and remote, and rises to less than 320 m above sea level, so once again, the key to finding it is likely to have lain in its enormous seabird populations, including a population of over two million Providence petrels (page 207).[74]

There seems little reason, then, to doubt the claim by Doubtless Bay Māori that their ancestors voyaged NNW. In autumn, flocks of departing godwits showed the way. And if voyagers had continued along this course beyond New Caledonia, they would have entered a region where the islands are more closely spaced and internavigable.[75] If Northland Māori did indeed see Polynesian pigs, then these, according to archaeologists, were present on nearby Ouvéa (a Polynesian Outlier of New Caledonia) and Tikopia (a Polynesian Outlier of the Solomons).[76]

Australia

New Zealand lies a lot closer to Australia than it does to Rarotonga,[77] and Māori must have been aware of its existence from smoke drifting across the Tasman Sea from large Australian bushfires; from storm-blown butterflies and moths;[78] and from the annual migratory flights of white-fronted terns, banded dotterels and Australasian gannets (Morus serrator, above left).[79] Actual evidence of Polynesian contact with Australia[80] has also been identified: a Polynesian adze (left) found in 1928 at Dark Point, NSW (length: 82 mm), shaped from

basalt whose source could be traced with X-ray fluorescence to Norfolk Island.[81] Archaeologist Peter White and co-workers believe that this item had almost certainly reached Australia before European contact. In terms of latitude, Dark Point lies about 200 km north of New Zealand's North Cape.

Cultural differences

Having explored prevailing winds, technological capacity, archaeological evidence and Māori tradition, we come now to the fourth point of scepticism toward a return voyage by Māori to the tropics. This refers to distinctive Māori cultural developments – several customs that are widespread in tropical East Polynesia but absent in New Zealand. Here we might include the existence in the tropics of stratified chiefdoms; the use of sharkskin drums and formal stone food pounders; the sport of archery; and the widespread construction of large ceremonial stone platforms – none of which are found in New Zealand.[82]

From such differences in culture one might infer either that little or no return voyaging occurred; or that major episodes of contact predate the period during which these cultural features became common in tropical East Polynesia.

In the case of archery, drums and food pounders, all reached the Hawaiian Islands, but not New Zealand or Easter Island; and in the case of stone platforms, these are unknown only in New Zealand – from which we might infer the order in which these islands might have broken away. If so, and insofar as any break in contact can be considered a discrete event, New Zealand may have been the first to break away – before about AD 1500, when stone marae platforms were first being constructed in the Society Islands.[83]

To sum up

In short, none of the four main objections that are commonly made toward return voyages by Māori is enough to discount traditions that refer to such voyages, especially so in the early period in which New Zealand was initially discovered and still in the process of being settled.

CHAPTER THIRTEEN

The Western Pacific

A Wider Range of Possibilities

Current orthodox archaeological thinking is that New Zealand's prehistory lies entirely with East Polynesia, but voyaging considerations suggest a wider range of possibilities.

Archaeologist Geoffrey Irwin, *The Prehistoric Exploration and Colonisation of the Pacific*, 1992

We have seen a wealth of evidence that the language and culture of New Zealand Māori is essentially East Polynesian, and will now widen our enquiry to consider whether any Pacific navigators reached New Zealand from other regions. As Geoffrey Irwin put it, on completion of his 1992 analysis of traditional voyaging strategies: 'current orthodox archaeological thinking is that New Zealand's prehistory lies entirely with East Polynesia, but voyaging considerations suggest a wider range of possibilities'.[1] What his computer-based study showed was that courses sailed to New Zealand from New Caledonia, Fiji, Tonga or Sāmoa were no less practicable than those sailed from East Polynesia.

In considering whether any voyages were made from this western quarter, we must bear in mind that myth, oral history, customs, language and material culture will, by their very nature, have little to say of antecedents who returned home, were conquered or absorbed; in the words of James Belich, 'failed migrations told no tales'.[2] Here then, our approach will be to explore potential motives for voyages from this western region of the Pacific, and the sailing capabilities of its inhabitants, before presenting evidence for and against contact.

Cultural regions of the Pacific

First, we should be clear what these cultural regions actually mean and what distinguishes them from one another.

The Pacific as a whole can be divided into three major cultural regions: **Polynesia** ('many islands'), **Micronesia** ('small islands and atolls'), and **Melanesia** (Fiji, New Caledonia, Vanuatu, the Solomons and New Guinea, where the people tend to have darker skin). Of these three, Polynesia can be further subdivided, on the basis of culture, beliefs and language, into **East** and **West Polynesia**, and the **Polynesian Outliers** (a chain of tiny Polynesian islands and atolls that extends to the west of the main so-called 'Polynesian Triangle').

Useful though these cultural categories can be at times, in reality the boundaries between them are frequently blurred due to ongoing voyaging contact between them.[3]

Distinguishing East and West Polynesia

> Oh, East is East and West is West, and never the twain shall meet . . .
> But there is neither East nor West, Border, nor Breed, nor Birth . . .

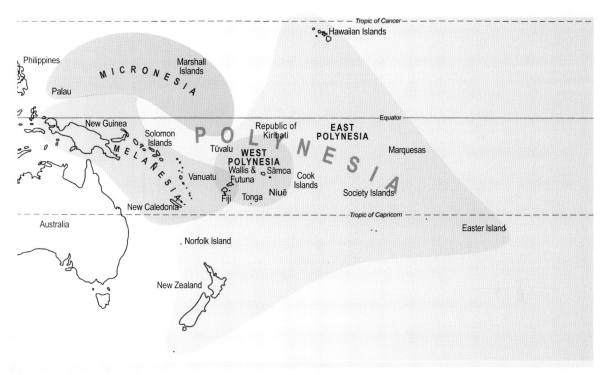

West and East Polynesia – 'same same but different'

	WEST POLYNESIA (Tonga, Sāmoa etc.)	EAST POLYNESIA
food pounders	formal food pounders very rare	formal food pounders made of stone or coral
stone adzes	adze heads not shaped to lock onto shaft	adze heads tanged (shaped to lock onto shaft)
tapa bark cloth	beaten strips joined by pasting	beaten strips joined by felting
coiled baskets	coiled baskets	no coiled baskets
kava-drinking	formal kava-drinking ceremonies	no formal kava ceremony
drums	large, canoe-shaped slit drums	skin drums and small bamboo slit gongs
canoe hulls	canoe hulls with low ends	canoe hulls often have a high, upturned stern
'nights of moon'	no individual 'nights of the moon'	'nights of the moon' individually named
marae	marae have no raised platform	marae built with a raised stone platform (ahu)
tiki	no human figures carved in stone	human figures carved in stone (tiki and mo`ai)
major gods	Tū, Tāne or Rongo unknown	Tū, Tāne and Rongo as major gods
Hawaiki/Pulotu	Pulotu named as the abode of the gods	origin identified as Hawaiki; Pulotu unknown

When Rudyard Kipling wrote these lines in *Ballad of East and West* (1889), he was thinking of British India, but his point remains valid for East and West Polynesia, where we find no real border between the two regions yet many striking differences in their myths, oral history, customs, language and material culture. The inhabitants of the two even chose to distribute different sets of plants and animals: the kūmara and bottle gourd – such important crops to East Polynesians – were never traditionally adopted in West Polynesia. The inhabitants of both regions also grew different strains of breadfruit and Pacific cabbage tree: while West Polynesian varieties produce viable seeds, those in East Polynesia generally don't.[4] And one

Māui hauled up many islands

*As Te Rangi Hīroa explains, Polynesians were 'deep-sea fishermen as well as able mariners'; they angled for fish and fished for islands. 'By adding magic powers to their tackle, semi-mythical fishermen were enabled to raise islands up from the depths of the sea.'[5] Māui, or Māui-Tikitiki-a-Taranga, is the great trickster of Polynesian mythology, famed for this feat and also for ensnaring the sun, obtaining fire and struggling to gain immortality for humankind. In the case of New Zealand, he fished up the North Island, which is traditionally known as Te Ika a Māui ('The Fish of Māui'). The territorial extent over which the exploits of **Māui** are known permits Polynesian origins to be traced to islands off New Guinea, north of Australia over 3000 years ago (see globe).[6]*

lineage of Pacific dog found in East Polynesia is unknown outside this region.[7] So how might such striking differences between these cultures have come about? The question is important, for it might enlighten us when it comes to issues of isolation, interaction and voyaging capability.

The first point to bear in mind is that the first settlers of these two regions arrived at completely different times, almost 2000 years apart. While the first known human settlement in West Polynesia, in Tonga, has been thorium-dated to 888 BC, give or take 8 years,[8] the more or less contemporaneous settlement of East Polynesia did not begin until around AD 1000.[9] This extraordinarily long pause has long puzzled archaeologists and linguists, who have put forward two main theories to explain it.

Two main theories

One theory holds that the origins of East Polynesians lie in West Polynesia (Sāmoa–Tūvalu); another places their origins in Micronesia. And, in a sense, both may be true.

In the first theory that the primary origin of East Polynesians lies in West Polynesia, the 2000-year pause may be attributable to the navigational skill required to sail against prevailing winds across the comparatively large water gap between Sāmoa and the Cook Islands.[10] If so, marked differences in culture and language, and even fishing technology, might be attributable to a subsequent period of isolation between the two groups. However, a large body of evidence has since emerged of ongoing contact,[11] which suggests that any strong differences actually developed elsewhere.

But where? Using shared innovations in vocabulary and grammar, Hawaiian linguist William Wilson has traced a northerly latitude-sailing route whereby, he believes, voyagers entered East Polynesia from further west, via the atolls of Tūvalu, Tokelau, Phoenix Islands, Northern Cook Islands and Line Islands.[12] Archaeologist David Addison and biological anthropologist Lisa Matoo-Smith, pursuing an independent line of evidence from the DNA of introduced chickens, dogs and rats, see evidence for an influx of a new people arriving in what we know of as Polynesia some time before AD 750, bringing with them new crops, material culture and ideas through Micronesia.[13] Geoscientist William Dickinson notes that almost all the northern atolls along their onward route into what is now East Polynesia lay beneath the sea until around AD 800–1000.[14] Archaeologist Mike Carson notes that this coincides with a dramatic population growth throughout Micronesia[15] of a seafaring people who specialised in locating and living in atoll environments.

In short, the contemporaneous onward spread of Polynesians to the east may have been rendered possible only at this point by a chain of uninhabited atolls being, in a sense, 'fished up from the sea',[16] as alluded to in the words of several Māui myths, including this chant from one of the northern atolls in this chain, Rakahanga:[17]

> The sea seethes,
> The sea recedes,
> It appears, the land appears
> And Maui stands upon it.

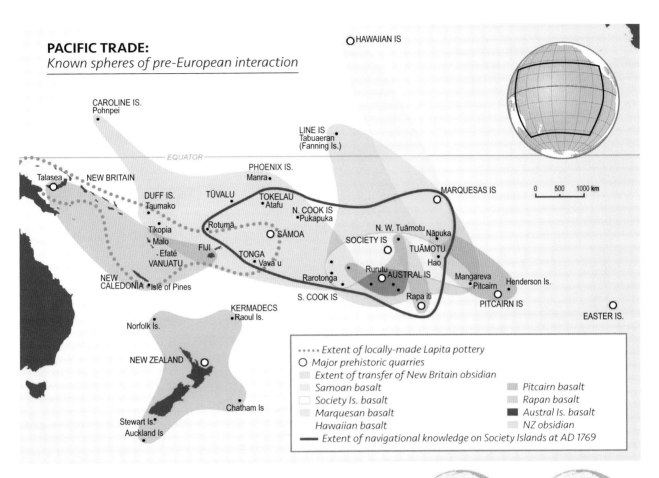

PACIFIC TRADE:
Known spheres of pre-European interaction

HAWAIIAN IS

CAROLINE IS.
Pohnpei

LINE IS
Tabuaeran
(Fanning Is.)

EQUATOR

PHOENIX IS.
Manra

Talasea · NEW BRITAIN

DUFF IS.
Taumako

TŪVALU

TOKELAU
· Atafu

N. COOK IS
·Pukapuka

MARQUESAS IS

0   500   1000 km

Tikopia

Rotumā

SĀMOA

N. W. Tuāmotu   Nāpuka

· Malo

FIJI

SOCIETY IS

TUĀMOTU

· Efaté

TONGA

· Vavaʻu

Hao

VANUATU

NEW
CALEDONIA   ·Isle of Pines

Rarotonga

Rurutu   AUSTRAL IS

Mangareva
· Pitcairn   Henderson Is.

S. COOK IS

Rapa iti

PITCAIRN IS

EASTER IS

KERMADECS
·Raoul Is.

Norfolk Is.

NEW ZEALAND

Chatham Is

Stewart Is.·
Auckland Is

····· *Extent of locally-made Lapita pottery*
O *Major prehistoric quarries*
▒ *Extent of transfer of New Britain obsidian*
▒ *Samoan basalt*   ▒ *Pitcairn basalt*
☐ *Society Is. basalt*   ▒ *Rapan basalt*
▒ *Marquesan basalt*   ■ *Austral Is. basalt*
    Hawaiian basalt   ▒ *NZ obsidian*
── *Extent of navigational knowledge on Society Islands at AD 1769*

This might explain how two distinct Polynesian populations came to intermingle; one with West Polynesian cultural traits more strongly influenced by Melanesia, and an East Polynesian one more strongly associated with the culture of Micronesia.[18] It might also help to account for a two-strand heritage in East Polynesian vocabulary, where we find both many terms that are shared between East and West Polynesia and many that are exclusively East Polynesian.

In any case, it is very clear that in the period during which tropical East Polynesia and New Zealand were being settled, boundaries between cultural regions were very fluid.

News travels

With no real barrier between East and West Polynesia, we might expect news of major uninhabited islands to have passed freely between the two cultural regions. The inhabitants of West Polynesia might also come to appreciate the existence of New Zealand through annual visits paid to most islands in this region by New Zealand's long-tailed cuckoo.[19] They would also find New Zealand closer to their islands than it is to any island in East Polynesia, with more favourable wind regimes to reach it.

The left globe shows the conventional delineation of the two major cultural regions of tropical Polynesia. In practice, however, these two regions overlap culturally and linguistically (right). The westward extension of East Polynesia shown here represents a likely route by which East Polynesian culture spread across the Pacific. The map above illustrates the known spheres of pre-European trade, showing the extent to which the interactions associated with archipelagos of different culture actually overlap.

0°

EQUATOR

0   250   500 km

Beru

**GILBERTESE
LANGUAGE**
(*Micronesian*)

Tabiteuea

Onotoa

Arorae

Tamana

K I R I B A T I

Kanton   Enderbury

Mc.Kean

Rawaki

Birnie

G I L B E R T   I S.

5° S

Nikumororo

Orona   Manra

P H O E N I X   I S.

Nanumea   Niutao

T U V A L U

Nanumanga

TUVALUAN LANGUAGE
(*Ellice Islands*)

Nui

Vaitupu

**GILBERTESE
LANGUAGE**
(*Micronesian*)

Nukufetau

Funafuti

**TOKELAUAN
LANGUAGE**

Atafu

Nukunonu

Fakaofo

T O K E L A U

10° S

Nukulaelae

Niulakita
(*previously uninhabited*)

Swains Is.

S A M O A

ROTUMĀ

Rotumā
(*Polynesian outlier of Fiji*)

ROTUMAN LANGUAGE

**WALLISIAN
LANGUAGE**

Wallis (`Uvea)

**SAMOAN
LANGUAGE**

Savai`i    `Upolu

Tutuila   Manu`a Group

**FUTUNIAN
LANGUAGE**

Futuna & Alofi

W A L L I S   &   F U T U N A

15° S

Rose Is.
(*uninhabited*)

F I J I

Niuafo`ou
(*Wallisian dialect?*)

Niuatoputapu & Tafahi Is.
(*language now extinct*)

Vanua Levu

Waya

Viti Levu

**WESTERN FIJIAN
LANGUAGE**
(*Polynesian*)

Kadavu Group

Lau Group

Vava`u Group

NIUĒ

Niuē

**NIUEAN
LANGUAGE**

Ha`apai Group

T O N G A

20° S

FIJIAN LANGUAGE
(*Melanesian languages including Fijian,
Lomaiviti and Lauan, and many dialects.*)

Tongatapu
Group

TONGAN LANGUAGE

`Ata

175° E

180°

175° W

170° W

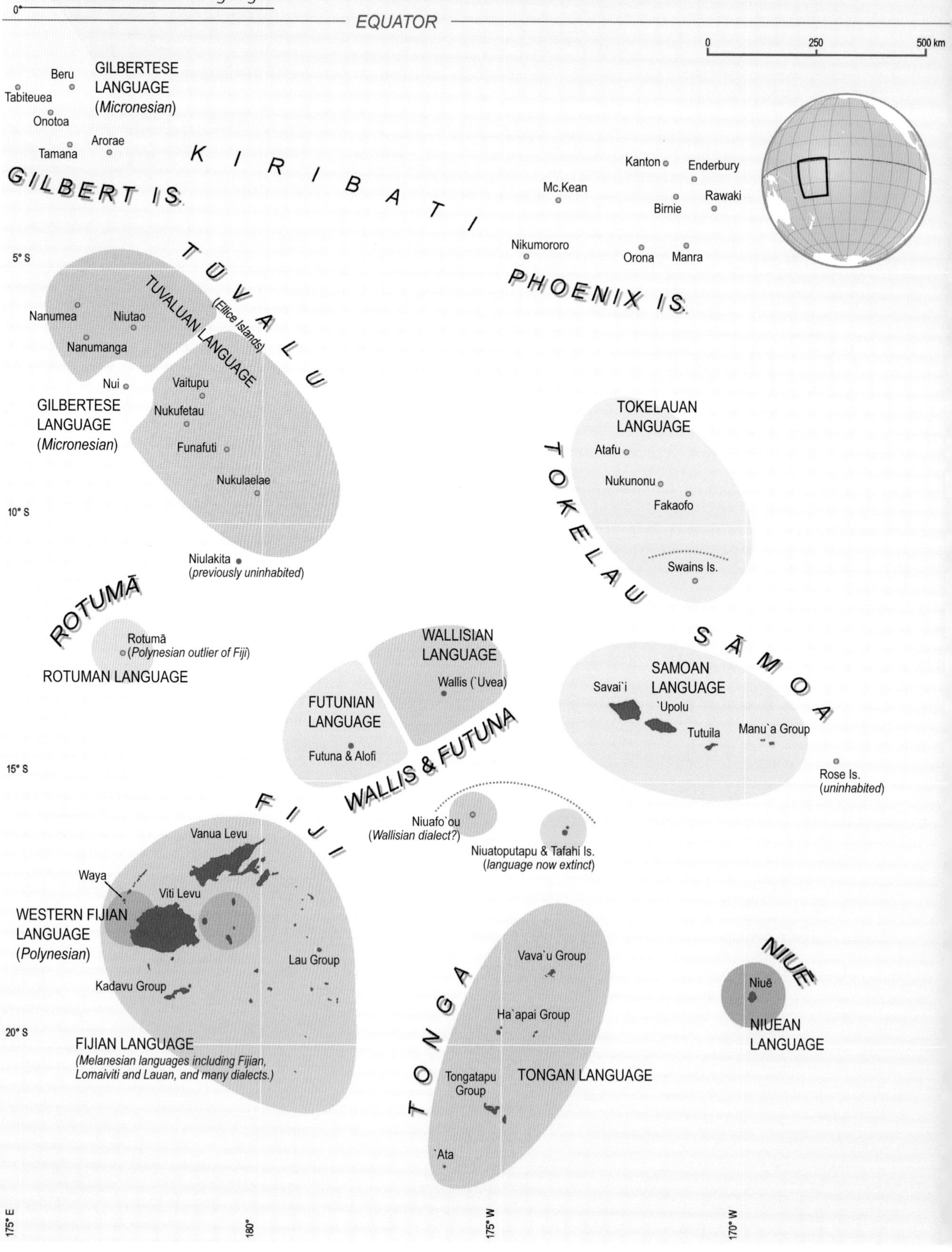

West Polynesian navigators

There is no question that several populations in West Polynesia possessed long-distance voyaging capabilities. This is evident in reports from Dutch explorers Willem Schouten and Jacob Le Maire: on reaching Tonga in 1616, they described Tongan craft as,

> very well fitted with sails, and run[ning] so well under sail, that there are very few ships in Holland which could beat them; they steer with two oars astern, having a man in the stern of each canoe, and they also run forward with their oars when they would put about; they go about very well of themselves, only taking the oars out of the water and letting them go, or all alone fly up in the wind.[20]

Tongans are known to have ranged throughout West Polynesia, as far west as the Polynesian Outliers (Tikopia, Anuta and Sikaiana), east to Niuē, and north into Micronesia (Gilbert Islands in Kiribati, and Pohnpei – some 4000 km away).[21] And, when Captain Cook reached Polynesia, he learned through Tupa`ia, that Tonga was in contact at that time with residents of the Society Islands, too.[22]

The voyaging capabilities of Samoans were no less impressive; indeed, the dexterity with which they manoeuvred their sailing canoes around the ships of French explorer Louis-Antoine de Bougainville in 1768 inspired him to name their islands *l'Archipel des Navigateurs* (archipelago of the navigators). Samoan basalt was distributed all over West Polynesia and reached the Cook Islands.[23] Contact with the Society Islands is also evident in directions to Sāmoa from Pukapuka (N. Cook Is) given to Cook by Tupa`ia.[24] Samoans are understood to have contributed toward the peopling of tropical East Polynesia in around AD 1000, so may well have had the requisite navigational capacity to reach New Zealand too.[25]

As for motives West Polynesians may have had to voyage south to New Zealand, the obvious one is to escape conflict at home – as referred to in many of the oral histories from this region. Those with the most compelling motives to move on, though, were the residents of low-lying atolls. With scant resources of soil, freshwater, volcanic rock and wood, and faced with the perennial threat of periodic drought and inundation from tsunami or tropical cyclones, they were obliged to live a more nomadic lifestyle. Consequently, atoll populations – such as those of Tūvalu and Tokelau,[26] – maintained 'a repertoire of strategies for successful transport and settlement of a founding population, as well as voyaging skills that enabled migrants to sustain regional social networks'.[27]

Indeed, Tokelauan traditions do speak of voyaging contact with Micronesia, Hawai`i, Sāmoa, Fiji, Tonga and the Cook Islands.[28] In proportion to the land area of Tokelau, their atolls also share considerably more place names with New Zealand than do other Polynesian archipelagos.[29]

West Polynesian navigators

For every one of the following western archipelagos, New Zealand lies closer than it does to either Rarotonga (3022 km) or Tahiti (4105 km).

Tonga; Fiji	*1875 km*
Niuē; Wallis & Futuna	*2400 km*
Rotumā	*2465 km*
Sāmoa	*2725 km*
Tokelau; Tūvalu	*3000 km*

Above: Large Tongan sailing canoe (1774).

Above: Fijian sailing canoe (c. 1839).

Above: Polynesian double hull sailing canoe seen between Tonga and Sāmoa by the Dutchman Schouten in 1616.

Similarly, the traditions of Tūvalu (Ellice Islands) tell of a voyaging corridor through their atolls from Rotumā, Wallis and Futuna, Sāmoa and Tonga up into Micronesia,[30] and language affiliations link them with several northern Polynesian Outlier atolls, almost 2000 km to the west. It seems that voyagers also passed through here en route to East Polynesia via Tokelau, Phoenix Islands, Northern Cook Islands and Southern Line Islands.[31] In proportion to land area, the number of New Zealand place names on Tuvaluan atolls is again high – similar to that of the Southern Cooks.[32]

So we can see that the inhabitants of several West Polynesian archipelagos had motives to migrate, and had proven abilities as long-distance voyagers. This brings us to the question of evidence, if any, for voyaging contact between this region and New Zealand.

Other navigators in the western Pacific

FIJI

Fiji can be distinguished from Polynesia on the basis of language, culture and racial appearance, which is largely Melanesian. There is little evidence in oral history or otherwise of Fijians as long-distance navigators,[33] and yet they played a significant role in Polynesia,[34] and were renowned shipbuilders.[35] Affinities in Pacific rat DNA suggest some minor contact between Waya Island (western Fiji) and New Zealand.[36]

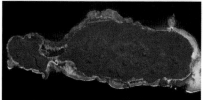

Top: Wallis Island (`Uvea), featuring Lake Lalolalo and surrounding forest. Rotumā, above, is just 13 km long.

NIUĒ

Contact between Niuē and East Polynesia is evident in language, nature names[37] and place names,[38] yet Niuē traditions have little, or nothing, to say of interarchipelago voyaging; this is consistent with archaeological evidence on the island.[39]

WALLIS (`UVEA) & FUTUNA

Uvean influence reached some 1600 km to the west, where the same island names `Uvea (Ouvéa) and Futuna recur,[40] and contact with the Society Islands to the east is known from directions given to Captain Cook by the Raiatean navigator Tupa`ia for reaching `Uvea from Savai`i (Sāmoa).[41] Between 1450 and 1540, Futuna was hit by a particularly catastrophic tsunami.[42]

ROTUMĀ *(left, seen from space)*
Rotumans are genetically more similar to Polynesian populations than are other Fijians.[43] Rotumā traditions speak of voyaging to Tonga, and contact with East Polynesia is known from the directions to here from Savai`i (Sāmoa) given by Tupa`ia to Cook.[44] Large double canoes remained in local use until at least the 1840s.[45]

Above: Niuē, showing its typically steep coastal cliffs.

MICRONESIA

Contact between Micronesia and West Polynesia is evident in artefact styles and language, and in Polynesian skeletal remains on the Marshall Islands (NNW of the Gilbert Is).[46] The boundary with Melanesia to the southwest is similarly blurred.[47] Micronesians were skilled navigators,[48] and their southernmost atoll (Arorae) lies closer to New Zealand than does Tahiti. Many of the islands in this region receive regular visits from the New Zealand long-tailed cuckoo.[49]

Evidence for and against contact

If we look for Māori names of plants and birds, we find them to be conspicuously absent in West Polynesia. For example, māhoe (hinahina or whiteywood) – a New Zealand native tree whose soft wood was highly valued by Māori as a rubbing board to generate fire by friction. Most New Zealand native trees are unique to the country, but māhoe is an exception: an identical species grows in Sāmoa, Tonga and Fiji, and yet here neither Māori name is known. This suggests that the people who coined both Māori names were unfamiliar with the forests of West Polynesia.[50]

A similar inference can be drawn from the name akeake (ake, page 125), a native tree of New Zealand that enjoys an even wider distribution across East and West Polynesia, but whose Māori name is clearly East Polynesian; in West Polynesia it goes by different names.[51]

The mangrove trees in New Zealand, known by Māori as mānawa, paetai or waikure, tell a similar story. Although no equivalent tree is found in East Polynesia, a similar mangrove does grow along West Polynesian shorelines, where it is known by the unrelated name of tongo. Likewise with the New Zealand kauri tree and its gum, kāpia: neither name is likely to have been coined by anyone already familiar with the closely related 'Fijian kauri', known as 'dakua', and its gum, 'makadre'.[52] The same is true of the Māori names recorded for New Zealand's chiefly podocarp trees: none is shared with the western Pacific, where corresponding trees are found.[53]

Māori bird names tell a similar story. While East Polynesia lacks any counterpart to the New Zealand fantail (pīwakawaka), in the western Pacific, where almost identical species do occur, none is known by a cognate of any of the 23 Māori fantail names recorded in New Zealand,[54] suggesting that all of these were coined by people from east of Sāmoa – the eastern limit of Pacific fantails. Similarly with the New Zealand pūkeko:[55] no equivalent bird is seen in East Polynesia; and in the western Pacific, where the almost identical purple swamphen is found, it is known by another name: karae (or kalae).[56] The implication is similar: that most migrants arriving in New Zealand came from islands east of Niuē.[57]

All this serves to emphasise an East Polynesian origin of Māori.

And yet a few intriguing exceptions do exist (see sidebar on page 218): names that are shared only with West Polynesia, thereby hinting at a very minor influence on the Māori language directly from West Polynesia. This is consistent with evidence from maternal DNA of Pacific rats collected from archaeological remains, which suggests a transfer from this western region to a site in the southern North Island, where one strain of DNA was found that is known only from rat populations in the western Pacific (see map, page 218).[58]

So, while it is clear that most of the canoes sailing to New Zealand did so from tropical East Polynesia, some direct contact with West Polynesia remains a possibility. On the other hand, such voyages must have been very few, as no West Polynesian-style adze heads have been found here.

This brings us to the third and final region of Polynesia: the intriguing and oft-overlooked Polynesian Outliers.

Tree and bird names *not* shared

New Zealand trees such as māhoe or hinahina (whiteywood, Melicytus ramiflorus); ake or akeake (Dodonaea viscosa); mānawa (mangrove, Avicennia marina subsp. australasica); and kauri (Agathis australis) have close relatives in West Polynesia, yet are known there by other names. The same is true of birds. The fantails of the western Pacific are almost identical to the pīwakawaka (New Zealand fantail, Rhipidura fuliginosa, above), yet none shares any of its 23 Māori fantail names. Likewise, New Zealand's pūkeko (purple swamphen, Porphyrio porphyrio, below) has an almost identical subspecies in West Polynesia but is known there by a different name.

Māori terms shared only with West Polynesia

However, Māori names of trees, birds, fish and insects include some that are known from West Polynesia and not from East Polynesia. This implies some minor, or indirect, cultural contact between West Polynesia and New Zealand Māori.

Above left: The tava (Pacific lychee, Pometia pinnata) of West Polynesia[59] evidently inspired the name for New Zealand's **tawa** (Beilschmiedia tawa); both are large timber trees with buttressed roots and a fruit whose seed is eaten roasted.

In West Polynesia, **tītoki** or **tokitoki** refers to trees with very hard wood,[60] a property shared with the tītoki or tokitoki (Alectryon excelsus) of New Zealand, below.[61] Both names are unknown in tropical East Polynesia.

Above: Māfai, a West Polynesian name for luffa vine (Luffa aegyptiaca) of the Cucumber family[62] is shared with New Zealand's **māwhai** (Sicyos australis, shown above), but is again unknown in tropical East Polynesia.

Above right: The West Polynesian name lulu for the barn owl (Tyto alba) is shared with the New Zealand morepork owl (**ruru**, Ninox novaeseelandiae), and yet owls are absent from tropical East Polynesia.[63]

Right: The Māori name **āwhato** for large edible beetle grubs or caterpillars, such as this 9-cm caterpillar of hīhue (convolvulus hawk moth, Agrius convolvuli),[64] is from West Polynesia. In tropical East Polynesia the term is unknown.

Right: The name **arāra** for local species of jack fish [Family: Carangidae], such as New Zealand's trevally (Pseudocaranx dentex), is likewise West Polynesian, and unknown in tropical East Polynesia.

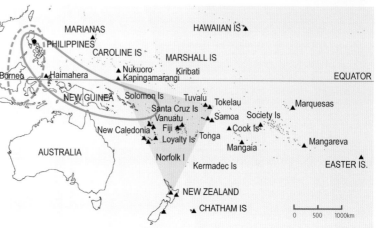

WEST POLYNESIAN RAT DNA

Further support for some (minor) contact between New Zealand and West Polynesia is found in the maternal DNA of the Pacific rat (Rattus exulans): one group from the North Island of New Zealand (red triangles) shares a maternal ancestry with this western region – from Kapingamarangi to Tokelau (an area depicted on this map as a large green triangle).

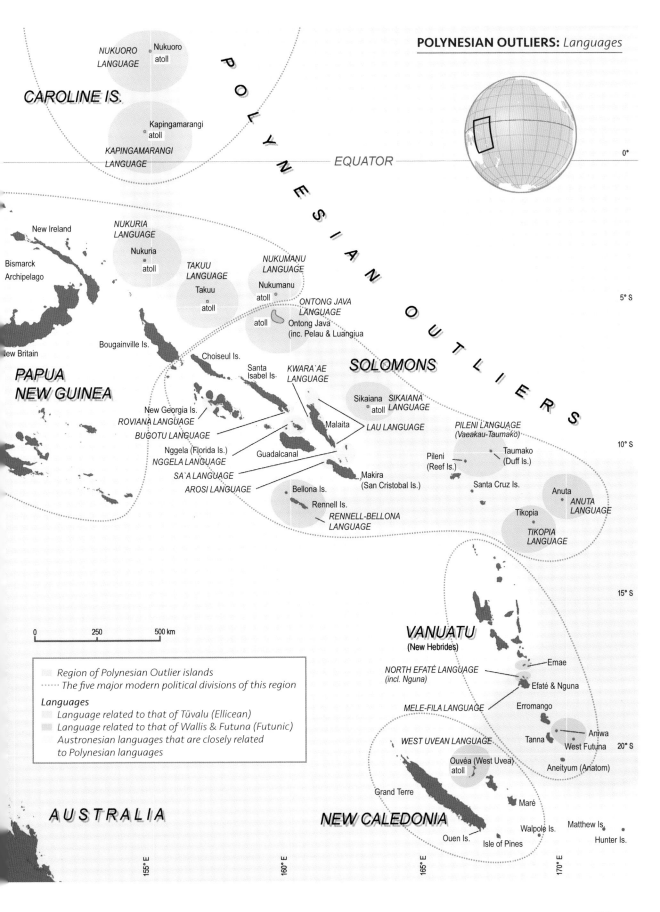

0°

CAROLINE IS.

NUKUORO
LANGUAGE

Nukuoro
atoll

Kapingamarangi
atoll

KAPINGAMARANGI
LANGUAGE

P O L Y N E S I A N   O U T L I E R S

EQUATOR

New Ireland

Bismarck
Archipelago

NUKURIA
LANGUAGE

Nukuria
atoll

TAKUU
LANGUAGE

Takuu
atoll

NUKUMANU
LANGUAGE

Nukumanu
atoll

ONTONG JAVA
LANGUAGE

Ontong Java
(inc. Pelau & Luangiua

5° S

New Britain

Bougainville Is.

Choiseul Is.

Santa
Isabel Is.

KWARA`AE
LANGUAGE

SOLOMONS

PAPUA
NEW GUINEA

New Georgia Is.
ROVIANA LANGUAGE

BUGOTU LANGUAGE

Nggela (Florida Is.)
NGGELA LANGUAGE

SA`A LANGUAGE

AROSI LANGUAGE

Malaita

LAU LANGUAGE

Guadalcanal

Makira
(San Cristobal Is.)

Sikaiana
atoll

SIKAIANA
LANGUAGE

PILENI LANGUAGE
(Vaeakau-Taumako)

Pileni
(Reef Is.)

Taumako
(Duff Is.)

Santa Cruz Is.

Anuta

ANUTA
LANGUAGE

Tikopia

TIKOPIA
LANGUAGE

10° S

Bellona Is.

Rennell Is.

RENNELL-BELLONA
LANGUAGE

15° S

VANUATU
(New Hebrides)

NORTH EFATÉ LANGUAGE
(incl. Nguna)

Emae

Efaté & Nguna

Erromango

MELE-FILA LANGUAGE

WEST UVEAN LANGUAGE

Ouvéa (West Uvea)
atoll

Tanna

Aniwa
West Futuna

Aneityum (Anatom)

20° S

0   250   500 km

Region of Polynesian Outlier islands
········· *The five major modern political divisions of this region*

Languages
Language related to that of Tūvalu (Ellicean)
Language related to that of Wallis & Futuna (Futunic)
Austronesian languages that are closely related
to Polynesian languages

AUSTRALIA

Grand Terre

NEW CALEDONIA

Maré

Ouen Is.   Isle of Pines

Walpole Is.

Matthew Is.

Hunter Is.

155° E

160° E

165° E

170° E

Opportunities in the NNW

Polynesian pigs have already been mentioned, but there were other potential benefits for Māori of contact with the NNW – opportunities for cultural exchange and the introduction of new crops.

Hue (bottle gourd) – DNA from original Māori varieties of hue (bottle gourd)[65] reveals hybridisation(s) between cultivars from both Asia and the Americas.[66] This fact, and a lack of pre-contact evidence of the plant in West Polynesia (the so-called 'bottle gourd gap'),[67] suggests that Asian seeds reaching New Zealand bypassed this region, for which the most direct route would be from the NNW.[68]

Karaka – Eating raw kernels of the New Zealand karaka tree (Corynocarpus laevigatus, below) leads to convulsions and paralysis, yet these kernels were quickly adopted by Māori as a food. By 1400 (within 150 years of settlement), seeds were being transported up to 1000 km from the North Island to

establish nut orchards as far afield as the Kermadecs and Chatham Islands, and karaka would become second only to kūmara among the vegetable foods of Māori.[69] Was their confidence in its safe preparation acquired by trial and error alone, or did Māori learn of a precedent elsewhere? Although the answer is not known, viable techniques were already in use for a closely related tree, Corynocarpus similis in Vanuatu and the Solomons, where locals have a long history of preparing its poisonous kernels by cooking and pounding.[70]

Taro – Early taro plants in New Zealand include stock with two different chromosome numbers – one shared with all of Polynesia; another with the region of New Caledonia and Timor.[71] The most direct route by which the latter might reach New Zealand is again from the NNW.

Kāpia – In the Pacific, the habit of chewing betel nut is largely a Melanesian one;[72] it is a sociable activity in which wads are shared.[73] On Pileni, Anuta, Tikopia and Rennell islands, the lime (or the container in which it is kept) is called kapia, a name unknown elsewhere in Polynesia, except New Zealand,[74] where **kāpia** refers to a soft white gum from the kauri tree (right) that was likewise kept in a special container for shared chewing.[75]

Poi dancing – The Māori performance art of **poi** dancing (above) – repeatedly hitting and swinging a lightweight ball attached to a cord, in time to music or a chant[76] – is reminiscent of the widespread Polynesian practice of juggling while chanting. However, the name and style link it more specifically with a very similar poi dance in Mele-Fila (a language spoken on Efate in Vanuatu) and with the poiloto of Pileni (Solomon Outliers).[77] A poi-like ball on a string (kā) is also used on nearby Ontong Java (Solomon Outliers), and an almost identical dance style is recorded in a pocket of southern coastal New Guinea (where related Austronesian languages are spoken).[78] Elsewhere in Polynesia, however, poi dances are unknown.[79]

Polynesian Outliers

The familiar term 'Polynesian Triangle' refers to Polynesia stretching from New Zealand to Hawai`i and Easter Island. However, this term obscures the fact that Polynesian culture actually extends much further, over an area shaped more like a stingray or eagle ray (see globe, left). That is, the 'Triangle' has a tail. This chain of little-known islets and atolls is not small; it extends some 4000 km northwest of Fiji along the eastern side of Vanuatu, Solomon Islands and New Guinea,[80] curling right up over the equator to Kapingamarangi and Nukuoro in the Caroline Islands.[81] Collectively, these 18 Polynesian societies are known as the Polynesian Outliers.[82]

   When it comes to the origins of New Zealand Māori, little attention has been paid to this region. This is surprising given that both accounts of

voyages collected from Māori by Cook's crew in 1769/70 – one at Doubtless Bay in the north of the North Island, the other at Queen Charlotte Sound at the top of the South Island – referred not to contact with East Polynesia, but with this NNW quarter.[83] En route lies Norfolk Island, which, as we saw in the last chapter, was formerly inhabited by Polynesians. Neither were the inhabitants of the Polynesian Outliers as isolated as they might seem today. Tikopia, for example, a Polynesian high island just north of Vanuatu, is known from archaeological evidence to have been in trading contact with islands as distant as Sāmoa, some 2000 km to the east.[84]

Northern Polynesian Outliers

Despite the apparent remoteness of these Polynesian Outliers from New Zealand today, the languages of many are surprisingly similar to Māori. On a visit to Kapingamarangi, a tiny atoll at the extreme northern tip of this chain, some 4400 km NNW of North Cape, Te Rangi Hīroa was surprised to find no need of an interpreter.[85] And again, when Māori doctor David Tipene-Leach of Ngāti Kere from Pōrangahau was working in the region in the 1990s, he found the language of Kapingamarangi even closer to Māori than Rarotongan 'as if from down the road in Aotearoa'.[86] Indeed, so striking are the similarities in vocabulary and grammar between the languages of these Northern Outliers and those of East Polynesia in general,[87] that William Wilson has proposed that these outliers lie on the route by which the ancestors of East Polynesians spread across the Pacific.[88]

If so, the inhabitants of Kapingamarangi may well have learnt of New Zealand's existence from visiting navigators, but perhaps also from annual visits paid to the atoll by the New Zealand long-tailed cuckoo and shining cuckoo.[89] With frequent droughts and periodic inundation from storms and tsunami, its inhabitants had ample motives to migrate.[90] The length of voyage required to reach New Zealand from here is not dissimilar to sailing from Tahiti to New Zealand. Nor is the course to New Zealand unduly difficult; the longest water gap to reach Grande Terre (New Caledonia) is less than 500 km, and two-way voyaging by Polynesians along at least half this route is supported by oral history.[91] This is in addition to two-way voyaging from New Zealand along much of this NNW route – at least as far as Ouvéa (`Uvea) or Tikopia – referred to in Māori oral history.

Archaeologists remain sceptical, though; they point to a lack of hard evidence.[92] For now, at least, contact along this route remains no more than a possibility. And yet, if this course was indeed sailed by the ancestors of Māori, it would provide an opportunity to introduce new varieties of taro and bottle gourd, tried and tested knowledge of how to prepare karaka kernels for safe consumption, and the Māori performance art of poi dancing (see box, 'Opportunities in the NNW').

Embarking on a course for New Zealand from this quarter would involve steering not by the setting sun, but by Canopus (Atutahi) on the horizon at sunset, a direction that was recorded for the *Māmari* canoe of Ngāpuhi.[93]

In summary, it is quite conceivable that the inhabitants of the Polynesian Outliers played a role, albeit a minor one, in the settlement of New Zealand.

Kapingamarangi Atoll

Kapingamarangi Atoll (Caroline Is) is located some 4400 km NNW of New Zealand's North Cape, a similar distance from New Zealand as is Tahiti, with a language that is more closely allied to Māori than Rarotongan is. Kapingamarangi even shares the same indigenous name for the New Zealand long-tailed cuckoo (below) as Tahitians use – as do the residents of many other tropical isles. Similarities between the language spoken here and New Zealand Māori are such that, when Māori anthropologist Te Rangi Hīroa visited the atoll in 1947, he found no need of an interpreter; he had only to substitute an occasional 'o' for an 'a', 'ti' for 'te' and 'nā' or 'nia' for 'ngā'. The current population of the atoll is around 500. Peak elevation: just 4 m above sea level; total land area: just 1.1 sq km.

A Mirror and a Window

Origins, Achievements and Loss

To remember is to laugh, to cry, to celebrate and to mourn.

Waikato skipper of the *Haunui*, Hoturoa Barclay-Kerr 2013

Origins of the Polynesian people

With our survey of the various cultural regions of Polynesia now complete, the question remains: Where did all these people – the ancestors of Polynesians in general – come from?

From close genetic and linguistic links between Polynesians and indigenous Taiwanese it is tempting to identify Taiwan as their origin;[1] but the issue is not quite that simple, for a strong genetic influence on the male side has also been found from Melanesia (e.g., New Guinea).[2] In reality, populations and customs rarely move as a single package over such enormous time scales – some 5000 years, in this case. People interact, assimilate, exchange ideas and goods, and occasionally cross cultural and racial boundaries in their choice of marriage partners.[3] To be more accurate, then, we really need to broaden the region of origin to encompass a triangle of islands bounded by Taiwan to the north, Philippines and New Guinea in the east and Indonesia in the south, a maritime domain in which two-way population movements between intervisible islands have been common for thousands of years[4] – 'a perfect nursery for learning seagoing skills', explains Geoffrey Irwin.[5] Within this maritime region, much of the genetic evidence points quite specifically to northern coastal New Guinea and the Bismarck Islands, immediately northeast of Australia.[6] As a homeland for the ancestors of Polynesians, this particular region can be traced back with some confidence for about 3500 years.[7]

From here, several lines of evidence can be used to trace onward human migration into the Pacific. One is archaeological finds of a distinctive kind of pottery known as Lapita, by which the spread of people who made this pottery can be traced right on through to the region of West Polynesia.[8] By about 3000 years ago, these potters had become sufficiently confident as sailors to voyage out of sight of land to reach the islands of Vanuatu and New Caledonia, from where they continued east to settle Tonga and Sāmoa. In fact, fragments of their pottery constitute the earliest evidence of human presence on these islands – appearing in the islands of Tonga around 900 BC. But were these people that we would today recognise as being Polynesian? Until 2016, it was hard to be sure.

The breakthrough came when 3000-year-old skeletal remains were unearthed from the oldest known cemetery in the Pacific, at Teouma on the south coast of Efate Island in Vanuatu. Not only did the DNA collected from three of the individuals turn out to be typically Polynesian, it was also similar to that found among indigenous populations in Taiwan and the Philippines. If these individuals are indeed typical of the period, then the ancestry of Polynesians at this point was primarily Asian, and much of the Melanesian ancestry we find among Polynesians today was introduced only later.[9]

Some 14 centuries later, in AD 500, the art of pottery-making suddenly and simultaneously all but disappears throughout West Polynesia. Indeed, in

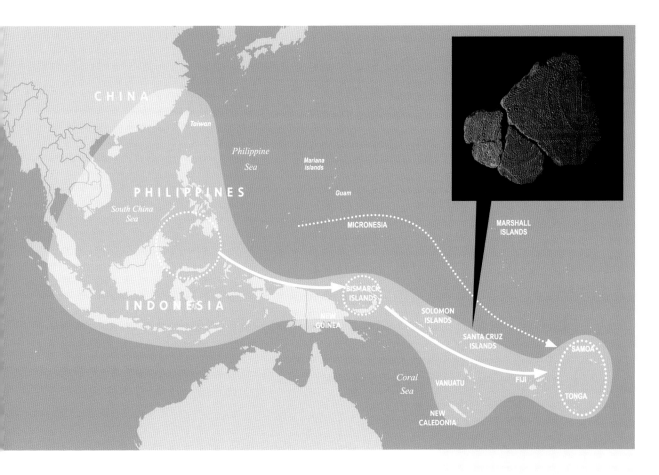

East Polynesia, which was settled some five centuries later still, almost no pottery has been found, even on islands where good potting clay is available. Instead, cooks opted to heat their food in underground cooking pits (umu or hāngī) – a practice adopted right across Polynesia to Easter Island, New Zealand and Hawai`i.

Given how useful pottery is, this sudden loss is intriguing. However, archaeologist David Addison and biological anthropologist Lisa Matisoo-Smith note that it coincides with what appears to be the influx of a new people arriving through Micronesia, bringing new crops, material culture and ideas.[10] It would seem that two or more populations came to settle in the West Polynesian region, one from land to the west with clay for making pots, the other more at home on atolls, such as most of Micronesia, where Lapita pottery is largely lacking.[11]

Multiple origins of Polynesians are also evident among their crops. While sugarcane, the fehi banana, Pacific plantains[12] and breadfruit can all be traced back to the New Guinea region, the paper mulberry tree (used for making tapa cloth) is traceable to the region of Taiwan/Japan. Indeed, in the case of Polynesian breadfruit, its DNA can be traced back to two parent species – a primary source in New Guinea, and a secondary input from the Mariana Islands and Palau via the atolls of Micronesia, Tūvalu and Tokelau.[13] A dual origin is equally evident for Polynesian dogs, chickens and rats: genetic analysis of their remains reveals at least two introductions out of Asia, with the timing of the second coinciding more or less with the disappearance in Polynesia of pottery.[14] This is consistent

Polynesian origins

Polynesian origins can be traced back to a triangle of intervisible islands bounded by Taiwan, Philippines, Indonesia and New Guinea, from where their ancestors began island-hopping into the Pacific. Archaeological finds of fragments of a distinctive kind of pottery (see photo) allow us to trace the route by which they, the first people to enter the region of Tonga and Sāmoa (West Polynesia), arrived from New Britain (in the Bismarck Is) almost 3000 years ago. Recent genetic research into the creatures the colonists brought with them has added a new strand to the story, though, telling of a second wave of migration over a thousand years later into the same region – and beyond, into East Polynesia – via the atolls of Micronesia (dotted line).

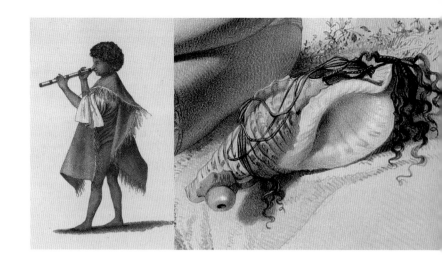

Evidence from musical instruments contributes to a more nuanced story, though. According to musicologist Mervyn McLean, an absence from island Melanesia of flutes played with the nose (right) points 'unequivocally to Micronesia as the area of origin for Polynesian nose flutes, with direct connection between Micronesia and Western Polynesia'; in Melanesia, flutes are blown with the mouth. McLean adds that Polynesian terms for trumpets made from conch shells (above far right) and Jew's harps from coconut leaves are likewise not shared with Melanesia. A dual origin for Polynesians therefore seems likely and is indeed consistent with the story told by human DNA.

with human DNA evidence,[15] and with the routes of introduction into Polynesia of various musical instruments, including slit gongs, nose flutes and mouth flutes, and the terms used for conch-shell trumpets and Jew's harps.[16] All likewise support at least two strands of immigration into what we now know as Polynesia.

Tempting though it is to try and portray these movements on a map as a series of one-way arrows, this tends to obscure the reality that returning to the west from Polynesia was no more difficult than reaching it. Interaction almost certainly continued in both directions, suggesting that the process of migration may be better characterised as one of expansion of the region over which two-way voyaging occurred. In an animated graphic, this might appear more as overlapping ripples in a pond. As each new route was opened up, those who sailed it are likely to have been defined less by race and language than by motive and capability.[17]

In that sense, any attempt to identify the origin for Polynesians should be content with identifying a region, rather than a place – namely, a region of Southeast Asia bounded by Indonesia, Taiwan and New Guinea.

Polynesia timeline

PERIOD	POLYNESIA	EUROPE
3000 BC	Ancestors of Polynesians on islands bounded by Indonesia, Taiwan and New Guinea.	Wheeled vehicles invented.
1000 BC	First people began to settle 'Remote Oceania', including Fiji & West Polynesia.	Druids in Britain. Iron replaced bronze for making tools and weapons.
AD 800	Austronesians from the region of Borneo reached Madagascar, over 7000 km away.[18]	Vikings attacked Britain.
AD 1000	Much of East Polynesia settled by Polynesians.	Vikings skirted the North Atlantic, obtaining a brief foothold in Newfoundland, North America.
AD 1250	Polynesians had fanned out and settled the rest of East Polynesia, including New Zealand, an area equivalent to all of North America.	Portuguese sailed to France, England, Spain and the Mediterranean.
15th century	Polynesian exploration over.	Europe's own 'Age of Exploration' begins.[19]

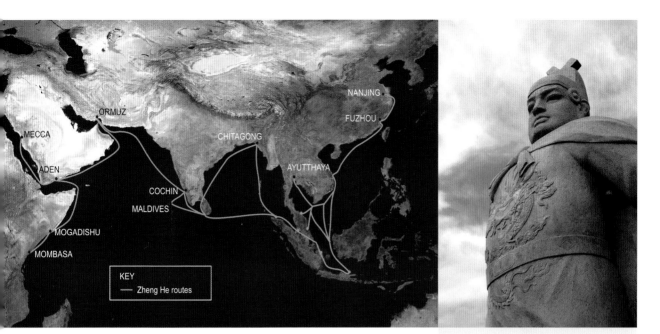

Zheng He (Cheng Ho)

The documented routes of trade that China's explorer and mariner Zheng He (Cheng Ho), above, sailed between 1405 and 1433 were ambitious – he ventured as far as India, Arabia and East Africa (see map above left); but this falls well short of the Polynesian achievement, for the Chinese voyages were not voyages of exploration.[24]

Extraordinary achievement

However one looks at this incredible phenomenon – the peopling of the Pacific – it is clear that the sea was not so much a barrier as a highway to Polynesians and Micronesians; not so much a vast oceanic wilderness with a scattering of islands randomly populated by the grace of prevailing winds, but rather a deliberately navigated and well travelled territory.

By around AD 1300 this activity is at its height. Polynesians are ready to engage in what is now known to have been one of the most rapid phases of human expansion in global prehistory, extending the boundaries of human exploration some 10,000 km to the east to reach Ecuador, pushing north to reach Necker Island in the Northwestern Hawaiian Islands and south to the subantarctic Auckland Islands. During this particular chapter of Polynesian history, they would discover almost every one of the 500 or so islands that lie strewn across a stretch of ocean the size of North America, despite many being tiny – mere specks on a map.[20] And it was during this era of expansion (c. AD 1000–1290), when Polynesians were venturing almost everywhere in this ocean that it was humanly possible for them to go,[21] that New Zealand was discovered.

At a time when no member of another culture is known to have deliberately ventured more than a few hundred kilometres from the shore, Polynesians had spread themselves over one fifteenth of the surface area of the globe. The territory they inhabited at that point was greater than that occupied by any other race.[22]

This golden era of Pacific exploration predates by almost two centuries Europe's own 'Age of Exploration' (1418–1620), and the more politically- or trade-motivated voyages of China's Zheng He (Cheng Ho) to India, Arabia and East Africa (1405–1433).[23] Te Rangi Hīroa would dub his people 'Vikings of the Sunrise', yet the preparedness of Polynesians to surrender to the wide ocean, their faith in their gods and their navigators goes well beyond the maritime achievements of the cold-hardy Norsemen, who are not

Christopher Columbus

When Italy's Christopher Columbus set out into the Atlantic from southern Spain in 1492, with a maritime compass, three ships and an all-male crew, he sought a new sea route to Japan – a potential gateway to the gold, spices, silks, perfumes and jewels of 'the Indies'. With the celestial navigation of Europeans still in its infancy, he estimated position by measuring time with a sandglass and throwing a piece of flotsam over the side to watch how fast it drifted by. Five weeks later, he reached land – not the land he hoped for, but a continent that lay in the way: America. For Europe it was a breakthrough.

known to have ventured more than 225 km from a coastline – even on their most daring voyages to North America.[25] When it comes to their ease and familiarity with the deep sea, their ability to make return voyages, and to successfully found new settlements almost everywhere they went, Polynesians and Micronesians excelled in founding what was in effect the world's first truly amphibious culture.

Māori are inheritors of this mana, linked to the achievements of their ancestors in the tropics by the traditional crops they brought, by their stories, customs and language – and very specifically by the names of places, plants and animals they introduced.

In their endeavours to criss-cross the Pacific from Southeast Asia to South America, the key to the success of the Polynesians lay in their hardiness, sense of adventure, adaptability, navigational skill, and two remarkable boat designs that were unfamiliar at that time in the West – the outrigger and the catamaran. Small and inefficient though their sails of pandanus may seem by modern standards, they can be shown to have given navigators an edge over the winds. Their hull designs were efficient and extraordinarily versatile, allowing crews to paddle for short distances when required. On entering shallow coastal waters close to reefs, or when hauling their canoes out onto beaches, the shallow draught of their craft and their superior manoeuvrability gave them a significant advantage over ships of European design.

To Europeans, such effective non-instrument methods of long-distance navigation would seem scarcely credible until they were explained and demonstrated by Micronesian navigators, who had maintained an unbroken lineage of navigational skills. It was they who helped 'modern man' (including Polynesians) to appreciate that an accurate course could be maintained with reference to a series of horizon stars, in combination with a highly refined observation of the background swell of the deep ocean. It was they who helped people of other cultures grasp how meticulous observation of the ocean and of the behaviour of local landfinding birds could serve to guide navigators between low-lying atolls that continue to wreck boats equipped with satellite navigation technology today.

Despite references in Polynesian mythology and poetry to the navigational role of migratory birds in long-distance exploration, the idea has often been dismissed as fanciful. And yet a survey of the natural history of the Pacific during the early period of human exploration, before the impact of humans and rats, finds no reason to doubt the poet. To this day, the presence of remote islands – including New Zealand, the Hawaiian Islands and Easter Island – is signalled from enormous distances by the return each spring of petrels and shearwaters. In this respect, New Zealand stands out not only as the so-called 'seabird capital of the world', but for its forest cuckoos, which converge on New Zealand in spring from almost every island in the tropical South Pacific.

Navigators knew of the presence of all these islands well before they reached them.

Tsunami

On 11 March 2011 this coastal community of Ōfunato, northeast Japan, was hit by a tsunami from the Great East Japan (Tōhoku) Earthquake. Although 'run-ups' of this wave in Japan rarely exceeded 10–15 m above sea level, funnelling and reflection into narrow valleys led to peaks of 20 m, or even 40 m in places. Over 15,000 people died.[26] In New Zealand, the run-up from a comparable tsunami in 1450 reached its highest point at around 32 m above sea level.

The long-distance voyaging stops

Despite this extraordinary period of exploration, much of the long-distance voyaging had stopped by the time Europeans arrived. Captain Cook found the inhabitants of Easter Island, New Zealand and the Hawaiian Islands isolated from their neighbours. A sudden contraction in long-distance voyaging had occurred, it seems – a phenomenon that has been variously attributed to the fact that Pacific exploration was by then complete; to stress on resources; conflict; a change in climate; and one or more tsunami. All may well have played a part, but here we will elaborate on two massive tsunami that are known to have occurred around this time.

Palaeotsunami researcher James Goff and associates have found evidence for at least two major inundation waves that struck many coastal settlements and low-lying atolls in the mid-15th century: one that affected the southwestern Pacific, including New Zealand; and another that caused damage across most, if not all, of the South Pacific.[27] The first is understood to have been triggered by the eruption of a submarine volcano known as Kuwae in Vanuatu, an event dateable with some precision from volcanic sulphates detected in ice-core samples taken from both hemispheres – from Antarctica and Greenland – to late 1452 or early 1453.[28] The coastal impact of the resulting tsunami has been identified by archaeologists in locations as distant as Fiji in the east and the northern coasts of New Zealand to the south.

The second major tsunami from this period is attributable to an earthquake that occurred around 1450 along the Tonga–Kermadec submarine trench. According to Goff, the marine shockwave set off by this event affected a much wider region: the resulting tsunami reached at least as far north as Pukapuka (N. Cook Is) and the Marquesas Islands, travelled east to the Pitcairn Islands, and south, striking with catastrophic force along the nearby northeast coast of New Zealand, where the resulting surge reached its highest at around 32 m above sea level, the height of an eight-

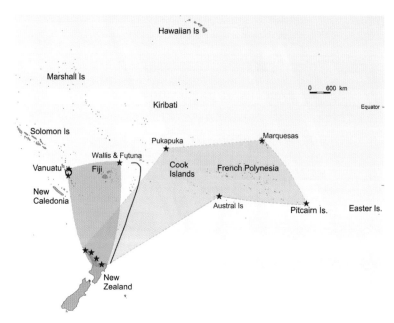

Megatsunami AD1450

Shown right is the estimated extent of two major mid-15th-century tsunami. The area in green shows the estimated regional extent of a tsunami generated by an earthquake around AD 1450 along the Tonga–Kermadec Trench (red line); and the blue area marks the major impact from another one, generated by the eruption in 1452/53 of a submarine volcano known as Kuwae in Vanuatu (red circle with yellow centre). Red stars indicate sites used to delimit the known impact of these tsunamis. The graphic above helps distinguish the 'run-up' from a tsunami, which refers specifically to the vertical rise in sea level, from the distance the inundation wave travels inland.

storey building. Here, above Doubtless Bay, archaeologist Bruce McFadgen[29] found a gravel sheet – a tsunami deposit – covering several tens of thousands of square metres of sand dunes. By the time the shockwave reached Cook Strait it was still generating run-ups of 10 m or more above sea level,[30] striking both sides of the strait and the northwest Nelson coast.

The full scale of loss to Māori is unknown, but their settlements were concentrated at the time in low-lying areas along the coasts of Northland, Auckland, Coromandel and Bay of Plenty – the very coasts that bore the full impact. The loss of lives, crops, stored supplies, canoes; the shellfish beds buried and the gardening soils poisoned by salt, is something we can only surmise. However, McFadgen notes that the timing coincides with a significant transformation in Māori life, including a sudden decline in long-distance trade[31] and an increased reliance on local sources of raw materials for making tools. No longer was obsidian from the northern North Island being carried the length of the country; the adze kit became simpler; and big sailing canoes were largely replaced by single-hulled canoes propelled by paddling.[32] An increase in conflict is evident at this point in the construction of pā (fortified sites);[33] and X-rays of limb bones begin to show visible evidence of malnutrition in the form of dense and numerous growth-arrest lines (Harris lines).[34]

Many graphic Māori oral traditions from around the coast do describe catastrophic inundations from the sea,[35] and yet some archaeologists remain sceptical. Atholl Anderson, for example, points out that many of these changes are not so readily dateable, and hence questions whether the evidence allows these events to be so clearly linked. In Anderson's view, 'it is much more probable that environmental influences on voyaging, migration and endemic cultural change came from slower but broader and more persistent variations in climate'.[36]

However much archaeologists may disagree on what brought this voyaging era to a close, we know that it did end. And the fact that it did so well before Europeans learned that the Pacific existed may well help explain why this phenomenal 'Age of Exploration' and colonisation has been largely overlooked in mainstream accounts of world history.

Memories bound

Polynesian tradition about much of this seems fragmentary. There is no clear account of those who undertook the remarkable voyages to South America and returned with the kūmara, for example.

To find out why, we might digress for a moment here to reflect on our dependence on the printed word; for by the time this extraordinary phase of oceanic exploration was complete, the first water-powered paper mills were just being developed in Europe, followed in about 1440 by the first Gutenberg printing press. These two developments alone would revolutionise the sharing of knowledge, but at the same time would rob us of much of our capacity to memorise. There are consequently very few today who can still recite Homer's 15,693-line *Iliad* or the 12,110-line *Odyssey* from memory. Meanwhile, in the Pacific, the arts of recollection endured. Polynesians continued to bind their memories into monuments of stone, body movement, sacred items and places. Oral narrative, proverb, chant and song endured as libraries of knowledge, along with patterns incised in gourd skins, body tattoo designs, and the carving of ancestral houses, paddles, canoe prows and genealogy staffs. Stories were 'stored in' the stars and in the transfigured landscape claimed by the ancestors.

Kupe 'marked' his passage along the New Zealand coastline with canoe paddles; and Rākaihautū carved out lakes with digging sticks. Cargo introduced on the canoe of Rokoitua was spilled and turned into rocks; and Pāoa urinated rivers into being to help float timbers to the coast.[37] Knowledge, incantations and sacredness were bound both physically and metaphorically with fibre,[38] while action chants (poi and haka) and string figures (whai) told their tales.

In other words, Polynesians had maintained their indigenous means of preserving and passing on knowledge, and would – for this skill – be deemed 'illiterate' by their colonisers, implying by definition in their own language that these people were 'ignorant'. The inference is unwarranted. For example, when Tamarau Waiari appeared before the Urewera Land Commission at Ruatoki in the 1890s to explain the claim of his hapū to certain lands, he demonstrated his ability to trace the descent of his people 'from an ancestor who flourished thirty-four generations ago' by reciting, over a period of three days, a genealogical table containing 'well over fourteen hundred names of persons'.[39] To know his history, he did not need books.

Waves of inundation

By the time Europeans reached the Pacific in 1520, the outer edges of this vast 'net' of Polynesian voyaging had frayed and broken. The first direct contact between the two cultures did not occur until 75 years later in 1595, when Marquesans would welcome Álvaro de Mendaña of Spain, unaware of the price they would pay from the landing of his 378 crew.

Above: In the 1890s, Ngāi Tūhoe leader Tamarau Waiari (1835–1904) demonstrated a prodigious memory by reciting a genealogical table containing the names of well over 1400 ancestors.

Population losses at a glance

Easter Island	**95%+**
Marquesas	**95%**
Rapa Iti *(Bass Is)*	**94%**
Tahiti *(Society Is)*	**93%**
Rurutu *(Austral Is)*	**90%**
Tubuai *(Austral Is)*	**90%**
Hawaiian Islands	**83%**
Tongareva *(N. Cook Is)*	**76%**
Rarotonga *(S. Cook Is)*	**70%**
New Zealand[40]	**60%**

Staggering losses among the Polynesian population occurred from European contact, ranging from a loss of 95 percent on Easter Island and the Marquesas to 60 percent in New Zealand. The percentage losses are based on original population estimates at contact, compared with physical head counts shortly after European contact.[41] Although doubts have been raised as to the accuracy of the original estimates, many of them are entirely consistent with recent archaeological findings.

This alien culture brought curio collectors who thought nothing of desecrating the sacred and mnemonic items. For example, when Cook's botanist Joseph Banks brazenly reached into one of the god houses at Taputapuātea marae on Ra`iātea to examine its contents, tearing at the sacred matting with his fingers as far he could go, puzzled by the offence he caused.[42] Missionaries followed, many seeking out symbols of divinity to remove or destroy. When Te Rangi Hīroa later attempted to trace the material heritage that had survived, he lamented: 'the regalia and symbols of spiritual and temporal power have been scattered among the museums of other peoples'.[43]

With these newcomers came so-called 'virgin soil epidemics' that took a particularly high toll on the elders, who were the repositories of cultural knowledge. In one flu outbreak in 1918 in which 20 percent of the Society Islands population died, losses among those older than 60 were almost 50 percent.[44] The demoralising aftermath of introduced disease running rampant across most of Polynesia was compounded by the introduction of firearms and alcohol, and – on many islands – the Peruvian slave trade. This is not to say that no efforts were made to allay the harm; they were.[45]

Despite these, on the worst affected islands the numbers that died during this early contact period represent an overwhelming proportion of the original population – up to 95 percent or even more, in some cases. If a comparable calamity struck Auckland, the survivors would all be able to find a seat in Eden Park stadium.[46] Death continued to come in waves on each island according to the timing and frequency of shipping contact. In New Zealand, where many Māori lived in remote areas, the losses were less, but still represent a devastating 60 percent of the original population.[47]

Although some historians, believing that the original population estimates may have been too high, suggested that the enormous losses were more apparent than real – 'the powerful myth of fatal impact' – many of the earliest estimates are consistent with subsequent counts of archaeological remains of dwelling sites and areas of land under cultivation at the time.[48] The losses were real, and effectively deprived a race of its 'cultural libraries' of oral narrative and inherited insights.[49] Sadly, the ensuing loss of cultural identity and its downstream effects is seldom acknowledged.

Rather, from the poor condition of Polynesians soon after contact with Europe, the newcomers were often quick to assume that their own arrival was a blessing – unaware, in many cases, that what they were witnessing was the effects of a crippling wave of unfamiliar diseases that they themselves had brought. In fact, the robust health of Polynesians at first contact drew comment from many early observers. In 1595, Quirós described Marquesans as 'a strong and healthy race, and indeed robust.'[50] Roggeveen's account of Rapanui in 1722 was, as we saw, very similar. No doubt there were exceptions, too; but Polynesian vigour would remain evident as late as 1778, when naturalist Johann Reinhold Forster concluded: 'The nations of the South-Sea-Isles generally enjoy a perfect state of health, and we saw many of them, who had attained to old age, for we observed grey and even white hairs on their heads; and all the symptoms and attendants of old age.'[51]

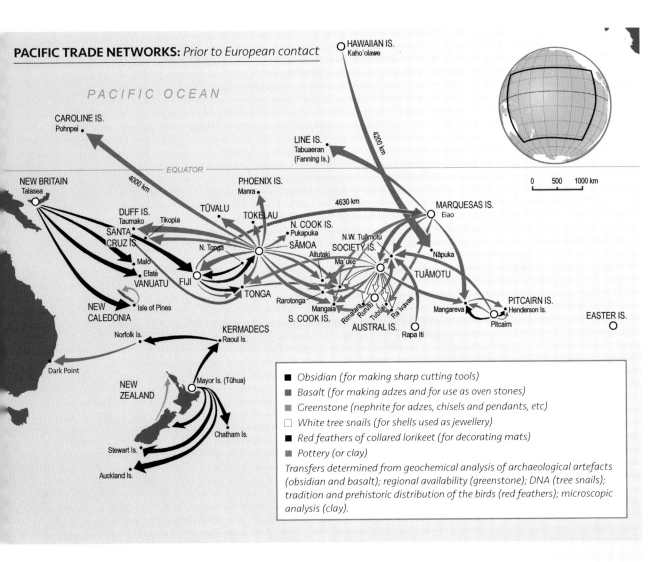

PACIFIC TRADE NETWORKS: *Prior to European contact*

PACIFIC OCEAN

HAWAIIAN IS.
Kahoʻolawe

CAROLINE IS.
Pohnpei

LINE IS.
Tabuaeran
(Fanning Is.)

4200 km

EQUATOR

NEW BRITAIN
Talasea

4000 km

PHOENIX IS.
Manra

DUFF IS.
Taumako · Tikopia

TŪVALU

TOKELAU

4630 km

MARQUESAS IS.
Eiao

SANTA
CRUZ IS.

N. Tonga

N. COOK IS.
Pukapuka

SĀMOA
Aitutaki

N.W. Tuāmotu

SOCIETY IS.
Maʻuke

Nāpuka

Malo
Efaté
VANUATU FIJI

TUĀMOTU

NEW
CALEDONIA Isle of Pines

TONGA

Rarotonga

Mangaia

Rimatara Rurutu Tubuai Ra ivavae

Mangareva

PITCAIRN IS.
Henderson Is.

Pitcairn

EASTER IS.

S. COOK IS.

AUSTRAL IS.
Rapa Iti

Norfolk Is.

KERMADECS
Raoul Is.

Dark Point

NEW
ZEALAND

Mayor Is. (Tūhua)

Chatham Is.

Stewart Is.

Auckland Is.

0   500   1000 km

- ■ Obsidian (for making sharp cutting tools)
- ■ Basalt (for making adzes and for use as oven stones)
- ■ Greenstone (nephrite for adzes, chisels and pendants, etc)
- ☐ White tree snails (for shells used as jewellery)
- ■ Red feathers of collared lorikeet (for decorating mats)
- ■ Pottery (or clay)

Transfers determined from geochemical analysis of archaeological artefacts (obsidian and basalt); regional availability (greenstone); DNA (tree snails); tradition and prehistoric distribution of the birds (red feathers); microscopic analysis (clay).

A shadowed history

Noting a conspicuous lack of long-distance voyaging craft at the margins of Polynesia, the newcomers were left with an enigma as to how most of this region had come to be settled by a single cultural group. Some went as far as to propose that a land bridge must have once connected all these islands.[52]

And yet Cook understood. In the Society Islands he had noted 'a great number of boathouses [housing craft for long-distance voyaging] all round the bays used only at particular seasons'. From such craft, from the navigational skills he witnessed and from close affinities in culture and language he had observed across Polynesia, he came to admire the magnificence of their achievement.

Cook's accounts of long-distance two-way voyaging would fade from memory, though, just as the glowing early descriptions of Polynesian health and well-being had done. Despite the remarkable capacity of these people to spread themselves over a region the size of Africa and Western

The myth of the 'primitive isolate'

The popular image of the indigenous inhabitants of the Pacific ending up on their home islands by accident and unable to return is firmly contradicted by the known extent of prehistoric trade (as shown in the map above), much of this trade in the reverse direction to the original voyages of settlement.[53] Isolation and a lack of requisite capability in the fields of navigation, sailing performance and boatbuilding are a myth.

A 'Stone Age' people?

Before iron was available to Polynesians, they mastered the use of stone tools to carve wood and stone. In the terminology of Europeans, they were living 'in the Stone Age' – with the implication, by definition, that they were living in 'an extremely backward or primitive era or state'. And yet, once iron was available to Polynesians, they quickly grasped the opportunity to use it. Indeed, so strong was the demand for iron among Polynesians that it casts doubt on any theories about the pre-Cook introduction of metal – such as that of the so-called 'Spanish helmet'.[54]

Giant stone statues on Easter Island, right, belie the myth of Polynesians as a primitive people.

Above: No sooner had Tupaʻia of the Society Islands been introduced to oils and watercolours than he took up painting: this one depicts a Māori fisherman with Joseph Banks, exchanging a crayfish for a piece of white cloth.

Europe combined, we would be told that the ability of a single people to find a thousand islands[55] scattered across the world's largest ocean could be attributed to chance and courage alone rather than skill.

Some suggested they had simply been blown off course while deep sea fishing[56] – overlooking the fact that, as Te Rangi Hiroa explains, 'Polynesian women did not go out fishing in canoes with their menfolk. The women's sphere of marine activity lay within the lagoon, and their boundary was the encircling reef. They did not pass beyond the reef except in transit with their families on visits to nearby islands or on organized expeditions.'[57]

Others, acknowledging that the women and crops Polynesians took with them implied a conscious choice to migrate, proposed that new islands had been discovered under duress on one-way voyages with families and seed material already onboard[58] – in effect divesting Polynesians of their extraordinary skill as explorers and navigators.

A 'Stone Age' people?

Polynesia, we were told by scholars, had 'remained in the Stone Age till Europeans broke into its isolated seas with their metal implements and weapons'.[59] This, with its pejorative use of the term 'Stone Age', implied, by definition, that before the arrival of Europeans, Polynesians had lived in 'an extremely backward or primitive era or state'. The irony of this association was not lost on Te Rangi Hīroa when it came to outlining the achievements of Rapanui: 'Because western people are now incapable of making stone images without steel tools and of transporting them without modern machinery, the very culture of the Easter Islanders has been attributed to a mythical people who never existed.'[60] Metal ores are, in fact,

Pre-contact industry

Though far less well known than the enormous stone statues of Rapanui on Easter Island, New Zealand Māori were responsible for many remarkable achievements of their own. This includes extensive gardens and fortifications, spectacularly long fishing nets, massive drainage systems and canal networks.

One example is illustrated in this aerial photograph (top left) taken in 1944, which shows a complex drainage system dug for gardening on the alluvial flats of the inner Rangaunu Harbour, near Kaitāia. A corresponding map of the same scene (left) depicts the canals as a vast network of solid black lines. The Herculean scale of this enterprise is evident from the fact that the main area drained here is about 4 sq km.

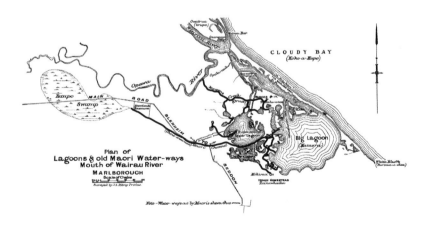

Shown in red on the map on the left is a network of over 19 km of canals that Māori cut by hand near the mouth of the Wairau River, South Island, to connect up local lagoons. These were designed to be navigable by small canoes and were used for catching eels and waterfowl. The level of engineering skill required and the scale of the project is reminiscent of aquaculture projects undertaken at the other end of the Pacific by the Hawaiians.

rare in tropical and subtropical Polynesia,[61] and once iron was available to Polynesians, they were swift to use it. This was already evident by 1767, when we find the *Dolphin* of the Wallis voyage in danger of falling apart in Tahiti because the crew had been extracting nails from it to trade with Polynesian women for sexual favours.[62]

Polynesians proved quick to adopt and adapt. Cook's Tahitian navigator Tupa`ia had only to see Cook's artist Sydney Parkinson with his oils and watercolours to take up two entirely new skills: he began painting and mapping his ocean world. With the arrival of Europeans, many Polynesians were quick to grab opportunities to crew on foreign ships while Māori promptly set up a trade in flax, and began raising potatoes, maize and pigs to help feed the new settlers. By 1801 Māori were supplying the missionaries, and by the 1850s they were transporting food and goods to and from Sydney in their own trading vessels.

The intellectual curiosity, quickness to learn, and tenacious memory of Polynesians drew comment from many early visitors to the Pacific.[63] Despite all this their culture has rarely been considered a 'civilisation' – because by definition, in the eyes of the colonisers, this required a 'stage of cultural development at which writing and the keeping of written records is attained'.[64] And so it would be culture, not science, that would shape our celebration of Polynesian accomplishments in the fields of navigation, boatbuilding, fishing, horticulture, megalithic construction and expansion of territory. Hence, someone raised in the Pacific today might easily remain oblivious of the fact that it was Polynesians who had carved, transported and erected the statues on Easter Island; the walled fishponds for aquaculture on the Hawaiian Islands; the massive 100-hectare networks of wetland agricultural ditches constructed in New Zealand;[65] or a complex of over 19 km of canals navigable by small canoes at the mouth of the Wairau River in the South Island.[66] Although remnants of all these remain archaeologically visible today, many other material products of this civilisation have long since disappeared – Māori fishing nets, for example, such as one made by a team of hundreds at Maketū in 1885 with fibre extracted from flax and cabbage-tree leaves, that extended for up to 1.9 km.[67]

'Noble savages' guilty of ecocide?

From the outset Polynesians were frequently portrayed as 'noble savages' living in a state of innocence in a 'Garden of Eden', descendants of those fortunate enough to land on natural paradises conveniently dotted by Providence with coconuts, bananas and breadfruit. But then, in the 21st century their alleged innocence would be turned against them. On Easter Island, for example, the impact of introduced rats, slavery and disease would be conflated with self-induced stress by imprudent inhabitants oblivious of the limits to their own resources, who were deemed guilty of 'ecocide'.[68] Suddenly, the victims of cultural and physical extermination had been turned into the perpetrators of their own demise.[69]

The wildlife extinctions and deforestation that followed Polynesian settlement throughout the Pacific were real enough; however, it is important to appreciate that there is little, if anything, to differentiate these 'first contact' impacts from those of European whalers, sealers or kauri loggers.[70] Just as conscientious citizens today work to rein in unsustainable exploitation of fossil fuels, deep-sea fisheries and old-growth forest, Polynesians made sincere attempts to manage their own impact. This is evident from the Polynesian term rāhui, which refers to a closed season declared on a resource – fish, birds, timber, bark, berries, etc. – in an effort to ensure ongoing supply and to protect its vitality. From the shared use of this term across most of Polynesia we can see that the practice and the philosophy behind it predate the settlement of New Zealand, Easter Island and the Hawaiian Islands. Then, as now, its effectiveness was limited by the immediate survival needs of a growing human population.

The myth of a single origin

Europeans have often sought to find a single origin for Māori in their traditions. But before the arrival of Europeans in New Zealand there was no unified historical account, and no need of one; tribal groups told their own stories. With good intentions perhaps, ethnologist Percy Smith attempted to 'tidy up' these diverse accounts in the late 19th century by amalgamating them, but this new history was not universally welcomed. By 1933, Sir Āpirana Ngata was already concerned: 'I think a lot of mischief has been done by Percy Smith in giving the impression of a great fleet, that bore down on New Zealand in the fourteenth century.'[71] The arrival of a single fleet had a heroic ring to it, but carried a misleading implication that the migratory canoes had all sailed from a single origin. In reality, some may have sailed in pairs,[72] as European ships often did, but there was nothing contained in the original traditions to suggest a fleet. As Margaret Orbell, a scholar of Māori texts, pointed out back in 1991, 'the range of mythological ideas, narratives and names known to have been brought to [New Zealand] may well turn out to have been too great to have been carried in the heads of people coming here from a single area in Central [East] Polynesia'.[73]

Their discovery of New Zealand must have been an important moment. In proportion to the land area hitherto settled by Polynesians, it was analogous to Europeans finding North America. (Although one important difference is that New Zealand was not already occupied.) The rigs, hull designs and wayfinding skills of Pacific navigators are fully consistent with two-way voyaging, allowing news of their discoveries to spread. There is little to suggest that New Zealand was a special case; hence, news of its discovery is likely to have drawn voyagers from many atolls and islands.[74]

In this early period, AD 1250–1450, canoes may have continued to arrive in New Zealand from a number of atolls and islands in the Society Islands, Southern Cook Islands, Austral Islands, Rapa Iti and the Tuamotus.[75] There is nothing to preclude individuals, or a whole canoeload, arriving via this central East Polynesian region from more distant isles, too, including the Marquesas, Mangareva, Pitcairn, Northern Cook and Line islands; or perhaps from the Hawaiian Islands or Easter Island. Others may have sailed here from northern atolls in West Polynesia, such as Tūvalu and

Shifting the credit

In the 1930s Thor Heyerdahl proposed that Polynesians were incapable of making and erecting the remarkable stone statues on Easter Island,[76] and that these can only have been made and placed there by white-skinned South Americans. In the 1960s Erich Von Däniken assured his readers that space aliens were responsible. In the 1990s, Gavin Menzies opined that credit should go to the Chinese, not only for the Easter Island statues, but for the introduction to New Zealand of pigs and horses.[77] By stretching out the impressive routes of trade sailed by Zheng He (Cheng Ho) 1405–1433 (page 225), Menzies had him circumnavigating the world. In 2012, Maxwell Hill went on to propose that credit for the discovery of New Zealand really lay with the Greeks.[78] This genre of 'alternative history' is hugely popular; its main hallmarks are: cherry-picking evidence to fit a theory; refusing to engage meaningfully with glaring gaps in 'their evidence' or with far simpler interpretations of the same facts; and a perceived conspiracy by others to destroy evidence and hide the truth.

Te Rangi Hīroa holding a taiaha, circa 1930.

Tokelau, or the Northern Polynesian Outliers. In reality, we may never know all their ports of departure, but this should not distract us from their overall achievement. From wherever the ancestors of Māori left, they crossed great expanses of ocean to reach New Zealand, out of sight of land for weeks – when others of their race were fanning out across the Pacific to find and settle all of East Polynesia.

At this point in European history, in AD 1250, Portuguese mariners had just begun making their first modest forays along the coastlines of France, England, Spain and the Mediterranean; it would be another 250 years before Europeans had the confidence to embark on ocean voyages of comparable length. Christopher Columbus sailed into the Atlantic in 1492, followed by Portuguese mariner Ferdinand Magellan who discovered a route into the Pacific via the south of South America in 1520.

One nation

Over the next three centuries, more European expeditions continued to arrive in the Pacific – from Spain, Portugal, Holland, France and England. By the time Captain James Cook reached the Pacific in 1769, some 48 expeditions and a total of 97 ships had gone before him.[79] What distinguished Cook's voyages through Polynesia was that they were unusually thorough, with a clear scientific focus. His three Pacific voyages gave him a uniquely broad firsthand perspective of the region before the full impact of European discovery was felt. For this reason, his impressions of Polynesia recorded in February 1778, not long before his death, provide us with a particularly lucid window into the past.

> How shall we account for this nation's having spread itself, in so many detached islands, so widely disjoined from each other, in every quarter of the Pacific Ocean? We find it, from New Zealand, in the South, as far as the Sandwich Islands [Hawai`i], to the North, and, in another direction, from Easter Island, to the Hebrides [Vanuatu]; that is, over an extent of sixty degrees of latitude, or twelve hundred leagues north and south, and eighty-three degrees of longitude, or sixteen hundred and sixty leagues east and west! How much farther in either direction its colonies reach is not known; but what we know already, in consequence of this and our former voyage, warrants our pronouncing it to be, though perhaps not the most numerous, certainly by far the most extensive, nation upon earth.[80]

Having opened this book with the words of Te Rangi Hīroa from *Vikings of the Sunrise*, let us hear his voice again in response to one of the many songs that honour the canoes that sailed for New Zealand:

> How can their fame be e'er forgot
> When they float for aye on memory's tide!

'Oh, poet's faith!' Te Rangi Hīroa replies, 'How indeed, unless our blood becomes so diluted that it fails to stir at the sound of our own speech?'[81]

Acknowledgements

The seed for this book was planted during a visit to the Hawaiian Islands in 1986, where I learnt that the forest vine known to native Hawaiians as `ie`ie is the direct equivalent of an almost identical vine in New Zealand known as kiekie. Shortly after this Dr Wendy Pond gave me a printed copy of a comparative dictionary of Polynesian languages, from which I learnt that these two terms are cognates (direct equivalents) of the same word and that such cognate words can be used to link languages spoken on islands right across the Pacific. I discovered that, although many Māori terms are widespread throughout the Pacific, others can be traced to quite specific regions; several are shared only with Rarotonga and/or Tahiti, for example, and others are shared exclusively with other archipelagos.

I was only dimly aware of where many of these islands were when friends Martine Cadet and Philippe Leroy invited me to join them on a trans-Pacific voyage through the Marquesas, the Tuamotus and Society Islands. Sailing through these atolls and islands over the next few months in 2006 gave me a fuller appreciation of Polynesian culture and history. Here, many others helped me: archaeologists, ornithologists and botanists, including Eric Olivier, Catherine Chavaillon, Dr Pierre Ottino and Dr Jean-Yves Meyer in the Marquesas Islands, and Dr Michael Poole and Dr Philippe Raust in the Society Islands. Others along the way introduced me to aspects of their own culture: Inatio Raveino and Jean Kape in the Tuamotus, George Estall on Tahiti, Henare, my guide to Taputapuātea marae on Ra`iātea, and Ed Saul, Man Unuia, George Mateariki, Bazza Ross and Gerald McCormack on Rarotonga and `Ātiu.

It was my interest in the origins of Māori plant names that really opened my eyes to the remarkable voyaging achievements of Polynesians and to the vast region over which their culture and heritage had spread.

On my return to New Zealand, many archaeologists, linguists, geneticists, botanists, ornithologists and anthropologists helped fill in more details. In particular, I would like to thank Drs Geoffrey Irwin, Nigel Prickett, Brian Gill, Art Whistler, Brian Molloy, Ewen Cameron, Geoff Chambers, Bruce McFadgen, David Addison, Jean-Christophe Galipaud, Ross Clark, Richard Moyle, Christophe Sand, Margaret Orbell, James Goff, Matiu Prebble, Paul Geraghty, Andrew Pawley, Melinda Allen, Marshall Weisler, Patrick McCoy, Susan Thorpe, Mara Mulrooney and Matt Rayner.

Non-specialists and friends helped in other ways: Jola Martysz interpreted many of my draft maps and graphics, while Anaru Leigh, Will Ord, Michael Highburger, Bob Kay, John Longden, David Corcoran, Richard McLachlan, Simon McDonald, Amy Ayres, Peter Whitmore, David Williams, Jean Rawlinson, John Lennane, Robbie Burton, Sam Elworthy, Catherine Montgomery and Juergen Heil all took time to read and comment on various sections or versions of draft manuscripts.

To transform a personal fascination into a finished book often requires a lot of support and encouragement. Here, I would particularly like to thank Drs David Tipene-Leach, Sally Abel and Rāwiri Taonui; also Glen Molesworth and Candice Paewai. They, and others who know me, know that this 'last mile' was particularly tough. Winning a place in the New Zealand Society of Authors Manuscript Assessment Programme in 2014 certainly helped, bringing science editor Susanna Lyle to my aid. However, it was philanthropist Dr Simon McDonald who provided the final push to bring the book to publication, when he informed me that it was his reading of an earlier draft of this book that moved him to provide financial backing and direction for the Māori Youth Development waka voyaging project *Hawaiki Rising*. One last hurdle remained, though: where to obtain funds for the book's production – an obstacle overcome at the eleventh hour through a substantial grant to the publishers from Creative New Zealand.

A heartfelt thanks to you all. Ehara taku toa, he takitahi, he toa takitini. (I acknowledge that my journey is not one that I walk alone, it is one that involves many.)

Andrew Crowe, Aotearoa New Zealand, 2018

Key to Language Globes

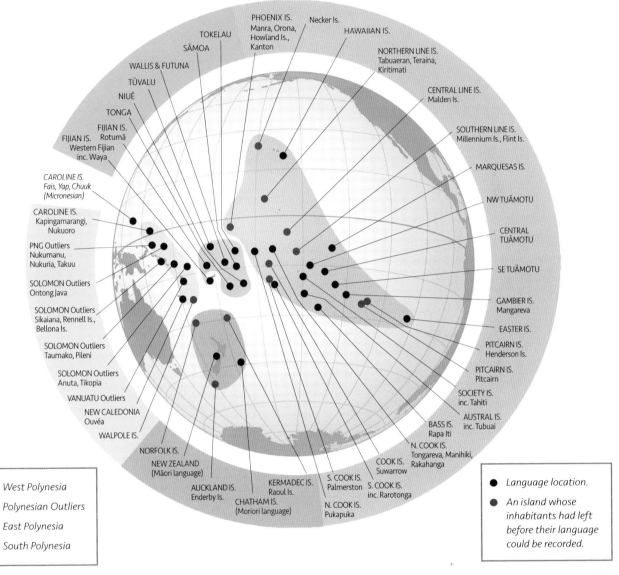

PHOENIX IS.
Manra, Orona, Howland Is., Kanton

Necker Is.

TOKELAU

HAWAIIAN IS.

SĀMOA

NORTHERN LINE IS.
Tabuaeran, Teraina, Kiritimati

WALLIS & FUTUNA

CENTRAL LINE IS.
Malden Is.

TŪVALU

NIUĒ

TONGA

SOUTHERN LINE IS.
Millennium Is., Flint Is.

FIJIAN IS.
Rotumā

FIJIAN IS.
Western Fijian inc. Waya

MARQUESAS IS.

CAROLINE IS.
Fais, Yap, Chuuk (Micronesian)

NW TUĀMOTU

CAROLINE IS.
Kapingamarangi, Nukuoro

CENTRAL TUĀMOTU

PNG Outliers
Nukumanu, Nukuria, Takuu

SE TUĀMOTU

SOLOMON Outliers
Ontong Java

GAMBIER IS.
Mangareva

SOLOMON Outliers
Sikaiana, Rennell Is., Bellona Is.

EASTER IS.

SOLOMON Outliers
Taumako, Pileni

PITCAIRN IS.
Henderson Is.

SOLOMON Outliers
Anuta, Tikopia

PITCAIRN IS.
Pitcairn

VANUATU Outliers

SOCIETY IS.
inc. Tahiti

NEW CALEDONIA
Ouvéa

AUSTRAL IS.
inc. Tubuai

WALPOLE IS.

BASS IS.
Rapa Iti

NORFOLK IS.

N. COOK IS.
Tongareva, Manihiki, Rakahanga

NEW ZEALAND
(Māori language)

COOK IS.
Suwarrow

AUCKLAND IS.
Enderby Is.

KERMADEC IS.
Raoul Is.

S. COOK IS.
Palmerston

S. COOK IS.
inc. Rarotonga

CHATHAM IS.
(Moriori language)

N. COOK IS.
Pukapuka

- West Polynesia
- Polynesian Outliers
- East Polynesia
- South Polynesia

- ● Language location.
- ● An island whose inhabitants had left before their language could be recorded.

The language globes found throughout this book tell a story of connections, showing how the language of New Zealand Māori is closely allied with that of other Polynesians, and especially so with East Polynesia. Each one maps the Pacific distribution of a particular Māori word used in the text and its recognisable equivalents (or cognates). The position of each dot corresponds with a dot on the larger globe above, which identifies the location where that particular cognate is recorded.

NEW ZEALAND MĀORI	ELSEWHERE IN POLYNESIA MAY BECOME
h as in haka (dance)	an s as in saka, or a 'glottal stop' as in `aka
k as in Hawaiki (homeland)	a 'glottal stop' as in Hawai`i
ng as in rangi (sky)	an n as in rani, or g as in ragi
p as in pipi (a kind of shellfish)	a b as in bibi
r as in marae (public meeting place)	an l as in malae, or a 'glottal stop' as in me`ae
t as in taro (a vegetable)	a d as in dalo, or k as in kalo
w as in weri (centipede)	a v as in veri
wh as in whai (stingray)	an f as in fai, v as in vai or h as in hai

Endnotes

Chance or Skill? [pp. 12–15]

1 Anderson (2014b: 26).
2 Te Rangi Hīroa (1938b: v).
3 Sharp (1964: 52).
4 Sharp (1956b: 155). Sharp's view was shared by the *Encyclopaedia of New Zealand*: 'present-day historians... believe that such arrivals were the result of accidental voyages rather than of organised attempts to migrate and colonise'. McLintock (ed.) (1966, Vol. 2: 88).
5 When more than 150 such voyages were tabulated and mapped by Golson (1962), almost all proved to be west-bound and within the tropical belt.
6 Sharp (1971: 35).
7 A quote from Sir William Deane, former Governor-General of Australia, Inaugural Vincent Lingiari Memorial Lecture, Aug 1996.
8 Anderson (2014b: 26), McLintock (ed.) (1966, Vol. 2: 88), Sharp (1971: 35).
9 McLintock (ed.) (1966, Vol. 1: 55): 'the study of adze types strongly suggests the Society Group of islands as the Hawaiki (or homeland) of the New Zealand Maori'. Sutton (ed.) (1994) gives: 'central East Pacific'. Davidson (1994: 216) gives: 'somewhere in Eastern Polynesia'.
10 King (2003: 46, 49): 'a significant number of migration canoes ... set out from an East Polynesian interaction sphere', 'including 'the Society, Marquesas, Austral and Cook groups'. To this, Prickett (2001: 19) adds the more distant Tuamotu and Marquesas groups, even Mangareva or Pitcairn Island as possibilities.

1 Out On a Limb [pp. 16–33]

1 Heyerdahl (1960: 84): 'One thing is certain: this was not the work of a canoe-load of Polynesian wood-carvers'; Heyerdahl (1960: 97): 'A wave of war and cannibalism swept over the island... When this genuine Polynesian wave arrived, all cultural life came to an abrupt end'; Heyerdahl (1960: 329): 'One thing is certain: they [Polynesians] must have reached Easter Island last, perhaps only a hundred years or so before the Europeans came'.
2 Visibility based on an elevation of 507 m, a calm sea and observer viewing from 3 m above sea level. (Isla Sala y Gómez, Manu Motu Motiro Hiva, about 400 km ENE of Easter Island, is no more than a rocky outcrop and uninhabitable.)
3 Palmer (1870). Fischer (2005: 91): Easter Islanders compared geographical notes with Rapans, 'thereby discovering that Rapa ("Extremity") was indeed only Rapa `Iti ("Lesser Extremity"), whereas Easter Island was Rapa Nui ("Greater Extremity/Land's End"). The name being incomprehensible as such in the Easter Island language, they translated this as Te Pito `o te Henua ("The End of the Land")'.
4 Roggeveen quoted in Corney (ed.) (1903).
5 Davis (2008). Much of Heyerdahl's 'evidence' has since been overturned; his conclusions regarding the introduction of plants proved invalid when the relevant pollen was shown to considerably predate the arrival of humans. See Fischer (1992) regarding linguistic conclusions of Langdon and Tryon (1983).
6 Raro`ia is some 3620 km from Easter Island; Callao to Easter Island is 3745 km.
7 Ostensibly to avoid coastal traffic, but through a very wide stretch of northbound current, flowing at 20 cm/ sec.
8 According to tests conducted by Irwin (1992: 164), notwithstanding the climate findings subsequent published by Goodwin et al. (2014) that a route from further south (Chile) to Easter Island was theoretically open between AD 910–950, 1140–1170, and 1230–1250.
9 The significance of non-Polynesian DNA in the modern population is discussed below.
10 A fathom is traditionally an arm-span (6 feet); the equivalent traditional unit of measurement used by Polynesians for measuring canoes and tapa cloth was the same, a ngafa or rofa (arm-span).
11 Ti (Pacific Island cabbage tree) is not listed by Cook, but is listed in the Rapanui dictionary by Englert (1993) as 'long, thick root, cooked in the earth oven, is deliciously sweet'. The remaining Easter Island names are known to New Zealand Māori as kūmara, māika (transferred to edible tubers of orchids and rengarenga lily), tō (transferred to the sweetish stem of raupō), moa, aute, taro, uwhi, hue and kiore.
12 Besides toromiro, ngā`atu, hauhau and tavai already mentioned, indigenous plants that cling to clothes are known here as piripiri, and a large fern species as nehenehe. Among birds, the red-tailed tropicbird (*Phaethon rubricauda*) is known here as tavake, sooty tern (*Onychoprion fuscatus* syn. *Sterna*) as manu-tara, white tern (*Gygis alba*) as kiakia, frigate bird (*Fregata* sp.) as makohe (a name shared only with the Tuamotus, Mangareva and the Marquesas), one species of petrel/shearwater as taīko, another as kumara (cognate with that for *Puffinus pacificus* on Tūvalu) and a booby (*Sula*) as kuia. For invertebrates, veri for centipede, pepa or peparere for butterfly, potupotu for beetles, takaure for fly and ngū for squid. Biggs and Clark (2006). For fish, see Randall and Egaña (1984).
13 A point discussed at length by Fischer (1992): 'Consistent with the archaeological, anthropological, and genetic data available to date is the verdict here that in the oldest Rapanui documents there is not a shred of linguistic evidence to justify considering a possible non-Polynesian substrate or a second Polynesian wave of settlers on the island.'
14 The 'not wholly authentic narrative' of Behrens did report: 'The natives prepare their meals in pots made of clay or earth. Each household appeared to us to have its own,' but Roggeveen's report is more credible and consistent with the archaeological evidence: 'It was incomprehensible to us how these people cook their food, for no one was able to perceive or find that they had any earthen pots, pans, or vessels.'
15 Hagelberg (1993). A small Native American influence has been detected in the DNA from blood samples collected from present-day Easter Islanders; however, most researchers attribute this to the Peruvian slave trade (1862) or to one or more crew members of Amerindian descent arriving here after Roggeveen (or perhaps earlier on a Polynesian sailing canoe). Hurles et al. (2003), Ghiani et al. (2005, 2006), Lie et al. (2007), Thorsby et al. (2009), Marshall (2011), Thorsby (2012).
16 Beck et al. (2003) quoted in Diamond (2005). Martinsson-Wallin and Crockford (2001) add that 'ceremonial sites with worked stones appear to be associated with activities occurring later than the initial settlement,' and see Table 2: Radiocarbon dates of ceremonial structures. See also Solsvik and Wallin (2007).
17 Lipo and Hunt (2005) estimate '14,000 tons' of stone was moved. According to Lipo et al. (2013), nearly 1000 statues were carved here, of which about 500 were transported along roads.
18 Best (1924b: 193) questioned the use of rollers by Māori, but individual rollers are named in tradition (Te Tahuri, Mounukuhia, Mouhapainga, and Manutawhio-rangi for the *Tākitimu*). This is reflected in the following Māori terms for roller: neke, ngaro, rango, tauru. The term rango is shared with several Polynesians languages, where it is often identified specifically as the rollers used for beaching or launching a canoe.
19 The trunk of the Tāne Mahuta kauri is estimated to be 244.5 m³, weighing (at 560 kg/m³) about 137 tonnes.
20 Best (1925c: 103). This property of whauwhaupaku (five finger, *Pseudopanax arboreus*) is alluded to in alternative Māori names, parapara ('spittle') and tauparapara (tau meaning 'suitable' or – in several Polynesian languages – 'to beach a canoe').
21 Best (1925c: 103). The number of haulers quoted here refers to a canoe being moved on Rarotonga.
22 Hunt and Lipo (2011), Lipo et al. (2013).
23 Best (1925c: 111).
24 Lipo and Hunt (2005).
25 In New Zealand, variations of this meaning of ahu as a sacred place occur in the terms ahumairangi, ahurewa and tūāahu (tūāhu).
26 Kirch (1990). On Savai`i (Sāmoa), 30,000 cubic metres were moved to construct a massive, tapering stone house platform of the Pulemelei Mound, some 50 m x 60 m at the base and 12 m high.
27 As described by Captain Cook.
28 Koskinen (1973), Crowe (2012, 2013, 2014). The Chatham Islands and Huahine (Society Is) link was identified by Skinner (1931), although clubs of comparable design are also found much further west, in Ontong Java (Solomons). Re sports and games, see Fischer (1992). Re place

names, see Barthel (1962), Koskinen (1973: 27). Many terms denoting human relationships (hina for grandchild, hinarere for great grandchild, koro for father) and important parts of the human body (rau`oho for hair, roro for brain, ketekete for belly, pātehe/petehe for castrate, vari for menstruation, henua or pū-henua for placenta) are also East Polynesian, as are the 'nights of the moon' (tireo, hiro, maharu, atua, ohua, hotu, maure, rākau, kokore, `orongo, mauri kero, `omutu). Biggs and Clark (2006).

29 Green (2000a), Jones et al. (eds) (2011). This conclusion is supported by closely related styles of religious sites found on South Marutea (SE Tuamotus), Mangareva (and neighbouring Temoe) and Pitcairn Island (Green 2000a), and maternal DNA from the earliest known remains of introduced Pacific rat on Easter Island, which finds its best match on Mangareva (Barnes et al. 2006). This scenario is consistent also with shared artefact styles and human skeletal characteristics (Green 2000a), and with simulated and actual voyaging demonstrating the practicability of locating Easter Island from the region of Mangareva, sailing via Henderson and Pitcairn Islands.

30 Steadman (2006: 251).

31 I find no direct reference to Polynesians making navigational use of pet petrels, but it would be surprising if they did not do so, for Herald petrels (*Pterodroma heraldica*) are sometimes kept as pets in Tonga, and one Manx shearwater (*Puffinus puffinus*) released in Boston was observed to home across the Atlantic to its colony on Skokholm Island, Wales within 13 days – a distance of over 4900 km. Jenkins (1973: 115). Note the fact that 'two pied titi, pet birds of Timu' are associated with the *Tākitimu* canoe.

32 E.g., the Juan Fernández petrel (*Pterodroma externa*), which still breeds on Juan Fernández Islands (Chile).

33 Steadman (2006: 251).

34 Subfossil evidence reveals that Easter Island and its offshore islets were formerly home to at least one species of heron, two rails, two parrots, and at least 25 nesting species of seabirds, including albatross, boobies, frigatebirds, fulmars, petrels, prions, shearwaters, storm petrels, terns and tropicbirds, and yet Easter Island and its surrounding islets nowadays support just 20 species of native birds, all either seabirds or shorebirds: petrels, shearwaters, tropicbirds, frigatebirds, boobies, terns, noddies, wandering tattler and sanderling. Invertebrates, including the island's endemic landsnails, suffered an equally grim fate. Kirch et al. (2009).

35 The positions given in his journal are 30° 30'S; 101° 45'W for the frigatebirds; and 27° 4'S; 103° 58'W for the terns ('egg birds'), noddies, tropicbirds and shearwaters.

36 Gould (1974), Flint (1991). On approach to Easter Island 6 Mar 1774, Cook began seeing sooty terns (near the close of their 'foraging for young' season) over 500 km east of the island (at 27° 4'S; 103° 58'W).

37 'Song of the Birds of the Sea Kings'. Stimson (1957: 215). The context removes any ambiguity as to whether this might alternatively refer to the bird's ability to locate shoals of fish.

38 The crew of the Polynesian-style *Hōkūle`a*, sailing to Easter Island from Hawai`i via Mangareva and Pitcairn Islands in 1999 describe another aid to finding the island. Approaching the island from the west (upwind) on 9 Oct with only non-instrument methods of navigation, they criss-crossed the island's known latitude until just before sunrise when their navigator reported seeing its shadow projected over the horizon.

39 According to http://www.windfinder.com/windstatistics/easter_island; although Goodwin et al. (2014) found evidence for persistent westerly wind anomalies AD 800–820, 830–910, 1010–1030, 1040–1060, 1080–1100, 1290–1440, 1500–1540, 1550–1570, and 1590–1610.

40 Steadman et al. (1994). Martinsson-Wallin and Crockford (2001): 'the majority of fish types found in the deposit live in habitats ranging from 500 m to over 1000 m offshore. This suggests the utilization of offshore fishing strategies, including seaworthy crafts, and fishing techniques such as trolling, long-line angling, and net fishing.' Harpoons were used to spear deep-water fish such as tuna. (Bones of seals also appear in middens here.) By around 1500, the dolphin bones have all but vanished from the refuse heaps. Steadman et al. (1994).

41 Roggeveen quoted in Corney (ed.) (1903: 150, 156): 'mother-of-pearl shells as ornaments about their necks' and 'the mother-of-pearl which was seen as a neck pendant is a flat shell of the same tint as the inner lip of our oysters'. Although species of Pterioidea (including a 3-cm wide *Isognomon incisum*) and Ostreoidea are found on Easter Island, no *Pinctada* or decorative equivalent has been recorded. Raines and Huber (2012). Reipā in Englert (1993), is unambiguously defined as 'mother-of-pearl'. Refer to several specimens collected from Easter Island held in the British Museum (Oc1920,0506.219, Oc1920,0506.220, Oc1920,0506.221). For *Pinctada margaritifera* on Ducie, see Rehder and Randall (1975).

42 According to Colenso quoted in Kirk (1889), toromiro is recorded as a name for miro chiefly from the East Cape. On Rarotonga, toromiro applies to *Schleinitzia insularum*; in Tahitian to *Thespesia populnea*.

43 Mieth and Bork (2010).

44 Diamond (1995: 68).

45 As Hunt (2007) puts it, Diamond's narrative turns 'the victims of cultural and physical extermination . . . into the perpetrators of their own demise'. By using what most now agree is an inflated pre-contact estimate of the human population of the island, Diamond not only exaggerates the population crash, but also shifts its timing back enabling him to link it more strongly with environmental degradation. In fact, the crash was caused by contact with Europeans.

46 Hunt and Lipo (2013) emphasise the damage caused by rats, whereas Mieth and Bork (2010) see fire as the primary cause of the palm forest's demise. Evidently, it was both. Cox and Elmqvist (2000) have also linked the palm's extinction to a demise in pollinating birds, such as a now-extinct parrot. The rat population figure is from Hunt and Lipo (2009a).

47 This slash and burn activity evidently reached a peak AD 1250–1500. In central Chile, small rodents and *Jubaea* palms do coexist and there is one area of Easter Island where evidence of palm regeneration follows first clearing and many *undamaged* seeds can be found. Mieth and Bork (2010), Prebble and Dowe (2008), Rull et al. (2010). Palm forest was evidently cleared for planting taro on the Hawaiian Islands, Rapa and Rimatara (Austral Is), too. Stevenson et al. (2006).

48 Elevitch (ed.) (2006). In Tonga, typical bole lengths on mature trees of 10 m and typical diameters at breast height of 30–50 cm permit trunks to be hewn into boards for traditional sewn-plank canoes. Another suitable local timber for paddles was Polynesian elaeocarpus (*Elaeocarpus tonganus*), a 20-m-tall tree with tough white timber, traditionally valued for this purpose in Rarotonga and the Austral Islands. Hunt and Lipo (2013: 177) assert that 'Palm trees are. . . not useful as sources of wood for canoes as their interior is soft and spongy with a brittle bark exterior'; however, coconut trunks were so used in the Marquesas Islands, Rakahanga (N. Cook Is) and elsewhere.

49 Anderson (2000b).

50 Small sails made from ngā`atu were occasionally used on Lake Titicaca (Heiser 1978); and leaves of its New Zealand namesake, ngatu, were laced together in a double layer as sails, but only for canoes sailed in sheltered waters. A shortage of sail-making fibre on Easter Island is consistent with the fact that Rapanui made mats of rushes sewn together with bast fibre, and banana bark for plaiting material – neither use recorded from elsewhere in Polynesia. Te Rangi Hīroa (1945: 15).

51 On Mangaia and `Ātiu (S. Cook Is) the use of this reed as sails is likewise unknown. Whistler (1990), McCormack (2007). On Easter Island, these rushes were sewn together with bast fibre – a technique unknown from elsewhere in Polynesia; similarly unique was the local method of plaiting rush baskets with the outer skins of the trunks of banana palms. Te Rangi Hīroa (1945: 15). But this material is again unlikely to have been serviceable at sea. Although the leaves of *Freycinetia* vines have been used elsewhere for sails, there is no evidence that these ever grew on Easter Island.

52 Despite the fact that the past presence of pandanus is easily picked up in the pollen record, no such evidence has been found here.

53 At least one of these pandanus varieties is thought likely to have been introduced by Polynesians. Florence et al. (1995). Pandanus is and was also present on Pitcairn Is Horrocks and Weisler (2006). Plant residues found on volcanic glass (ignimbrite) artefacts on Henderson by Weisler and Haslam (2005) revealed uses that 'included slicing soft plant materials (possibly leaves or green plant stems)'. According to Rehder and Randall (1975) and Florence et al. (1995), Pandanus does not occur on Ducie.

54 The prehistoric presence of coconuts and candlenut trees on Henderson Is has been determined from remains in habitation sites. Waldren et al. (1999). (Coconut was subsequently planted on Easter Island, though few produce mature fruit.) Roggeveen observes that caulking was a problem for Easter Islanders: 'But as they lack the knowledge and particularly the materials for caulking and making tight the great number of seams of the canoes, these are accordingly very leaky, for which reason they are compelled to spend half the time in bailing.'

55 Anderson (2009b).

56 Green (2001: 71–72), Weisler and Green (2001: 420, 423, 440) support the idea that Easter Island maintained contact with East Polynesia through Henderson, Pitcairn and Mangareva, based partly on 'one-piece fishhook type in stone shared between Pitcairn and Rapa Nui', which suggest to them 'a post-settlement period linkage of Pitcairn with Rapa Nui. The strong indication is that these kinds of stone fishhooks may have been

invented on Rapa Nui, where there are no natural supplies of pearl shell, and then taken to Pitcairn to which pearl shells, or fishhooks in that material, were being imported from Mangareva.' Likewise, Solsvik and Wallin (2007) 'suggest that the development of ritual architecture in East Polynesia, or of the so-called marae-ahu complex might have occurred in the south-eastern edge of the region rather than in the central archipelagos of the Cooks, Tuamotus, and Societies'. Anderson and Kennett (eds) (2012: 254) also acknowledge that 'Easter Island had sweet potato, taro, yam, banana and sugarcane, a range sufficiently large to suggest that initial colonisation might have involved a number of canoes or some two-way voyaging'.

57 A computer drift simulation was set up by Montenegro et al. (2007) to illustrate the potential mechanism of natural transfer; however, this did not take into account how long the seeds remain viable inside a capsule while buoyant in saltwater. Green (2005: 43). Some early bottle-gourd seeds of Polynesians have a genetic profile consistent with a source in South America (page 187). Some researchers might add soapberry (*Sapindus saponaria*) to the list – a small tree of the American tropics that may also have reached Polynesia in pre-European times.

58 The same would apply to the claim by Anderson et al. (2007) that known contact between Polynesia and South America was instigated by Amerindians aboard Ecuadorian sailing rafts.

59 Green (2005: 43): setting out 'from the Mangarevan–Pitcairn-Rapa Nui (Easter Island) region'.

60 This site is on the Arauco Peninsula in south central Chile. The first chicken bone, radiocarbon dated to AD 1304–1424, revealed a mtDNA sequence typical of the mtDNA of chickens from Tonga, Sāmoa, Niuē, Hawai`i and Easter Island. Similar results followed. Storey et al. (2007), critique by Gongora et al. (2008a, 2008b) and responses by Storey et al. (2008, 2011, 2013). The finding was again challenged by Thomson et al. (2014a), with various counter-challenges later that same year (Beavan 2014, Bryant 2014, Storey and Matisoo-Smith 2014, Thomson et al. 2014b). Matisoo-Smith and Ramirez (2010) present craniometric analyses for the six complete crania from Mocha Island, Chile, three of which are identified as having some Polynesian ancestry, Mocha being a windswept island some 30 km off the Chilean coast and just 100 km from where the chicken bones were found.

61 Ramírez-Aliaga (2011: 103). (The Mapuche language is also known as Mapudungun.) Polynesian-style sewn-plank canoes were in use nearby in pre-Spanish times, and the term 'oué-lée' for 'a spear or harpoon' in the Kawésqar language (spoken by the maritime Alakaluf people further south along the Chilean coast) may be ultimately derived from the Polynesian term 'welo' for 'stab or spear' from the Hawaiian term for a short spear, `ēlau. Klar (2011: 205). Striking stylistic similarities have been identified between the Chilean 'clava mere okewa' of this region and the Polynesian patu hand clubs (known in Māori also as mere), though none yet from a 'secure archaeological context'. Anderson (2014b: 25) is sceptical.

62 At the southern end – off the Chilean coast – this upwelling is at its strongest in spring and summer.

63 For example by Anderson et al. (2007).

64 Ballard et al. (eds) (2005) and Jones et al. (eds) (2011).

65 Roullier et al. (2013). Further support for this as a source region of Polynesian tubers is found in a historic variety of kūmara in the Hawaiian and Society islands whose distinctive leaf form is evidently shared only along the coast of northern Peru. Green (2005: 56). The genetic diversity of the vegetable in the Pacific suggests to researchers multiple introductions of this vegetable to the Pacific and from more than one source in tropical America. Scaglion (2005: 40), Green (2005: 47). Likewise, for Polynesian bottle-gourd seeds, more than one American source for Pacific plants is considered plausible.

66 Scaglion and Cordero (2011: 177), Scaglion (2005: 36).

67 Green (2005: 54) observed that 'only in Rapanui language does kumara with the short u occur as an ancient introduction, a factor militating against this island as the ultimate source of the term in proto-CEP or as the place where it was initially introduced to east Polynesia'. Again quoting Green (2005: 51) – 'a large number of inland field systems and 'rock gardens' [on Easter Island], where the sweet potato is inferred to have been the main plant under cultivation during the Expansion Phase from 1100 to 1600 AD'.

68 Although Green (2005: 48–49) concluded that the vegetable may have been of rather marginal importance in the Marquesas and in the Society Is, more 'as a supplementary food crop in times of scarcity', starch residue from shell tools on the Marquesas reveal the use of kūmara from the 14th century AD onward. Allen and Ussher (2013).

69 According to Green (2005: 48–53), kūmara may have been traditionally grown on Rurutu (Austral Is) and was known (though perhaps not

grown) in the Tuamotus, yet evidently not grown on Rarotonga (S. Cook Is) prior to 1832. Horrocks and Weisler (2006) identified 'starch grains and xylem cells of *Ipomoea* sp., possibly introduced *I. batatas*, in Pitcairn Island deposits dated to the last few centuries before European contact in 1790'. Tubers were not introduced to Tonga, etc. until the late 18th century and no European references have been found to the presence of sweet potato in late 18th and 19th century sources on Niuē. Green (2005: 60).

70 Ballard et al. (eds) (2005).

71 Irwin (pers. comm. 28.05.2016). Irwin (1992: 164): in the case of simulated voyages aboard Polynesian-style canoes sailing to South America from the Marquesas, only two canoes (out of 3450) from this quarter reached South America.

72 Fischer (1992) concludes, 'Nothing in Rap's phonology would appear to support a "non-Polynesian substrate" or "second Polynesian wave" hypothesis – the Rap glottal stop /?/, for example, is wonderfully vestigial, proving a profound EPn time-depth . . .'

73 Much less than on, say, the Kermadec Islands or the Chatham Islands. Barnes et al. (2006) concede that this may be simply the result of 'arrivals to Rapa Nui from colonists who did not bring Pacific rats with them . . . [or] sustained migration to Rapa Nui by Polynesians bringing with them rats of a single genetic population'. It is noteworthy, too, that, as Anderson (2009b: 1510) points out, Pacific rats do not appear to have arrived on Mangareva until some 200 years after people.

74 Re drums, see Te Rangi Hīroa (1944: 456); re formal food pounders, see Te Rangi Hīroa (1944: 417); re archery, see Patole-Edoumba (1999: Figs 1 and 2).

75 Note that a collapse in regional trade is also evident in the region of Mangareva – around 1450.

76 Froyd et al. (2010).

77 Goff (2011).

78 Prof. James Goff (pers. comm. 25.11.2013), perhaps 'somewhere off the southern coast. . . and to the west of the southeast ridge'. Geologist and anthropologist Charles Love (2007) suggests that 'there may have been two paleo-tsunamis from the north, the older of which lambasted the main wall of the original platform [of Ahu Te Pito Kura] at the head of the bay'.

79 Okal et al. (2002).

80 The impact on Easter Island of the 1960 event, as recorded by Cristino (2002), Hamilton (2008) and Fritz et al. (2011), is judged comparable with that from one recorded in 1575. Fritz et al. (2011). The Tongariki platform was reconstructed with the aid of a crane and fortunately survived another tsunami from an earthquake off the Chilean coast in 2010, which generated a smaller run-up here of 4 m.

81 Comte and Pardo (1991), Cisternas et al. (2005). And – after Roggeveen's and Cook's visits – in 1868 and 1877.

82 Hamilton (2007).

83 Permanent and widespread settlement on the island is thought to have occurred by at least AD 1200 (Mulrooney 2013) (or AD 1200–1253 according to Wilmshurst et al. 2011). There is as yet no compelling evidence to support the much earlier dates widely quoted in popular sources.

84 Interestingly, early kūmara is not known from Rapa Iti. Anderson and Kennett (eds) (2012: 247). Ballard et al. (eds) (2005: 85) have linked the introduction of this drought-resistant tuber to Easter Island to the human energy required to achieve the island's megalithic grandeur.

85 Unlike individual items of obsidian or greenstone, New Zealand flax plants tend to remain highly visible. When introduced to the Hawaiian Islands (Hawai`i and Kaua`i) in the 1930s as an ornamental plant, it spread quickly to become a weed.

86 This is consistent with a recent review of linguistic evidence by Walworth (2014), which finds evidence of interarchipelago contact across much of East Polynesia, but not Easter Island, which was more isolated.

87 Of over 1000 Easter Island place names listed by Barthel (1962), at least 90 are found in New Zealand, occurring at a density far higher than that recorded for the Society Islands. Crowe (2012). The surprising strength of this link was picked up by Koskinen (1973: 27).

88 A population that, according to Hunt (2007), is likely to have been maintained for many centuries prior to that.

89 Pollard et al. (2010). More than 400 at a time came onto the frigate of Gonzales' expedition – according to officer Don Francisco Antonio, Chief Pilot, quoted in Corney (ed.) (1903: 303).

90 A conventional route for modern sailors (Wood and Wood 2005). Another route was demonstrated by the *Hōkūle`a* navigating without instruments in Nov 1999 to Tahiti via the Marquesas, from where trade winds ensure a relatively straightforward onward voyage to New Zealand.

91 See www.wakatapu.maori.nz, along with text reports by satellite phone from chief navigator Jack Thatcher reporting position en route, e.g. on 20 Sep 'about 560 n/miles off Tipuai' [sic]. [accessed 6-Mar-13]. For the original navigators, knowing where to turn north was probably heavily dependant on the presence of seabirds nesting on these islands in numbers that are scarcely imaginable now.

92 In New Zealand, for example, the leaves and namesake stems (ngatu) of the equivalent bulrush (raupō, *Typha orientalis*) were similarly used for making rafts, its leaves as thatching, for kites or laced together in a double layer as sails for canoes sailed in sheltered waters. Although the name 'raupō' links the New Zealand plant with the Cook Islands and Rapa Iti, 'ngatu' is a term shared with Easter Island (and – in a different form – with Hawaiʻi). In New Zealand Māori and the Tuāmotu islands, ngatu means 'crushed or mashed'. In Peru, however, where the Rapanui name is unknown, the giant bulrush is known as totora.

93 In New Zealand, tawai or tawhai refers to silver beech (*Nothofagus menziesii*), a tree whose bark was used by Māori to produce a black dye for colouring flax and cabbage tree leaves. This property may account for the origin of the Rapanui name as several overseas *Polygonum* species are used for dye. e.g., the leaves of Japanese indigo (*Polygonum tinctorium*) for a blue pigment, and other knotweeds (*Polygonum aviculare* and *Polygonum hydropiper*) used worldwide to produce indigo and yellow-gold pigments, respectively.

94 Prior to the 1870s, the term 'rongorongo' was evidently unknown in the Rapanui language, when it was adopted from the Mangarevan word for 'ritual chanters'. Fischer (1997), Flenley and Bahn (2002), Fischer (2005).

95 Using inflated estimates of the pre-contact population – 15,000 'up to 20,000' – enabled Diamond (1995, 2005) to shift the timing of this crash to predate European contact. Such a high population is far in excess of that which archaeological evidence supports. Hunt (2007), Fischer (2005), Hunt and Lipo (2007, 2009a, 2009b), Mulrooney (2009). Stevenson et al. (2015) note a pre-contact abandonment of leeward and interior locations, which they link with drought and loss of fertility.

96 When obsidian is chipped, water vapour begins to penetrate the fresh surface. Artefacts can be dated by measuring the depth of this 'hydration rind'. Re their use for cutting and scraping, see Hunt and Lipo (2007). The shape of the flakes was shown to be inconsistent with their use as effective weapons. Lipo et al. (2010). Mulrooney (2013) found no evidence of a major pre-European collapse.

97 Mulrooney et al. (2007).

98 Roggeveen quoted in Corney (ed.) (1903), Mulrooney et al. (2007).

99 Ghiani et al. (2006).

100 Corney (ed.) (1903: 153).

101 Quoted from Officer Don Francisco Antonio. Lieut. Alberto Olaondo quoted in Langdon (1995) estimated at that time of 'about 1000 to 1200'. Corney (ed.) (1903: 299). A thought-provoking account of the Spanish ritual from a Rapanui point of view is given by Edwards (2011).

102 Pollard et al. (2010); as documented by the slavers at the time. Maude (1981).

2 Dark Horses of the South [pp. 34–49]

1 Captain Cook's *Journal* 17 Mar 1774 (Beaglehole (ed.) 1967). Cook was aware that Henderson Is and Ducie Is (Pitcairn group) had been sighted in 1606 by Portuguese sailor Pedro Fernandez de Quirós. Lying within a six degree band of latitude, a loose chain of islands reaches from Easter Island across the Pacific to the Kermadecs and Norfolk Island.

2 At least, probably not in August or September, when westerlies are more common.

3 Easter Island at 27°S; Ducie at 25°S; Henderson at 24°S; Pitcairn Island at 25°S; Oeno at 24°S; Mangareva (Gambier Is) at 23°S, Rapa Iti (Bass Is) at 27°S, and Raʻivavae (Austral Is) at 24°S.

4 He named it 'Luna-puesta'. Markham (ed.) 1904: 192.

5 Including breeding pairs of petrels, Christmas shearwaters, white terns and red-tailed tropicbirds. http://www.birdlife.org/datazone/sitefactsheet.php?id=19788

6 Namely, the blue-tailed skink (*Emoia cyanura*) and the mourning gecko (*Lepidodactylus lugubris*) – both spread throughout most of the Pacific by Polynesians. Gill (1993), Rehder and Randall (1975). Although this gecko is parthenogenetic (i.e., a new population may theoretically be founded from a single egg rafting here), human-mediated transport is considered more likely. Brian Gill (pers. comm. 28.06.2012). Ducie was described by the Quirós crew as 'well-wooded', presumably in reference to *Heliotropium foertherianum* (= *Argusia argentea*), which can reach 5 m.

7 Although species of Pterioidea and Ostreoidea are found on Easter Island (namely, *Malleus regulus, Isognomon incisum, Isognomon nucleus,*

Parahyotissa inermis and *Neopycnodonte cochlear*), no *Pinctada* nor decorative equivalent has been recorded there. Raines and Huber (2012). Re *Pinctada margaritifera* on Ducie, see Rehder and Randall (1975).

8 Brooke (1995). This estimate is from 1991.

9 Gill and Hauber (2013).

10 Five million pairs. Brooke et al. (2010).

11 Gill (1993): The mourning gecko (*Lepidodactylus lugubris*), snake-eyed skink (*Cryptoblepharus poecilopleurus*), white-bellied skink (*Emoia cyanura*) and moth skink (*Lipinia noctua*).

12 The jumping spider is *Frigga crocata*. Benton and Lehtinen (1995). The landsnails are *Gastrocopta pediculus, Lamellidea oblonga* and *Pupisoma orcula*. Preece (1998). Also widely distributed with the aid of Polynesian canoes is the slightly larger 'graceful awl snail' (*Lamellaxis gracilis*), which can be up to 11 mm high.

13 Hather and Weisler (2000). Waldren et al. (1999) report coconut shell, wood, and husk at several sites on the North and East beaches: 'The earliest associated radiocarbon dates are calibrated between AD 1000 to 1390'.

14 Stefan et al. (2002).

15 Weisler (2002). A link to the northwest, too, was identified here by American anthropologist Yosihiko Sinoto in the style of the oldest stone tools from five natural caves and rockshelters that displayed a 'close affiliation with the early Marquesan culture'. Sinoto (1983a). Ducie Atoll some 360 km to the east would seem to be another possible source of pearl shell found on Henderson.

16 Turtles and red feathers harvested on Henderson are thought to have been sent to the larger island of Mangareva, Pitcairn sent fine-grained basalt for adzes to Henderson and to Mangareva, whose huge lagoon in turn supplied large, black-lipped pearl shell for fishhooks and ornaments, and inferior volcanic rocks for fashioning into tools or for use in cooking pits. Bone found on Henderson Is include those of Pacific rat and pig, and several now extinct birds: two endemic Henderson Island pigeons, an endemic ground dove and an endemic sandpiper (all of which had reduced powers of flight), whose loss is attributable at least partly to hunting by the Polynesian settlers, but probably also to introduction of the rats. Steadman and Olson (1985); Wragg and Weisler (1994); and Weisler and Woodhead (1995), whose first date of AD 1000 was subsequently brought forward. The turtle meat from Henderson was of green sea turtle (*Chelonia mydas*), which breeds on its shores Jan–Mar, and the source of the red feathers was the Henderson Island lorikeet (*Vini stepheni*). Weisler and Green (2001). The feathers may have served as gifts to be taken to other islands, including Easter Island.

17 Weisler (2005).

18 Goff et al. (2011a), narrowed down by Goff et al. (2012) to a tsunami around AD 1450 generated from the Tonga-Kermadec Trench, rather than from the coast of South America.

19 Gill and Hauber (2013).

20 Emory (1928b): 'This tool, however, was obviously designed for hafting. Though far more finely finished, it calls to mind the hafted knives of Easter Island and Chatham Islands described by Skinner'.

21 Te Rangi Hiroa (1938b: 223). Cook never visited the Pitcairn group. At least one of these statues (made of local volcanic tuff) had a trunk without legs and two five-fingered hands clasped on the abdomen in a characteristic Polynesian pose. (In some districts of New Zealand, carvings with five-fingered hands are common; in others, three-fingered hands, as found in the Cook Is)

22 Anderson (2009b).

23 Weisler (1994), Collerson and Weisler (2007).

24 This is mentioned here despite the distance (some 2075 km), not dissimilar to 2050 km to NW Tuamotus.

25 Gill and Hauber (2013).

26 Davidson (1984): '. . .The similarity between adzes from early New Zealand sites such as Wairau Bar and the undated collections from Pitcairn is particularly striking.' According to Emory (1928b) Pitcairn adzes 'are diversified beyond a range which might be expected from the various uses to which they are put. Differences in the cultures reaching out to Pitcairn alone will account for certain of the wide distinctions'.

27 The lizards are the blue-tailed skink (*Emoia cyanura*) and mourning gecko (*Lepidodactylus lugubris*). Gill (1993). Re adze head, see Emory (1928b); this was found by a crew member of the *Wild Wave*, which wrecked here in that year. At the southeast end, a patch of cannibal tomato (*Solanum viride*) is considered to be 'probably a Polynesian introduction'. Florence et al. (1995).

28 A stand of coconut trees at the north of the island is the result of a later introduction by the Pitcairn Islanders.

29 http://www.iucnredlist.org/details/22698039/0 Today, the atoll supports

12,500 breeding pairs of Murphy's petrel and 500–1000 breeding pairs of red-tailed tropicbird.

30 Gill and Hauber (2013).

31 English is related to most languages spoken from Iceland to India, with earthy or concrete words generally derived from German, overlaid with an intellectual influence from French. Thus a cow in the field (German 'Kuh') becomes beef (French 'bœuf'), while a sheep (German 'Schaf') arrives at the table of the aristocrat as 'mutton' (French 'mouton').

32 Fischer (2001). New Zealand Māori is also rich in doublets. The East Tuamotuan connection is supported by a high incidence on Mangareva of Tuamotuan bird names. Emory (1947a).

33 Clark et al. (eds) (2008), Anderson et al. (2003), Kirch et al. (2010).

34 Green and Weisler (2002), who add that 'recent linguistic reworking of the early subgrouping of Eastern Polynesia suggests that the languages of Easter Island, Original Mangarevan, and probably the extinct Polynesian languages of Henderson and Pitcairn were the first in the region'. A major secondary contact with Marquesan speakers is inferred, changing Mangarevan into a Marquesic language, of a form then taken to Rapa Iti. Deguilloux et al. (2011): Analysis of ancient human remains (at least 400 years old) from a burial site on one atoll in the group, Temoe, revealed a dual genetic heritage, with a maternal Melanesian genetic component among the original Polynesian settlers. A Melanesian influence in Polynesians had previously been reported only on the male side.

35 Te Rangi Hīroa (1938b: 213). Green and Weisler (2004). Mangareva is the eastern limit of dogs known prehistorically for Oceania.

36 Weisler (2002), Di Piazza and Pearthree (2001c). The source material of basalt tools on Mangareva has been geochemically traced back to Pitcairn, Eiao (Marquesas Is) and Ra`iātea (Society Is). Its own local basalt was exported to Henderson Island.

37 Green and Weisler (2002).

38 Conte and Kirch (eds) (2004).

39 Weisler (2002: 267). This is consistent with dating evidence showing that both archipelagos were settled at around AD 1000 – slightly earlier than some of the other East Polynesian islands. Wilmshurst et al. (2011), Kirch et al. (2015b), Stevenson et al. (2017).

40 Weisler (2002: 268). A contraction in voyaging that coincides roughly with extensive fortifications (pā) first built on Rapa Iti and New Zealand around 1500.

41 Rolett (2002). As on Easter Island, the loss of forest is likely to be linked to rats.

42 Goff et al. (2012), Sladen et al. (2007).

43 Waite (1993) – includes photos.

44 Beechey's estimate at contact in 1825 was 1500; a head count by French missionaries in 1834 revealed 2121; a subsequent post-impact census in 1871 by a French army doctor found just 936. (No grounds were found for accepting higher estimates of the original inhabitants – up to 9000 and more.) Dutton and Tryon (1994), Te Rangi Hīroa (1938a: 207). The 1996 census puts the inhabitants at some 870.

45 Tregear (1899: In the introduction).

46 Te Rangi Hīroa (1938b: 203), including the native greeting here 'Ena koe' (There you are), the exact equivalent of the Rarotongan and New Zealand one, 'Tēnā koe'.

47 Koskinen (1963) found 88 place names on Mangareva shared with New Zealand. Archaeologist Nigel Prickett (2001: 19) also identifies Mangareva as a possible point of origin for New Zealand Māori.

48 See, for example, https://www.windfinder.com/windstatistics/rikitea_mangareva and https://www.windfinder.com/windstatistics/rapa_iti

49 Taonui (2006: 46).

50 Walworth (2015). Re linguistic links with Mangareva, see also Fischer (2001), Green and Weisler (2002).

51 Anderson and Kennett (eds) (2012).

52 Schmidt (1996), Kennett et al. (2006).

53 As recorded by Taonui (2006: 45). Hiro here is thought to be the same womanising, thieving navigator as the one known in the Society Islands and Tuamotus (and on other East Polynesian islands: Hilo on Hawai`i, `Iro on Rarotonga and Whiro in New Zealand). Although Amerindian Y chromosomes have been found among the current population, most scholars now attribute this to the offloading here of smallpox and dysentery victims at the close of the Peruvian slave trade. Hurles et al. (2003).

54 Di Piazza (2010: 390).

55 Collerson and Weisler (2007). No evidence has yet been found, though, of contact with Pitcairn or Easter Island; for example, no obsidian flakes found here could be sourced back to these islands. Anderson and Kennett (eds) (2012: 248).

56 Hutton and Priddel (2002).

57 Anderson and Kennett (eds) (2012: 201) give AD 1100–1200. Including one widespread little species, Desjardin's flat beetle (Cryptamorpha desjardinsi) [Family: Silvanidae], that feeds on the surface mildews of plants. Prebble and Porch (2009).

58 Te Rangi Hīroa (1938b: 181); plus gourd fragments from archaeological finds by Kennett's team (above). For the animal introductions, see Anderson (2009b).

59 Richards (2004). A recent study of the agricultural carrying capacity per watershed (Anderson and Kennett (eds) 2012: 242) concluded that 2027 is a conservative estimate of the original population.

60 Prebble (pers. comm. 12.03.2011).

61 The distinctive culture, history and language of Rapa all display strong links, not only with Mangareva, Easter Island and the East Tuamotus, but also with New Zealand. 'The frequent use of the K and the ng or gn, [in Rapan] appears more to resemble New Zealand [Māori] or [the language of] the Marquesans'. (Missionaries George Pritchard and Alexander Simpson quoted in Richards 2004). Richards (2004) identifies Mangarevan influences. Anderson and Kennett (ed.) (2012) link Rapan also with Easter Island and east Tuamotuan.

62 At least 21 place names on Rapa (or Oparo) are shared with New Zealand. Crowe (2012, 2014).

63 According to Hugh Cuming in May 1828, quoted in Richards (2004).

64 Edwards (2003, 2006, 2011). Like Mangareva, 1300 km upwind to the east, where at least one major marae platform is also thought to be astronomically orientated. Kirch (2004a).

65 Rolett et al. (2015).

66 Also a conch shell trumpet, pearl shell fishhooks, ornaments, coral and sea urchin spine abraders and Terebra shell chisels (gouge-like, made from the tip portion of the shell filed flat to form a bevel). Bollt (2008, 2009). See also Wilmshurst et al. (2011).

67 Middens reveal coastal waters rich in turtles and Pacific fruit bats on the land. Five bat bones dating to around AD 1100 were recovered in archaeological context on Rurutu from animals that – on current evidence – were introduced by people. If so, the likely source is Mangaia. Weisler et al. (2006). Three species of land birds – a flightless rail and two species of ground-dove – were also lost to extinction as a result of Polynesian occupation. Steadman and Bollt (2010).

68 Cook's crew, on rowing ashore in 1769, were challenged by several men on the shoreline armed with long spears. Cook, preferring not to land, continued toward New Zealand, but his botanist Joseph Banks commented on the deforestation: 'more barren than any thing we have seen in these seas'.

69 Pollen research from Prebble and Wilmshurst (2009). Indeed, 19th century Tahitians called these and the S. Cook Is the Paroquet Is It may have been these red feathers that inspired an old name for the Austral Islands, Fenua `ura ('Red Land'). Henry (1928).

70 The Austral Is are readily distinguishable from Rapa on account of having a distinct culture and language, for, although dialects spoken on the Australs are mutually intelligible, Rapan is not. Rapa is nevertheless often included nowadays in the Australs for administrative purposes.

71 Rolett et al. (2015).

72 According to anthropologist Donald Stanley Marshall, regular voyages were made from the Austral Islands and from the Southern Cooks to the tiny, intermediate atoll of Maria (or Nurotu), 'to collect exotic bird feathers and other natural products'. An East Polynesian adze has been found on Nuroto. Marshall (1954). According to Dening (1962), residents of Ma`uke (S. Cook Is) voyaged to Nurotu for fishing, turtle hunting and coconuts.

73 Shared nature vocabulary includes the term 'ngaio' for Myoporum stokesii, a small coastal tree on Ra`ivavae, shared for Myoporum species on New Zealand, Rapa Iti and Mangaia (S. Cook Is), but not on the Society Is, where the tree is absent. See also Zamponi (1996). Koskinen (1973: 26) remarks on finding more place names shared between these islands and the Cook Is, than with the Society Is.

74 Collerson and Weisler (2007). Similarly, Stimson and Marshall (1964: 23) have linked the language of Ra`ivavae to that of Fangatau (central Tuamotus).

75 Lee et al. (2007).

76 Taonui (2006: 46). Intricately carved, ceremonial fly-whisks found in Tahiti were either imported from the Austral Island or copied from Austral Island models. Tahitians continued to navigate between these two island groups without navigational instruments until at least the 1930s. Wray (1939).

77 Te Rangi Hīroa (1938b: 178). Although low-lying coastal areas on Rurutu were severely affected by a tsunami in around 1450, any long-term impact on long-distance voyaging is likely to be less, because of the availability of protected natural harbours nearby. According to Goff et

al. (2011a), this tsunami occurred AD 1450–1600; it was subsequently assigned by Goff et al. (2012) to a major earthquake in the Tonga–Kermadec Trench c.1450.
78 Wilmshurst et al. (2011), Hermann et al. (2016).
79 To be publicly derided from the pulpit on Ra`iatea as 'gods of the heathen'. Te Rangi Hiroa (1938b: 178).
80 Lavondès (1957), Hooper (2007).
81 Te Rangi Hiroa (1938b: 178).
82 In the 1830s, the population on Rurutu fell some 90 percent from an estimated 3000 to 200–300. Seabrook quoted in Bollt (2008). (By the 1920s its population had recovered to 1240, and stands today at 2000.) On Tupua`i (Tubuai), in the 30 years following the landing of the *Bounty* in 1789, introduced diseases led to a population crash from 3000 to 900, and by 1823 to just 300. (The population of the Australs is now about 6500.)
83 'All the available evidence of artefacts, language, biology and tradition suggests that. . . the Māori homeland. . . consists of the Society Islands, the southern Cook Islands and the Austral Islands in French Polynesia.' Irwin (2012). Davidson (1984) proposed that the Austral Islands 'may have been more important in the settlement of New Zealand than is recognised at present', and Bollt (2008) described one adze from Rurutu in 2008 as 'thought-provoking in terms of a potential Austral Islands–New Zealand connection'. Crowe (2012, 2014) lists 47 New Zealand place names on the Austral Islands and Rapa Iti combined (21 on Rapa Iti, and 26 on the Austral Islands proper). Combining both groups, Koskinen (1963) identified slightly more (53).
84 Raoul Island and Norfolk Island lie at 29°S.
85 For this reason, Mangareva is referred to by Tuamotuans as 'Raroata' ('below-shadow'), for at the height of summer – for nine days either side of the summer solstice – midday shadows fall to the north (rather than to the south). Young (1899). The position of the sun overhead is likewise noted on the atoll of Ouvéa (at 21°S), a Polynesian Outlier island of New Caledonia, where the term sapa means '*Soleil passer son zenith*' ('sun reaches its zenith'). Edwards (2006) has proposed that this phenomenon may account for the astronomical orientation of religious structures on islands situated elsewhere along this latitude – on Easter Island, Mangareva and Ra`ivavae, at least.
86 The latter route more practicable prior to AD 1500 than now, according to Goodwin et al. (2014).
87 Te Rangi Hiroa (1938a: 414).
88 Kirch (2004a), Kirch and Conte (2009).
89 Declinations for AD 1250–1450.

3 Maui's Hook [pp. 50–65]

1 The rhumbline distance between the two is about 7200 km and the Earth's circumference is about 40,000 km.
2 Surfing in small canoes and body surfing was recorded by early ethnographers at Tahiti, Tonga and Sāmoa, and in New Zealand where Māori used surfboards about 3 ft long (not long enough to stand on). Ngāi Tahu are also said to have used blades of kelp seaweed for surfing. However, the sport was more fully developed in Hawai`i – the only place where Polynesians are known to have *stood* on their boards.
3 Kirch and Rallu (2007: 112): '300,000 and above' for the Hawaiian Islands. For comparison, David Burley (in Kirch and Rallu 2007: 186) states that 'the maximum population threshold [for Tonga] is estimated at between 30,000 and 40,000 individuals for the archipelago as a whole'. For Sāmoa, Green (in Kirch and Rallu 2007: 330, 331) estimated around 70,000. Population estimates for other islands, as presented elsewhere in this book, are also lower.
4 Kirch (1985: 7).
5 Green (2005: 46).
6 Kirch (1985: 6, 7).
7 Cook in Beaglehole (ed.) 1967 (Vol 3, Part 1: 265).
8 Together, the Hawaiian Islands cover 16,692 sq km.
9 Beaglehole (ed.) (1967: 279).
10 Kamakau (1961: 92).
11 On hearing of the arrival of Cook's strange ship, the local chiefs are said to have exclaimed, in the words of local historian Samuel Kamakau (1961: 97): 'That was surely Lono! He has come back from Kahiki'. Other accounts suggest that he was initially deified.
12 Beaglehole (1974: 672).
13 A critical examination of these population figures appears elsewhere in the book.
14 Gilbert (1982: 101).
15 McCoy et al. (2009). At least two other basalt quarries are found on this island, with more on all the other major Hawaiian islands. This is in addition to quarries of obsidian-like volcanic glass found on the 'Big Island', Moloka`i and Kaho`olawe, which supplied the raw material for making cutting tools.
16 Some begun in the 13th century and developed over 500 years. Kolb (2006).
17 The platform was built in four distinct stages, beginning c.1400. Kolb (1999).
18 Ahu Tongariki on Easter Island was originally 220 m long, but much narrower.
19 Consistent with recent thorium dating results showing multiple temple forms constructed simultaneously on Maui between AD 1550 and 1700. Kirch, Mertz-Kraus and Sharp (2015).
20 Kolb (1991: 130, 160).
21 Kolb (1994).
22 Kirch (1985: 6).
23 Samwell quoted in Best (1925c: 327)
24 A conclusion supported by a number of words common to Hawaiian and Marquesan but not recorded elsewhere, e.g. a`ea`e (ake) for a variety of banana; pa`iuma (pakiuma) for a chest-slapping dance; pe`ahi (pekahi) for a fan. Further examples are given by Green (1966).
25 References to voyaging to Hawai`i can also be found in the oral history of Tokelau (Macgregor 1937: 26). The high incidence of place names shared between the Hawaiian Islands and the Northern Polynesian Outliers suggests contact between these regions (Koskinen 1973: 18), consistent with a link identified by Hawaiian linguist Wilson (2012). Pearce and Pearce (2011: 167) speculate on immigration from Maluku Islands (Indonesia/ New Guinea region) via Micronesia.
26 Allen (2014). Although some Hawaiian traditions are judged to be potentially post-European constructs, those migration traditions bearing the hallmarks of authenticity generally refer to Tahitian homelands. Taonui (2006: 45).
27 Koskinen (1973: 27).
28 Matisoo-Smith (2009a).
29 Many of which Hawaiians subsequently harvested for food, including one small, unnamed (now extinct) petrel and several other species whose colonies were subsequently wiped out on the main islands. Olson and James (1982b).
30 Bulwer's petrel (*Bulweria bulwerii*), Hawaiian petrel (`ua`u, *Pterodroma sandwichensis*), Hawaiian shearwater (or Newell's shearwater, *Puffinus newelli*) and wedge-tailed shearwater (*Ardenna pacifica* syn *Puffinus pacificus*).
31 Irwin (1992: 167).
32 Arcturus served as a zenith star in 1500 for Kaua`i at 22°N, 5 Jan–24 Jun (and in 2000 for 19°N).
33 In 1976, the *Hōkūle`a* made a return trip from Hawai`i to Tahiti – some 5000 km each way – navigating the first leg to Tahiti solely by non-instrument methods.
34 Earlier carbon dates were skewed by samples that included charcoal from trees that may have incorporated atmospheric carbon well before the arrival of humans. The archaeological and palaeoenvironmental estimates of the date of colonisation evidently show a striking convergence, with the first settlement dates for these islands now understood to be around AD 940–1130 (at 95 percent confidence), Athens et al. (2014). Previous to this thorough review, even later figures had been proposed by Wilmshurst et al. 2011 (AD 1220–1261), and Reith et al. 2011 (AD 1220–1261).
35 Kirch (1982). Like New Zealand, the Hawaiian Islands have only one native land mammal – a forest bat (Hawaiian hoary bat, *Lasiurus cinereus semotus*) – and an unusually high proportion of unique birds, many of which proved highly vulnerable to introduced predators (including humans).
36 Dubbed 'moa-nalo' or 'Hawaiian superducks', many flightless, weighing up to 7.6 kg. There is some doubt as to whether the extinction of flightless ibises here predates the arrival of humans.
37 Habitat change was well underway in dryland forest before the forest was burnt or major agriculture began, implicating the Pacific rat, which halted plant regeneration by eating seeds. Olson and James (1982a).
38 Athens (2009).
39 The dogs were raised for food and pigs bred as sacrificial offerings and as a chiefly luxury food. Ellis (1827). According to Kirch and O'Day (2003), the domestic archaeological record reveals that the diet of commoners differed from that of the elite. The latter had preferential access to fatty, oily or greasy flesh foods, including large limpets and cowries, large fish and sharks, birds, pigs and dogs, while the commoners' diet focussed on smaller shellfish and Pacific rat.
40 Whistler (2009). Pollen analysis confirms that many other local plants once thought to have been introduced by Polynesians (intentionally or

otherwise) were already present prior to the arrival of humans, e.g., milo (*Thespesia populnea*) and kou (*Cordia subcordata*), both now known to be indigenous.

41 Kelly (1989: 82).

42 Kurashima and Kirch (2011).

43 By AD 1600. Athens et al. (2002).

44 Observation made in Mar 1779. Captain Cook and Midshipman Trevenen quoted in Green (2005: 52).

45 King in Beaglehole (ed.) (1967. Vol 3: 618).

46 According to Handy quoted in Yen (1960). The other region of Polynesia where seeding is known is Easter Island. Yen (1960).

47 One exception is a minor variation on Ni`ihau, where speakers use k and t; and r and l, interchangeably.

48 As determined through Wavelength Dispersive X-Ray Fluorescence (WDXRF) and microscopic analysis.

49 Emory (1928a), DLNR (2008). The island's ceremonial use may have been linked to its location on the Tropic of Cancer, the northernmost point at which the sun's path reaches its zenith at midday in the middle of the northern summer – and therefore an important reference latitude for traditional navigators. Rooney et al. (2008). See corresponding islands in the southern hemisphere – Ra`ivavae and Mangareva – on the Tropic of Capricorn. See also Alexander (1894).

50 Anderson (2006a), on the other hand – writing on the theme of Polynesians in exile – proposes that evidence of human presence on Nihoa and Necker Islands is the result of early dispersals of exile communities.

51 Klar and Jones (2005), Jones and Klar (2005).

52 Jones proposes two periods of contact: one around AD 700, introducing the technology of the sewn-plank canoe and composite harpoon from elsewhere in Polynesia; with a second from Hawai`i circa AD 1300, bringing the Hawaiian-style compound bone fishhook, along with grooved and barbed fishhooks of bone and shell. Note, though, that Californian evidence for the sewn-plank canoe and composite harpoon predates other known evidence of Polynesians in the Hawaiian region. Jones (2011: 91). Jones et al. in Jones et al. (ed.) (2011: 274) suggests that bottle gourds may have reached Hawai`i by this route, drawing attention to cosmological belief systems shared between the two regions – although this last would seem to imply more than a brief visit.

53 Anderson (2006b), Arnold (2007).

54 Some of which carried fifty or more crew. Brigham (1903: 59).

55 Best (1925c: 331).

56 It is acknowledged here that although the term Kahiki is often translated as Tahiti, it also has the wider meaning of 'distant land'. The interpretation given here is that of Rāwiri Taonui (2006: 46), a specialist in the authenticity and meaning of Polynesian oral tradition. See also Cachola-Abad (1993).

57 Kirch and Green (2001: 80, 87).

58 Matisoo-Smith et al. (1998).

59 Matisoo-Smith (2009b). Multiple interaction is also supported by the distribution of freshwater fingernail clams in ancient Hawaiian taro ponds, the spat of which evidently continued to arrive on root stock from elsewhere in Polynesia. Burky et al. (2000).

60 Irwin (1992: 167).

61 Collerson and Weisler (2007); provenance questioned by Anderson (2008d) with responses by Weisler (2008), Kirch (2008) and others. Consequently, Weisler (pers. comm. 15.06.2016) suggests that 'it is best to say that this adze was originally from Hawaii, not specially Kaho'olawe island'.

62 Te Rangi Hīroa (1938b: 143). In the case of Teraina, Fanning did not actually land. See also Di Piazza and Pearthree (2001c).

63 Watling (1995), King (1973). The presence of Pacific rats on the Line Islands indicates that even tiny Starbuck, Vostok and Jarvis were visited.

64 Di Piazza and Pearthree (2001a).

65 Flint (1991), Weimerskirch et al. (2005).

66 At this latitude, the South Celestial Pole lies beneath the horizon.

67 Dated from ritual offerings of branch coral, found with the nearby cairn (ahu). Kirch et al. (2013). In 1865, Hawaiian historian Samuel Kamakau maintained that navigational directions had been passed down to him for a southbound voyage from the Hawaiian Islands. 'If you sail for Kahiki [here interpreted as Tahiti or the Society Islands], you will discover new constellations and strange stars over the deep ocean. When you arrive at the "Piko o Wakea" [equatorial region], you will lose sight of "Hoku-paa" (North Star); and the "Newe" will be the southern guiding star, and the constellation of "Humu" [Altair] will stand as a guide above you.' Alexander (1891), also quoted in Smith (1899, 1904), Best (1923), Te Rangi Hīroa (1926b). Altair rises to its zenith on this course during the hours of darkness from mid-April to mid-September.

Running a star navigation programme for that period, one finds that, on reaching the latitude of the first of the Equatorial Islands (or Line Islands), the bright star of Altair [Humu] is at its zenith. Continuing south until the North Star disappears below the horizon at the latitude of Kiritimati (Christmas Is at 2°N), the Southern Cross [Newe] is rising; however, it does so at night only October to early March, so, although Newe rises in the SSE, at about 145–150°, a marker for the course from this point through to Tahiti, it does so at a different time of year. Thus, these directions refer either to a split voyage, continued after a sojourn in the Line Islands or were invented after European contact. Note that the authenticity of other aspects of Kamakau's traditional navigational knowledge have been questioned by Alexander (1891), Lewis (1972: 45, 383), and Bruce (1976), namely the traditional use of a water-filled 'sacred calabash' for gauging the elevation of stars.

68 A palaeotsunami deposit (indicating 120 m inundation, landward of 3 m high dune) in Māhā'ulepū Caves on Kaua`i (Hawaiian Is) is dateable to AD 1430–1665. Goff et al. (2011a).

69 Te Rangi Hīroa (1944: 456), Patole-Edoumba (1999), Taonui (2006: 46).

70 The fact that ceremonial stone platforms are found all over East Polynesia but not in New Zealand would seem to suggest that any major contact dates only from the earliest settlement period, before the custom of building such platforms became widespread. According to Kolb (2006), the earliest stone platforms on the Hawaiian Islands date to the 13th century.

71 Smith (1899), Best (1923), Te Rangi Hīroa (1926b).

72 As referred to in Smith (1898).

73 Based on informal questioning by the present author over a number of years: 'So where do you think Māori came from?'

74 Matisoo-Smith et al. (1998).

75 On Mangareva (Gambier Is), archaeological evidence shows the first settlers arriving some 200 years before Pacific rats, and visits by Polynesians to the Snares and Auckland Islands likewise did not result in rats becoming established there (Anderson 2009b). Similarly, despite the known transfer of Marquesan basalt from Eiao to Mo`orea in the Society Is (Di Piazza and Pearthree 2001c), mtDNA from Marquesan rats has not been picked up among Society Is rat populations (Matisoo-Smith et al. 1998).

76 Dixon (1916: 93). Many traditions are more widespread. Traditions concerning Rātā – a canoe builder who seeks agreement of the gods to fell trees, are traceable some 2500 years back to the region of Fiji, Tonga and Sāmoa; he is known as Laka in Hawai`i; elsewhere as Lata (Sāmoa, Tokelau and Pukapuka); Lasa (Tonga); Raka (Rarotonga); Aka (Marquesas); Rātā (Tuamotus, Tahiti and New Zealand) and Rata on Takuu. Likewise, Tāwhaki – known across East and West Polynesia for ascending into the heavens – is known here as Kaha`i; elsewhere as Tafahi (Sāmoa); Tahaki (Tuamotus and Mangareva); Tafa`i (Tahiti); and Ta`aki (Rarotonga).). Among Polynesian gods, Tū (or Tūmatauenga, god of war, known here as Kū) and Rongo (god of agriculture in New Zealand, but here as Lono, god of rain and weather) are recognised throughout East Polynesia. Others – such as Tangaroa, god of the ocean (known here as Kanaloa) – are known over a much wider area: across West and East Polynesia to Easter Island. Stories about the Polynesian god of land-based nature, Tāne (known here as Kāne), separating sky and Earth are traceable even further back to Borneo and the Philippines some 6000 years ago. (The areas of responsibility of these gods differ slightly between island groups.) Taonui (2006: 25–33).

77 Hawaiian and Māori were originally assigned to different linguistic subgroups – Marquesic and Tahitic respectively – a distinction now questioned by Walworth (2014). Many terms are shared only between New Zealand Māori and Hawaiian, e.g. arawhata (alahaka, *bridge or ladder*); hamo (hamo, *a sweet potato variety*); hau tea (hau kea, *snow*); hūwai (hūwai, *edible shellfish, shell used as a scraping tool*); kao (`ao, *dried sweet potato*); kau-moana (`au-moana, *sailor*); moi (moi, *a sweet potato variety*); ngaro – in western dialects (ngaro, *blowfly*); oha or owha (oha, *a common greeting*); omo (omo, *gourd*); pāha`aha`a (pāhaka, *a variety of gourd with short fruit*); pairua (pailua, *nausea*); pūkoro (pū`olo, *container, bag*); taumaha (kaumaha, *heavy*). Over 500 New Zealand place names can be recognised on the Hawaiian Islands, considerably more than on any other Polynesian archipelago. Crowe (2013). A substantial number of these names are not shared with the Society Islands. Koskinen (1963, 1973: 18, 26, 27). Rogers et al. (2009: 3840, 3838 Fig. 1) also find a link in their analysis of the evolution of Polynesian canoe design traits: 'one conclusion it yields: that Hawaii was the primary cultural origin for New Zealand'.

78 In 2014, *Hōkūle`a* sailed to New Zealand via Tahiti and the Cook Islands to approach it from Sāmoa via Tonga.

79 Kirch and Rallu (2007: 112): '300,000 and above' and Kirch and Rallu

(2007: 126): 'Perhaps the 300,000 figure is not that far off'. See also Kirch and Rallu (2007: 53).

80 Census figures from Marques (1893), Schmitt (1967). The 2010 census gives 80,337 (5.9% of the total) for ('pure') native Hawaiians and 355,816 (26.2%) for Pacific Islanders.

81 The consequent loss of surviving Hawaiian traditions includes some purportedly authentic traditions that may be post-European constructs. Taonui (2006: 45).

82 Williams (1971): Hau 'appears as an element in many words denoting dew, frost, snow, etc. ? hauku, etc.'.

83 On the Hawaiian Islands, the 'sled' could be either a branch of cabbage tree or a board with two runners 'up to five yards long'. Its equivalent in New Zealand was a simple flat board or, more usually, a fan of flax leaves or the branch of a cabbage tree with a short piece of stem attached.

4 Statues in the Forest [pp. 66–79]

1 The height above ground of Takaiʻi is about 235 cm. Genealogical dating suggests that it was carved no earlier than about 1750. Ottino-Garanger (1957), Ottino and de Bergh-Ottino (1991: 1). Many other statues were removed, including the very large stone head of one that weighed over three tons, taken some years prior to 1920 by a German trading company.

2 Heyerdahl (1974: 217, 235).

3 Taonui (2006: 45).

4 Kirch (2012: 59).

5 Heyerdahl (1974: 166).

6 Ferdinand Magellan preceded Mendaña in Polynesia by 74 years. He was the first European to find the Tuamotus, but, although he sighted the atoll of Pukapuka in 1521, he remained oblivious of its residents; he dismissed it as inhospitable and did not land.

7 Quirós quoted in Markham (ed.) (1904: 17).

8 Hughes and Fischer (eds) (1998: xxx).

9 Te Rangi Hīroa (1938b: 152). Many descendants of the survivors subsequently moved to Papeʻete (Tahiti) for work, leaving some 8600 inhabitants today, spread across six of the 12 main islands.

10 Based on the most conservative estimates of the original population, introduced disease, arms and alcohol led to a population crash on the Marquesas 1804–80 from an estimated 45,000 to 4865, reaching a low point of 2255 by the early 1900s. Hughes and Fischer (eds) (1998: xiii), Kirch and Rallu (2007: 30), Rallu (1992). See also Craig (ed.) 1980.

11 Te Rangi Hīroa (1938b: 168).

12 Morinda pollen is present on Mangaia (S. Cook Is) in the oldest soil samples, dated to 5300 BC.

13 In Tahitian, two varieties are recognised: a white-fruited one (ʻahiʻa tea) and a red-fruited one (ʻahiʻa ʻura).

14 Known in the Western Pacific and Polynesian Outliers as nonu.

15 Data compiled from the Smithsonian Institute – Wagner and Lorence (2011, accessed 2014), omitting all species whose prehistoric introduction by Polynesians is disputed.

16 Allen (2004). Starch residue from shell tools on the Marquesas reveals kūmara from the 14th century onward. Allen and Ussher (2013).

17 Zerega et al. (2004). The New Zealand climate is too cool for breadfruit, and yet memory of it survives in its Polynesian name, kuru, which occurs in a few ancient Māori songs and in at least one classic lament as 'an edible, tree-borne fruit in tradition'.

18 Found on Hivaʻ Oa, Nuku Hiva and ʻUa Huka. The term 'plainware' distinguishes these pots from decorated Lapita pottery. Analysis of some potsherds from Nuku Hiva reveals quartz in the clay, consistent with importation from the Rewa Delta, Viti Levu, Fiji, over 4500 km to the west. Sinoto (1957), Dickinson et al. (1998). According to Allen et al. (2012) and Allen (2014), the remaining sherds are now thought likely to be Fijian imports too.

19 Rolett (1993).

20 As identified by Finnish ethnologist Aarne Koskinen (1973: 26), who found links with both the NW and SE dialect areas of the Marquesas.

21 Wilson (2012).

22 Different origins are consistent with findings from cranial and cranio-facial measurements, and with the overlap in linguistic grouping of ʻUa Huku. Stefan and Chapman (2003).

23 For example, the moth skink (Lipinia noctua), which lives near humans on islands over much of the Pacific and gives birth to live young. It is unable to swim, so can have reached these islands only with the aid of canoes. When samples of its DNA were collected from 15 Pacific island groups and analysed, moth skinks from Kapingamarangi were found to belong to the same lineage as those distributed across tropical Polynesia

to the east (as opposed to those on the neighbouring Micronesian islands of Pohnpei and Kosrae, belonging to a population found in New Guinea to the west). Austin (1999).

24 Fisher (1997), from an analysis of the protein variation in populations of stump-toed gecko (Gehyra mutilata) and oceanic gecko (Gehyra oceanica). Although the latter is reasonably well adapted for rafting on floating mats of vegetation, this mode of transport can be discounted on account of the prevailing easterly winds and currents.

25 Teleogryllus oceanicus. Tinghitella et al. (2011). In the Marquesas, crickets and their cry are known as vivī.

26 Shelley (2004). Scolopendra morsitans.

27 In New Zealand Māori, regional differences in pronunciation, vocabulary, idiom and grammar were previously more pronounced. Indeed, based on percentages of shared basic vocabulary of eight North Island dialects, these are technically classified as separate languages. (Exceptions are Tūhoe and Ngāti Porou; and Te Aupōuri and Ngāpuhi.) Māori 'dialects' are classified as a single language only because of their high level of mutual intelligibility. Harlow (2007: 53).

28 Harlow (2007: 56), Clark (2014).

29 Stone tools, personal ornaments and ancient sherds of plainware pottery were found – similar to those on Hivaʻ Oa. Sinoto and Kellum (1965). In the 1950s, American archaeologist Robert Suggs (1961) and collaborators had made what seemed like similarly early finds on Nuku Hiva.

30 Pierre Ottino of the Orstom Research Centre in Tahiti. Ottino and de Bergh-Ottino (1991: 16), Kirch (2000).

31 Ottino (1992).

32 Allen and McAlister (2010), Wilmshurst et al. (2011), Mulrooney et al. (2011), Allen (2014), Athens et al. (2014), Conte and Molle (2014), Kirch et al. (2015b), Stevenson et al. (2017).

33 Although Ficus marquisensis is indigenous on western Nuku Hiva, other species have been planted. This veneration for fig trees extends well beyond Polynesia, through Southeast Asia to India, and even West Africa. Aoʻa is a common tree across the tropical Pacific. For Northland Māori, its shamanic equivalent is the gnarly old pūriri tree, around which the bones of the dead were sometimes buried, or placed inside the hollow trunk. Orbell (1996) and Wendy Pond (unpublished field research). On atolls, the equivalent reliquary tree is the gnarly old pukatea (Pisonia grandis), whose New Zealand namesake pukatea (Laurelia novae-zelandiae) was also used for this purpose.

34 Evidence that toa (ironwood) seeds were introduced from Southeast Asia includes the abundance of its pollen in recent soil samples here, and yet its absence from samples dating from prior to human settlement. (The local variety, Casuarina equisetifolia var. equisetifolia, is thought to be native also to Australia.)

35 An alternative name, tānekaha ('strong man') is another likely reference to the warrior.

36 The red colouring derived from the tropical Casuarina comes from the sap; that of the tānekaha from its bark.

37 Collected by German ethnographer Karl von den Steinen, with destination interpreted by Handy (1930: 130) as 'Aotona (Rarotonga)'; ʻAʻ otona or Oautona is the Marquesan rendering of Rarotonga.

38 Oral histories collected by Beaglehole and Beaglehole (1938) on Pukapuka (N. Cook Is) speak of contact maintained with Witi (Fiji), Tonga, Niuē, Yamoa (Sāmoa), Tokelau and Yiva (which is presumed to be the Marquesas Is).

39 WDXRF (wavelength dispersive X-ray fluorescence analysis).

40 Rupe is also an alternative name of Hina's brother Māui-mua, who turned himself into a pigeon. 'Rupe seems to be a kind of honorific term,' explains Best (1942: 226), 'occasionally used by Māori folk, as when the pigeon is personified in certain myths, but not when speaking of the birds in any ordinary way.'

41 Weisler (1998).

42 Di Piazza and Pearthree (2001c).

43 Hermann (2013) quoted in Rolett et al. (2015).

44 McAlister et al. (2013), Rolett et al. (2015).

45 Matisoo-Smith et al. (1998), Matisoo-Smith and Robins (2009), Matisoo-Smith (2009a). The ectoparasitic rat mite, Laelaps hawaiiensis, which is said by some authors to have travelled with it, turns out to be conspecific with the widespread Laelaps nuttalli.

46 Porter quoted in Best (1925c: 320).

47 Druett (2011: 229). (The original pidgin Tahitian noted against the name Ohevatoutouai on the map is here corrected for clarity.)

48 Out of some 100 endemic plants recorded for the Marquesas, only seven are not classified as rare. The Marquesan kiekie is Freycinetia impavida and/or F. arborea; the Marquesan kohai is Sesbania marchionica (or Sophora tomentosa). The Marquesan naʻu is Lepidium bidentatum; the

Marquesan okaoka is a nettle [Urticaceae]; the Marquesan pa`a fern is *Marattia salicina*; the Marquesan feki is one of three native species of Cyatheaceae tree ferns (*Alsophila tahitensis*, *Sphaeropteris feani* or *S. medullaris*); and oupo`o, porohito is *Solanum viride* (introduced by Polynesians). Names updated according to Wagner and Lorence (2011).

49 Names recorded for the vine in the Marquesas are pohue and paniaoe. Pétard (1986: 258).

50 In New Zealand and across the tropical Pacific, the term is generic for vines. Other pōhuehue or pōhue in New Zealand include muehlenbeckia vines (*Muehlenbeckia* species), clematis vines (*Clematis* species), New Zealand passionfruit vine (*Passiflora tetrandra*), and native cucumber vine (*Sicyos australis*).

51 Tutu actually means 'a hoop used as a net spreader'. Its flexible stems were also used for making fish traps; however, no comparable use is recorded for the flexible stems of New Zealand tutu.

52 The main motive for Polynesians consuming human flesh was not nutritional: on atolls such as Tongareva and Pukapuka (N. Cook Is), Tikopia (Solomon Is) and Kapingamarangi (Caroline Is), where comparable protein from pigs was often in short supply, the practice was rare. Oliver (2002: 102). On the Marquesas most of the meat came from native birds, particularly seabirds, but also parrots, rails, pigeons and doves. Fish and turtles were harvested, too – mostly from the deep sea. European commentators frequently embellished their accounts of cannibalism in the Pacific, failing to acknowledge comparable practices at the time in Europe of consuming human body parts for their perceived 'medical' benefit (Gordon-Grube 1988: 406). The irony of this European fascination and revulsion for the practice reached new heights in 1820, when the crew from the whaleship *Essex*, shipwrecked nearby and chose to sail away from the Marquesas to escape its cannibals, only to resort in the end to eating their own fellows.

53 On the occasion when a cooked human knee was brought to German botanist Berthold Carl Seemann in Fiji in the early 1860s, he reported that the fruit of this plant is 'occasionally prepared like tomato sauce'. Seemann (1862). Large-fruited cultivars are now also available. Also known as *Solanum uporo*.

54 Despite the original dialectical variations in New Zealand Māori having been very poorly documented, at least eight regional dialects are distinguished in the North Island and one from the South Island. Harlow (2007: 41–61).

55 A high proportion of basic vocabulary is shared only between South Island and East Coast (NI) Māori (Ngāti Porou and Kahungunu; this is thought to be a consequence of a later incursion by East Coast tribes into the South Island (Harlow 2007: 55). Harlow (1994) finds links in the dialects of East Coast Māori and the Southern Cooks – evident also in South Island Māori 'over the top of' a Marquesan influence.

56 Harlow (2007: 55–56). Green (1966: 31) likewise 'call[s] attention to possible linguistic evidence from some dialects in New Zealand and the Chathams that may point to contact with the languages of the [Marquesas] rather than [Tahitian or Rarotongan]'. Otherwise, linguists tend to set Marquesan apart from New Zealand Māori (and Tahitian, Tuamotuan and Rarotongan), categorising it as closer to the languages of Mangareva and Easter Island, which suggests that, if the Marquesas did play a role in the settlement of New Zealand, it was probably a relatively minor one. Gray et al. (2009: online supporting material).

57 However, Handy (1923) notes that Marquesan place names were frequently changed. Koskinen (1963) counted 70 New Zealand place names in the Marquesas; Crowe (2014) lists 63, of which most occur on Hiva `Oa. In proportion to land area, though, the highest concentration is found on `Ua Huka.

58 More examples are given by Green (1966) and Harlow (2007: 41), who elaborate on their overall significance.

59 Beattie (1920: 71).

60 The first record of the maritime use of a compass in Europe is 1187. In China its first use *at sea* may predate this to around 1110, or possibly earlier.

61 From Millennium Atoll, some 2140 km to the west, Eiao presents a target arc of just 0.268 degrees.

5 Expanding the Target [pp. 80–93]

1 Horvath and Finney (1969) describe an experiment in which a reconstructed Hawaiian double canoe was paddled by a crew of physically fit and experienced paddlers at slightly more than 3 knots, sustained for two eight-hour stints over two days, covering almost 50 km per day. Although this would have provided the means to cross the doldrums and to maintain progress through other calms and light airs, they nevertheless concluded that 'paddling, as the sole propulsive force

of a double-canoe, would have been of extremely limited value for long-range voyaging'.

2 According to Taonui (2012) 'the most manageable long-distance canoes were about 20 metres long'.

3 In 1606, Quirós (in Markham (ed.) 1904: 216) reports seeing at Rakahanga (N. Cook Is) 'some very large vessels, twenty yards in length and two wide, more or less, in which they navigate for great distances. They hold about fifty persons.' Taonui (1994: 329) reviews the evidence for smaller crews on long-distance voyages. Although some twin-hulled Tahitian canoes seen by Cook were longer still (108 ft; 33 m), these were war canoes manoeuvred by paddling.

4 As quoted in Di Piazza and Pearthree (2001b).

5 See Irwin, in Jones et al. (ed.) (2011: 249).

6 Sinoto (1983b) dated the remains as being from around AD 1000–1100, a date revised by Anderson and Sinoto (2002) to about AD 1050–1450. A reconstruction of the Anaweka canoe from New Zealand's South Island is shorter: about 16 m. Johns et al. (2014).

7 Best (1925c: 400), Te Rangi Hīroa (1950b: 45): 'When I had the chance of visiting the spot, I took a chain tape with me to make an accurate measurement of the reputed length of Tainui. It was 70 feet.' This may in fact be near the upper length limit for a Polynesian deep-sea voyaging canoe, as craft longer than the wavelength of the waves are thought to be too prone to breaking up in stormy weather.

8 The old Polynesian word for mast, 'tira', is remembered in Māori, suggesting that masts were used on migration voyages to New Zealand.

9 Captain Moi of Sāmoa and Jacques Koah of Bora Bora, quoted in Barr (2006: 163, 166).

10 The latitude of Tahanea (NW Tuamotus), and Ra`iātea, Mo`orea and Huahine (in the Society Is). In 1250, the zenith of Sirius was at 16°S, the latitude of Fakarava (NW Tuamotus) and Maupiti (Society Is).

11 Finney (1979: 213).

12 Makemson (1941). Other stars, such as Rehua (Antares), were seen as both a god and a star (Tautahi and Taipuhi 1900). Lewis (1964): 'the zenith star was regarded as the star of the land; it belonged to the island over which it passed'. Spica can be used in this way only in those months during which it rises this high in the hours of darkness.

13 This 'star-on-top' technique is known to have been used by Tongan, Tahitian and Tikopian navigators. In 1350, Spica reached its zenith during the hours of darkness only 4 Jan–20 June. Although this limits its usefulness in the period during which westerlies tend to blow in this region (Nov–Jan), it may in practice have been possible to use the declination of Spica just before dawn (before it reached the zenith) as early as 15 December, bearing in mind David Lewis's finding that, when a star was more than 5° from vertical, he could not judge its zenith to nearer than one degree (equivalent to 60 nautical miles).

14 Lewis (1964).

15 Gould (1974).

16 Best (1922a: 28).

17 Although James Barr (2006: 162) writes of 'several occasions in the early 1980s [when he] chose to study with four men who held the craft of open sea navigation . . . Tranhei Theki (Maori), J. W. Kei (Tahiti), Jacques Koah (Bora Bora), and Matthew Burke Moi (Rorotonga and Western Samoa)' of whom only Moi was under age 60. Lewis (1972: 199) refers to the Tongan Ve`ehala.

18 Recorded in Rarotongan as 'a morning star' (which Vega is in summer in January); and in Tuamotuan as 'the name of a star'. Vega is not mentioned in Māori navigational lore, presumably because it remains below the horizon from late spring to early summer, when most of the voyages to New Zealand are thought to have occurred.

19 Recorded also on Pukapuka (N. Cook Is), with an archaic meaning of 'bright or shining'.

20 Two forms of this term survive in Māori – rapa (flash, or sheet lightning) and kāraparapa (flashing) – both with cognates elsewhere in Polynesia.

21 Lewis (1972: 198).

22 This recalls the naming of Mangareva as 'Raro-ata the Land-of-faint-light-beneath-the-waves' – see Young (1899) and the chant 'Voyaging' in Stimson (1957). Also 'the bright or gleaming current' (te au-kānapanapa) that is said to have guided Kupe, the navigator, to land his canoe near New Zealand's Bay of Islands.

23 Beaglehole (ed.) (1962: 368).

24 Lewis (1964).

25 In around AD 1250, their coincident rising occurred at 22°S – the latitude of Mangaia (S. Cook Is) and Mururoa Atoll (Tuamotus). As a navigational aid, this can be useful Feb–July, the period for which these two stars are above the eastern horizon during the hours of darkness.

26 Lewis (1972).

27 Further detail is provided by Lewis (1972).

28 According to Barr (2006: 164), Polynesian navigators speak of being able to distinguish more than twenty distinct types of waves, each with its own name and function, providing the navigator with information about direction, distance from landmasses, and speed.

29 In Māori, karekare also means 'agitated or disturbed', as in pōkarekare in the famous New Zealand folk song 'Pōkarekare Ana', in reference to agitated waters at Waiapū.

30 As demonstrated to Lewis (1972).

31 Kotzebue quoted in D'Arcy (2006: 73).

32 Barr (2006: 165).

33 Beaglehole (ed.) (1962: 208). On 27 Dec 1769.

34 Cook (1846: 448).

35 See figs 12 and 13 in Lewis (1972), or maps 6 and 7 in 2nd ed. (1994: 142, 143).

36 Gooding and Magnuson (1967).

37 Wood (1875).

38 Because of its elevation, Tahiti can be seen in clear conditions from 95 km away even without a capping cloud, a distance that drops in less favourable weather to 30–40 km or less.

39 In New Zealand (which lacks coral reefs), this term refers to either a rocky reef or a shore generally.

40 A comparable phenomenon is evident at close range on the underside of the wings of white terns flying over shallow water.

41 The name `Ana`a means 'bright' or 'glowing'. Other lagoons in the region known for turning the underside of clouds green are those of Fakahina and Fangatau (Tuamotus).

42 A local fisherman on Fa`aite (Tuamotus) confirmed for me the distance over which such a sighting of `Ana`a might be made: 'we used to see [the tinted cloud] from here [70 km away]. But the [1983] cyclone changed the lagoon. Now, we can't see it until 30 kilometres.'

43 Lewis (1972: 218).

44 Also reported by Lewis (1972: 198) and others.

45 Heyerdahl (1950: 166).

46 From 30 nautical miles according to Lewis (1972: 198, 213, 273).

47 Although birds seen around sunset are likely to be returning home from their fishing grounds for the night to rest, the odd individual may still be seen a long way from land, obliging one to take into account the size of the flocks and to discount any young birds without family responsibilities.

48 From the songs, 'Voyaging' and 'Song of the Birds of the Sea Kings' in Stimson (1957). On outlying islands of Polynesia they are fed with fish and still kept as pets. Hadden (2004). Tame frigatebirds were reportedly also used in Polynesia and Micronesia for carrying simple cord-messages or pearl fishhooks between the islands. Lewis (1972: 208, 209). Its Polynesian names, mokohe or kōtaha, are not recorded in New Zealand, doubtless due to the extreme rarity of the bird in southern waters.

49 Nevertheless, Cook (1846: 448) sighted frigatebirds over 800 km before reaching Easter Island, and Thor Heyerdahl recorded seeing small frigatebird flocks as much as 1000 nautical miles (1850 km) from land at both ends of his journey (Peru and Polynesia). Also, one banded on Tern Island near Johnston Atoll was seen in the Philippines, 7627 km from where it was marked. Dearborn (2003). Their reliability as landfinders may therefore be overstated.

50 'Song of the Birds of the Sea Kings'. Stimson (1957: 214). Lewis (1972: 211), on the other hand, dismisses the tropicbird 'as too erratic in its range and homing characteristics to be of much use to seamen'.

51 Wodzicki and Laird (1970).

52 The common brown noddy (Anous stolidus) is more pelagic than the smaller black noddy (Anous minutus). (In tropical Polynesia, both species were commonly eaten.)

53 That is, if we put aside here the issue of Heyerdahl's raft having been towed a long way to sea to make his start.

6 Crossroads of East Polynesia [pp. 94–109]

1 In Tahitian, Tuāmotu is known as Pa`umotu, from pa`u (Tahitian for 'shallow place', or 'bright spot in the sky, corresponding to a shallow lagoon in which the clear blue sky is reflected'). Académie Tahitiennne (1999).

2 The islanders rarely eat this plant nowadays, but do pull up whole plants to feed to their pigs – hence the English name.

3 Photo taken on Palmerston Atoll (Cook Is).

4 Information from the Beagleholes (1938) working on Pukapuka (N. Cook Is).

5 But not Pacific golden plover or reef heron. A similar range of birds is eaten on the Tokelau Is, where the reef heron is again a conspicuous

exception. Wodzicki and Laird (1970).

6 This plant is found in full sun across Micronesia, Cook Islands and French Polynesia. Its roots can be baked as a bland kind of famine food, and its tender young leaves and shoots cooked as a vegetable.

7 Giant swamp taro (Cyrtosperma merkusii; syn. C. chamissonis). Hather and Weisler (2000).

8 Pigs were a later introduction, possibly because of the limited availability of plant food for them. Prior to 1880, chickens were likewise absent – except on Mataiva in the extreme west.

9 According to radiocarbon dating evidence from archaeological excavations in the region, the surrounding archipelagos – Society, Gambier and Marquesas islands. Wilmshurst et al. (2011), Allen (2014), Conte and Molle (2014), Kirch et al. (2015b), Stevenson et al. (2017). This date is consistent with the 1000 years of habitation inferred from extensive genealogies collected by researchers at the Bishop Museum in Hawai`i, who used the high incidence of intermarriage between members of neighbouring atolls to cross-check remembered lines of descent for accuracy, and from these estimated the number of generations of continuous occupation.

10 Dickinson (2009).

11 Dupon (1986). And, if predictions about global warming, rising sea levels, and increasingly frequent storms are correct, most of these atolls will be permanently swallowed up again by the end of this century.

12 Chauvet (1935), who gives specific examples of major inundations on `Ana`a in 1877, and on Hikueru, Paraoa, and Hao (on the last of which 500 were drowned).

13 Smith (1903), Emory (1934b, 1940, 1947c), Weisler (2002).

14 Sugarcane is intolerant of severe frosts and does not appear to have been successfully grown by pre-European Māori in New Zealand, where its name was transferred to the stem of raupō (Typha orientalis), which is likewise valued for roof thatching.

15 In New Zealand, the name was transferred to a look-alike cousin, rengarenga (renga lily, Arthropodium cirratum).

16 Little and Skolmen (2003), Larrue et al. (2010). Polynesian bamboo was almost certainly brought to New Zealand, where sensitivity to frost would have hampered propagation. Although linked by name to New Zealand's kohekohe tree (Dysoxylum spectabile), the reason remains obscure. Biggs (1991: 68).

17 Danielsson (1952).

18 John Byron quoted in Emory (1934b: 14). Father Fierens, visiting a marae on Tātakoto in 1870, likewise referred to altars 'furnished with small boxes resembling coffins and enclosing hair of ancestors or feathers of rare birds. The whole box is covered with pandanus leaves and feathers of sea birds. I saw a few idols of wood. . .' (Fierens quoted in Emory 1934b: 14.)

19 Coconut cream was traditionally rendered into oil in a wooden bowl; the cream was curdled by 'stone boiling' (immersing hot stones in the liquid – a method practised in New Zealand for cooking bull kelp and the kernels of hinau berries).

20 Although most of the palms growing here today were planted in the 19th century to meet an international demand for copra (dried coconut).

21 Coconut palm pollen found in lake sediments on `Ātiu (Cook Is) in the 1990s was dated at 6600 BC; similarly, in the lake sediments on Mangaia at 5300 BC. Both greatly predate human settlement of these islands. Some 16 million years ago, a much smaller species (with nuts just 3 cm long) also grew in Northland, New Zealand.

22 Ward and Brookfield (1992). Europeans saw the thin-husked kind in Colombia in 1513. Zizumbo-Villarreal and Quero (1998). DNA research appears to link these early coconuts to those from the Philippines, rather than to any other Pacific region – 'an origin [that] rules out the possibility of natural dissemination by the sea currents'. Baudouin and Lebrun (2009) add that the morphology and the physiology of fruit from this Panama Tall cultivar belongs to the domesticated niu vai type that is poorly adapted to long-distance dissemination by sea currents. Clement et al. (2013), who reviewed the evidence, conclude that introduction to Panama occurred after Spanish conquest.

23 This coconut term survives in the Māori names kahakaha (Collospermum species) and kakaha (Astelia species), the strap-like leaves of which supplied a generally inferior alternative source of fibre.

24 Specifically, foods prepared from kūmara (sweet potato) and bracken fern rhizome.

25 Elsewhere, the name is known only in other forms. In the Tuamotus, Laportea ruderalis grows on most of the atolls and certainly goes by this name on Raro`ia, Hao and on Tepoto-Nord (as 'ogaoga').

26 Riley (1994: 374).

27 'Quant aux pirogues, j'en voyais partout de différentes formes et de différentes grandeurs; mais les plus considérables étaient celles qu'ils

nomment pahi (navire), et qui ne servent que pour les longs voyages en mer. Elles sont toujours attachées deux ensemble, avec une plate forme au milieu. Ce sont des bâtiments immenses, dont un mesurait soixante quinze pieds de long sur vingt-huit de large.' Moerenhout (1837, vol. 1: 179). Tuamotuans were adept at building double-hulled craft from small pieces of timber ingeniously fitted and lashed together – see Emory (1975) and detailed engravings of one 13 m long by Pâris (1841).

28 Hornell (1945), in reference to *The Canoes of Oceania*, Haddon & Hornell, 3 vols, Honolulu, 1936–38.

29 William Ellis (1829-32) quoted in Di Piazza and Pearthree (2001b). On atolls in the Line and Phoenix Islands, tool-making basalt was shown to have been brought from no fewer than seven sources, some of it from over 2400 km (over 1300 nautical miles) away, a feat that was probably achieved with locally built outriggers. Di Piazza and Pearthree (2001c).

30 Di Piazza and Pearthree (2001b).

31 Di Piazza and Pearthree (2001b), Anderson (2014b: 35).

32 As observed by Banks in the Society Islands in 1769, quoted in Beaglehole (ed.) (1962: 320).

33 Worn fragments of these urchin spines found in archaeological sites continue to serve as a useful indicator of levels of prehistoric human activity.

34 Emory (1975: 141). If a manta ray was available, its tail skin was used for heavy sanding and skin from its sides for lighter finishing.

35 Sharks' teeth were also used as cutting and carving instruments, adding a sharp edge to war clubs and spears; or drilled as pendants and ear ornaments. In New Zealand, shark teeth (or ear ornaments made from them) are known by the same names as the sharks themselves: makao, mako, mōtoi or ngutukao.

36 The rig suggests that it may have been influenced by European contact.

37 Emory (1975: 140).

38 Stimson and Marshall (1964).

39 Used by Māori for scraping vegetables and preparing leaves for weaving or rope-making, and as a tool for cutting hair, flax and meat, and for fashioning fishhooks. On the atoll of `Ana`a (Tuamotus) and in Mangarevan, the term refers also to a tool made from this shell or from a piece of mother-of-pearl.

40 On Pukapuka (N. Cook Is.), at least, also as lancets for surgery. Beaglehole and Beaglehole (1938).

41 Emory and Ottino (1967).

42 Taonui (2006: 45). The centre of French colonial administration for the Tuamotus shifted to Fakarava from nearby `Ana`a in 1878. Fakarava was Havaiki (homeland) to the renowned navigator Pere, who voyaged from here to Tahiti. The regional prominence of this atoll is reflected in the naming of its own Taputapuātea marae.

43 Taonui (2006: 45).

44 Emory (1975), Moerenhout (1837).

45 Re the Hawaiian Islands, see Collerson and Weisler (2007), whose conclusions were subsequently challenged by Anderson (2008a), with responses from Weisler (2008) and Kirch (2008).

46 This is reflected in early Polynesia–European contact and the early introduction of iron to the Tuamotuans. In 1521 Magellan passed within sight of Pukapuka Atoll, followed by the *San Lesmes* (which sank off Āmanu in 1526), then the Portuguese Quirós in 1606. Next came the ships of the Dutch, Schouten and Le Maire, who made contact on Takapoto in 1616, and then five crew deserting Roggeveen's Easter Island expedition on Takaroa in 1722. (The *San Lesmes* is one of seven caravel that left Spain in 1524. After three were lost or turned back, the remaining four rounded Cape Horn and were separated in a storm. In 1929 and 1968/69, iron cannons believed to be from the *San Lesmes* were recovered off Āmanu (Tuamotus), giving rise to conjecture regarding the early impact across the South Pacific of Spanish crew who survived the shipwrecks.)

47 In 1976, 1980 and 1985, when the traditional-style Hawaiian waka *Hōkūle`a* sailed from Hawai`i to Tahiti, it made first landfall here. On approach from the north, Rangiroa, Mataiva and Tikehau all serve as dependable landing sites, from where the navigator can obtain a bearing for the closing leg. Similarly, voyaging from Mangareva to the Marquesas through these atolls (including Taenga, Vahitahi and Marutea) is recorded in the traditional Tuamotuan chant 'Voyaging'. Stimson (1957: 61).

48 Wilkes (1852: 123), who produced the first complete map of the archipelago in 1845.

49 Consistent with the insect's short flight range – 92 m through forest in one experiment, Once egg development is complete, the eggs are resistant to desiccation. Failloux et al (1997), McCormack (2007).

50 Transferred in New Zealand to the similar-looking New Zealand falcon

(kārewarewa, *Falco novaeseelandiae*), a transfer that had already occurred before the publication of Williams, *A Dictionary of the Maori Language* – as evident in traditional sayings: 'Kia ata kai, kaua e kainga kārearea tia' (Eat slowly; don't eat like a falcon); and 'He kārewarewa koe kia whakatopatia ki te kiore?' (Are you like the falcon who swoops onto the rat?).

51 The term kivi has been recorded for other shorebirds from the Polynesian Outliers.

52 Chorus of 'Pathway of the Birds' translated from Huauri's 'Lament for Tahaki' by Stimson (1957: 73–75).

53 Although their return south in August may have helped with the location or relocation of islands in the tropical Pacific itself. In Samoan tradition, Tagaloa sent his daughter Sina to Earth in the form of a bird, Tuli, to find dry land. Tuli refers specifically to landfinding waders, often to the Pacific golden plover (Clark 1982) – a species mentioned also in one old Tuamotuan voyaging song, 'Song of the Birds of the Sea Kings': 'O Soaring bird-god of the heavens! Thou art. . . the eyes of the plover'. Stimson (1957: 214).

54 Of Tuamotuan bird names, nearly 80 percent are shared with East Polynesia and none exclusively with West Polynesia. Emory (1947a).

55 Bogert (1937), Philippe Raust, Société d'Ornithologie de Polynésie (pers. comm.).

56 Best (1929:57) identifies the Māori ngutukao as a tiger shark. The term ngutukao is also found in Tonga for a much smaller fish, with a similarly pointed nose: the longface emperor (*Lethrinus olivaceus*). In the Rennell Islands (Solomons), ngutukao is a kind of porpoise, as is nu`ao in Hawai`i. The related name ulukao for great white shark is also recorded on Nukumanu (PNG).

57 Tuamotuans find an analogous link between tides, sharks and ferocious monsters, especially near the mouth of lagoons, where the tidal flow of marine life brings most shark attacks on fishermen.

58 Rongo et al. (2009). The name of the primary dinoflagellate responsible for ciguatera, *Gambierdiscus toxicus*, derives from the acuteness of the problem in the Gambier Is, near the nuclear test sites. However, although the tests are likely to have aggravated the problem, the presence of ciguatera in the Pacific predates the tests by hundreds of years.

59 Orbell (1995: 226). Rona – a woman who dared curse the moon for going behind a cloud – is a Tuamotuan story that is shared with New Zealand's Far North – and, in this case, also with Tahiti.

60 Tapsell (2006). In the North Island, Taputapuātea also refers to a sacred site at Whitianga.

61 Crowe (2014) found 146 New Zealand place names on the Tuamotus, compared with 108 on S. Cooks and 43 on N. Cooks. Koskinen (1973: 27) identified a strong link also between Tuamotuan place names and those of the Cook Is – more than with the Society Is. In this respect, several atolls in the southeastern Tuamotus stand out, particularly in proportion to land area. The density of shared names on Rēao Atoll, for example, is comparable with that found on Rarotonga, while the concentrations on Akiaki, Pīnaki and Vāhitahi all considerably exceed it. The link is interesting in that many Polynesian place names refer to distinctive geographical features, and New Zealand and the Tuamotus are geographically dissimilar.

62 Biggs (1965: 378). Likewise, Emory (1940): 'the Tuamotuan dialects are closer to the Maori than the Tahitian'. Of eight Tuamotuan dialects, those of the northwestern atolls are judged to be more strongly allied to the Society Islands and New Zealand, while southeastern ones display stronger affinities with the Marquesas and Mangareva.

63 As acknowledged by Sinoto (1983a).

64 As has been proposed by archaeologist Nigel Prickett (2001: 19), and by historian James Belich (1996: 19), who ranks the Tuamotus a 'dark-horse possibility'.

65 In the case of departures from the southern Tuamotuan atolls, departures may have been through the Austral Islands.

7 One Hawaiki Among Many [pp. 110–21]

1 Cook (1846: 117): 'To these six islands, Ulietea, Otaha, Bolabola, Huaheine, Tubai, and Maurua, as they lie contiguous to each other, I gave the names of Society Islands.'

2 Wilmshurst et al. (2011), Mulrooney et al. (2011). According to Stevenson et al. (2017), an analysis of sediment cores from Lake Temae – pollen, accelerator mass spectrometry (AMS) dating, and charcoal particle counts – are indicative of human presence on the island of Mo`orea by at least 1060–980 cal. yr BP.

3 Lepofsky (2003); although bottle gourds do seem to have entered the Pacific from both sides.

4 See also Henry (1912).

5 Salmond (2004: 38), Taonui (2006: 45).

6 Taonui (2006: 45).

7 Henry (1912).

8 Di Piazza and Pearthree (2007a).

9 Banks in Beaglehole (ed.) (1962, vol 1: 319), 21 July 1769.

10 Parkinson (1773: 74), 4 Aug 1769.

11 A nautical league is 3 nautical miles or 5.556 km.

12 Cook's Journal entry for 9 Aug 1769. 200–300 leagues is equivalent to 1100–1600 km; Rotumā (for which Tupa`ia gave directions) is 3400 km from Ra`iātea.

13 Rolett (2002). From this point, a few regions of the Pacific remained in contact with one another nonetheless, e.g., (1) the Society Islands and western Tuamotus; (2) the region of Fiji, Sāmoa and Tonga; and (3) Micronesia.

14 This refers to ENSO (El Niño–Southern Oscillation), which may have played a role in the timing of the initial colonisation of East Polynesia, too. See Rockman and Steele (eds) (2003), Anderson et al. (2006), Allen (2006), Goodwin et al. (2014).

15 In 1521 and 1526, Spanish ships had begun passing through the Tuamotus, followed by a violent visit to the Marquesas in 1595, news of which is likely to have led to a heightened wariness of newcomers. A conflict on the Society Islands, centred on a sacred drum, Ta`i-moana, led to two priests being killed – a quarrel that is remembered both in New Zealand and in the S. Cook Islands.

16 Goff et al. (2011a) refer to specific inundation events on Rurutu (Austral Is) AD 1450–1600, on Henderson Is AD 1260–1430, on the Marquesas AD 1450–1500, and on Pukapuka and Aitutaki AD 1500–1600. Goff et al. (2012) show that similar impacts were felt at this time on the Society and Cook Islands.

17 According to archaeologist Yosihiko Sinoto, the building of a canoe on Huahine was interrupted by a major tsunami. Sinoto's (1983b) original dates for this event were AD 1000–1100, subsequently revised by Anderson and Sinoto (2002) to about AD 1050–1450.

18 Known alternatively as kaweau, kawekaweā, kawekaweau, koehoperoa, koekoeā, koekoeau, kōhoperoa or kuekuea.

19 *Parsonsia heterophylla* in New Zealand; *Jasminum didymum* in Tahitian.

20 Académie Tahitiennne (1999: 404).

21 Robertson (1948), 18 June 1767.

22 Another estimate for Tahiti made seven years later in 1774 by Johann Forster, now judged to be more reliable, placed the figure even higher at 121,500. For New Zealand, see the estimates of Pool (1991) and Lewthwaite (1999): 'not much exceeding 100,000'.

23 Cook (1846, vol. 1: 71). It measured 267 ft by 71 ft at the base, rising in a stepped pyramid to 44 ft high.

24 Banks in Beaglehole (ed.) (1962: entry for 29 June 1769).

25 A fact that ethnologist Percy Smith used to support his conclusion that the Society Islands must be 'the immediate home from whence [Māori] came to New Zealand'. Smith (1898, 1904: 391).

26 Although Te Rangi Hīroa (1950b: 37) concedes that Tawhiti in the Māori phrases 'Tawhitinui, Tawhitiroa, Tawhitipamamao te hono-i-wairua' 'probably refers also to Tahiti'. See also Taonui (2006: 53).

27 As Belich (1996: 63) suggests, 'Hawaiki may have been goal as well as source, Promised Land as well as Paradise Lost . . . Parts, perhaps even the whole of New Zealand, were also originally named for it.' See also Simmons (1976), Groube (1965).

28 To Hawaiki nui, Hawaiki roa, Hawaiki pāmamao. Phillips et al. (eds) (2006: 41).

29 To this list, Taonui (2009) adds Havaiki on Niuē and Savaiki on Tongareva. Gifford (1923) explains that Havaiki in the Tongan archipelago applies to various tracts of land, where its meaning may refer directly to the island of Savai`i, or be derived from 'small' (iki) 'passage' (hava).

30 And various physical locations in New Zealand, including at Maketū Harbour, Lake Rotongaio, Kāwhia Harbour, Aotea Harbour and, on the eastern side, Rangitoto Is. Te Pou-hawaiki is a volcanic cone in central Auckland.

31 Tuamotuans use the term for homelands – either local or distant – as in the words of one traditional voyaging chant: 'The peaks of Havaiki are banked in clouds! . . . May the headland break through the shrouding mists! . . . Gliding, sweep in through the sacred pass . . .' From a traditional voyaging chant recorded by Stimson (1957: 57–61). An earlier translation appears in Stimson (1932). This clearly refers to a reef-encircled high island, such as one of the Society Islands.

32 An old name for Fakarava Atoll according to Association Culturelle, 'Te Reo o te Tuāmotu' (2001). Other forms of the same word are recorded on the Tuamotus as denoting celestial or subterranean hemispheres.

33 Based on local Cook Island genealogies and traditional history, Te Rangi

Hīroa (1950b) interprets the Rarotongan use of this term as referring to the Society Islands; however, Rarotongan traditions also give `Avaiki as an old name for Rarotonga and for various islands further west (Taonui 2006: 43, 49, 50).

34 Taonui (2006: 49).

35 Taonui (2006: 45). Just prior to Cook's visit, this hub had moved from Porapora to Taputapuātea.

36 Taputapuātea Stream, which drains the hills behind Whitianga, survives on modern maps and signage. Other New Zealand sites bearing this name include one on Maunganui Bluff (given as 'Mangonui Bluff' in Salmond) and another in Tauranga. Taputapuātea is also the ancient name of Mokoia Island in Lake Rotorua. Salmond (2004: 479).

37 Tapsell (2006).

38 Charcoal from one archery platform at the Taputapuātea site returned a radiocarbon date of about 1600. Emory and Sinoto (1965). Nine marae in the `Opunohu Valley, Mo`orea, were carbon dated to 1400–1650, while three large coastal marae and 19 inland marae platforms here – with remains of religious offerings made largely of coral – were found, by means of a precision technique called thorium dating, to be newer still; they were constructed between 1620 and 1760. Solsvik and Wallin (2007), Sharp et al. (2010). Wallin (1997): 'Concerning the chronological aspects of the archery platforms, there are indications that they developed in a quite late phase, possibly around A.D. 1400-1600.' A clear sequence was identified in local marae construction styles, starting with simple structures that lack an enclosing wall, progressing through walled enclosures with raised platforms to the grandest and most recent style with many steps, like the monumental one on Tahiti that Banks described in 1769. Temple architecture on Mo`orea using coral evidently developed rapidly over a period of approximately 140 years from around 1620 to 1760, culminating in large 'royal' marae with stepped ahu, such as those built in 1743 at Umarea, with the two larger ones of Nu`urua and Nu`upure approximately 20 years later. See also Wallin and Solsvik (2010).

39 This would help account for such stone platforms being unknown in New Zealand. Conversely, it would seem to imply that the Society Islands were still in contact at this point with other distant isles, such as the Marquesas, Easter Island and Hawai`i, where the custom of building these platforms was indeed adopted.

40 Rangiātea is given by Tapsell (2006) as the origin of *Te Arawa* and *Tainui*; by Taonui (2012a) as the origin of *Aotea*; and by Harvey (2012) as the origin of *Mātaatua*.

41 And to a spiritual realm. Royal (2012): 'Like Hawaiki, Rangiātea is seen as both a physical place and a spiritual realm – the fount of wisdom about the nature of existence.'

42 Best (1917), Davis et al. (1990). *Kurahaupō* and *Tākitimu* traditions refer to departures from the canoe-racing lagoon of Pikopiko-i-Whiti [Pi`opi`o-i-hiti]. Best (1917) places this lagoon at Taha`a, and as an ancient name of the lagoon encircling Tahiti. Jones and Biggs (1995) refer to the lagoon that encircles Ra`iātea.

43 Parkinson (1773: 70). The Polynesian custom of caging herons as pets is also recorded elsewhere (Wodzicki and Laird, 1970) and is perhaps linked to their use for landfinding, too.

44 Parkinson (1773), Salmond (2004: 101–2).

45 Charcoal from one archery platform here returned a radiocarbon date of about 1600. Emory and Sinoto (1965). The development on the Society Is of this type of massive marae architecture has been dated to 1620–1760 by Sharp et al. (2010), consistent with the suggestion by Solsvik and Wallin (2007) that these temple sites may not have played an important part in Society Is religious practices or socio-political structure until after 1500. The larger standing stones ('backrests for the chiefs') are evidently original, but few portable artefacts remain; many were removed by missionaries, colonists and souvenir hunters. The present cairn or altar is, of course, the product of a recent cultural revival.

46 For a detailed assessment of the early population estimates for Tahiti, see Kirch and Rallu (2007).

47 An analysis of Polynesian place names by Koskinen (1963: 10) found that 'the connection between New Zealand and certain island groups around Tahiti is not so marked as could be supposed'; nonetheless, over 250 Society Island place names are found in New Zealand – which is still high (Crowe 2014).

48 Wilson (2012) identifies language innovations that support a distinctive unified history of the languages of the Cooks, Australs, Tuamotus and New Zealand; he adds that Tahitian reflects 'innovations that are not only absent from Rapanui but also absent from Marquesan, Mangarevan, and sometimes Hawaiian . . . The number of such distinctive Tahitic innovations is substantial: POLLEX (2012) lists 212 of them'. So, although it is true that Tahitian is less readily understood

by modern Māori than Rarotongan or Tuamotuan, this may be partly attributable to ongoing interarchipelago influence on Tahitian after New Zealand's isolation.
49 Matisoo-Smith et al. (1998).

8 En Route to New Zealand [pp. 122–37]

1 According to Evans (1997), *Te Arawa*, *Kurahaupō*, *Mātaatua*, *Tainui* and *Tākitimu* settlement canoes all stopped off at Rarotonga on their way through to New Zealand, but the *Aotea* did not.
2 Te Rangi Hīroa (1944: 411). In some traditions a district in Tahiti is specified.
3 Wilmshurst et al. (2011), Mulrooney et al. (2011), Kirch (ed.) (2017), Stevenson et al. (2017).
4 Crombie and Steadman (1986). *Gehyra oceanica* and *Lepidodactylus lugubris* [Gekkonidae], and *Cryptoblepharus* cf. *poecilopleurus*, *Emoia cyanura* and *Lipinia noctua* [Scincidae].
5 Brook (2010). These include *Allopeas gracile* from Asia, 2 mm *Pupisoma orcula* from Asia, *Costigo saparuana* from he Banda Sea region, and 2.5 mm long *Gastrocopta pediculus* from tropical western Pacific.
6 Di Piazza and Pearthree (2001c), McAlister et al. (2013), Rolett et al. (2015), Weisler et al. (2016).
7 Walter and Sheppard (1996), Best et al. (1992).
8 Walter and Dickinson (1989).
9 Te Rangi Hīroa (1944: 176). As we saw (page 48), this last contact between the Southern Cook Is and Austral Is has since been confirmed by means of the known transfer of stone tools.
10 Campbell (2002).
11 Sheppard (1997).
12 A name unknown elsewhere, except in Tahitian, where it refers to a species of banana.
13 Here, ʻAvaiki is generally taken to be Rarotonga (Taonui 2006: 43), though others have interpreted Rū's homeland variously as Raʻiātea, Tubuai (Austral Is), Tubuai-manu (Maiʻao, Society Is) or Savaiʻi (Sāmoa). Halbert (1999).
14 Radiocarbon-dating evidence from Aitutaki. Allen and Wallace (2007). According to the findings of geoscientist William Dickinson (2009), Aitutaki did not appear above sea level until around AD 800.
15 Allen and Steadman (1990), Steadman (1991), Allen (1992).
16 Sinoto (1983a), Di Piazza and Pearthree (2001c). In 1990, 'the first archaeologically recorded quarry for the Southern Cooks' was identified on an islet in the southeast of the lagoon (Moturākau): the quarry 'was an important basalt resource area [for making adze heads] throughout much of the island's prehistory'. Allen and Schubel (1990).
17 Skinner (1933). 'Found by a native called Panga Rio in a small creek called Vaitekea, on Aitutaki . . .' The piece, which was '4¾ inches long and 1¾ inches in maximum width [with] one surface show[ing] a small amount of grinding', was sent to the Otago University Museum and judged by geologist Dr F. J. Turner as follows: 'in its macroscopic properties, microstructure, and especially in the presence of talc secondarily deposited along shear-zones, the rock perfectly resembles the typical tangiwai serpentines from Anita Bay, Milford Sound'.
18 See Stoddart et al. (1990).
19 The total population of Rarotonga in 2006 was 14,153, and yet in that same year, 58,008 inhabitants of New Zealand identified themselves as Cook Island Māori, illustrating the scale of the regional exodus.
20 Salmond (2004: 321).
21 In the latter name, local historian Tou Unuia identifies a cultural link with namesake marae sites on neighbouring Aitutaki, Mangaia, Maʻuke and Mitiʻāro, and with the main ceremonial centre of ʻOrongo on Easter Island. The name is derived from Rongo, the East Polynesian god of peace and agriculture, to whom it was dedicated. The local ariki title of Rongomatāne can likewise be linked with Rongomātāne (a god of the forest) in New Zealand.
22 Where the bright red feathers of honeyeaters were pasted onto a bark strip and coiled for use as currency; as many as ten coils (each 5–9 m long, with feathers from 300–350 birds) being typically required by a man to present to his bride's family.
23 When Cook reached the Marquesas in 1774, his crew found that, as soon as they offered red parrot feathers from Tonga in exchange for local pigs, Marquesans would trade for nothing less. Oral accounts collected in the Marquesas by German ethnographer Karl Von Den Steinen in 1897, speak of voyagers sailing west from here to collect red feathers from Rarotonga.
24 While these names may originate in the Society Islands, parrots may have been previously known on the Cook Islands as kākā, too. (Compare Malay kaka-tuwah = cockatoo.)

25 And among the native cultures of Indonesia, Australia, Eskimo and Africa.
26 Known in West Polynesia as tika.
27 Indeed, among useful coastal plants of the Pacific, beach hibiscus ranks second only to coconut. Fishing line and nets were also made from the bark from another shrub, *Pipturus argenteus*, known by cognate names, fau sogā (in Sāmoa) and wao (on Pukapuka).
28 Indeed, 'ama' in this tree's alternative names (whauama, hauama, houama) refers to the outrigger – as in 'waka ama'. Whau/ hou recurs in names for another New Zealand sandal-making tree, whauwhaupaku or puahou (five finger, *Pseudopanax arboreus*), whose inner bark served to make padded footwear in the cooler South Island climate. Horwood and Wilson (2008).
29 Or with leaves folded over them and sewn as roofing thatch. The term 'kaʻo' refers to these 'rafters' that support the thatch.
30 Best (1925c: 195, 253).
31 A term that also appears in Tahitian for a sedge, mōuʻu raupo.
32 The Polynesian name is used for octopus right across the Pacific, but is recorded for both squid and octopus only in the Society Islands, here in the Cooks and in New Zealand (as wheke).
33 Christian (1924).
34 Best (1899), Pendergrast (1987), Cooper and Cambie (1991), Maysmor (2001), Scheele and Sweetapple (2011).
35 Ngata (1950).
36 Green (2005: 53).
37 The authors' original estimate of 'around AD 1000' (Hather and Kirch 1991) was adjusted by Wilmshurst et al. (2011) and subsequently by Kirch (ed.) (2017) to 'by AD 1400'. Kūmara is understood to have reached Rarotonga much later (and later again the Philippines, thence New Guinea and Melanesia – on 16th-century Spanish ships).
38 Te Rangi Hīroa (1944: 178), McCormack (2007).
39 Te Rangi Hīroa (1944: 177).
40 Bonar (1901): 'nearly 60 feet long, or perhaps more'.
41 Kirch and Green (2001) argue that a Pacific-wide use of the word Māori for indigenous predates this, but see Williams (1971: 179), Atkinson (1892) and Sorrenson (1979: 59) for its first use in New Zealand.
42 First known record in 1852, according to Pukui and Elbert (1985).
43 Davies (1851), and see Saura (2011).
44 Biggs (1994), Crowe (2014).
45 At least 45 Rarotongan place names are shared with New Zealand. Crowe (2014).
46 Depicted in carving in the marakihau style – with a serpent-like body and hollow tongue. At least 22 New Zealand place names can be recognised on Mangaia, a number that is again high in proportion to its size; on ʻĀtiu, Maʻuke and Mitiʻāro, New Zealand place names are scattered more thinly, but at a density that is still equivalent to that found on Society Islands such as Raʻiātea and Tahaʻa. Crowe (2014).
47 Ngata (1950).
48 Matisoo-Smith et al. (1998).
49 Smith's story can be traced back to an earlier account published by Sir George Grey in 1853, in which Smith (1898) subsequently identified their port of departure with Rarotonga. Relying on diverse sources, Grey (1853, 1854: 101) had given this same list of canoes in a chapter entitled 'Construction of canoes to emigrate to New Zealand'. S. Percy Smith elaborated on this, attributing the initial discovery of the country to Kupe, followed by a single 'Great Fleet' of canoes some four centuries later. In 1976, this so-called orthodox version of New Zealand's discovery and settlement was dubbed by ethnologist David Simmons 'the Great New Zealand Myth'. A detailed analysis of the original traditions led Simmons (1976) to the conclusion that 'Kupe is most definitely contemporary' with other founding canoes. Tribal historian Rongowhakaata Halbert (1999) agrees, 'Kupe's voyaging was probably confined to the coastal waters of Aotearoa [New Zealand]'. A critical analysis of the traditions is provided by Taonui (1994: 264–67). Sorrenson (1979) provided another very readable summary. Likewise, New Zealand historian Michael King (2003: 42): 'It is . . . unlikely that [Kupe] was the discoverer of the country.' Despite the diverse genealogies recorded for Kupe, these are now believed to refer to the same man (Taonui 2011: 6).
50 King (2003: 38–41). Smith's narrative did not match the genealogies and stories he collected. His interpretation was challenged by Stokes (1930), by Ngata (1933) quoted in Belich (1996: 25), by Sharp (1964: 88), by Simmons (1969, 1976) and others. Smith had effectively 'cut and pasted' diverse tribal stories, selectively ignoring significant details to generate his own version. Smith's story was nonetheless widely accepted as authentic, even by Māori, particularly from 1910 until 1970. Taonui (2006: 35). Even an attempt by Anderson (2014b: 42, 67) to argue

'that the concept of a fleet, or fleets, of migration canoes is no Pākehā invention', came to the conclusion that 'migration occurred in many more canoes than are included in the "Great Fleet", and some of them probably travelled together'. As to how Smith's story came to be so widely accepted, the answer lies partly in the timing, for its publication coincided with catostrophic population losses and land alienation among Māori during the so-called 'Decades of Despair' (1840–1900). Smith's heroic narrative provided a welcome counterpoint to the resulting loss of morale, serving as 'a source of pride for Māori and an antidote to the concurrent and widespread view that Tasman and Cook "discovered" New Zealand.' King (2003: 35). On Rarotonga likewise, during the dysentery epidemic of 1830, mass burials were occuring at a rate of 10 to 20 people a day. And from 1827 to 1867 introduced epidemics of influenza, measles, smallpox, tuberculosis, dysentery and whooping cough took around 70 percent of the Rarotongan population. Crocombe (1961: 135).

51 Contact along this latitude is consistent with the facts that an Ellicean (Tuvaluan) language is spoken on Sikaiana, and that Sikaiana lies in a region identified by linguist William Wilson (2012) as a major origin of East Polynesians.

52 Sāmoa (at 13°S) and Pukapuka (at 11°S) lie at similar latitudes, as do Tongareva (at 9°S) and Nuku Hiva (at 9°S). With Rigel, the brightest star in the constellation of Orion, as a zenith star, navigators could explore upwind and downwind along this latitude relatively safely. In AD 1000, Rigel was zenith star for 10°S; in 2000 for 8°S.

53 Contact from Sāmoa to the Marquesas via Manihiki is supported by the evolution of Polynesian canoe design traits. Rogers et al. (2009: 3838, Fig. 2). Contact along this route is consistent with settlement of East Polynesia through Tokelau, Phoenix Islands, Line Islands and N. Cook Islands. Addison et al. (2009), Koskinen (1973: 18).

54 Beaglehole and Beaglehole (1938: 413, 415). This includes an influence from both West and East Polynesia in the musical instruments of Pukapuka. McLean (1999: 100).

55 Based on the fact that a raid in 1863 by Peruvian slave traders took 145 men and women, and that a population estimate three years later in 1866 still gave 750. Oliver (2002: 33), Maude (1981: 192).

56 An adze found on nearby Nassau that was provisionally sourced on the basis of style to Mangaia suggests contact with Mangaia. Skinner (1940).

57 Beaglehole and Beaglehole (1938: 351), Di Piazza and Pearthree (2001c), Chikamori and Yoshida (1988).

58 Specifically, directions via Pukapuka to Atafu, Swains Is, Savai`i, `Upolu, Tutuila, Manu`a, Vava`u and `Uiha. Di Piazza and Pearthree (2007a).

59 Chikamori quoted in Kirch (2000: 232) gives radiocarbon dates for Pukapuka of '2310 ± 65 to 1540 ± 70 BP'.

60 Markham (ed.) (1904: 216).

61 Emory (1934a: 8).

62 Te Rangi Hiroa (1932a: 5, 22, 1932b: 16).

63 Quoted in Roscoe (1987). And this was already 30 years after first contact with Europe in 1788.

64 Roscoe (1987). A detailed study in 1987 by anthropologist Paul Roscoe provided some support for this figure: he estimated a peak of around 1750 inhabitants, 'unambiguously establish[ing] the atoll as one of the most densely populated in the Pacific for its size range', and added that 'the population of Tongareva suffered a spectacular decline during the period 1853–1862'.

65 Beaglehole and Beaglehole (1938: 388–93).

66 Goff et al. (2011a) postulates that this may be the same tsunami event that can be dated on Aitutaki to AD 1500–1600.

67 Oliver (2002: 33), Maude (1981: 192).

68 In 1769, Tahitian navigator Tupa`ia was able to give Captain Cook accurate course directions from Meheti`a (Society Is) to Pukapuka. Di Piazza and Pearthree (2007a).

69 Bogert (1937), McCormack (2007).

70 Contact by Pukapuka and Rakahanga with Rarotonga is referred to in oral tradition. Taonui (2006: 41).

71 Jones (2001).

72 Te Rangi Hiroa (1932a: 189).

73 Cook landed on Palmerston Atoll on 13 April 1777. In 1863 the island was reoccupied and currently supports about 50 residents.

74 Gill (1885).

75 Te Rangi Hiroa (1932a: 11). New Zealand place names can be recognised on both atolls – more in proportion to land area than are found on most other islands in Polynesia. Crowe (2012, 2014).

76 Te Rangi Hiroa (1932b: 13, 14,15) observed that the local 'tch' sound also 'appears in the Chatham Islands where the *t* undergoes a change in sound before all the vowels except o'; a similar pronunciation of the 't' is

found in the Tongan archipelago (as noted by Tregear 1891).

77 Note that comparable scores for Pukapuka, Manihiki and Rakahanga are all similarly high. Crowe (2014) found 43 New Zealand place names shared with the *Northern* Cook Islands. This represents a total for all the Cook Is (N. and S.) of 151 (108+43), for which Koskinen (1963: 8) found 133.

78 Skinner (1933). The adze was 'about five inches long and about three inches wide at the cutting edge, and . . . not very well finished'.

79 Pukapuka to NZ is 3380 km; Rakahanga to NZ 3750 km, Tongareva to NZ 4050 km, and Tahiti to NZ 4090 km.

9 Nature's Signposts [pp. 138–57]

1 According to Te Rangi Hiroa (1950b: 38), 'practically all the canoe traditions give accounts of the bitter fighting that took place before their departure'.

2 Dening (1962).

3 Te Rangi Hiroa (1938b: 42).

4 Notably by Andrew Sharp (1956a, 1956b).

5 When more than 150 such voyages were tabulated and mapped by Golson (1962), almost all proved to be west-bound and within the tropical belt. (Leonardo Pakarati's story here of steering from Easter Is to Tahiti by aiming his bow at Venus after sunset in Jan 1949 is clearly fabricated, for at that time and location, Venus was not even visible.)

6 Levison et al. (1972).

7 In the Northern Hemisphere, the corresponding phenomenon is a mirror image of this.

8 Past wind directions in the tropical Pacific can be ascertained by studying changes in the geochemistry of coral skeletons growing on Line Island reefs. Variations in the coral growth rates, combined with more general climate modelling, have enabled scientists to identify a peak in El Niño events around AD 1200. This would have resulted in weakening trade winds and strengthening equatorial westerlies, coinciding roughly with the earliest archaeological dates of human presence in East Polynesia. Increased frequency of episodes of ENSO may therefore have played a role in the discovery and settlement of the eastern Pacific. Cobb et al. (2003), Rockman and Steele (eds) (2003), Anderson et al. (2006), Allen (2006), Wilmshurst et al. (2011). See also Goodwin et al. (2014).

9 Williams (1837: 363): 'two hundred miles west of [Niuē to Tahiti]. . . in the short space of fifteen days, a distance of about seventeen or eighteen hundred miles to the eastward'. See also Finney (1989).

10 Lewis (1972: 4).

11 The indigenous name, Rangitahua, is thought to refer to Raoul. Note that Rangi-ta`ua is also a marae name in the Keia district of Mangaia (S. Cook Is).

12 Larrue et al. (2010).

13 A British crew aboard the *Lady Penrhyn* came upon two of these islands en route to Tahiti from Sydney.

14 As alluded to in the migration narratives of *Mātaatua, Kurahaupō* and *Aotea*.

15 Known Polynesian sites and artefact finds are on the north side of the island, though, an area facing away from prevailing westerly winds, with some offshore shelter from the Herald Islands. Landing on this side – nowadays, at least – involves negotiating a difficult boulder beach.

16 Duff (1968).

17 Candlenut (*Aleurites moluccana*) is native to Indo-Malaysia, aboriginally introduced to the Pacific Islands, including Raoul Is, where the Bell family found it already established in 1878 at Coral Bay – a site used by Polynesians. West (1996). The Pacific Island cabbage tree (tī, *Cordyline fruticosa*) on Raoul Is is a sterile cultivar and hence not only a Polynesian introduction, but specifically from East Polynesia. Hinkle (2004).

18 MacPhail et al. (2001), McBreen et al. (2003), Wehi and Clarkson (2007). However, introduction of flax in the European era cannot be ruled out.

19 Anderson and McFadgen (1990), Anderson (2000a). In 2010, another obsidian flake from Tūhua was found 110 km to the southwest on Macauley Island (Furey et al. 2015).

20 Matisoo-Smith et al. (1998, 1999), Atkinson and Towns (2001). Matisoo-Smith et al. (1998): 'Genetic diversity among rats from the Kermadecs supports their role as intermediary islands in two-way and multiple voyaging between the New Zealand archipelago and the tropics.'

21 In fact, in good conditions, Raoul can sometimes be seen from a distance of up to 110 km.

22 Based on Raoul being 9.5 km wide and some 900 km distant from the (now uninhabited) island of `Ata (Tonga).

23 Based on the first census of the *Onychoprion fuscatus* population here, made by the 1966/67 OSNZ expedition, which estimated 40,000 pairs at Denham Bay, about 40,000 along the southern side of Hutchinson Bluff,

2500+ pairs on North Meyer, 4000+ pairs on South Meyer and up to 3000 pairs on Dayrell (Veitch et al. 2004).

24 From Macauley Is, another one of the Kermadecs.

25 The same is true of populations based on Norfolk Is and Rapa Iti.

26 According to 1908 estimates. Veitch et al. (2004). More than 12,000 Kermadec petrels were harvested and preserved here by Europeans for winter food in 1889 alone. At the end of the breeding season, the birds range north across the tropical Pacific – usually flying low to the water – some reaching as far north as Hawai`i.

27 June–July, white-naped petrels head north from these islands for winter, ranging across the tropical Pacific as far as the Hawaiian Is In October, the entire population (nowadays, some 50,000 pairs of birds) converges on the one tiny island here (Macauley Is, Kermadecs) to breed.

28 Kōwhai seeds from New Zealand float to Chile, too. Markham and Godley (1972), the phylogeny of various populations of the species confirms transport in this direction. Hurr et al. (1999). Their colour clearly distinguishes them from seed produced by any equivalent tropical shrub, for the `ōhai of Tonga (*Delonix regia*); `ōfai of French Polynesia (*Sesbania grandiflora*; syn. *S. coccinea* ssp. *atollensis*); and *Sophora tomentosa* of tropical Polynesia are dark brown and/or much larger.

29 Adams (1994: 13,114).

30 The nearest region where this kelp grows naturally and plentifully is the Three Kings Islands, north of New Zealand's North Cape. Over 70 million rafts of it are estimated to be afloat at any one time – borne on the Antarctic Circumpolar Current, or West Wind Drift. Smith (2002).

31 Terms for specific species of driftwood (fukafuka or maota), and for whole floating trees (afatea) are recorded on Takuu (a Polynesian Outlier of New Guinea), and terms for *specific species* of driftwood (ahadea and ahabagua) on Nukuoro (Caroline Is).

32 As New Zealand botanist Thomas Cheeseman (1888) learnt from Thomas Bell, who had been living with his family on Raoul Island since 1878 – and this is well before the felling of kauri reached its peak around 1900. According to Halkett and Sale (1986), kauri logs are 'reported to have floated with prevailing winds as far as Chile'.

33 In the first formal estimate of sooty shearwater numbers within New Zealand territory, Newman et al. (2009) 'estimated the total population over 1994–2005 to be 21.3 (19.0–23.6) million individual birds in the New Zealand region'.

34 Determined from subfossil and midden evidence. Here, as elsewhere, the fat chicks supplied a traditional food harvested in spring by Māori who had only to reach into their nesting burrows to grab them.

35 Shaffer et al. (2006).

36 In Tuamotuan tītī also means 'to flock or congregate together'. This name is recorded on Rarotonga and Mangaia (S. Cook Is) for the black-winged petrel (*Pterodroma nigripennis*), a bird that on Mangaia was harvested to extinction. Steadman and Kirch (1990). On Rapa Iti, 'oioi' applies to petrels.

37 Although 300,000–400,000 pairs of mottled petrels breed on offshore islands around Stewart Island now, they previously bred in large numbers also in North Island forest. Māori reached into burrows to harvest the fat chicks and, on foggy nights, made fires on high hills near their burrows to attract the adults, killing them with sticks.

38 The total population nowadays is about 1,300,000, but would have been considerably higher prior to the introduction of Pacific rats, as reflected in a six-fold explosion in the Cook's petrel population on Little Barrier Island after the eradication of rats, from around 50,000 pairs in 2004 to an estimated 286,000 pairs the following year. Again, this bird formerly bred far more widely, as indicated by subfossil midden evidence of at least 11 extinct forest colonies on the North and South Island mainland. Imber (2003).

39 Nowadays some 3000–4000 black petrels nest in burrows on Little Barrier and Great Barrier Islands, but numbers would again have been far higher, given that they previously nested also on mountain ranges in the North Island and northwestern South Island. Despite large numbers of chicks taken from their burrows by Māori, the size of flocks witnessed by Cook off New Zealand in 1769 impressed him. By Mar–July, most are heading off from here over East Polynesia to waters off southern Mexico and Peru.

40 Tennyson and Martinson (2006). Although most of New Zealand's original 88 seabird species still survive, many do so in greatly reduced numbers.

41 Turbott (ed.) (1967: 142).

42 Nowadays, these birds face significant additional risks from the infilling of mudflats for building development around the Yellow Sea, where they make an annual stop to feed on their way north to nest.

43 Based on flock sizes of 30–80 given in Woodley (2009: 79) and 700 to 1200 given by Captain Mair quoted in Buller (1877).

44 Riegen (2005). To perform this extraordinary 10,600-km feat of crossing the Pacific in a single non-stop flight, godwits have evolved a wind-sensitive migration strategy with a timing that is precise. When setting off on their non-stop southbound flight to New Zealand (lasting just 6–10 days), their peak departure dates from Alaska rarely vary by more than two or three weeks.

45 Gill et al. (2009).

46 According to Woodley (2009: 34), traditions of Ngāti Awa (eastern Bay of Plenty) and Ngāi Tāhuhu (Northland) refer to godwits guiding their ancestral canoes to New Zealand; however, Gudgeon (1903: 126) did distinguish the migratory bird concerned as one that leaves from, and returns to, small islands in the Pacific – which would seem to preclude the godwit.

47 By Henry Mair (brother of Captain Gilbert Mair) and quoted in Buller (1888: 44).

48 Higgins (ed.) (1999: 776).

49 According to natural history writer Craig Robertson (2011) and http://nzbirdsonline.org.nz/species/long-tailed-cuckoo.

50 Fulton (1903), Bogert (1937).

51 Quoted in Turbott (ed.) (1967: 76).

52 In New Zealand, kārewarewa, kārewarewa tara etc. refer to the New Zealand falcon, a look-alike bird clearly distinguishable from the cuckoo by its agile hunting behaviour, hooked bill and non-migratory habits.

53 Which could be translated as kā ('screech') + rewa ('depart').

54 For example, 'Song of the Birds of the Sea Kings' in Stimson (1957: 214).

55 Which were up to about 6 m long, 4.5 m wide and 3 m high. Emory (1934b). Here, the name Vairaatea is used, an orthography atypical of the Marangai dialect.

56 Gill and Hauber (2012).

57 Iceland had been settled by about AD 700, and Madagascar as early as 350 BC, evidence for which includes a sudden decline at this point in local megafauna followed closely by a sudden increase in *Sporormiella* fungus, which specialises in living in the dung of herbivores, including grazing livestock. Burney et al. (2004). The island seems to have been visited at least intermittently by Africans prior to the arrival of Austronesian-speaking maritime travellers from Island Southeast Asia.

58 King (2003:42).

59 Simmons (1969) distinguishes between locally born Toikairākau ('Toi the wood eater') of Bay of Plenty–Tūhoe, and Toitehuatahi ('Toi the first') – an ancestor of Arawa who never came to New Zealand.

60 Of course, being able to identify such points of contact now would seem to imply that Kupe's visit was witnessed by prior inhabitants and that knowledge of the relevant locations was subsequently passed on by them.

61 Swarbrick (2012). By 1840, Māori clearance by fire of New Zealand's indigenous forest had reduced the total cover to 53 percent.

62 Although dead, the stump of the largest kauri seen by Europeans (near Thames) measured 8.3 m across.

63 Best (1925c: 93).

64 Banks in Beaglehole (ed.) (1962: 320). Journal entry from 21 July 1769.

65 Europeans were slow to see the connection between ambergris and whales. On finding pieces of kauri gum washed up in mangrove swamps, they also assumed that mangrove trees were the origin, recording their confusion for posterity in the original scientific name for mangroves, *Avicennia resinifera* (now *A. marina* spp. *australasica*). In their efforts to define the Māori terms pakake, pakaka and mīmiha, Europeans could state only that these words referred to 'a black bituminous substance on the sea beach', overlooking the knowledge by Māori of its true origin, implied by the fact that all are Māori terms for whales.

66 An adult sperm whale may be up to 20 m long and about 13 m in girth; the *trunk* of Tāne Mahuta (the largest living kauri in terms of bulk) is 17.68 m high and 13.77 m in girth.

67 Adze heads, chisels, gouges, knives and scrapers, fish hook barbs, awls, points of drills and bird spears.

68 Although perhaps not in great quantities; indeed, none of these has yet been found in a secure archaeological context in the tropics. Despite reference to greenstone (bowenite and nephrite) in some traditional narratives, evidence for its long-distance transport by South Island Māori does not begin until the late 1300s. McKinnon (ed.) (1997).

69 Oliver (2002: 58).

70 From kiwi, weka and long-tailed cuckoo.

71 Other feathers used include those of pūkeko (blue) and albatross (white) and, for ornamentation of boxes, the hair and neck, etc., the feathers of shining cuckoo, white heron, bittern, harrier, gannet and paradise shelduck. Interestingly, the attractive blue feathers of kōtare (kingfisher) were not traditionally used.

72 Based on reconstructions from bones, taller estimates were made, but had failed to take account of the likely stance of moa as deduced from the natural S-shaped pose of related birds. Latest maximum weight estimates of the largest species put females at 242 kg (Tennyson and Martinson 2006) and here compared with average weight of an adult human at 62 kg.

73 The largest intact moa eggshell so far discovered was 24 cm x 17.8 cm. Worthy (2012). Moa bones also proved highly useful for fashioning fishhooks, harpoon heads and ornaments.

74 It is sometimes claimed that a sample of moa flesh – either dried or preserved in a gourd skin – was taken back to 'Hawaiki' (by Kupe or Ngāhue). Dansey (1947), Nelson (1991).

75 Kekeno ('to look about') and ihupuku ('hesitating').

76 Subfossil remains from early archaeological sites on the Kermadecs, Norfolk Island and the Southern Cook Islands reveal that they previously migrated further north still, in winter. Pup bones in archaeological sites reveal that fur-seal and sealion breeding ranges retreated southward from the Northland coast around 1300; to Cook Strait by about 1600; and to East Otago by 1800 (Anderson 2002a). When William Wyatt Gill recorded one on Mangaia (S. Cook Is) in the 1880s, locals had no name for it. Polynesians occasionally encountered seals sleeping on Nāpuka (Tuamotus) too, where they were known as humi or torotoro (Emory 1947c), and where a local marae was dedicated to butchering them for food.

77 Although the term poaka used by Māori today for 'pig' is evidently derived from the English 'porker' (Williams 1971: 505); when Cook arrived in New Zealand in 1769, the original Polynesian name 'puaka' was already known to Northland Māori – transcribed at the time as booah (pua`a, or puaka). See also Williams (1971: 301).

78 Even on small islands, pigs proved capable of wreaking havoc among crops, as occurred when they were introduced to the Austral Islands in 1789 by the mutineers of the *Bounty*. On Tikopia (Solomon Outliers) Polynesians even went so far as to deliberately kill off their own animals. Oliver (2002: 80). Although most Polynesians kept pigs untethered, Samoans kept theirs in enclosures.

79 Collins et al. (2014) used ancient DNA to differentiate midden remains of a now-extinct New Zealand endemic sealion (*Phocarctos* species), whose range was later replaced by that of *Phocarctos hookeri*.

80 Belich (1996: 54).

81 During his visit to Dusky Sound in 1773. Forster (1982). Seal teeth proved useful for making fishhooks and needles, and their skins would be worn inside out for warmth as cloaks (kahu-kekeno), which are likely to have been particularly useful in the first few years of Māori settlement, when there were not many dogs.

82 Polynesians sailing up the west coast of South America may have encountered one of several penguin species off the coasts of Chile and Peru.

83 This miniature species is known to Māori as kororā ('grey'), describing the colour seen as it dips and dives among the waves.

84 Boessenkool et al. (2009). Kororā (blue penguin, *Eudyptula minor*), hoiho (yellow-eyed penguin, *Megadyptes antipodes*, right), tawaki (pokotiwha, Fiordland crested penguin, *Eudyptes pachyrhynchus*) and now-extinct Waitaha penguin (*Megadyptes waitaha*) were all eaten by Māori.

85 Wilson (ed.) (1987: 78).

86 Larson et al. (2007).

87 Dobney et al. (2008) find a complete absence of 'Pacific Clade' haplotypes (sets of linked genes) in modern and ancient pig specimens from mainland China, Taiwan, the Philippines, Borneo and Sulawesi. A study of tooth outline and mtDNA shows a second prehistoric introduction to Micronesia through the Philippines. Piper et al. (2009) found evidence to suggest that 'domestic pigs were possibly introduced from Taiwan to the northern Philippines prior to the translocation of the 'Pacific Clade' from the mainland through ISEA'.

88 Archaeological evidence of pig has been found on Mangareva and Henderson Is, but those on the Tuamotus are thought to have arrived post-European-contact.

89 Kirch and Green (2001).

10 Planned Voyages of Settlement [pp. 158–75]

1 According to Goodwin et al. (2014), this may have been less of an issue prior to AD 1300.

2 Accumulated wind data indicates that the optimum time for sailing this route is in the southern spring (Oct–Dec), when the incidence of calms in this region is at its lowest (the chances of being left becalmed at sea between the S. Cook Is and New Zealand at this time is around 5 percent) and the frequency of easterly winds at its highest (blowing almost 80 percent of the time). McKinnon (ed.) 1997.

3 The South Pacific hurricane season is often given as Oct/Nov–April, but the highest cyclone risk in this region is Dec–Mar; even then, as Irwin (1992: 66) points out, the chances of any individual voyage being struck by a cyclone are slim.

4 Referred to as tūtara-kauika in Best (1922a: 29) and defined by Williams (1971) as 'a school of whales' (or as the 'right whale').

5 Although canoes sailing to New Zealand did not do so as a single fleet, *Tainui* and *Te Arawa* evidently sailed together. Belich (1996: 33). Legend links their voyages through their respective narratives and genealogies, a link 'reinforced by early marriage between the two groups'. Simmons (1969: 28).

6 'There are more kura in this land than there are kura in Hawaiki', he declared, 'kura' here meaning 'red' – specifically red feathers, from parakeets or the tail of red-tailed tropicbirds. Te Rangi Hiroa (1950b: 49). The practice of a navigator wearing crimson plumes as an insignia of rank was evidently widespread. Stimson (1932).

7 Williams (1837: 97). Similarly, standing stones were erected for this purpose in Kiribati and Tonga, and in the Tuamotus, where the use of similar stones is recorded for craft plying between the atolls of Nukutavake and Vairangatea (Vaira`atea). Emory (1934b).

8 According to Māori ethnologist Te Rangi Hiroa (1950b: 8), 'some traditions say that the correct sailing directions [for reaching New Zealand from Rarotonga] were to the left of the setting sun and others toward the rising sun'. However, prehistorian Atholl Anderson (2008d) cautions that 'traditions are seldom literal and ancient; they have been continually manipulated for various ends by Polynesians and Europeans'.

9 Lines from the traditional song 'Departure' as recorded and translated by Stimson (1957: 52).

10 Evans (1998: 49, 1997: 80).

11 According to Best (1922a: 44), 'Tradition states that the stars relied on during the voyage hither of the "Takitumu" were Atutahi (Canopus), Tautoru (Orion's Belt), Puanga (Rigel), Karewa [ID unknown], Takarua (Sirius), Tawera (Venus as Morning Star), Meremere (Venus as Evening Star), Matariki (Pleiades), Tama-rereti (Tail of Scorpion?), Te Ikaroa [the Milky Way].' (With respect to the conventional definition of Tāwera as 'The morning star, the planet Venus', this is hard to reconcile with the alignment of Tāwera with Antares given by Tautahi and Taipuhi, 1900.)

12 This is confirmed by the non-random placement of the rising and setting points of the chosen stars – as depicted on page 151. The programme was set for the location of Rarotonga (21°S; 160°W) on 23 Oct 1250; however, the change in positions of the stars is sufficiently slow that the observations generated by it remain valid to c1450. A start by 23 Oct represents a reasonable fit for the most complete known navigational star sequence – that of the *Tākitimu*. For recorded sets of navigational stars, see Best (1922a: 28, etc.) and Evans (1998).

13 Assuming that the record favours prow and stern stars. The date is governed by the visibility of Pleiades and Antares, suggesting a voyage commenced by about 23 Oct in 1250, or 25 Oct in 1450. In the case of the *Aotea* the instruction to rest the prow on Antares is specific; similarly, Pleiades serves until around this date each year as a stern star. Not all recorded 'sky ropes' are consistent with voyages along this bearing, though. For example, *Māmari* of Ngāpuhi steered toward Canopus 'when night falls' (see footnote 93, chapter 13), suggesting an approach from the NNW.

14 The navigational importance of Matariki is recorded for both the *Tākitimu* and *Tainui* canoes.

15 Three weeks later, Matariki (Pleiades) reappears as a morning horizon star at WNW off the starboard bow – which it does until 8 April.

16 Because the orbit of Venus around the sun is closer than ours, it always sets into, or rises from, the same quarter of the horizon as the sun. For about 10 months, it crosses the heavens ahead of the sun (during which time it is a morning star), and behind it for another 10 months (as an evening star).

17 That is, a maximum of 45°, or three hours interval, between the setting of Venus and the sun.

18 Canopus features prominently in the navigational lore of *Te Arawa*, *Tākitimu* and *Māmari*. Best (1922a: 45). As a horizon star, Canopus is useful only before the end of Oct (though it remains visible, close to the horizon soon after sunset, as late as Nov), marking 147° – a compass point that would need to be kept aligned with the port beam for this particular course.

19 'Nga turanga whatu o Rehua' ('on the place of Rehua's eyes'). Tautahi and Taipuhi (1900). (Rehua is also portrayed as a bird whose wings arch out on either side of Antares.) At the beginning of the sailing season, resting the course of the canoe on the place of Antares would serve as an almost perfect guide for a WSW course at the start of each night. According to

Evans (1998), Antares is also listed for *Te Arawa*. As it must set at least an hour later than the sun to be worthy of a place in the navigational instructions, and this occurs in 1250–1450 only prior to 23 Oct, this is chosen as our starting date for the simulation.

20 Mention of Puanga (Rigel) in the *Tākitimu* navigational instructions lends further support to a departure before 31 Oct. After this date, it is too high above the horizon by the time the sun has set to be useful as a guiding star.

21 Name given by Best (1922a: 38) for the same three stars of Orion's Belt in the Cook Islands. On East Futuna (Wallis & Futuna) and Tokelau, Tolu ('three') is said to refer to Orion's Belt, too; however, their Tokelauan use at their zenith as a direct guide on voyages from Nukunonu to Atafu at 8–9°S would suggest the three bright stars of Orion's sword at 6°S. (Orion's Belt at zenith signals 2°S.) Māori likened this, in combination with another short string of neighbouring stars, to an adze, Te Kakau a Māui.

22 Even in New Zealand, where deep-sea navigation had long fallen into disuse, '[t]he late chief Hone Mohi Tawhai [d.1894] informed Mr. J. B. Lee that he knew about three hundred star-names, but no one took the trouble to collect them'. Best (1922a: 46). As we saw, Lewis (1964) is more conservative; he tells us that Polynesian wayfinders had names for, and knew the courses of, some 150 stars.

23 More specifically: (1) For *Te Arawa* to follow close to the setting point of the sun, its voyage must have been underway in late spring/early summer. (2) For the crew of *Te Arawa* and *Tainui* to see the pōhutukawa in resplendent bloom, they must have reached New Zealand in the last two weeks of December. (3) For *Tākitimu* to make use of Canopus and Rigel, it had set out for New Zealand by 23 Oct; and, to make navigational use of the sun and rainbows, part of this course was sailed near the end of December. (4) In following the eyes of Rehua (Antares), *Aotea* must have set out before 1 November. (5) Other waka coming to New Zealand may have sailed other courses.

24 Because the rising and setting points of the sun drift cyclically back and forth along the horizon through the year, the navigator must constantly 'recalibrate' its bearing against that of other horizon stars.

25 In the Tuamotus at least, though Best (1922a: 51) gives also Sāmoa and Tahiti.

26 Best (1922a: 33, 45, 109).

27 A navigator following the morning rainbows would be led on quite a different course (WNW), and would be guided to New Zealand only from the Chatham Islands.

28 With an elevation of less than 40°.

29 Or 17th night, depending on the tribe.

30 Which a navigator may judge by how fast the sea is flowing past the hull, factoring in an educated guess as to the effect of local currents (which are not normally discernible in the open sea), and the sideways push of the wind discerned from the angle of deviation between the wake of the canoe and its hull.

31 Forster (1778: 509, 531 [note 18]).

32 The moon may also serve as a direct navigational aid, for at night its illuminated face continues to point to the hidden whereabouts of the sun.

33 Precision is aided by the fact that the moon rises each night some 50 minutes later than the night before – a lag that translates roughly to the span of thumb to forefinger with the arm outstretched. 'Nights of the moon' can thus be confidently identified not only by checking the moon's shape but also by its height in the heavens at sunset or sunrise.

34 As observed by Joseph Banks in 1769, during his visit with Cook to Tahiti. Banks in Beaglehole (ed.) (1962).

35 At this level, seven percent of the crew of 121 life-raft voyages died. At lower levels of water consumption, deaths jump dramatically. Golden and Tipton (2002).

36 Aboard *Te Aurere* and *Ngāhiraka Mai Tawhiti*, sailing to Easter Island from New Zealand via the Austral Islands. The 43 days here refers to the first leg of this voyage, 17 Aug to 29 Sep 2012.

37 Crozet quoted in Best (1925b: 252): 'Some [Māori] calabashes will hold as much as from ten to twelve pints of water.' The much larger sizes quoted elsewhere are thought to have been less well suited for water storage. See also Erickson et al. (2005).

38 Ideal for this purpose because of the sodium and potassium, vitamin C and sugars content. When blood plasma was scarce during World War II, this liquid was administered intravenously to patients suffering from loss of blood. Campbell-Falck et al. (2000). And from the 1950s, it was given in the same way to rehydrate patients suffering from diarrhoea.

39 In reality, the number of coconuts required to obtain this quantity of liquid may have been still higher due to fermentation of water in green coconuts, necessitating that some be supplied from more mature (and

therefore drier) nuts. Note that this minimum ration of 500 ml a day for survival represents a quarter (or less) of a more normal consumption of 2–4 litres, depending on climate and levels of physical activity.

40 Lounsbury and Bellamy (eds) (2002).

41 Thor Heyerdahl's recommendation was no stronger than 20–40 percent; even so, his raft *Kon-Tiki* carried over 1000 litres (275 gallons in 56 water cans) for a crew of six for 101 days – again, one tonne of freshwater.

42 The point is not only relevant to the voyaging range of Polynesians, it may be of medical interest, too. Mechanisms for excreting excess salt are known to exist in marine birds such as albatross and shags, through glands just behind their eye sockets; and also in some marine reptiles.

43 Emory (1934a: 38).

44 Beaglehole (1966).

45 Cook (1784). Likewise, wells on Polynesian atolls such as Malden Is contain only brackish water. Many other examples are given in Norton (1992). Experiments have shown that the ability of individuals to tolerate the salt levels found in seawater does vary; also, that it is only after three days that the cost to the body generally becomes evident. Barrington (1959).

46 Tregear (1899). In 1952, French physician Alain Bombard (1953) claimed, during one 23-day rainless period of a 65-day voyage across the Atlantic, to have drunk only seawater supplemented with fluid obtained from fish; however, significant aspects of his claim were subsequently challenged by German physician Hannes Lindemann. Another curious claim is that 'early [Samoan] voyagers always took a supply of leaves of a certain kind of herb or plant, as a means of lessening thirst ... By chewing [these] they declared that, to a certain extent, they could drink sea water with some kind of impunity, and thus assuage thirst.' The Rev. J. B. Stair, a missionary based in Sāmoa 1838–45, went to some lengths to try and identify the shrub. He reported: 'The natives I asked, said that they themselves did not know what it was, as the custom had grown into disuse; but they were confident such a custom had prevailed in the past ... I questioned many men of intelligence about the matter ...The constant reply was, "We do not know what it was ourselves, but we are certain our forefathers were accustomed to use the plant."' Stair (1895).

47 Similarly, the blood of turtles can be drunk, as its salt concentration is similar to ours: a 20-kg animal provides about one litre – a day's lifeboat ration for five.

48 Most of this is inferred from ethnographic evidence, but this last is inferred from the widespread distribution of the Polynesian terms tauraki ('to dry in air or by exposure to the sun') and kao – a term that, on Pukapuka (N. Cook Is), refers specifically to sun-dried fish, and in the Hawaiian Islands to baked taro or kūmara dried for sea journeys. Best (1923). In New Zealand, kao refers to a preparation of grated kūmara cooked and dried in the sun – a voyaging food referred to in tradition. Dried kūmara was reportedly brought by Hoaki and Taukata from Hawaiki on the *Hīnakipākau-o-te-rupe*. Taonui (2012a). For atoll dwellers, Te Rangi Hīroa (1938b: 40) adds 'ripe pandanus fruit grated into a coarse flour, cooked, dried, and packed in cylindrical bundles with an outer wrapping of dried pandanus leaves'.

49 Te Rangi Hīroa (1938b: 40). See also Rowe (1930: 268) re Samoan canoes: 'fire was carried under cover on a tray of earth and stones'.

50 Babayan et al. (1987: 196).

51 Houghton (1995). In winter at latitudes of 22°, the effects of exposure resulted in the deaths of every member of the Hawaiian group, too. By the time they reached the Kermadecs – even in summer – more than 80 percent succumbed to hypothermia. Although inadequate allowance may have been made in the trials for the protection afforded by traditional shelter and clothing (e.g. thick layers of pleated bark cloth), this does not detract from the *comparative* value of the trials. This adaptation to cold by Polynesians has been linked to a high incidence of obesity, type II diabetes and gout, resulting from a widespread change in diet.

52 Te Rangi Hīroa (1938b: 100).

53 From 'Storm', recorded and translated by Stimson (1957: 75).

54 'Rotu' in the Tuamotus (Vāhitahi) means to 'render the sea calm by use of a spell'; while karakia in the Tuamotus and S. Cook Is refers to 'a pre-Christian prayer'.

55 Twin-hulled craft are notoriously difficult to right; once overturned they are doomed, according to early observers in Hawai`i, unless they are towed to shallow water where they can be righted and bailed. The other option was to dismantle and reassemble the craft at sea. Outrigger canoes enjoy a far better chance of recovery.

56 Summer water temperatures at this latitude are typically 21–22°C, temperatures at which most adults can be expected to succumb to exhaustion or unconsciousness within 2–12 hours. US Coast Guard (2003). Here again, the dominant Polynesian body type would have helped.

57 From the Tuamotuan song 'Voyaging', recorded and translated by Stimson (1957: 47).

58 Which are likewise recorded in old Yankee whaling logs in enormous numbers here – at least from the Kermadecs south – and which have no trouble keeping up with modern yachts sailing at 6–7 knots. These nutrient-rich waters also attract pygmy sperm whales, beaked whales and pilot whales.

59 The name is recorded also from the N. Cook Is, but here applies to local species of dolphin.

60 July–Oct, humpbacks are just outside the reefs of Rarotonga, Mangaia and Aitutaki (S. Cook Is), also around Tonga (Tongatapu, Ha`apai group and Vava`u group), Mo`orea (near Tahiti) and Rurutu (Austral Is). Tracking research shows that many belong to distinct populations. Garrigue et al. (2002). In spring, they head down to their summer feeding grounds off Antarctica, some passing along the east coast of New Zealand.

61 Best (1925c: 406). Namely tūtara-kauika (that is, a school of whales, leader of a school of whales, or personification of whales) and Te Wehenga-kauki.

62 North American deep-sea whale vessel logbooks (1761–1920) estimate around 120,000 animals in the region of Sāmoa-Tonga alone – as compared with a population for the Tongan region now of some 1840. Branch (2011).

63 With lengths of 12–16 m, many would have been more than half the length of a voyaging canoe and, if travelling at average speeds of around 8 kph (4 knots), are likely to have been slowly streaming past the heavily laden migration waka. (Canoe speed is discussed more fully on page 174.)

64 In winter and early spring, many venture as far north of New Zealand as 25°S – north of the Kermadecs.

65 In the Tuamotus, toroa may refer to either a booby or an albatross, the smaller species of which are known in New Zealand as mollymawks. Another Māori albatross name that has its roots in the tropical Pacific, kōputu (for the light-mantled sooty albatross), refers in East Polynesia (Cook Is, Society Is and Marquesas) to other black birds of the deep ocean, particularly petrels such as the herald petrel.

66 The black-browed mollymawk (Diomedea melanophrys) ranges north to the Tropic of Capricorn; stragglers sometimes reach the Tuāmotu and Pitcairn Islands. The wandering albatross (Diomedea exulans) ranges north to around 20°S, occasionally as far north as Fiji.

67 Evans (1998: 120).

68 As confirmed by records from fishing vessels: http://data.dragonfly. co.nz/seabird-counts/explore/counts/xbg/black-backed-gull.html

69 Evans (1998: 120), on his approach to New Zealand aboard the Hawaiki-Nui in 1985, noted a distinct drop in temperature, a heavy dew in the morning, and insects beginning to land on the canoe – all at about 300 km out.

70 Beaglehole (1974: 161).

71 Evans (1998: 120) reports seeing 'the long cloud that often sits over New Zealand' at around 180 km. The crew of the Hōkūle`a, almost due east of the Bay of Islands, reported first seeing 'an image refracted over the horizon of long grey land mass or a dark cloud bank hovering above it' some 100 nautical miles (185 km) from land.

72 Although 'Aotearoa', explains King (2003: 41), is perhaps more properly rendered as 'Long Clear Day' or 'Long White Cloud'.

73 King (2003: 41), Salmond (2004: 459; 2008:16; 2009: 232, 356), Orbell (1998), Cook (1846: 169).

74 One Rarotongan name recorded for New Zealand, `Avaiki Tautau, could be translated as 'burning homeland'. Evidence for the scale of this burning is presented in the next chapter.

75 Based on NASA satellite images taken over the sea, showing smoke from large Australian bushfires.

76 Lewis (1972) aboard the Rehu Moana reports finding such vegetation some 280–370 km off New Zealand.

77 Mangrove propagules are released in northern New Zealand in late December; in fact, this tree is believed to have reached New Zealand originally as propagules floating much further – across the Tasman Sea from Australia.

78 Evans (1998). Joseph Banks aboard the Endeavour spotted seaweed over 500 km east of East Cape. Banks in Beaglehole (ed.) (1962): 3 Oct 1769.

79 'Land Sighted' as translated by Stimson (1957: 76).

80 Based on coastal cliff heights of 150 m, a calm sea and observer's eye at elevation of 3 m above sea level.

81 Journal entry from 17 Jan 1770. Beaglehole (ed.) (1962).

82 In two separate incidents – Louis-Antoine de Bougainville in Sāmoa and Cook in Tonga. In Tonga, Cook ran a series of tests using a 'ship log' payed out from on board one of the local sailing canoes: close-hauled in

83 As this overlooks likely advances in Polynesian maritime technology, particularly with respect to their rigs. The converse argument has also been made: that Polynesian maritime technology regressed in this time. See Anderson (2008d).

84 Although the Hōkūle`a covered around 185 km a day on this leg in 1985, Anderson (2002b) points out that such 'reconstructions' are modern designs, 'combining favourable features from different Oceanic boatbuilding traditions to create vessels of superior sailing and seakeeping qualities. Hokule`a has a Hawaiian hull plan but Tahitian sails and two masts, not recorded from Hawai`i, while her masts and rigging are of a Tongan design unrecorded in East Polynesia. She has watertight compartments, glass-over-ply construction, nylon rope rigging and terylene sails of massive area. East Polynesian vessels observed at contact set either one large sail as in Hawaii, or two small sails as in Tahiti. The sails used on Hokule`a and other such vessels are about twice the area, relative to waterline length, of those recorded on historical canoes'. (See response by Finney 2006: 132). Also, the deployment of watertight compartments on modern reconstructions permits them to be driven harder without sinking. See also Anderson (2008d).

85 Anderson in Byrnes (ed.) (2009).

86 Irwin (2010: 138); Irwin in Jones et al. (eds) (2011: 250).

87 Irwin and Flay (2015).

88 Anderson (2000b) observes that traditional outrigger vessels fitted with pandanus-leaf lateen sail have 'showed average sailing speeds, excluding periods of calm when vessels were paddled or poled, [of] about 2.5 knots, with the figures falling to less than 2 knots on most of the longer passages'. Tupa`ia told Cook of late 18th-century Tahitian canoes taking 10–12 days to reach northern Tonga and at least 30 days to get back, suggesting mean speeds of voyaging canoes even at that time of about 2.6 knots. If, as Anderson (2008b) suggests, Polynesian vessels from up to five centuries prior indeed carried a simpler rig, 'mean passage speeds may have been only 1kt or so'. See also Rockman and Steele (eds) (2003: 173). Irwin (pers. comm. 13.12.2016) cautions that 'speed is very variable and so is voyage duration. For canoes sailing over a known route (one that has been crossed by explorers) I think Atholl [Anderson]'s estimate for an average speed would often be too low, but not always'.

89 That is, if Tākitimu was indeed guided by Canopus and Rigel, it must have set sail from the direction of Rarotonga by around 23 Oct and yet, for the sun and rainbows to be navigationally relevant, it is likely to have still been at sea in late November. The departure point given by Te Rangi Hīroa (1950b) is Pikopikoiwhiti (generally taken to be in the Society Is); however, Halbert (1999) tells us that Tākitimu had nine names in the course of its travels, and that it was from Rarotonga to New Zealand that it sailed under this name. If commencing on this course from Rarotonga, and the star record is correct, its average speed may have been around one and a half knots.

11 Adapting to a Cool Land [pp. 176–95]

1 McWethy et al. (2010).

2 Dated, that is, from associated marine shell.

3 Schmidt and Higham (1998), Prickett (2001: 29).

4 Davidson et al. (2011).

5 Jock Phillips. 'Beach culture: Travellers on the beach', Te Ara – The Encyclopedia of New Zealand, updated 13-Jul-12. www.TeAra.govt.nz/mi/beach-culture/page-1.

6 Taonui in Phillips et al. (eds) (2006: 58), McKinnon (ed.) (1997), Evans (1997). Waka, the Māori word for a canoe, refers not only to the craft and its crew, but also to an iwi (tribe). Another canoe listed by Taylor (1855:123) that is 'reported to have brought the first settlers to the island' is the waka Ringaringa.

7 Te Rangi Hīroa (1950b: 23, 26, 34) gives crew numbers of 60 (with Toi), 66 (aboard the Kurahaupō) and 70 (aboard the Horouta). For the Māmari, Kaamira (1957: 242) gives 42.

8 Taonui in Phillips et al. (eds) (2006: 58). See also Taonui (1994). Belich (1996: 59) and others make a similar point.

9 Markham (ed.) (1904: 216).

10 Martin (1981): 22 Feb 1847.

11 Some claim tainui branches acted as portage rollers, but they are too thin for use as actual rollers. Rather, its branches would have been laid green as a slipway.

12 Te Rangi Hīroa (1926b: 52) gives the local Kāwhia version of the account, but acknowledges that, due to the plant's distribution, the tainui branches must have been gathered locally. See also Best (1925c: 400).

13 This species appears to favour wind-shorn coastal forest and scrub, and is known from Oligocene-age pollen fossils in Te Kuiti Group limestones, and in Southland from Miocene-age leaf impressions. MacPhail (1981). Despite its natural rarity, wherever it is planted, it generally thrives – for example, in the drier parts of the eastern South Island, at Hawke's Bay and Hamilton.

14 A tradition on voyaging canoes, according to Te Rangi Hīroa (1938b: 40). An outrigger could be expected to have carried fewer crew again. (The *Tainui*, for example, is referred to in several accounts as a single-hulled vessel.)

15 Taonui (2012). Previously, Taonui (1994) cited Lewis (1972) for open-sea canoes in the 17th and 18th centuries carrying larger crew numbers (24 and 35).

16 Or, to include the researchers' margin of error, 170–230 women. Whyte et al. (2005). 'The high probability that members of voyaging parties were related indicates that our calculated population estimates are on the conservative side, because genetic effective population size could remain small while the actual number of founders could be much larger.' Whyte also identified four rare and novel types of Māori maternal DNA not known elsewhere in Polynesia. See also earlier estimate by Penny et al. (2002) of 50–100 founding females.

17 Marshall et al. (2005). If some of the original DNA brought here was lost as a consequence of massacres, exodus, tsunami and volcanic eruptions, this estimate would again be conservative. However, geneticist Geoff Chambers (pers. comm. 6.8.2013) cautions that 'estimates of founding population sizes based on genetic data are just that – estimates (including ours). As such they are vulnerable to assumptions within the calculations, e.g. regarding the rate and mode of population growth.' Application of the latest DNA technology to ancient human remains from Marlborough's Wairau Bar may well increase this estimate.

18 McKinnon (ed.) (1997: Plate 12), Williams (2009). Likewise, core samples from tidal mudflat sediments show changes around this time in microscopic marine life (foraminifera) as a result of an increased run-off of freshwater from land cleared of its forest cover. Hayward et al. (2006).

19 Swarbrick (2012). Leaving 68 percent total forest cover, which has since been reduced to about 25 percent.

20 Peat and macrofossils from bogs (less vulnerable to contamination than lakes, swamps and coastlines) have produced no earlier human environmental impact dates than 1200–1400. McGlone and Wilmshurst (1999). A sudden rise in bracken spores over much of lowland country appears in the pollen fossil record around 1250–1300, reflecting massive forest clearance as this fern spread from its original coastal dune habitat. Such studies have now involved identification of pollen from more than 100 species or plant groups.

21 Hogg et al. (2003), Lowe and Newnham (2004).

22 Thomson et al. (2014).

23 Holdaway (1996, 1999), Brook (2000), Wilmshurst and Higham (2004), Wilmshurst et al. (2008), Irwin and Walrond (2009).

24 News of the discovery of New Zealand by Abel Tasman in 1642 went unheeded until competition from neighbouring powers and a shortage of timber for shipbuilding spurred the exploitation of resources further afield. And then the immigrants were largely British, rather than Dutch. A similar scenario is theoretically conceivable for Pacific peoples, with different groups responsible at different times for discovery and settlement.

25 Holdaway (1996, 1999), Brook (2000), Wilmshurst and Higham (2004), Wilmshurst et al. (2008), Irwin and Walrond (2009).

26 Or AD 1230–1282 according to Wilmshurst et al. (2011), and put back slightly by Mulrooney et al. (2011).

27 Irwin and Walrond (2009). Anderson (2014b: 67) reached a very similar conclusion from Māori genealogy: 'On the evidence of length-frequency in a sample of whakapapa, the period of migration was in the late thirteenth to late fourteenth centuries.'

28 Anderson (2014b: 73).

29 Rolett (2002).

30 Schmidt (1996). However, the fact that Māori of Queen Charlotte Sound and Doubtless Bay were able to give directions to Cook and Banks in 1769–70 for voyages to and from the NNW suggests some minor voyaging may have continued along this route as late as the 1600s. Cook (1846: 170), Geraghty and Tent (2010), Tent and Geraghty (2011). These discussions with Cook's crew date from 9 Dec 1769 at Doubtless Bay and 5/6 Feb 1770 at Queen Charlotte Sound.

31 Breeding in the Far North at that time, as we have seen. Archaeological evidence confirms that seals were a significant component of the early diet of Māori dogs. Clark (1997).

32 Quoted in Yadav (2004). Lt Henry Lidgbird Ball of the *Supply* had already gone ashore in March that year.

33 Steadman (1995, 1999), Pimm et al. (2006), Duncan et al. (2013).

34 With the arrival of European sealers in the late 18th and early 19th centuries, hundreds of thousands more were clubbed to death, taking the species to near extinction.

35 McKinnon (ed.) (1997: Plate 12), Berentson (2012: 240, 244), and Anderson (2003: 124) who subsequently rounded the number of moa butchered up to 'about 90,000' (2003: 133).

36 Belich (1996: 34, 51).

37 Estimates of the total population range wildly. Berentson (2012: 251).

38 Of these, the first to succumb to extinction by Polynesian hunters was the heavy New Zealand coot (2 kg) and the largest was the North Island takahē. Evidence that all these birds were eaten is found in Māori kitchen middens. The same is true of the now-extinct NZ raven (*Corvus antipodum*) – almost three times the weight of an Australian magpie – but the demise of many others, like the 240-g snipe-rail (*Capellirallus karamu*) – a small flightless soil-probing rail living in the forest in much the same way as the kiwi – may be attributable to the Pacific rat.

39 Steadman (1995) gave an informal estimate of 2000 species – a figure he extrapolated from remains of extinct birds so far recovered and identified from a selection of these islands, many of which supported unique species. Subsequent estimates by Pimm et al. (2006) arrived at slightly lower figures. In New Zealand alone, at least 11 species of rails were lost.

40 Their population has since been heavily reduced to less than 70,000 birds.

41 The diet that Georg Forster (son of J. R. Forster) observed was mainly fish, but archaeological evidence indicates also moa and seals. Colenso (1877: 12), Titcomb (1969), Clark (1997).

42 Colenso (1877), Savolainen (2004), Matisoo-Smith (2009a), Oskarsson et al. (2012), Greig et al. (2015). One of these breeds is evidently confined to East Polynesia, having probably arrived via a different route.

43 As proposed by Haami (1994), for example.

44 'Genetic diversity among rats from the Kermadecs supports their role as intermediary islands in two-way and multiple voyaging between the New Zealand archipelago and the tropics'. Matisoo-Smith et al. (1998).

45 Especially when not universally regarded as food, for though they were eaten on Mangaia (S. Cook Is); by commoners in the Hawaiian Is (Kirch and O'Day 2003); and on Easter Island (observed by Cook), they were not eaten on Mangareva (Conte and Kirch 2008).

46 Unlike common ship rats, Pacific rats have a marked aversion to wet conditions. Since each female can give birth to six or more at a time, with more than one litter per female possible on a long voyage, they may have even doubled as an emergency food supply en route.

47 On Mangareva (Gambier Is), archaeological evidence shows settlers arriving some 200 years before the rats; and similarly, visits by Polynesians to the Snares and Auckland Islands did not result in their introduction there. Neither has DNA from Marquesan rat populations been picked up among Pacific rats in the Society Islands – despite the transfer of Marquesan basalt along this same route. Anderson (2009b), Di Piazza and Pearthree (2001c), Matisoo-Smith et al. (1998).

48 Roberts (1990: 24, 116).

49 *Sarcoptes scabiei*. First Lieutenant Pottier de L'Horne gave an accurate description of the malady among Māori in 1769. The Pacific dog is likely to have been host to fleas and lice, too. Based on the known cargo of Polynesian canoes elsewhere in the Pacific, ants and tiny snails were probably also onboard, but if so, they do not seem to have survived the change in climate.

50 Walter et al. (2010).

51 Lepofsky (2003), Whistler (2009).

52 Grant (1994). Some early attempts to settle were made near the warmer northern tip of the North Island, where the best chance of trialling tropical crops lay; but the earliest recorded gardening sites in New Zealand lie further south, at Palliser Bay, near Wellington. Walter et al. (2010), Bassett et al. (2004), Furey (2006: 119).

53 As referred to in *Māhuhu* canoe tradition, quoted in Te Rangi Hīroa (1950b: 62).

54 King (2003: 32). As for finding archaeological evidence for these in New Zealand, 'sugar cane pollen and its phytoliths are difficult to distinguish from many other grasses, [however] kape, other yams, bananas and especially tumeric have potentially distinctive starch grains, and bananas have distinctive leaf phytoliths'. Horrocks et al. (2008).

55 Also known as other wort, and elsewhere in Polynesia as kamika. Leach (2005).

56 Other weeds occasionally considered Polynesian introductions and discounted here are: the true beggar's ticks, *Bidens pilosa* (as it was unknown from tropical Polynesia); the fern, *Cyclosorus interruptus*

(now considered native); *Hibiscus trionum* and *Oxalis corniculata* (now considered European introductions.)

57 Horrocks (2004).

58 Confirmed from microfossil pollen evidence from this site (Horrocks et al. 2008). Te Aute, south of Napier, is said to be so named to commemorate an unsuccessful attempt at growing the tree. In the west, its southern limit of cultivation is thought to be marked by archaeological finds of tapa beaters in Taranaki. Leach (1984). The last local aute plants are thought to have died out in the 1840s, but memory of them survives in songs, several northern place names and in the name, aute-taranga (sand pimelea, *Pimelea arenaria*), whose slippery inner bark was beaten to supply similarly strong white cloth-like strips for tying up hair or likewise worn as an ornament in the ears (also as aute for a Northland shrub, *Hebe diosmifolia*).

59 As Joseph Banks observed, they may have kept longer if they had been dried well first. Banks in Beaglehole (ed.) (1962): 17 Aug 1769.

60 Furey (2006: 17).

61 Even so, more detail of the plant's dispersal across Polynesia is anticipated from ongoing research into lineages of specific cultivars. Seelenfreund et al. (2010), Moncada et al. (2013), Chang et al. (2015), González-Lorca et al. (2015).

62 Hinkle (2007). Thirteen varieties of tī have been recorded on the Society Is (Lepofsky 2003), and more than 50 cultivars are traditionally recognised in the Bismarck Archipelago.

63 Kreike et al. (2004), Lebot and Aradhya (1991).

64 Names include akarewa, awanga, hanina, haukopa, taro hoia, whakahekerangi, kahuorangi, kākātarahae, kauere, kinakina, kōareare, kohurangi/ kohuorangi, makatiti, mamaku, matatiti (makatiti), ngāue, paeangaanga, pātai, pehu, pongi, pōtango, takatakapo, tanae, tautaumahei, whakatauare, tokotokohau, turitaka, upokotiketike and wairuaārangi, but Best (1931) refers to 41 Māori taro variety names (including duplicates). See also taro DNA evidence, page 220. In the Hawaiian Islands, according to Handy and Handy 1972 (quoted in Irwin 1998), approximately 300 varieties are reported.

65 Coates et al. (1988) who observe that 'explanations of direct transmission in prehistory from Melanesia to New Zealand [of 42 chromosome forms] are generally unacceptable on cultural grounds'. This anomalous material was collected from untended plants on the Cavalli Islands, Great Barrier Is, and Spirits Bay. Yen and Wheeler (1968).

66 Traditions concerning return trips include those by the *Te Aratāwhao*, *Horouta* and *Mātaatua* canoes and the *Mānuka* and *Āraiteuru* canoes. Kūmara tubers were also reportedly introduced on the *Māhuhu-ki-te-rangi* (*Māhuhu*) canoe and the *Tainui* and *Te Arawa* canoes (*Ngā Māhanga-a-Tuamatua*).

67 According to archaeologist Helen Leach, who specialises in prehistoric horticulture. Leach (1984: 103) quoted in Furey (2006: 12). Green (2005: 54) discusses difficulties inherent in identifying which are genuine ancient introductions.

68 Green (2005: 53): Mangaia is 'the most probable source for the kuumara plants of New Zealand'.

69 Hinkle (2007).

70 Best (1931: 13).

71 Also known as tī māhonge, tī papa or tī tahanui – an edible cultivar bred by Māori from *Cordyline australis*, developed by continually selecting plants that suckered (Hinkle 2007).

72 Horrocks et al. (2004), Horrocks and Barber (2005), Furey (2006). In 1769, Joseph Banks observed taro growing at Anaura Bay on the East Coast. In New Zealand, both 'dryland' and wetland cultivation were used.

73 Taylor (1855: 123).

74 Horrocks (2004), Best (1931).

75 Cardinal direction given as hau-tiu. Graham (1939). When the *Āraiteuru* canoe was wrecked at Matakaea (Shag Point), Otago, its cargo is said to have petrified to form the Moeraki Boulders, which, in some versions, included gourds.

76 Clarke et al. (2006).

77 Best (1931). Names recorded for Māori gourd varieties include arero-uru, whakahaumatua, ikaroa (or ikaroa a rauru), kōkakoware, mānukaroa (for bowls), paretarakihi, pūau, and upokotaipu (= upokotaupō). Gourd skins were also used for making musical instruments and canoe bailers.

78 Erickson et al. (2005). The original wild plants from Africa bear thin-walled, non-durable fruit.

79 Firth and Best quoted in Belich (1996: 45). Crozet (quoted in Best 1925b: 252) gives a more conservative figure of 'ten to twelve pints of water'. Larger gourds were deemed less suited to water-carrying.

80 Horrocks and Barber (2005), Horrocks et al. (2008).

81 Best (1931: 5).

82 Ahmed and Urooj (2008).

83 Green (2005: 54): New Zealand varieties 'thought on increasingly good grounds to be ancient, all have elongated edible roots that display a white skin colour and possess a white to creamy internal flesh'.

84 Best (1931). Jones (1994: 70). See also Yen (1961) for success/ failure data from experimental plantings.

85 Furey (2006: 20, 119). For example, learning to pick off harmful caterpillars by hand or encouraging tame seagulls to do the same or deterring these with smoke from burning kauri gum or the insecticidal leaves of kawakawa.

86 For south Wairarapa and Marlborough, and in the present-day climate, at least (Burtenshaw 2009). Māori traditionally planted whole kūmara tubers (as with the common potato), rather than the stem cuttings planted nowadays from more vigorous-growing varieties introduced by Europeans. Yen (1961).

87 Furey (2006: 20).

88 Yen (1961), Bassett et al. (2004). Grown prehistorically also on Rurutu (Austral Is) and possibly on Pitcairn Is Archaeological evidence shows it have been an early introduction to Easter Is (by 1526±100) and to Hawai`i (1290–1430).

89 A claim made by Brailsford (1997: 6), for example, who interprets one of the Māori names for it, peruperu, as a 'very obvious reference to Peru, one of the homelands that hosted the potato', claiming that it was introduced by Waitaha.

90 The single exception is uwhi (the traditional term for yam). Other Māori names recorded in New Zealand include: riwai, hīwai, huiwaiwaka, kapana, mahetau, parareka, parate, taewa (or taewha), taiwa (or taiwha), urenika, karuparera, peruperu, purupuru, kōtīpō, pāpaka, rokoroko and araro.

91 The swift uptake of potatoes resulted from their high yield, being easy to store and tolerant of far cooler climates than kūmara (e.g., around Invercargill). By 1803, Māori were producing sufficient surplus to trade.

92 Cameron (1964), Harris (2005).

93 Best (1922b: 27 etc.).

94 In the tropics, ritual kilts were also made from leaves of the tropical cabbage tree, or the fine bark fibre of *Hibiscus* trees.

95 Te Rangi Hīroa (1938b: 508), Colenso (1884: 48).

96 Horwood and Wilson (2008).

97 Best (1924b: 558–570).

98 Williams (2009), who argues that 'vegetation changes occurred not as a result of indifference, but as a direct result of the introduction of a culture for which fire was a dominant tool in a flammable environment'. Many of these early southern inhabitants subsequently died out or moved to the North Island, where 80 percent of Māori were living by the time Europeans arrived.

99 Presumably named after the bright orange pīngao dragonfly of the tropical South Pacific (*Pantala flavescens*).

100 Horwood and Wilson (2008).

101 For bamboo spike sedge, see Best (1899). Fireside details from Williams (2009: 178). Such vines include mangemange fern, rātā, kaihou (NZ jasmine), split kareao (supplejack) and kōhia (NZ passionfruit).

102 From 'kākā' for the cloth-like fibre surrounding base of coconut fronds + mā (white).

103 De Lisle (1965). From 1842, a small party of Māori and their Moriori slaves again settled here for 12–14 years, joined by British colonists, 1849–1852, but the climate proved too harsh for them.

104 Anderson (2005). Although NZ flax is found here, it was probably introduced later – in the 1800s.

105 Anderson (2005).

106 Newman et al. (2009).

107 The winds at Enderby are predominantly westerly and strong, averaging 16 knots. Favourable winds from the south or southeast blow with a frequency of just 12.7 percent – at least nowadays. De Lisle (1965).

108 Or Mōriori with a long initial vowel according to linguist Bruce Biggs (POLLEX).

109 Wood et al. (2014): 'the presence of archaic adzes and Mayor Island obsidian flakes on the islands point to settlement contemporaneous or shortly after mainland New Zealand in the 13th century AD'. Later dates for initial settlement have also been proposed: AD 1500. Anderson (2014b: 36).

110 POLLEX.

111 Davis and Solomon (2017).

112 Rangatira (South East Is) and Māngere were uninhabited.

113 Variously translated as 'misty sun' (Susan Thorpe, pers. comm. 2018) or 'garlands of the mist' (Solomon and Forbes, 2010).

114 Based on current populations, some one million pairs of white-faced storm petrels (*Pelagodroma marina*) and some 300,000 pairs of broad-billed prion (pararā, *Pachyptila vittata*).

115 David and Solomon (2017).

116 Clark (1994). See also Sutton (1980).

117 No fossilised karaka wood has been found here and groves all coincide with archaeological sites; hence botanists agree that karaka is almost certainly not native to these islands. Leach and Stowe (2005), Costall (2006). The *name* karaka originates in tropical Polynesia, where it applies to look-alike trees.

118 Unless heading for elsewhere and arriving with them on the Chathams by accident.

119 For obsidian see McKinnon (ed.) (1997: Plate 14); for voyaging see Irwin (1992: 171).

120 A post-European influence in the language from the Ngāti Mutunga invaders of Taranaki in 1835 was excluded from the analysis. Harlow (2007: 57–59). The dialect in the South Island may, of course, reflect one that was once more widely spoken.

121 Matisoo-Smith et al. (1999).

122 Anderson (2014b: 80).

123 Atkinson and Towns (2001). The ancestors of many South Island Māori did, however, come from the East Coast of the North Island.

124 King (1989), Anderson (2014b: 55), Hokotehi Moriori Trust (2018), Davis and Solomon (2017).

125 Pollen evidence suggests a lack of substantial trees prior to human settlement, with about 80 percent of the main island covered with sedges, rushes, ferns, swamp grasses and shrubs. As Anderson concedes, there was 'considerable deforestation' here nonetheless. Anderson (2014b: 83).

126 It is estimated that Chatham Island tāiko bones constituted 53 percent and 49 percent respectively of total bone mass material in the two Moriori kitchen middens. Taken for food in Jan; in winter, these birds disappear from the island, most migrating to feed in subantarctic waters. Although the name tāiko for petrels or shearwaters occurs in Sāmoa and much of East Polynesia (p. 147), it was most likely transferred to the Chatham Is directly from New Zealand – where it applies to the black petrel. For the inhabitants of Waihora village, Anderson (2014b: 83) estimates that most of food energy (85 percent) came from seal meat.

127 Here, as on mainland New Zealand, bracken fern 'roots' (eruhe, aruhe) were eaten.

128 Kōpi according to Susan Thorpe (Hokotehi Moriori Trust); and kopi or kopī in POLLEX.

129 The term köpī has also been recorded on Rarotonga (S. Cook Is) for plants of the ginger family (whose roots have a similar colour and consistency to the kernels).

130 Orthography from Susan Thorpe (Hokotehi Moriori Trust); POLLEX gives tchāik. The 'tch' in Moriori represents the distinctive pronunciation of 't'; and 'h' replaces 'wh'; final vowels are often clipped (King, 1989).

131 Green flax leaves were also formed into a horn-shaped utensil for carrying water (in place of the Polynesian gourd, which could not be grown here). Shand (1894). Smissen and Heenan's (2010) conclusion on whether planting material was ever introduced from the mainland was, 'We found no evidence of hybridism with *Phormium* introduced from New Zealand'.

132 Moriori had their own local sources of fine-grained basalt for making adze heads and chisels, and chert for drills and flake tools. Meat was plentiful, primarily from seabirds, including penguins, but also from ducks and forest birds (including a kākā-like parrot and at least three species of rails), fur seals, sealions, stranded sperm whales, fish, eels and crayfish. Shand (1894), McFadgen (1994).

133 Power (compiler) (2013: 168), Goff et al. (2011a).

134 Six-metre-high waves from another tsunami in 1924 led to the loss of one trawler here and smashed another.

135 Dr Brian Molloy (pers. comm. 2006): *C. laevigatus* is known to be endemic to New Zealand (with fossil evidence of karaka fruit in Southland dating to the Miocene (over 5 million years ago). See also Costall (2006).

136 Evans (1997: 20, 107), Phillips et al. (eds) (2006: 178). According to Best (1931: 18), the 'Aotea, Nukutere, Matahorua, Taki-tumu, and Tainui, are credited with having so brought it'. Te Rangi Hīroa (1938b: 282) speculated that, since karaka occurs on the Kermadecs, the *Aotea* left Hawaiki (implying here Raʻiātea) and was driven west to the Kermadecs (Rangitahua) 'in March when the karaka was covered with its golden berries', from whence the fruit was introduced to New Zealand. However, scientists have since determined that seed was introduced to the Kermadecs by humans from the North Island of New Zealand. Molloy (1990). Factors used to distinguish these from karaka trees of 'natural' origin include their proximity to registered archaeological sites. In general, trees found on windier sites close to the coast tended to be of 'cultivated' origin.

12 The Cuckoos Depart [pp. 196–209]

1 Rolett (2002).

2 For example, Cook quoted in Best (1925b: 255) notes that, 'The gourds [of the Hawaiian Islands] grow to so enormous a size that some of them are capable of containing from ten to twelve gallons' and Ellis (1827: 183), who remarks that the drinking water of the Tahitians 'is contained in calabashes, which are much larger than any I ever saw used for the same purpose in the [Hawaiian] Islands'.

3 Sharp (1971) – a sentiment echoed rather more softly by New Zealand historian James Belich in 1996: 'return voyaging is not very credible'. Belich (1996: 33). However, Belich (1996: 59) goes on to concede the possibility of a return by people with *Takitimu* associations. Likewise, Adds (2012) argues against 'the possibility of contact with the tropical Polynesian homelands in the prehistoric past'.

4 King (2003: 71–76), Adds (2012), Anderson (2014a: 72).

5 King (2003: 49).

6 Adds (2012).

7 Sutton (1987: 23).

8 Sutton (1987: 23) goes on to point out the cultural ramifications, emphasising that it is 'possible that innovations were brought into [the tropical] homeland region from New Zealand, as well as taken there'.

9 Keane (2012). Refer also to caption of photograph here of 'migrating kuaka'.

10 Woodley (2009: 79).

11 Oliver (1955: 535).

12 Gill (1989).

13 Phillips (ed.) et al. (2006: 108).

14 Barthel (1962).

15 Captain Mair quoted in Buller (1877).

16 Buller (1877).

17 Lewis (1972: Figs. 12, 13).

18 Fell (1947), Gill (1983, 1989).

19 This rather liberal translation is from Best (1942: 340).

20 Garrigue et al. (2002).

21 Now about 1.3 million, although this bird formerly bred far more widely, as indicated by subfossil midden evidence of at least 11 extinct forest colonies on the mainland of both the North and South Islands. Imber (2003).

22 Newman et al. (2009) estimated the current New Zealand population of sooty shearwater (1994–2005) to be 21.3 (19.0–23.6) million individuals.

23 Gill and Hauber (2012) suggest that birds leaving New Zealand in autumn may leave to the northeast on westerly winds, before turning north and then heading west through the tropics with the southeasterly trade winds. In spring, they conclude, some return south and southeast to New Zealand through the region of the Kermadec Islands.

24 Gill and Hauber (2012).

25 White quoted in Williams (1971: 111).

26 Using flight routes of shining cuckoo leaving New Zealand for the Solomons as directional guides may be impractical, for although some depart toward Norfolk Is, others fly to (or via) Australia. Their return flights from Norfolk Is to the SSE in September would be less ambiguous indicators of the whereabouts of forested land (i.e. New Zealand). Some have interpreted the pet cuckoo (Te Kawa) of Whātonga the navigator as a shining cuckoo, but the diet of this bird (about 50 percent caterpillars plus ladybirds) would be hard to emulate. A more likely candidate is the long-tailed cuckoo – because of its more catholic tastes: invertebrates, lizards, small birds, chicks, eggs and a range of fruit.

27 An increased frequency of ENSO (El Niño–Southern Oscillation) is evident in the fossil-coral record for a period around AD 1380–1400, for example – as determined by fossil-coral oxygen isotopic records from Palmyra Is. Cobb et al. (2003).

28 From Dusky Sound via the Chatham Is to Tahiti.

29 See Irwin (1992: 110), who discusses both route options, noting that without instruments, the navigator cannot ascertain longitude (east–west position) with any accuracy.

30 For a discussion of critical differences between this and voyaging renaissance replica craft, see Anderson (2008a).

31 Forster (1778: 509).

32 Forster (1778: 531, n. 18).

33 According to climatologist Ian Goodwin, in the period AD 1280–1300, Māori may even have made a direct return to the Southern Cooks. Goodwin et al. (2014).

34 Traditions of new arrivals being killed are common to much of East Polynesia, including the Tuamotus, Northern Cooks, Rarotonga, Mangaia and Mangareva. Taonui (1994: 258).

35 'Voyaging' in Stimson (1957: 61). In the chant, these extend some 1700

km from Mangareva through the entire Tuamotuan archipelago to Nuku Hiva and `Ua Pou in the Marquesas Islands. Specific Tuamotuan atolls identifiable in this chant include Taenga, Vāhitahi and Marutea. Similarly, when Quirós's crew sought coconut water to quench their thirst on the Tuamotuan atoll of Hao in 1606, they were greeted by inhabitants armed with clubs and spears. In 1767, Wallis was likewise challenged on Pīnaki (Tuamotus), and Cook received a similar reception at Rurutu (Austral Is) in 1769.

36 Taonui (1994: 257).
37 For example, at Queen Charlotte Bay. Banks's journal entry for 5 Feb 1770, in Beaglehole (ed.) (1962).
38 Forster (1777).
39 On the same occasion, near Whale Island off the Bay of Plenty coast on 1 Nov. 1769, one of the *Endeavour*'s journal keepers described the sail carried by this canoe as 'a sail of an odd construction, which was made from a kind of matting, and of a triangular figure, the hypothenuse, or broadest part, being placed at the top of the mast, and ending in a point at the bottom. One of its angles was marled to the mast, and another to a spar with which they altered its position according to the direction of the wind, by changing it from side to side.'
40 Other varieties supplied fleshy fibrous keys that were canoe fare (on Kiribati), eaten either raw or mashed into a paste. The prop-roots are split to make walls of traditional houses.
41 As discussed earlier. See Irwin and Flay (2015).
42 Johns et al. (2014). Other materials used for caulking the topstrake (gunwale, or rauawa) of Māori canoes are flax fibre smeared with the jelly-like gum from five finger (whauwhaupaku), and the seed fluff from raupō (hune). Best (1925c).
43 Johns et al. (2014).
44 Johns et al. (2014).
45 Occasionally, New Zealand sails were made from the leaves of kiekie, kutakuta (bamboo spike-sedge, *Eleocharis sphacelata*) or raupō (bulrush).
46 Best (1942: 285). Although Best (1942: 283) noted the use of water containers made from ingeniously folded bark of various native trees (tōtara and mānuka in particular, but also makomako and miro), such containers would have had a very short life. Belich (1996) and others suggest that water may have been carried in moa eggshells, too, but these – at around 1.4 mm thick for those of the South Island giant moa (and often less for the others) – are now considered to have been too fragile for this purpose.
47 As evidenced in language: whakahunga (dried inanga whitebait), mahiti (dried crayfish tails), maraki (dried fish), paka, pakapaka or paku (dried provisions, fish, birds etc.), hinu or huahua (pigeons and rats preserved in their own fat). Dried kūmara (kao) would have been available only after Māori gardens were already well established.
48 Anderson and McFadgen (1990), Walter et al. (2010).
49 While Tonga, Sāmoa, Pitcairn and Easter Island do all have obsidian of their own (as do the Kermadecs), through much of tropical Polynesia this resource is scarce. It could, though, be argued that obsidian was not carried far by Polynesians in general – perhaps because of the local availability of alternative raw materials to make knives, e.g. oyster shells and bamboo.
50 Only after the 16th century did greenstone become the most prized and widely moved resource in the country, and it was not until shortly before European contact that ornaments made from it took on a ceremonial significance. Walter et al. (2010). Nathan (2012). Although there are accounts of Ngāhue and/or Kupe taking greenstone from the Arahura River (north of Hokitika), along with axes and neck and ear pendants fashioned from it, back 'home' to their compatriots (Best 1924a: 456, Dansey 1947: 7, Nelson 1991:10), these accounts are unlikely to pass tests for historic authenticity.
51 Holden and Qualtrough (1884).
52 In the case of the Millennium Atoll find, for example, they may conceivably have arrived with 'several native families' dropped off on this atoll on 4 July 1848 by Edward Lucett along with a consignment of 'pigs, fowls, turkeys &c., to form an establishment for rearing stock'. Merchant (1851). Note that nephrite also occurs in NSW (Australia), Île Ouen (New Caledonia) and SE Asia.
53 In 1998, Lisa Matisoo-Smith and colleagues found archaeological support for return voyaging; they determined from the DNA of Pacific rats that 'genetic diversity among rats from the Kermadecs supports their role as intermediary islands in two-way and multiple voyaging between the New Zealand archipelago and the tropics'. Matisoo-Smith et al. (1998).
54 King (2003: 41), Salmond (2004: 459; 2008:16; 2009: 232, 356), Orbell (1998), Cook (1846: 169).
55 Salmond (2006: 262, 266; 2008: 16; 2009: 356).
56 Irwin (pers. comm. 31.8.2015).

57 Finding archaeological evidence for voyages of return is inherently more difficult than for discovery and settlement, since the latter can be picked up from a clear signature left by the first presence of humans in a 'virgin environment'.
58 Kirch and Green (2001), based on the durability of 100–300 types of objects known from ethnographic sources that could 'be expected in any comprehensive account of material culture on a Polynesian island'.
59 Taonui (2012a): 'One day Kahukura, a visitor from Hawaiki, arrived with some dried kūmara (sweet potato), which the locals had never eaten before. Toi gave the canoe to Kahukura to go and obtain the kūmara back in Hawaiki. After retrieving the vegetables, Kahukura sent them back on the *Horouta*, which was commanded by Pāoa (or Pāwa).' 'The *Mānuka* canoe set out for Hawaiki, the Polynesian homeland, and successfully returned with a cargo of kūmara (sweet potato).' 'It is said that Roko, or Rongo-i-tua, aware of the frailties of the kūmara, then set forth from Hawaiki on the *Ārai-te-uru* with new varieties of the vegetable.'
60 In the event of a voyage to South America, the route is unlikely to have been a direct one, despite the fact that Mocha and Arauco lie at about the same latitude (38° S) as Gisborne (New Zealand) on account of the strong cold westerlies of the Southern Ocean, correspondingly large waves, the immense distance (almost 9000 km) and lack of any stopovers for repairs or supplies. Likewise the old clipper route that once carried much of the wool, grain and gold from Australia via Cape Horn to Europe is improbable due to extreme conditions encountered that far south (in the so-called 'Furious Fifties'). Prevailing winds would suggest an outbound route instead via the Austral Islands or the Tuamotus, with a return voyage via Mangaia and/or the Society Islands. (Although it might perhaps be argued that some or all of the tubers were being brought from an established kūmara nursery as close to home as on one of New Zealand's offshore islands.)
61 Banks in Beaglehole (ed.) (1962: 446–47).
62 Quick though the crew of Cook's ship were to acknowledge Tupaia's genius, they wearied of his pride and his habit of extorting homage from those around him. Tupa`ia was high born and wanted everyone around him to know it – at least according to witness John Marra (1775), quoted in Salmond (2004: 112).
63 As they did with pigs were introduced to Tupua`i (Tubuai, Austral Is).
64 None of the tropical-bred pigs and chickens that Cook's ship carried from Tahiti survived the cold en route, and no evidence of Polynesian pig has ever been found south of Henderson and Pitcairn Islands.
65 On 5 Feb 1770 at Queen Charlotte Sound: 'Of Ulimaroa we had heard something before, from the people about the Bay of Islands.'
66 Cook's Ulimaroa or Olhemaroa and Banks's Olimaroa both translate as Rimaroa, the article '`o' having been added by the Tahitian-speaking Tupa`ia. Geraghty and Tent (2010), Tent and Geraghty (2011, 2012). Although rima can mean 'five' or 'hand', in this NNW region the meaning of 'arm' or 'hand-arm' is widespread. Another possibility is that this 'long arm' referred to an island-hopping route, in this case the whole NNW chain of internavigable Polynesian Outliers.
67 Note that the pigs were not necessarily encountered on this expedition in the 'large countrey' itself.
68 Although MacPhail et al. (2001) and Coyne (2009) argue in favour of human introduction of flax, other botanists (Mills 2009, Smissen and Heenan 2010) argue against this. It is now generally considered native here.
69 Human skeletons were found both in caves and in raised burial mounds up on the plateau. From these two different ways of disposing of the remains of the dead, and from stone artefacts traceable to two distinct regions, archaeologists deduce that the island was occupied in two distinct phases. Although the earlier artefacts can be traced to the west (Grande Terre, for example), the style of two black basaltic adzes is stylistically Fijian/West Polynesian. The first group (probably Melanesian) appear to have arrived at least 2500 years ago, and abandoned the island after 1000 years. Then, around AD 1250–1500, this 'mystery island' was used by a different people, at least some of whom were Polynesian, as deduced from a single jaw found in 1967 among the remains of eight former inhabitants (young children, adolescents, adult men and women) that displayed 'characteristics more common in Polynesian than Melanesian populations . . .'. Sand (2004).
70 From a charcoal-rich layer in an adjacent bay, consistent with the age of subfossil bone deposits of Pacific rat introduced by humans around 1200. Matisoo-Smith et al. (2001). See also Anderson et al. (2001).
71 Turner et al. (2001): 'The non-Raoul Island piece . . . was in a high-quality, translucent green obsidian which has a specific gravity and major elements profile consistent with the Mayor Island source (New Zealand) . . . However, the trace element analysis by PIXE/PIGME and NAA contains some anomalous data, and the origin of this piece remains in question.'

72 Turner et al. (2001), Anderson (2000a), Anderson and White (2001a, 2001b).

73 Matisoo-Smith *et al.* (2001).

74 Medway (2002). From archaeological remains of identifiable bones, we know that these and other birds were harvested by the original inhabitants and that they include the land birds described in 1788 by Lieutenant King: 'pigeons, parrots, parroquets, doves, and a variety of other birds, in great numbers, and so very tame, that they might be knocked down with a stick'.

75 Sailing via these internavigable Polynesian Outlier islands, they might reach Sikaiana or neighbouring atolls, where they could alternatively turn east to head along an established voyaging route back into East Polynesia via the atolls of Tūvalu and Tokelau to Pukapuka (N. Cook Is).

76 In this vicinity, Polynesian pigs are known to have been archaeologically present in this period only on Ouvéa and Tikopia. 'A pig-bone has been found here on Ouvéa in a stratigraphic context without European goods,' says Christophe Sand, Institut de Recherche pour le Développement (IRD) (pers. comm. 2006). From AD 1200, the inhabitants of Tikopia were known to import pigs and arrows from Melanesian areas in the nearby Solomon Islands. Feinberg and Scaglion (eds) (2012: 34). Pigs were also present on non-Polynesian islands of Erromango, Malakula and Malo in Vanuatu. Anderson (2009b).

77 Some 2000 km as compared with 3000 km.

78 Conspicuous butterflies and moths appearing from across the Tasman nowadays include the Australian painted lady butterfly (*Vanessa kershawi*), Australian blue tiger (*Tirumala hamata hamata*), blue moon butterfly (*Hypolimnas bolina nerina*) and bogong moth (*Agrotis infusa*).

79 It is sometimes erroneously claimed that Māori of Queen Charlotte Sound and Doubtless Bay knew of Australia as Ulimaroa (as first transcribed by Cook). However, the original references clearly refer to land to the north or north-northwest of New Zealand, a direction altered by subsequent writers to northwest and most recently to west – an error promulgated on an early Swedish map of Australia (1769) and repeated by Pearce and Pearce (2011: 154). For discussion of the true location of Ulimaroa, see Geraghty and Tent (2010), and Tent and Geraghty (2011, 2012).

80 At least 40,000 years of human habitation in Australia renders the task of differentiating evidence of Polynesian landfall difficult, and yet, as Irwin (1992: 100) points out, 'Australia was so easy [to reach that] it is inconceivable that this did not happen many times, accidentally or otherwise.'

81 Thorpe (1929), with an alternative explanation for how this adze might have reached here in Thorpe (1931). Geochemical research in White et al. (2014).

82 Despite the sizable population of North Island, Māori did not traditionally amalgamate into large political groups. Kirch (2000: 283).

83 Sharp et al. (2010).

13 A Wider Range of Possibilities [pp. 210–21]

1 Irwin (1992: 170).

2 Belich (1996: 65).

3 Due to significant overlaps in culture, language and DNA, many scholars distinguish the regions of Oceania not by race but by the relative ease with which each can be reached from a continental landmass, thus distinguishing Near Oceania from Remote Oceania. Humans did not reach islands in Remote Oceania until less than 4000 years ago, when an ambitious leap occurred across a relatively large stretch of open ocean to reach the region of Polynesia, Vanuatu, New Caledonia, Fiji, Palau and Micronesia.

4 Hinkle (2004).

5 Te Rangi Hīroa (1938b: 52).

6 Taonui (2006: 29). Lessa (1956) reports the story of Motikitik fishing up islands from Pulo Anna (and Palau generally), Ulithi, Fais, Lamotrek and Yap, and Chuuk (Truk).

7 Matisoo-Smith (2009a).

8 Burley et al. (2012). Based on an *Acropora* coral file (abrader) found at Nukuleka on the Tongan island of Tongatapu, dated by high-precision uranium/thorium (U/Th) dating to 2838±8 BP. (BP means before 1950.)

9 Wilmshurst et al. (2011), Mulrooney et al. (2011), Allen (2014), Athens et al. (2014), Conte and Molle (2014), Kirch et al. (2015), Stevenson et al. (2017), Kirch (ed.) (2017).

10 Making landfall in East Polynesia hinged on relatively small target arcs of exploration. Di Piazza et al. (2007b).

11 This includes (1) the ongoing transfer of Samoan stone to Mangaia and Rarotonga (S. Cook Is), Pukapuka (N. Cook Is) and Manra Island (Phoenix Is); (2) a cultural overlap between the two regions in Niuē, Pukapuka

(N. Cook Is), Tokelau and Tūvalu, acknowledged by Burrows (1940) in his original classification: 'some islands I classified as "intermediate," namely, the Ellice and Tokelau group and Niue,' and shared place names (Koskinen 1973: 18); (3) the more or less contemporaneous expansion of East Polynesian settlement; and (4) the familiarity shown in 1769 by Tahitian navigator Tupa`ia with West Polynesia, when he provided Cook with accurate star bearings for voyages from Savai`i (Sāmoa) via `Uvea (Wallis and Futuna) to Rotumā (north of Fiji).

12 Wilson (2012). See Addison and Matisoo-Smith (2010) and other papers by archaeologist David Addison.

13 Irwin (1981), Addison and Matisoo-Smith (2010).

14 Emergence dates given by Dickinson (2009): Tūvalu (AD 1100), Tokelau (AD 1000), Phoenix Is (AD 900), N. Cook Is (AD 900) and Line Is (AD 800).

15 Carson (2013): 'Within the last 1000 years, life-changing population growth and other transformations occurred throughout Micronesia. Resident populations vastly increased, as witnessed in widespread formalized villages.'

16 Another important factor may have been the development of the double canoe.

17 Te Rangi Hīroa (1938b: 122).

18 A case most recently and comprehensively argued by McLean (2014), but not dissimilar from the case put by Te Rangi Hiroa (1938b: 314-5), with archaeological and DNA support for a second strand through Micronesia 1500–2000 years ago, argued by Addison and Matisoo-Smith (2010).

19 Islanders in this region, except those of Fiji, New Caledonia and Vanuatu, know this bird by the same name.

20 Their two journals were reduced to one by Dalrymple (1770: 22): see journal entry 11 May 1616.

21 Geraghty (1994), Aswani and Graves (1998). From the Tongans, Cook obtained the names of 153 islands, including Futuna, Rotumā and Vaitupu (1650 km to the NNW, in Tūvalu). Dening (1962: 110). Egan and Burley (2009) note striking similarities in style between petroglyph motifs at Houmale`eia on the Tongan island of Foa and those on the Hawaiian archipelago.

22 As revealed in directions to Vava`u given by Tupa`ia to Cook. Di Piazza and Pearthree (2007a). The route from Tonga to New Zealand is used by many yachts today; however, Tongans may have been reluctant to leave the region of southeast trade winds (26°S in summer; 20°S in winter) to venture this far south. Irwin (2010). Koskinen (1963) counted some 474 Tongan place names shared with New Zealand (most of them widely shared across tropical Polynesia); however, Gifford (1923) points out that the Tongan village is a post-European phenomenon and that many village tract names have been borrowed in recent times from other islands. Many appear superficially similar but do not qualify as true cognates due to orthography and/or etymology.

23 Di Piazza and Pearthree (2001c). The basalt came from Tutuila (American Sāmoa) – much of it from a single large fortified quarry, Tātaga Matau, but also from other quarries on the same island – Fagasa, Faga`itua, and several smaller ones. Some of this basalt is judged to have been transported 1000 or more years ago.

24 To Savai`i, `Upolu and Tutuila. Di Piazza and Pearthree (2007a).

25 From a comparative study of Polynesian myth-incidents, anthropologist Roland Dixon concluded that 'New Zealand's affiliation with Samoa is nearly as strong as with Hawaii.' Dixon (1916: 94). Koskinen (1963) found 146 place names shared with New Zealand (27.8 percent of the Samoan total – a lower percentage than for East Polynesian archipelagos). Origin traditions of Māori include references to Kuparu – an old name for `Upolu (Taonui 2006: 53); Nu`utele on `Upolu (as *Nukutere*, one of the ancestral migration canoes); Savai`i (as Hawaiki, ancestral homeland); Vavau on `Upolu (as Wawau, in origin traditions); and Si`ulagi point on Ta`ū (as Hikurangi); however, all these names are also shared with tropical East Polynesia.

26 Where the distinction between East and West Polynesia is weak. Burrows (1940).

27 Green and Green, in Kirch and Rallu (2007: 253).

28 Macgregor (1937: 5, 28, 90, 174), Taonui (2006: 40), Di Piazza and Pearthree (2007a: 133), Burrows (1923). Many aspects of Tokelauan language and culture are East Polynesian.

29 Even after discounting the many names that are shared with elsewhere in Polynesia (here represented by a bullet point), this proportion remains high. Shared Tokelauan place names are followed here by their New Zealand equivalent.
Avalau—Awarau ● / Falafala—Te Wharawhara / Fenualoa—Whenuaroa ● / Malatea—Maratea ● / Matangi—Matangi / Motu Iti—Motuiti ● / Motufala—Motuwhara ● / Motuloa—Moturoa ● / Muli—Muri ● / Mulifenua—Muriwhenua ● / Na Taulaga—Tauranga ● / Onepoto—Onepoto ● / Otoka—Otoka / Palea—Parea ● / Pilipili—Piripiri /

Pukava—Pukawa / Taulaga—Tauranga ● / Tafata—Tawhata / Te Fala—Te Whara ● / Te Maile—Te Maire ● / Te One—Te One / Te Oneloa—Oneroa ● / Te Palaoa—Paraoa ● / Te Papaloa—Paparoa ● / Te Puka—Te Puka ● / Tokelau—Tokerau ● / Vaipapa—Waipapa ● / Vaitupu—Waitupu ●

30 Taonui (2006: 40). Basalt adze heads here are traceable to Sāmoa.

31 Addison et al. (2009), Koskinen (1973: 18).

32 New Zealand place names occurring in Tūvalu are listed, with bullet points representing those names that are also shared with elsewhere: Avalau—Awarau ● / Fagalei—Whāngārei [? cognate] ● / Fale—Whare ● / Motala—Motara / Motuloa—Moturoa ● / Motulua—Moturua ● / Motutanifa—Motutaniwha / Tefala—Te Whara / Telele—Te Rere / Tepuka—Te Puka ● / Tokelau—Tokerau ● / Vaiatoa—Waiatoa

33 A minority Polynesian population lives on the western half of Viti Levu and adjacent Waya Is (Yasawa Group).

34 As evident in DNA, for example. Kayser et al. (2006). Mirabal et al. (2012) put the Melanesian component of the Samoan and Tongan Y chromosomes at 23–42 percent. Among Fijians, Shipley et al. (2015) note maternal lineages more strongly associated with Polynesian populations. Fiji exported red feathers from Fijian lorikeets (for adorning fine mats and ornaments); Fijian hardwood for Tongan canoes from exceptionally large specimens of kwila (vesi, Intsia bijuga); and Fijian sandalwood (ahi, Santalum species) for Tongan incense to honour their dead. Sāmoa contributed fine mats and basalt adze-heads; and Tonga exported fine bark cloth and highly prized whale teeth. Barnes and Hunt (2005). Taylor (2012).

35 Although voyages to New Zealand from Ulimaroa have also been interpreted as referring to Fiji. See Geraghty and Tent (2010).

36 Matisoo-Smith et al. (1998). 'Fiji' is a corruption of Fisi, the Tongan form of Viti. Although references in the origin traditions of East Coast tribes of New Zealand Māori to Whiti may be Fiji, Fiti is a widespread traditional name, particularly in the western Pacific. Te Fiti is also a name used for Tahiti. Taonui (2006).

37 Such Niuean names include: akeake (a native tree, Dodonaea species), whose Māori equivalent is akeake; fou hele (plants yielding useful fibre), whose Māori equivalent is houhere; palatao (a large ground fern [Marattiaceae]), whose Māori equivalent is para; talaō (grouper, a reef fish), whose Māori equivalent is tarao.

38 Koskinen (1973: 18) identified a particularly strong link between place names of Niuē and the Tuamotus. Koskinen (1963) gives the number of place names shared between Niuē and New Zealand as 36 (33.6 percent of the total 107 Niuean place names he found); however, most of these are shared widely across much of tropical Polynesia.

39 From a paucity of basalt artefacts, and almost none of pearl shell, Walter and Anderson (1995) conclude that 'Niuean prehistory has been characterised by isolation, rather than interaction with other islands or archipelagos.'

40 To avoid confusion, Futuna (Wallis & Futuna) is sometimes referred to as East Futuna. Two kilometres SE of East Futuna lies the small, now-uninhabited island of Alofi, which rises to 365 m and was previously also densely inhabited and cultivated. Related languages are spoken on Polynesian Outlier islands in the Solomons, Vanuatu and New Caledonia.

41 Di Piazza and Pearthree (2007a).

42 Goff et al. (2011b). Koskinen (1963) gives 26 New Zealand place names for Futuna and 24 for ʻUvea.

43 With respect to mtDNA. Shipley et al. (2015).

44 Rotumā was annexed by Fiji in 1881, and a large proportion of its original Polynesian inhabitants subsequently moved.

45 Best (1923: 36).

46 Weisler and Swindler (2002). Typically, such skeletal remains are identified as Polynesian from a 'rocker jaw' bone, the corner of which is curved, rather than angular. Lum and Cann (2000) identify 'genetic similarities among Micronesian and Polynesian populations result[ing], in some cases, from a common origin, and in others, from extensive gene flow'. This blurring between Polynesia and Micronesia has led archaeologists to group this central-eastern Micronesia and Polynesia region as 'Remote Oceania'. See also O'Shaughnessy et al. (1990). Archaeological evidence from Manra and Orona (Phoenix Is) link them to both cultural regions. The origin of basalt adze heads recovered from Manra can be geochemically traced to Sāmoa (Di Piazza and Pearthree 2001c), and a reciprocal Micronesian influence is evident in the DNA of breadfruit grown on Tūvalu and Tokelau. Zerega et al. (2004).

47 A blurred boundary with Melanesia is evident in language, human DNA, ethnology (e.g., kite fishing) and archaeology (e.g., pottery remains and shell adzes), suggesting that interaction continued long after initial settlement. Intoh (1999).

48 A region that is still known for the non-instrument skills of its navigators, in particular those of Satawal (Caroline Is, Federated States of Micronesia).

49 Although this cuckoo is known to visit islands in Micronesia from Palau in the west, through the Caroline Is, Nauru, Marshall Is to Kiribati or Gilbert Is, no cognates of its Polynesia-wide name are recorded from this region. See cuckoo map on page 149.

50 Māhoe (Melicytus ramiflorus) also occurs on Norfolk Is and on Tonga (where it is known as pualiki). Botanist Arthur Whistler (pers. comm. 11.09.2008) found no name for it in Sāmoa. (Although four subspecies of M. ramiflorus are currently distinguished – subsp. ramiflorus of New Zealand, subsp. oblongifolius of Norfolk Is, subsp. fastigiata of Fiji and subsp. samoensis of Sāmoa and Tonga – all are similar.)

51 Lala vao on Sāmoa; wase in Fiji; and osi on Waya (Fiji).

52 Pacific kauri (Agathis macrophylla) goes by unrelated names of dakua or makadre in Fiji, duro in Solomons, and khoe, nejev or nendu in Vanuatu.

53 Although brown pine (Podocarpus neriifolius) is known in Fiji as kuasi or gagali, and Podocarpus pallidus is called uhiuhi in Tonga, a novel tree term was coined for the corresponding tree in New Zealand: tōtara (Podocarpus totara). Likewise, names like yaka and tagitagi (used in Fiji for Dacrydium nidulum and nausoriense with purple-black fruit) or amunu (for Dacrycarpus imbricatus with feathery leaves like a miro) are unknown for corresponding trees in New Zealand.

54 The Samoan fantail is seʻu, and the spotted fantail of Fiji is manu sa or sesi, and yet no cognate terms in Māori – heku, ha and hehi – are known in New Zealand.

55 The same is true of its alternative Māori names: pākura and tangata tawhito.

56 Or manualiʻi in Sāmoa.

57 Though remains of a close relative were found by Steadman (1988) on the Marquesas Islands.

58 Refers to haplogroup IIIa found at the Washpool archaeological site, whose distribution includes Vanuatu, New Caledonia, Fiji, Sāmoa, Tokelau and Kapingamarangi (Caroline Is). Matisoo-Smith and Robins (2004).

59 Tava was introduced to the East Polynesian region only after European contact. Its Tahitian name kava is identifiable as a 'borrowing' by an absence of the 'k' sound in Tahitian.

60 Often Alectryon species or, on Niuē, Cryptocarya species.

61 The hard wood of the New Zealand tree was used for making toki (adze) handles. Scheele (2013).

62 Applied in the tropics to island luffa vine or dish-cloth gourd (Luffa aegyptiaca; syn. L. cylindrica).

63 With the exception of the Hawaiian Islands, owls are archaeologically absent in East Polynesia, where the name was sometimes applied to a local seabird. On Rarotonga the term is recorded, but the owl itself is not. On the Hawaiian Is, which likewise lacked barn owls (until introduced in 1958), the native short-eared owls are known by other names, such as pueo. An absence of owl remains dating from before human settlement on those islands where barn owls do occur suggests that they colonised only after the introduction of the Pacific rat, a favourite food. (The so-called 'Easter Island barn owl' presumed from subfossil evidence has turned out to be a procellarid. Steadman 2006.) Note that the owl name 'ruru' is not onomatopoeic in origin, for the main call of the barn owl is a drawn-out, rasping screech. As Geraghty (2009) observes, 'the most likely explanation [for the transfer] is simply that the Eastern Polynesians who colonised New Zealand were familiar with owls, and their name, from voyaging to Western Polynesia.'

64 E.g., the fat, timber-eating grub of the giant longhorn beetle eaten in the Sāmoa/Tonga/Fiji region, and the edible sago grub in swampy areas of Melanesia. On the other hand, cognates of the New Zealand term, huhu (a large, white, edible beetle grub that tunnels into the rotten wood of old damp logs) and tunga (a dialect variation for this grub) are shared across tropical Polynesia (East and West), where tunga refers to a kind of edible beetle grub in dead wood or sugarcane.

65 The bottle gourd had reached Huahine (Society Is) by around AD 1050 and within 300–400 years had reached Hawaiʻi, Marquesas, New Zealand (and Easter Island?), where its thick waterproof shell was highly valued as a water container. Clarke (2009: 154) was 'unable to find any reports of dated prehistoric bottle gourd remains' on Easter Island. The bottle gourd is native to Africa, but has been grown in the Americas for at least 9900 years, and in China and Japan for at least 7000 years.

66 Asian DNA (chloroplast haplotypes) were found in all samples, with other DNA (nuclear markers) indicating a significant genetic contribution from the Americas, representing two morphologically distinct subspecies: L. siceraria ssp. siceraria (African and American/New World bottle gourds) and L. siceraria ssp. asiatica (Asian bottle gourds). It remains to be seen whether further research turns up dual-origin

material from other islands. Clarke et al. (2006). See also Green (2000b). As Clarke (2009) points out, 'It is [also] possible that the New Zealand bottle gourds used for this study have been contaminated by gene flow (especially pollen-mediated) from post-European contact introductions'.

67 Gourds recorded in Sāmoa, Tonga and Fiji in 1860s have all been re-identified as the Polynesian wax gourd (*Benincasa hispida* var. *pruriens*).

68 Of course, the plant may have bypassed West Polynesia to the north of it, or passed through West Polynesia without being adopted there by a pottery-based culture with no need for the plant.

69 Colenso quoted in Crowe (2004: 24). New Zealand karaka kernels were traditionally cooked in a pit (earth oven), then placed in a basket and trampled in water to remove the surrounding pulp before steeping in water for at least three weeks to remove the last vestiges of poison. The taste is like sweet chestnut.

70 *Corynocarpus similis*, the most widely distributed species, is found in Vanuatu, Solomon Is (where it is known as ibo kwao or ibo bala), New Britain, New Ireland, and the Bismarck Archipelago. Likewise, the Kanak people of New Caledonia had learned the safe preparation of the tree's locally endemic cousin, *Corynocarpus dissimilis*. Walter and Sam (1990), Wagstaff and Dawson (2000), Blench et al. 2002.

71 Coates et al. (1988), who observe that 'explanations of direct transmission in prehistory from Melanesia to New Zealand [of 42 chromosome forms] are generally unacceptable on cultural grounds'. This anomalous material was collected from untended plants on the Cavalli Islands, Great Barrier Island and Spirits Bay. Yen and Wheeler (1968).

72 A psychoactive stimulant nut from the areca palm (*Areca catechu*), mixed with lime from burnt coral or pounded shells, and wrapped in a leaf of the betel vine (*Piper betle*).

73 These wads are shared at least in the Solomons, including on the Polynesian Outlier island of Tikopia.

74 Because of the difference in recorded vowel length, some might attribute this to coincidence.

75 Of New Zealand's kāpia, Yate (1835: 110) writes, 'Often have I, most politely, been offered, out of the toothless mouth of an old woman, or of a tobacco-chewing old man, this precious morsel, to have my share of its sweets.'

76 The poi is about the size of a tennis ball and traditionally made from a flax-fibre bag filled with the fluff from raupō (bulrush) seed heads or from doubled-up raupō leaves.

77 In Polynesian languages, the meaning of poi includes 'to flinch' and 'to leap about'. Paringatai (2005) links the dance name with a second, unrelated meaning – poi puddings of pounded banana, taro or breadfruit traditionally eaten by tropical Polynesians (cognate with paoi, to mash, in Māori).

78 Here, at Hood Point, east of Port Moresby, British anthropologist and ethnologist, Alfred Haddon (1901: 217) watched girls use a 'three foot' long cord with a small netted bag at one end, the other attached to their waist belt, walking up and down, swinging the ball 'with the right hand, causing it to make a graceful sweep behind the back round to the left side, where it was caught with the left hand. During this whole manoeuvre the whole body made a half turn. The action was then repeated with the left hand, the tassel being caught with the right hand …' A similar eyewitness account from the same region comes from Elkington (1907: 54), of 'a score of girls' practising such a dance, 'swinging in their hands a long string at the end of which is a ball'.

79 H. D. Skinner (1931) noted shared styles of curvilinear carving and in the style of ceremonial patu-style weapons or clubs (patu) on Ontong Java.

80 The existence of this long arm of Polynesia was anticipated by Cook back in 1778. 'We may safely conclude,' he wrote, '[that the islands of this "Nation"] extend to the west beyond [Vanuatu].'

81 Stories of the famed Māui fishing up islands are found still further north to Yap, Fais and Palau.

82 Kirch (1984).

83 As recorded by Cook on 6 Feb 1770 at Queen Charlotte Sound, their ancestors 'had once [witnessed coming] to this place a small vessel, from a distant country, called ULIMAROA, in which were four men, who, upon their coming on shore, were all killed: upon being asked where this distant land lay, he pointed to the northward.' Cook (1846: 170). 'Something of this land was mentioned by the people of the Bay of Islands, who said that some of their Ancestors had been there.' In Beaglehole (1967), the spelling is Olhemaroa. A question was raised at the time whether this referred to the four men of Tasman's crew killed here in 1642. However, 'to this he replied in the negative'. Another tradition was collected in which '2 large vessels, much larger than theirs, which some time or other came here and were totally destroyd by the inhabitants and all the people belonging to them kill'd. This Tupia

says is a very old tradition, much older than his great grandfather, and relates to two large canoes which [also] came from Olimaroa, one of the Islands he has mentioned to us.' Banks's journal entry for 5 Feb 1770, in Beaglehole (ed.) (1962). As we saw, Ulimaroa, Olhemaroa or Olimaroa were subsequently transliterated by linguists to Rimaroa. (Geraghty and Tent 2010).

84 Whence basalt was imported. Best et al. (1992).

85 Te Rangi Hīroa (1950a). Emory (1947b) identified a strong link in the language of these atolls with those of the distant Tuamotus.

86 Medical doctor David Tipene-Leach (pers. comm.), who worked in the region in the 1990s. Linguists classify the language of these two atolls as Ellicean, thereby linking them with Tūvalu some 2500 km to the southeast.

87 Identified by Wilson (2012) on the basis of 51 shared lexical and 22 grammatical innovations that suggest tiny atolls such as Takuu, Nukuria, Nukumanu and Luangiua (Ontong Java) are the home of East Polynesian languages, although he concedes that the Northern Outliers and the Eastern Polynesian islands may alternatively have both been peopled from islands where a language has since fallen into disuse. From old atoll and high island vocabulary in East Polynesia, other linguists had also proposed initial colonisation of East Polynesia from the Northern Outliers followed by one or more migrations from the region of Sāmoa. Kirch (2000: 245), Geraghty (2009). According to Feinberg and Scaglion (eds) (2012: 41), the settlement of these Outliers by Polynesians began as early as AD 1000.

88 According to archaeologist Patrick Kirch, 'the first colonists on both Nukuoro and Kapingamarangi appear to have already been adapted to atoll conditions, suggesting that we look to the other equatorial Outlier atolls and to the Tuvalu group for the immediate sources of the Nukuoro and Kapingamarangi populations'. Kirch (1984).

89 In July 1996, Buden (1998) reported at least two members of the New Zealand subspecies of shining cuckoo, and noted the New Zealand long-tailed cuckoo as a 'regular but uncommon visitor to Kapingamarangi'. In late September these birds are drawn south to lay their eggs, a timing that coincides with the main sailing season to avoid South Pacific cyclones. In the reverse direction, flocks of godwits departing from New Zealand in February for the Yellow Sea are flying non-stop over here, but mostly at high altitudes.

90 One of its islets, Touhou, has been built up to its present height only with the aid of sea walls. In 1858, a storm washed off all vegetation and most of the land surface of another islet, followed in 1896 by a tsunami, and another storm in 1947, which destroyed a large part of what remained. The arrival of five seagoing canoes of Marshallese in about 1870 set off a slaughter that is estimated to 'have reduced the population by as much as two-thirds or more', with extended periods of drought following in 1890 and 1916–18. Wiens (1956).

91 From the high island of Tikopia to the atoll of Ontong Java. Bayliss-Smith (1978: 54, 57). Contact between Ontong Java–Nukumanu and Tikopia was also witnessed by Europeans in 1606. Feinberg and Scaglion (eds) (2012: 92).

92 Archaeologists point to a lack of hard evidence for contact along this route; they observe that although obsidian from Talasea, New Britain, was distributed as far south as New Caledonia, none of this valued commodity has been found on either Norfolk Island or New Zealand. Likewise, no New Zealand obsidian is known to have reached these islands to the NNW, the majority of whose inhabitants are Melanesian. Geoffrey Irwin (pers. comm. 31.03.2013).

93 Kaamira (1957: 241) of Te Aupōuri and Te Rarawa iwi gives the following navigational instruction for the *Māmari* canoe to reach Hokianga: 'When night falls lay the bow of the canoe on the star called Atua-tahi (One god). Hold to the left of Te Mangoo-roa (The long shark) and travel on.' Bruce Biggs translates 'Atua-tahi' as 'perhaps Atutahi (Canopus)' and 'Te Mangoo-roa' as 'The Milky Way'. If he and Evans (1998: 49) are correct, this waka approached New Zealand from the direction of New Caledonia and Norfolk Island before 1 November on a 149° course (or, in the highly unlikely event of sailing in winter 28 June–19 July, on a 212° course from Tonga). The former interpretation is consistent with the fact that, from midnight until dawn, steering to the left of the Milky Way – which now stands vertical like a pillar of cloud – would lead one from this NNW quarter to North Cape.

14 Origins, Achievements and Loss [pp. 222–37]

1 Specifically in maternal DNA. Trejaut et al. (2005). Blust (1988). Gray et al. (2009) found support in language for a pulse–pause migration from Taiwan approximately 5230 years ago.

2 Su et al. (2000), Hurles et al. (2002), Lum et al. (2002), Kayser et al. (2008).

Soares et al. (2011) found evidence of 'two-way maternal gene flow between Island Southeast Asia and Near Oceania, likely reflecting movements along a "voyaging corridor" between them'. Underhill et al. (2001) identified a similarly complex ancestry among Māori: 'The Y-chromosome results [from NZ Māori men] support a pattern of complex interrelationships between Southeast Asia, Melanesia, and Polynesia, in contrast to mtDNA and linguistic data, which uphold a rapid and homogeneous Austronesian expansion.' Bellwood et al. (2011: 347) agrees that the direction of influence from Taiwan remains in question, for 'genetics still has to come to terms with the large error ranges inherent in molecular clock dating, as does linguistics with glottochronology, and archaeology with the often fragmentary and tangential nature of its data set with regard to human population migration'. See also Oppenheimer and Richards (2001), Oppenheimer (2004), Mirabal et al. (2012).

3 Just as Māori in New Zealand today do not necessarily speak Māori, and the Cham people of southern Vietnam speak Austronesian languages, yet do not share Austronesian genes. We run into similar difficulties in Europe if we attempt to go back 5000 years, for while we do know that wheeled carts were first being used around this time and stone circles like Stonehenge were being built, we know little of the movements, culture and language of the people that made them.

4 Archaeological evidence for which is summarised in some detail by Bulbeck (2008). Evidence of trade 2200–1500 BC from Taiwan to the Philippines includes two bracelets of Taiwan nephrite found in Nagsabaran.

5 Irwin (1989: 168).

6 Trejaut et al. (2011), Friedlaender et al. (2007). According to Trejaut et al. (2011), the so-called 'Polynesian motif' of maternal DNA (haplogroup B4a1a1a) 'has never been seen in Taiwan, and had its major expansion approximately 6650 years [ago] in the Bismarck Archipelago'. The female ancestors of Polynesians were generally less mobile though than the men, who carry more Melanesian DNA.

7 Anderson (2014b: 22).

8 In the other direction, one can trace the origin of Lapita even further back through comparable pottery styles in use around 2000 BC in the northern Philippines. Bellwood et al. (2011: 332–36). McNiven et al. (2011) recently found Lapita also on the south coast of New Guinea. See also Specht et al. (2014).

9 Skoglund et al. (2016) obtained three mitochondrial DNA sequences from Vanuatu and all were found to be haplogroup B4a1a1a, the classic 'Polynesian motif', similar to indigenous Taiwanese populations such as the Ami and Atayal as well as to populations from the Philippines such as the Kankanaey, who have no detectable Papuan ancestry. The possible range of Papuan ancestry in the Vanuatu individuals was estimated to be 0–11%, suggesting that the Papuan admixture found among Polynesians came later. The actual routes of movement are not known. See also Valentin et al. (2016), who came to a similar conclusion from an analysis of skull shape from the same cemetery.

10 Irwin (1981), Addison and Matisoo-Smith (2010).

11 At least at the eastern end of Micronesia; see Takayama (1981). Pottery is, however, found on high islands at the western end, on Chuuk, Pohnpei and Kosrae.

12 Kennedy (2008). More specifically, the Pacific plantain is thought to originate from along the north coast of New Guinea or in the Bismarck Archipelago (Perrier et al. 2011).

13 Zerega et al. (2004). Primarily, *Artocarpus camansi* from New Guinea, but with a minor genetic input from *A. mariannensis*, a strain from the Mariana Islands and Palau.

14 'After ≈2000 cal BP', at least. Addison and Matisoo-Smith (2010).

15 O'Shaughnessy et al. (1990): 'The globin gene data are not inconsistent with a Polynesia colonization scenario that includes routes through both Melanesia and Micronesia, perhaps meeting in the melting pot of Fiji-Samoa-Tonga, from which the final later migrations to the far reaches of the eastern Pacific took place.' Lum and Cann (2000): 'Thus genetic similarities [in MtDNA] among Micronesian and Polynesian populations result, in some cases, from a common origin, and in others, from extensive gene flow.'

16 McLean (1974, 1996, 2008, 2010, 2014). Nose flutes refer to flutes played with one nostril, the other blocked off with the thumb. Although Māori played nose flutes too (made from soft stone, whale tooth, various woods and the stems of gourds), McLean doubts that this playing method 'was much used' here (notwithstanding a few accounts of this from the 1880s and 1890s). In the tropics, the flutes are traditionally made of bamboo.

17 Matisoo-Smith (2012: 408) likewise notes that 'There seems to be the implication in many genetic studies of Pacific peoples that populations are static and unchanging and thus events that occurred thousands, if

not tens of thousands, of years ago are easily reconstructed from the DNA of peoples, their languages, and their cultural affiliations today.' Specht et al. (2014) have been more explicit in deconstructing Lapita as a valid cultural complex.

18 Burney et al. (2004), Hurles et al. (2005), Cox et al. (2012).

19 Portuguese sail around Africa. Christopher Columbus reaches the Americas (1492).

20 Wilmshurst et al. (2011), Mulrooney et al. (2011), Allen (2014), Athens et al. (2014), Conte and Molle (2014), Kirch et al. (2015b), Stevenson et al. (2017).

21 The few exceptions include Lord Howe Is off Australia; Guadalupe Is, Revillagigedo, Clipperton, Cocos and Juan Fernández islands off the American coast; and Midway Is northwest of Hawai`i; most of these islands lie in regions that experience little or no wind for much of the year.

22 King (2003: 37). Based on the conventional 'Polynesian Triangle', with an extension to include Tūvalu and the Polynesian Outliers, but excluding Melanesia and Micronesia, an ocean area of 35,000,000 km² is estimated. The whole of Africa is about 30,000,000 km² and Western Europe is about 4,000,000 km². Admittedly, members of land-based cultures might prefer to discount the oceanic component of this territory.

23 Unprecedented though voyages under the command of Zheng He (Cheng Ho) were for the size and military capacity of their fleets, their routes to reach India, Arabia and East Africa (1405–1433) were not new, and fall well short of the fanciful claims by Gavin Menzies in his book *1421: The Year China Discovered the World* that the Chinese discovered Australia, New Zealand, the Americas and Antarctica.

24 Viviano (2005); notwithstanding claims by Menzies (2002).

25 Although the Vikings reached North America, they did so via the Faroe Islands, skirting the coasts of Iceland and Greenland. They were thus not required to cross vast stretches of ocean or to develop methods of navigation anywhere near as sophisticated as those of Polynesians. (Faroe Islands to Iceland is 450 km.)

26 Lekkas et al. (2011).

27 Goff et al. (2012: Figure 1). Evidenced by a sandwiched, archaeologically sterile layer of sand.

28 Gao et al. (2006).

29 At Henderson Bay in Doubtless Bay. McFadgen (2007: 163). 'At the only site on the Aupōuri Peninsula that has been well-studied'. Dr Bruce McFadgen (pers. comm. 20.08.2013).

30 McFadgen (2007: 226). Although the evidence in some low-lying locations could be interpreted as effects from storm surge, at specific locations elsewhere along this range detailed research permits a stronger inference.

31 'An explanation for why trading or distribution of various rock types stopped (Nelson mineral belt argillites especially), and why the archaic adze kit changed to a generalised single type, often made of local stone.' Bruce McFadgen (pers. comm. 24.08.2013).

32 McFadgen (2007: 232), King (2003: 71–73).

33 According to Belich (1996: 54), Māori are at this point migrating into hitherto thinly-peopled inland and western regions of the country, a point disputed by Anderson (2014b: 120), citing lack of evidence.

34 Of both children and adults in Palliser Bay, dated to the late 15th century. Leach (1981).

35 King and Goff (2006: 8–13). Indeed, floods, tsunamis and avalanches (caused by earthquakes) were of sufficient import to Māori that a god – Parawhenuamea, wife of Kiwa – is associated with them.

36 Anderson (2009c, 2014b: 120).

37 Indentations were left in the cliff-face of Paratutae Rock by Kupe's paddle; Rākaihautū carved out several South Island lakes; and Pāoa urinated into being the Waipāoa, Waioeka and Mōtū rivers.

38 Kaeppler (2007). In the tropics, the traditional material for this was sennit. Its New Zealand equivalent is flax fibre, which is traditionally used for binding cultural knowledge into weaving designs.

39 Best (1922c: 5).

40 This is based on a population estimate for New Zealand of 100,000. Te Rangi Hīroa (1924) writes that: 'It does not seem improbable [that there was] a pre-European population of from 200,000 to 500,000', but professional demographers think it was less. Ian Pool (1991) leans toward 100,000, while Lewthwaite (1999) (abandoning his earlier estimate of 250,000), writes, 'critical evaluations of historical sources, demographic analysis, archaeological calculations based on settlement-sites, residues of fish and shellfish consumed, and analyses of past evaluations, generally suggest estimates not much exceeding 100,000'.

41 By 1872, the original population of Easter Island (3000–4000) had plummeted to just 111. On the Marquesas, it crashed from an estimated 45,000 (in 1804) to 4865 in 1880, reaching a low of 2255 by the early 1900s. On Tahiti, it fell from an estimate of 121,500 (in 1774) to 16,050

in 1799; and to just 8658 by 1829. Kirch and Rallu (2007: 3). On Rurutu, introduced disease led to a fall in population in the 1830s from an estimated 3000 to 200–300. On Tubuai, in the 30 years following the landing of the *Bounty* in 1789, introduced diseases saw the population fall from 3000 to 900, and by 1823 to just 300. On Rapa Iti, introduced disease led to a crash from around 2000 to 120 by 1867. In New Zealand, an estimated population of up to 100,000 (in 1769) had fallen to 42,000 by 1896. On Mangareva, a loss of more than half the 2100 inhabitants in the 10 years following 1834 is attributed to the cruel missionary zeal of Father Laval. In the Hawaiian Islands, an estimated population of 300,000 (in 1779) fell to 142,050 in 1823, to just 70,000 by 1853, and to around 51,000 by 1872. Kirch and Rallu (2007), Marques (1893), Schmitt (1967). From 1790 to 1850 on Sāmoa, the loss was from about 68,000 to 30,000. Kirch and Rallu (2007: 206, 230). For Rarotonga, see Crocombe (1961: 135). For Tongareva, see Roscoe (1987).

42 *Banks Journal*, 20 July 1769, 'Here were also 4 or 5 Ewharre no Eatua or god houses which were made to be carried on poles. One of these I examind by putting my hand into it: within was a parsel about 5 feet long and one thick wrappd up in matts, these I tore with my fingers till I came to a covering of mat made of platted Cocoa nut fibres which it was impossible to get through so I was obligd to desist, especialy as what I had already done gave much offence to our new friends.'

43 Te Rangi Hīroa (1938b: 582). See, for example, wrappers and containers of divinity illustrated in Kaeppler (2007).

44 The Society Islands figures of loss from the 1918 flu epidemic are 191/1000, and 400–500/1000 for those older than 60. Greater vulnerability to flu viruses among older Polynesians – over Europeans and Chinese – continued for at least 150 years after contact with Europeans. Kirch and Rallu (2007: 26).

45 For example, in Tonga in Oct 1773, where Captain Cook writes in his *Journal*: 'as we had yet some venereal complaints on board, I took all possible care to prevent the disorder being communicated to them'.

46 Based on a seating capacity of 60,000 for Eden Park stadium and a population of 1.5 million for urban Auckland.

47 For a critical appraisal of these figures, see population sidebar and associated footnotes.

48 Kirch and Rallu (2007). This is consistent with similar losses among Amerindians from European disease of 90–95 percent. Mann (2005). See also Belich (1996: 174).

49 On many islands, this loss is ongoing with a postcolonial diaspora to New Zealand and elsewhere.

50 Quirós quoted in Markham (ed.) (1904: 17).

51 Forster (1778: 477).

52 In *Maori and Polynesian: Their origin, history and culture*, Brown (1907: 252–63), for example, judged Polynesians incapable of long-distance navigation, so proposed a land bridge – a subsiding belt of islands – running from Japan through to Easter Island. 'There must have been a more or less incontinuous land-bridge from the coast of Asia . . . a primitive route from Japan, with Islands separated only by narrow straits.'

53 References for transfers shown: Addison (2007), Allen (2014), Anderson (2000a, 2005, 2008a, 2008b), Barnes and Hunt (2005), Barnes and Hunt (2005), Best et al. (1992), Burley and Dickinson (2001), Carson (2002), Collerson and Weisler (2007), Di Piazza and Pearthree (2001c), Dickinson et al. (1998), Kirch (2000), Lee et al. (2007), McAlister et al. (2013), McKinnon (ed.) (1997), Rolett et al. (2015), Sand (1998), Summerhayes (2009), Walter and Dickinson (1989), Walter et al. (2010), Weisler (1994, 1998, 2002, 2008), Weisler and Kirch (1996), Clark et al. (2014), White et al. (2014), Weisler et al. (2016).

54 For example, the so-called 'Tamil Bell' (a broken bronze bell identified in Northland in 1836); and an iron helmet (known as the 'Spanish helmet'), found in Wellington Harbour some time before 1904.

55 Based on some 1600 named islands in the region listed by Motteler (1986).

56 Notably by Sharp (1961, 1964).

57 Te Rangi Hīroa (1938b: 63).

58 Anderson (2014b: 26).

59 Professor John Macmillan Brown, one-time chancellor of the University of New Zealand. Brown (1907: 147).

60 Te Rangi Hīroa (1938b: 245).

61 Though gold and copper ore are present in Fiji.

62 One of many reasons why the 'Spanish helmet' found in Wellington Harbour around 1904 is unlikely to be anything other than an item of colonial baggage.

63 As noted by John Charlot (2004), Professor of Polynesian Religions at the University of Hawaiʻi, 'wherever and whenever regular schools were established, Polynesians flocked to them'.

64 Ethnocentricity is likewise evident in abhorrence reserved for human sacrifice and cannibalism in Polynesia, at a time when being 'hanged, drawn and quartered' (drawn on a sled through the streets, hanged until almost dead, chopped into four pieces while still alive, and then emasculated and disembowelled) remained an official punishment in England until 1870. Likewise with slavery (as evidenced in traditional Polynesian terms for slaves): this practice was not officially abolished in the US until 1865; and indeed it is a practice that continues today, with over 20 million slaves worldwide, according to the UN.

65 Some in the Kaitāia floodplain extend over 100 hectares and have since been drained for pasture. Horrocks and Barber (2005).

66 For catching eels and waterfowl. Skinner (1912).

67 Witnessed by Captain Gilbert Mair. Best (1929: 11).

68 Diamond (2005), but also by Flenley and Bahn (2002).

69 In the words of archaeologist Terry Hunt (2007). In the alternative view, Swiss anthropologist Alfred Métraux characterised the fate of Rapanui instead as: 'one of the most hideous atrocities committed by white men in the South Seas'. Métraux (1957: 38).

70 By the time of European settlement, New Zealand had already lost about 40 percent of its original forest cover, all its big flightless birds and northern seal colonies – a pattern of loss that followed first human arrivals across the world. Some 45,000 years earlier, Australia's indigenous megafauna had suffered similarly sudden losses on arrival of the first wave of human inhabitants there.

71 Ngata (1933) quoted in Belich (1996: 25).

72 As acknowledged earlier, for example, the *Tainui* and *Te Arawa* evidently sailed together.

73 Orbell (1991: 5).

74 Consistent with the maternal DNA of Pacific rats brought to New Zealand, and with the range of origins of Māori terms for specific plants and animals, etc. Knapp et al. (2012), testing maternal DNA from human remains excavated in one of New Zealand's earliest archaeological sites at Wairau Bar, also found two different DNA types, which they say 'indicates that the founding populations were unlikely to be from a single matrilocal source'. However, geneticist Geoff Chambers (pers. comm. 6.8.2013) cautions that 'finding two mtDNA types does not mean that they came from different places'.

75 Consistent with human mtDNA results which 'support an East Polynesian origin for Māori'. Penny et al. (2002).

76 Heyerdahl (1974: 166).

77 On ABC's *Four Corners* (McDermott 2006), Menzies modified his earlier view of where Māori had come from, bringing this event forward some 1600 years: 'Around 200 BC, Chinese miners sailed from Taiwan and they collected, on their way, Melanesian, I say, indentured labourers, or slaves, took them to New Zealand, and these Melanesians, in due course, rose up, murdered the Maori men, kept their wives as their own wives.' Menzies' claim (2002) that China explored the open Pacific in the 15th century is dismissed by professional Chinese historians as fiction – 'fantastic speculation' and frequently 'factually wrong'. Menzies' response to the historians on ABC's *Four Corners was to point out that*, 'The public are on my side, and they are the people that count.'

78 Maxwell Hill and co-authors of *To the Ends of the Earth*.

79 Including expeditions aboard merchant and naval vessels, and those by European buccaneers and missionaries. Quanchi and Robson (2005: xxx). Figures include 11 ships in the Nassau Fleet and *San Cristóbal* and *San Martin* under Ruy Lopez de Villalobos.

80 Cook (1846 vol. 2: 256).

81 Te Rangi Hīroa (1938b: 279).

References

ABC | Four Corners. 2006. TV transcript. See McDermott.

Académie Tahitiennne. 1999. Dictionnaire Tahitien–Français: Fa'atoro Parau Tahiti–Farāni. Fare Vāna`a, Pape`ete.

Adams, N. M. 1994. *Seaweeds of New Zealand.* CUP, Christchurch.

Addison, D. J. 2007. The Tutuila basalt export industry and the 5600 km distribution of Samoan adzes at ~700–600 BP. In *The Gotland Papers.* Gotland Uni. with Easter Is. Foundation, Sweden, 20–25 Aug: 347–58.

Addison, D. J. and Matisoo-Smith, E. 2010. Rethinking Polynesians origins: A West-Polynesia triple-I model. *Archaeol. Oceania* 45: 1–12.

Addison, D. J. et al. 2009. Archaeology of Atafu, Tokelau: Some initial results from 2008. *Rapa Nui J.* 23(1): 5–9.

Adds, P. 2012. Long-distance prehistoric two-way voyaging: The case for Aotearoa and Hawaiki. *J. Roy. Soc. NZ* 42(2): 99–103.

Ahmed, F. and Urooj, A. 2008. In vitro starch digestibility characteristics of *Dioscorea alata* tuber. *World J. Dairy & Food Sci.* 3(2): 29–33.

Alexander, W. D. 1891. Instructions in ancient Hawaiian astronomy as taught by Kaneakahoowaha. *Hawaiian Annual for 1891*, pp. 142–43 (trans. from Kamakau, S. M. Ku`oko`a newspaper, 5 Aug 1865).

— 1894. Stone idols from Necker Island. *JPS* 3(3): 153–54.

Allen, M. S. 1992. Temporal variation in Polynesian fishing strategies: The Southern Cook Islands in regional perspective. *Asian Perspectives* 31(2): 183–204.

— 1996. Patterns of interaction in Southern Cook Island prehistory. *Bull. Indo-Pacific Prehistory Assn* 15: 13–21.

— 2004. Revisiting and revising Marquesan culture history: New archaeological investigations at Anaho Bay, Nuku Hiva Island. *JPS* 113(2): 143–96.

— 2006. New ideas about Late Holocene climate variability in the Central Pacific. *Current Anthropol.* 47(3): 521–35.

— 2014. Marquesan colonisation chronologies and post-colonisation Interaction: Implications for Hawaiian origins and the 'Marquesan Homeland' hypothesis. *J. Pac. Archaeol.* 5(2): 1–17.

Allen, M. S. and Johnson, K. T. M. 1997. Tracking ancient patterns of interaction: Recent geochemical studies in the Southern Cook Islands. In Weisler, M. I. (ed.) 1997: 111–33.

Allen, M. S. and McAlister, A. J. 2010. The Hakaea Beach site, Marquesan colonisation and models of East Polynesian settlement. *Archaeol. Oceania* 45(2): 54–65.

Allen, M. S. and Schubel, S. E. 1990. Recent archaeological research on Aitutaki, Southern Cooks: The Moturakau shelter. *JPS* 99(3): 265–96.

Allen, M. S. and Steadman, D. W. 1990. Excavations at the Ureia Site, Aitutaki, Cook Islands: Preliminary results. *Archaeol. Oceania* 25(1): 24–37.

Allen, M. S. and Ussher, E. 2013. Starch analysis reveals prehistoric plant translocations and shell tool use, Marquesas Islands, Polynesia. *J. Archaeol. Sci.* 40(6): 2799–812.

Allen, M. S. and Wallace, R. 2007. New evidence from the East Polynesian gateway: Substantive and methodological results from Aitutaki, Southern Cook Islands. *Radiocarbon* 49(3): 1163–79.

Allen, M. S. et al. 2012. The anomaly of Marquesan ceramics: A fifty year retrospective. *J. Pac. Archaeol.* 3(1): 90–104.

Anderson, A. 2000a. Implications of prehistoric obsidian transfer in South Polynesia. *Bull. Indo-Pacific Prehistory Assn* 20: 117–23.

— 2000b. Slow boats from China: Issues in the prehistory of Indo-Pacific seafaring. *Mod. Quaternary Res. SE Asia* 16: 13–50.

— 2002a. Faunal collapse, landscape change and settlement history in Remote Oceania. *World Archaeol.* 33(3): 375–90.

— 2002b. Taking to the boats: The prehistory of Indo-Pacific colonization. Public lecture for the National Institute of Asia and the Pacific, 18 Dec. (As PDF at http://apo.org.au/node/6475.)

— 2003. *Prodigious Birds: Moas and moa-hunting in prehistoric New Zealand.* CUP, Cambridge.

— 2005. Subpolar settlement in South Polynesia. *Antiquity* 79(306): 791–800.

— 2006a. Islands of exile: Ideological motivation in maritime migration. *J. Is. & Coastal Archaeol.* 1(1): 33–47.

— 2006b. Polynesian seafaring and American horizons: A response to Jones and Klar. *American Antiquity* 71(4): 759–63.

— 2008a. Problems of the 'traditionalist' model of long-distance Polynesian voyaging. *Insights* 1(12): 2–12. Durham Uni.

— 2008b. Response to comments on 'Traditionalism, interaction and long-distance seafaring in Polynesia'. *J. Is. & Coastal Archaeol.* 3(2): 268–70.

— 2008c. Short and sometimes sharp: Human impacts on marine resources in the archaeology and history of South Polynesia. Ch. 2 in Torben, C. R. and Erlandson, J. M. (eds) *Human Impacts on Ancient Marine Ecosystems: A global perspective.* Uni. California Press, Berkeley.

— 2008d. Traditionalism, interaction, and long-distance seafaring in Polynesia. *J. Is. & Coastal Archaeol.* 3(2): 240–50.

— 2009a. Origins, settlement and society of pre-European South Polynesia. Ch. 2 in Byrnes, G. (ed.) *The New Oxford History of New Zealand.* OUP, Melbourne.

— 2009b. The rat and the octopus: Initial human colonization and the prehistoric introduction of domestic animals to Remote Oceania. *Biol. Invasions* 11: 1503–19.

— 2009c. Epilogue: Changing archaeological perspectives upon historical ecology in the Pacific Islands. *Pac. Sci.* 63(4): 747–57.

— 2014a. *Catching the Wind.* New Zealand Aronui Lecture. (Video at https://vimeo.com/106239820).

— 2014b. Speaking of migration, AD 1150–1450. Ch. 2. in Anderson, A. et al. 2014.

— 2017. Changing perspectives upon Māori colonisation voyaging. *J. Roy. Soc. NZ* 47(3): 1–10.

Anderson, A. and Kennett, D. J. (eds) 2012. *Taking the High Ground: The archaeology of Rapa, a fortified island in remote East Polynesia.* ANU Press, Canberra.

Anderson, A. and McFadgen, B. 1990. Prehistoric two-way voyaging between New Zealand and East Polynesia: Mayor Island obsidian on Raoul Island, and possible Raoul Island obsidian in New Zealand. *Archaeol. Oceania* 25(1): 37–42.

Anderson, A. and Sinoto, Y. H. 2002. New radiocarbon ages of colonization sites in East Polynesia. *Asian Perspectives* 41(2): 242–57.

Anderson, A. and White, P. 2001a. Approaching the prehistory of Norfolk Island. *Rec. Aust. Mus.*, Supplement 27: 1–9.

—— 2001b. Prehistoric settlement on Norfolk Island and its oceanic context. *Rec. Aust. Mus.*, Supplement 27: 135–41.

Anderson, A. et al. 2001. The radiocarbon chronology of the Norfolk Island archaeological sites. *Rec. Aust. Mus.*, Supplement 27: 33–42.

— 2003. Cultural chronology in Mangareva (Gambier Islands), French Polynesia: Evidence from recent radiocarbon dating. *JPS* 112(2): 119–40.

— 2006. Prehistoric maritime migration in the Pacific Islands: An hypothesis of ENSO forcing. *Holocene* 16(1): 1–6.

— 2007. Ecuadorian sailing rafts and Oceanic landfalls. In *Vastly Ingenious: The archaeology of Pacific material culture in honour of Janet M. Davidson.* Otago Uni. Press, Dunedin.

— 2014. *Tangata Whenua: An illustrated history.* Bridget Williams Books, Wellington.

Archey, G. 1926. A recently-discovered carved stone figure. *JPS* 35(138): 150–52.

Arnold, J. E. 2007. Credit where credit is due: The history of the Chumash oceangoing plank canoe. *American Antiquity* 72: 196–209.

Association Culturelle 'Te Reo o te Tuāmotu'. 2001. *Tuāmotu te Kāiga: Langues and Culture: Quête identitaire et affirmation culturelle: Premier festival du 22 au 24 Septembre 2000.* Ed. Haere Po, Papeete.

Aswani, S. and Graves, M. W. 1998. The Tongan maritime expansion: A case in the evolutionary ecology of social complexity. *Asian Perspectives* 37(2): 135–64.

Athens, J. S. 2009. *Rattus exulans* and the catastrophic disappearance of Hawai`i's native lowland forest. *Biological Invasions* 11: 1489–501.

Athens, J. S. et al. 2002. Avifaunal extinctions, vegetation change, and Polynesian impacts in prehistoric Hawai`i. *Archaeol. Oceania* 37: 57–78.

Athens, J. S. et al. 2014. A paleoenvironment and archeological model-based age estimate for the colonization of Hawai`i. *American Antiquity* 79(1): 144–155.

Atkinson, A. S. 1892. What is a Tangata Maori? *JPS* 1(3): 133–136.

Atkinson, I. A. E. and Towns, D. R. 2001. Advances in New Zealand mammalogy 1990–2000: Pacific rat. *J. Roy. Soc. NZ* 31(1): 99–109.

Austin, C. C. 1999. Lizards took express train to Polynesia. *Nature* 397: 113–114.

Babayan, C. et al. 1987. Voyage to Aotearoa. *JPS* 96(2): 161–200.

Bahn, P. and Flenley, J. 1992. *Easter Island: Earth Island*. Thames & Hudson, London.

Ballard, C. et al. (eds) 2005. *The Sweet Potato in Oceania: A reappraisal.* Ethnology Monographs 19. Oceania Monograph 56. Uni. Pittsburgh, Pittsburgh and Uni. Sydney, Sydney.

Banks, J. 1962 – see Beaglehole, J. C. (ed.) 1962.

Barnes, S. S. and Hunt, T. L. 2005. Sāmoa's pre-contact connections in West Polynesia and beyond. *JPS* 114(3): 227–66.

Barnes, S. S. et al. 2006. Ancient DNA of the Pacific rat (*Rattus exulans*) from Rapa Nui (Easter Island). *J. Archaeol. Sci.* 33: 1536–40.

Barr, J. 2006. Of metaphysics and Polynesian navigation. Ch. 10 in McDonald, B. (ed.) *Seeing God Everywhere: Essays on nature and the sacred.* Indica Books, Varanasi.

Barrington, P. C. 1959. Sea water drinking in survival at sea. *Proc. Roy. Soc. Med.* 52: 448–50.

Barthel, T. S. 1962. Easter Island place-names. *J. Société Océanistes* 18: 100–07.

Bassett, K. N. et al. 2004. Gardening at the edge: Documenting the limits of tropical Polynesian kumara horticulture in southern New Zealand. *Geoarchaeology* 19(3): 185–218.

Baudouin, L. and Lebrun, P. 2009. Coconut (*Cocos nucifera* L.) DNA studies support the hypothesis of an ancient Austronesian migration from Southeast Asia to America. *Genet. Resour. Crop. Evol.* 56: 257–62.

Bayliss-Smith, T. 1978. Changing patterns of inter-island mobility in Ontong Java atoll. *Archaeol. and Physical Anthropol. in Oceania* 13(1): 40–73.

Beaglehole, E. and Beaglehole, P. 1938. *Ethnology of Pukapuka*. Bishop Mus. Bull. 150, Honolulu.

Beaglehole, J. C. (ed.) 1962. *The Endeavour Journal of Joseph Banks 1768–1771*, vol. 1. Angus & Robertson, Sydney.

— 1967. *The Journals of Captain James Cook. The Voyage of the Resolution and Discovery, 1776–1780.* Hakluyt Soc., Cambridge.

Beaglehole, J. C. 1966. *The Exploration of the Pacific.* (Pioneer histories vol. 3.) Stanford Uni. Press, Stanford.

— 1974. *The Life of Captain James Cook.* A. & C. Black, London.

Beattie, H. 1920. The Southern Maori, and greenstone. *Trans. Proc. NZ Inst.* 52: 45–72.

Beavan, N. 2014. No evidence for sample contamination or diet offset for pre-Columbian chicken dates from El Arenal. *PNAS* 111(35): E3582.

Beechey, F. W. 1831. *Narrative of a Voyage to the Pacific and Beering's Strait, to Cooperate with the Polar Expeditions: Performed in His Majesty's ship Blossom . . . in the years 1825, 26, 27, 28.* Colburn & Bentley, London.

Behrens, C. F. 1903. In Corney, B. G. (ed.): 131–37.

Belich, J. 1996. *Making Peoples: A history of the New Zealanders from Polynesian settlement to the end of the nineteenth century.* Penguin, Auckland.

Bellwood, P. et al. 2011. Are 'cultures' inherited? Multidisciplinary perspectives on the origins and migrations of Austronesian-speaking peoples prior to 1000 BC. Ch. 16 in Roberts, B. W. and Linden, M. V. (eds). *Investigating Archaeological Cultures: Material culture, variability, and transmission.* Springer, NY.

Benton, T. G. and Lehtinen, P. T. 1995. Biodiversity and origin of the non-flying terrestrial arthropods of Henderson Island. *Biol. J. Linnean Soc.* 56: 261–72.

Berentson, Q. 2012. *Moa: The Life and Death of New Zealand's Legendary Bird.* Craig Potton Publishing, Nelson.

Besnier, N. et al. 1998. Polynesian Outliers. In Kaeppler, A. L. and Love, J. W. (eds) *The Garland Encyclopedia of World Music*, vol. 9: *Australia and the Pacific Islands*. Garland, NY.

Best, E. 1899. The art of the whare pora: Notes on the clothing of the ancient Maori . . . *Trans. NZ Inst.* 31: 625–58.

— 1917. Some place names of islands of the Society Group. *JPS* 26(3): 111–15.

— 1918. Polynesian navigators: Their exploration and settlement of the Pacific. *Geographic Review* 5(3): 169–82.

— 1922a. *Astronomical Knowledge of the Maori, Genuine and Empirical.* Dom. Mus. Monograph 3, Wellington.

— 1922b. *The Maori Division of Time.* Dom. Mus. Monograph 4, Wellington.

— 1922c. *Some Aspects of Maori Myth and Religion.* Dom. Mus. Monograph 1, Wellington.

— 1923. *Polynesian Voyagers: The Maori as a Deep-Sea Navigator, Explorer and Colonizer.* Dom. Mus. Monograph 5, Wellington.

— 1924a. *Maori Religion and Mythology. Part II.* Dom. Mus. Bull. 11, Wellington.

— 1924b. *The Maori*, vol. 2. Govt. Printer, Wellington.

— 1925a. *Games and Pastimes of the Maori.* Dom. Mus. Bull. 8, Wellington.

— 1925b. *Maori Agriculture.* Dom. Mus. Bull. 9, Wellington.

— 1925c. *The Maori Canoe.* Dom. Mus. Bull. 7, Wellington.

— 1929. *Fishing Methods and Devices of the Maori.* Dom. Mus. Bull. 12, Wellington.

— 1931. Maori agriculture. *JPS* 40(157): 1–22.

— 1942. *Forest Lore of the Maori.* Dom. Mus. Bull. 14, Wellington.

Best, S. B. et al. 1992. Necromancing the stone: Archaeologists and adzes in Samoa. *JPS* 101(1): 45–84.

Biggs, B. 1965. Reviews: *A Dictionary of Some Tuamotuan Dialects of the Polynesian Language. JPS* 74(3): 375–89.

— 1985. *The Complete English–Maori Dictionary.* AUP, Auckland.

— 1991. A linguist revisits the New Zealand bush. In Pawley, A. (ed.) *Man and a Half: Essays in Pacific anthropology and ethnobiology in honour of Ralph Bulmer.* Memoir 48. Poly. Soc., Auckland.

— 1994. Does Maori have a closest relative? In Sutton, D. G. (ed.) 1994: 96–105.

Biggs, B. and Clark, R. 2006. *Comparative Polynesian Lexicon* (POLLEX). Originally a privately circulated computer file – now updated online by Greenhill and Clark: http://pollex.org.nz.

Blench, R. et al. 2002. Fruits and arboriculture in the Indo-Pacific region. Paper presented at the 17th Congress of the Indo-Pacific Prehistory Assn, Taipei, Taiwan, 9–15 Sep.

Blust, R. 1988. The Austronesian homeland: A linguistic perspective. *Asian Perspectives* 26(1): 45–67.

Boessenkool, S. et al. 2009. Relict or colonizer? Extinction and range expansion of penguins in southern New Zealand. *Proc. R. Soc. B.* 276(1658): 815–21.

Bogert, C. 1937. Birds collected during the Whitney South Sea Expedition. XXXIV: The distribution and migration of the long-tailed cuckoo (*Urodynamis taitensis* Sparrman). *Am. Mus. Novitates* 933.

Bollt, R. 2008. Excavations in Peva Valley, Rurutu, Austral Islands (East Polynesia). *Asian Perspectives* 47(1): 156–87.

— 2009. Artifact: Tiki pendant. *Archaeol.* 62(3): 68.

Bombard, A. 1953. *The Bombard Story.* A. Deutsch, London.

Bonar, W. 1901. Ancient Polynesian canoe. *JPS* 10(4): 205.

Bougainville de, L. A. 1772. *A Voyage Round the World Performed by Order of His Most Christian Majesty in the Years 1766, 1767, 1768, and 1769.* (Transl. J. R. Forster.) Nourse and Davies, London.

Brailsford, B. 1997. *The Tattooed Land* (2nd edn). Stoneprint Press, Hamilton.

Branch, T. A. 2011. Humpback whale abundance south of 60°S from three complete circumpolar sets of surveys. *J. Cetacean Res. Manage.* Special Issue 3: 53–69.

Bridgman, H. A. 1983. Could climatic change have had an influence on the Polynesian migrations? *Palaeogeography, Palaeoclimatology, Palaeoecology* 41(3): 193–206.

Brigham, W. T. 1903. *A Handbook for Visitors to the Bernice Pauahi Bishop Museum of Polynesian Ethnology and Natural History.* Bishop Mus. Special Pub. vol. 3.

Brook, F. J. 2000. Prehistoric predation of the landsnail *Placostylus ambagiosus* Suter (Stylommatophora: Bulimulidae), and evidence for the timing of establishment of rats in northernmost New Zealand. *J. Roy. Soc. NZ* 30: 227–41.

— 2010. Coastal landsnail fauna of Rarotonga, Cook Islands. *Tuhinga* 21: 161–252.

Brooke, M. de L. 1995. The breeding biology of the gadfly petrels *Pterodroma* spp. of the Pitcairn Islands: characteristics, population sizes and controls. *Biol. J. Linnean Soc.* 56(12): 213–31.

Brooke, M. de L. et al. 2010. Potential for rat predation to cause decline of the globally threatened Henderson petrel *Pterodroma atrata. Endangered Species Research* 11(1): 47–59.

Brown, J. M. 1907. *Maori and Polynesian: Their origin, history and culture.* Hutchinson & Co., London.

Bruce, L. 1976. Preliminary study of three Polynesian sources for celestial navigation. In *Micronesian and Polynesian Voyaging: Three readings*: 1–23. Pac. Is. Studies Program, Uni. Hawai`i.

Bryant, D. 2014. Statistical flaws undermine pre-Columbian chicken debate. *PNAS* 111(35): E3584.

Buck, Sir Peter Henry – see Te Rangi Hiroa.

Buden, D. W. 1998. The birds of Kapingamarangi Atoll, including first record of the shining cuckoo (*Chrysococcyx lucidus*) from Micronesia. *Notornis* 45: 141–53.

Bulbeck, D. 2008. An integrated perspective on the Austronesian diaspora: The switch from cereal agriculture to maritime foraging in the colonisation of Island Southeast Asia. *Australian Archaeol.* 67: 31–51.

Buller, W. L. 1877. Art. XIX. Notes on the ornithology of New Zealand. *Trans. Proc. Roy. Soc. NZ* 10: 191–201.

— 1888. *A History of the Birds of New Zealand.* John Van Voorst, London.

— 1967. – see Turbott, E. G. (ed.) 1967.

Burky, A. J. et al. 2000. The occurrence of the freshwater clams, *Musculium partumeium* (Say) and *Pisidium casertanum* (Poli) (Bivalvia: Sphaeriidae), in the Hawaiian Islands. *Micronesica* 33(1/2): 161–64.

Burley, D. V. and Dickinson, W. R. 2001. Origin and significance of a founding settlement in Polynesia. *PNAS* 98(20): 11829–31.

Burley, D. V. et al. 2012. High precision U/Th dating of first Polynesian settlement. *PLoS One* 7(11): e48769.

Burney, D. A. et al. 2004. A chronology for late prehistoric Madagascar. *J. Human Evolution* 47: 25–63.

Burrows, E. G. 1940. Culture-areas in Polynesia. *JPS* 49(195): 347–64.

Burrows, W. 1923. Some notes and legends of a south sea island. Fakaofo of the Tokelau or Union Group. *JPS* 32(127): 143–73.

Burtenshaw, M. 2009. *A Guide to Growing Pre-European Māori Kūmara in the Traditional Manner.* Open Polytechnic NZ, Lower Hutt.

Buse, J. and Taringa, R. 1995. *Cook Islands Maori Dictionary.* Cook Is Min. Ed., Rarotonga.

Cachola-Abad, C. K. 1993. Evaluating the orthodox dual settlement model for the Hawaiian Islands: An analysis of artefact distribution and Hawaiian oral traditions. In Graves, M. W. and Green, R. C. (eds) *The Evolution and Organization of Prehistoric Society in Polynesia.* NZ Archaeol. Assn Monograph 19: 13–32.

Cameron, R. J. 1964. Destruction of the indigenous forests for Maori agriculture during the nineteenth century. *NZ J. For.* 9: 98–109.

Campbell, M. 2002. Ritual landscape in late pre-contact Rarotonga: A brief reading. *JPS* 111(2): 147–70.

Campbell-Falck, D. et al. 2000. The intravenous use of coconut water. *Am. J. Emergency Med.* 18(1): 108–11.

Carson, M. T. 2002. Inter-cultural contact and exchange in Ouvea (Loyalty Islands, New Caledonia). PhD dissertation, Uni. Hawai`i.

— 2013. Austronesian migrations and developments in Micronesia. *J. Austronesian Studies* 4(1): 25–52.

Caviedes, C. N. and Waylen, P. R. 1993. Anomalous westerly winds during El Niño events: The discovery and colonization of Easter Island. *Applied Geography* 13(2): 123–34.

Chang, C.-S. et al. 2015. A holistic picture of Austronesian migrations revealed by phylogeography of Pacific paper mulberry. *PNAS* 112(44): 13537–42.

Charlot, J. 2004. Classical Polynesian thinking. Ch. 3 in Deutsch, E. and Bontekoe, R. A. (eds). *Companion to World Philosophies.* Wiley-Blackwell, Malden, Mass.

Chauvet, S.-C. 1935. *L'Île de Pâques et Ses Mystères.* TEL, Paris. (English translation, *Easter Island and Its Mysteries,* online at www.chauvet-translation.com).

Cheeseman, T. F. 1888. On the flora of the Kermadec Islands. *Trans. NZ Inst.* 20: 151–81.

Chikamori, M. 1996. Development of coral reefs and human settlement: Archaeological research in the Northern Cook Islands and Rarotonga. *Bull. Indo-Pacific Prehistory Assn* 15: 45–52.

Chikamori, M. and Yoshida, S. 1988. *An archaeological survey of Pukapuka atoll (Preliminary Report).* Dept Archaeol. and Ethnology, Keio Uni., Tokyo.

Christian, F. W. 1924. *A vocabulary of the Mangaian language.* Bishop Mus. Bull. 2, Honolulu.

Cisternas, M. et al. 2005. Predecessors to the giant 1960 Chile earthquake. *Nature* 437: 404–07.

Clark, G. and Martinsson-Wallin, H. 2007. Monumental architecture in West Polynesia: Origins, chiefs and archaeological approaches. *Archaeol. Oceania* 42, Supplement.

Clark, G. et al. (eds) 2008. *Islands of Inquiry: Colonisation, seafaring and the archaeology of maritime landscapes.* ANU, Canberra.

Clark, G. R. 1997. Maori subsistence change: Zooarchaeological evidence from the prehistoric dog of New Zealand. *Asian Perspectives* 36(2): 200–19.

Clark, G. R. et al. 2014. Stone tools from the ancient Tongan state reveal prehistoric interaction centers in the Central Pacific. *PNAS* 111(29): 10491–96.

Clark, R. 1982. Proto-Polynesian birds. In Siikala, J. (ed.) *Oceanic Studies (Essays in Honour of Aarne A. Koskinen).* Finnish Anthropol. Soc., Helsinki.

— 1994. Moriori and Maori: The linguistic evidence. In Sutton, D. G. (ed.) 1994.

— 2014. Arhotica: Notes on a former r-less dialect of Māori. In Onysko, A. et al. *He Hiringa He Pūmanawa.* Huia, Wellington.

Clarke, A. C. 2009. Origins and dispersal of the sweet potato and bottle gourd in Oceania: Implications for prehistoric human mobility. PhD thesis, Massey Uni., Palmerston North.

Clarke, A. C. et al. 2006. Reconstructing the origins and dispersal of the Polynesian bottle gourd (*Lagenaria siceraria*). *Mol. Biol. Evol.* 23(5):

893–900.

Clement, C. R. et al. 2013. Coconuts in the Americas. *Bot. Rev.* 79(3): 342–70.

Coates, D. J. et al. 1988. Chromosome variation in taro, *Colocasia esculenta*: Implications for origin in the Pacific. *Cytologia* 53(3): 551–60.

Cobb, K. M. et al. 2003. El Niño/Southern Oscillation and tropical Pacific climate during the last millennium. *Nature* 424: 271–76.

Colenso, W. 1877. *Notes on the Ancient Dog of the New Zealanders.* Kiwi Publishers, Christchurch.

— 1884. *An Account of Visits to, and Crossings over, the Ruahine Mountain Range, Hawke's Bay, New Zealand; and of the natural history of that region, 1845–1847.* Napier.

Collerson, K. D. and Weisler, M. I. 2007. Stone adze compositions and the extent of ancient Polynesian voyaging and trade. *Science* 317: 1907–11.

Collins, C. J. et al. 2014. Extinction and recolonization of coastal megafauna following human arrival in New Zealand. *Proc. R. Soc. B.* 281(1786): 1471–2954.

Comte, D. and Pardo, M. 1991. Reappraisal of great historical earthquakes in the Northern Chile and Southern Peru seismic gaps. *Natural Hazards* 4: 23–44.

Conte, E and Kirch, P. V. 2008. One thousand years of human environmental transformation in the Gambier Islands (French Polynesia). Ch. 16 in Clark, G. et al. (eds) 2008.

Conte, E. and Kirch, P. V. (eds) 2004. *Archaeological Investigations in the Mangareva Islands (Gambier Archipelago), French Polynesia.* Uni. California, Berkeley.

Conte, E. and Molle, G. 2014. Reinvestigating a key site for Polynesian prehistory: new results from the Hane dune site, Ua Huka (Marquesas). *Archaeol. Oceania* 49(3): 121–136.

Cook, J. 1784. *A Voyage Towards the South Pole, and Round the World,* vol. 1. W. Strahan & T. Cadell, London.

— 1846. *The Voyages of Captain James Cook.* William Smith, London. 2 vols.

Cooper, R. C. and Cambie, R. C. 1991. *New Zealand's Economic Native Plants.* OUP, Auckland.

Corney, B. G. (ed.) 1903. *The Voyage of Captain don Felipe González in the ship of the line San Lorenzo, with the frigate Santa Rosalia in company, to Easter Island in 1770–1; Preceded by an extract from Mynheer Jacob Roggeveen's Official Log of His Discovery of and Visit to Easter Island, in 1722.* Hakluyt Soc., Cambridge.

Costall, J. A. 2006. The endemic tree *Corynocarpus laevigatus* (karaka) as a weedy invader in forest remnants of southern North Island, New Zealand. *NZ J. Bot.* 44: 5–22.

Cox, M. P. et al. 2012. A small cohort of Island Southeast Asian women founded Madagascar. *Proc. R. Soc. B* 279: 2761–68.

Cox, P. A. and Elmqvist, T. 2000. Pollinator extinction in the Pacific Islands. *Conserv. Biol.* 14(5): 1237–39.

Coyne, P. 2009. *Phormium tenax* (New Zealand flax) – Norfolk Island native? *Cunninghamia* 11(2): 167–70.

Craig, R. D. (ed.) 1980. *The Marquesas Islands – Their Description and Early History by Reverend Robert Thomson (1816–1851)* (2nd edn). Inst. Poly. Studies, Hawai`i.

Craig, R. D. 1989. *Dictionary of Polynesian Mythology.* Greenwood Press, NY.

Cristino, C. 2002. Archaeological excavations and reconstruction of Ahu Tongariki – Easter Island. *Revista de Urbanismo* N° 5. 10 pp.

Crocombe, R. G. 1961. Land tenure in the Cook Islands. PhD thesis, ANU, Canberra.

Crombie, R. I. and Steadman, D. W. 1986. The lizards of Rarotonga and Mangaia, Cook Island Group, Oceania. *Pac. Sci.* 40(1–4): 44–57.

Crook, W. P. et al. – see Hughes, H. G. A. and Fischer, S. R. (eds) 1998.

Crowe, A. 2004. *A Field Guide to the Native Edible Plants of New Zealand.* Penguin, Auckland.

— 2012. New Zealand place names in South Polynesia. *Rapa Nui J.* 26(2): 43–53.

— 2013. New Zealand place names shared with the Hawaiian Archipelago. *Rapa Nui J.* 27(1): 21–36.

— 2014. New Zealand place names shared with Central East Polynesia. *Rapa Nui J.* 28(1): 5–21.

D'Arcy, P. 2006. *The people of the sea: Environment, identity and history in Oceania.* UHP, Honolulu.

Dalrymple, A. 1770. *An Historical Collection of the Several Voyages and Discoveries in the South Pacific Ocean,* vol. 1. Alexander Dalrymple, London.

Danielsson, B. 1952. A recently discovered marae in the Tuamotu Group. *JPS* 61(3 & 4): 222–29.

— 1957. Unique Tahitian stone figure. *JPS* 66(4): 396–97.

Dansey, H. D. B. 1947. *How the Maoris Came to New Zealand.* Reed, Wellington.

Davidson, J. 1984. *The Prehistory of New Zealand.* Longman Paul, Auckland.

— 1994. The Eastern Polynesian origins of the New Zealand Archaic. In Sutton, D. G. (ed.) 1994.

Davidson, J. et al. 2011. Connections with Hawaiki: The evidence of a shell tool from Wairau Bar, Marlborough, New Zealand. *J. Pac. Archaeol.* 2(2): 93–102.

Davies, J. 1851. *A Tahitian and English Dictionary.* London Missionary Soc. Press, Tahiti.

Davis, D. and Solomon, M. 2017. Moriori – Origins of the Moriori people. In *Te Ara – the Encyclopedia of New Zealand.* Updated 1-Mar-17: http://www.TeAra.govt.nz/en/moriori/page-1.

Davis, Te Aue et al. 1990. *Ngā Tohu Pūmahara – The Survey Pegs of the Past: understanding Māori place names.* NZ Geographic Board, Wellington.

Davis, W. 2008. *The Wayfinders: Why ancient wisdom matters in the modern world.* Anansi Press, Toronto.

De Lisle, J. F. 1965. The climate of the Auckland Islands, Campbell Island and Macquarie Island. *Proc. NZ Ecol. Soc.* 12: 37–44.

Dearborn, D. C. 2003. Inter-island movements and population differentiation in a pelagic seabird. *Molecular Ecol.* 12: 2835–43.

Deguilloux, M.-F. et al. 2011. Human ancient and extant mtDNA from the Gambier Islands (French Polynesia): Evidence for an early Melanesian maternal contribution and new perspectives into the settlement of easternmost Polynesia. *Am. J. Phys. Anthropol.* 144: 248–57.

Dening, G. M. 1962. The geographical knowledge of the Polynesians and the nature of inter-island contact. In Golson, J. (ed.) 1962: 102–31.

— *Islands and Beaches, Discourse on a Silent Land: Marquesas 1774–1880.* Melbourne Uni. Press, Melbourne.

Di Piazza, A. 2010. A reconstruction of a Tahitian star compass based on Tupaia's 'Chart for the Society Islands with Otaheite in the Center'. *JPS* 119(4): 377–92.

Di Piazza, A. and Pearthree, E. 2001a. An island for gardens, an island for birds and voyaging: A settlement pattern for Kiritimati and Tabuaeran, two 'mystery islands' in the northern Lines, Republic of Kiribati. *JPS* 110(2): 149–70.

— 2001b. L'art d'être pirogues de voyage en Océanie insulaire. *J. Société Océanistes* 112: 61–72.

— 2001c. Voyaging and basalt exchange in the Phoenix and Line archipelagoes: The viewpoint from three mystery islands. *Archaeol. Oceania* 36: 146–52.

— 2007a. A new reading of Tupaia's chart. *JPS* 116(3): 321–40.

Di Piazza, A. et al. 2007b. Sailing virtual canoes across Oceania: Revisiting island accessibility. *J. Archaeol. Sci.* 34(8): 1219–25.

Diamond, J. 1995. Easter's End. *Discover* 9: 62–9.

— 2005. *Collapse: How societies choose to fail or survive.* Penguin, London.

Dickinson, W. R. 2009. Pacific atoll living: How long already and until when? *GSA Today* 19(3): 4–10.

Dickinson, W. R. et al. 1998. Temper sands in exotic Marquesan pottery and the significance of their Fijian origin. *J. Société Océanistes* 107(2): 119–33.

Dixon, R. B. 1916. *Oceanic Mythology.* (Vol. 9 of Gray, L. H. (ed.) *The mythology of all races.*) Marshall Jones Co., Boston.

DLNR (State of Hawai`i Dept of Land & Natural Resources). 2008. *Papahānaumokuākea Marine National Monument Management Plan.* Vol. 2, Final environmental assessment. Appendix A. DLNR, Honolulu.

Dobney, K. et al. 2008. The pigs of Island Southeast Asia and the Pacific: New evidence for taxonomic status and human-mediated dispersal. *Asian Perspectives* 47(1): 59–74.

Dordillon, R. I. 1931. *Grammaire et Dictionnaire de la Langue des Iles Marquises. Marquisien–Français.* Institut d'Ethnologie, Paris.

Druett, J. 2011. *Tupaia: The remarkable story of Captain Cook's Polynesian navigator.* Random House, Auckland.

Duff, R. 1968. Stone adzes from Raoul, Kermadec Islands. *JPS* 77(4): 386–401.

Duncan, R. P. et al. 2013. Magnitude and variation of prehistoric bird extinctions in the Pacific. *PNAS* 110(16): 6436–41.

Dupon, J. F. 1986. *Atolls and the Cyclone Hazard: A case study of the Tuamotu Islands.* South Pacific Study 3, S. Pac. Reg. Env. Programme, S. Pac. Comm., Noumea.

Edwards, E. 2003. *Ra`ivavae: Archaeological survey of Ra`ivavae, French Polynesia.* Easter Island Foundation, Los Osos, California.

— 2006. *Raivavae Archaeological Project: Preliminary report of fieldwork: Island of Raivavae, Austral Islands, French Polynesia, May–June 2006.* (As PDF at http://www.academia.edu/2629624.)

— 2011. Astronomically aligned religious structures on Raiatea and Raivavae and the Matariki festival of 1770 on Easter Island. *Proc. International Astronomical Union* 7: 275–81.

Egan, S. and Burley, D. V. 2009. Triangular men on one very long voyage: The context and implications of a Hawaiian-style petroglyph site in the Polynesian kingdom of Tonga. *JPS* 118(3): 209–32.

Elbert, S. H. 1941. Chants and love songs of the Marquesas Islands, French Oceania. *JPS* 50(198): 53–91.

Elevitch, C. R. (ed.) 2006. *Traditional Trees of Pacific Islands: Their culture, environment, and use.* Permanent Agric. Resources, Hawai`i: http://www.traditionaltree.org.

Elkington, E. W. 1907. *The Savage South Seas.* A. & C. Black, London.

Ellis, W. 1827. *Narrative of a Tour through Hawaii.* H. Fisher, son, & P. Jackson, London.

Emory, K. P. 1928a. *Archaeology of Nihoa and Necker Islands.* Bishop Mus. Bull. 53, Honolulu.

— 1928b. Stone implements of Pitcairn Island. *JPS* 37(146): 125–35.

— 1934a. Archaeology of the Pacific Equatorial Islands. Bishop Mus. Bull. 123, Honolulu.

— 1934b. *Tuamotuan Stone Structures.* Bishop Mus. Bull. 118, Honolulu.

— 1940. Tuamotuan concepts of creation. *JPS* 49(193): 69–136.

— 1947a. Tuamotuan bird names. *JPS* 56(2): 188–96.

— 1947b. Tuamotuan plant names. *JPS* 56(3): 266–77.

— 1947c. *Tuamotuan Religious Structures and Ceremonies.* Bishop Mus. Bull. 191, Honolulu.

— 1975. *Material Culture of the Tuamotu Archipelago.* Pacific Anthropological Records, no. 22. Dept Anthropol., Bishop Mus., Honolulu.

Emory, K. P. and Ottino, P. 1967. Histoire ancienne de `Ana`a, atoll des Tuāmotu. *J. Société Océanistes* 23: 29–57.

Emory, K. P. and Sinoto, Y. H. 1965. *Preliminary Report on the Archaeological Investigations in Polynesia.* Bishop Mus., Honolulu. (Unpublished typescript.)

Englert, Padre S. 1993. *La Tierra de Hotu Matu`a – Historia y Etnología de la Isla de Pascua: Gramática y Diccionario del Antiguo Idioma de la Isla,* 6th edn. Editorial Universitaria, Santiago de Chile.

Erickson, D. L. et al. 2005. An Asian origin for a 10,000-year-old domesticated plant in the Americas. *PNAS* 102(51): 18315–20.

Evans, J. 1997. *Ngā Waka o Neherā: The First Voyaging Canoes.* Reed, Auckland.

— 1998. *The Discovery of Aotearoa.* Reed, Auckland.

Failloux, A.-B et al. 1997. Genetic differentiation associated with commercial traffic in the Polynesian mosquito, *Aedes polynesiensis* Marks 1951. *Biol. J. Linnean Soc.* 60(1): 107–18.

Feinberg, R. and Scaglion, R. (eds) 2012. *Polynesian Outliers: The state of the art.* Ethnology Monographs 21. Uni. Pittsburgh, Pittsburgh.

Fell, H. B. 1947. The migration of the New Zealand bronze cuckoo, *Chalcites lucidus lucidus* (Gmelin). *Trans. Proc. Roy. Soc. NZ* 76: 504–15.

Finney, B. 1979. *Hokulea: The way to Tahiti.* Dodd, Mead & Co., NY.

— 1989. Wait for the west wind. *JPS* 98(3): 261–302.

— 2001. Voyage to Polynesia's land's end. *Antiquity* 75(287): 172–81.

— 2006. In Howe, K. R. (ed.) 2006.

Finney, B. et al. 1986. Re-learning a vanishing art. *JPS* 95(1): 41–90.

Fischer, S. R. 1992. Homogeneity in Old Rapanui. *Oceanic Linguistics* 31(2): 181–190.

— 1997. *Rongorongo, the Easter Island script: History, traditions, texts.* OUP, Oxford.

— 2001. Mangarevan doublets: Preliminary evidence for Proto-Southeastern Polynesian. *Oceanic Linguistics* 40(1): 112–124.

— 2005. *Island at the End of the World.* Reaktion Books, London.

Fisher, R. N. 1997. Dispersal and evolution of the Pacific Basin Gekkonid lizards *Gehyra oceanica* and *Gehyra mutilata.* *Evolution* 51(3): 906–21.

Fitzpatrick, S. M. and Callaghan, R. 2009. Examining dispersal mechanisms for the translocation of chicken (*Gallus gallus*) from Polynesia to South America. *J. Archaeol. Sci.* 36(2): 214–23.

Flenley, J. and Bahn, P. 2002. *The Enigmas of Easter Island: Island on the edge.* OUP, NY.

Flenley, J. R. et al. 1991. The Late Quaternary vegetational and climatic history of Easter Island. *J. Quaternary Sci.* 6(2): 85–115.

Flint, E. N. 1991. Time and energy limits to the foraging radius of sooty terns *Sterna fuscata. Ibis* 133(1): 43–46.

Florence, J. et al. 1995. The flora of the Pitcairn Islands: A review. *Biol. J. Linnean Soc.* 56: 79–119.

Forster, G. 1777. *A Voyage Round the World in His Britannic Majesty's Sloop, Resolution, Commanded by Capt. James Cook, during the Years 1772, 3, 4, and 5.* B. White, London. 2 vols.

Forster, J. R. 1778. *Observations Made During a Voyage Round the World* [*in HMS* Resolution]. G. Robinson, London.

— 1982. *The* Resolution *Journal of Johann Reinhold Forster, 1772–1775,* vol. 2. Hakluyt Soc., London.

Freeman, R. et al. 2010. Black petrels (*Procellaria parkinsoni*) patrol the ocean shelf-break: GPS tracking of a vulnerable Procellariiform seabird. *PLoS One* 5(2): e9236.

Friedlaender, J. S. et al. 2007. Melanesian mtDNA complexity. *PLoS One* 2(2): e248.

Fritz, H. M. et al. 2011. Field survey of the 27 February 2010 Chile tsunami. *Pure Appl. Geophys.* 168: 1989–2010.

Froyd, C. A. et al. 2010. Historic fuel wood use in the Galápagos Islands: Identification of charred remains. *Veget. Hist. Archaeobot.* 19(3): 207–17.

Fulton, R. 1903. The kohoperoa or koekoea, long-tailed cuckoo (*Urodynamis taitensis*). *Trans. NZ Inst.* 36: 133–48.

Furey, L. 2006. *Maori Gardening: An archaeological perspective.* DoC, Wellington.

Furey, L. 2015. Obsidian from Macauley Island: A New Zealand connection. *Bull. Auck. Mus.* 20: 511–18.

Galipaud, J.-C. and Lilley, I. (eds) 1999. *The Pacific from 5000 to 2000 BP: Colonisation and transformation.* Ed. de IRD, Paris.

Gao, C. et al. 2006. The 1452 or 1453 A.D. Kuwae eruption signal derived from multiple ice core records: Greatest volcanic sulfate event of the past 700 years. *J. Geophys. Res.* 111.D12.

Gardner, R. 2005. A botanist follows a linguist through the New Zealand bush: Origins of Māori plant-names. *Auck. Bot. Soc. J.* 60(1): 28–31.

Garrigue, C. et al. 2002. Movements of humpback whales in Oceania, South Pacific. *J. Cetacean Res. Manage.* 4(3): 255–60.

Geraghty, P. 1994. Linguistic evidence for the Tongan Empire. In Dutton, T. E. and Tryon, D. T. *Language Contact and Change in the Austronesian World.* Walter de Gruyter, Berlin.

— 2009. Words of Eastern Polynesia: Is there lexical evidence for the origin of the East Polynesians? Ch. 26 in Adelaar, A. and Pawley, A. (eds). *Austronesian Historical Linguistics and Culture History: A festschrift for Bob Blust.* Pac. Linguistics, Res. Sch. Pac. Asian Studies, ANU, Canberra.

Geraghty, P. and Tent, J. 2010. Two unusual early names for the Australian continent. Part 2. *Placenames Australia,* June: 4–7.

Ghiani, M. E. et al. 2005. Migration and isolation effects on the Rapanui population (Easter Island) through the analysis of STRs on the Y chromosome. *Human Evolution* 20(2–3): 85–92.

— 2006. Y-chromosome-specific STR haplotype data on the Rapanui population (Easter Island). *Human Biology* 78(5): 565–78.

Gifford, E. W. 1923. *Tongan Place Names.* Bishop Mus. Bull. 6, Honolulu.

Gilbert, G. 1982. *Captain Cook's Final Voyage: The journal of midshipman George Gilbert.* Caliban Books, London.

Gill, B. J. 1983. Morphology and migration of *Chrysococcyx lucidus,* an Australasian cuckoo. *NZ J. Zool.* 10: 371–82.

— 1989. The secret life of the shining cuckoo. *Forest & Bird* 20(3): 34–36.

— 1993. The lizards of the Pitcairn Island Group, South Pacific. *NZ J. Zool.* 20(3): 161–64.

Gill, B. J. and Hauber, M. E. 2012. Piecing together the epic transoceanic migration of the long-tailed cuckoo (*Eudynamys taitensis*): An analysis of museum and sighting records. *Emu* 112: 326–32.

— 2013. Distribution and age-specific plumage states of the long-tailed cuckoo (*Eudynamys taitensis*). *Notornis* 60: 158–70.

Gill, R. E. et al. 2009. Extreme endurance flights by landbirds crossing the Pacific Ocean: Ecological corridor rather than barrier? *Proc. R. Soc. B.* 276(1656): 447–57.

Gill, W. W. 1885. *Jottings from the Pacific.* Religious Tract Soc., London.

Goff, J. 2011. Evidence of a previously unrecorded local tsunami, 13 April 2010, Cook Islands: Implications for Pacific Island countries. *Nat. Hazards Earth Syst. Sci.* 11: 1371–79.

Goff, J. et al. 2011a. Palaeotsunamis in the Pacific Islands. *Earth-Science Reviews* 107(1–2): 141–146.

— 2011b. Predecessors to the 2009 South Pacific tsunami in the Wallis and Futuna Archipelago. *Earth-Science Reviews* 107(1–2): 91–106.

— 2012. Palaeotsunamis and their influence on Polynesian settlement. *Holocene* 22(9): 1067–1069.

Goff, J. R. and McFadgen, B. G. 2002. Seismic driving of nationwide changes in geomorphology and prehistoric settlement—a 15th Century New Zealand example. *Quaternary Science Reviews* 21(20–22): 2229–36.

Golden, F. and Tipton, M. 2002. *Essentials of Sea Survival.* Human Kinetics Publishers, Champaign, Illinois.

Golson, J. (ed.) 1962. Polynesian navigation. *JPS* 71 (Memoir 34).

Golson, J. 1962. A table of accidental and deliberate voyages in the South Pacific. In Golson, J. (ed.) 1962: 137–53.

Gonçalves, V. F. et al. 2013. Identification of Polynesian mtDNA haplogroups in remains of Botocudo Amerindians from Brazil. *PNAS* 110(16): 6465–69.

Gongora, J. et al. 2008a. Indo-European and Asian origins for Chilean and Pacific chickens revealed by mtDNA. *PNAS* 105(30): 10308–13.

— 2008b. Reply to Storey et al.: More DNA and dating studies needed for ancient El Arenal-1 chickens. *PNAS* 105(48): 100.

González-Lorca, J. et al. 2015. Ancient and modern introduction of *Broussonetia papyrifera* ([L.] Vent.; Moraceae) into the Pacific: Genetic, geographical and historical evidence. *NZ J. Bot.* 53(2): 75–89.

Gooding, R. M. and Magnuson, J. J. 1967. Ecological significance of a drifting object to pelagic fishes. *Pac. Sci.* 21(4): 486–97.

Goodwin, I. A. et al. 2014. Climate windows for Polynesian voyaging to New Zealand and Easter Island. *PNAS* 111(41): 14716–21.

Gordon-Grube, K. 1988. Anthropophagy in post-Renaissance Europe: The tradition of medicinal cannibalism. *American Anthropol.* 90(2): 405–09.

Gould, P. J. 1974. Sooty tern (*Sterna fuscata*). In King, W. B. (ed.) *Pelagic Studies of Seabirds in the Central and Eastern Pacific Ocean.* Smithsonian Contrib. Zool. 158.

Graham, G. 1939. *Mahuhu:* The ancestral canoe of Ngati-Whatua (Kaipara). *JPS* 48(192): 186–91.

Grant, P. J. 1994. Late Holocene histories of climate, geomorphology and vegetation, and their effects on the first New Zealanders. In Sutton, D. G. (ed.) 1994.

Gray, R. D. et al. 2009. Language phylogenies reveal expansion pulses and pauses in Pacific settlement. *Science* 323: 479–83.

Green, R. C. 1966. Linguistic subgrouping within Polynesia: The implications for prehistoric settlement. *JPS* 75(1): 6–38.

— 2000a. Origins for the Rapanui of Easter Island before European contact: Solutions from holistic anthropology to an issue no longer much of a mystery. *Rapa Nui J.* 14(3): 71–76.

— 2000b. Shorter communication: A range of disciplines support a dual origin for the bottle gourd in the Pacific. *JPS* 109(2): 191–98.

— 2001. Commentary on the sailing raft, the sweet potato and the South American connection. *Rapa Nui J.* 15(2): 69–77.

— 2005. Sweet potato transfers in Polynesian prehistory. In Ballard, C. et al. (eds) 2005.

Green, R. C. and Weisler, M. I. 2002. The Mangarevan sequence and dating of the geographic expansion into Southeast Polynesia. *Asian Perspectives* 41(2): 213–41.

— 2004. Prehistoric introduction and extinction of animals in Mangareva, Southeast Polynesia. *Archaeol. Oceania* 39: 34–41.

Greig, K. et al. 2015. Complete mitochondrial genomes of New Zealand's first dogs. *PloS One* 10(10): e0138536.

Grey, G. 1853. *Ko Nga Moteatea, Me Nga Hakirara O Nga Maori.* Robert Stokes, Wellington.

— 1854. *Polynesian Mythology and Ancient Traditional History of the New Zealanders as Furnished by their Priests and Chiefs.* J. Murray, London. (Also 2nd edn 1885.)

Groube, L. M. 1965. *Settlement Patterns in New Zealand Prehistory.* Anthropol. Dept, Uni. Otago.

Gudgeon, Lieut.-Col. 1902. The whence of the Maori. Parts I & II. *JPS* 11(3): 179–90; 11(4): 247–56.

— 1903. The whence of the Maori. Parts III & IV. *JPS* 12(1): 51–61; 12(2): 120–30; 12(3): 166–79.

Haami, B. J. T. M. 1994. The kiore rat in Aotearoa: A Maori perspective. Ch. 5 in Morrison, J. et al. (eds). *Science of Pacific Island Peoples,* vol. 3: *Fauna, Flora, Food and Medicine.* Inst. Pac. Studies, USP, Suva.

Hadden, D. W. 2004. Birds of the northern atolls of the North Solomons Province of Papua New Guinea. *Notornis* 51: 91–102.

Haddon, A. C. 1901. *Head-hunters, Black, White, and Brown.* AMS Press, NY.

Hagelberg, E. 1993. Ancient DNA studies. *Evolutionary Anthropol.* 2: 199–207.

Halbert, R. 1999. *Horouta: The history of the* Horouta *canoe, Gisborne and East Coast.* Reed, Auckland.

Halkett, J. and Sale, E. V. 1986. *The World of the Kauri.* Reed Methuen, Auckland.

Hamilton, S. 2007. Back to the sea: Rapa Nui's ahu seascapes. In *The Gotland Papers.* Gotland Uni. with Easter Is. Foundation, Sweden, 20–25 Aug: 167–80.

— 2008. Rapa Nui landscapes of construction. *Archaeol. International* 10: 49–53.

Handy, E. S. C. 1923. *The Native Culture in the Marquesas.* Bishop Mus. Bull. 9, Honolulu.

— 1930. *Marquesan Legends.* Bishop Mus. Bull. 69, Honolulu.

Handy, W. C. 1922. *Tattooing in the Marquesas.* Bishop Mus. Bull. 1, Honolulu.

Harlow, R. 1994. Maori dialectology and the settlement of New Zealand. In Sutton, D. G. (ed.) 1994: 106–22.

— 2007. *Māori: A linguistic introduction.* CUP, Cambridge.

Harris, G. 2005. An indigenous Māori potato or unique Māori cultivars. *JPS* 114(1): 69–77.

Harvey, L. 2012. Ngāti Awa – Origins. In *Te Ara – the Encyclopedia of New Zealand.* Updated 22-Sep-12: http://www.TeAra.govt.nz/en/ngati-awa/page-1.

Hather, J. and Kirch, P. V. 1991. Prehistoric sweet potato (*Ipomoea batatas*) from Mangaia Island, Central Polynesia. *Antiquity* 65: 887–93.

Hather, J. G. and Weisler, M. I. 2000. Prehistoric giant swamp taro (*Cyrtosperma chamissonis*) from Henderson Island, Southeast Polynesia. *Pac. Sci.* 54(2): 149–56.

Hayward, B. W. et al. 2006. Effect and timing of increased freshwater runoff into sheltered harbor environments around Auckland City, New Zealand. *Estuaries & Coasts* 29(2): 165–82.

Heiser, C. B. 1978. The totora (*Scirpus californicus*) in Ecuador and Peru. *Econ. Bot.* 32(3): 222–36.

Henry, T. 1912. The Tahitian version of the names Ra`iatea and Taputapu-atea. *JPS* 21(2): 77–78.

— 1928. *Ancient Tahiti Based on Material Recorded by J. M. Orsmond.* Bishop Mus. Bull. 48, Honolulu.

Hermann, A. et al. 2016. The Atiahara site revisited: An early coastal settlement in Tubuai (Austral Islands, French Polynesia). *Archaeol. Oceania* 51(1): 31–44.

Heyerdahl, T. 1950. *The Kon-Tiki Expedition: By raft across the South Seas.* Allen & Unwin, London.

— 1960. *Aku-Aku: The secret of Easter Island.* Penguin, Middlesex.

— 1974. *Fatu-Hiva: Back to nature.* Allen & Unwin, London.

Higgins, P. J. (ed.) 1999. *Handbook of Australian, New Zealand & Antarctic Birds.* Vol. 4, *Parrots to Dollarbird.* OUP, Melbourne.

Higham, T. F. G. and Hogg, A. G. 1997. Evidence for late Polynesian colonization of New Zealand: University of Waikato radiocarbon measurements. *Radiocarbon* 39: 149–92.

Hilder, B. 1962. Primitive navigation in the Pacific. Part II. In Golson, J. (ed.) 1962: 80–97.

Hinkle, A. E. 2004. The distribution of a male sterile form of ti (*Cordyline fruticosa*) in Polynesia: A case of human selection? *JPS* 113: 263–90.

— 2007. Population structure of Pacific *Cordyline fruticosa* (Laxmanniaceae) with implications for human settlement of Polynesia. *Am. J. Botany* 94(5): 828–39.

Hogg, A. G. et al. 2003. A wiggle-match date for Polynesian settlement of New Zealand. *Antiquity* 77: 116–25.

Hokotehi Moriori Trust. 2018. https://www.moriori.co.nz/.

Holdaway, R. N. 1996. Arrival of rats in New Zealand. *Nature* 384: 225–26.

— 1999. A spatio-temporal model for the invasion of the New Zealand archipelago by the Pacific rat *Rattus exulans.* *J. Roy. Soc. NZ* 29(2): 91–105.

Holden, E. S. and Qualtrough, E. F. 1884. Report of the Eclipse Expedition to Caroline Island. *Natl. Acad. Sci. Memoir* 2: 22–26.

Hooper, S. 2007. Embodying divinity: The life of A`a. *JPS* 116(2): 131–80.

Hornell, J. 1945. Was there pre-Columbian contact between the peoples of Oceania and South America? *JPS* 54(4): 167–91.

Horrocks, M. 2004. Polynesian plant subsistence in prehistoric New Zealand: A summary of the microfossil evidence. *NZ J. Bot.* 42(2): 321–34.

Horrocks, M. and Barber, I. 2005. Microfossils of introduced starch cultigens from an early wetland ditch in New Zealand. *Archaeol. Oceania* 40(3): 106–14.

Horrocks, M. and Weisler, M. 2006. Analysis of plant microfossils in archaeological deposits from two remote archipelagos: The Marshall Islands, Eastern Micronesia, and the Pitcairn Group, Southeast Polynesia. *Pac. Sci.* 60(2): 261–80.

Horrocks, M. et al. 2004. Microbotanical remains reveal Polynesian agriculture and mixed cropping in early New Zealand. *Review of Palaeobotany & Palynology* 131(3–4): 147–57.

— 2008. Sediment, soil and plant microfossil analysis of Maori gardens at Anaura Bay, eastern North Island, New Zealand: Comparison with descriptions made in 1769 by Captain Cook's expedition. *J. Archaeol. Sci.* 35(9): 2446–64.

Horvath, S. and Finney, B. 1969. Paddling experiments and the question of Polynesian voyaging. *American Anthropol.* 71(2): 271–76.

Horwood, M. and Wilson, C. 2008. *Te Ara Tapu: Sacred Journeys.* (Whanganui Regional Museum Taonga Māori Collection.) Random House, Auckland.

Houghton, P. 1995. Polynesian body size: An adaptation to environmental temperature? *Asia Pac. J. Clin. Nutr.* 4: 354–56.

Howe, K. R. 2003. *The Quest for Origins.* Penguin, Auckland.

— 2009. Ideas of Māori origins – 1920s–2000: New understanding. In *Te Ara – the Encyclopedia of New Zealand.* Updated 4-Mar-09: http://www.TeAra.govt.nz/en/ideas-of-maori-origins/5.

Howe, K. R. (ed.) 2006. *Vaka Moana: Voyages of the ancestors – The discovery and settlement of the Pacific.* David Bateman, Auckland.

Hughes, H. G. A. and Fischer, S. R. (eds) 1998. *An Essay Toward a Dictionary and Grammar of the Lesser-Australian Language, according to the Dialect used at the Marquesas (1799).* Inst. Poly. Languages and Literatures, Auckland.

Hunt, T. L. 2007. Rethinking Easter Island's ecological catastrophe. *J. Archaeol. Sci.* 34: 485–502.

Hunt, T. L. and Lipo, C. P. 2006. Late colonisation of Easter Island. *Science* 311(5767): 1603–06.

— 2007. Chronology, deforestation, and collapse: Evidence vs. faith in Rapa Nui prehistory. *Rapa Nui J.* 21(2): 85–97.

— 2008. Evidence for a shorter chronology on Rapa Nui (Easter Island). *J. Is. & Coastal Archaeol.* 3(1): 140–48.

— 2009a. Ecological catastrophe, collapse, and the myth of 'ecocide' on Rapa Nui (Easter Island). Ch. 2 in McAnany, P. A. and Yoffee, N. (eds). *Questioning Collapse: Human resilience, ecological vulnerability, and the aftermath of empire.* CUP, NY.

— 2009b. Revisiting Rapa Nui (Easter Island) 'ecocide'. *Pac. Sci.* 63(4): 601–16.

— 2011. *The Statues that Walked: Unraveling the mystery of Easter Island.* Free Press, NY.

— 2013. The human transformation of Rapa Nui (Easter Island, Pacific Ocean). Ch. 8 in Larrue, S. (ed.) *Biodiversity and Societies in the Pacific Islands.* Presses Universitaires de Provence.

Hurles, M. E. et al. 2002. Y chromosomal evidence for the origins of Oceanic-speaking peoples. *Genetics* 160: 289–303.

— 2003. Native American Y chromosomes in Polynesia: The genetic impact of the Polynesian slave trade. *Am. J. Hum. Genet.* 72(5): 1282–87.

— 2005. The dual origin of the Malagasy in Island Southeast Asia and East Africa: Evidence from maternal and paternal lineages. *Am. J. Hum. Genet.* 76(5): 894–901.

Hurr, K. A. et al. 1999. Evidence for the recent dispersal of *Sophora* (Leguminosae) around the Southern Oceans: Molecular data. *J. Biogeography* 26(3): 565–77.

Hutton, I. and Priddel, D. 2002. Breeding biology of the black-winged petrel, *Pterodroma nigripennis,* on Lord Howe Island. *Emu* 102(4): 361–65.

Imber, M. J. 2003. Cook's petrel (*Pterodroma cookii*): Historic distribution, breeding biology and effects of predators. *Notornis* 50: 221–30.

Intoh, M. 1999. Cultural contacts between Micronesia and Melanesia. In Galipaud, J.-C. and Lilley, I. (eds) 1999: 407–22.

Irwin, G. J. 1981. How Lapita lost its pots: The question of continuity in the colonisation of Polynesia. *JPS* 90(4): 481–95.

— 1989. Against, across and down the wind: A case for the systematic exploration of the remote Pacific islands. *JPS* 98(2): 167–206.

— 1992. *The Prehistoric Exploration and Colonisation of the Pacific.* CUP, Cambridge.

— 2010. Pacific voyaging and settlement: Issues of biogeography and archaeology, canoe performance and computer simulation. Ch. 10 in Anderson et al. (eds). *The Global Origins and Development of Seafaring.* McDonald Inst., Cambridge.

— 2012. Pacific migrations – East to the empty Pacific. In *Te Ara – the Encyclopedia of New Zealand.* Updated 22-Sep-12: http://www.TeAra.govt.nz/en/pacific-migrations/page-6.

Irwin, G. J. and Flay, R. G. J. 2015. Pacific colonisation and canoe performance: Experiments in the science of sailing. *JPS* 124(4): 419.

Irwin, G. J. and Walrond, C. 2009. When was New Zealand first settled? – The date debate. In *Te Ara – the Encyclopedia of New Zealand.* Updated 4-Mar-09: http://www.TeAra.govt.nz/en/when-was-new-zealand-first-settled.

Irwin, S. V. 1998. Molecular characterization of taro (*Colocasia esculenta*) using RAPD markers. *Euphytica* 99: 183–89.

Jacomb, C. et al. 2014. High-precision dating and ancient DNA profiling of moa (Aves: Dinornithiformes) eggshell documents a complex feature and refines the chronology of New Zealand settlement by Polynesians. *J. Archaeol. Sci.* 50: 24–30.

Jefferson, C. 1955. The dendroglyphs of the Chatham Islands. *JPS* 64(4): 367–441.

Jenkins, J. A. F. 1973. Seabird observations around the Kingdom of Tonga. *Notornis* 20(2): 113–19.

Johns, D. A. et al. 2014. An early sophisticated East Polynesian voyaging canoe discovered on New Zealand's coast. *PNAS* 111(41): 14728–33.

Jones, K. L. 1994. *Ngā Tohuwhenua Mai Te Rangi: A New Zealand archaeology in aerial photographs.* VUP, Wellington.

Jones, P. and Biggs, B. 1995. *Nga Iwi o Tainui: The traditional history of the Tainui people.* AUP, Auckland.

Jones, R. J. 2001. The status of seabird colonies on the Cook Islands atoll of Suwarrow. *Bird Conservation International* 11: 309–17.

Jones, T. L. 2011. The artefact record from North America. In Jones, T. L. et al. (eds) 2011.

Jones, T. L. and Klar, K. A. 2005. Diffusionism reconsidered: Linguistic and archaeological evidence for prehistoric Polynesian contact with Southern California. *American Antiquity* 70(3): 457–84.

Jones, T. L. et al. (eds) 2011. *Polynesians in America: Pre-Columbian contacts with the New World.* AltaMira Press, Lanham.

Julien, M. et al. 1957. *Mémoire de pierre, mémoire d`homme: Tradition et archéologie en Océanie.* Université de Paris.

Kaamira, H. 1957. The story of Kupe. *JPS* 66(3): 232–48.

Kaeppler, A. L. 2007. Containers of divinity. *JPS* 116(2): 97–130.

Kahn, J. G. et al. 2014. Re-dating of the Kuli`ou`ou rockshelter, O`ahu,

Hawai`i: Location of the first radiocarbon date from the Pacific Islands. *JPS* 123(1): 67–90.

Kamakau, S. M. 1865 – see Alexander, W. D. 1891.

— 1961. *Ruling Chiefs of Hawai`i*. Kamehameha Schools Press, Honolulu.

Katayama, K. 1994. Biological affinity between Southern Cook Islanders and New Zealand Māori: Implications for the settlement of New Zealand. In Sutton, D. G. (ed.) 1994: 230–42.

Kayser, M. et al. 2006. Melanesian and Asian origins of Polynesians: MtDNA and Y chromosome gradients across the Pacific. *Mol. Biol. Evol.* 23(11): 2234–44.

— 2008. Genome-wide analysis indicates more Asian than Melanesian ancestry of Polynesians. *Am. J. Hum. Genet.* 82: 194–98.

Keane, K. 2012. Ngā manu – birds: Birds associated with death. In *Te Ara – the Encyclopedia of New Zealand*. Updated 22-Sep-12: http://www.teara.govt.nz/en/nga-manu-birds/page-2

Kelly, L. G. 1955. Cook Island origin of the Maori. *JPS* 64(2): 181–96.

Kelly, M. 1989. Dynamics of production intensification in pre-contact Hawai`i. Ch. 5 in van der Leeuw, S. E. and Torrence, R. (ed.) *What's New?: A closer look at the process of innovation*. Unwin Hyman, London.

Kennedy, J. 2008. Pacific bananas: Complex origins, multiple dispersals? *Asian Perspectives* 47(1): 75–94.

Kennett, D. et al. 2006. Prehistoric human impacts on Rapa, French Polynesia. *Antiquity* 80(308): 340–54.

King, J. 1967. Journal of Lieutenant James King. In Beaglehole, J. C. (ed.) 1967.

King, M. 1989. *Moriori: A people rediscovered*. Viking, Auckland.

— 2003. *The Penguin History of New Zealand*. Penguin, Auckland.

King, W. B. 1973. Conservation status of birds of Central Pacific Islands. *Wilson Bull.* 85(1): 89–103.

Kirch, P. V. 1976. Ethno-archaeological investigations in Futuna and Uvea (Western Polynesia). *JPS* 85(1): 27–70.

— 1982. The impact of the prehistoric Polynesians on the Hawaiian ecosystem. *Pac. Sci.* 36: 1–14.

— 1984. The Polynesian Outliers: Continuity, change, and replacement. *J. Pac. History* 19(4): 224–38.

— 1985. *Feathered Gods and Fishhooks: An introduction to Hawaiian archaeology and prehistory*. UHP, Honolulu.

— 1986. Rethinking East Polynesian prehistory. *JPS* 95(1): 9–40.

— 1989. *The Evolution of the Polynesian Chiefdoms*. CUP, Cambridge.

— 1990. Monumental architecture and power in Polynesian chiefdoms: A comparison of Tonga and Hawaii. *World Archaeol.* 22(2): 206–22.

— 1996. Late Holocene human-induced modifications to a central Polynesian island ecosystem. *PNAS* 93(11): 5296–300.

— 2000. *On the Road of the Winds*. Uni. California Press, Berkeley.

— 2004a. Solstice observation in Mangareva, French Polynesia: New perspectives from archaeology. *Archaeoastronomy* 18: 1–9.

— 2004b. Temple sites in Kahikinui, Maui, Hawaiian Islands: Their orientations decoded. *Antiquity* 78(299): 102–14.

— 2008. Comment on Atholl Anderson's 'Traditionalism, interaction and long-distance seafaring in Polynesia'. *J. Is. & Coastal Archaeol.* 3(2): 260–61.

— 2012. *A Shark Going Inland is My Chief: The Island civilization of ancient Hawai`i*. UCP, Berkeley.

Kirch, P. V. (ed.) 2017. *Tangatatau Rockshelter: The Evolution of an Eastern Polynesian Socio-Ecosystem*. Cotsen Inst. Archaeol., UCLA.

Kirch, P. V. and Conte, E. 2009. Combler une lacune dans la préhistoire de la Polynésie orientale: Nouvelles données sur l'archipel des Gambier (Mangareva). *J. Société Océanistes* 128: 91–116.

Kirch, P. V. and Green, R. C. 2001. *Hawaiki, Ancestral Polynesia: An essay in historical anthropology*. CUP, Cambridge.

Kirch, P. V. and McCoy, M. D. 2007. Reconfiguring the Hawaiian cultural sequence: Results of re-dating the Halawa Dune site (MO-A1-3), Moloka`i Island. *JPS* 116(4): 385–406.

Kirch, P. V. and O'Day, S. J. 2003. New archaeological insights into food and status: A case study from pre-contact Hawai`i. *World Archaeol.* 34(3): 484–97.

Kirch, P. V. and Rallu, J.-L. 2007. *The Growth and Collapse of Pacific Island Societies: Archaeological and demographic perspectives*. UHP, Honolulu.

Kirch, P. V. et al. 2009. Subfossil land snails from Easter Island, including *Hotumatua anakenana*, new genus and species (Pulmonata: Achatinellidae). *Pac. Sci.* 63(1): 105–22.

— 2010. The Onemea Site (Taravai Island, Mangareva) and the human colonization of Southeastern Polynesia. *Archaeol. Oceania* 45: 66–79.

— 2013. The 'pānānā' or 'sighting wall' at Hanamauloa, Kahikinui, Maui: Archaeological investigation of a possible navigational monument. *JPS* 122(1): 45–68.

— 2015a. Precise chronology of Polynesian temple construction and use for

southeastern Maui, Hawaiian Islands determined by 230 Th dating of corals. *J. Archaeol. Sci.* 53: 166–77.

— 2015b. Human ecodynamics in the Mangareva Islands: a stratified sequence from Nenega–Iti Rock Shelter (site AGA-3, Agakauiti Island). *Archaeol. Oceania* 50(1): 23–42.

Kirk, T. 1889. *The Forest Flora of New Zealand*. Govt Printer, Wellington.

Klar, K. A. 2011. Words from furthest Polynesia: North and South American linguistic evidence for prehistoric contact. In Jones, T. L. et al. (eds) 2011.

Klar, K. A. and Jones, T. L. 2005. Linguistic evidence for a prehistoric Polynesia–Southern California contact event. *Anthropological Linguistics* 47(4): 369–400.

Knapp, M. et al. 2012. Complete mitochondrial DNA genome sequences from the first New Zealanders. *PNAS* 109(45): 18350–54.

Kolb, M. J. 1991. Social power, chiefly authority, and ceremonial architecture, in an island polity, Maui, Hawai`i. (Doctoral dissertation, Uni. California, LA).

— 1994. Monumentality and the rise of religious authority in precontact Hawai`i. *Current Anthropol.* 35(5): 521–33.

— 1999. Monumental grandeur and political florescence in pre-contact Hawai`i: Excavations at Pi`ilanihale Heiau, Maui. *Archaeol. Oceania* 34: 71–82.

— 2006. The origins of monumental architecture in Ancient Hawai`i. *Current Anthropol.* 47(4): 657–65.

Koskinen, A. A. 1963. A preliminary statistical study of Polynesian place names. *Studia Missiologica Fennica* II (Finnish Soc. Missionary Research, Helsinki) 8: 7–11.

— 1973. *Place Name Types and Cultural Sequence in Polynesia: Report of a simple statistical study of an investigation still in progress*. Finnish Soc. Missiology and Ecumenics, Helsinki.

Kreike, C. M. et al. 2004. Genetic diversity of taro, *Colocasia esculenta* (L.) Schott, in Southeast Asia and the Pacific. *Theor. Appl. Genet.* 109: 761–68.

Kurashima, N. and Kirch, P. V. 2011. Geospatial modeling of pre-contact Hawaiian production systems on Moloka`i Island, Hawaiian Islands. *J. Archaeol. Sci.* 38(12): 3662–74.

Lang, A. 2011. *Die Pflanzenwelt Polynesiens* website. Updated 7-Aug-2011: http://www.polynesien.minks-lang.de.

Langdon, R. 1995. New light on Easter Island prehistory in a 'censored' Spanish report of 1770. *J. Pac. History* 30(1): 112–20.

Langdon, R. and Tryon, D. 1983. *The Language of Easter Island: Its development and Eastern Polynesian relationships*. Inst. Poly. Studies, Hawai`i.

Larrue, S. et al. 2010. Anthropogenic vegetation contributions to Polynesia's social heritage: The legacy of candlenut tree (*Aleurites moluccana*) forests and bamboo (*Schizostachyum glaucifolium*) groves on the island of Tahiti. *Econ. Bot.* 64(4): 329–39.

Larson, G. et al. 2007. Phylogeny and ancient DNA of *Sus* provides new insights into Neolithic expansion in island Southeast Asia and Oceania. *PNAS* 104(12): 4834–39.

Lavondès, A. 1957. L'histoire de A`a de Rurutu et l'évolution des mythes. Ch. 4 in Julien, M. et al. 1957.

Law, R. G. 1970. The introduction of kumara into New Zealand. *Archaeol. and Physical Anthropol. in Oceania* 5(2): 114–27.

Leach, B. F. 1981. The prehistory of the Southern Wairarapa. *J. Roy. Soc. NZ* 11(1): 11–33.

Leach, H. 1984. *1000 Years of Gardening in New Zealand*. Reed, Wellington.

— 2005. Gardens without weeds? Pre-European Maori gardens and inadvertent introductions. *NZ J. Bot.* 43: 271–84.

Leach, H. and Stowe, C. 2005. Oceanic arboriculture at the margins: The case of the karaka (*Corynocarpus laevigatus*) in Aotearoa. *JPS* 114(1): 7–27.

Lebot, V. and Aradhya, K. M. 1991. Isozyme variation in taro (*Colocasia esculenta* (L.) Schott) from Asia and Oceania. *Euphytica* 56(1): 55–66.

Lee, T. et al. 2007. Prehistoric inter-archipelago trading of Polynesian tree snails leaves a conservation legacy. *Proc. R. Soc. B.* 274(1627): 2907–14.

Lekkas, E. et al. 2011. Critical factors for run-up and impact of the Tohoku earthquake tsunami. *International J. Geosciences* 2: 310–17.

Lepofsky, D. 2003. The ethnobotany of cultivated plants of the Maohi of the Society Islands. *Econ. Bot.* 57(1): 73–92.

Lessa, W. A. 1956. Myth and blackmail in the Western Carolines. *JPS* 65(1): 67–74.

Levison, M. et al. 1972. *The Settlement of Polynesia: A computer simulation*. Uni. Minnesota Press, Minneapolis.

Lewis, D. 1964. Polynesian navigational methods. *JPS* 73(4): 364–74.

— 1972. *We, the Navigators: The ancient art of landfinding in the Pacific*. Reed, Wellington. (Also 2nd edn, UHP, Honolulu 1994.)

Lewis, M. P. (ed.) 2009. *Ethnologue: Languages of the World*. SIL International, Dallas, 16th edn: http://www.ethnologue.com.

Lewthwaite, G. R. 1999. Rethinking Aotearoa's human geography. *Social Sci. J.* 36(4): 641–58.

Lie, B. A. et al. 2007. Molecular genetic studies of natives on Easter Island: Evidence of an early European and Amerindian contribution to the Polynesian gene pool. *Tissue Antigens* 69(1): 10–18.

Linton, R. 1925. *Archaeology of the Marquesas Islands.* Bishop Mus. Bull. 23, Honolulu.

Lipo, C. P. and Hunt, T. L. 2005. Mapping prehistoric statue roads on Easter Island. *Antiquity* 79: 1–11.

— 2009. A.D. 1680 and Rapa Nui prehistory. *Asian Perspectives* 48(2): 309–17.

Lipo, C. P. et al. 2010. Stylistic variability of stemmed obsidian tools (mata`a), frequency seriation, and the scale of social interaction on Rapa Nui (Easter Island). *J. Archaeol. Sci.* 37: 2551–61.

— 2013. The 'walking' megalithic statues (moai) of Easter Island. *J. Archaeol. Sci.* 40(6): 2859–66.

Little, E. L. Jr. and Skolmen, R. G. 2003. *Agriculture Handbook,* no. 679. Coll. Trop. Agric. & Human Resources, Uni. Hawai`i, Manoa.

Lounsbury, D. E. and Bellamy, R. F. (eds) 2002. *Medical Aspects of Harsh Environments,* vol. 2. Washington, DC: Office of the Surgeon General, Dept of the Army, USA. (Ch. 29 'Shipboard medicine'.)

Love, C. 2007. The Easter Island cultural collapse. In *The Gotland Papers.* Gotland Uni. with Easter Is. Foundation, Sweden, 20–25 Aug: 67–86.

Lowe, D. J. and Newnham, R. M. 2004. Role of tephra in mitochondrial DNA evidence for the spread of Pacific rats through Oceania dating Polynesian settlement and impact, New Zealand. *PAGES (Past Global Changes) News* 12(3): 5–7.

Lum, J. K. and Cann, R. L. 2000. MtDNA lineage analyses: Origins and migrations of Micronesians and Polynesians. *Am. J. Phys. Anthropol.* 113(2): 151–68.

Lum, J. K. et al. 2002. Affinities among Melanesians, Micronesians, and Polynesians: A neutral, biparental genetic perspective. *Human Biology* 74(3): 413–30.

Macgregor, G. 1937. *Ethnology of Tokelau Islands.* Bishop Mus. Bull. 146, Honolulu.

MacPhail, M. K. 1981. Fossil *Pomaderris apetala*-type pollen in North-West Nelson: Reflecting extension of wet sclerophyll forests in south-eastern Australia? *NZ J. Bot.* 19: 17–22.

MacPhail, M. K. et al. 2001. Polynesian plant introductions in the Southwest Pacific: Initial pollen evidence from Norfolk Island. *Rec. Aust. Mus.,* Supplement 27: 123–34.

Makemson, M. W. 1941. *The Morning Star Rises: An account of Polynesian astronomy.* Yale Uni. Press, New Haven.

Mann, C. 2005. *1491: New Revelations of the Americas Before Columbus.* Knopf, NY.

Markham, C. (ed.) 1904. *The Voyages of Pedro Fernandez de Quiros, 1595 to 1606.* Hakluyt Soc., London.

Markham, K. R. and Godley, E. J. 1972. Chemotaxonomic studies in *Sophora. NZ J. Bot.* 10: 627–40.

Marques, A. 1893. The population of the Hawaiian islands. Is the Hawaiian a doomed race? *JPS* 2(4): 253–70.

Marra, J. 1775. *Journal of the* Resolution's *Voyage in 1772, 1773, 1774, and 1775, on discovery to the southern hemisphere.* F. Newberry, London.

Marshall, D. S. 1954. Seabrook adze. *JPS* 63(3–4): 251–52.

Marshall, M. 2011. Early Americans helped colonise Easter Island. *New Scientist* 22: 34.

Marshall, S. J. et al. 2005. Austronesian prehistory and Polynesian genetics: A molecular view of human migration across the Pacific. *NZ Science Review* 62(3): 75–80.

Martin, H. B. 1981. *The Polynesian Journal of Captain Henry Byam Martin, R.N., in command of H.M.S. Grampus-50 guns at Hawaii and on station in Tahiti and the Society Islands, August 1846 to August 1847.* ANU Press, Canberra.

Martinsson-Wallin, H. and Crockford, S. J. 2001. Early Settlement of Rapa Nui (Easter Island). *Asian Perspectives* 40(2): 244–78.

Matisoo-Smith, E. 2009a. The commensal model for human settlement of the Pacific 10 years on: What can we say and where to now? *J. Is. & Coastal Archaeol.* 4(2): 151–63.

— 2009b. David Penny: Man on the edge. *NZ Science Review* 66(1): 16–20.

— 2012. The great blue highway: Human migration in the Pacific. Ch. 19 in Crawford, M. H. and Campbell, B. C. (eds). *Causes and Consequences of Human Migration: An Evolutionary Perspective.* CUP, Cambridge.

Matisoo-Smith, E. and Ramirez, J.-M. 2010. Human skeletal evidence of Polynesian presence in South America? Metric analyses of six crania from Mocha Island, Chile. *J. Pac. Archaeol.* 1(1): 76–88.

Matisoo-Smith, E. and Robins, J. H. 2004. Origins and dispersals of Pacific peoples: Evidence from mtDNA phylogenies of the Pacific rat. *PNAS* 101(24): 9167–72.

— 2009. Mitochondrial DNA evidence for the spread of Pacific rats through Oceania. *Biol. Invasions* 11: 1521–27.

Matisoo-Smith, E. et al. 1998. Patterns of prehistoric human mobility in Polynesia indicated by mtDNA from the Pacific rat. *PNAS* 95(25): 15145–50.

— 1999. Prehistoric mobility in Polynesia: MtDNA variation in *Rattus exulans* from the Chatham and Kermadec Islands. *Asian Perspectives* 38(2): 186–99.

— 2001. Genetic variation in archaeological *Rattus exulans* remains from the Emily Bay settlement site, Norfolk Island. *Rec. Aust. Mus.,* Supplement 27: 81–84.

— 2009. On the rat trail in Near Oceania: Applying the commensal model to the question of the Lapita colonization. *Pac. Sci.* 63(4): 465–75.

Maude, H. E. 1981. *Slavers in Paradise: The Peruvian labour trade in Polynesia, 1862–1864.* USP, Suva.

Maysmor, B. 2001. *Te Manu Tukutuku: The Maori kite.* Steele Roberts, Wellington.

McAlister, A. et al. 2013. The identification of a Marquesan adze in the Cook Islands. *JPS* 122(3): 257–73.

McBreen, K. et al. 2003. The use of molecular techniques to resolve relationships among traditional weaving cultivars of *Phormium.* NZ J. Bot. 41: 301–10.

McCormack, G. 2007. *Cook Islands Biodiversity Database.* Cook Islands Natural Heritage Project. Updated July 2007: http://cookislands. bishopmuseum.org.

McCoy, P. C. et al. 2009. 230Th dates for dedicatory corals from a remote alpine desert adze quarry on Mauna Kea, Hawai`i. *Antiquity* 83: 445–57.

McDermott, Q. 2006. *Junk History.* Australian Broadcasting Corporation's *Four Corners.* 31/07/2006. Transcript: http://www.abc.net.au/4corners/content/2006/s1702333.htm.

McFadgen, B. G. 1994. Archaeology and Holocene sand dune stratigraphy on Chatham Island. *J. Roy. Soc. NZ* 24(1): 17–44.

— 2007. *Hostile Shores: Catastrophic events in prehistoric New Zealand and their impact on Maori coastal communities.* AUP, Auckland.

McGlone, M. S. and Wilmshurst, J. M. 1999. Dating initial Maori environmental impact in New Zealand. *Quaternary International* 59(1): 5–16.

McKinnon, M. (ed.) 1997. *Bateman New Zealand Historical Atlas.* David Bateman, Auckland.

McLean, M. 1974. The New Zealand nose flute: Fact or fallacy? *Galpin Soc. J.* 27: 79–94.

— 1996. *Maori Music.* AUP, Auckland.

— 1999. *Weavers of Songs: Polynesian music and dance.* AUP, Auckland.

— 2008. *Were Lapita Potters Ancestral to Polynesians? A view from ethnomusicology.* Occasional papers in Pacific Ethnomusicology, no. 7. Archive of Maori & Pacific Music, Auckland.

— 2010. *Music, Dance, and Polynesian Origins: The evidence from Poc and Ppn.* Occasional papers in Pacific Ethnomusicology, no. 8. Archive of Maori & Pacific Music, Auckland.

— 2014. *Music, Lapita, and the Problem of Polynesian Origins.* The author, Auckland. (As PDF at http://polynesianorigins.org.)

McLintock, A. H. (ed.) 1966. *An Encyclopaedia of New Zealand.* Govt Printer, Wellington. 3 vols.

McNiven, I. J. et al. 2011. New direction in human colonisation of the Pacific: Lapita settlement of South Coast New Guinea. *Australian Archaeol.* 72: 1–6.

McWethy, D. B. et al. 2010. Rapid landscape transformation in South Island, New Zealand, following initial Polynesian settlement. *PNAS* 107(50): 21343–48.

Medway, D. G. 2002. History and causes of the extirpation of the Providence petrel (*Pterodroma solandri*) on Norfolk Island. *Notornis* 49: 246–58.

Menzies, G. 2002. *1421: The Year China Discovered the World.* Bantam Press, London.

Merchant, A. 1851. *Rovings in the Pacific from 1837 to 1849; with a glance at California.* Longman, Brown, Green & Longmans, London.

Métraux, A. 1957. *Easter Island: A stone-age civilization of the Pacific.* (Transl. from French.) A. Deutsch, London.

Mieth, A. and Bork, H.-R. 2010. Humans, climate or introduced rats: Which is to blame for the woodland destruction on prehistoric Rapa Nui (Easter Island)? *J. Archaeol. Sci.* 37(2): 417–26.

Mills, K. 2009. Was *Phormium tenax* introduced to Norfolk Island by the Polynesians? *Cunninghamia* 11(2): 171–75.

Mirabal, S. et al. 2012. Increased Y-chromosome resolution of haplogroup O suggests genetic ties between the Ami aborigines of Taiwan and the Polynesian islands of Samoa and Tonga. *Gene* 492(2): 339–48.

Moerenhout, J.-A. 1837. *Voyages aux îles du Grand Océan.* Arthus Bertrand, Paris. 2 vols.

Molloy, B. P. J. 1990. The origin, relationships, and use of karaka or kopi (*Corynocarpus laevigatus*). Ch. 2.8 in Harris, W. and Kapoor, P. (eds). *Nga Mahi Maori o te Wao Nui a Tane: Contributions to an international workshop on ethnobotany, Te Rehua Marae.* Bot. Divn, DSIR, Christchurch: 48–53.

Moncada, X. et al. 2013. DNA extraction and amplification from contemporary Polynesian bark-cloth. *PloS One* 8(2): e56549.

Montenegro, Á. et al. 2007. Modelling the prehistoric arrival of the sweet potato in Polynesia. *J. Archaeol. Sci.* 20: 1–130.

Motteler, L. S. 1986. *Pacific Island Names: A map and name guide to the new Pacific.* Bishop Mus., Honolulu.

Mulrooney, M. A. 2009. The myth of A.D. 1680: New evidence from Hanga Ho`onu, Rapa Nui (Easter Island). *Rapa Nui J.* 23(2): 94–105.

— 2013. An island-wide assessment of the chronology of settlement and land use on Rapa Nui (Easter Island) based on radiocarbon data. *J. Archaeol. Sci.* 40(12): 4377–99.

Mulrooney, M. A. et al. 2007. Empirical assessment of a pre-European societal collapse on Rapa Nui (Easter Island). In *The Gotland Papers.* Gotland Uni. with Easter Is. Foundation, Sweden, 20–25 Aug: 141–53.

— 2011. High-precision dating of colonization and settlement in East Polynesia. *PNAS* 108(23): 192–94.

— 2014. *New Dates from Old Samples: A revised chronology for the Wai`ahukini rockshelter site (H8), Ka`u district, Hawaii Island.* Soc. Hawaiian Archaeol. Special Pub. 4: 17–26.

Murray-McIntosh, R. P. et al. 1998. Testing migration patterns and estimating founding population size in Polynesia by using human mtDNA sequences. *PNAS* 95(15): 9047–52.

Nathan, S. 2012. West Coast region – Māori exploration and settlement. *Te Ara – the Encyclopedia of New Zealand.* Updated 13-Jul-12: http://www.TeAra.govt.nz/en/west-coast-region/4.

Nelson, A. 1991. *Nga Waka Māori: Maori canoes.* Macmillan, Auckland.

Newman, J. et al. 2009. Estimating regional population size and annual harvest intensity of the sooty shearwater in New Zealand. *NZ J. Zool.* 36: 307–23.

Ngata, A. T. 1950. The Io Cult – early migration – puzzle of the canoes. *JPS* 59(4): 335–46.

Norton, S. A. 1992. Salt consumption in ancient Polynesia. *Perspect. Biol. Med.* 35(2): 160–81.

Nunn, P. D. 2003. Fished up or thrown down: The geography of Pacific island origin myths. *Annals Assn Am. Geographers* 93(2): 350–64.

Okal, E. A. et al. 2002. A field survey of the 1946 Aleutian tsunami in the far field. *Seismological Research Letters* 73(4): 490–503.

Oliver, D. L. 2002. *Polynesia in Early Historic Times.* Bess Press, Honolulu.

Oliver, W. R. B. 1955. *New Zealand Birds.* Reed, Wellington.

Olson, S. L. and James, H. F. 1982a. Fossil birds from the Hawaiian Islands: Evidence for wholesale extinction by man before Western contact. *Science* 217: 633–35.

— 1982b. *Prodromus of the Fossil Avifauna of the Hawaiian Islands.* Smithsonian Contributions to Zool., no. 365.

Oppenheimer, S. 2004. The 'Express Train from Taiwan to Polynesia': On the congruence of proxy lines of evidence. *World Archaeol.* 36(4): 591–600.

Oppenheimer, S. and Richards, M. 2001. Fast trains, slow boats, and the ancestry of the Polynesian islanders. *Science Progress* 84(3): 157–81.

Orbell, M. 1991. *Hawaiki: A New Approach to Maori Tradition.* CUP, Christchurch.

— 1995. *The Illustrated Encyclopedia of Maori Myth and Legend.* CUP, Christchurch.

— 1996. *The Natural World of the Maori.* David Bateman, Auckland.

— 1998. *A Concise Encyclopedia of Maori Myth and Legends.* CUP, Christchurch.

O'Shaughnessy, D. F. et al. 1990. Globin genes in Micronesia: Origins and affinities of Pacific Island peoples. *Am. J. Hum. Genet.* 46: 44–155.

Oskarsson, M. C. R. et al. 2012. Mitochondrial DNA data indicate an introduction through Mainland Southeast Asia for Australian dingoes and Polynesian domestic dogs. *Proc. R. Soc. B.* 279(1730): 967–74.

Ottino, P. 1992. Anapua: Abri-sous-roche de pêcheurs. Etude des hameçons. *J. Société Océanistes* 94: 57–79; 95: 201–26.

Ottino, P. and de Bergh-Ottino, M.-N. 1991. *Hiva Oa – Glimpses of an Oceanic Memory.* Dépt Archéologie, Centre Polynesién des Sciences Humaines Te Anavaharau.

Ottino-Garanger, P. 1957. Archéologie et restauration à Hiva Oa: le 'me`ae' Iipona de Puamau, aux îles Marquises. Ch. 5(2) in Julien, M. et al. 1957.

Palmer, J. L. 1870. A visit to Easter Island, or Rapa Nui, in 1868. *J. Roy. Geog. Soc. London* 40: 167–81.

Paringatai, K. 2005. *Poia atu / mai (?) taku poi – The Polynesian origins of poi.* World Indigenous Peoples Conference on Education, Uni. Waikato, Hamilton.

Pâris, F.-E. 1841. *Essai sur la Construction Navale des Peuples Extra-Européens.* Arthus Bertrand, Paris.

Parkinson, S. 1773. *A Journal of a Voyage to the South Seas.* Stanfield Parkinson, London.

Patole-Edoumba, E. 1999. L'archerie en Océanie. *J. Société Océanistes* 108: 57–70.

Pearce, C. E. M. and F. M. 2011. *Oceanic Migration: Paths, sequence, timing and range of prehistoric migration in the Pacific and Indian oceans.* Springer, Heidelberg.

Pendergrast, M. 1987. *Te Aho Tapu – The Sacred Thread: Traditional Maori weaving.* Reed, Auckland.

Penny, D. et al. 2002. Estimating the number of females in the founding population of New Zealand: Analysis of mtDNA variation. *JPS* 111(3): 207–22.

Perrier, X. et al. 2011. Multidisciplinary perspectives on banana (*Musa* spp.) domestication. *PNAS* 108(28): 11311–18.

Pétard, P. 1986. *Plantes Utiles de Polynésie Française (Ra`au Tahiti).* Éditions Haere Pô, Pape`ete.

Phillips, J. et al. (eds) 2006. *Māori Peoples of New Zealand – Ngā Iwi o Aotearoa.* Te Ara – the Encyclopedia of New Zealand. David Bateman, Auckland.

Pimm, S. et al. 2006. Human impacts on the rates of recent, present, and future bird extinctions. *PNAS* 103(29): 10941–46.

Piper, P. J. et al. 2009. A 4000 year-old introduction of domestic pigs into the Philippine Archipelago: Implications for understanding routes of human migration through island Southeast Asia and Wallacea. *Antiquity* 83(3): 687–95.

Pocock, M. (ed.) 1997. *The Pacific Crossing Guide.* Adlard Coles Nautical, London.

Pollard, J. et al. 2010. Te Miro o`one: The archaeology of contact on Rapa Nui (Easter Island). *World Archaeol.* 42(4): 562–80.

POLLEX – see Biggs, B. and Clark, R. 2006.

Pool, I. 1991. *Te Iwi Maori: A New Zealand population past, present & projected.* AUP, Auckland.

Pool, I. and Kukutai, T. 2011. Taupori Māori – Māori population change. In *Te Ara – the Encyclopedia of New Zealand.* Updated 10-May-11: http://www.TeAra.govt.nz/en/taupori-maori-maori-population-change.

Power, W. L. (compiler). 2013. *Review of Tsunami Hazard in New Zealand (2013 update)*, GNS Science Consultancy Report 2013/131. 222 pp.

Pratt, H. D. et al. *A Field Guide to the Birds of Hawaii and the Tropical Pacific.* Princeton Uni. Press, NJ, 1987.

Prebble, M. and Dowe, J. L. 2008. The Late Quaternary decline and extinction of palms on oceanic Pacific islands. *Quaternary Science Reviews* 27: 2546–67.

Prebble, M. and Porch, N. 2009. Documenting the Downstream Ecological Consequences of Human Colonisation of the Austral Archipelago (French Polynesia) using Palaeoecological Records. Paper presented at the 11th Pacific Science Inter-congress, Papeete. Dept Archaeol. & Nat. Hist., ANU, Canberra.

Prebble, M. and Wilmshurst, J. M. 2009. Detecting the initial impact of humans and introduced species on island environments in Remote Oceania using palaeoecology. *Biol. Invasions* 11: 1529–56.

Preece, R. C. 1998. Impact of early Polynesian occupation on the land snail fauna of Henderson Island, Pitcairn group (South Pacific). *Phil. Trans. R. Soc. Lond. B* 353: 347–68.

Prickett, N. 2001. *Maori Origins: From Asia to Aotearoa.* David Bateman & Auckland Museum, Auckland.

Pukui, M. K. and Elbert, S. H. 1985. *Hawaiian Dictionary.* UHP, Honolulu.

Quanchi, M. and Robson, J. 2005. *Historical Dictionary of the Discovery and Exploration of the Pacific Islands.* The Scarecrow Press, Lanham, Maryland.

Rainbird, P. 2004. *The Archaeology of Micronesia.* CUP, Cambridge.

Raines, B. and Huber, M. 2012. Biodiversity quadrupled – Revision of Easter Island and Salas y Gómez Bivalves. *Zootaxa* 3217: 1–106.

Rallu, J. -L. 1992. From decline to recovery: The Marquesan population 1886–1945. *Health Transition Review* 2(2): 177–94.

Ramírez-Aliaga, J. 2011. The Mapuche connection. In Jones, T. L. et al. (eds) 2011.

Randall, J. E. and Egaña, A. C. 1984. *Native Names of Easter Island Fishes: With comments on the origin of the Rapanui people.* Occasional papers of the Bishop Mus. 25(12), Honolulu.

Rayner, M. J. et al. 2011. Contemporary and historical separation of transequatorial migration between genetically distinct seabird populations. *Nature Communications* 2: 332.

Rehder, H. A. and Randall, J. E. 1975. *Ducie Atoll: Its history, physiography and biota.* Atoll Res. Bull. 183, Washington.

Rensch, K. H. 1988. *Fish Names of Eastern Polynesia.* Pacific Linguistics series, no. 106. Dept Linguistics, Res. Sch. Pac. Studies, ANU, Canberra.

Richards, R. 2004. The earliest foreign visitors and their massive depopulation of Rapa Iti from 1824 to 1830. *J. Société Océanistes* 118(1): 3–10.

Riegen, A. 2005. How do bar-tailed godwits migrate from Alaska to New Zealand? *Miranda News* 58: 14–17.

Rieth, T. M. et al. 2011. The 13th century Polynesian colonization of Hawai`i Island. *J. Archaeol. Sci.* 38(10): 2740–49.

Riley, M. 1994. *Māori Healing and Herbal.* Viking Sevenseas, Paraparaumu.

Roberts, M. 1990. The Ecological Parasitology of the Polynesian rat (*Rattus exulans*) on Tiritiri Matangi Island. PhD thesis, Uni. Auckland.

Robertson, C. 2011. *Long-tailed Cuckoo: Pathfinding in paradise.* Museum Victoria, Melbourne: http://www.thestudy.net.au/projects/museum-victoria-blogs.html.

Robertson, G. 1948. *The Discovery of Tahiti: A journal of the second voyage of HMS Dolphin round the World.* Hakluyt Soc., London.

Rockman, M. and Steele, J. (eds) 2003. *Colonization of Unfamiliar Landscapes: The archaeology of adaptation.* Routledge, Abingdon.

Rogers, D. S. et al. 2009. Inferring population histories using cultural data. *Proc. R. Soc. B* 276: 3835–43.

Rolett, B. V. 1993. Marquesan prehistory and the origins of East Polynesian culture. *J. Société Océanistes* 96(1): 29–47.

— 2002. Voyaging and interaction in ancient East Polynesia. *Asian Perspectives* 41(2): 182–94.

Rolett, B. V. et al. 1997. Marquesan voyaging: Archaeometric evidence for inter-island contact. In Weisler (ed.) 1997: 134–48.

— 2015. Ancient East Polynesian voyaging spheres: New evidence from the Vitaria Adze Quarry (Rurutu, Austral Islands). *J. Archaeol. Sci.* 53: 459–71.

Rongo, T. et al. 2009. Did ciguatera prompt the late Holocene Polynesian voyages of discovery? *J. Biogeography* 36(8): 1423–32.

Rooney J. et al. 2008. Geology and geomorphology of coral reefs in the northwestern Hawaiian Islands. In Riegl, B. M. and Dodge, R. E. (eds). *Coral Reefs of the USA.* Coral Reefs of the World, vol. 1: 515–67.

Roscoe, P. B. 1987. Of canoes and castaways: Reassessing the population of Tongareva (Penrhyn Island) at contact. *Pacific Studies* 11(1): 43–61.

Rossel, G. et al. 1999–2000. From Latin America to Oceania: The historic dispersal of sweet potato re-examined using AFLP. *CIP Program Report.* pp. 315–21.

Roullier, C. et al. 2013. Historical collections reveal patterns of diffusion of sweet potato in Oceania obscured by modern plant movements and recombination. *PNAS* 110(6): 2205–10.

Rowe, N. A. 1930. *Samoa under the Sailing Gods.* Putnam, London.

Royal, C. 2012. Hawaiki – Location and associations. In *Te Ara – the Encyclopedia of New Zealand*, updated 22-Sep-12: http://www.TeAra.govt.nz/en/hawaiki/page-3.

Rull, V. et al. 2010. Paleoecology of Easter Island: Evidence and uncertainties. *Earth-Science Reviews* 99(1–2): 50–60.

Salmond, A. 2004. *The Trial of the Cannibal Dog: Captain Cook in the South Seas.* Penguin, Auckland.

— 2006. Two worlds. Ch. 7 in Howe, K. R. (ed.) 2006.

— 2008. *Voyaging Worlds.* Hakluyt Soc., London.

— 2009. *Aphrodite's Island: The European discovery of Tahiti.* Penguin, Auckland.

Sand, C. 1998. Recent archaeological research in the Loyalty Islands of New Caledonia. *Asian Perspectives* 37: 194–223.

— 2004. Walpole, A "Mystery Island" in Southeast New Caledonia? *Rec. Aust. Mus.*, Supplement 29: 109–22.

Saura, B. 2011. Saying 'Indigenous' in Tahiti: The term Mā`ohi. *Shima* 5(2). 18 pp.

Savage, S. 1980. *A Dictionary of the Maori Language of Rarotonga.* Suva Printing & Publishing Co, Suva.

Savolainen, P. 2004. A detailed picture of the origin of the Australian dingo, obtained from the study of mitochondrial DNA. *PNAS* 101(33): 12387–90.

Scaglion, R. 2005. *Kumara* in the Ecuadorian Gulf of Guayaquil? In Ballard, C. et al. (eds) 2005.

Scaglion, R. and Cordero, M. 2011. Did ancient Polynesians reach the New World? In Jones, T. L. et al. (eds) 2011.

Scheele, S. 2013. Ngā Tipu Whakaoranga database. http://maoriplantuse.landcareresearch.co.nz.

Scheele, S. and Sweetapple, P. 2011. Kuta and kāpūngāwhā: Reeds and sedges used for weaving. Landcare Research: http://www.landcareresearch.co.nz/science/plants-animals-fungi/plants/ethnobotany/weaving-plants/information-sheets.

Schmidt, M. 1996. The commencement of pa construction in New Zealand prehistory. *JPS* 105(4): 441–60.

Schmidt, M. and Higham, T. 1998. Sources of New Zealand's east Polynesian culture revisited: The radiocarbon chronology of the Tairua

archaeological site, New Zealand. *JPS* 107(4): 395–404.

Schmitt, R. C. 1965. Garbled population estimates of Central Polynesia. *JPS* 74(1): 57–62.

— 1967. How many Hawaiians? *JPS* 76(4): 467–76.

Scofield, P. et al. 2003. What birds were New Zealand's first people eating? Wairau Bar's avian remains re-examined. *Rec. Canterbury Mus.* 17: 17–35.

Scott, D. et al. 2008. Decline of sooty shearwaters, *Puffinus griseus*, on The Snares, New Zealand. *Papers Proc. Roy. Soc. Tasmania* 142(1): 185–96.

Seelenfreund, D. et al. 2010. Paper mulberry (*Broussonetia papyrifera*) as a commensal model for human mobility in Oceania: Anthropological, botanical and genetic considerations. *NZ J. Bot.* 48(3–4): 231–47.

Seemann, B. 1862. *Viti: An account of a government mission to the Vitian or Fijian Islands, in the years 1860–61.* Macmillan, Cambridge.

Shaffer, S. A. et. al. 2006. Migratory shearwaters integrate oceanic resources across the Pacific Ocean in an endless summer. *PNAS* 103(34): 12799–802.

Shand, A. 1894. The Moriori people of the Chatham Islands: Their traditions and history. *JPS* 3(2): 76–92.

Sharp, A. 1956a. *Ancient Voyagers in the Pacific.* Poly. Soc. Memoir 32.

— 1956b. The prehistory of the New Zealand Maoris. Some possibilities. *JPS* 65(2): 155–60.

— 1961. Polynesian navigation to distant islands. *JPS* 70(2): 219–26.

— 1964. *Ancient Voyagers in Polynesia.* Uni. California Press, Berkeley.

— 1971. Polynesian ancestors settle the Pacific. In Knox, R. (ed.) *New Zealand's Heritage.* Paul Hamlyn, Wellington, vol. 1: 33–36.

Sharp, W. D. et al. 2010. Rapid evolution of ritual architecture in central Polynesia indicated by precise 230Th/U coral dating. *PNAS* 107(30): 13234–39.

Shelley, R. M. 2004. Occurrences of the centipedes, *Scolopendra morsitans* L. and *S. subspinipes* Leach, on Pacific Islands (Chilopoda: Scolopendromorpha: Scolopendridae). *Entomological News* 115(2): 78–83.

Sheppard, P. J. et al. 1997. Basalt sourcing and the development of Cook Island exchange systems. In Weisler, M. I. (ed.) 1997: 85–110.

Shipley, G. P. et al. 2015. Genetic structure among Fijian island populations. *J. Human Genetics* 60: 69–75.

Simmons, D. R. 1969. A New Zealand myth: Kupe, Toi and the 'Fleet'. *NZ J. History* 3(1): 14–31.

— 1976. *The Great New Zealand Myth: A study of the discovery and origin traditions of the Maori.* Reed, Wellington.

Sinoto, Y. H. 1957. Tracing human movement in East Polynesia. Ch. 2(3) in Julien, M. et al. 1957.

— 1983a. An analysis of Polynesian migrations based on the archaeological assessments. *J. Société Océanistes* 76(39): 57–67.

— 1983b. Huahine: Heritage of the great navigators. *Museum International* 35(1): 70–73.

Sinoto, Y. H. and Kellum, M. 1965. Preliminary report on excavations in the Marquesas Islands, French Polynesia. Bishop Mus., Honolulu. (Unpublished report.)

Skinner, H. D. 1931. On the patu family and its occurrence beyond New Zealand. *JPS* 40(160): 183–96.

— 1933. Notes and queries: Greenstone in the Cook Group. *JPS* 42(167): 225–26.

— 1940. Provenance of the Nassau Island adze. *JPS* 49(194): 272–81.

Skinner, W. H. 1912. Ancient Maori canals. Marlborough, N. Z. *JPS* 21(3): 105–08.

Skoglund, P. et al. 2016. Genomic insights into the peopling of the Southwest Pacific. *Nature* 538: 510–26.

Sladen, A. et al. 2007. Evaluation of far-field tsunami hazard in French Polynesia based on historical data and numerical simulations. *Nat. Hazards Earth Syst. Sci.* 7: 195–206.

Smissen, R. D. and Heenan, P. B. 2010. A taxonomic appraisal of the Chatham Islands flax (*Phormium tenax*) using morphological and DNA fingerprint data. *Australian Systematic Botany* 23(5): 371–80.

Smith, S. D. A. 2002. Kelp rafts in the Southern Ocean. *Global Ecology & Biogeography* 11: 67–9.

Smith, S. P. 1898. Hawaiki: The whence of the Maori: Being an introduction to Rarotongan history, Part II. *JPS* 7(4): 185–223.

— 1899. Art. XXX.–The Tohunga-Maori: A sketch. *Trans. Proc. Roy. Soc. NZ* 32: 253–70.

— 1903. Some Paumotu chants. *JPS* 12(4): 221–42.

— 1904. *Hawaiki: The original home of the Maori.* Whitcombe & Tombs, Christchurch.

Soares, P. et al. 2011. Ancient voyaging and Polynesian origins. *Am. J. Hum. Genet.* 88(2): 239–47.

Solomon, M. and Forbes, S. 2010. Indigenous archaeology: a Moriori case study. In: Phillips, C. and Allen, H. (eds). *Bridging the Divide: Indigenous Communities and Archaeology into the 21st Century.* Left Coast Press, CA. pp. 213–232.

Solsvik, R. and Wallin, P. 2007. Time and temples: Chronology of marae structures in the Society Islands. In *The Gotland Papers*. Gotland Uni. with Easter Is. Foundation, Sweden, 20–25 Aug: 269–84.

Sorrenson, M. P. K. 1979. *Māori Origins and Migrations: The genesis of some Pākehā myths and legends*. AUP, Auckland.

Specht, J. et al. 2014. Deconstructing the Lapita cultural complex in the Bismarck Archipelago. *J. Archaeol. Res.* 22(2): 89–140.

Spennemann, D. H. R. 1997. *Distribution of Rat Species (Rattus spp.) on the Atolls of the Marshall Islands: Past and present dispersal*. Atoll Res. Bull. 446, Washington.

Spriggs, M. and Anderson, A. 1993. Late colonization of East Polynesia. *Antiquity* 67: 200–17.

Stair, J. B. 1895. Floatsam and jetsam from the great ocean: Or, summary of early Samoan voyages and settlement. *JPS* 4(2): 99–131.

Steadman, D. W. 1988. A new species of *Porphyrio* (Aves: Rallidae) from archaeological sites in the Marquesas Islands. *Proc. Biol. Soc. Washington* 101(1): 162–70.

— 1991. Extinct and extirpated birds from Aitutaki and Atiu, Southern Cook Islands. *Pac. Sci.* 45: 325–47.

— 1995. Prehistoric extinctions of Pacific Island birds: Biodiversity meets zooarchaeology. *Science* 267(5201): 1123–31.

— 1999. The prehistoric extinction of South Pacific birds: Catastrophe versus attrition. In Galipaud, J.-C. and Lilley, I. (eds) 1999: 375–86.

— 2006. *Extinction and Biogeography of Tropical Pacific Birds*. UCP, Chicago.

Steadman, D. W. and Bollt, R. 2010. Prehistoric birds from Rurutu, Austral Islands, East Polynesia. *Pac. Sci.* 64(2): 315–25.

Steadman, D. W. and Kirch, P. V. 1990. Prehistoric extinction of birds on Mangaia, Cook Islands, Polynesia. *PNAS* 87(24): 9605–09.

Steadman, D. W. and Olson, S. L. 1985. Bird remains from an archaeological site on Henderson Island, South Pacific: Man-caused extinctions on an 'uninhabited' island. *PNAS* 82(18): 6191–95.

Steadman, D. W. et al. 1994. Stratigraphy, chronology, and cultural context of an early faunal assemblage from Easter Island. *Asian Perspectives* 33(1): 79–96.

Stefan, V. H. and Chapman, P. M. 2003. Cranial variation in the Marquesas Islands. *Am. J. Phys. Anthropol.* 121(4): 319–31.

Stefan, V. H. et al. 2002. Shorter communication: Henderson Island crania and their implication for southeastern Polynesian prehistory. *JPS* 111(4): 371–84.

Stevenson, C. M. et al. 2006. Prehistoric and early historic agriculture at Maunga Orito, Easter Island (Rapa Nui), Chile. *Antiquity* 80: 919–36.

— 2015. Variation in Rapa Nui (Easter Island) land use indicates production and population peaks prior to European contact. *PNAS* 112(4): 1025–30.

Stevenson, J. et al. 2017. Polynesian colonization and landscape changes on Mo`orea, French Polynesia: The Lake Temae pollen record. *Holocene* 27(12):1963–1975.

Stimson, J. F. 1932. Songs of the Polynesian voyagers. *JPS* 41(163): 181–201.

— 1957. *Songs and Tales of the Sea Kings: Interpretations of the oral literature of Polynesia*. Peabody Mus. Salem, Mass.

Stimson, J. F. and Marshall, D. S. 1964. *A Dictionary of some Tuamotuan Dialects of the Polynesian Language*. Peabody Mus. Salem, Mass., & Royal Inst. of Linguistics and Anthropology, The Hague.

Stoddart, D. R. et al. 1990. *Mauke, Mitiaro and Atiu: Geomorphology of makatea islands in the Southern Cooks*. Smithsonian Inst., Washington.

Stokes, J. F. G. 1930. An evaluation of early genealogies used for Polynesian history. *JPS* 39(153): 1–42.

— 1955. Language in Rapa. *JPS* 64(3): 315–40.

Storey, A. A. and Matisoo-Smith, E. A. 2014. No evidence against Polynesian dispersal of chickens to pre-Columbian South America. *PNAS* 111(35): E3583.

Storey, A. A. et al. 2007. Radiocarbon and DNA evidence for a pre-Columbian introduction of Polynesian chickens to Chile. *PNAS* 104(25): 10335–39.

— 2008. Pre-Columbian chickens, dates, isotopes and mtDNA. *PNAS* 105(48): 99.

— 2011. A reappraisal of the evidence for pre-Columbian introduction of chickens to the Americas. In Jones, T. L. et al. (eds) 2011.

— 2013. Polynesian chickens in the New World: A detailed application of a commensal approach. *Archaeol. Oceania* 48: 101–19.

Su, B. et al. 2000. Polynesian origins: Insights from the Y chromosome. *PNAS* 97(15): 8225–28.

Suggs, R. C. 1961. *The Archaeology of Nuku Hiva, Marquesas Islands, French Polynesia*. Monograph 49(1) Anthropol. Papers Am. Mus. Nat. Hist., NY.

Summerhayes, G. R. 2009. Obsidian network patterns in Melanesia – Sources, characterisation and distribution. *Bull. Indo-Pacific Prehistory Assn* 29: 110–24.

Sutton, D. G. 1980. A culture history of the Chatham Islands. *JPS* 89(1): 67–94.

— 1987. Time-place systematics in New Zealand archaeology: The case for a fundamental revision. *J. Société Océanistes* 84: 23–29.

Sutton, D. G. (ed.) 1994. *The Origins of the First New Zealanders*. AUP, Auckland.

Swarbrick, N. 2012. Logging native forests – Centuries of change. In *Te Ara – the Encyclopedia of New Zealand*. Updated 13-Jul-12: http://www.TeAra.govt.nz/en/logging-native-forests/page-1.

Takayama, J. 1981. Early pottery and population movements in Micronesian prehistory. *Asian Perspectives* 24(1): 1–10.

Taonui, R. 1994. Te Haerenga waka: Polynesian origins, migrations and navigation. Masters thesis, Uni. Auckland.

— 2006. Polynesian oral traditions. Ch. 2 in Howe, K. R. (ed.) 2006.

— 2009. Tapa whenua – Naming places. In *Te Ara – the Encyclopedia of New Zealand*. Updated 1-Mar-09: http://www.TeAra.govt.nz/en/tapa-whenua-naming-places/2.

— 2011. Whakapapa – Genealogy – Whakapapa with links to Polynesia. In *Te Ara – the Encyclopedia of New Zealand*. Updated 3-May-11: http://www.TeAra.govt.nz/en/whakapapa-genealogy/3

— 2012. Canoe navigation – Ocean voyaging. In *Te Ara – the Encyclopedia of New Zealand*. Updated 22-Sep-12: http://www.TeAra.govt.nz/en/canoe-navigation/page-2.

— 2012a. Canoe traditions. In *Te Ara – the Encyclopedia of New Zealand*. Updated 22-Sep-12: http://www.TeAra.govt.nz/en/canoe-traditions.

Tapsell, P. 2006. Te Arawa. Ch. 35 in Phillips, J. et al. (eds) 2006. Or http://www.teara.govt.nz/en/te-arawa/page-1.

Tautahi, H and Taipuhi, W. 1900. Ko 'Aotea' waka. *JPS* 9(4): 200–33.

Taylor, D. A. 2012. Mitochondrial DNA variation in the Fijian Archipelago. MA thesis, Uni. Kansas, KS.

Taylor, R. 1855. *Te Ika a Maui, or, New Zealand and its inhabitants*. Wertheim and Macintosh, London.

Te Ahukaramū Charles Royal. See Royal, Charles.

Te Rangi Hiroa (Buck, P. H.) 1924. The passing of the Maori. *Trans. Proc. Roy. Soc. NZ* 55: 362–75.

— 1926b. The value of tradition in Polynesian research. *JPS* 35(139): 181–203.

— 1927. *The Material Culture of the Cook Islands (Aitutaki)*. Thomas Avery & Sons, New Plymouth.

— 1932a. *Ethnology of Manihiki and Rakahanga*. Bishop Mus. Bull. 99, Honolulu.

— 1932b. *Ethnology of Tongareva*. Bishop Mus. Bull. 92, Honolulu.

— 1938a. *Ethnology of Mangareva*. Bishop Mus. Bull. 157, Honolulu.

— 1938b. *Vikings of the Sunrise*. Frederick A. Stokes Co., NY.

— 1944. *The Arts and Crafts of the Cook Islands*. Bishop Mus. Bull. 179, Honolulu.

— 1945. *An Introduction to Polynesian Anthropology*. Bishop Mus. Bull. 187, Honolulu.

— 1950a. *Material Culture of Kapingamarangi*. Bishop Mus. Bull. 200, Honolulu.

— 1950b. *The Coming of the Maori*. Whitcombe & Tombs, Wellington.

Tennyson, A. and Martinson, P. 2006. *Extinct Birds of New Zealand*. Te Papa Press, Wellington.

Tent, J. and Geraghty, P. 2011. Ulimaroa unveiled? *The Globe* 69: 29–40.

— 2012. Where in the world is Ulimaroa? Or, how a Pacific island became the Australian continent. *J. Pac. History* 47(1): 1–20.

Thomson, V. A. et al. 2014. Molecular genetic evidence for the place of origin of the Pacific rat, *Rattus exulans. PloS One* 9(3): e91356.

— 2014a. Using ancient DNA to study the origins and dispersal of ancestral Polynesian chickens across the Pacific. *PNAS* 111(13): 4826–31.

— Reply to Beavan, Bryant, and Storey and Matisoo-Smith: Ancestral Polynesian 'D' haplotypes reflect authentic Pacific chicken lineages. *PNAS* 111(35): E3585-86.

Thorpe, W. W. 1929. Evidence of Polynesian culture in Australia and Norfolk Island. *JPS* 38(150): 123–26.

— 1931. Correspondence. *JPS* 40(160): 252.

Thorsby, E. 2012. The Polynesian gene pool: An early contribution by Amerindians to Easter Island. *Phil. Trans. R. Soc. B* 367(1590): 812–19.

Thorsby, E. et al. 2009. Further evidence of an Amerindian contribution to the Polynesian gene pool on Easter Island. *Tissue Antigens* 73(6): 582–85.

Tinghitella, R. M. et al. 2011. Island hopping introduces Polynesian field crickets to novel environments, genetic bottlenecks and rapid evolution. *J. Evolution Biol.* 24: 1199–211.

Titcomb, M. A. 1969. *Dog and Man in the Ancient Pacific, with Special Attention to Hawaii*. Bishop Mus. Special Pub. 59, Honolulu.

Tregear, E. 1891. *Maori–Polynesian Comparative Dictionary*. Lyon & Blair, Wellington.

— 1892. The Polynesian bow. *JPS* 1(1): 56–59.

— 1899. *A Dictionary of Mangareva (or Gambier Islands)*. Govt Printer, Wellington.

Trejaut, J. A. et al. 2005 Traces of archaic mitochondrial lineages persist in Austronesian-speaking Formosan populations. *PLoS Biol* 3(8): e247.
— 2011. Modern human migrations in insular Asia according to mitochondrial DNA and non-recombining Y chromosome. *ISBT Science Series* 6: 361–65.
Turbott, E. G. (ed.) 1967. *Buller's Birds of New Zealand*. Whitcoulls Publishers, Christchurch. (Reproduced from 2nd edn 1888.)
Turner, M. et al. 2001. Stone artefacts from the Emily Bay settlement site, Norfolk Island. *Rec. Aust. Mus.*, Supplement 27: 53–66.
US Coast Guard. 2003. *Boat Crew Seamanship Manual* (COMDTINST M16114.5C) USCG, Washington.
Underhill, P. A. et al. 2001. Maori origins, Y-chromosome haplotypes and implications for human history in the Pacific. *Human Mutation* 17: 271–80.
Valentin, F. et al. 2016. Early Lapita skeletons from Vanuatu show Polynesian craniofacial shape: Implications for Remote Oceanic settlement and Lapita origins. *PNAS* 113(2): 292–97.
Veitch, C. R. et al. 2004. Birds of the Kermadec Islands, south-west Pacific. *Notornis* 51: 61–90.
Viviano, F. 2005. China's great armada: six hundred years ago China's Admiral Zheng He led a mighty fleet on the first of seven voyages that reshaped an empire. *National Geographic* 208: 28.
Von Däniken, E. and Heron, M. 1970. *Return to the Stars*. Souvenir Press, London.
Wagner, W. L. and Lorence, D. H. 2011. *Flora of the Marquesas Islands*. Smithsonian Inst.: http://botany.si.edu/pacificislandbiodiversity/marquesasflora.
Wagstaff, S. J. and Dawson, M. I. 2000. Classification, origin, and patterns of diversification of *Corynocarpus* (Corynocarpaceae) inferred from DNA sequences. *Systematic Botany* 25(1): 134–49.
Waite, D. 1993. Three images from Mangareva: A reappraisal. Ch. 13 in Dark, P. J. C. *Artistic Heritage in a Changing Pacific*. UHP, Honolulu.
Waldren, S. et al. 1999. *The Non-Native Vascular Plants of Henderson Island, South Central Pacific Ocean*. Atoll Res. Bull. 463, Washington.
Wallin, P. 1997. Archery platforms (vahi te`a) in the Society Islands, Polynesia: A contextual interpretation. *Current Swedish Archaeol.* 5: 193–201.
Wallin, P. and Solsvik, R. 2010. Marae reflections: On the evolution of stratified chiefdoms in the Leeward Society Islands. *Archaeol. Oceania* 45(2): 86–93.
Walter, A. and Sam, C. 1990. Rapport d'une enquête préliminaire sur l'exploitation traditionnelle des arbres fruitiers à Vanuatu. *Notes et Documents D'Ethnographie* 3, ORSTOM, Port Vila.
Walter, R. 1994. The Cook Islands–New Zealand connection. In Sutton, D. G. (ed.) 1994: 220–29.
Walter, R. and Anderson, A. 1995. Archaeology of Niue Island: Initial results. *JPS* 104(4): 471–81.
Walter, R. and Dickinson, W. R. 1989. A ceramic sherd from Ma`uke in the Southern Cook Islands. *JPS* 98(4): 465–70.
Walter, R. and Sheppard, P. J. 1996. The Ngati Tiare adze cache: Further evidence of prehistoric contact between West Polynesia and the Southern Cook Islands. *Archaeol. Oceania* 31: 33–39.
Walter, R. et al. 2010. Colonisation, mobility and exchange in New Zealand prehistory. *Antiquity* 84(324): 497–513.
Walworth, M. E. 2014. Eastern Polynesian: The linguistic evidence revisited. *Oceanic Linguistics* 53(2): 256–72.
— 2015. Classifying Old Rapa: Linguistic evidence for prehistoric contact networks in South-East Polynesia. *Thirteenth International Conference on Austronesian Linguistics (13-ICAL)*: 163–64.
Ward, R. G. and Brookfield, M. 1992. The dispersal of the coconut: Did it float or was it carried to Panama? *J. Biogeography* 19(55): 467–80.
Watling, D. 1995. Notes on the status of Kuhl's lorikeet *Vini kuhlii* in the Northern Line Islands, Kiribati. *Bird Conservation International* 5: 481–89.
Wehi, P. M. and Clarkson B. D. 2007. Biological flora of New Zealand 10. *Phormium tenax*, harakeke, New Zealand flax. *NZ J. Bot.* 45: 521–44.
Weimerskirch, H. et al. 2005. Foraging strategy of a tropical seabird, the red-footed booby, in a dynamic marine environment. *Marine Ecology-Progress Series* 288: 251–61.
Weisler, M. I. (ed.) 1997. *Prehistoric Long-Distance Interaction in Oceania: An interdisciplinary approach*. NZ Archael. Assn Monograph 21.
Weisler, M. I. 1994. The settlement of marginal Polynesia: New evidence from Henderson Island. *J. Field Arch.* 21(1): 83–102.
— 1997. Prehistoric long-distance interaction at the margins of Oceania. In Weisler, M. I. (ed.) 1997: 149–72.
— 1998. Hard evidence for Prehistoric interaction in Polynesia. *Current Anthropol.* 39(4): 521–30.
— 2002. Centrality and the collapse of long-distance voyaging in East Polynesia. Ch. 13 in Glascock, M. D. (ed.) *Geochemical Evidence for Long-Distance Exchange*. Bergin & Garvey, Westport, CT.
— 2005. *Life on the Margins of the Great Ocean*. ABC | Perspective. 13 April. Program transcript. http://www.abc.net.au/radionational/programs/perspective/marshall-weisler/3448842.
— 2008. Sourcing studies are best done in collaboration with geochemists. Comment on Atholl Anderson's 'Traditionalism, interaction and long-distance seafaring in Polynesia'. *J. Is. & Coastal Archaeol.* 3(2): 265–67.
Weisler, M. I. and Green, R. C. 2001. Holistic approaches to interaction studies: A Polynesian example. In Jones, M. and Sheppard P. (eds). *Australasian Connections and New Directions*. Research in Anthropol. and Linguistics, no. 5, Uni. Auckland.
Weisler, M. I. and Haslam, M. 2005. Determining the function of Polynesian volcanic glass artifacts: Results of a residue study. *Hawaiian Arch.* 10: 1–17.
Weisler, M. I. and Kirch, P. V. 1996. Interisland and interarchipelago transfer of stone tools in prehistoric Polynesia. *PNAS* 93(4): 1381–85.
Weisler, M. I. and Swindler, D. 2002. Rocker jaws from the Marshall Islands: Evidence for interaction between eastern Micronesia and west Polynesia. *People and Culture in Oceania* 18: 23–33.
Weisler, M. I. and Woodhead, J. D. 1995. Basalt Pb isotope analysis and the prehistoric settlement of Polynesia. *PNAS* 92(6): 1881–1885.
Weisler, M. I. et al. 2006. A new eastern limit of the Pacific flying fox, *Pteropus tonganus* (Chiroptera: Pteropodidae), in prehistoric Polynesia: A case of possible human transport and extirpation. *Pac. Sci.* 60(3): 403–11.
— 2016. Cook Island artifact geochemistry demonstrates spatial and temporal extent of pre-European interarchipelago voyaging in East Polynesia. *PNAS* 113(29): 8150–55.
West, C. J. 1996. *Assessment of the Weed Control Programme on Raoul Island, Kermadec Group*. DoC, Wellington, Sci. & Res. series, no. 98.
Whistler, W. A. 1990. *Ethnobotany of the Cook Islands: The plants, their Maori names, and their uses*. Allertonia: A series of occasional papers, Natl Trop. Bot. Gdn, Lawai, Hawai`i.
— 2009. *Plants of the Canoe People: An ethnobotanical voyage through Polynesia*. Natl Trop. Bot. Gdn, Lawai, Hawai`i.
White, J. 1887–90. *The Ancient History of the Maori: His mythology and traditions*. G. Didsbury, Wellington. 6 vols.
White, P. et al. 2014. A Norfolk Island basalt adze from coastal New South Wales. *Australian Arch.* 79: 131–36.
Whyte, A. L. H. et al. 2005. Human evolution in Polynesia. *Human Biology* 77(2): 157–77.
Wiens, H. J. 1956. *The Geography of Kapingamarangi Atoll in the Eastern Carolines*. Atoll Res. Bull. 48, Washington.
Wilkes, C. 1852. *Narrative of the United States Exploring Expedition: During the years 1838, 1839, 1840, 1841, 1842*. Ingram, Cooke, and Co., London.
Williams, E. 2009. Māori fire use and landscape changes in southern New Zealand. *JPS* 118(2): 175–89.
Williams, H. W. 1919. Some notes on the language of the Chatham Islands. *Trans. Proc. Roy. Soc. NZ* 51: 415–22.
— 1971. *A Dictionary of the Maori Language*. Govt Printer, Wellington.
Williams, J. 1837. *A Narrative of Missionary Enterprises in the South Sea islands: With remarks upon the natural history of the islands, origin, languages, traditions, and usages of the inhabitants*. J. Snow, London.
Wilmshurst, J. and Higham, T. F. G. 2004. Using rat-gnawed seeds to independently date the arrival of Pacific rats and humans in New Zealand. *Holocene* 14: 801–06.
Wilmshurst, J. M. et al. 2008. Dating the late prehistoric dispersal of Polynesians to New Zealand using the commensal Pacific rat. *PNAS* 105(22): 7676–80.
— 2011. High-precision radiocarbon dating shows recent and rapid initial human colonization of East Polynesia. *PNAS* 108(5): 1815–20.
Wilson, J. (ed.) 1987. *From the Beginning: The archaeology of the Maori*. Penguin, Auckland.
Wilson, W. H. 2012. Whence the East Polynesians?: Further linguistic evidence for a Northern Outlier source. *Oceanic Linguistics* 51(2): 289–359.
Wodzicki, K. and Laird, M. 1970. Birds and bird lore in the Tokelau Islands. *Notornis* 17(4): 247–276.
Wood, C. and Wood, M. 2005. *Charlie's Charts of Polynesia*. Charlie's Charts, Surrey, Canada.
Wood, C. F. 1875. *A Yachting Cruise in the South Seas*. H. S. King & Co., London.
Wood, J. R. et al. 2014. An extinct nestorid parrot (Aves, Psittaciformes, Nestoridae) from the Chatham Islands, New Zealand. *Zool. J. Linnean Soc.* 172(1): 185–99.

Woodhead, J. and Weisler, M. I. 1997. Accurate sourcing of basaltic artefacts by radiogenic isotope analysis. In Weisler, M. I. (ed.) 1997: 212–23.

Woodley, K. 2009. *Godwits: Long-haul champions.* Penguin, Auckland.

Worthy, T. H. 2012. 'Moa – Appearance and breeding', *Te Ara – the Encyclopedia of New Zealand*, updated 13-Jul-12: http://www.TeAra.govt.nz/en/moa/page-3

Worthy, T. H. et al. 2011. Prehistoric birds and bats from the Atiahara site, Tubuai, Austral Islands, East Polynesia. *Pac. Sci.* 65(1): 69–85.

Wragg, G. M. and Weisler, M. I. 1994. Extinctions and new records of birds from Henderson Island, Pitcairn Group, South Pacific Ocean. *Notornis* 41: 61–70.

Wray, J. W. 1939. *South Sea Vagabonds.* Collins, Auckland.

Yadav, P. R. 2004. *Vanishing and Endangered Species.* Discovery Pub. House, New Delhi.

Yate, W. 1835. *An Account of New Zealand and of the Formation and Progress of the Church Missionary Society's Mission in the Northern Island.* Seeley & Burnside, London.

Yen, D. E. 1960. The sweet potato in the Pacific: The propagation of the plant in relation to its distribution. *JPS* 69(4): 368–75.

— 1961. The adaptation of kumara by the New Zealand Maori. *JPS* 70(3): 338–48.

Yen, D. E. and Wheeler, J. M. 1968. Introduction of taro into the Pacific: The indications of the chromosome numbers. *Ethnology* 7(3): 259–67.

Young, J. L. 1899. Names of the Paumotu Islands. *JPS* 8(4): 264–68.

Zamponi, R. 1996. Multiple sources of glottal stop in Ra`ivavaean. *Oceanic Linguistics* 35(1): 6–20.

Zerega, N. J. C. et al. 2004. Complex origins of breadfruit (*Artocarpus altilis*, Moraceae): Implications for human migrations in Oceania. *Am. J. Bot.* 91(5): 760–66.

Zhang, D. et al. 2000. Assessing genetic diversity of sweet potato (*Ipomoea batatas* (L.) Lam.) cultivars from tropical America using AFLP. *Genet. Resour. Crop. Evol.* 47(6): 659–65.

Zizumbo-Villarreal, D. and Quero, H. J. 1998. Re-evaluation of early observations on coconut in the New World. *Econ. Bot.* 52(1): 68–77.

Picture Credits

Every endeavour has been made to contact the copyright holders of images used in this book. Please contact the publisher if you are the copyright holder and have not been correctly identified.

Abbreviations

CINHT = Cook Islands Natural Heritage Trust
NZETC = New Zealand Electronic Text Centre
PD/WC = Pubic domain from Wikimedia Commons
Te Papa/MONZ = Te Papa Tongarewa/Museum of New Zealand
WC = from Wikimedia Commons

Front cover: Rui Camilo/Hauser Fotografen
Back cover: (clockwise from top left) Martine Cadet; Candice Paewai; Andrew Crowe; Andrew Crowe; Jola Martysz; Nigel Milius; Yves Picq CC by SA 3.0, WC; Jola Martysz; Tom Grey.

Prelims

1: Candice Paewai.
5: (from left to right) Jola Martysz; Jola Martysz; Mrogex, CC by SA 3.0, WC.
7: (map) Andrew Crowe/Jola Martysz.
8–9: (map) Andrew Crowe/Alice Bell.
10: Nigel Milius.

Chance or Skill? [pp. 12–15]

13: Sir Peter Henry Buck. S P Andrew Ltd :Portrait negatives. Ref: 1/1-019099-F. Alexander Turnbull Library, Wellington, New Zealand.

1 Out On a Limb [pp. 16–33]

17: (top) Jola Martysz; (bottom) Guy Wenborne, Fotógrafo, www.guy.cl.
18: (top) William Hodges, A Man of Easter Island, David Rumsey Map Collection, www.davidrumsey.com; (bottom) Jola Martysz.
19: (top) Courtesy of the Kon-Tiki Museum, Oslo.
20: (top) From 'On the patu family and its occurrence beyond New Zealand', by H. D. Skinner, http://www.jps.auckland.ac.nz/popup.php?wid=1792&fig=JPS_040_189_a.jpg&action=figure. With permission of the *Journal of the Polynesian Society*; (bottom) WE000903. Bequest of Kenneth Athol Webster, 1971, Te Papa/MONZ.
21: (top) Terry L. Hunt, Professor and Dean, University of Arizona; (centre) map Carl Lipo; (bottom) Jola Martysz.
22: Duncan Wright, USFWS, PD/WC.
23: Consultaplantas (Own work) CC by SA 4.0, WC.
24: Scott Zona, CC by SA 4.0, WC
25: (both) G. McCormack/CINHT.
26: (top) Ti`a, Ornament. Aitutaki, Cook Islands. Auckland War Memorial Museum Tāmaki Paenga Hira. AM14488; (bottom) OL000114. Oldman Collection. Gift of the New Zealand Government, 1992, Te Papa/MONZ.
27: (top) Jola Martysz; (bottom) Courtesy of the Kon-Tiki Museum, Oslo.
28: (map) Andrew Crowe/Jola Martysz.
29: (top) Diego Delso, CC by SA 3.0, WC; (bottom) FE008557. Gift of F. C. Gentry, 1947, Te Papa/MONZ.
30: (top) The Estate of Lorenzo Dominguez; (bottom) NGDC Tsunami Travel Time Maps/NOAA.
32: (top) Rivi, CC by SA 3.0, WC; (bottom left) G. McCormack/CINHT; (bottom middle) Pedro Tenorio Lezama; (bottom right) Museo Nacional de Historia Natural de Santiago de Chile, PD/WC.
33: (top) Carl Lipo; (bottom) Duché de Vancy, *Population de l'île de Pâques et statues Moai lors de la visite de l'expédition La Pérouse en 1786*, PD-Art (PD-old-100), WC.

2 Dark Horses of the South [pp. 34–49]

35: (top) NASA; (bottom) Angela K. Kepler, PD-author, WC.
36: (both) Jola Martysz.
37: (top) Tara Proud; (bottom) set of four stamps designed by Lucas Kukler.

38: (top) from 'Stone implements of Pitcairn Island', by Kenneth P. Emory, http://www.jps.auckland.ac.nz/document//Volume_37_1928/Volume_37,_No._146/Stone_implements_of_Pitcairn_Island,_by_Kenneth_P_Emory,_p_125-135/p1. With permission of the *Journal of the Polynesian Society*; (bottom) set of four stamps designed by Lucas Kukler.
39: (top left) Jola Martysz; (top right) Marshall Weisler; (middle) NASA; (bottom) from 'Stone implements of Pitcairn Island', by Kenneth P. Emory, http://www.jps.auckland.ac.nz/document//Volume_37_1928/Volume_37,_No._146/Stone_implements_of_Pitcairn_Island,_by_Kenneth_P_Emory,_p_125-135/p1.With permission of the *Journal of the Polynesian Society*.
40: (top) FRED, CC-by-SA 3.0, WC; (bottom) NASA.
41: Louis Le Breton, from *Voyage au Pôle Sud et dans l'Océanie sur les corvettes L'Astrolabe et La Zélée*, Jules Dumont d'Urville, 1846, PD-Art (PD-old-100).
42: (top left) The Michael C. Rockefeller Memorial Collection, Bequest of Nelson A. Rockefeller, 1979, accession no. 1979.206.1466, The Met, CC0 1.0 Universal; (top right) Andrew Crowe; (bottom left and right) Jola Martysz.
43: (top left) Douglas Kennett; (top right) Courtesy DigitalGlobe Inc.
44: (left) Andrew Crowe; (right) Júlio Reis, CC by SA 3.0, WC.
45: Collections of the State Library of New South Wales, CC by SA 3.0.
46: (top left) NASA; (top middle) Pierre Verger, 1933; (top right) NASA; (middle left and right) NASA; (bottom left) Robert Bollt; (bottom right) G. McCormack/CINHT.
47: (top) G. McCormack/CINHT; (bottom) Thomas Cockrem/Alamy Stock Photo.
48: (map) Andrew Crowe/Jola Martysz.

3 Maui's Hook [pp. 50–65]

51: (top) NASA; (bottom) Brian Snelson.
52: (top) Justforasecond, CC by 2.5, WC; (middle) Forest & Kim Starr, USGS, PD/WC; (bottom) Andrew Crowe.
53: (top) John Webber, collections of the State Library of New South Wales; (middle) PD/ WC; (bottom) Daniel Ramirez from Honolulu, USA, 'King Kamehameha Parade, 2012 (7435717490)', CC by 2.0 WC.
54: 1992-0035-1725. Gift of Horace Fildes, 1937, Te Papa/MONZ.
55: (top left) Ron Dahlquist Photography, www.rondahlquist.com; (top right) McCoy et al (2009); (middle) Marshall Weisler and Pat McCoy; (bottom) McCoy et al (2009).
56: Forest & Kim Starr, USGS, PD/WC.
57: (top) Julian Hume; (bottom) Carl Buell.
58: Forest & Kim Starr, USGS, PD/ WC.
59: (top) H. Zell, CC by SA 3.0, WC; (middle) Steve Hurst; (bottom left) Andrew Crowe; (bottom right) from *Maori Agriculture*, Elsdon Best, NZETC, CC by SA 3.0 NZ license; (map) Andrew Crowe/Jola Martysz.
60: (top) G. Wallace, USFWS Pacific Region, PD/WC; (top right) 'Stone tiki from Necker Island', p 152, *Journal of the Polynesian Society*; (bottom) LCDR Eric Johnson, NOAA Corps, PD/ C.
61: (top left) Bishop Museum; (top right) David Rumsey Map Collection, www.davidrumsey.com; (bottom) adze, Marshall Weisler/Bishop Museum.
62: (top) G. McCormack/CINHT; (middle) Jiny Kim, USFWS, PD/WC; (bottom) Angela K. Kepler, PD-author, WC.
63: (map) Andrew Crowe/Jola Martysz; (all photos) NASA.
64: (top) Patrick V. Kirch; (bottom) Andrew Crowe.
65: (top) Aiden Relkoff , CC by SA 4.0, WC; (bottom) With permission of Tom Pōhaku Stone.

4 Statues in the Forest [pp. 66–79]

67: (top) Monster4711, CC by SA 4.0, WC; (bottom) Yves Picq CC by SA 3.0, WC.
68: (top) Martine Cadet; (bottom) Andrew Crowe.
69: (top left) Martine Cadet; (top right) Unknown, PD-0ld, WC; (middle right) David Rumsey Map Collection, www.davidrumsey.com; (bottom) 85/1061. Courtesy of the Division of Anthropology, American Museum of Natural History.

70: (middle left and right) G. McCormack/CINHT; (bottom) Eric Guinther, CC by SA 3.0 WC.

71: (top) © Hans Hillewaert, CC by SA 4.0, WC; (bottom) Pubic domain, WC.

72: (top) Martine Cadet; (bottom) Madame S. Hoare, PD-US, WC; (map) Andrew Crowe/Jola Martysz.

73: (top) G. McCormack/CINHT; (middle left) Andrew Crowe; (top right) G. McCormack/CINHT; (bottom) Andrew Crowe.

74: Andrew Crowe.

75: (all) Andrew Crowe.

76: (top left) FE006538, Te Papa Tongarewa/Museum of New Zealand; (top right) NASA; (bottom left) Samuel Etienne, CC by SA 3.0 WC; (bottom middle) Céline Labaume, CC by SA 3.0 WC; (bottom right) G. McCormack/CINHT.

77: (top) Andrew Crowe; (bottom) G. McCormack/CINHT.

78: G. McCormack/CINHT.

79: (Marquesan ceremony) Martine Cadet; (three flower photos) G. McCormack/CINHT.

5 Expanding the Target [pp. 80–93]

81: Candice Paewai.

82: (top) David Lewis, photographer unknown; (bottom) Creator unknown: Photograph of stones marking bow and stern of Tainui (canoe), Kawhia. Ref: PAColl-8245. Alexander Turnbull Library, Wellington, New Zealand.

83: (top) USGS Museum Staff, United States Geological Survey, PD/WC; (middle) Pearson Scott Foresman, PD/WC.

84: (top) Pearson Scott Foresman, PD/WC; (bottom) Photograph by Mike Peel (www.mikepeel.net), CC by SA 4.0, WC.

85: (top) G. McCormack/CINHT; (bottom) Andrew Crowe /Jola Martysz.

86: (top) Photo by alessandrobol on Foter.com/CC by 2.0; (bottom) Sander van der Wel from Netherlands, CC by SA 2.0, WC.

87: Phillip Capper, CC by SA, WC.

88: (top) Jola Martysz; (middle) Andrew Crowe; (bottom) Wing-Chi Poon, CC by SA 3.0, WC.

89: (top) NASA; (bottom) NASA/GSFC/JPL-Caltech.

90: (top) NOAA; (bottom) From Schott, 1935, in We, the Navigators, David Lewis (University of Hawaii Press, 1972).

91: (top) NASA; (middle) Sémhur, CC by SA 4.0 WC; (bottom) Anonymous CC0-PD/WC.

92: (top left) Andrew Crowe; (top middle) Gregg Yan, CC by SA 3.0, WC; (top right) Martine Cadet; (below left) DickDaniels (http://carolinabirds.org/), CC by SA 3.0, WC; (below right) JJ Harrison (jjharrison89@facebook.com), CC by SA 3.0, WC.

93: (top) Forest and Kim Starr, USGS, PD/WC; (bottom) Andrew Crowe.

6 Crossroads of East Polynesia [pp. 94–109]

95: (top left) NASA; (top right) Jean Kape; (bottom right) Andrew Crowe.

96: (top) G. McCormack/CINHT; (middle above) Andrew Crowe; (middle below) Jola Martysz; (bottom) G. McCormack/CINHT.

97: (top, all) G. McCormack/CINHT; (right centre) Andrew Crowe; (bottom) NASA.

98–99: (map) Andrew Crowe/Jola Martysz.

100: (top left) Andrew Crowe; (top right) EJavanainan, PD/WC; (bottom) F. Munkert, PD/WC.

101: (top left) G. McCormack/CINHT; (top centre) Andrew Crowe; (top right) G. McCormack/CINHT; (middle) Andrew Crowe; (bottom left) Jola Martysz; (bottom right) Andrew Crowe.

102: (top left) CC by SA 3.0 NZ license, The New Zealand Electronic Text Collection, http://nzetc.victoria.ac.nz/tm/scholarly/BucViki-fig-BucViki_P015b.html; (top right) G. McCormack/CINHT; (bottom) Lionel Rich, CC by SA 2.5 WC.

103: (top) Capt Henry Byam Martin, 1847; (middle) G. McCormack/CINHT; (bottom) Liné1, CC by SA 4.0, WC.

104: (left, top to bottom) Jola Martysz; (insert) Andrew Crowe; Martin Kohl; anon.; Andrew Crowe; (right, top to bottom) Andrew Crowe, Veronidae, CC by SA 3.0, WC; Andrew Crowe.

105: G. McCormack/CINHT

106: (top left) G. McCormack/CINHT; (top right) Bryan Harry, PD/WC; (bottom) Dick Daniels, CC by SA 3.0, WC.

107: (left, from top) Photo 2222 at the English Language Wikipedia, CC by SA 3.0; Andrew Crowe; Richard Ling, CC by SA 2.0, WC; Jack Randall; (right, from top) Andrew Crowe; Richard Field.

108: (from top) Terry Goss, CC by SA 3.0, via WC; Brocken Inaglory, CC by SA 3.0, WC; Thomas Ehrensperger CC by SA 3.0, WC; Albert Kok, CC by SA 3.0, WC; Jola Martysz.

109: Jola Martysz.

7 One Hawaiki Among Many [pp. 110–21]

111: (top right) Jola Martysz; (bottom) Samuel Etienne, CC by SA 3.0, WC.

112: Andrew Crowe; (map) Andrew Crowe/Jola Martysz.

113: (top) David Rumsey Map Collection. www.davidrumsey.com; (bottom) Yosihiko Sinoto.

114: (top left) By Daniel Julie from Paris, France (DSC00031/French Polynésia/Mooréa Island/), CC by 2.0, WC; (top right) David Rumsey Map Collection. www.davidrumsey.com; (middle) NASA; (bottom) NASA.

115: (top) NASA; (bottom) David Rumsey Map Collection. www.davidrumsey.com.

116: (top) Andrew Crowe; (middle left) G. McCormack/CINHT; (middle right) G. McCormack/CINHT; (bottom) Keisotyo, CC by SA 3.0, WC.

117: (top) T. Chapman, based on a sketch by Capt. W. Wilson, from Wilson, J. (1799) *A Missionary Voyage to the Southern Pacific Ocean*; (bottom) NASA.

118: From photo, Andrew Crowe.

119: (top) Glen Fergus, CC-by-SA 2.5, WC; (bottom) G. McCormack/CINHT.

120: (top) Andrew Crowe; (bottom left) Andrew Crowe; (bottom right) RB000268/071a. Gift of Charles Rooking Carter, Te Papa/MONZ.

121: After Wilson (1799).

8 En Route to New Zealand [pp. 122–37]

123: (top) Andrew Crowe; (bottom) NASA.

124: (top) jaxshells.org; (middle) G. McCormack/CINHT; (bottom) G. McCormack/CINHT.

125: (top row, from left) G. McCormack/CINHT; G. McCormack/CINHT; Andrew Crowe; (middle row, from left) Andrew Crowe; G. McCormack/CINHT; (right) Kahuroa, PD/WC; (bottom) Andrew Crowe.

126: (from the top) Andrew Crowe; G. McCormack/CINHT; Philippe Bourjon, CC by SA 3.0, WC; (bottom left) Andrew Crowe; (bottom right) G. McCormack/CINHT.

127: (top left) NASA; (top right) Andrew Crowe.

128: (left) G. McCormack/CINHT; (right) FE011763/1, Te Papa/MONZ; (map) Andrew Crowe/Jola Martysz.

129: (top row) NASA; (middle left) David Rumsey Map Collection, www.davidrumsey.com; (bottom) G. McCormack/CINHT.

130: (top left) Andrew Crowe; (top right) Andrew Crowe; (centre left) Andrew Crowe; (bottom left) G. McCormack/CINHT; (bottom right) Ibsut (Ian Sutton).

131: (top left) Andrew Crowe; (top right) G. McCormack/CINHT; (centre left) Jola Martysz; (centre right) G. McCormack/CINHT; (bottom above and below) Andrew Crowe.

132: (top left) Andrew Crowe; (top right) Andrew Crowe; (middle right) G. McCormack/CINHT; (bottom) OL000423. Oldman Collection. Gift of the New Zealand Government, 1992, Te Papa/MONZ.

133: Andrew Crowe.

134: (map) Andrew Crowe/Jola Martysz; (all photos) NASA.

135: Ewan Smith, CC by SA 3.0, WC.

136: (left) G. McCormack/CINHT; (right) Ewan Smith, CC by SA 3.0, WC; (bottom) G. McCormack/CINHT.

137: (top) Magy357, CC by SA 3.0, WC; (bottom) NASA.

9 Nature's Signposts [pp. 138–57]

139: (top) NASA; (bottom) CC-by-2.0, Department of Conservation, New Zealand.

140: David Rumsey Map Collection, www.davidrumsey.com.

141: Candice Paewai.

142: (left) G. Irwin; (middle) Andrew Crowe and Jola Martysz; (right) Wood, C. and M. *Charlie's Charts of Polynesia.*

143: (left) G. McCormack/CINHT; (middle) G. McCormack/CINHT; (top right) Auckland War Memorial Museum/Kath Prickett.

144: (top) Christopher Watson (http://www.comebirdwatching.blogspot.com/), CC by SA 3.0, WC; (middle) G. McCormack/CINHT; (bottom) JJ Harrison, CC by SA 3.0, WC.

145: (all) Andrew Crowe.

146: (both) Aviceda at English Wikipedia, CC by SA 3.0.

147: (top left) Tom Grey; (top right) Map from Shaffer et al. 2006. Migratory shearwaters integrate ocean resources across the Pacific Ocean in an endless summer. *PNAS* 103 (34): 12799–12802. © National Academy of Sciences, U.S.A.; (bottom) Aviceda at English Wikipedia, CC by SA 3.0.

148: (top map) Matt Rayner/Alice Bell; (globe) Matt Rayner et al.

149: (top) © Tony Whitehead, WildLight Photography, www.wildlight.co.nz; (middle) USGS, PD/WC; (bottom) Andrew Crowe/Jola Martysz

150: G. McCormack/CINHT

151: (top left) Karora, PD, WC; (top right) Heather Cuthill, CC by SA 2.0, WC;

152: (top) Andrew Crowe; (bottom left) Mr Tickle, CC by SA 3.0, WC; (centre inserts left and right) Andrew Crowe; (bottom right) Gabriel Barathieu, CC by SA 2.0, WC.

153: OR.024148/1, Te Papa Tongarewa/Museum of New Zealand; (middle left) Ti`a, Ornament. Aitutaki, Cook Islands. Auckland War Memorial Museum Tāmaki Paenga Hira. AM14488; (middle insert) Andrew Crowe; (bottom right) JShook, en.wikipedia.org, CS by SA 2.5.

154: (top) Paul Martinson, South Island Giant Moa. *Dinornis robustus*. From the series: *Extinct Birds of New Zealand*, 2006-0010-1/18, Purchased 2006. Te Papa/MONZ; (centre left) Robyn Eyles holding a moa egg ca 1970, Canterbury Museum. 19XX.2.5049; (centre middle) Photo of Paul Scofield at Canterbury Museum, courtesy of Quinn Berentson; (centre right) G. McCormack/CINHT.

155: Conty, CC by 3.0, WC.

156: (top left) Andrew Crowe; (top right) Karora, PD/WC; (right) Richard Giddins from London, UK, CC by 2.0, via WC.

157: (top) Andrew Crowe/Jola Martysz; (middle) G. McCormack/CINHT; (bottom) Sydney Parkinson, collections of the State Library of New South Wales, CC by SA 3.0.

10 Planned Voyages of Settlement [pp. 158–75]

159: (top) G. McCormack/CINHT; (bottom) Andrew Crowe.

160: Andrew Crowe/Jola Martysz.

161: (map) Andrew Crowe/Jola Martysz.

162: (both) Andrew Crowe/Jola Martysz.

163: European Southern Observatory, CC by 4.0, WC.

164: (top) Andrew Crowe; (middle) Arne-Kaiser, CC by SA 4.0, WC; (bottom) Stephen Balaban, CCO 1.0 PD/WC.

165: Andrew Crowe.

166: ME000441. Purchased 1904, Te Papa/MONZ.

167: (top) Andrew Crowe; (bottom) Jo Langeneck, CC by SA 4.0, WC.

168: Original Edward S. Curtis (restored), PD-US, WC.

169: CSIRO, CC by 3.0.

170: (top left) Nigel Milius; (top right) Cianc, CC by 2.0, WC; (bottom); NOAA Fisheries (TBjornstad), PD/WC.

171: (both) Nigel Milius.

172: (top) Amada44, PD-self, WC; (centre left) JJ Harrison (jjharrison89@facebook.com), CC by SA 3.0, WC; (centre right) Sabine's Sunbird, CC by SA 3.0, WC; (bottom) J. P. Bennett from Yamato, Japan, CC by 2.0, WC.

173: (top) Charles E. Wildbore, Palmerston North, circa 1904, 2008N_Bf2_WOR_1408 A bush fire in Pohangina Valley Public Photograph Collection Bf 2, Palmerston North Libraries and Community Services; (bottom) VIIRS/Suomi NPP/NASA.

174: Sid Mosdell from New Zealand, CC by 2.0, WC.

175: (both) Geoff Irwin.

11 Adapting to a Cool Land [pp. 176–95]

177: (top left) Tairua lure, Pearl shell (*Pinctada margaritifera*). Coromandel District. Auckland War Memorial Museum Tāmaki Paenga Hira. AU1785; (top right) shell, Janet Davidson/ Shell artefact, Wairau Bar, Marlborough, J. R. Eyles Collection, Canterbury Museum 1947.35.1099; (bottom) Andy king50, CC by SA 3.0, WC.

178: Krzysztof Golik, CC by 4.0, WC.

179: (photo) Porlob, PD/WC; (maps) from *Bateman New Zealand Historical Atlas*, Malcolm McKinnon ed. (Bateman, 1997).

180: (top) G. McCormack/CINHT; (bottom) F J Brook.

181: (top, all) Paul Martinson, From the series: *Extinct Birds of New Zealand*. Purchased 2006. (from left) North Island Adzebill. *Aptornis otidiformis*. 2006-0010-1/40, North Island Goose. *Cnemiornis gracilis*. 2006-0010-1/28, New Zealand Coot. *Fulica prisca*. 2006-0010-1/50. Te Papa/MONZ; (bottom) John Megahan, CC by 2.5, WC.

182: Representation of a Bird of the Coot kind, found at Lord Howe Island A604008h, collections of State Library of New South Wales, CC-by-SA 3.0.

183: (top left) Frankzed, CC-by- 2.0, WC; (top right) Peter Halasz, CC-by-SA 3.0, WC; (bottom) Murray Dawson, CC-by-SA 3.0, WC.

184: (top) LM000828. Gift of Mr Anderson, 1876. Te Papa/MONZ; (bottom) Andrew Crowe.

185: (top) G. McCormack/CINHT; (bottom) Forest & Kim Starr (USGS), PD/WC.

186: G. McCormack/CINHT.

187: G. McCormack/CINHT.

188: (top three) G. McCormack/CINHT; (bottom) Graham Harris.

189: Andrew Crowe.

190: (top left) Andrew Crowe; (top centre) Avenue, CC by SA 3.0, WC; (top right and bottom) Andrew Crowe.

191: (top left) Ngarangi Kaihuia wearing a tag cloak. Photograph taken by William Henry Thomas Partington. Ref: 1/1-003113-G. Alexander Turnbull Library, Wellington, New Zealand; (top centre above) Tomas Sobek, CC by 2.0, WC; (top centre below) Andrew Crowe; (top right) flax sandals, D24.576 Pāraerae, courtesy Otago Museum; (bottom) David Rumsey Map Collection, www.davidrumsey.com.

192: (top) Jo Hiscock, Crown copyright © Department of Conservation CC by 4.0; (bottom) Charles Chilton, Freshwater and Marine Image Bank , University of Washington, PD-UWASH-FMIB, WC.

193: (top) NASA; (bottom) Dragonfly Science. Crown copyright © DOC CC by 3.0 accompanying report Yvan Richard, Edward R. Abraham, Finlay N. Thompson & Katrin Berkenbusch (2011). Counts of seabirds around commercial fishing vessels within New Zealand waters. 30 pages. (Unpublished report prepared for the Department of Conservation, retrieved from https://seabird-counts.dragonfly.co.nz/seabirds-around-fishing-vessels.pdf, Nov 19, 2013.)

194: (top) Houi/GFDL, CC by SA 3.0, WC; (bottom left) B. Navez (Kerguelen) CC by SA 3.0, WC; (bottom right) F004324/03,04,07,08, Te Papa/MONZ.

195: (map) Andrew Crowe/Jola Martysz, (map pic) Andrew Crowe; (bottom) Dendroglyph, Chatham Islands. Silcock, Kathleen Joan: Photographs and postcards of the Chatham Islands. Ref: PAColl-1964-27. Alexander Turnbull Library, Wellington, New Zealand.

12 The Cuckoos Depart [pp. 196–209]

197: (top) Phil Battley; (right) Aviceda, CC by SA 3.0, WC.

198: Andrew Crowe.

199: (map) Andrew Crowe/Jola Martysz; (photos) Andrew Crowe.

200: (top left) Mgiganteus.1, CC by SA 3.0, WC; (top centre left) E. Javanainen, PD-self, WC; (top centre right) Granitethighs, CC by SA 3.0, WC; (top right) Didier Descouens, CC by SA 4.0, WC; (map) Matt Rayner/Alice Bell.

201: (map) Andrew Crowe/Jola Martysz; (graphic) James Renwick, NIWA, 2009. Image courtesy of NIWA.

202: (top right) Add_ms_23920_f048r. Source: Add. 23920, f.48. Herman Spöring from *A Collection of Drawings made in the Countries visited by Captain Cook in his First Voyage, 1768-1771.* © The British Library Board; (bottom) David Rumsey Map Collection, www.davidrumsey.com.

203: (all) Reprinted with permission from Johns, D. et al. 2014. An early sophisticated East Polynesian voyaging canoe discovered on New Zealand's coast. *PNAS* 111 (41): 14728.

204: (top sketches), CC by SA 3.0 NZ license, NZETC; (far left) G. McCormack/CINHT; (left) Andrew Crowe.

205: (map) From Matisoo-Smith, E. et al. (2009). *Pacific Science* 63 (4): 465–75; (left) ME00696. Purchased 1931, Te Papa/MONZ; (right) ME002965. Gift of Alexander Turnbull, 1913. Te Papa/MONZ.

207: (bottom left) Inas, CC by SA 4.0, WC; (bottom right) JJ Harrison (jjharrison89@facebook.com), CC by SA 3.0, WC.

208: (top) Papier K, CC by SA 3.0, WC; (bottom) Christopher Watson (http://www.comebirdwatching.blogspot.com/), CC by SA 3.0, WC.

209: (top left) JJ Harrison (jjharrison89@facebook.com), CC by SA 3.0, WC; (bottom left) From Sutherland, L. G. (1929). Study of the Maori mind. *JPS* 38 (150):127–47. With permission of the *Journal of the Polynesian Society*.

13 A Wider Range of Possibilities [pp. 210–21]

211: (map) Andrew Crowe/Alice Bell.

212: Dittmer, Wilhelm, 1866-1909: Maui fishing New Zealand out of the ocean. Ref: PUBL-0088-049. Alexander Turnbull Library, Wellington, New Zealand.

213: (map) Andrew Crowe/Jola Martysz.

214: (map) Andrew Crowe/Jola Martysz.

215: (top) William Hodges, collections of State Library of New South Wales, CC by SA 3.0; (middle) Louis Le Breton, PD-old, WC; (bottom) Willem Schouten, PD-old, WC.

216: (left above) Jola Martysz; (left below) NASA; (right) Jola Martysz.

217: (top) CC by SA 3.0 New Zealand license, NZETC, http://nzetc.victoria.ac.nz/etexts/BulBird/Bul01BirdP008.jpg. By J. G. Keulemans, in W.L. Buller's *A History of the Birds of New Zealand*. 2nd edition. Published 1888; (bottom) EfAston , CC-by-SA 3.0, WC.

218: (top left) G. McCormack/CINHT; (top middle) Kahuroa, PD-user, WC; (top right) Peter Trimming from Croydon, England, CC by 2.0, WC; (middle right) Kristian Peters, Fabelfroh 15:17, 12 September 2007 (UTC), CC by SA 3.0, WC; (bottom left) Andrew Crowe; (bottom right) Ian Skipworth, PD-author, WC; (map) Adapted from Matisoo-Smith, E. and Robins, J. H. (2004). Origins and dispersals of Pacific peoples: Evidence from mtDNA phylogenies of the Pacific rat. *PNAS* 101(24): 9169. Copyright (2004) National Academy of Sciences, U.S.A.

Index

(Main entries in **bold**)